P9-CLO-879

THE USE
OF FORCE

THE USE OF FORCE

Military Power and International Politics, Third Edition

Edited by

Robert J. Art and
Kenneth N. Waltz

UNIVERSITY
PRESS OF
AMERICA

Lanham • New York • London

Copyright © 1983, 1988 by

Robert J. Art and Kenneth N. Waltz

Second Edition published in 1983. Third Edition 1988

University Press of America,® Inc.

4720 Boston Way
Lanham, MD 20706

3 Henrietta Street
London WC2E 8LU England

All rights reserved

Printed in the United States of America

British Cataloging in Publication Information Available

First Edition © 1971 by Little, Brown & Co., Inc.

Library of Congress Cataloging-in-Publication Data

The Use of Force : international politics and foreign policy / edited
by Robert J. Art and Kenneth N. Waltz.—3rd ed.
p. cm.
Bibliography: p.
1. War. 2. International relations. 3. Arms race. 4. Arms
control. 5. World politics—20th century. 6. Peace. I. Art,
Robert J. II. Waltz, Kenneth Neal, 1924–
U21.2.U83   1988
327.1'17—dc 19   88–17198 CIP
ISBN 0–8191–7002–X (alk. paper)
ISBN 0–8191–7003–8 (pbk. : alk. paper)

All University Press of America books are produced on acid-free paper.
The paper used in this publication meets the minimum requirements of
American National Standard for Information Sciences—Permanence of Paper
for Printed Library Materials, ANSI Z39.48–1984.

Preface

In the third edition of this book, we have retained the perspective of the first two editions. We have continued to emphasize the relation between technology on the one hand and military strategy and foreign policy on the other. The selections reprinted here are of two types. Some treat general principles guiding the direct use of force; others deal with specific applications of force and, in doing so, illustrate the general principles. In choosing either type of selection, we have continued to keep three questions in mind: (1) What role has the threatened or actual use of military force played in international politics?; (2) How has military power changed in the twentieth century?; and (3) How have changes in the instruments of force affected the use of force by twentieth century statesmen?

We have also made significant changes in this edition. First, we have reorganized the book into three major divisions that deal, respectively, with strategies for the use of force (or what today is often termed "grand strategy"), with case studies about some significant twentieth century applications of force, and with contemporary dilemmas and disputes about how force should be used. More than the first two editions, the third provides a broad, although still not comprehensive, survey of the impact that new technologies have had on military strategy and statecraft in this century. The third edition combines classic pieces with contemporary analyses and thereby yields historical perspective.

Second, we have expanded the coverage of contemporary problems. The selections in Part III are organized under five headings: nuclear strategy, the European theater, power projection, arms races and arms control, and nuclear proliferation. Apart from counterinsurgency warfare and terrorism, which have been omitted because of space limitations, these five topics cover the main issues in the use of force that the United States has faced in the eighties and will continue to face in the nineties. In each of the sections of Part III, we have taken account of differences in view among strategists by selecting pieces that take issue with one another.

Third, in order to keep the book at a manageable length, we have omitted the editors' introduction that appeared in the first two editions. We believe that our introductions to each major division set forth the important themes and draw attention to important points subsequently covered. We hope that both beginning and advanced students will continue to find this edition helpful in understanding the many dilemmas faced by statesmen when contemplating the use of force.

Contents

Part I
Strategies for the Use of Force

States coexist in a condition of anarchy. If a state is attacked, it has to defend itself with whatever means it can muster. Because no authoritative agency can be called on to resolve disputes among states, statesmen often find it convenient, and sometimes necessary, to threaten the use of force or actually to use force. Military force is important, if not central, in international politics. It brings some order out of chaos, and it helps to make and enforce the rules of the game.

Because force is so important internationally, the following questions arise: How can states most effectively employ military force in pursuit of national goals? What effects has the growth in national military power had on the ways in which force has been used? What kinds of military threats are productive, and what kinds counterproductive? What are the factors that influence the strategies that states devise to have their military forces support their larger foreign policies? Have nuclear weapons changed the nature of international politics or drastically altered the ways in which states can use military power? These are the questions that the authors of the selections in Part I explore.

In his essay, Thomas C. Schelling makes a distinction between coercive violence and brute force and shows how nuclear weapons have reversed the relation of victory to coercion; military victory need not precede doing violence to the enemy country. In his selection Glenn H. Snyder delineates the functions of pre-attack deterrence and post-attack defense and argues that nuclear weapons produce an inherent conflict between the two. Barry R. Posen examines the factors that influence the strategies that states develop for using force and thereby devises a set of propositions about the determinants of grand strategy. Robert Jervis looks at the different ways defensive and offensive strategies affect the probabilities that cooperation and peace or conflict and war will prevail. Finally, the selections under the heading "Nuclear Strategies: The Record" deal with the choices that statesmen have made in their plans for the use of nuclear weapons.

1

The Diplomacy of Violence

THOMAS C. SCHELLING

The usual distinction between diplomacy and force is not merely in the instruments, words or bullets, but in the relation between adversaries —in the interplay of motives and the role of communication, understandings, compromise, and restraint. Diplomacy is bargaining; it seeks outcomes that, though not ideal for either party, are better for both than some of the alternatives. In diplomacy each party somewhat controls what the other wants, and can get more by compromise, exchange, or collaboration than by taking things in his own hands and ignoring the other's wishes. The bargaining can be polite or rude, entail threats as well as offers, assume a status quo or ignore all rights and privileges, and assume mistrust rather than trust. But whether polite or impolite, constructive or aggressive, respectful or vicious, whether it occurs among friends or antagonists and whether or not there is a basis for trust and goodwill, there must be some common interest, if only in the avoidance of mutual damage, and an awareness of the need to make the other party prefer an outcome acceptable to oneself.

With enough military force a country may not need to bargain. Some things a country wants it can take, and some things it has it can keep, by sheer strength, skill, and ingenuity. It can do this *forcibly*, accommodating only to opposing strength, skill and ingenuity and without trying to appeal to an enemy's wishes. Forcibly a country can repel and expel, penetrate and occupy, seize, exterminate, disarm and disable, confine, deny access, and directly frustrate intrusion or attack. It can, that is, if it has enough strength. "Enough" depends on how much an opponent has.

There is something else, though, that force can do. It is less military, less heroic, less impersonal, and less unilateral; it is uglier, and has received less attention in Western military strategy. In addition to seizing and holding, disarming and confining, penetrating and obstructing, and all that, military force can be used *to hurt*. In addition to taking and protecting things of value it can *destroy* value. In

From *Arms and Influence* by Thomas C. Schelling. Copyright © 1966 by Yale University, pp. 1–10 and 12–34. Reprinted by permission of the publisher, Yale University Press. Portions of the text and some footnotes have been omitted.

addition to weakening an enemy militarily it can cause an enemy plain suffering.

Pain and shock, loss and grief, privation and horror are always in some degree, sometimes in terrible degree, among the results of warfare; but in traditional military science they are incidental, they are not the object. If violence can be done incidentally, though, it can also be done purposely. The power to hurt can be counted among the most impressive attributes of military force.

Hurting, unlike forcible seizure or self-defense, is not unconcerned with the interest of others. It is measured in the suffering it can cause and the victims' motivation to avoid it. Forcible action will work against weeds or floods as well as against armies, but suffering requires a victim that can feel pain or has something to lose. To inflict suffering gains nothing and saves nothing directly; it can only make people behave to avoid it. The only purpose, unless sport or revenge, must be to influence somebody's behavior, to coerce his decision or choice. To be coercive, violence has to be anticipated. And it has to be avoidable by accommodation. The power to hurt is bargaining power. To exploit it is diplomacy—vicious diplomacy, but diplomacy.

THE CONTRAST OF BRUTE FORCE WITH COERCION

There is a difference between taking what you want and making someone give it to you, between fending off assault and making someone afraid to assault you, between holding what people are trying to take and making them afraid to take it, between losing what someone can forcibly take and giving it up to avoid risk or damage. It is the difference between defense and deterrence, between brute force and intimidation, between conquest and blackmail, between action and threats. It is the difference between the unilateral, "undiplomatic" recourse to strength, and coercive diplomacy based on the power to hurt.

The contrasts are several. The purely "military" or "undiplomatic" recourse to forcible action is concerned with enemy strength, not enemy interests; the coercive use of the power to hurt, though, is the very exploitation of enemy wants and fears. And brute strength is usually measured relative to enemy strength, the one directly opposing the other, while the power to hurt is typically not reduced by the enemy's power to hurt in return. Opposing strengths may cancel each other, pain and grief do not. The willingness to hurt, the credibility of a threat, and the ability to exploit the power to hurt will indeed depend on how much the adversary can hurt in return; but there is little or nothing about an adversary's pain or grief that directly reduces one's own. Two sides cannot both overcome each other with superior strength; they may both be able to hurt each other. With strength they can dispute objects of value; with sheer violence they can destroy them.

And brute force succeeds when it is used, whereas the power to hurt is most successful when held in reserve. It is the *threat* of damage, or of more damage to come, that can make someone yield or comply. It is *latent* violence that can influence someone's choice—violence that can still be withheld or inflicted, or that a victim believes can be withheld or inflicted. The threat of pain tries to structure someone's motives, while brute force tries to overcome his strength. Unhappily, the power to hurt is often communicated by some performance of it. Whether it is sheer terroristic violence to induce an irrational response, or cool premeditated violence to persuade somebody that you mean it and may do it again, it is not the pain and damage itself but its influence on somebody's behavior that matters. It is the expectation of *more* violence that gets the wanted behavior, if the power to hurt can get it at all.

To exploit a capacity for hurting and inflicting damage one needs to know what an adversary treasures and what scares him and one needs the adversary to understand what behavior of his will cause the violence to be inflicted and what will cause it to be withheld. The victim has to know what is wanted, and he may have to be assured of what is not wanted. The pain and suffering have to appear *contingent* on his behavior; it is not alone the threat that is effective—the threat of pain or loss if he fails to comply—but the corresponding assurance, possibly an implicit one, that he can avoid the pain or loss if he does comply. The prospect of certain death may stun him, but it gives him no choice.

Coercion by threat of damage also requires that our interests and our opponent's not be absolutely opposed. If his pain were our greatest delight and our satisfaction his greatest woe, we would just proceed to hurt and to frustrate each other. It is when his pain gives us little or no satisfaction compared with what he can do for us, and the action or inaction that satisfies us costs him less than the pain we can cause, that there is room for coercion. Coercion requires finding a bargain, arranging for him to be better off doing what we want—worse off not only doing what we want—when he takes the threatened penalty into account.

It is this capacity for pure damage, pure violence, that is usually associated with the most vicious labor disputes, with racial disorders, with civil uprisings and their suppression, with racketeering. It is also the power to hurt rather than brute force that we use in dealing with criminals; we hurt them afterward, or threaten to, for their misdeeds rather than protect ourselves with cordons of electric wires, masonry walls, and armed guards. Jail, of course, can be either forcible restraint or threatened privation; if the object is to keep criminals out of mischief by confinement, success is measured by how many of them are gotten behind bars, but if the object is to *threaten* privation, success will be measured by how few have to be put behind bars and success then depends on the subject's understanding of the consequences. Pure damage is what a car threatens when it tries to hog the road or to keep its rightful share, or to go first through an intersection. A tank or a bulldozer can force its way regardless of others' wishes; the rest of us have to threaten damage, usually mutual damage, hoping the other driver values his car or his limbs enough to give way, hoping he sees us, and hoping he is in control of his own car. The threat of pure damage will not work against an unmanned vehicle.

This difference between coercion and brute force is as often in the intent as in the instrument. To hunt down Comanches and to exterminate them was brute force; to raid their villages to make them behave was coercive diplomacy, based on the power to hurt. The pain and loss to the Indians might have looked much the same one way as the other; the difference was one of purpose and effect. If Indians were killed because they were in the way, or somebody wanted their land, or the authorities despaired of making them behave and could not confine them and decided to exterminate them, that was pure unilateral force. If *some* Indians were killed to make *other* Indians behave, that was coercive violence—or intended to be, whether or not if was effective. The Germans at Verdun perceived themselves to be chewing up hundreds of thousands of French soldiers in a gruesome "meatgrinder." If the purpose was to eliminate a military obstacle— the French infantryman, viewed as a military "asset" rather than as a warm human being—the offensive at Verdun was a unilateral exercise of military force. If instead the object was to make the loss of young men—not of impersonal "effectives," but of sons, husbands, fathers, and the pride of French manhood—so anguishing as to be unendurable, to make surrender a welcome relief and to spoil the foretaste of an Allied victory, then it was an exercise in coercion, in applied violence, intended to offer relief upon accommodation. And of course, since any use of force tends to be brutal, thoughtless, vengeful, or plain obstinate, the motives themselves can be mixed and confused. The fact that heroism and brutality can be either coercive diplomacy or a contest in pure strength does not promise that the distinction will be made, and the strategies enlightened by the distinction, every time some vicious enterprise gets launched.

The contrast between brute force and coercion is illustrated by two alternative strategies attributed to Genghis Khan. Early in his career he pursued the war creed of the Mongols: the vanquished can never be the friends of the victors, their death is necessary for the victors' safety. This was the unilateral extermination of a menace or a liability. The turning point of his career, according to Lynn Montross, came later when he discovered how to use his power to hurt for diplomatic ends. "The great Khan, who was not inhibited by the usual mercies, conceived the plan of forcing captives—women, children, aged fathers, favorite sons—to march ahead of his army as the first potential victims of resistance."[1] Live captives have often proved more valuable than enemy dead; and the technique discovered by the Khan in his maturity remains contemporary. North Koreans and Chinese were reported to have quartered prisoners of war near strategic targets to inhibit bombing attacks by United Nations aircraft. Hostages represent the power to hurt in its purest form.

COERCIVE VIOLENCE IN WARFARE

This distinction between the power to hurt and the power to seize or hold forcibly is important in modern war, both big war and little war, hypothetical war and real war. For many years the Greeks and the Turks on Cyprus could hurt each other indefinitely but neither could quite take or hold forcibly what they wanted or protect themselves from violence by physical means. The Jews in Palestine could not expel the British in the late 1940s but they could cause pain and fear and frustration through terrorism, and eventually influence somebody's decision. The brutal war in Algeria was more a contest in pure violence than in military strength; the question was who would first find the pain and degradation unendurable. The French troops preferred—indeed they continually tried—to make it a contest of strength, to pit military force against the nationalists' capacity for terror, to exterminate or disable the nationalists and to screen off the nationalists from the victims of their violence. But because in civil war terrorists commonly have access to victims by sheer physical propinquity, the victims and their properties could not be forcibly defended and in the end the French troops themselves resorted, unsuccessfully, to a war of pain.

Nobody believes that the Russians can take Hawaii from us, or New York, or Chicago, but nobody doubts that they might destroy people and buildings in Hawaii, Chicago, or New York. Whether the Russians can conquer West Germany in any meaningful sense is questionable; whether they can hurt it terribly is not doubted. That the United States can destroy a large part of Russia is universally taken for granted; that the United States can keep from being badly hurt, even devastated, in return, or can keep Western Europe from being devastated while itself destroying Russia, is at best arguable; and it is virtually out of the question that we could conquer Russia territorially and use its economic assets unless it were by threatening disaster and inducing compliance. It is the power to hurt, not military strength in the traditional sense, that inheres in our most impressive military

[1] Lynn Montross, *War Through the Ages* (3rd ed., New York, Harper, and Brothers, 1960), p. 146.

capabilities at the present time. We have a Department of *Defense* but emphasize *retaliation*—"to return evil for evil" (synonyms: requital, reprisal, revenge, vengeance, retribution). And it is pain and violence, not force in the traditional sense, that inhere also in some of the least impressive military capabilities of the present time—the plastic bomb, the terrorist's bullet, the burnt crops, and the tortured farmer.

War appears to be, or threatens to be, not so much a contest of strength as one of endurance, nerve, obstinacy, and pain. It appears to be, and threatens to be, not so much a contest of military strength as a bargaining process—dirty, extortionate, and often quite reluctant bargaining on one side or both—nevertheless a bargaining process.

The difference cannot quite be expressed as one between the *use* of force and the *threat* of force. The actions involved in forcible accomplishment, on the one hand, and in fulfilling a threat, on the other, can be quite different. Sometimes the most effective direct action inflicts enough cost or pain on the enemy to serve as a threat, sometimes not. The United States threatens the Soviet Union with virtual destruction of its society in the event of a surprise attack on the United States; a hundred million deaths are awesome as pure damage, but they are useless in stopping the Soviet attack—especially if the threat is to do it all afterward anyway. So it is worthwhile to keep the concepts distinct—to distinguish forcible action from the threat of pain—recognizing that some actions serve as both a means of forcible accomplishment and a means of inflicting pure damage, some do not. Hostages tend to entail almost pure pain and damage, as do all forms of reprisal after the fact. Some modes of self-defense may exact so little in blood or treasure as to entail negligible violence; and some forcible actions entail so much violence that their threat can be effective by itself.

The power to hurt, though it can usually accomplish nothing directly, is potentially more versatile than a straightforward capacity for forcible accomplishment. By force alone we cannot even lead a horse to water—we have to drag him—much less make him drink. Any affirmative action, any collaboration, almost anything but physical exclusion, expulsion, or extermination, requires that an opponent or a victim *do* something, even if only to stop or get out. The threat of pain and damage may make him want to do it, and anything he can do is potentially susceptible to inducement. Brute force can only accomplish what requires no collaboration. The principle is illustrated by a technique of unarmed combat: one can disable a man by various stunning, fracturing, or killing blows, but to take him to jail one has to exploit the man's own efforts. "Come-along" holds are those that threaten pain or disablement, giving relief as long as the victim complies, giving him the option of using his own legs to get to jail. . . .

The fact that violence—pure pain and damage—can be used or threatened to coerce and to deter, to intimidate and to blackmail, to demoralize and to paralyze, in a conscious process of dirty bargaining, does not by any means imply that violence is not often wanton and meaningless or, even when purposive, in danger of getting out of hand. Ancient wars were often quite "total" for the loser, the men being put to death, the women sold as slaves, the boys castrated, the cattle slaughtered, and the buildings leveled, for the sake of revenge, justice, personal gain, or merely custom. If an enemy bombs a city, by design or by carelessness, we usually bomb his if we can. In the excitement and fatigue of warfare, revenge is one of the few satisfactions that can be savored. . . . Pure violence, like fire, can be harnessed to a purpose; that does not mean that behind every holocaust is a shrewd intention successfully fulfilled.

But if the occurrence of violence does not always bespeak a shrewd purpose, the absence of pain and destruction is no sign that violence was idle. Violence is most purposive and most successful when it is threatened and not used. Successful threats are those that do not have to be carried out. By European standards, Denmark was virtually unharmed in the Second World War; it was violence that made the Danes submit. Withheld violence—successfully threatened violence— can look clean, even merciful. The fact that a kidnap victim is returned unharmed, against receipt of ample ransom, does not make kidnapping a nonviolent enterprise. The American victory at Mexico City in 1847 was a great success; with a minimum of brutality we traded a capital city for everything we wanted from the war. We did not even have to say what we could do to Mexico City to make the Mexican government understand what they had at stake. (They had undoubtedly got the message a month earlier, when Vera Cruz was being pounded into submission. . . .)

Whether spoken or not, the threat is usually there. . . .

THE STRATEGIC ROLE OF PAIN AND DAMAGE

Pure violence, nonmilitary violence, appears most conspicuously in relations between unequal countries, where there is no substantial military challenge and the outcome of military engagement is not in question. Hitler could make his threats contemptuously and brutally against Austria; he could make them, if he wished, in a more refined way against Denmark. It is noteworthy that it was Hitler, not his generals, who used this kind of language; proud military establishments do not like to think of themselves as extortionists. Their favorite job is to deliver victory, to dispose of opposing military force and to leave most of the civilian violence to politics and diplomacy. But if there is no room for doubt how a contest in strength will come out, it may be possible to bypass the military stage altogether and to proceed at once to the coercive bargaining.

A typical confrontation of unequal forces occurs at the *end* of a war, between victor and vanquished. Where Austria was vulnerable before a shot was fired, France was vulnerable after its military shield had collapsed in 1940. Surrender negotiations are the place where the threat of civil violence can come to the fore. Surrender negotiations are often so one-sided, or the potential violence so unmistakable, that bargaining succeeds and the violence remains in reserve. But the fact that most of the actual damage was done during the military stage of the war, prior to victory and defeat, does not mean that violence was idle in the aftermath, only that it was latent and the threat of it successful. . . .

. . . The Russians crushed Budapest in 1956 and cowed Poland and other neighboring countries. There was a lag of ten years between military victory and this show of violence, but the principle was the one [just] explained. . . . Military victory is often the prelude to violence, not the end of it, and the fact that successful violence is usually held in reserve should not deceive us about the role it plays.

What about pure violence during war itself, the infliction of pain and suffering as a military technique? Is the threat of pain involved only in the political use of victory, or is it a decisive technique of war itself?

Evidently between unequal powers it has been part of warfare. Colonial conquest has often been a matter of "punitive expeditions" rather than genuine military engagements. If the tribesmen escape into the brush you can burn their villages without them until they assent to receive what, in strikingly modern language, used to be known as the Queen's "protection." . . .

Pure hurting, as a military tactic, appeared in some of the military actions against the plains Indians. In 1868, during the war with the Cheyennes, General Sheridan decided that his best hope was to attack the Indians in their winter camps. His reasoning was that the Indians could maraud as they pleased during the seasons when their ponies could subsist on grass, and in the winter hide away in remote places. "To disabuse their minds from the idea that they were secure from punishment, and to strike at a period when they were helpless to move their stock and villages, a winter campaign was projected against the large bands hiding away in the Indian territory."[2]

These were not military engagements; they were punitive attacks on people. They were an effort to subdue by the use of violence, without a futile attempt to draw the enemy's military forces into decisive battle. They were "massive retaliation" on a diminutive scale, with

---

[2] Paul I. Wellman, *Death on the Prairie* (New York, Macmillan, 1934), p. 82.

local effects not unlike those of Hiroshima. The Indians themselves totally lacked organization and discipline, and typically could not afford enough ammunition for target practice and were no military match for the cavalry; their own rudimentary strategy was at best one of harassment and reprisal. Half a century of Indian fighting in the West left us a legacy of cavalry tactics; but it is hard to find a serious treatise on American strategy against the Indians or Indian strategy against the whites. The twentieth is not the first century in which "retaliation" has been part of our strategy, but it is the first in which we have systematically recognized it.

Hurting, as a strategy, showed up in the American Civil War, but as an episode, not as the central strategy. For the most part, the Civil War was a military engagement with each side's military force pitted against the other's. The Confederate forces hoped to lay waste enough Union territory to negotiate their independence, but hadn't enough capacity for such violence to make it work. The Union forces were intent on military victory, and it was mainly General Sherman's march through Georgia that showed a conscious and articulate use of violence. "If the people raise a howl against my barbarity and cruelty, I will answer that war is war. . . . If they want peace, they and their relatives must stop the war," Sherman wrote. And one of his associates said, "Sherman is perfectly right. . . . The only possible way to end this unhappy and dreadful conflict . . . is to make it terrible beyond endurance."[3]

Making it "terrible beyond endurance" is what we associate with Algeria and Palestine, the crushing of Budapest, and the tribal warfare in Central Africa. But in the great wars of the last hundred years it was usually military victory, not the hurting of the people, that was decisive; General Sherman's attempt to make war hell for the Southern people did not come to epitomize military strategy for the century to follow. To seek out and to destroy the enemy's military force, to achieve a crushing victory over enemy armies, was still the avowed purpose and the central aim of American strategy in both world wars. Military action was seen as an *alternative* to bargaining, not a *process* of bargaining.

The reason is not that civilized countries are so averse to hurting people that they prefer "purely military" wars. (Nor were all of the participants in these wars entirely civilized.) The reason is apparently

[3] J. F. C. Fuller reproduces some of this correspondence and remarks, "For the nineteenth century this was a new conception, because it meant that the deciding factor in the war—the power to sue for peace—was transferred from government to people, and that peace-making was a product of revolution. This was to carry the principle of democracy to its ultimate stage. . . ." *The Conduct of War: 1789–1961* (New Brunswick, Rutgers University Press, 1961), pp. 107–12.

that the technology and geography of warfare, at least for a war between anything like equal powers during the century ending in World War II, kept coercive violence from being decisive before military victory was achieved. Blockade indeed was aimed at the whole enemy nation, not concentrated on its military forces; the German civilians who died of influenza in the First World War were victims of violence directed at the whole country. It has never been quite clear whether blockade—of the South in the Civil War or of the Central Powers in both world wars, or submarine warfare against Britain—was expected to make war unendurable for the people or just to weaken the enemy forces by denying economic support. Both arguments were made, but there was no need to be clear about the purpose as long as either purpose was regarded as legitimate and either might be served. "Strategic bombing" of enemy homelands was also occasionally rationalized in terms of the pain and privation it could inflict on people and the civil damage it could do to the nation, as an effort to display either to the population or to the enemy leadership that surrender was better than persistence in view of the damage that could be done. It was also rationalized in more "military" terms, as a way of selectively denying war material to the troops or as a way of generally weakening the economy on which the military effort rested.

But terrorism—as violence intended to coerce the enemy rather than to weaken him militarily—blockade and strategic bombing by themselves were not quite up to the job in either world war in Europe. (They might have been sufficient in the war with Japan after straightforward military action had brought American aircraft into range.) Airplanes could not quite make punitive, coercive violence decisive in Europe, at least on a tolerable time schedule, and preclude the need to defeat or to destroy enemy forces as long as they had nothing but conventional explosives and incendiaries to carry. Hitler's V-1 buzz bomb and his V-2 rocket are fairly pure cases of weapons whose purpose was to intimidate, to hurt Britain itself rather than Allied military forces. What the V-2 needed was a punitive payload worth carrying, and the Germans did not have it. Some of the expectations in the 1920s and the 1930s that another major war would be one of pure civilian violence, of shock and terror from the skies, were not borne out by the available technology. The threat of punitive violence kept occupied countries quiescent; but the wars were won in Europe on the basis of brute strength and skill and not by intimidation, not by the threat of civilian violence but by the application of military force. Military victory was still the price of admission. Latent violence against people was reserved for the politics of surrender and occupation.

The great exception was the two atomic bombs on Japanese cities. These were weapons of terror and shock. They hurt, and promised more hurt, and that was their purpose. The few "small" weapons we had were undoubtedly of some direct military value, but their enormous advantage was in pure violence. In a military sense the United States could gain a little by destruction of two Japanese industrial cities; in a civilian sense, the Japanese could lose much. The bomb that hit Hiroshima was a threat aimed at all of Japan. The political target of the bomb was not the dead of Hiroshima or the factories they worked in, but the survivors in Tokyo. The two bombs were in the tradition of Sheridan against the Comanches and Sherman in Georgia. Whether in the end those two bombs saved lives or wasted them, Japanese lives or American lives; whether punitive coercive violence is uglier than straightforward military force or more civilized; whether terror is more or less humane than military destruction; we can at least perceive that the bombs on Hiroshima and Nagasaki represented violence against the country itself and not mainly an attack on Japan's material strength. The effect of the bombs, and their purpose, was not mainly the military destruction they accomplished but the pain and shock and the promise of more.

THE NUCLEAR CONTRIBUTION TO TERROR AND VIOLENCE

Man has, it is said, for the first time in history enough military power to eliminate his species from the earth, weapons against which there is no conceivable defense. War has become, it is said, so destructive and terrible that it ceases to be an instrument of national power. "For the first time in human history," says Max Lerner in a book whose title, *The Age of Overkill*, conveys the point, "men have bottled up a power . . . which they have thus far not dared to use." And Soviet military authorities, whose party dislikes having to accommodate an entire theory of history to a single technological event, have had to re-examine a set of principles that had been given the embarrassing name of "permanently operating factors" in warfare. Indeed, our era is epitomized by words like "the first time in human history," and by the abdication of what was "permanent."

For dramatic impact these statements are splendid. Some of them display a tendency, not at all necessary, to belittle the catastrophe of earlier wars. They may exaggerate the historical novelty of deterrence and the balance of terror.[4] More important, they do not help to iden-

---

[4] Winston Churchill is often credited with the term, "balance of terror," and the following quotation succinctly expresses the familiar notion of nuclear mutual deterrence. This, though, is from a speech in Commons in November 1934. "The fact remains that when all is said and done as regards defensive methods, pending some new discovery the only direct measure of defense upon a great scale is the certainty of being able to inflict simultaneously upon the enemy as great damage as he can inflict upon ourselves. Do not let us undervalue the efficacy of this procedure. It may well prove in

tify just what is new about war when so much destructive energy can be packed in warheads at a price that permits advanced countries to have them in large numbers. Nuclear warheads are incomparably more devastating than anything packaged before. What does that imply about war?

It is not true that for the first time in history man has the capability to destroy a large fraction, even the major part, of the human race. Japan was defenseless by August 1945. With a combination of bombing and blockade, eventually invasion, and if necessary the deliberate spread of disease, the United States could probably have exterminated the population of the Japanese islands without nuclear weapons. . . .

It is a grisly thing to talk about. We did not do it and it is not imaginable that we would have done it. We had no reason; if we had had a reason, we would not have had the persistence of purpose, once the fury of war had been dissipated in victory and we had taken on the task of executioner. If we and our enemies might do such a thing to each other now, and to others as well, it is not because nuclear weapons have for the first time made it feasible.

Nuclear weapons can do it quickly. . . . To compress a catastrophic war within the span of time that a man can stay awake drastically changes the politics of war, the process of decision, the possibility of central control and restraint, the motivations of people in charge, and the capacity to think and reflect while war is in progress. It *is* imaginable that we might destroy 200,000,000 Russians in a war of the present, though not 80,000,000 Japanese in a war of the past. It is not only imaginable, it is imagined. It is imaginable because it could be done "in a moment, in the twinkling of an eye, at the last trumpet."

This may be why there is so little discussion of how an all-out war might be brought to a close. People do not expect it to be "brought" to a close, but just to come to an end when everything has been spent. It is also why the idea of "limited war" has become so explicit in recent years. Earlier wars, like World Wars I and II or the Franco-Prussian War, were limited by *termination*, by an ending that occurred before the period of greatest potential violence, by negotiation that brought the *threat* of pain and privation to bear but often precluded the massive *exercise* of civilian violence. With nuclear weapons available, the restraint of violence cannot await the outcome of a contest of military strength; restraint, to occur at all, must occur during war itself.

This is a difference between nuclear weapons and bayonets. It is not in the number of people they can eventually kill but in the speed

---

practice—I admit I cannot prove it in theory—capable of giving complete immunity. If two Powers show themselves equally capable of inflicting damage upon each other by some particular process of war, so that neither gains an advantage from its adoption and both suffer the most hideous reciprocal injuries, it is not only possible but it seems probable that neither will employ that means. . . ."

with which it can be done, in the centralization of decision, in the divorce of the war from political processes, and in computerized programs that threaten to take the war out of human hands once it begins.

That nuclear weapons make it *possible* to compress the fury of global war into a few hours does not mean that they make it *inevitable*. We have still to ask whether that is the way a major nuclear war would be fought, or ought to be fought. Nevertheless, that the whole war might go off like one big string of firecrackers makes a critical difference between our conception of nuclear war and the world wars we have experienced.

There is no guarantee, of course, that a slower war would not persist. The First World War could have stopped at any time after the Battle of the Marne. There was plenty of time to think about war aims, to consult the long-range national interest, to reflect on costs and casualties already incurred and the prospect of more to come, and to discuss terms of cessation with the enemy. The gruesome business continued as mechanically as if it had been in the hands of computers (or worse: computers might have been programmed to learn more quickly from experience). One may even suppose it would have been a blessing had all the pain and shock of the four years been compressed within four days. Still, it was terminated. And the victors had no stomach for doing then with bayonets what nuclear weapons could do to the German people today.

There is another difference. In the past it has usually been the victors who could do what they pleased to the enemy. War has often been "total war" for the loser. With deadly monotony the Persians, Greeks, or Romans "put to death all men of military age, and sold the women and children into slavery," leaving the defeated territory nothing but its name until new settlers arrived sometime later. But the defeated could not do the same to their victors. The boys could be castrated and sold only after the war had been won, and only on the side that lost it. The power to hurt could be brought to bear only after military strength had achieved victory. The same sequence characterized the great wars of this century; for reasons of technology and geography, military force has usually had to penetrate, to exhaust, or to collapse opposing military force—to achieve military victory—before it could be brought to bear on the enemy nation itself. The Allies in World War I could not inflict coercive pain and suffering directly on the Germans in a decisive way until they could defeat the German army; and the Germans could not coerce the French people with bayonets unless they first beat the Allied troops that stood in their way. With two-dimensional warfare, there is a tendency for troops to confront each other, shielding their own lands while attempting to press into each other's. Small penetrations could not do major damage to the people; large penetrations were so destructive of military organization that they usually ended the military phase of the war.

Nuclear weapons make it possible to do monstrous violence to the enemy without first achieving victory. With nuclear weapons and to-day's means of delivery, one expects to penetrate an enemy homeland without first collapsing his military force. What nuclear weapons have done, or appear to do, is to promote this kind of warfare to first place. Nuclear weapons threaten to make war less military, and are respon-sible for the lowered status of "military victory" at the present time. *Victory is no longer a prerequisite for hurting the enemy.* And it is no assurance against being terribly hurt. One need not wait until he has won the war before inflicting "unendurable" damages on his enemy. One need not wait until he has lost the war. There was a time when the assurance of victory—false or genuine assurance—could make na-tional leaders not just willing but sometimes enthusiastic about war. Not now.

Not only *can* nuclear weapons hurt the enemy before the war has been won, and perhaps hurt decisively enough to make the military engagement academic, but it is widely assumed that in a major war that is *all* they can do. Major war is often discussed as though it would be only a contest in national destruction. If this is indeed the case—if the destruction of cities and their populations has become, with nuclear weapons, the primary object in an all-out war—the sequence of war has been reversed. Instead of destroying enemy forces as a prelude to imposing one's will on the enemy nation, one would have to destroy the nation as a means or a prelude to destroying the enemy forces. If one cannot disable enemy forces without virtually destroy-ing the country, the victor does not even have the option of sparing the conquered nation. He has already destroyed it. Even with blockade and strategic bombing it could be supposed that a country would be defeated before it was destroyed, or would elect surrender before an-nihilation had gone far. In the Civil War it could be hoped that the South would become too weak to fight before it became too weak to survive. For "all-out" war, nuclear weapons threaten to reverse this sequence.

So nuclear weapons do make a difference, marking an epoch in warfare. The difference is not just in the amount of destruction that can be accomplished but in the role of destruction and in the decision process. Nuclear weapons can change the speed of events, the control of events, the sequence of events, the relation of victor to vanquished, and the relation of homeland to fighting front. Deterrence rests today on the threat of pain and extinction, not just on the threat of military defeat. We may argue about the wisdom of announcing "uncondi-tional surrender" as an aim in the last major war, but seem to expect "unconditional destruction" as a matter of course in another one.

Something like the same destruction always *could* be done. With nuclear weapons there is an expectation that it *would* be done. . . .

What is new is . . . the idea that major war might be just a contest in the killing of countries, or not even a contest but just two parallel exercises in devastation.

That is the difference nuclear weapons make. At least they *may* make that difference. They also may not. If the weapons themselves are vulnerable to attack, or the machines that carry them, a successful surprise might eliminate the opponent's means of retribution. That an enormous explosion can be packaged in a single bomb does not by itself guarantee that the victor will receive deadly punishment. Two gunfighters facing each other in a Western town had an unquestioned capacity to kill one another; that did not guarantee that both would die in a gunfight—only the slower of the two. Less deadly weapons, permitting an injured one to shoot back before he died, might have been more conducive to a restraining balance of terror, or of caution. The very efficiency of nuclear weapons could make them ideal for starting war, if they can suddenly eliminate the enemy's capability to shoot back.

And there is a contrary possibility: that nuclear weapons are not vulnerable to attack and prove not to be terribly effective against each other, posing no need to shoot them quickly for fear they will be destroyed before they are launched, and with no task available but the systematic destruction of the enemy country and no necessary reason to do it fast rather than slowly. Imagine that nuclear destruction *had* to go slowly—that the bombs could be dropped only one per day. The prospect would look very different, something like the most terroristic guerrilla warfare on a massive scale. It happens that nuclear war does not have to go slowly; but it may also not have to go speedily. The mere existence of nuclear weapons does not itself determine that everything must go off in a blinding flash, any more than that it must go slowly. Nuclear weapons do not simplify things quite that much.

In recent years there has been a new emphasis on distinguishing what nuclear weapons make possible and what they make inevitable in case of war. The American government began in 1961 to emphasize that even a major nuclear war might not, and need not, be a simple contest in destructive fury. Secretary McNamara gave a controversial speech in June of 1962 on the idea that "deterrence" might operate even in war itself, that belligerents might, out of self-interest, attempt to limit the war's destructiveness. Each might feel the sheer destruction of enemy people and cities would serve no decisive military purpose but that a continued *threat* to destroy them might serve a purpose. The continued threat would depend on their not being destroyed yet. Each might reciprocate the other's restraint, as in limited wars of lesser scope. Even the worst of enemies, in the interest of reciprocity, have often not mutilated prisoners of war; and citizens might deserve comparable treatment. The fury of nuclear attacks might fall mainly on each other's weapons and military forces.

"The United States has come to the conclusion," said Secretary McNamara,

> that to the extent feasible, basic military strategy in a possible general war should be approached in much the same way that more conventional military operations have been regarded in the past. That is to say, principal military objectives . . . should be the destruction of the enemy's military forces, not of his civilian population . . . giving the possible opponent the strongest imaginable incentive to refrain from striking our own cities.[5]

This is a sensible way to think about war, if one has to think about it and of course one does. But whether the Secretary's "new strategy" was sensible or not, whether enemy populations should be held hostage or instantly destroyed, whether the primary targets should be military forces or just people and their source of livelihood, this is not "much the same way that more conventional military operations have been regarded in the past." This is utterly different, and the difference deserves emphasis.

In World Wars I and II one went to work on enemy military forces, not his people, because until the enemy's military forces had been taken care of there was typically not anything decisive that one could do to the enemy nation itself. The Germans did not, in World War I, refrain from bayoneting French citizens by the millions in the hope that the Allies would abstain from shooting up the German population. They could not get at the French citizens until they had breached the Allied lines. Hitler tried to terrorize London and did not make it. The Allied air forces took the war straight to Hitler's territory, with at least some thought of doing in Germany what Sherman recognized he was doing in Georgia; but with the bombing technology of World War II one could not afford to bypass the troops and go exclusively for enemy populations—not, anyway, in Germany. With nuclear weapons one has that alternative.

To concentrate on the enemy's military installations while deliberately holding in reserve a massive capacity for destroying his cities, for exterminating his people and eliminating his society, on condition that the enemy observe similar restraint with respect to one's own society, is not the "conventional approach." In World Wars I and II the first order of business was to destroy enemy armed forces because that was the only promising way to make him surrender. To fight a purely military engagement "all-out" while holding in reserve

---

[5] Commencement Address, University of Michigan, June 16, 1962.

a decisive capacity for violence, on condition the enemy do likewise, is not the way military operations have traditionally been approached. Secretary McNamara was proposing a new approach to warfare in a new era, an era in which the power to hurt is more impressive than the power to oppose.

FROM BATTLEFIELD WARFARE TO THE DIPLOMACY OF VIOLENCE

Almost one hundred years before Secretary McNamara's speech, the Declaration of St. Petersburg (the first of the great modern conferences to cope with the evils of warfare) in 1868 asserted, "The only legitimate object which states should endeavor to accomplish during war is to weaken the military forces of the enemy." And in a letter to the League of Nations in 1920, the President of the International Committee of the Red Cross wrote: "The Committee considers it very desirable that war should resume its former character, that is to say, that it should be a struggle between armies and not between populations. The civilian population must, as far as possible, remain outside the struggle and its consequences."[6] His language is remarkably similar to Secretary McNamara's.

The International Committee was fated for disappointment, like everyone who labored in the late nineteenth century to devise rules that would make war more humane. When the Red Cross was founded in 1863, it was concerned about the disregard for noncombatants by those who made war; but in the Second World War noncombatants were deliberately chosen as targets by both Axis and Allied forces, not decisively but nevertheless deliberately. The trend has been the reverse of what the International Committee hoped for.

In the present era noncombatants appear to be not only deliberate targets but primary targets, or at least were so taken for granted until about the time of Secretary McNamara's speech. In fact, noncombatants appeared to be primary targets at both ends of the scale of warfare; thermonuclear war threatened to be a contest in the destruction of cities and populations; and, at the other end of the scale, insurgency is almost entirely terroristic. We live in an era of dirty war.

Why is this so? Is war properly a military affair among combatants, and is it a depravity peculiar to the twentieth century that we cannot keep it within decent bounds? Or is war inherently dirty, and was the Red Cross nostalgic for an artificial civilization in which war had become encrusted with etiquette—a situation to be welcomed but not expected?

---

[6] International Committee of the Red Cross, *Draft Rules for the Limitation of the Dangers Incurred by the Civilian Population in Time of War* (2nd ed., Geneva, 1958), pp. 144, 151.

To answer this question it is useful to distinguish three stages in the involvement of noncombatants—of plain people and their possessions —in the fury of war. These stages are worth distinguishing; but their sequence is merely descriptive of Western Europe during the past three hundred years, not a historical generalization. The first stage is that in which the people may get hurt by inconsiderate combatants. This is the status that people had during the period of "civilized warfare" that the International Committee had in mind.

From about 1648 to the Napoleonic era, war in much of Western Europe was something superimposed on society. It was a contest engaged in by monarchies for stakes that were measured in territories and, occasionally, money or dynastic claims. The troops were mostly mercenaries and the motivation for war was confined to the aristocratic elite. Monarchs fought for bits of territory, but the residents of disputed terrain were more concerned with protecting their crops and their daughters from marauding troops than with whom they owed allegiance to. They were, as Quincy Wright remarked in his classic *Study of War*, little concerned that the territory in which they lived had a new sovereign.[7] Furthermore, as far as the King of Prussia and the Emperor of Austria were concerned, the loyalty and enthusiasm of the Bohemian farmer were not decisive considerations. It is an exaggeration to refer to European war during this period as a sport of kings, but not a gross exaggeration. And the military logistics of those days confined military operations to a scale that did not require the enthusiasm of a multitude.

Hurting people was not a decisive instrument of warfare. Hurting people or destroying property only reduced the value of the things that were being fought over, to the disadvantage of both sides. Furthermore, the monarchs who conducted wars often did not want to discredit the social institutions they shared with their enemies. Bypassing an enemy monarch and taking the war straight to his people would have had revolutionary implications. Destroying the opposing monarchy was often not in the interest of either side; opposing sovereigns had much more in common with each other than with their own subjects, and to discredit the claims of a monarchy might have produced a disastrous backlash. It is not surprising—or, if it is surprising, not altogether astonishing—that on the European continent in that particular era war was fairly well confined to military activity.

One could still, in those days and in that part of the world, be concerned for the rights of noncombatants and hope to devise rules that both sides in the war might observe. The rules might well be observed because both sides had something to gain from preserving social order

---

[7] Chicago, University of Chicago Press, 1942, p. 296.

and not destroying the enemy. Rules might be a nuisance, but they restricted both sides the disadvantages might cancel out.

This was changed during the Napoleonic wars. In Napoleon's France, people cared about the outcome. The nation was mobilized. The war was a national effort, not just an activity of the elite. It was both political and military genius on the part of Napoleon and his ministers that an entire nation could be mobilized for war. Propaganda became a tool of warfare, and war became vulgarized.

Many writers deplored this popularization of war, this involvement of the democratic masses. In fact, the horrors we attribute to thermonuclear war were already foreseen by many commentators, some before the First World War and more after it; but the new "weapon" to which these terrors were ascribed was people, millions of people, passionately engaged in national wars, spending themselves in a quest for total victory and desperate to avoid total defeat. Today we are impressed that a small number of highly trained pilots can carry enough energy to blast and burn tens of millions of people and the buildings they live in; two or three generations ago there was concern that tens of millions of people using bayonets and barbed wire, machine guns and shrapnel, could create the same kind of destruction and disorder.

That was the second stage in the relation of people to war, the second in Europe since the middle of the seventeenth century. In the first stage people had been neutral but their welfare might be disregarded; in the seond stage people were involved because it was *their* war. Some fought, some produced materials of war, some produced food, and some took care of children; but they were all part of a war-making nation. When Hitler attacked Poland in 1939, the Poles had reason to care about the outcome. When Churchill said the British would fight on the beaches, he spoke for the British and not for a mercenary army. The war was about something that mattered. If people would rather fight a dirty war than lose a clean one, the war will be between nations and not just between governments. If people have an influence on whether the war is continued or on the terms of a truce, making the war hurt people serves a purpose. It is a dirty purpose, but war itself is often about something dirty. The Poles and the Norwegians, the Russians and the British, had reason to believe that if they lost the war the consequences would be dirty. This is so evident in modern civil wars—civil wars that involve popular feelings—that we expect them to be bloody and violent. To hope that they would be fought cleanly with no violence to people would be a little like hoping for a clean race riot.

There is another way to put it that helps to bring out the sequence of events. If a modern war were a clean one, the violence would not be ruled out but merely saved for the postwar period. Once the army has been defeated in the clean war, the victorious enemy can be as brutally coercive as he wishes. A clean war would determine which side gets to use its power to hurt coercively after victory, and it is likely to be worth some violence to avoid being the loser.

"Surrender" is the process following military hostilities in which the power to hurt is brought to bear. If surrender negotiations are successful and not followed by overt violence, it is because the capacity to inflict pain and damage was successfully used in the bargaining process. On the losing side, prospective pain and damage were averted by concessions; on the winning side, the capacity for inflicting further harm was traded for concessions. The same is true in a successful kidnapping. It only reminds us that the purpose of pure pain and damage is extortion; it is *latent* violence that can be used to advantage. A well-behaved occupied country is not one in which violence plays no part; it may be one in which latent violence is used so skillfully that it need not be spent in punishment.

This brings us to the third stage in the relation of civilian violence to warfare. If the pain and damage can be inflicted during war itself, they need not wait for the surrender negotiation that succeeds a military decision. If one can coerce people and their governments while war is going on, one does not need to wait until he has achieved victory or risk losing that coercive power by spending it all in a losing war. General Sherman's march through Georgia might have made as much sense, possibly more, had the North been losing the war, just as the German buzz bombs and V-2 rockets can be thought of as coercive instruments to get the war stopped before suffering military defeat.

In the present era, since at least the major East-West powers are capable of massive civilian violence during war itself beyond anything available during the Second World War, the occasion for restraint does not await the achievement of military victory or truce. The principal restraint during the Second World War was a temporal boundary, the date of surrender. In the present era we find the violence dramatically restrained during war itself. The Korean War was furiously "all-out" in the fighting, not only on the peninsular battlefield but in the resources used by both sides. It was "all-out," though, only within some dramatic restraints: no nuclear weapons, no Russians, no Chinese territory, no Japanese territory, no bombing of ships at sea or even airfields on the United Nations side of the line. It was a contest in military strength circumscribed by the threat of unprecedented civilian violence. Korea may or may not be a good model for speculation on limited war in the age of nuclear violence, but it was dramatic evidence that the capacity for violence can be consciously restrained even under the provocation of a war that measures its military dead in tens of thousands and that fully preoccupies two of the largest countries in the world.

A consequence of this third stage is that "victory" inadequately expresses what a nation wants from its military forces. Mostly it wants, in these times, the influence that resides in latent force. It wants the bargaining power that comes from its capacity to hurt, not just the direct consequence of successful military action. Even total victory over an enemy provides at best an opportunity for unopposed violence against the enemy population. How to use that opportunity in the national interest, or in some wider interest, can be just as important as the achievement of victory itself; but traditional military science does not tell us how to use that capacity for inflicting pain. And if a nation, victor or potential loser, is going to use its capacity for pure violence to influence the enemy, there may be no need to await the achievement of total victory.

Actually, this third stage can be analyzed into two quite different variants. In one, sheer pain and damage are primary instruments of coercive warfare and may actually be applied to intimidate or to deter. In the other, pain and destruction *in* war are expected to serve little or no purpose but *prior threats* of sheer violence, even of automatic and uncontrolled violence, are coupled to military force. The difference is in the all-or-none character of deterrence and intimidation. Two acute dilemmas arise. One is the choice of making prospective violence as frightening as possible or hedging with some capacity for reciprocated restraint. The other is the choice of making retaliation as automatic as possible or keeping deliberate control over the fateful decisions. The choices are determined partly by governments, partly by technology. Both variants are characterized by the coercive role of pain and destruction—of threatened (not inflicted) pain and destruction. But in one the threat either succeeds or fails altogether, and any ensuing violence is gratuitous; in the other, progressive pain and damage may actually be used to threaten more. The present era, for countries possessing nuclear weapons, is a complex and uncertain blend of the two.

Coercive diplomacy, based on the power to hurt, was important even in those periods of history when military force was essentially the power to take and to hold, to fend off attack and to expel invaders, and to possess territory against opposition—that is, in the era in which military force tended to pit itself against opposing force. Even then, a critical question was how much cost and pain the other side would incur for the disputed territory. The judgment that the Mexicans would concede Texas, New Mexico, and California once Mexico City was a hostage in our hands was a diplomatic judgment, not a military one. If one could not readily take the particular territory he wanted or hold it against attack, he could take something else and trade it. Judging what the enemy leaders would trade—be it a capital city or national survival—was a critical part of strategy even in the past. Now we are in an era in which the power to hurt—to inflict pain and shock and privation on a country itself, not just on its military forces—is commensurate with the power to take and to hold, perhaps more than commensurate, perhaps decisive, and it is even more necessary to think of warfare as a process of violent bargaining. This is not the first era in which live captives have been worth more than dead enemies, and the power to hurt has been a bargaining advantage; but it is the first in American experience when that kind of power has been a dominant part of military relations.

The power to hurt is nothing new in warfare, but for the United States modern technology has drastically enhanced the strategic importance of pure, unconstructive, unacquisitive pain and damage, whether used against us or in our own defense. This in turn enhances the importance of war and threats of war as techniques of influence, not of destruction; of coercion and deterrence, not of conquest and defense; of bargaining and intimidation.

Quincy Wright, in his *Study of War*, devoted a couple of pages (319–320) to the "nuisance value" of war, using the analogy of a bank robber with a bomb in his hand that would destory bank and robber. Nuisance value made the threat of war, according to Wright, "an aid to the diplomacy of unscrupulous governments." Now we need a stronger term, and more pages, to do the subject justice, and need to recognize that even scrupulous governments often have little else to rely on militarily. It is extraordinary how many treatises on war and strategy have declined to recognize that the power to hurt has been, throughout history, a fundamental character of military force and fundamental to the diplomacy based on it.

War no longer looks like just a contest of strength. War and the brink of war are more a contest of nerve and risk-taking, of pain and endurance. Small wars embody the threat of a larger war; they are not just military engagements but "crisis diplomacy." The threat of war has always been somewhere underneath international diplomacy, but for Americans it is now much nearer the surface. Like the threat of a strike in industrial relations, the threat of divorce in a family dispute, or the threat of bolting the party at a political convention, the threat of violence continuously circumscribes international politics. Neither strength nor goodwill procures immunity.

Military strategy can no longer be thought of, as it could for some countries in some eras, as the science of military victory. It is now equally, if not more, the art of coercion, of intimidation and deterrence. The instruments of war are more punitive than acquisitive. Military strategy, whether we like it or not, has become the diplomacy of violence.

Deterrence and Defense

GLENN H. SNYDER

National security still remains an "ambiguous symbol," as one scholar described it almost a decade ago.[1] Certainly it has grown more ambiguous as a result of the startling advances since then in nuclear and weapons technology, and the advent of nuclear parity between the United States and the Soviet Union. Besides such technological complications, doctrine and thought about the role of force in international politics have introduced additional complexities. We now have, at least in embryonic form, theories of limited war, of deterrence, of "tactical" vs. "strategic" uses of nuclear weapons, of "retaliatory" vs. "counterforce" strategies in all-out war, of "limited retaliation," of the mechanics of threat and commitment-making, of "internal war," "protracted conflict," and the like. Above all, the idea of the "balance of terror" has begun to mature, but its relation to the older concept of the "balance of power" is still not clear. We have had a great intellectual ferment in the strategic realm, which of course is all to the good. What urgently remains to be done is to tie together all of these concepts into a coherent framework of theory so that the end-goal of national security may become less ambiguous, and so that the military means available for pursuance of this goal may be accumulated, organized, and used more efficiently. This book can claim to make only a start in this direction.

The central theoretical problem in the field of national security policy is to clarify and distinguish between the two central concepts of *deterrence* and *defense*. Essentially, deterrence means discouraging the enemy from taking military action by posing for him a prospect of cost and risk outweighing his prospective gain. Defense means reducing our own prospective costs and risks in the event that deterrence fails. Deterrence works on the enemy's *intentions*; the *deterrent value*

From *Deterrence and Defense: Toward a Theory of National Security* by Glenn H. Snyder, pp. 3-16, 31, 33-40, 50, 97-109. Copyright © 1961 by Princeton University Press. Reprinted by permission of Princeton University Press. Portions of the text and some footnotes have been omitted.

[1] Arnold Wolfers, " 'National Security' as an Ambiguous Symbol," *Political Science Quarterly*, Vol. LXVII, No. 4 (December 1952), pp. 481ff.

of military forces is their effect in reducing the likelihood of enemy military moves. Defense reduces the enemy's *capability* to damage or deprive us; the *defense value* of military forces is their effect in mitigating the adverse consequences for us of possible enemy moves, whether such consequences are counted as losses of territory or war damage. The concept of "defense value," therefore, is broader than the mere capacity to hold territory, which might be called "denial capability." Defense value is denial capability plus capacity to alleviate war damage.

It is commonplace, of course, to say that the primary objectives of national security policy are to deter enemy attacks and to defend successfully, at minimum cost, against those attacks which occur. It is less widely recognized that different types of military force contribute in differing proportions to these two objectives. Deterrence does not vary directly with our capacity for fighting wars effectively and cheaply; a particular set of forces might produce strong deterrent effects and not provide a very effective denial and damage-alleviating capability. Conversely, forces effective for defense might be less potent deterrents than other forces which were less efficient for holding territory and which might involve extremely high war costs if used.

One reason why the periodic "great debates" about national security policy have been so inconclusive is that the participants often argue from different premises—one side from the point of view of deterrence, and the other side from the point of view of defense. For instance, in the famous "massive retaliation" debate of 1954, the late Secretary of State Dulles and his supporters argued mainly that a capacity for massive retaliation would deter potential Communist mischief, but they tended to ignore the consequences should deterrence fail. The critics, on the other hand, stressed the dire consequences should the threat of massive retaliation fail to deter and tended to ignore the possibility that it might work. The opposing arguments never really made contact because no one explicitly recognized that considerations of reducing the probability of war and mitigating its consequences must be evaluated simultaneously, that the possible consequences of a failure of deterrence are more or less important depending on the presumed likelihood of deterrence. Many other examples could be cited.

Perhaps the crucial difference between deterrence and defense is that deterrence is primarily a peacetime objective, while defense is a wartime value. Deterrent value and defense value are directly enjoyed in different time periods. We enjoy the deterrent value of our military forces prior to the enemy's aggressive move; we enjoy defense value after the enemy move has already been made, although we indirectly profit from defense capabilities in advance of war through our knowledge that if the enemy attack occurs we have the means of mitigating its consequences. The crucial point is that *after* the enemy's attack takes place, our military forces perform different functions and yield wholly different values than they did as deterrents prior to the attack. As deterrents they engaged in a psychological battle—dissuading the enemy from attacking by attempting to confront him with a prospect of costs greater than his prospective gain. After the enemy begins his attack, while the psychological or deterrent aspect does not entirely disappear, it is partly supplanted by another purpose: to resist the enemy's onslaught in order to minimize *our* losses or perhaps maximize *our* gains, not only with regard to the future balance of power, but also in terms of intrinsic or non-power values. That combination of forces which appeared to be the optimum one from the point of view of deterrence might turn out to be far inferior to some other combination from the point of view of defense should deterrence fail. In short, maximizing the enemy's cost expectancy may not always be consistent with minimizing our own. Thus we must measure the value of our military forces on two yardsticks, and we must find some way of combining their value on *both* yardsticks, in order accurately to gauge their aggregate worth or "utility" and to make intelligent choices among the various types of forces available.

Before launching into a theoretical analysis of the concepts of deterrence and defense, it may be useful to present a sampling of policy issues involving a need to choose between deterrence and defense; the examples will be treated in more detail in subsequent chapters.

EXAMPLES OF CHOICES AND CONFLICTS BETWEEN DETERRENCE AND DEFENSE

A strategic retaliatory air force sufficient only to wreak minimum "unacceptable" damage on Soviet cities—to destroy, say, 20 cities—after this force has been decimated by a surprise Soviet nuclear attack, would have great value for deterring such a surprise attack and might be an adequate deterrent against that contingency. But if deterrence were to fail and the Soviet attack took place, it would then not be rational to *use* such a minimum force in massive retaliation against Soviet cities, since this would only stimulate the Soviets to inflict further damage upon us and would contribute nothing to our "winning the war." If we are interested in defense—i.e., in winning the war and in minimizing the damage to us—as well as in deterrence, we may wish to have (if technically feasible) a much larger force and probably one of different composition—a force which can strike effectively at the enemy's remaining forces (thus reducing our own costs) and, further, either by actual attacks or the threat of attacks, force the enemy to surrender or at least to give up his territorial gains.

The threat of massive nuclear retaliation against a Soviet major ground attack in Western Europe may continue to provide considerable deterrence against such an attack, even if actually to carry out the threat would be irrational because of the enormous costs we would suffer from Soviet counterretaliation. Strategic nuclear weapons do not provide a rational means of defense in Western Europe unless they not only can stop the Russian ground advance but also, by "counterforce" strikes, can reduce to an acceptable level the damage we would suffer in return. We may not have this capability now and it may become altogether infeasible as the Soviets develop their missile technology. For a means of rational defense, therefore, NATO may need enough ground forces to hold Europe against a full-scale attack by Soviet ground forces. This does not mean, however, that we necessarily must maintain ground forces of this size. If we think the probability of attack is low enough, we may decide to continue relying on nuclear deterrence primarily, even though it does not provide a rational means of defense. In other words, we might count on the Soviet uncertainties about whether or not nuclear retaliation is rational for us, and about how rational we are, to inhibit the Soviets from attacking in the face of the terrible damage they *know* they would suffer if they guessed wrong.

An attempt to build an effective counterforce capability, in order to have both a rational nuclear defense and a more credible nuclear deterrent against ground attack in Europe, might work against the *deterrence* of direct nuclear attack on the United States. Since such a force, by definition, would be able to eliminate all but a small fraction of the Soviet strategic nuclear forces if it struck first, the Soviets might, in some circumstances, fear a surprise attack and be led to strike first themselves in order to forestall it.

Tactical nuclear weapons in the hands of NATO forces in Europe have considerable deterrent value because they increase the enemy's cost expectation beyond what it would be if these forces were equipped only with conventional weapons. This is true not only because the tactical weapons themselves can inflict high costs on the enemy's forces, but also because their use (or an enemy "preemptive" strike against them) would sharply raise the probability that the war would spiral to all-out dimensions. But the defense value of tactical nuclear weapons against conventional attack is comparatively low against an enemy who also possesses them, because their use presumably would be offset by the enemy's use of them against our forces, and because in using such weapons we would be incurring much greater costs and risks than if we had responded conventionally.

For deterrence, it might be desirable to render automatic a response which the enemy recognizes as being costly for us, and communicate the fact of such automation to the enemy, thus reducing his doubts that we would actually choose to make this response when the occasion for it arose. For example, a tactical nuclear response to conventional aggression in Europe may be made semi-automatic by thoroughly orienting NATO plans, organization, and strategy around this response, thus increasing the difficulty of following a non-nuclear strategy in case of a Soviet challenge. But such automation would not be desirable for defense, which would require flexibility and freedom to choose the least costly action in the light of circumstances at the time of the attack.

The Continental European attitude toward NATO strategy is generally ambivalent on the question of deterrence vs. defense; there is fear that with the Soviet acquisition of a substantial nuclear and missile capability, the willingness of the United States to invoke massive retaliation is declining, and that therefore the deterrent to aggression has weakened. Yet the Europeans do not embrace the logical consequence of this fear: the need to build up an adequate capacity to defend Europe on the ground. A more favored alternative, at least in France, is the acquisition of an independent strategic nuclear capability. But when European governments project their imaginations forward to the day when the enemy's divisions cross their borders, do they really envisage themselves shooting off their few missiles against an enemy who would surely obliterate them in return? One doubts that they do, but this is not to say that it is irrational for them to acquire such weapons; they might be successful as a deterrent because of Soviet uncertainty as to whether they would be used, and Soviet unwillingness to incur the risk of their being used.

Further examples easily come to mind. For the sake of deterrence in Europe, we might wish to deploy the forces there as if they intended to respond to an attack with nuclear weapons; but this might not be the optimum deployment for defense once the attack has occurred, if the least-cost defense is a conventional one. For deterrence of limited aggressions in Asia, it might be best to deploy troops on the spot as a "plate-glass window." But for the most efficient and flexible defense against such contingencies, troops might better be concentrated in a central reserve, with transport facilities for moving them quickly to a threatened area.

As Bernard Brodie has written,[2] if the object of our strategic air forces is only deterrence, there is little point in developing "clean" bombs; since deterrence is to be effected by the threat of dire punishment, the dirtier the better. But if we also wish to minimize our own costs once the war has begun, we might wish to use bombs producing minimum fall-out, to encourage similar restraint in the enemy.

[2] Bernard Brodie, *Strategy in the Missile Age*, Princeton: Princeton University Press, 1959, p. 295.

For deterrence, it might be desirable to disperse elements of the Strategic Air Command to civilian airfields, thus increasing the number of targets which the enemy must hit if he is to achieve the necessary attrition of our retaliatory power by his first strike. However, this expedient might greatly increase the population damage we would suffer in the enemy's first strike, since most civilian airfields are located near large cities, assuming that the enemy would otherwise avoid hitting cities.

THE TECHNOLOGICAL REVOLUTION

The need to *choose* between deterrence and defense is largely the result of the development of nuclear and thermonuclear weapons and long-range airpower. Prior to these developments, the three primary functions of military force—to *punish* the enemy, to *deny* him territory (or to take it from him), and to *mitigate damage* to oneself— were embodied, more or less, in the same weapons. Deterrence was accomplished (to the extent that military capabilities were the instruments of deterrence) either by convincing the prospective aggressor that his territorial aim was likely to be frustrated, or by posing for him a prospect of intolerable cost, or both, but both of these deterrent functions were performed by the *same* forces. Moreover, these same forces were also the instruments of defense if deterrence failed.

Long-range airpower partially separated the function of punishment from the function of contesting the control of territory, by making possible the assault of targets far to the rear whose relation to the land battle might be quite tenuous. Nuclear weapons vastly increased the relative importance of prospective *cost* in deterring the enemy and reduced (relatively) the importance of frustrating his aggressive enterprise. It is still true, of course, that a capacity to deny territory to the enemy, or otherwise to block his aims, may be a very efficient deterrent. And such denial *may* be accomplished by strategic nuclear means, though at high cost to the defender. But it is now conceivable that a prospective aggressor may be deterred, in some circumstances at least, solely or primarily by threatening and possessing the capability to inflict extreme punishment on his homeland assets and population, even though he may be superior in capabilities for contesting the control of territory. Nuclear powers must, therefore, exercise a conscious choice between the objectives of deterrence and defense, since the relative proportion of "punishment capacity" to "denial capacity" in their military establishments has become a matter of choice.

This is the most striking difference between nuclear and prenuclear strategy: the partial separation of the functions of pre-attack deterrence and post-attack defense, and the possibility that deterrence may now be accomplished by weapons which might have no rational use for defense should deterrence fail.

DETERRENCE

Deterrence, in one sense, is simply the negative aspect of political power; it is the power to dissuade as opposed to the power to coerce or compel. One deters another party from doing something by the implicit or explicit threat of applying some sanction if the forbidden act is performed, or by the promise of a reward if the act is not performed. Thus conceived, deterrence does not have to depend on military force. We might speak of deterrence by the threat of trade restrictions, for example. The promise of economic aid might deter a country from military action (or any action) contrary to one's own interests. Or we might speak of the deterrence of allies and neutrals as well as potential enemies—as Italy, for example, was deterred from fighting on the side of the Dual Alliance in World War I by the promise of substantial territorial gains. In short, deterrence may follow, first, from any form of control which one has over an opponent's present and prospective "value inventory"; secondly, from the communication of a credible threat or promise to decrease or increase that inventory; and, thirdly, from the opponent's degree of confidence that one intends to fulfill the threat or promise.

In an even broader sense, however, deterrence is a function of the *total* cost-gain expectations of the party to be deterred, and these may be affected by factors other than the apparent capability and intention of the deterrer to apply punishments or confer rewards. For example, an incipient aggressor may be inhibited by his own conscience, or, more likely, by the prospect of losing moral standing, and hence political standing, with uncommitted countries. Or, in the specific case of the Soviet Union, he may fear that war will encourage unrest in, and possibly dissolution of, his satellite empire, and perhaps disaffection among his own population. He may anticipate that his aggression would bring about a tighter welding of the Western alliance or stimulate a degree of mobilization in the West which would either reduce his own security or greatly increase the cost of maintaining his position in the arms race. It is also worth noting that the benchmark or starting point for the potential aggressor's calculation of costs and gains from military action is not his *existing* value inventory, but the extent to which he expects that inventory to be changed if he refrains from initiating military action. Hence, the common observation that the Russians are unlikely to undertake overt military aggression because their chances are so good for making gains by "indirect" peaceful means. Conceivably the Soviets might attack the United States, even though they foresaw greater costs than gains, if the alternative of not attacking seemed to carry within it a strong possibility that the United States would strike them first and, in doing so, inflict greater costs on the Soviet Union than it could by means of retaliation after the Soviets had struck first. In a (very abstract) nutshell, the potential aggressor presumably is deterred from a military move not simply when his expected cost exceeds his expected gain, but when the net gain is less or the net loss is more than he can expect if he refrains from the move. But this formulation must be qualified by the simple fact of inertia: deliberately to shift from a condition of peace to a condition of war is an extremely momentous decision, involving incalculable consequences, and a government is not likely to make this decision unless it foresees a very large advantage in doing so. The great importance of *uncertainty* in this context will be discussed below.

In a broad sense, deterrence operates during war as well as prior to war. It could be defined as a process of influencing the enemy's *intentions*, whatever the circumstances, violent or non-violent. Typically, the outcome of wars has not depended simply on the clash of physical capabilities. The losing side usually accepts defeat somewhat before it has lost its physical ability to continue fighting. It is deterred from continuing the war by a realization that continued fighting can only generate additional costs without hope of compensating gains, this expectation being largely the consequence of the previous application of force by the dominant side. In past wars, such deterrence usually has been characteristic of the terminal stages. However, in the modern concept of limited war, the intentions factor is more prominent and pervasive; force may be threatened and used partly or even primarily, as a bargaining instrument to persuade the opponent to accept terms of settlement or to observe certain limitations. Deterrence in war is most sharply illustrated in proposals for a strategy of limited retaliation, in which initial strikes, in effect, would be *threats* of further strikes to come, designed to deter the enemy from further fighting. In warfare limited to conventional weapons or tactical nuclear weapons, the strategic nuclear forces held in reserve by either side may constitute a deterrent against the other side's expanding the intensity of its war effort. Also, limited wars may be fought in part with an eye to deterring future enemy attacks by convincing the enemy of one's general willingness to fight.

The above observations were intended to suggest the broad scope of the concept of deterrence, its non-limitation to military factors, and its fundamental affinity to the idea of political power. In the discussion following, we shall use the term in a narrower sense, to mean the discouragement of the *initiation* of military aggression by the threat (implicit or explicit) of applying military force in response to the aggression. We shall assume that when deterrence fails and war begins, the attacked party is no longer "deterring" but rather "defending." Deterrence in war and deterrence, by military action, of subsequent aggressions will be considered as aspects of defense and will be treated later in this chapter.

The logic of deterrence. The object of military deterrence is to reduce the probability of enemy military attacks, by posing for the enemy a sufficiently likely prospect that he will suffer a net loss as a result of the attack, or at least a higher net loss or lower net gain than would follow from his not attacking. If we postulate two contending states, an "aggressor" (meaning potential aggressor) and a "deterrer," with other states which are objects of conflict between these two, the probability of any particular attack by the aggressor is the resultant of essentially four factors which exist in his "mind." All four taken together might be termed the aggressor's "risk calculus." They are (1) his valuation of his war objectives; (2) the cost which he expects to suffer as a result of various possible responses by the deterrer; (3) the probability of various responses, including "no response"; and (4) the probability of winning the objectives with each possible response. We shall assume, for simplicity's sake, that the deterrer's "response" refers to the deterrer's entire strategy of action throughout the war precipitated by the aggressor's move—i.e., not only the response to the initial aggressive move, but also to all subsequent moves by the aggressor. Thus the aggressor's estimate of costs and gains is a "whole war" estimate, depending on his image of the deterrer's entire sequence of moves up to the termination of the war, as well as on his own strategic plans for conducting the war, plans which may be contingent on what moves are made by the deterrer during the war.

Obviously, we are dealing here with factors which are highly subjective and uncertain, not subject to exact measurement, and not commensurate except in an intuitive way. Nevertheless, these are the basic factors which the potential aggressor must weigh in determining the probable costs and gains of his contemplated venture.

Certain generalizations can be made about the relationship among these factors. Factor 3 in the aggressor's calculus represents the "credibility" of various possible responses by the deterrer. But credibility is only one factor: it should not be equated with the deterrent *effectiveness* of a possible or threatened response, which is a function of all four factors—i.e., the net cost or gain which a response promises, discounted by the probability (credibility) of its being applied. An available response which is very low in credibility might be sufficient to deter if it poses a very severe sanction (e.g., massive retaliation) or if the aggressor's prospective gain carries very little value for him. Or a threatened response that carries a rather high credibility but poses only moderate costs for the aggressor—e.g., a conventional response, or nuclear retaliation after the aggressor has had the advantage of the first strategic strike—may not deter if the aggressor places a high value on his objective and anticipates a good chance of attaining it.

The credibility factor deserves special attention because it is in terms of this component that the risk calculus of the aggressor "interlocks" with that of the deterrer. The deterrer's risk calculus is similar to that of the aggressor. If the deterrer is rational, his response to aggression will be determined (within the limits, of course, of the military forces he disposes) largely by four factors: (1) his valuation of the territorial objective and of the other intangible gains (e.g., moral satisfaction) which he associates with a given response; (2) the estimated costs of fighting; (3) the probability of successfully holding the territorial objective and other values at stake; and (4) the change in the probability of future enemy attacks on other objectives which would follow from various responses. Variations on, and marginal additions to, these factors may be imagined, but these four are the essential ones. The deterrer will select the response which minimizes his expectation of cost or maximizes his expectation of gain. (As in the case of the aggressor's calculus, we assume that the deterrer's estimates of cost and gain are "whole war" estimates—i.e., the aggregate effects not only of the deterrer's initial response, but also of all the aggressor's countermoves, combined with the deterrer's counter-countermoves, over the entire progress of the war.) The credibility of various possible responses by the deterrer depends on the aggressor's image of the deterrer's risk calculus—i.e., of the latter's net costs and gains from each response—as well as on the aggressor's assessment of the deterrer's capacity to act rationally.

The aggressor, of course, is not omniscient with respect to the deterrer's estimates of cost and gain. Even the deterrer will be unable to predict in advance of the attack how he will visualize his cost-gain prospects and, hence, exactly what response he will choose once the aggression is under way. (Witness the United States response to the North Korean attack in 1950, which was motivated by values which apparently did not become clear to the decision-makers until the actual crisis was upon them.) Nor can the aggressor be sure the deterrer will act rationally according to his own cost-gain predictions. Because of these uncertainties, the aggressor's estimate of credibility cannot be precise. More than one response will be possible, and the best the aggressor can do is attempt to guess how the deterrer will visualize his gains and losses consequent upon each response, and from this guess arrive at a judgment about the likelihood or probability of each possible response.

The deterrer evaluates the *effectiveness* of his deterrent posture by attempting to guess the values of the four factors in the aggressor's risk calculus. In estimating the credibility factor, he attempts to guess how the aggressor is estimating the factors in *his* (the deterrer's) calculus. He arrives at some judgment as to whether the aggresor is likely to expect a net cost or net gain from the aggressive move and, using this judgment and his degree of confidence in it as a basis, he determines the probability of aggression. Happily, the spiral of "guesses about the other's guesses" seems to stop here. In other words, the aggressor's decision whether or not to attack is not in turn affected by his image of the deterrer's estimate of the likelihood of attack. He knows that once the attack is launched the deterrer will select the response which promises him the least cost or greatest gain—at that point, the deterrer's previous calculations about "deterrence" of that attack become irrelevant.

Denial vs. punishment. It is useful to distinguish between deterrence which results from capacity to deny territorial gains to the enemy, and deterrence by the threat and capacity to inflict nuclear punishment. Denial capabilites—typically, conventional ground, sea, and tactical air forces—deter chiefly by their effect on the fourth factor in the aggressor's calculus: his estimate of the probability of gaining his objective. Punishment capabilities—typically, strategic nuclear power for either massive or limited retaliation—act primarily on the second factor, the aggressor's estimate of possible costs, and may have little effect on his chances for territorial gain. Of course, this distinction is not sharp or absolute; a "denial" response, especially if it involves the use of nuclear weapons tactically, can mean high direct costs, plus the risk that the war may get out of hand and ultimately involve severe nuclear punishment for both sides. This prospect of cost and risk may exert a significant deterring effect. A "punishment" response, if powerful enough, may foreclose territorial gains, and limited reprisals may be able to force a settlement short of complete conquest of the territorial objective. However, there are some differences worth noting between these two types or strategies of deterrence.

Apart from their differential impact on the cost and gain elements of the aggressor's calculations, the two types of response are likely to differ also in their credibility or probability of application. As a response to all-out nuclear attack on the deterrer, the application of punishment will be highly credible. But for lesser challenges, such as a conventional attack on an ally, a threat to inflict nuclear punishment normally will be less credible than a threat to fight a "denial" action —assuming, of course, that denial capabilities are available. While the making of a *threat* of nuclear punishment may be desirable and rational, its *fulfillment* is likely to seem irrational after the aggressor has committed his forces, since punishment alone may not be able to hold the territorial objective and will stimulate the aggressor to make counterreprisals. The deterrer therefore has a strong incentive to renege on his threat. Realizing this in advance, the aggressor may not think the threat a very credible one. A threat of denial action will seem more credible on two counts: it is less costly for the deterrer and it may be effective in frustrating the aggressor's aims, or at least in reducing his gains. A denial response is more likely than resprisal action to promise a rational means of *defense* in case deterrence fails; this consideration supports its credibility as a deterrent.

A related difference is that the threat of denial action is likely to be appraised by the aggressor in terms of the deterrer's *capabilities*; threats of nuclear punishment require primarily a judgment of *intent*. It is fairly certain that the deterrer will fight a threatened denial action if he has appropriate forces;[3] the essential question for the aggressor, therefore, is whether these forces are strong enough to prevent him from making gains. In the case of nuclear reprisals, however, the capability to inflict unacceptable punishment is likely to be unquestioned, at least for large nuclear powers; here the aggressor must attempt to look into the mind of the deterrer and guess whether the will to apply punishment exists. Thus a denial threat is much more calculable for the aggressor than a reprisal threat—assuming that a comparison of military capabilities is easier than mind-reading. This may make a denial strategy the more powerful deterrent of the two if the deterrer has strong denial forces; but if he obviously does not have enough ground and tactical forces to block conquest, the threat may be weaker than a nuclear reprisal threat. Even if there is doubt in the aggressor's mind that the reprisals will be carried out, these doubts may be offset by the possible severity of his punishment if he miscalculates and the threat is fulfilled. . . .

DEFENSE[4]

The deterrer, in choosing his optimum military and threat posture in advance of war, must estimate not only the effectiveness of that posture for deterrence, but also the consequences for himself should deterrence fail. In short, he is interested in defense as well as in deterrence; his security is a function of both of these elements. Capabilities and threats which produce a high level of deterrence may not yield a high degree of security because they promise very high costs and losses for the deterrer should war occur. . . .

Strategic value and deterrent value. Much of the inconclusiveness of the recurring "great debates" about military policy might be avoided if the concept of "strategic value" could be clarified and clearly separated from the deterrent effects of military action. The strategic

---

[3] It is possible that the aggressor may be able to deter "denial" resistance by threatening to take punitive action if resistance occurs. This is perhaps most feasible with respect to allies of the country attacked whose troops are not deployed on the territory of the victim.

[4] The reader is reminded that I am using the word "defense" in a rather special sense, which is narrower than one ordinary usage of the term and broader than another. Obviously it is narrower than the usage which makes "defense" synonymous with all military preparedness. It is broader, however, than "capacity to hold territory in case of attack," which I would prefer to call "denial capability."

value of a particular piece of territory is the effect which its loss would have on increasing the enemy's *capability* to make various future moves, and on decreasing our own capacity to resist further attacks. The deterrent value of defending or attempting to defend that piece of territory is the effect of the defense on the enemy's *intention* to make future moves. The failure to recognize this distinction contributed to the apparent about-face in United States policy toward South Korea, when we decided to intervene after the North Korean attack in June 1950. Earlier, the Joint Chiefs of Staff had declared that South Korea had no strategic value—apparently meaning that its loss would have no significant effect on the U.S. capacity to fight a general war with the Soviet Union. This determination was thought to justify—or at least was used as a rationalization for—the withdrawal of U.S. combat forces from the Korean peninsula in 1948 and 1949. Secretary of State Dean Acheson strengthened the impression that "no strategic value" meant "no value" when, in a speech early in 1950, he outlined a U.S. "defense perimeter" in the Far East which excluded Korea. Then when the North Koreans, perhaps encouraged by these high-level U.S. statements, attacked in June 1950, the United States government suddenly discovered that it had a deterrent interest, as well as strong political and intrinsic interests, in coming to the rescue of South Korea. The dominant theme in the discussions leading up to the decision to intervene was that if the Communists were "appeased" this time, they would be encouraged to make further attacks on other areas.[5] The chief motive behind the intervention was to prevent such encouragement from taking place, and positively to deter similar attempts in the future.

[5] As former President Truman has stated: "Our allies and friends abroad were informed through our diplomatic representatives that it was our feeling that it was essential to the maintenance of peace that this armed aggression against a free nation be met firmly. We let it be known that we considered the Korean situation vital as a symbol of the strength and determination of the West. Firmness now would be the only way to deter new actions in other portions of the world. Not only in Asia but in Europe, the Middle East, and elsewhere the confidence of peoples in countries adjacent to the Soviet Union would be very adversely affected, in our judgment, if we failed to take action to protect a country established under our auspices and confirmed in its freedom by action of the United Nations. If, however, the threat to South Korea was met firmly and successfully, it would add to our successes in Iran, Berlin and Greece a fourth success in opposition to the aggressive moves of the Communists. And each success, we suggested to our allies, was likely to add to the caution of the Soviets in undertaking new efforts of this kind. Thus the safety and prospects for peace of the free world would be increased." Harry S. Truman, *Years of Trial and Hope*, New York: Doubleday and Co., 1956, pp. 339-40.

The primary political value of the intervention, as U.S. decisionmakers saw it, was that it would give other free nations confidence that they could count on U.S. aid in resisting aggression. The most salient intrinsic values were moral value in opposing the aggressive use of force, support for the "rule of law" in international affairs, support for the collective security system embodied in the United Nations Charter, and the special responsibility the United States felt for the Republic of Korea, whose government it had played a major role in establishing. "Support for the collective security system" of course had deterrent and political as well as moral overtones.

Another case in point was the debate about the desirability of a United States commitment to defend the Chinese offshore islands of Quemoy and Matsu. Those who took the negative in this debate stressed that these two small islands held no "strategic value" for the United States, that they were not "vital" to the defense of Formosa, etc. Former Secretary of State Dean Acheson declared that the islands were not worth a single American life.[6] Administration spokesmen, on the other hand, emphasized the political and deterrent value of defending Quemoy and Matsu. President Eisenhower, for example, said that this country's allies "would be appalled if the United States were spinelessly to retreat before the threat of Sino-Soviet armed aggression."[7] Secretary of State Dulles asserted that the stakes were not "just some square miles of real estate," but the preservation of confidence in other countries—both allies and enemies—that the United States would resist aggression. It was better to meet the challenge at the beginning, Mr. Dulles said, than after "our friends become disheartened and our enemies overconfident and miscalculating."[8]

Power values are sometimes discussed in terms of the "falling domino" theory. According to this reasoning, if one objective is lost to the enemy, other areas contiguous to the first one inevitably will be lost as well, then still additional areas contiguous to these, etc., as a whole row of dominoes will fall when the first one is knocked over.[9] In its extreme form, the domino thesis would value any objective, no matter how small, as dearly as the value which the United States placed on the continued independence of all other non-Communist countries. Thus we should be as willing to fight for one place as another, since a failure to resist once inevitably means future losses. The important thing is to "draw a line" and resist violations of the line, whatever their dimensions and wherever and whenever they may occur.

The domino theory tends to overstate power values: since the enemy may have limited aims and may be satisfied with a small gain, his increase in capability from a single small conquest may not significantly shift the balance of capabilities in his favor, and the loss of single small areas may not have adverse political effects among

[6] *New York Times,* October 3, 1958, p. 3.
[7] *Ibid.,* October 5, 1958, p. 1.
[8] *Ibid.,* September 26, 1958, p. 1.
[9] Apparently the domino theory was first given public expression by President Eisenhower on April 7, 1954, when he said, in reply to a request that he explain the strategic value of Indo-China to the United States: "You had a row of dominoes set up, and you knocked over the first one, and what would happen to the last one was the certainty that it would go over very quickly. So you could have a beginning of a disintegration that would have the most profound influences." The President then referred to "the possible sequence of events, the loss of Indo-China, of Burma, of Thailand, of the peninsula, and Indonesia following." *Ibid.,* April 8, 1954, p. 18.

neutrals and allies. [10] Nevertheless, the domino image does highlight an important truth: the strategic and intrinsic value of the immediate territorial prize is not a sufficient criterion for evaluating the wisdom of resisting aggression, or for estimating the forces necessary for successful resistance. The enemy's possible ultimate objective must also be considered, as well as the effect of resistance in discouraging him from attempting further progress toward that objective, and in forestalling political changes among other countries which would tend to further that ultimate objective.

There is a relationship between the strategic, political, and intrinsic value which the enemy believes one attaches to a given objective, and the deterrent value which can be realized by responding to an attack on that objective. For example, a failure to resist effectively a Communist attack on the offshore islands of Quemoy and Matsu might not increase perceptibly the chances of Chinese Communist attacks on other non-Communist countries in Asia, if the Communists did not believe we placed a high intrinsic and strategic value on these islands. On the other hand, it could be argued that a determined and costly response to an attack on an objective which the enemy thinks means little to us in strategic and intrinsic terms is likely to give him greater pause with respect to his future aggressive intentions. Thus, if the objective is to "draw a line" to deter future aggression, perhaps the best place to draw it is precisely at places like Quemoy and Matsu. The enemy would reason that if the United States were willing to fight for a place of such trivial intrinsic and strategic value to itself, it must surely be willing to fight for other places of greater value. Thus, the deterrent value of defending any objective varies inversely with the enemy's perception of its value to us on other accounts. There is a further consideration: if it is thought necessary to fight a certain amount of war, or risk a certain amount of war, to convince the other side of our willingness to fight generally, what better place to do it than at places like Quemoy and Matsu, where it is least likely that the war will spiral to all-out dimensions?

Mutually shared expectations are extremely important in determining the deterrent value of military actions. The United States did not lose much in deterrent utility by failing to intervene in Hungary in 1956, because both sides regarded Hungary as part of the Communist camp. But a failure to defend Berlin would severely undermine the U.S. capability to deter future Communist incursions in Europe or elsewhere.

[10] It is hard to believe, for example, that a Communist Chinese conquest of Quemoy and Matsu would have reduced the confidence of the European allies in the willingness of the United States to defend Europe. The solidarity of NATO might have been weakened by a U.S. attempt to defend the islands.

The consequences of enemy moves, and the defense value of forces for resisting them, are subject to modification by policy declarations. Threats and commitments may involve one's honor and prestige in a particular area or objective, and this involvement increases the deterrent, political, and intrinsic value of defending such places and the value of forces which are able to defend. Thus the adverse consequences of an unresisted Communist attack on Quemoy and Matsu were increased by the various official statements, including the Formosa Resolution passed by Congress, to the effect that these offshore islands were "related" to the defense of Formosa. But these consequences were not increased as much as they might have been, had the United States made an unequivocal commitment to defend the islands.

Of course, losses of power values through the loss of an ally or neutral to the enemy may be offset by increased mobilization of domestic resources. The cost of the additional mobilization required might be taken as a measure of the power value of the territory in question. Thus the defending power might ask itself: "If I let this piece of territory or this ally be taken over by the enemy, how many additional resources will I have to spend for military weapons to have the same degree of security I have been enjoying?"

Once war is entered into, consideration of deterrent possibilities may call for a different strategy than would be the case if we were interested only in the strategic and intrinsic values of the particular area attacked. If the latter were our only interest, our war aims might be limited to restoration of the *status quo ante*; deterrence of future aggressions, however, might dictate more ambitious aims. In the Korean War, for example, it is possible that if closer consideration had been given to deterrent benefits, the U.N. armies might have pushed on farther than they did—if not to the Yalu, then perhaps at least to the "narrow neck" of the Korean peninsula. The opportunity was not taken to show the Communists that their aggressions were likely to result in losses not only of manpower but also of territory; that in future limited wars they could not hope to end up at least where they started.

In general, we will be willing to suffer higher costs in fighting a limited war if deterrence is an objective than if it is not. In other words, it may be desirable to fight on longer and in the face of a higher cost expectancy if an important objective is to assure the enemy of our willingness to suffer costs in future contingencies.

The objective of deterrence may call for the use of different weapons than would the simple objective of blocking enemy conquest of an area at least cost. Our use of nuclear weapons probably would support the Communist estimate of our willingness to use them in the future; and, conversely, to refrain from using them when such use would be militarily advantageous would weaken that estimate.

However, as in the decision whether or not to fight at all, the strategic and intrinsic value of the immediate objective is relevant to the deterrent effects: the use of nuclear weapons to defend highly valued objectives might support but little the probability that they would be used to meet lesser challenges;[11] the failure to use them when the prize was small would not necessarily signal a reluctance to do so when the object of the conflict was vital.

Finally, for deterrent reasons it might be desirable to *attempt* resistance against a particular limited enemy attack even though we knew in advance that our resistance would fail. The purpose would be to inform the enemy, for future reference, that although he could expect to make gains from limited aggression in the future, these gains could be had only at a price which (we hoped) the enemy would not want to pay. Proposals for limited nuclear retaliation against one or a few enemy cities in response to limited ground aggression may draw on this kind of reasoning.

Of course, the concept of "deterrence by action" has no relevance in determining the appropriate response to a direct thermonuclear attack on the United States, or in valuing the forces for the response. In that event there would be no future contingencies which would seem worth deterring or worrying about at all, compared with the magnitude of the catastrophe which had already taken place. The primary values would be intrinsic values associated with reducing war damage, perhaps limiting the enemy's territorial gains in Eurasia, and preserving the independence of the United States itself.[12]

Power values lost by the defender represent power values gained by the attacker, although the values may not be equally important to each side. For example, the Middle East has strategic value for the United States because its geographic location and resources add significantly to the West's capacity to fight limited war in Europe and elsewhere, and because the area, in the hands of the Soviets, would increase the Soviets' capacity to fight such wars—because of its position athwart vital transportation routes if not because of its oil resources. Our strategic loss if the Middle East should fall under Communist control would be the sum of the deprivation to the West's future military capabilities and the increment to the Soviet capabilities. Similarly, the strategic gain to the Soviets would be the sum of their own direct gain in military resources plus the losses for the West.

[11] On the other hand, any use of nuclear weapons would set a precedent. The symbolic or psychological barrier to their use which had rested on their previous non-use would be eroded. The Russians might believe, after they had been used once, that the probability of their use in *any* future conflict had increased.

[12] We might, of course, attempt to "deter" the enemy from continuing his attacks, thus reducing our war costs and perhaps preserving our independence and the essential fabric of our society, by a discriminating use of the weapons we had left after absorbing a surprise attack, accompanied by appropriate bargaining tactics. . . .

It is less obvious that deterrent values also have this reciprocal character. When, by fighting in Korea, we demonstrated our willingness to defend free institutions in Asia, not only did we gain "deterrent value" with respect to other possible Communist moves in Asia; the Communists lost something analogous to it in their own value system. Presumably they became less confident that overt aggression could be attempted again without U.S. intervention. Their "expected value" from future aggressive moves declined perhaps below what it was before Korea, and certainly below what it would have been if the North Korean aggression had been unopposed by the United States.

When an aggressor state successfully completes a conquest, or has its demands satisfied short of war, its willingness in the future to make war, or to make demands at the risk of war, presumably is strengthened by the reduction of expected cost or risk which it perceives in such future moves. This reduction in the perceived chances of being opposed in the future we might label "expectation value," to differentiate it from "deterrent value," which is peculiarly associated with *status quo* powers. Deterrent and expectational values are in obverse relationship—i.e., when the defender loses deterrent value by failing to fight or to carry out a threat, the aggressor gains expectational value, and vice versa—although again the gain or loss may have a stronger psychological impact on one side than on the other, since the value in question is highly subjective.

This distinction is similar to Thomas Schelling's distinction between "compellent" and "deterrent" threats.[13] A compellent threat is used in an aggressive way; it is designed to persuade the opponent to give up some value. A deterrent threat, on the other hand, is intended to dissuade the opponent from initiating some positive action. A successful conquest would increase an aggressor's compellent power with respect to other possible victims, especially if the fighting had included the use of nuclear weapons; other countries would lose deterrent power, since their psychological capacity to resist demands would be weakened by the aggressor's demonstration of willingness to risk or to undertake nuclear war.

Strategic gains by the Soviets might appear in their risk calculus as an increased probability that future attacks on other areas would be successful, or perhaps as a decreased expectation of cost in making future conquests. Gains in expectational value would appear as a decreased probability of resistance to future attacks, or perhaps as a reduced probability of a high-cost response by the defender or its allies. The aggregate of strategic gains and expectational gains pro-

[13] Thomas C. Schelling, *The Strategy of Conflict*, Cambridge: Harvard University Press, 1960, pp. 195-196.

duces an increase in "expected value" to be gained from future moves (or a reduction in "expected cost").

This might not always be the case if the consequence of a successful aggression were to stimulate an increased level of military mobilization by the United States and its allies and/or an increased determination to resist future attacks. Thus a successful limited attack might backfire and *reduce* the Soviets' strategic position as well as their expectational value, although of course they would retain whatever intrinsic values they had gained by their conquest. . . .

THE NEW BALANCE OF POWER

. . . The existence of a balance of power, or the capabilities requirements for balancing, can hardly be determined without attempting to look into the "mind" of the enemy. One might say that a subjective "balance of intentions" has become at least as important as the more objectively calculable "balance of capabilities."

A corollary of the increased relative importance of intentions is that methods of communicating intent have become more important *means* in the balancing process than they have been in the past. First, nations are becoming more sensitive to what they say to each other about their intentions; the psychological importance of threats and other declarations is on the increase. Secondly, the function of military forces themselves may be shifting in the direction of a demonstrative role: the signaling of future intentions to use force in order to influence the enemy's intentions, as opposed to being ready to use, or using force simply as a physical means of conquest or denial. Hence the enhanced importance of *deterrence* in the modern balance of power as compared with *defense*. We are likely to see more imaginative and subtle uses of "force demonstration" in time of peace. . . . Warfare itself may in the future become less a raw physical collision of military forces and more a contest of wills, or a bargaining process, with military force being used largely to demonstrate one's willingness to raise the intensity of fighting, with the object of inducing the enemy to accept one's terms of settlement. While direct conflict or competition is going on at a low level of the spectrum of violence, selective force demonstrations using means appropriate to higher levels may take place as threats to "up the ante." . . .

Explaining Military Doctrine

BARRY POSEN

MILITARY ORGANIZATIONS AND MILITARY DOCTRINE

Hypotheses—Offense, Defense, and Deterrence

Most soldiers and many civilians are intuitively attracted to the offense as somehow the stronger form of war. Clausewitz, often misconstrued as the apostle of the offensive, was very mindful of the advantages of a defensive strategy. He called defense "the stronger form of war." However, every aspect of his work that *could be taken* as offensive advocacy has been so taken. What accounts for such systematic misinterpretation?

Uncertainty Reduction

Military organizations will generally prefer offensive doctrines because they *reduce uncertainty* in important ways.

1. The need for standard scenarios encourages military organizations to prefer offensive doctrines. In order to have a set of SOPs* and programs, they must plan for a "standard scenario." Once SOPs and programs have been tailored to such a scenario, the organization, in order to be "fought"—used in combat—must be used with those SOPs and programs. If the organization is to be "fought" successfully, it must respond to command in predictable ways. Commanders must have orders to give that generate predictable responses. Thus, it is strongly in the interests of a military organization to impose its "standard scenario" on the adversary through offensive action before the adversary does the same to it.

2. Warfare is an extremely competitive endeavor. Its most successful practitioners strive for even the smallest advantages. Thus, military organizations seem to prefer offensive doctrines not only because they appear to guarantee the side on the offense its standard scenario, but because they also *deny* the enemy his standard scenario. A military organization prefers to fight its own war and

From *The Sources of Military Doctrine: France, Britain and Germany Between the World Wars* by Barry R. Posen, pp. 47–80. Copyright 1984 by Cornell University Press. Used by permission of the publisher, Cornell University Press. Portions of the text and some footnotes have been omitted.
*Editors' Note: SOPs are shorthand for Standard Operating Procedures.

prevent its adversary from doing so. Taking the offensive, exercising the initiative, is a way of structuring the battle. The advantages seen to lie with surprise are more than psychological. An organization fighting the war that it planned is likely to do better than one that is not. For example, in the Arab attack on Israel in 1973, Egyptian and Syrian preparations were aimed at imposing an uncongenial style of warfare on Israel.

Defensive warfare might also seem to allow an organization to structure the battle. However, the defending organization is often in a reactive position, improvising new programs to cope with the adversary's initiative. If the defending organization is, for whatever reasons, a fast learner, it may rapidly improvise countermeasures that destroy the offender's programs. (The Israel Defense Forces achieved this with their Suez Canal crossing in 1973.) This leaves both organizations fighting a battle of improvisation which both would probably prefer to avoid. Victory goes to the most flexible command structure. Generally, however, professional soldiers appear to believe that striking the first blow is beneficial because, at least initially, it reduces the attacker's necessity to improvise and the defender's ability to improvise. This military judgment may reflect an implicit understanding that military organizations are not fast learners, precisely because they are the structured systems portrayed earlier. The perceived advantage of taking the offensive is thus magnified.

3. Because predicting whose national will can be broken first is a political task, not susceptible to the analytical skills of a military organization, military organizations dislike deterrent doctrines. Punishment warfare, conventional or nuclear, tends not to address an adversary's capabilities, but his will. Calculating in advance of a war whose will is likely to break first is inherently somewhat more difficult for a military organization than devising plausible scenarios for destroying enemy capabilities. Calculations of enemy determination demand an entirely different set of skills than those commanded by a military organization. Calculations about military outcomes are at least somewhat susceptible to "engineering" criteria; calculations of relative will are not. However, this argument may be a weak one. There are more powerful reasons why military organizations do not favor deterrent doctrines.

4. Military organizations will prefer offensive doctrines because they help increase organizational size and wealth. Size and wealth help reduce internal uncertainty by increasing the rewards that the organization can distribute to its members. Size and wealth help reduce external uncertainty by providing a buffer against unforeseen events such as huge losses or partial defeats.

While the offensive allows the attacking force to be more certain of how its organization will perform, and to deny that certainty to an adversary, the offensive is likely to be technically more complex, quantitatively more demanding. There are many extra contingencies for which an offensive military instrument must be prepared. An attacking army encounters natural obstacles that must be crossed, creating a demand for engineers. Fortifications encountered may demand more and heavier artillery for their reduction. The offensive army may have to go anywhere, requiring special technical capabilities in its equipment. Nothing can be specialized for the environment of the home country. Aircraft need greater range and payload. All of these factors require an extensive logistics capability to uncoil behind the advancing military force. Troops will be required to guard and defend this line of communication. Operations at range will impose greater wear and tear on the equipment—demanding large numbers in reserve, and still more support capability. While various characteristics of geography, politics, and technology might place these same demands on a defensive force, as a general rule offensive doctrines impose them to a greater extent. Deterrent doctrines offer the most minimal material opportunities for military organizations. This is partly because they are more dependent on political will than on military capabilities. Partly it is a result of the clarity of the punishment mission, which allows rather extreme specialization.

5. Military organizations will prefer offensive doctrines because they enhance military autonomy. As noted earlier, civilian intervention in operational matters can be a key source of uncertainty for military organizations. Offensive doctrines tend to be more complicated than defensive or deterrent doctrines, and thus increase the difficulties for civilians who wish to understand military matters. Defense and deterrence are relatively easy for civilians to master. Deterrent warfare with nuclear weapons has consistently proved to be the easiest form of warfare for civilian analysts to understand in the post-war period. Deterrent warfare by means of popular resistance—extended guerrilla action, for example—depends so heavily on the legitimacy of the government and its authority over its people that it may be the highest form of political-military warfare. Defense or denial does not present the complications of the offensive, and again includes such strong cooperation with civilian authorities as to restrict the operational autonomy of the army. The offensive, however, can be waged off national soil, and therefore immediately involves less civilian interference. Offensive operations are elaborate combinations of forces and strategems—more art than science. Denial is more straightforward, and punishment is simplest of all. From specialists in victory, defense turns soldiers into specialists in attrition, and deterrence makes them specialists in slaughter.

There is little in organization theory or the civil-military relations literature to suggest that modern militaries will prefer anything but offensive doctrines, if such doctrines are in any way feasible.

Geography

6. Organization theory suggests a somewhat muted geographical influence on military doctrine. (The influence of technology will be discussed below.) Where geography can plausibly be argued to favor an offensive doctrine, it reinforces the organizational tendencies outlined above. For instance, it has become commonplace to explain the affinity of Prussia-Germany (in the past) and Israel (in the present) for offensive doctrines by their a) being surrounded and outnumbered by powerful enemies and b) enjoying the advantage of interior lines (with the ability to shift forces quickly from one front to another). Thus, the sequential defeat of the members of an enemy coalition with a series of rapid offensives, before they can pull their forces together and coordinate an attack, is deemed to be very attractive. Presumably, any state finding itself in a similar position would agree.

One less often finds the reverse argued—that some particular geographic configuration generally and sensibly leads to a defensive military doctrine. At the level of grand strategy, of course, both Britain and the United States have exploited the defensive advantage bestowed by ocean barriers. Yet, the navies of both powers have periodically argued for offensive military strategies to achieve "command of the sea." They usually have been constrained to operate in a more limited fashion, but the preference for the offensive, even in situations where it seems unreasonable, is striking.

Numerous examples of military organizations that undervalue the defensive utility of geography can be found. British colonial soldiers in India viewed Afghanistan as a potential Russian invasion route, and sought to control it. Yet, one British military expedition after another met with disaster brought on by wild Afghan raiders, treacherous terrain and weather, and long distances. This stark evidence of the area's unsuitability as an invasion route was ignored, as subsequent expeditions were deemed necessary. In World War I the Russians underrated the defensive value of the Masurian Lakes to the Germans. The lakes ultimately split the large Russian force, allowing a smaller German army to defeat it piecemeal. At the outset of World War I the British dispatched a small force to Persia, to guard the Abadan oil facilities. Its commanders opted for an attack on Baghdad, a distant objective for which the force was woefully inadequate. Currently, the U.S. Navy advocates an offensive strategy against Soviet Naval forces based in the Barents Sea and Murmansk—a tough and distant target. NATO has geographic choke points off the Norwegian North Cape, and in the Greenland-Iceland-United Kingdom Gap, that provide a powerful defensive advantage against any Soviet naval offensive, and all but obviate the need for an offensive against the north. In short, organization theory suggests that geographic factors that support offensive doctrines will more often be correctly assessed than those that support a defensive doctrine. History seems to confirm this observation.

*Hypotheses—Integration**

It was over a century and a half ago that Clausewitz made his now famous remarks on the relationship of war to policy. Most simply, "war is not a mere act of policy but a true political instrument, a continuation of political activity by other means." Political considerations reach into the military means, to influence *"the planning of war, of the campaign, and often even of the battle"* (my emphasis). Clausewitz clearly believed that statesmen could and should ensure that policy infuse military operations. Those in charge of policy require "a certain grasp of military affairs." They need not be soldiers, however. "What is needed in the post is distinguished intellect and character. He [the statesman] can always get the necessary military information somehow or other." Clausewitz was over-optimistic on this score. Few have challenged his judgment that policy must infuse acts of war, but the achievement of this goal has proven more difficult than he imagined. . . .

Functional specialization between soldiers and statesmen, and the tendency of soldiers to seek as much independence from civilian interference as possible, combine to make political-military integration an uncertain prospect. These two fundamental aspects of state structure and organization lead to the following deductions:

1. As a rule, soldiers are not going to go out of their way to reconcile the means they employ with the ends of state policy. This is not necessarily to argue that they deliberately try to disconnect their means from political ends. Often, however, soldiers will elevate the narrow technical requirements of preferred operations above the needs of civilian policy. In the case of the European militaries prior to World War I, the single-minded pursuit of battlefield advantage closed off diplomatic options for statesmen.

2. This cause of disintegration is exacerbated because military organizations are unwilling to provide civilian authorities with information that relates to doctrinal questions, especially those having the most to do with the actual conduct of operations. Thus, civilians

---

*Editors' Note: By integration (and disintegration), Posen means how well (and how poorly) suited a nation's military forces and doctrine are to its foreign policy goals.

are simply unaware of the ways military doctrine may conflict with the ends of state policy. Policy-makers may simply not know enough about the operational practices of their military organizations to either alter their political strategy or force changes in military doctrine that would bring it in line with the existing political strategy. Nevertheless, in spite of the limits of information, organization theory would seem to suggest that if political-military integration is to be achieved, civilian intervention into doctrinal matters is essential. The question is, given the obstacles, what is sufficient to cause civilian intervention? This is a question better answered by balance of power theory.

3. The setting of priorities among military forces and missions is a key aspect of political-military integration. In multiservice military organizations, civilian intervention is critical to the setting of priorities. This is another way civilian intervention causes integration. In chapter 1 it was argued that one of the tasks of grand strategy is to set priorities among threats and opportunities in the environment, and to set priorities among forces to match these threats and opportunities. Interpreting the external environment is the specialty of civilians. Building and operating military forces is the task of services. Setting priorities among the services, and among forces or branches within services, is a central task of grand strategy. Yet, the tendency of individuals within organizations to preserve the task and power of their organization or sub-organization suggests that *among* or *within* services the goal of autonomy should be just as strong as it is for the military as a whole. Thus, it is very difficult for a group of services to accomplish the task of setting priorities. The inclination of a group of services or sub-services to set priorities among themselves is going to be low.

In the absence of civilian intervention, and the exercise of the legitimate authority that only the civilians possess, militaries will arrange a "negotiated environment." This is likely to take the form of either preserving a customary budgetary split or dividing shares equally. Each service will prepare for its own war. Forces will not cooperate effectively. Neither will they be well balanced. A tendency will emerge for each service to set requirements as if it were fighting the war alone. This can easily result in misallocation of the scarce security resources of the state.

Left to themselves, a group of services cannot make a military doctrine that will be well integrated with the political aspects of the state's grand strategy. They can simply assemble a batch of service doctrines. This is less true within services, where higher authority can make allocation decisions. Even within services, priorities may not be set according to strategic criteria. A service doctrine may be as difficult to produce as an overall grand strategy. . . .

Hypotheses—Innovation in Military Doctrine

Obstacles

1. Because of the process of institutionalization, innovation in military doctrine should be rare. It will only occasionally be sponsored by the military organization itself. As already remarked, according to organization theory organizations try to control the behavior of their members in order to achieve purposes. One way of doing this is by distributing power through the organization so as to ensure that certain tasks will be accomplished. Individuals develop a vested interest in the distribution of power and in the purposes it protects. Generally, it is not in the interests of most of an organization's members to promote or succumb to radical change.

2. Innovations in military doctrine will be rare because they increase operational uncertainty. While innovation is in process, the organization's SOPs and programs will be in turmoil. The ability of commanders to "fight" the organization with confidence will decline. Should a war come during the transition, the organization will find itself between doctrines. Under combat conditions, even a bad doctrine may be better than no doctrine. It is possible to argue that the Prussians at Jena, the French in 1940, and the Russians in 1941 were taken in the midst of doctrinal transition.

3. Because of the obstacles to innovation discussed above, a technology that has not been tested in war can seldom function by itself as the catalyst for doctrinal innovation. Military organizations often graft new pieces of technology on to old doctrines. As Bernard Brodie has noted, "Conservatism of the military, about which we hear so much, seems always to have been confined to their adaptation to new weaponry rather than their acceptance of it."[1] . . . A new technology will normally be assimilated to an old doctrine rather than stimulate change to a new one. . . . This problem stems from the difficulty of proving anything about a new military technology without using it in a major war.

Causes of Innovation

In the military sphere, there are two exceptions to the preceding proposition that military organizations generally fail to innovate in response to new technology:

4. Military organizations do seem willing to learn from wars fought by their client states—with the weapons and perhaps the doctrine of the patron. Both the U.S. and Soviet militaries are willing to draw lessons from the 1973 Arab-Israeli war, although many of the "lessons" are not entirely clear.

[1] Bernard Brodie, "Technological Change, Strategic Doctrine, and Political Outcomes," in *Historical Dimensions,* ed. Knorr, p. 299.

5. Military organizations are even better able to learn about technology by using it in their own wars. Perhaps the best example of direct experience leading to correct appraisal of technology is found in the evolution of Prussian doctrine from 1850 to 1870. Prussia's attempted railroad mobilization against Austria in 1850 was a fiasco. Learning from the experience, the Prussians turned the railroad into an efficient war instrument by 1866. There are limits to the power of this proposition. In the American Civil War, frontline soldiers adjusted rapidly to the technological facts of modern firepower. They "dug in" whenever they had the chance. The generals understood the least, ordering frontal assaults against prepared positions throughout the war. The same occurred in World War I, with generals ordering repeated costly offensives. Bernard Brodie notes that the generals "seemed incapable of learning from experience, largely because of the unprecedented separation of the high command from the front lines." This seems a plausible explanation, and again is entirely consistent with organization theory. . . .

The preceding examples also offer insights into the relationship between technology and the offensive, defensive, or deterrent character of military doctrine. Most simply, if a military organization has adopted an offensive doctrine, or is bent on adopting one, technological lessons on the advantage of defense are likely to be ignored, corrupted, or suppressed. This is consistent with the argument advanced earlier concerning the probable offensive preferences of most military organizations.

Organization theory predicts at least two causes of innovation that are much stronger and more reliable in their operation than experience with new technology: (6) military organizations innovate when they have failed—suffered a defeat—and (7) they innovate when civilians intervene from without. These hypotheses can be deduced from the basic survival motive of large organizations. Failure to achieve their organizational purpose, the successful defense of the state, can cause military organizations to reexamine their basic doctrinal preferences. Similarly, soldiers may respond to the civilian intervention that defeat often precipitates in order to defend the organization's autonomy, which is under attack.

Failure and civilian intervention often go hand in hand. Soldiers fail; civilians get angry and scared; pressure is put on the military. Sometimes the pressure is indirect. Civilian leaders become disenchanted with the performance of one service and shift resources to another. These resources may provide the "slack" for the newly favored service to attempt some innovations. The loser strives to win back his lost position. Interservice rivalry in postwar America may have produced some benefits—a menu of innovations for policymakers. Arguably, interservice rivalry has been a major factor in the growth of the "Triad," which has on the whole increased U.S. security. Similarly, aggrandizement at the expense of another service may be a motive for innovation.

Although civilian intervention into military doctrine would seem to be a key determinant of innovation, it involves special problems. The division of labor between civilians and soldiers is intense. Civilians are not likely to have the capability to dream up whole new doctrines. Thus, civil intervention is dependent on finding sources of military knowledge. Civil intervention should take the form of choosing from the thin innovation menu thrown up by the services. In multiservice defense establishments, civilians have the possibility, depending on the strategic position of the state, of choosing among competing services. Within services, hierarchy and the chain of command should tend to suppress the emergence of new doctrinal alternatives at levels where the civilians cannot find them. None of this is to say that innovation in military doctrine is impossible. These are merely tendencies. . . .

Summary: Organization Theory Hypotheses

Offense, Defense, and Deterrence

1. The need for standard scenarios to reduce operational uncertainty encourages military organizations to prefer offensive doctrines.

2. The incentive, arising from the highly competitive nature of warfare, to deny an adversary his "standard scenario" encourages offensive doctrines.

3. The inability of military organizations to calculate comparative national will causes them to dislike deterrent doctrines.

4. Offensive doctrines will be preferred by military organizations because they increase organizational size and wealth.

5. Offensive doctrines will be preferred by military organizations because they enhance organizational independence from civilian authority.

6. Because the organizational incentives to pursue offensive doctrines are strong, military organizations will generally fix on geographic and technological factors that favor the offensive, but underrate or overlook such factors that favor defense or deterrence.

Integration

1. Because military organizations seek independence from civilian authority in order to reduce the uncertainties of combat, military doctrines tend to be poorly integrated with the political aspects of grand strategy. Soldiers will avoid including political criteria in their

military doctrine if such criteria interfere with strictly instrumental military logic.

2. Because of functional specialization, civilians and soldiers tend to know too little about each other's affairs. Soldiers, again in the quest for autonomy, will exacerbate this problem by withholding important military information from civilians. Inadequate civilian understanding of military matters creates obstacles to political-military integration.

3. Technical specialization within military organizations works against a strategically rational setting of priorities among different services, further contributing to disintegration.

In spite of the obstacles, civilian intervention into military doctrine is likely to be the primary cause of political-military integration of grand strategy, simply because civilians alone have the interest and the authority to reconcile political ends with military means and set priorities among military services according to some rational calculus.

Innovation

Most propositions about military innovation are negative.

1. Because of the process of institutionalization, which gives most members of an organization a stake in the way things are, doctrinal innovation will only rarely be sponsored by the organization itself.

2. Because doctrinal innovation increases operational uncertainty, it will rarely be sponsored by the organization itself.

3. New technology, when it has not been tried in combat, is seldom by itself a catalyst of doctrinal innovation.

4. A client state's combat experience with a new technology can cause innovation.

5. Direct combat experience with a new technology can cause innovation.

6. Failure on the battlefield can cause doctrinal innovation.

7. Civilian intervention can cause military innovation.

BALANCE OF POWER THEORY AND MILITARY DOCTRINE

Organization theory suggests a tendency toward offensive, stagnant military doctrines, poorly integrated with the political elements of a state's grand strategy. Balance of power theory predicts greater heterogeneity in military doctrine, dependent on reasonable appraisals by each state of its political, technological, economic, and geographical problems and possibilities in the international political system. The three case studies will show that although organization theory does accurately predict certain tendencies in military doctrine, overall outcomes are more consistent with balance of power theory predictions.

From balance of power theory specific propositions about the variables offense-defense-deterrence, innovation-stagnation, and integration-disintegration can be deduced. Balance of power theory also describes the circumstances under which these propositions are most likely to hold true. In times of relative international calm, when statesmen and soldiers perceive the probability of war as remote, the organizational dynamics outlined above tend to operate. When threats appear greater, or war appears more probable, balancing behavior occurs. A key element of that behavior is greater civilian attention to matters military.

Such attention puts the more ossified, organizationally self-serving, and politically unacceptable aspects of military doctrine under a harsher light. Fear of disaster or defeat prompts statesmen to question long-standing beliefs, to challenge service preferences, to alter budget shares, and to find new sources of military advice and leadership. Civilians intervene to change details, including posture and doctrine, not merely general principles. Organization theory would view civilian influence at such a level as unlikely. Moreover, soldiers, fearful that policies long preferred for their peacetime utility may be found wanting in war, are (according to balance of power theory) somewhat more amenable to outside criticism than in times of international calm. Soldiers themselves are more likely to examine their traditional premises. They will not abandon them, but they may hedge against their failure. These military tendencies are insufficiently strong in their own right to produce military doctrines consistent with balance of power theory predictions. It is the combination of civilian intervention and increased military open-mindedness that produces the results predicted. . . .

Hypotheses—Offense, Deterrence, and Defense

Discussion of individual hypotheses on the causes of offensive, defensive, and deterrent doctrines must be prefaced with a defense of the overarching hypothesis that balance of power theory implies heterogeneity rather than homogeneity on this dimension. I have argued that organization theory suggests that most militaries will prefer the offensive. If balance of power theory also suggested homogeneity on this dimension—the predominance among doctrines of *one* of the three categories—that could make the task of competitive theory testing either simpler or more difficult. The task would be simple if balance of power theory implied that states would prefer defensive doctrines, since we could easily examine a large number of military doctrines and discover if they were usually offensive or usually defensive. On the other hand, if balance of power theory predicted offensive doctrines, then both theories would be predicting the same outcome, and one could hardly test them against each other. In cases where we found offensive doctrines, we would have an "overdetermination" problem—explanation of over 100 percent of the outcome. Of course, in cases where defensive or deterrent doctrines were found, both theories would be discredited. Balance of power theory does not predict homogeneous outcomes, however, although a misreading of the theory might suggest this.

Several students of state behavior whose analyses reflect the balance of power perspective have predicted state policies that would seem to demand offensive doctrines. Hans Morgenthau, John Herz, and to a lesser extent Robert Gilpin predict that states will generally try to expand their power. States will seek not simply equality, but superiority. States are likely to behave this way because power is the key to survival in an anarchical system; since relative power is difficult to measure, the state never knows when it has enough, and it should therefore logically strive for a fairly wide margin of superiority. Basically, these theorists argue, as I have argued, that the security dilemma is always present. Effectively, they also argue, as I have *not*, that the security dilemma is usually quite intense. If this view of the system and its effects on actors were complete, then it would seem logical to deduce that all states will prefer offensive doctrines in order to be ready to expand their power. Because an offensive doctrine may allow the conquest of one's neighbors and the seizure of power assets that lie beyond one's borders, it might appear to be the military option that provides the most security.

This view, however, is not complete. It is *ahistorical* in the most fundamental sense, assuming that states are effectively newborn children, thrust into the jungle of international politics with nothing more than an orientation briefing on the "law of tooth and claw" to guide their actions. Under such conditions the security dilemma might indeed operate with extraordinary intensity. Robert Gilpin, however, admits that states make cost-benefit calculations when deliberating about whether or not to attempt expansion, and that perceptions of cost are affected by the state's historical experience. Of particular importance are the consequences of its own or others' attempts at expansion, and the lessons learned from those episodes. While states, or those who act for them, frequently misread the lessons of history, balance of power theory itself suggests that expanding hegemons will be opposed and stopped. *We have ample historical evidence that this is the case.* This is a lesson that is easy to learn. Indeed, such learning is consistent with Kenneth Waltz's prediction that states will become socialized to the norms of the system that they inhabit. Not all states learn the lesson—not well enough to sustain perpetual peace—but enough learning takes place to make violent, unlimited, expansionist policies the exception rather than the rule. Status quo policies are the rule rather than the exception. France under Louis XIV and Napoleon, Germany under the Kaiser and Hitler, are already too many would-be European hegemons for those who have had to oppose them, but surprisingly few for a three-century game that has often involved as many as six major players.

A status quo policy, of course, need not lead to a defensive military doctrine, but it certainly need not lead to an offensive one either. Instead, status quo powers will assess their political, geographical, and technological positions and possibilities, and devise a military doctrine that preserves their interests at the lowest costs and risks. Thus, an inference from balance of power theory is that military doctrines will be heterogeneous along the dimension of offense-defense deterrence.

Offense

1. States bent on conquest will prefer offensive military doctrines. This proposition is not deduced from balance of power theory, but rather is a matter of common sense. Louis XIV, Napoleon Bonaparte, and Adolph Hitler all had expansionist foreign policies, and required offensive instruments to pursue those policies.

2. States will try to pass on the costs of war to others. Offensive operations are one way to accomplish this. If war seems to involve high collateral damage, states will try to arrange that the war will be fought on the territory of the enemy, of neutrals, or even of allies. Nicholas Spykman once admonished, "Only in periods of weakness and decline have states fought at home. In periods of vitality and strength, they fight on other people's territory."[2] Of course, not all states have the option of fighting abroad, but those that do tend to avail themselves of it. . . .

3. States will support offensive doctrines when power appears to be shifting against them. Offensive doctrines are necessary to fight "preventive" wars. It also seems probable that in environments where power might rapidly shift, statesmen will want to keep an offensive capability "in the hole." A particularly intense arms race would seem to promote offensive doctrines. (We have already seen how the reverse can be true.) Preventive war is a peculiar sort of balancing behavior. "Because I cannot keep you from catching up I will cut you down now." Israel's cooperation in the Franco-British

[2] Spykman, *America's Strategy in World Politics*. New York: Harcourt, Brace, and World, 1942 p. 29.

attack on Egypt in 1956 is explained in part by the fear that Egypt's new claim on the arsenals of the Eastern bloc would give her a permanent arms-race advantage. Hitler preferred an offensive doctrine partly because he believed that he had rearmed more quickly than his putative adversaries, but that they would soon catch up. An offensive doctrine would allow him to prevent this by permitting Germany to strike the Allies before they could remedy their military deficiencies.

4. Similarly, states without allies, *facing multiple threats*, will be attracted to offensive doctrines. An offensive doctrine allows the state to choose the time and place of battle. If the joint capabilities of the adversaries are superior, offensive doctrines will be particularly attractive. In an offensive move, an isolated state can attack and defeat its adversaries sequentially, minimizing the effect of the imbalance of capabilities. This is a variety of preventive war. Instead of waging one dangerous war against a superior coalition, the offender elects to wage what amounts to a separate war against each of the members of the opposing coalition in turn. An offensive doctrine is thus a method of power balancing.

5. The force of the preceding hypothesis is increased if the geographic factor of encirclement is added. The military history of Prussia and later of Germany reveals a constant affinity for offensive doctrines. This is explained in part by the frequent threats of multifront wars. Israel's offensive doctrine allows her to defeat the Arab states sequentially. It may be that the offensiveness of the Soviet military doctrine—both in the rocket forces and in the ground forces—is partially a response to the existence of hostile states on every border.

6. Statesmen will prefer offensive military doctrines if they lack powerful allies, because such doctrines allow them to manipulate the threat of war with credibility. Offensive doctrines are best for making threats. States can use both the threat of alliance and the threat of military force to aid diplomacy in communicating power and will. In the absence of strong allies, the full burden of this task falls on the state's military capabilities. This was the major characteristic of Hitler's early diplomacy. It provided the motivation for former Secretary of Defense James Schlesinger's merchandising of substantial nuclear counterforce capability in the guise of "flexible strategic options." To some extent, this motivation appears to have been behind the offensive aspects of Strategic Air Command doctrine in the 1950s. Military demonstrations and an offensive doctrine are also important elements of Israeli grand strategy.

7. A state need not be politically isolated or geographically encircled to find defensive doctrines unattractive. States with far-flung security dependencies may find it advisable to defend such

allies by concentrating offensive, disarming military power, or deterrent, punitive military power, against its adversary (or adversaries) rather than dispersing its scarce military capabilities in futile denial efforts in many places. Such dependencies, like NATO Europe in the 1950s, may be far from the guarantor, close to a major power adversary, and too weak to contribute much to their own defense. The security of such states is difficult to guarantee by defensive/denial means alone. If the United States had had to secure postwar Europe with conventional denial means, there would probably have been a great many more American troops in Europe than there were. The Soviet adversary had to be dissuaded from going to war against U.S. dependencies. The same was true if French allies in eastern Europe were going to be protected during the interwar period.

How is dissuasion to be accomplished if defensive/denial means are ruled out? Only deterrence and offense remain. While the United States has relied mainly on deterrence in the Cold War, offense has also played an important role. Many have argued against reliance on deterrence alone, since the adversary could punish the United States in return for any strike we might deliver. Extended deterrence is difficult because, whereas a state's readiness to inflict punishment on an adversary that aggresses directly against it might be unquestionable, its willingness to punish the same adversary for offenses against far-removed dependencies, and so to draw fresh fire and suffering on itself, is less likely to be credited. The credibility of the commitment is believed to go up with an ability to limit damage to ourselves by disarming the adversary. . . .

Deterrence

8. Far-flung security dependencies and powerful adversaries can lead a great power to either deterrent or offensive doctrines. Offensive doctrines will be preferred, but often the sheer scope of the problem and the capabilities of the adversary (or adversaries) make offensive capabilities hard to get. Technology and geography are frequently the key determinants of the scope of the problem. Before World War II Britain hoped to hold possessions half a globe away. She lacked the raw capability to project much power such a distance—particularly after ensuring the homeland against more immediate adversaries. Even if she could have mustered the capabilities and mastered the distances, Britain lacked a military technology that could disarm Japan and keep her disarmed. When states face such a situation, they will accept, although they may not embrace, deterrent doctrines.

The political organisms that most often find themselves in this situation seem to be the great empires of history. The British found it advantageous in the 1920s and '30s to police Arabian tribesmen not by pitched battle, but by bombing from the air. They could either obey the rules or be punished. A close examination of British defense policy in the 1930s shows a pronounced inclination toward deterrence. The politicians of the period frequently used the term. Due to economic, industrial, and technological constraints, the actual operations envisioned were more of the denial than the punishment variety. However, dissuasion was the goal, and one finds a constant concern with the manipulation of military capability and potential military capability to discourage aggression. Only with the short-lived commitment to the population bombing doctrine of Bomber Command were any punitive operations planned in the 1930s. . . .

9. As noted previously, small states threatened by powerful adversaries often make recourse to deterrent doctrines. The peculiar coincidence of doctrines among the very strong and the very weak is easy to explain. In both cases, insufficient capabilities drive states to such doctrines. When a state's capabilities fall short of its aims or needs, it may throw its political "will" into the balance. Will is as much a product of a state's political cohesion as it is a product of any material source. Thus, whenever states face security threats and are, by reason of the magnitude of the task or their own poverty, short of resources, we can expect to see deterrent doctrines.

Defense

I have argued that coalition formation is a common method both of enhancing perceived power for diplomacy and mustering real power for war. Yet, coalition management has its problems. Napoleon once declared that if he had to make war, he would prefer to make it against a coalition. Alfred Vagts observes, "Of all types of war, this is the one in which it is most likely that political aims will crowd out and repress strategic aims. And even if this is not intended, the other partner or partners will still suspect it, will try to spare their own forces and sacrifice those of the ally."

10. Defensive doctrines, or doctrines with strong defensive elements, will be preferred by statesmen with status quo policies who are preparing to fight in coalitions. Such doctrines give the states in the coalition more time to settle the division of costs and benefits of the war. This phenomenon will be particularly pronounced if the costs of going on the offensive are seen to be high. One paradoxical example is found in Egyptian behavior during the 1973 Arab-Israeli war. Although the Egyptians had mounted a successful offensive to cross the Suez Canal, after crossing they chose a low-risk strategy of staying behind their air and anti-tank defenses. By so doing, they allowed Israel the luxury of concentrating the bulk of her military

capability on the dangerous Syrian offensive. Egypt passed on the costs of the war to the Syrians. Egypt only left her defensive positions when frenzied Syrian protests suggested Israel's imminent victory. When Egypt finally attacked, its offensive was shattered. Britain and France were guilty of similar "buck-passing" in the 1930s. In both the Egyptian-Syrian case and the British-French case, the costs of going on the offensive were seen to be high. In the case of the 1914 powers, the cost of the offensive was seen to be low. This explains the less cautious behavior in the earlier period.

11. The preceding hypothesis may be attenuated by another constraint. Although states may seek military doctrines that allow them to pass some of their defense costs onto coalition partners, they must in some measure please these present or potential allies in order to attract them. Thus, alliance suitors may adopt the doctrines of their intended allies. A given military doctrine may fail to achieve both the goal of buck-passing and the goal of alliance-making, and when it does, a state can face difficult choices. In 1973, Egypt appears to have portrayed her military doctrine one way to achieve Syrian cooperation in the initial attack; operated another to spare her own forces early in the war; and finally shifted back to a strategy more accommodating to the Syrians in the abortive offensive against Israeli forces in the Sinai passes. France in the 1930s, on the other hand, could both attract British support and control her own contribution to any ultimate war effort with a defensive doctrine. Britain did not want any provocation of Germany, and that was fine with France.

12. Status quo states will generally prefer defensive doctrines if geography or technology makes such doctrines attractive. They are more likely to correctly interpret such factors than are non-status quo states, and since their goal is to conserve power, they are more likely to exploit them militarily.

13. Status quo states may prefer defensive doctrines simply because those states know that they are unlikely to strike the first blow. Since they expect to suffer the first blow, it is reasonable for them to expend their military effort learning how to parry it.

Hypotheses—The Causes of Civilian Intervention and Its Effects on Integration and Innovation

I have discussed some causes of the character of military doctrine. Organization theory identifies external intervention as a key source of integration and innovation, but also predicts that such intervention will be very difficult. Balance of power theory predicts that, difficult or not, such intervention will occur if it is necessary to secure the state. If balance of power theory successfully predicts not only intervention, but also the circumstances under which it occurs, then the theory gains in credibility relative to organization theory. Thus, it is important to address the causes of civilian intervention into military matters.

1. Political leaders with aggression in mind will often take a look at their military forces to see if they are ready to go. Hitler was most attentive to his military capabilities and, as we shall see, was a prime mover in the development of Blitzkrieg. This is not so much a proposition deduced from balance of power theory as a matter of common sense. The anarchy of international politics permits mischief. The military value of the object in view may or may not be a motive for mischief. If political leaders contemplate aggression for the purpose of expanding their resources for security, then their intervention can be loosely explained in terms of structural constraints. Otherwise, we must fall back on avarice and "bloody-mindedness" as an explanation.

For whatever reasons civilian policy-makers choose a path of aggression, soldiers must either carry out the orders of their chiefs or resign. The prospect of war can have a catalytic effect on the behavior of soldiers whose lives or careers will inevitably be put into jeopardy. The final steps to the Blitzkrieg doctrine were taken by the commanders of the Germany Army only late in 1939 and early in 1940, when it became clear that Hitler was committed to an offensive against the Allies.

2. If planned aggression for political ends is one general cause of civilian intervention in military matters, the other is fear. This is consistent with balance of power theory. It is easy for statesmen to become frightened by events in the international environment. Many different kinds of events may threaten the state's security. Just as states "balance" materially by arms-racing or coalition formation, they "balance" qualitatively by taking a close look at the doctrine, competence, and readiness of their military organizations. They do not do so all the time, but when they do, fear is most often the driving force.

3. The same fear increases military organizations' receptivity to outside criticism and also sharpens their own self-critical faculties. The force of this proposition is attenuated in multipolar systems, however, if a given state perceives itself to have alliance possibilities. Under conditions of threat, civilians may divide their energies between chasing allies and reviewing their military posture. This may so reduce the pressure on a given military organization as to allow organizational dynamics to triumph. More specific propositions on this matter can be generated.

4. In the face of any sort of security problem, states without allies will tend to pay a good deal of attention to their military organizations. This is true of states that are politically isolated.

Israel is a good current example: military leaders retire to become key political leaders, and politicians are generally well versed in military matters. This sort of attention is also characteristic of both poles in a bipolar system. Since the dawn of the Cold War American leaders have paid more attention to military matters than in any prior period of our history.

Examples of military innovation caused by civilian intervention and stimulated by political isolation are the development of the standing army in France under Louis XIV and the mass army during the French Revolution. Recall the important role played by Cardinal Richelieu and the civilian war minister Michel Le Tellier in the development of France's first all-professional, standing army. What had driven France in this direction? Historian Michael Howard writes, "On the death of Gustavus, . . . Richelieu saw himself faced with the necessity of improvising an army and entering the field himself if Habsburg power, Spanish and Austrian, was not to become dominant in Europe." Le Tellier's son, the Marquis de Louvois, completed his father's work, creating the army with which Louis XIV waged war on nearly all of Europe.

The case of Revolutionary France is similar. The Directory had accumulated six major adversaries, and by August 23, 1793, the danger had become so great that the Committee on Public Safety ordered universal conscription for the first time in any modern European state. By the following summer, the French army fielded three-quarters of a million men, the largest armed force in Europe since the barbarian invasions. The Committee did not simply invent the mass army. Lazare Carnot, a former military professional and a man with new ideas about military organizations and tactics, had joined the Revolution. It was his hand that guided French military innovation.

While political isolation provides an added spur to civilian intervention, even states with alliance possibilities show tendencies to civilian intervention in the face of new or growing threats. The best example of this is found in British behavior in 1934–1940. The rising military power of Germany brought not only a return to substantial defense spending, but greater civilian attention to the plans of the military. In spite of a military organization committed to an offensive doctrine, civilians intervened to promote a major defensive innovation—the development of the country's integrated air defense system, the first of its kind in history. . . . While the RAF did not wholeheartedly embrace air defense, and jealously guarded Bomber Command, that organization's support for air defense increased as the possibility of war loomed larger.

5. Disasters fresh in a state's memory are great promoters of civilian intervention, even if no immediate threat appears on the

horizon. (This proposition and those that follow have their counterparts at the organizational level.) If a threat is apparent, the tendency will be more pronounced. The most recent example is the apparently very thorough review by Israel's Agranat Commission of all the events leading up to and including the 1973 war. While the Commission included two former chiefs of staff, the chairman and the other two members were civilians. Most of the report remains secret, but it is known to have generated wide-ranging reform in Israel's armed forces.

Another example is found in the case of Prussia. Between October 7 and November 7, 1806, Napoleon Bonaparte completely destroyed the armies of the heirs of Frederick the Great. The "army with a country" was swept aside by the superior numbers and methods of the French. Following this disaster, both civilian and military reformers came to the fore. Before the war, reforms of either bureaucracy or army were practically impossible. After the war, under the leadership of the soldiers Gerhard Scharnhorst and Count August Gneisenau, a commission was set up to reform the army. Opposition was not wanting, and in fact was suppressed only by the direct intervention of the king, who removed the opponents of reform from the commission.

6. Some civilian intervention is produced not by disaster but by the high costs expected of a particular military exercise. A victorious but very costly war can substantially weaken a state. Even in the context of a superiority that provided some damage-limiting capability, U.S. civilian policy-makers in the 1950s watched their nuclear forces more closely than they had ever watched military forces before. Though the United States might have "prevailed" in a nuclear conflict, the game was not likely to be worth the candle. . . .

The experience or expectation of military disaster provides a key avenue by which technology can influence military doctrine. Civilians especially are moved to interpret new technology and integrate such interpretations into military doctrine when the technology presents some very clear and unambiguous threat to the state's survival. The threat may be of defeat or the probability of high collateral damage. Civilian intervention is unlikely unless demonstration of the technology, by test or combat-use, is sufficiently stark and frightening to shake civilians' faith in the ability of their own military organizations to handle it. The attitudes of French civilians to any chance of a replay of World War I, British civilians to the spectre of bombs falling on London, and American civilians to nuclear weapons are all good examples. Even here, though, the impact of technology is not determinative. In the French case technology was seen to be largely immutable, a force to be accepted and dealt with. In the British case, technology was seen as something to be changed.

Simple fear of defeat provides another motivation for civilian intervention. If an adversary appears particularly impressive, potentially capable of a decisive victory, civilians will pay considerable attention to their military instrument. The intervention of British civilians into the doctrine of the RAF, for instance, was driven by fear of the German "knock-out-blow-from-the-air."

Summary: Balance of Power Theory Hypotheses

Offense, Defense, and Deterrence

In general, the theory predicts heterogeneity along the dimension offense-defense-deterrence.

1. Expansionist powers will prefer offensive doctrines.

2. States will prefer offensive doctrines when war appears to involve very high collateral damage, because offense allows the state to take the war somewhere else.

3. States with a favorable power position that is suffering erosion will prefer offensive doctrines. (Offensive doctrines are a vehicle for preventive war.)

4. States that face several adversaries may prefer offensive doctrines. (Again, offensive doctrines are the vehicle for preventive war.)

5. Similarly, geographically encircled states may prefer offensive doctrines.

6. States without allies will prefer offensive doctrines because they must exploit military power for diplomacy, a purpose best served by offensive capabilities.

7. States with widely distributed security dependencies will prefer offensive doctrines because they allow the concentration of scarce military assets.

8. States with far-flung security dependencies will accept deterrent doctrines when it is not feasible to sustain offensive or defensive doctrines. Deterrent doctrines are a vehicle for throwing political will into the military balance.

9. Similarly, small states may opt for deterrent doctrines because their capabilities are insufficient to support any other kind.

10. The possibility of coalition warfare can lead a state to a defensive doctrine because such doctrines permit a pace of warfare that allows allies to settle the division of the risks, costs, and benefits of war.

11. States preparing to fight in coalitions must also please their prospective coalition partners. This dilutes the power of proposition

10. If, for its own special reasons, a state adopts an offensive doctrine, its suitors may find it necessary to conform. By the same token, however, conformity to a defensive doctrine is likely if the state being wooed adopts a defensive doctrine.

12. Status quo states will generally prefer defensive doctrines if geography or technology makes such doctrines attractive.

13. Status quo states may prefer defensive doctrines simply because they know that they are unlikely to strike first.

Integration and Innovation

1. Statesmen contemplating aggression will tend to intervene in their military organizations.

2. Generally, anything that increases the perceived threat to state security is a cause of civilian intervention in military matters and hence a possible cause of integration and innovation.

3. Soldiers themselves tend to be more amenable to external prodding when the threat of war looms larger.

4. In states that are either politically isolated or geographically surrounded, civilians tend to intervene in military matters more frequently, and soldiers tend to approach war more seriously than in states with more favorable security conditions. Thus, both integration and innovation should be more frequent in such states.

5. Recent military disasters can be causes of integration and innovation.

6. Anticipated high costs of warfare can be a cause of civilian intervention. Because new technology (e.g., nuclear weapons) can greatly affect anticipated costs, this is one way technology can exert an influence on integration and innovation.

All of the preceding possible causes can be weakened in multipolar systems, where allies appear to be easy to come by. States and statesmen may spend too much time chasing allies, and not enough time auditing their war machines.

SUMMARY

In this chapter I have offered brief surveys of organization theory and balance of power theory, and from these theories I have inferred hypotheses about what causes military doctrine to vary along the dimensions offense-defense-deterrence, innovation-stagnation, and integration-disintegration. I have integrated with these hypotheses a small group of propositions that concern the influence of technology and geography upon military doctrine. Most of these propositions are consistent with one or the other of the two theories introduced.

As argued in the opening pages of this chapter, these are structural theories. They are appropriate for the examination of the cases that follow. These theories will be used in combination to explain the military doctrines of France, Britain, and Germany. Because in some of the cases contradictory hypotheses about doctrine are generated by the two theories, a comparison of these military doctrines allows us to examine and weigh the explanatory power of each theory.

In the broadest sense military doctrine should, according to *organization theory,* show a tendency to be offensive, disintegrated, and stagnant. This is suggested both by the character of military organizations and by their functional separation from the political decision-makers of the state. *Balance of power theory* predicts somewhat different outcomes, depending on the state's situation. In general, anything that makes the civilian leaders of a state more fearful should encourage political-military integration and operational innovation. Civilian preferences for offense, defense, or deterrence will be influenced by the international environment. Finally, if the two theories introduced here have any validity at all, we should find that *technology* and *geography* are rarely determinative in their own right, although they should often have an important effect on doctrine.

Under what conditions will organization theory enjoy its greatest explanatory power? Under what conditions will the international environment have the greatest influence? In times of relative international calm we should expect a high degree of organizational determinism. In times of threat we should see greater accommodation of doctrine to the international system—integration should be more pronounced, innovation more likely. Among states, doctrines should show more heterogeneity. However, even under such circumstances all will not necessarily be well. Multipolar structures, although they exert an important influence on doctrine, may so confuse decisionmakers as to allow organizational determinants to come to the fore once again. The effects can be disastrous.

Cooperation Under The
Security Dilemma

ROBERT JERVIS

I. ANARCHY AND THE SECURITY DILEMMA

The lack of an international sovereign not only permits wars to occur, but also makes it difficult for states that are satisfied with the
status quo to arrive at goals that they recognize as being in their common interest. Because there are no institutions or authorities that can
make and enforce international laws, the policies of cooperation that
will bring mutual rewards if others cooperate may bring disaster if
they do not. Because states are aware of this, anarchy encourages
behavior that leaves all concerned worse off than they could be, even
in the extreme case in which all states would like to freeze the status
quo. This is true of the men in Rousseau's "Stag Hunt." If they
cooperate to trap the stag, they will all eat well. But if one person
defects to chase a rabbit—which he likes less than stag—none of the
others will get anything. Thus, all actors have the same preference
order, and there is a solution that gives each his first choice: (1)
cooperate and trap the stag (the international analogue being cooperation and disarmament); (2) chase a rabbit while others remain at their
posts (maintain a high level of arms while others are disarmed); (3) all
chase rabbits (arms competition and high risk of war); and (4) stay at
the original position while another chases a rabbit (being disarmed
while others are armed).[1] Unless each person thinks that the others
will cooperate, he himself will not. And why might he fear that any
other person would do something that would sacrifice his own first
choice? The other might not understand the situation, or might not be
able to control his impulses if he saw a rabbit, or might fear that some

From "Cooperation Under the Security Dilemma," *World Politics,* Vol. 30, no. 2
(January 78). Copyright © 1978 by Princeton University Press. Excerpts, pp. 167–170,
186-214, reprinted by permission of Princeton University Press.
    * I am grateful to Robert Art, Bernard Brodie, and Glenn Snyder for comments,
and to the Committee on Research of the UCLA Academic Senate for financial support. An earlier version of this essay appeared as Working Paper No. 5, UCLA Program in Arms Control and International Security.
    [1] This kind of rank-ordering is not entirely an analyst's invention, as is shown by the
following section of a British army memo of 1903 dealing with British and Russian
railroad construction near the Persia-Afghanistan border:

other member of the group is unreliable. If the person voices any of these suspicions, others are more likely to fear that he will defect, thus making them more likely to defect, thus making it more rational for him to defect. Of course in this simple case—and in many that are more realistic—there are a number of arrangements that could permit cooperation. But the main point remains: although actors may know that they seek a common goal, they may not be able to reach it.

Even when there is a solution that is everyone's first choice, the international case is characterized by three difficulties not present in the Stag Hunt. First, to the incentives to defect given above must be added the potent fear that even if the other state now supports the status quo, it may become dissatisfied later. No matter how much decision makers are committed to the status quo, they cannot bind themselves and their successors to the same path. Minds can be changed, new leaders can come to power, values can shift, new opportunities and dangers can arise.

The second problem arises from a possible solution. In order to protect their possessions, states often seek to control resources or land outside their own territory. Countries that are not self-sufficient must try to assure that the necessary supplies will continue to flow in wartime. This was part of the explanation for Japan's drive into China and Southeast Asia before World War II. If there were an international authority that could guarantee access, this motive for control would disappear. But since there is not, even a state that would prefer the status quo to increasing its area of control may pursue the latter policy.

When there are believed to be tight linkages between domestic and foreign policy or between the domestic politics of two states, the quest for security may drive states to interfere pre-emptively in the domestic politics of others in order to provide an ideological buffer zone. Thus, Metternich's justification for supervising the politics of the Italian states has been summarized as follows:

The conditions of the problem may . . . be briefly summarized as follows:

a) If we make a railway to Seistan while Russia remains inactive, we gain a considerable defensive advantage at considerable financial cost;

b) If Russia makes a railway to Seistan, while we remain inactive, she gains a considerable offensive advantage at considerable financial cost;

c) If both we and Russia make railways to Seistan, the defensive and offensive advantages may be held to neutralize each other; in other words, we shall have spent a good deal of money and be no better off than we are at present. On the other hand, we shall be no worse off, whereas under alternative (b) we shall be much worse off. Consequently, the theoretical balance of advantage lies with the proposed railway extension from Quetta to Seistan.

W. G. Nicholson, "Memorandum on Seistan and Other Points Raised in the Discussion on the Defence of India," (Committee of Imperial Defence, March 20, 1903). It should be noted that the possibility of neither side building railways was not mentioned, thus strongly biasing the analysis.

Every state is absolutely sovereign in its internal affairs But this implies that every state must do nothing to interfere in the internal affairs of any other. However, any false or pernicious step taken by any state in its internal affairs may disturb the repose of another state, and this consequent disturbance of another state's repose constitutes an interference in that state's internal affairs. Therefore, every state—or rather, every sovereign of a great power—has the duty, in the name of the sacred right of independence of every state, to supervise the governments of smaller states and to prevent them from taking false and pernicious steps in their internal affairs.[2]

More frequently, the concern is with direct attack. In order to protect themselves, states seek to control, or at least to neutralize, areas on their borders. But attempts to establish buffer zones can alarm others who have stakes there, who fear that undesirable precedents will be set, or who believe that their own vulnerability will be increased. When buffers are sought in areas empty of great powers, expansion tends to feed on itself in order to protect what is acquired, as was often noted by those who opposed colonial expansion. Balfour's complaint was typical: "Every time I come to a discussion—at intervals of, say, five years—I find there is a new sphere which we have got to guard, which is supposed to protect the gateways of India. Those gateways are getting further and further away from India, and I do not know how far west they are going to be brought by the General Staff."[3]

Though this process is most clearly visible when it involves territorial expansion, it often operates with the increase of less tangible power and influence. The expansion of power usually brings with it an expansion of responsibilities and commitments; to meet them, still greater power is required. The state will take many positions that are subject to challenge. It will be involved with a wide range of controversial issues unrelated to its core values. And retreats that would be seen as normal if made by a small power would be taken as an index of weakness inviting predation if made by a large one.

The third problem present in international politics but not in the Stag Hunt is the security dilemma: many of the means by which a state tries to increase its security decrease the security of others. In domestic society, there are several ways to increase the safety of one's person and property without endangering others. One can move to a safer neighborhood, put bars on the windows, avoid dark streets, and keep a distance from suspicious-looking characters. Of course these

[2] Paul Schroeder, *Metternich's Diplomacy at Its Zenith, 1820–1823* (Westport, Conn.: Greenwood Press 1969), 126.

[3] Quoted in Michael Howard, *The Continental Commitment* (Harmondsworth, England: Penguin 1974), 67.

measures are not convenient, cheap, or certain of success. But no one save criminals need be alarmed if a person takes them. In international politics, however, one state's gain in security often inadvertently threatens others. In explaining British policy on naval disarmament in the interwar period to the Japanese, Ramsey MacDonald said that "Nobody wanted Japan to be insecure."[4] But the problem was not with British desires, but with the consequences of her policy. In earlier periods, too, Britain had needed a navy large enough to keep the shipping lanes open. But such a navy could not avoid being a menace to any other state with a coast that could be raided, trade that could be interdicted, or colonies that could be isolated. When Germany started building a powerful navy before World War I, Britain objected that it could only be an offensive weapon aimed at her. As Sir Edward Grey, the Foreign Secretary, put it to King Edward VII: "If the German Fleet ever becomes superior to ours, the German Army can conquer this country. There is no corresponding risk of this kind to Germany; for however superior our Fleet was, no naval victory could bring us any nearer to Berlin." The English position was half correct: Germany's navy was an anti-British instrument. But the British often overlooked what the Germans knew full well: "in every quarrel with England, German colonies and trade were . . . hostages from England to take." Thus, whether she intended it or not, the British Navy constituted an important instrument of coercion. . . .[5]

II. OFFENSE, DEFENSE, AND THE SECURITY DILEMMA

Another approach starts with the central point of the security dilemma—that an increase in one state's security decreases the security of others—and examines the conditions under which this proposition holds. Two crucial variables are involved: whether defensive weapons and policies can be distinguished from offensive ones, and whether the defense or the offense has the advantage. The definitions are not always clear, and many cases are difficult to judge, but these two variables shed a great deal of light on the question of whether status-quo powers will adopt compatible security policies. All the variables discussed so far leave the heart of the problem untouched. But when defensive weapons differ from offensive ones, it is possible for a state

[4] Quoted in Gerald Wheeler, *Prelude to Pearl Harbor* (Columbia: University of Missouri Press 1963), 167.

[5] Quoted in Leonard Wainstein, "The Dreadnought Gap," in Robert Art and Kenneth Waltz, eds., *The Use of Force* (Boston: Little, Brown 1971), 155; Raymond Sontag, *European Diplomatic History, 1871-1932* (New York: Appleton-Century-Croits 1933), 147. The French had made a similar argument 50 years earlier; see James Phinney Baxter III, *The Introduction of the Ironclad Warship* (Cambridge: Harvard University Press 1933), 149. For a more detailed discussion of the security dilemma, see Jervis, *Perception and Misperception in International Politics* (Princeton: Princeton University Press 1976), 62-76.

to make itself more secure without making others less secure. And when the defense has the advantage over the offense, a large increase in one state's security only slightly decreases the security of the others, and status-quo powers can all enjoy a high level of security and largely escape from the state of nature.

OFFENSE-DEFENSE BALANCE

When we say that the offense has the advantage, we simply mean that it is easier to destroy the other's army and take its territory than it is to defend one's own. When the defense has the advantage, it is easier to protect and to hold than it is to move forward, destroy, and take. If effective defenses can be erected quickly, an attacker may be able to keep territory he has taken in an initial victory. Thus, the dominance of the defense made it very hard for Britain and France to push Germany out of France in World War I. But when superior defenses are difficult for an aggressor to improvise on the battlefield and must be constructed during peacetime, they provide no direct assistance to him.

The security dilemma is at its most vicious when commitments, strategy, or technology dictate that the only route to security lies through expansion. Status-quo powers must then act like aggressors; the fact that they would gladly agree to forego the opportunity for expansion in return for guarantees for their security has no implications for their behavior. Even if expansion is not sought as a goal in itself, there will be quick and drastic changes in the distribution of territory and influence. Conversely, when the defense has the advantage, status-quo states can make themselves more secure without gravely endangering others.[6] Indeed, if the defense has enough of an advantage and if the states are of roughly equal size, not only will the security dilemma cease to inhibit status-quo states from cooperating, but aggression will be next to impossible, thus rendering international anarchy relatively unimportant. If states cannot conquer each other, then the lack of sovereignty, although it presents problems of collective goods in a number of areas, no longer forces states to devote their primary attention to self-preservation. Although, if force were not usable, there would be fewer restraints on the use of nonmilitary instruments, these are rarely powerful enough to threaten the vital interests of a major state.

Two questions of the offense-defense balance can be separated. First, does the state have to spend more or less than one dollar on defensive forces to offset each dollar spent by the other side on forces

---

[6] Thus, when Wolfers (fn. 10) 126, argues that a status-quo state that settles for rough equality of power with its adversary, rather than seeking preponderance, may be able to convince the other to reciprocate by showing that it wants only to protect itself, not menace the other, he assumes that the defense has an advantage.

that could be used to attack? If the state has one dollar to spend on increasing its security, should it put it into offensive or defensive forces? Second, with a given inventory of forces, is it better to attack or to defend? Is there an incentive to strike first or to absorb the other's blow? These two aspects are often linked: if each dollar spent on offense can overcome each dollar spent on defense, and if both sides have the same defense budgets, then both are likely to build offensive forces and find it attractive to attack rather than to wait for the adversary to strike.

These aspects affect the security dilemma in different ways. The first has its greatest impact on arms races. If the defense has the advantage, and if the status-quo powers have reasonable subjective security requirements, they can probably avoid an arms race. Although an increase in one side's arms and security will still decrease the other's security, the former's increase will be larger than the latter's decrease. So if one side increases its arms, the other can bring its security back up to its previous level by adding a smaller amount to its forces. And if the first side reacts to this change, its increase will also be smaller than the stimulus that produced it. Thus a stable equilibrium will be reached. Shifting from dynamics to statics, each side can be quite secure with forces roughly equal to those of the other. Indeed, if the defense is much more potent than the offense, each side can be willing to have forces much smaller than the other's, and can be indifferent to a wide range of the other's defense policies.

The second aspect—whether it is better to attack or to defend—influences short-run stability. When the offense has the advantage, a state's reaction to international tension will increase the chances of war. The incentives for pre-emption and the "reciprocal fear of surprise attack" in this situation have been made clear by analyses of the dangers that exist when two countries have first-strike capabilities.[7] There is no way for the state to increase its security without menacing, or even attacking, the other. Even Bismarck, who once called preventive war "committing suicide from fear of death," said that "no government, if it regards war as inevitable even if it does not want it, would be so foolish as to leave to the enemy the choice of time and occasion and to wait for the moment which is most convenient for the enemy."[8] In another arena, the same dilemma applies to the policeman in a dark alley confronting a suspected criminal who appears to be holding a weapon. Though racism may indeed be present, the security dilemma can account for many of the tragic shootings of innocent people in the ghettos.

---

[7] Schelling (fn. 20), chap. 9.
[8] Quoted in Fritz Fischer, *War of Illusions* (New York: Norton 1975), 377, 461.

ROBERT JERVIS 73

Beliefs about the course of a war in which the offense has the advantage further deepen the security dilemma. When there are incentives to strike first, a successful attack will usually so weaken the other side that victory will be relatively quick, bloodless, and decisive. It is in these periods when conquest is possible and attractive that states consolidate power internally—for instance, by destroying the feudal barons—and expand externally. There are several consequences that decrease the chance of cooperation among status-quo states. First, war will be profitable for the winner. The costs will be low and the benefits high. Of course, losers will suffer; the fear of losing could induce states to try to form stable cooperative arrangements, but the temptation of victory will make this particularly difficult. Second, because wars are expected to be both frequent and short, there will be incentives for high levels of arms, and quick and strong reaction to the other's increases in arms. The state cannot afford to wait until there is unambiguous evidence that the other is building new weapons. Even large states that have faith in their economic strength cannot wait, because the war will be over before their products can reach the army. Third, when wars are quick, states will have to recruit allies in advance.[9] Without the opportunity for bargaining and re-alignments during the opening stages of hostilities, peacetime diplomacy loses a degree of the fluidity that facilitates balance-of-power policies. Because alliances must be secured during peacetime, the international system is more likely to become bipolar. It is hard to say whether war therefore becomes more or less likely, but this bipolarity increases tension between the two camps and makes it harder for status-quo states to gain the benefits of cooperation. Fourth, if wars are frequent, statesmen's perceptual thresholds will be adjusted accordingly and they will be quick to perceive ambiguous evidence as indicating that others are aggressive. Thus, there will be more cases of status-quo powers arming against each other in the incorrect belief that the other is hostile.

When the defense has the advantage, all the foregoing is reversed. The state that fears attack does not pre-empt—since that would be a wasteful use of its military resources—but rather prepares to receive an attack. Doing so does not decrease the security of others, and several states can do it simultaneously; the situation will therefore be stable, and status-quo powers will be able to cooperate. When Herman Kahn argues that ultimatums "are vastly too dangerous to give because . . . they are quite likely to touch off a pre-emptive strike,"[10] he incorrectly assumes that it is always advantageous to strike first.

[9] George Quester, *Offense and Defense in the International System* (New York: John Wiley 1977), 105–06; Sontag (fn. 5), 4–5.
[10] Kahn (fn. 23), 211 (also see 144).

More is involved than short-run dynamics. When the defense is dominant, wars are likely to become stalemates and can be won only at enormous cost. Relatively small and weak states can hold off larger and stronger ones, or can deter attack by raising the costs of conquest to an unacceptable level. States then approach equality in what they can do to each other. Like the .45-caliber pistol in the American West, fortifications were the "great equalizer" in some periods. Changes in the status quo are less frequent and cooperation is more common wherever the security dilemma is thereby reduced.

Many of these arguments can be illustrated by the major powers' policies in the periods preceding the two world wars. Bismarck's wars surprised statesmen by showing that the offense had the advantage, and by being quick, relatively cheap, and quite decisive. Falling into a common error, observers projected this pattern into the future.[11] The resulting expectations had several effects. First, states sought semi-permanent allies. In the early stages of the Franco-Prussian War, Napoleon III had thought that there would be plenty of time to recruit Austria to his side. Now, others were not going to repeat this mistake. Second, defense budgets were high and reacted quite sharply to increases on the other side. It is not surprising that Richardson's theory of arms races fits this period well. Third, most decision makers thought that the next European war would not cost much blood and treasure.[12] That is one reason why war was generally seen as inevitable and why mass opinion was so bellicose. Fourth, once war seemed likely, there were strong pressures to pre-empt. Both sides believed that whoever moved first could penetrate the other deep enough to disrupt mobilization and thus gain an insurmountable advantage. (There was no such belief about the use of naval forces. Although Churchill made an ill-advised speech saying that if German ships "do not come out and fight in time of war they will be dug out like rats in a hole,"[13] everyone knew that submarines, mines, and coastal fortifications made this impossible. So at the start of the war each navy prepared to

---

[11] For a general discussion of such mistaken learning from the past, see Jervis (fn. 5), chap. 6. The important and still not completely understood question of why this belief formed and was maintained throughout the war is examined in Bernard Brodie, *War and Politics* (New York: Macmillan 1973), 262–70; Brodie, "Technological Change, Strategic Doctrine, and Political Outcomes," in Klaus Knorr, ed., *Historical Dimensions of National Security Problems* (Lawrence: University Press of Kansas 1976), 290–92; and Douglas Porch, "The French Army and the Spirit of the Offensive, 1900–14," in Brian Bond and Ian Roy, eds,. *War and Society* (New York: Holmes & Meier 1975), 117–43.

[12] Some were not so optimistic. Gray's remark is well-known: "The lamps are going out all over Europe; we shall not see them lit again in our life-time." The German Prime Minister, Bethmann Hollweg, also feared the consequences of the war. But the controlling view was that it would certainly pay for the winner.

[13] Quoted in Martin Gilbert, *Winston S. Churchill, III, The Challenge of War, 1914–1916* (Boston: Houghton Mifflin 1971), 84.

defend itself rather than attack, and the short-run destabilizing forces that launched the armies toward each other did not operate.)[14] Furthermore, each side knew that the other saw the situation the same way, thus increasing the perceived danger that the other would attack, and giving each added reasons to precipitate a war if conditions seemed favorable. In the long and the short run, there were thus both offensive and defensive incentives to strike. This situation casts light on the common question about German motives in 1914: "Did Germany unleash the war deliberately to become a world power or did she support Austria merely to defend a weakening ally," thereby protecting her own position?[15] To some extent, this question is misleading. Because of the perceived advantage of the offense, war was seen as the best route both to gaining expansion and to avoiding drastic loss of influence. There seemed to be no way for Germany merely to retain and safeguard her existing position.

Of course the war showed these beliefs to have been wrong on all points. Trenches and machine guns gave the defense an overwhelming advantage. The fighting became deadlocked and produced horrendous casualties. It made no sense for the combatants to bleed themselves to death. If they had known the power of the defense beforehand, they would have rushed for their own trenches rather than for the enemy's territory. Each side could have done this without increasing the other's incentives to strike. War might have broken out anyway, just as DD is a possible outcome of Chicken, but at least the pressures of time and the fear of allowing the other to get the first blow would not have contributed to this end. And, had both sides known the costs of the war, they would have negotiated much more seriously. The obvious question is why the states did not seek a negotiated settlement as soon as the shape of the war became clear. Schlieffen had said that if his plan failed, peace should be sought.[16] The answer is complex, uncertain, and largely outside of the scope of our concerns. But part of the reason was the hope and sometimes the expectation that breakthroughs could be made and the dominance of the offensive restored. Without that hope, the political and psychological pressures to fight to a decisive victory might have been overcome.

The politics of the interwar period were shaped by the memories of the previous conflict and the belief that any future war would resemble it. Political and military lessons reinforced each other in ameliorating the security dilemma. Because it was believed that the First World War had been a mistake that could have been avoided by

---

[14] Quester (fn. 33), 98–99. Robert Art, *The Influence of Foreign Policy on Seapower,* II (Beverly Hills: Sage Professional Papers in International Studies Series, 1973), 14–18, 26–28.

[15] Konrad Jarausch, "The Illusion of Limited War: Chancellor Bethmann Hollweg's Calculated Risk, July 1914," *Central European History, II* (March 1969), 50.

[16] Brodie (fn. 8), 58.

skillful conciliation, both Britain and, to a lesser extent, France were highly sensitive to the possibility that interwar Germany was not a real threat to peace, and alert to the danger that reacting quickly and strongly to her arms could create unnecessary conflict. And because Britain and France expected the defense to continue to dominate, they concluded that it was safe to adopt a more relaxed and nonthreatening military posture.[17] Britain also felt less need to maintain tight alliance bonds. The Allies' military posture then constituted only a slight danger to Germany; had the latter been content with the status quo, it would have been easy for both sides to have felt secure behind their lines of fortifications. Of course the Germans were not content, so it is not surprising that they devoted their money and attention to finding ways out of a defense-dominated stalemate. *Blitzkrieg* tactics were necessary if they were to use force to change the status quo.

The initial stages of the war on the Western Front also contrasted with the First World War. Only with the new air arm were there any incentives to strike first, and these forces were too weak to carry out the grandiose plans that had been both dreamed and feared. The armies, still the main instrument, rushed to defensive positions. Perhaps the allies could have successfully attacked while the Germans were occupied in Poland.[18] But belief in the defense was so great that this was never seriously contemplated. Three months after the start of the war, the French Prime Minister summed up the view held by almost everyone but Hitler: on the Western Front there is "deadlock. Two Forces of equal strength and the one that attacks seeing such enormous casualties that it cannot move without endangering the continuation of the war or of the aftermath."[19] The Allies were caught in a dilemma they never fully recognized, let alone solved. On the one hand, they had very high war aims; although unconditional surrender had not yet been adopted, the British had decided from the start that the removal of Hitler was a necessary condition for peace.[20] On the other hand, there were no realistic plans or instruments for allowing the Allies to

---

[17] President Roosevelt and the American delegates to the League of Nations Disarmament Conference maintained that the tank and mobile heavy artillery had reestablished the dominance of the offensive, thus making disarmament more urgent (Boggs, fn. 28, pp. 31, 108), but this was a minority position and may not even have been believed by the Americans. The reduced prestige and influence of the military, and the high pressures to cut government spending throughout this period also contributed to the lowering of defense budgets.

[18] Jon Kimche, *The Unfought Battle* (New York: Stein 1968); Nicholas William Bethell, *The War Hitler Won: The Fall of Poland, September 1939* (New York: Holt 1972); Alan Alexandroff and Richard Rosecrance, "Deterrence in 1939," *World Politics*, XXIX (April 1977), 404–24.

[19] Roderick Macleod and Denis Kelly, eds., *Time Unguarded: The Ironside Diaries, 1937–1940* (New York: McKay 1962), 173.

[20] For a short time, as France was falling, the British Cabinet did discuss reaching a negotiated peace with Hitler. The official history ignores this, but it is covered in P. M. H. Bell, *A Certain Eventuality* (Farnborough, England: Saxon House 1974), 40–48.

impose their will on the other side. The British Chief of the Imperial General Staff noted, "The French have no intention of carrying out an offensive for years, if at all"; the British were only slightly bolder.[21] So the Allies looked to a long war that would wear the Germans down, cause civilian suffering through shortages, and eventually undermine Hitler. There was little analysis to support this view—and indeed it probably was not supportable—but as long as the defense was dominant and the numbers on each side relatively equal, what else could the Allies do?

To summarize, the security dilemma was much less powerful after World War I than it had been before. In the later period, the expected power of the defense allowed status-quo states to pursue compatible security policies and avoid arms races. Furthermore, high tension and fear of war did not set off short-run dynamics by which each state, trying to increase its security, inadvertently acted to make war more likely. The expected high costs of war, however, led the Allies to believe that no sane German leader would run the risks entailed in an attempt to dominate the Continent, and discouraged them from risking war themselves.

Technology and Geography. Technology and geography are the two main factors that determine whether the offense or the defense has the advantage. As Brodie notes, "On the tactical level, as a rule, few physical factors favor the attacker but many favor the defender. The defender usually has the advantage of cover. He characteristically fires from behind some form of shelter while his opponent crosses open ground."[22] Anything that increases the amount of ground the attacker has to cross, or impedes his progress across it, or makes him more vulnerable while crossing, increases the advantage accruing to the defense. When states are separated by barriers that produce these effects, the security dilemma is eased, since both can have forces adequate for defense without being able to attack. Impenetrable barriers would actually prevent war; in reality, decision makers have to settle for a good deal less. Buffer zones slow the attacker's progress; they thereby give the defender time to prepare, increase problems of logistics, and reduce the number of soldiers available for the final assault. At the end of the 19th century, Arthur Balfour noted Afghanistan's "non-conducting" qualities. "So long as it possesses

---

[21] Macleod and Kelly (fn. 43), 174. In flat contradiction to common sense and almost everything they believed about modern warfare, the Allies planned an expedition to Scandinavia to cut the supply of iron ore to Germany and to aid Finland against the Russians. But the dominant mood was the one described above.

[22] Brodie (fn. 8), 179.

few roads, and no railroads, it will be impossible for Russia to make effective use of her great numerical superiority at any point immediately vital to the Empire.'' The Russians valued buffers for the same reasons; it is not surprising that when Persia was being divided into Russian and British spheres of influence some years later, the Russians sought assurances that the British would refrain from building potentially menacing railroads in their sphere. Indeed, since railroad construction radically altered the abilities of countries to defend themselves and to attack others, many diplomatic notes and much intelligence activity in the late 19th century centered on this subject.[23]

Oceans, large rivers, and mountain ranges serve the same function as buffer zones. Being hard to cross, they allow defense against superior numbers. The defender has merely to stay on his side of the barrier and so can utilize all the men he can bring up to it. The attacker's men, however, can cross only a few at a time, and they are very vulnerable when doing so. If all states were self-sufficient islands, anarchy would be much less of a problem. A small investment in shore defenses and a small army would be sufficient to repel invasion. Only very weak states would be vulnerable, and only very large ones could menace others. As noted above, the United States, and to a lesser extent Great Britain, have partly been able to escape from the state of nature because their geographical positions approximated this ideal.

Although geography cannot be changed to conform to borders, borders can and do change to conform to geography. Borders across which an attack is easy tend to be unstable. States living within them are likely to expand or be absorbed. Frequent wars are almost inevitable since attacking will often seem the best way to protect what one has. This process will stop, or at least slow down, when the state's borders reach—by expansion or contraction—a line of natural obstacles. Security without attack will then be possible. Furthermore, these lines constitute salient solutions to bargaining problems and, to the extent that they are barriers to migration, are likely to divide ethnic groups, thereby raising the costs and lowering the incentives for conquest.

Attachment to one's state and its land reinforce one quasi-geographical aid to the defense. Conquest usually becomes more difficult the deeper the attacker pushes into the other's territory. Nationalism spurs the defenders to fight harder; advancing not only

---

[23] Arthur Balfour, ''Memorandum,'' Committee on Imperial Defence, April 30, 1903, pp. 2–3; see the telegrams by Sir Arthur Nicolson, in G. P. Gooch and Harold Temperley, eds., *British Documents on the Origins of the War*, Vol. 4 (London: H.M.S.O. 1929), 429, 524. These barriers do not prevent the passage of long-range aircraft; but even in the air, distance usually aids the defender.

lengthens the attacker's supply lines, but takes him through unfamiliar and often devastated lands that require troops for garrison duty. These stabilizing dynamics will not operate, however, if the defender's war materiel is situated near its borders, or if the people do not care about their state, but only about being on the winning side. In such cases, positive feedback will be at work and initial defeats will be insurmountable.[24]

Imitating geography, men have tried to create barriers. Treaties may provide for demilitarized zones on both sides of the border, although such zones will rarely be deep enough to provide more than warning. Even this was not possible in Europe, but the Russians adopted a gauge for their railroads that was broader than that of the neighboring states, thereby complicating the logistics problems of any attacker—including Russia.

Perhaps the most ambitious and at least temporarily successful attempts to construct a system that would aid the defenses of both sides were the interwar naval treaties, as they affected Japanese-American relations. As mentioned earlier, the problem was that the United States could not defend the Philippines without denying Japan the ability to protect her home islands.[25] (In 1941 this dilemma became insoluble when Japan sought to extend her control to Malaya and the Dutch East Indies. If the Philippines had been invulnerable, they could have provided a secure base from which the U.S. could interdict Japanese shipping between the homeland and the areas she was trying to conquer.) In the 1920's and early 1930's each side would have been willing to grant the other security for its possessions in return for a reciprocal grant, and the Washington Naval Conference agreements were designed to approach this goal. As a Japanese diplomat later put it, their country's "fundamental principle" was to have "a strength insufficient for attack and adequate for defense."[26] Thus, Japan agreed in 1922 to accept a navy only three-fifths as large as that of the United States, and the U.S. agreed not to fortify its Pacific islands.[27] (Japan had earlier been forced to agree not to fortify the islands she had taken from Germany in World War I.) Japan's navy would not be large enough to defeat America's anywhere other than close to the home islands. Although the Japanese could still take the Philippines,

---

[24] See, for example, the discussion of warfare among Chinese warlords in Hsi-Sheng Chi, "The Chinese Warlord System as an International System," in Morton Kaplan, ed., *New Approaches to International Relations* (New York: St. Martin's 1968), 405–25.

[25] Some American decision makers, including military officers, thought that the best way out of the dilemma was to abandon the Philippines.

[26] Quoted in Elting Morrison, *Turmoil and Tradition: A Study of the Life and Times of Henry L. Stimson* (Boston: Houghton Mifflin 1960), 326.

[27] The U.S. "refused to consider limitations on Hawaiian defenses, since these works posed no threat to Japan." Braisted (fn. 27), 612.

not only would they be unable to move farther, but they might be weakened enough by their efforts to be vulnerable to counterattack. Japan, however, gained security. An American attack was rendered more difficult because the American bases were unprotected and because, until 1930, Japan was allowed unlimited numbers of cruisers, destroyers, and submarines that could weaken the American fleet as it made its way across the ocean.[28]

The other major determinant of the offense-defense balance is technology. When weapons are highly vulnerable, they must be employed before they are attacked. Others can remain quite invulnerable in their bases. The former characteristics are embodied in unprotected missiles and many kinds of bombers. (It should be noted that it is not vulnerability *per se* that is crucial, but the location of the vulnerability. Bombers and missiles that are easy to destroy only after having been launched toward their targets do not create destabilizing dynamics.) Incentives to strike first are usually absent for naval forces that are threatened by a naval attack. Like missiles in hardened silos, they are usually well protected when in their bases. Both sides can then simultaneously be prepared to defend themselves successfully.

In ground warfare under some conditions, forts, trenches, and small groups of men in prepared positions can hold off large numbers of attackers. Less frequently, a few attackers can storm the defenses. By and large, it is a contest between fortifications and supporting light weapons on the one hand, and mobility and heavier weapons that clear the way for the attack on the other. As the erroneous views held before the two world wars show, there is no simple way to determine which is dominant. "[T]hese oscillations are not smooth and predictable like those of a swinging pendulum. They are uneven in both extent and time. Some occur in the course of a single battle or campaign, others in the course of a war, still others during a series of wars." Longer-term oscillations can also be detected:

> The early Gothic age, from the twelfth to the late thirteenth century, with its wonderful cathedrals and fortified places, was a period during which the attackers in Europe generally met serious and increasing difficulties, because the improvement in the strength of fortresses outran the advance in the power of destruction. Later, with the spread of firearms at the end of the fifteenth century, old fortresses lost their power to resist. An age ensued during which the offense possessed, apart from short-term setbacks, new advantages. Then, during the seventeenth century, especially after about 1660, and until at least at the outbreak of the War of the Austrian Succession in 1740, the defense regained much of the ground it had lost

---

[28] That is part of the reason why the Japanese admirals strongly objected when the civilian leaders decided to accept a seven-to-ten ratio in lighter craft in 1930. Stephen Pelz, *Race to Pearl Harbor* (Cambridge: Harvard University Press 1974), 3.

since the great medieval fortresses had proved unable to meet the bombardment of the new and more numerous artillery.[29]

Another scholar has continued the agrument: "The offensive gained an advantage with new forms of heavy mobile artillery in the nineteenth century, but the stalemate of World War I created the impression that the defense again had an advantage; the German invasion in World War II, however, indicated the offensive superiority of highly mechanized armies in the field."[30]

The situation today with respect to conventional weapons is unclear. Until recently it was believed that tanks and tactical air power gave the attacker an advantage. The initial analyses of the 1973 Arab-Israeli war indicated that new anti-tank and anti-aircraft weapons have restored the primacy of the defense. These weapons are cheap, easy to use, and can destroy a high proportion of the attacking vehicles and planes that are sighted. It then would make sense for a status-quo power to buy lots of $20,000 missiles rather than buy a few half-million dollar tanks and multi-million dollar fighter-bombers. Defense would be possible even against a large and well-equipped force; states that care primarily about self-protection would not need to engage in arms races. But further examinations of the new technologies and the history of the October War cast doubt on these optimistic conclusions and leave us unable to render any firm judgment.[31]

Concerning nuclear weapons, it is generally agreed that defense is impossible—a triumph not of the offense, but of deterrence. Attack makes no sense, not because it can be beaten off, but because the attacker will be destroyed in turn. In terms of the questions under consideration here, the result is the equivalent of the primacy of the defense. First, security is relatively cheap. Less than one percent of the G.N.P. is devoted to deterring a direct attack on the United States; most of it is spent on acquiring redundant systems to provide a lot of insurance against the worst conceivable contingencies. Second, both sides can simultaneously gain security in the form of second-strike

---

[29] John Nef, *War and Human Progress* (New York: Norton 1963), 185. Also see *ibid.*, 237, 242–43, and 323; C. W. Oman, *The Art of War in the Middle Ages* (Ithaca, N.Y.: Cornell University Press 1953), 70–72; John Beeler, *Warfare in Feudal Europe, 730–1200* (Ithaca, N.Y.: Cornell University Press 1971), 212–14; Michael Howard, *War in European History* (London: Oxford University Press 1976), 33–37.

[30] Quincy Wright, *A Study of War* (abridged ed.; Chicago: University of Chicago Press 1964), 142. Also see 63–70, 74–75. There are important exceptions to these generalizations—the American Civil War, for instance, falls in the middle of the period Wright says is dominated by the offense.

[31] Geoffrey Kemp, Robert Pfaltzgraff, and Uri Ra'anan, eds., *The Other Arms Race* (Lexington, Mass.: D. C. Heath 1975); James Foster, "The Future of Conventional Arms Control," *Policy Sciences*, No. 8 (Spring 1977), 1–19.

capability. Third, and related to the foregoing, second-strike capability can be maintained in the face of wide variations in the other side's military posture. There is no purely military reason why each side has to react quickly and strongly to the other's increases in arms. Any spending that the other devotes to trying to achieve first-strike capability can be neutralized by the state's spending much smaller sums on protecting its second-strike capability. Fourth, there are no incentives to strike first in a crisis.

Important problems remain, of course. Both sides have interests that go well beyond defense of the homeland. The protection of these interests creates conflicts even if neither side desires expansion. Furthermore, the shift from defense to deterrence has greatly increased the importance and perceptions of resolve. Security now rests on each side's belief that the other would prefer to run high risks of total destruction rather than sacrifice its vital interests. Aspects of the security dilemma thus appear in a new form. Are weapons procurements used as an index of resolve? Must they be so used? If one side fails to respond to the other's buildup, will it appear weak and thereby invite predation? Can both sides simultaneously have images of high resolve or is there a zero-sum element involved? Although these problems are real, they are not as severe as those in the prenuclear era: there are many indices of resolve, and states do not so much judge images of resolve in the abstract as ask how likely it is that the other will stand firm in a particular dispute. Since states are most likely to stand firm on matters which concern them most, it is quite possible for both to demonstrate their resolve to protect their own security simultaneously.

OFFENSE-DEFENSE DIFFERENTIATION

The other major variable that affects how strongly the security dilemma operates is whether weapons and policies that protect the state also provide the capability for attack. If they do not, the basic postulate of the security dilemma no longer applies. A state can increase its own security without decreasing that of others. The advantage of the defense can only ameliorate the security dilemma. A differentiation between offensive and defensive stances comes close to abolishing it. Such differentiation does not mean, however, that all security problems will be abolished. If the offense has the advantage, conquest and aggression will still be possible. And if the offense's advantage is great enough, status-quo powers may find it too expensive to protect themselves by defensive forces and decide to procure offensive weapons even though this will menace others. Furthermore, states will still have to worry that even if the other's military posture shows that it is peaceful now, it may develop aggressive intentions in the future.

Assuming that the defense is at least as potent as the offense, the differentiation between them allows status-quo states to behave in ways that are clearly different from those of aggressors. Three beneficial consequences follow. First, status-quo powers can identify each other, thus laying the foundations for cooperation. Conflicts growing out of the mistaken belief that the other side is expansionist will be less frequent. Second, status-quo states will obtain advance warning when others plan aggression. Before a state can attack, it has to develop and deploy offensive weapons. If procurement of these weapons cannot be disguised and takes a fair amount of time, as it almost always does, a status-quo state will have the time to take countermeasures. It need not maintain a high level of defensive arms as long as its potential adversaries are adopting a peaceful posture. (Although being so armed should not, with the one important exception noted below, alarm other status-quo powers.) States do, in fact, pay special attention to actions that they believe would not be taken by a status-quo state because they feel that states exhibiting such behavior are aggressive. Thus the seizure or development of transportation facilities will alarm others more if these facilities have no commercial value, and therefore can only be wanted for military reasons. In 1906, the British rejected a Russian protest about their activities in a district of Persia by claiming that this area was "only of [strategic] importance [to the Russians] if they wished to attack the Indian frontier, or to put pressure upon us by making us think that they intend to attack it."[32]

The same inferences are drawn when a state acquires more weapons than observers feel are needed for defense. Thus, the Japanese spokesman at the 1930 London naval conference said that his country was alarmed by the American refusal to give Japan a 70 percent ratio (in place of a 60 percent ratio) in heavy cruisers: "As long as America held that ten percent advantage, it was possible for her to attack. So when America insisted on sixty percent instead of seventy percent, the idea would exist that they were trying to keep that possibility, and the Japanese people could not accept that."[33] Similarly, when Mussolini told Chamberlain in January 1939 that Hitler's arms program was motivated by defensive considerations, the Prime Minister replied that "German military forces were now so strong as to make it impossible for any Power or combination of Powers to attack her successfully.

---

[32] Richard Challener, *Admirals, Generals, and American Foreign Policy, 1898–1914* (Princeton: Princeton University Press 1973), 273; Grey to Nicolson, in Gooch and Temperley (fn. 47), 414.

[33] Quoted in James Crowley, *Japan's Quest for Autonomy* (Princeton: Princeton University Press 1966), 49. American naval officers agreed with the Japanese that a ten-to-six ratio would endanger Japan's supremacy in her home waters.

She could not want any further armaments for defensive purposes; what then did she want them for?"[34]

Of course these inferences can be wrong—as they are especially likely to be because states underestimate the degree to which they menace others.[35] And when they are wrong, the security dilemma is deepened. Because the state thinks it has received notice that the other is aggressive, its own arms building will be less restrained and the chances of cooperation will be decreased. But the dangers of incorrect inferences should not obscure the main point: when offensive and defensive postures are different, much of the uncertainty about the other's intentions that contributes to the security dilemma is removed.

The third beneficial consequence of a difference between offensive and defensive weapons is that if all states support the status quo, an obvious arms control agreement is a ban on weapons that are useful for attacking. As President Roosevelt put it in his message to the Geneva Disarmament Conference in 1933: "If all nations will agree wholly to eliminate from possession and use the weapons which make possible a successful attack, defenses automatically will become impregnable, and the frontiers and independence of every nation will become secure."[36] The fact that such treaties have been rare—the Washington naval agreements discussed above and the anti-ABM treaty can be cited as examples—shows either that states are not always willing to guarantee the security of others, or that it is hard to distinguish offensive from defensive weapons.

Is such a distinction possible? Salvador de Madariaga, the Spanish statesman active in the disarmament negotiations of the interwar years, thought not: "A weapon is either offensive or defensive according to which end of it you are looking at." The French Foreign Minister agreed (although French policy did not always follow this view): "Every arm can be employed offensively or defensively in turn. . . . The only way to discover whether arms are intended for purely defensive purposes or are held in a spirit of aggression is in all cases to enquire into the intentions of the country concerned." Some evidence for the validity of this argument is provided by the fact that much time in these unsuccessful negotiations was devoted to separating offensive from defensive weapons. Indeed, no simple and unambiguous definition is possible and in many cases no judgment can be reached. Before the American entry into World War I, Woodrow Wilson wanted to arm merchantmen only with guns in the back of the

---

[34] E. L. Woodward and R. Butler, eds., *Documents on British Foreign Policy, 1919–1939,* Third series, III (London: H.M.S.O. 1950), 526.

[35] Jervis (fn. 5), 69–72, 352–55.

[36] Quoted in Merze Tate, *The United States and Armaments* (Cambridge: Harvard University Press 1948), 108.

ship so they could not initiate a fight, but this expedient cannot be applied to more common forms of armaments.[37] There are several problems. Even when a differentiation is possible, a status-quo power will want offensive arms under any of three conditions. (1) If the offense has a great advantage over the defense, protection through defensive forces will be too expensive. (2) Status-quo states may need offensive weapons to regain territory lost in the opening stages of a war. It might be possible, however, for a state to wait to procure these weapons until war seems likely, and they might be needed only in relatively small numbers, unless the aggressor was able to construct strong defenses quickly in the occupied areas. (3) The state may feel that it must be prepared to take the offensive either because the other side will make peace only if it loses territory or because the state has commitments to attack if the other makes war on a third party. As noted above, status-quo states with extensive commitments are often forced to behave like aggressors. Even when they lack such commitments, status-quo states must worry about the possibility that if they are able to hold off an attack, they will still not be able to end the war unless they move into the other's territory to damage its military forces and inflict pain. Many American naval officers after the Civil War, for example, believed that "only by destroying the commerce of the opponent could the United States bring him to terms."[38]

A further complication is introduced by the fact that aggressors as well as status-quo powers require defensive forces as a prelude to acquiring offensive ones, to protect one frontier while attacking another, or for insurance in case the war goes badly. Criminals as well as policemen can use bulletproof vests. Hitler as well as Maginot built a line of forts. Indeed, Churchill reports that in 1936 the German Foreign Minister said: "As soon as our fortifications are constructed [on our western borders] and the countries in Central Europe realize that France cannot enter German territory, all these countries will begin to feel very differently about their foreign policies, and a new constellation will develop."[39] So a state may not necessarily be reassured if its neighbor constructs strong defenses.

More central difficulties are created by the fact that whether a weapon is offensive or defensive often depends on the particular situation—for instance, the geographical setting and the way in which the weapon is used. "Tanks . . . spearheaded the fateful German thrust through the Ardennes in 1940, but if the French had disposed of

---

[37] Boggs (fn. 28), 15, 40.
[38] Kenneth Hagan, *American Gunboat Diplomacy and the Old Navy, 1877–1889* (Westport, Conn.: Greenwood Press 1973), 20.
[39] Winston Churchill, *The Gathering Storm* (Boston: Houghton 1948), 206.

a properly concentrated armored reserve, it would have provided the best means for their cutting off the penetration and turning into a disaster for the Germans what became instead an overwhelming victory."[40] Anti-aircraft weapons seem obviously defensive—to be used, they must wait for the other side to come to them. But the Egyptian attack on Israel in 1973 would have been impossible without effective air defenses that covered the battlefield. Nevertheless, some distinctions are possible. Sir John Simon, then the British Foreign Secretary, in response to the views cited earlier, stated that just because a fine line could not be drawn, "that was no reason for saying that there were not stretches of territory on either side which all practical men and women knew to be well on this or that side of the line." Although there are almost no weapons and strategies that are useful only for attacking, there are some that are almost exclusively defensive. Aggressors could want them for protection, but a state that relied mostly on them could not menace others. More frequently, we cannot "determine the absolute character of a weapon, but [we can] make a comparison . . . [and] discover whether or not the offensive potentialities predominate, whether a weapon is more useful in attack or in defense."[41]

The essence of defense is keeping the other side out of your territory. A purely defensive weapon is one that can do this without being able to penetrate the enemy's land. Thus a committee of military experts in an interwar disarmament conference declared that armaments "incapable of mobility by means of self-contained power," or movable only after long delay, were "only capable of being used for the defense of a State's territory."[42] The most obvious examples are fortifications. They can shelter attacking forces, especially when they are built right along the frontier,[43] but they cannot occupy enemy territory. A state with only a strong line of forts, fixed guns, and a small army to man them would not be much of a menace. Anything else that can serve only as a barrier against attacking troops is similarly defensive. In this category are systems that provide warning of an attack, the Russian's adoption of a different railroad gauge, and nuclear land mines that can seal off invasion routes.

If total immobility clearly defines a system that is defensive only, limited mobility is unfortunately ambiguous. As noted above, short-

[40] Brodie, *War and Politics* (fn. 35), 325.

[41] Boggs (fn. 28), 42, 83. For a good argument about the possible differentiation between offensive and defensive weapons in the 1930's, see Basil Liddell Hart, "Aggression and the Problem of Weapons," *English Review*, Vol. 55 (July 1932), 71–78.

[42] Quoted in Boggs (fn. 28), 39.

[43] On these grounds, the Germans claimed in 1932 that the French forts were offensive (*ibid.*, 49). Similarly, fortified forward naval bases can be necessary for launching an attack; see Braisted (fn. 27), 643.

ROBERT JERVIS   87

range fighter aircraft and anti-aircraft missiles can be used to cover an attack. And, unlike forts, they can advance with the troops. Still, their inability to reach deep into enemy territory does make them more useful for the defense than for the offense. Thus, the United States and Israel would have been more alarmed in the early 1970's had the Russians provided the Egyptians with long-range instead of short-range aircraft. Naval forces are particularly difficult to classify in these terms, but those that are very short-legged can be used only for coastal defense.

Any forces that for various reasons fight well only when on their own soil in effect lack mobility and therefore are defensive. The most extreme example would be passive resistance. Noncooperation can thwart an aggressor, but it is very hard for large numbers of people to cross the border and stage a sit-in on another's territory. Morocco's recent march on the Spanish Sahara approached this tactic, but its success depended on special circumstances. Similarly, guerrilla warfare is defensive to the extent to which it requires civilian support that is likely to be forthcoming only in opposition to a foreign invasion. Indeed, if guerrilla warfare were easily exportable and if it took ten defenders to destroy each guerrilla, then this weapon would not only be one which could be used as easily to attack the other's territory as to defend one's own, but one in which the offense had the advantage: so the security dilemma would operate especially strongly.

If guerrillas are unable to fight on foreign soil, other kinds of armies may be unwilling to do so. An army imbued with the idea that only defensive wars were just would fight less effectively, if at all, if the goal were conquest. Citizen militias may lack both the ability and the will for aggression. The weapons employed, the short term of service, the time required for mobilization, and the spirit of repelling attacks on the homeland, all lend themselves much more to defense than to attacks on foreign territory.[44]

Less idealistic motives can produce the same result. A leading student of medieval warfare has described the armies of that period as follows: "Assembled with difficulty, insubordinate, unable to maneuver, ready to melt away from its standard the moment that its short period of service was over, a feudal force presented an assemblage of unsoldierlike qualities such as have seldom been known to coexist. Primarily intended to defend its own borders from the Magyar, the Northman, or the Saracen . . . , the institution was utterly unadapted to take the offensive."[45] Some political groupings can be similarly

[44] The French made this argument in the interwar period; see Richard Challener, *The French Theory of the Nation in Arms* (New York: Columbia University Press 1955), 181–82. The Germans disagreed; see Boggs (fn. 28), 44–45.
[45] Oman (fn. 53), 57–58.

described. International coalitions are more readily held together by fear than by hope of gain. Thus Castlereagh was not being entirely self-serving when in 1816 he argued that the Quadruple Alliance "could only have owed its origin to a sense of common danger; in its very nature it must be conservative; it cannot threaten either the security or the liberties of other States."[46] It is no accident that most of the major campaigns of expansion have been waged by one dominant nation (for example, Napoleon's France and Hitler's Germany), and that coalitions among relative equals are usually found defending the status quo. Most gains from conquest are too uncertain and raise too many questions of future squabbles among the victors to hold an alliance together for long. Although defensive coalitions are by no means easy to maintain—conflicting national objectives and the free-rider problem partly explain why three of them dissolved before Napoleon was defeated—the common interest of seeing that no state dominates provides a strong incentive for solidarity.

Weapons that are particularly effective in reducing fortifications and barriers are of great value to the offense. This is not to deny that a defensive power will want some of those weapons if the other side has them: Brodie is certainly correct to argue that while their tanks allowed the Germans to conquer France, properly used French tanks could have halted the attack. But France would not have needed these weapons if Germany had not acquired them, whereas even if France had no tanks, Germany could not have foregone them since they provided the only chance of breaking through the French lines. Mobile heavy artillery is, similarly, especially useful in destroying fortifications. The defender, while needing artillery to fight off attacking troops or to counterattack, can usually use lighter guns since they do not need to penetrate such massive obstacles. So it is not surprising that one of the few things that most nations at the interwar disarmament conferences were able to agree on was that heavy tanks and mobile heavy guns were particularly valuable to a state planning an attack.[47]

Weapons and strategies that depend for their effectiveness on surprise are almost always offensive. That fact was recognized by some of the delegates to the interwar disarmament conferences and is the principle behind the common national ban on concealed weapons. An earlier representative of this widespread view was the mid-19th-century Philadelphia newspaper that argued: "As a measure of defense, knives, dirks, and sword canes are entirely useless. They are fit only for attack, and all such attacks are of murderous character.

[46] Quoted in Charles Webster, *The Foreign Policy of Castlereagh, II, 1815–1822* (London: G. Bell and Sons 1963), 510.
[47] Boggs (fn. 28), 14–15, 47–48, 60.

Whoever carries such a weapon has prepared himself for homicide."[48]

It is, of course, not always possible to distinguish between forces that are most effective for holding territory and forces optimally designed for taking it. Such a distinction could not have been made for the strategies and weapons in Europe during most of the period between the Franco-Prussian War and World War I. Neither naval forces nor tactical air forces can be readily classified in these terms. But the point here is that when such a distinction is possible, the central characteristic of the security dilemma no longer holds, and one of the most troublesome consequences of anarchy is removed.

Offense-Defense Differentiation and Strategic Nuclear Weapons. In the interwar period, most statesmen held the reasonable position that weapons that threatened civilians were offensive.[49] But when neither side can protect its civilians, a counter city posture is defensive because the state can credibly threaten to retaliate only in response to an attack on itself or its closest allies. The costs of this strike are so high that the state could not threaten to use it for the less-than-vital interest of compelling the other to abandon an established position.

In the context of deterrence, offensive weapons are those that provide defense. In the now familiar reversal of common sense, the state that could take its population out of hostage, either by active or passive defense or by destroying the other's strategic weapons on the ground, would be able to alter the status quo. The desire to prevent such a situation was one of the rationales for the anti-ABM agreements; it explains why some arms controllers opposed building ABM's to protect cities, but favored sites that covered ICBM fields. Similarly, many analysts want to limit warhead accuracy and favor multiple re-entry vehicles (MRV's), but oppose multiple independently targetable re-entry vehicles (MIRV's). The former are more useful than single warheads for penetrating city defenses, and ensure that the state has a second-strike capability. MIRV's enhance counterforce capabilities. Some arms controllers argue that this is also true of cruise missiles, and therefore do not want them to be deployed either. There is some evidence that the Russians are not satisfied with deterrence and are seeking to regain the capability for defense. Such an effort, even if not inspired by aggressive designs, would create a severe security dilemma.

What is most important for the argument here is that land-based ICBM's are both offensive and defensive, but when both sides rely on Polaris-type systems (SLBM's), offense and defense use different weapons. ICBM's can be used either to destroy the other's cities in

---

[48] Quoted in Philip Jordan, *Frontier Law and Order* (London: University of Nebraska Press 1970), 7; also see 16–17.

[49] Boggs (fn. 28), 20, 28.

retaliation or to initiate hostilities by attacking the other's strategic missiles. Some measures—for instance, hardening of missile sites and warning systems—are purely defensive, since they do not make a first strike easier. Others are predominantly offensive—for instance, passive or active city defenses, and highly accurate warheads. But ICBM's themselves are useful for both purposes. And because states seek a high level of insurance, the desire for protection as well as the contemplation of a counterforce strike can explain the acquisition of extremely large numbers of missiles. So it is very difficult to infer the other's intentions from its military posture. Each side's efforts to increase its own security by procuring more missiles decreases, to an extent determined by the relative efficacy of the offense and the defense, the other side's security. That is not the case when both sides use SLBM's. The point is not that sea-based systems are less vulnerable than land-based ones (this bears on the offense-defense ratio) but that SLBM's are defensive, retaliatory weapons. First, they are probably not accurate enough to destroy many military targets.[50] Second, and more important, SLBM's are not the main instrument of attack against other SLBM's. The hardest problem confronting a state that wants to take its cities out of hostage is to locate the other's SLBM's, a job that requires not SLBM's but anti-submarine weapons. A state might use SLBM's to attack the other's submarines (although other weapons would probably be more efficient), but without anti-submarine warfare (ASW) capability the task cannot be performed. A status-quo state that wanted to forego offensive capability could simply forego ASW research and procurement.

There are two difficulties with this argument, however. First, since the state's SLBM's are potentially threatened by the other's ASW capabilities, the state may want to pursue ASW research in order to know what the other might be able to do and to design defenses. Unless it does this, it cannot be confident that its submarines are safe. Second, because some submarines are designed to attack surface ships, not launch missiles, ASW forces have missions other than taking cities out of hostage. Some U.S. officials plan for a long war in Europe which would require keeping the sea lanes open against Russian submarines. Designing an ASW force and strategy that would meet this threat without endangering Soviet SLBM's would be difficult but not impossible, since the two missions are somewhat different.[51] Furthermore, the Russians do not need ASW forces to combat submarines carrying out conventional missions; it might be in

---

[50] See, however, Desmond Ball, "The Counterforce Potential of American SLBM Systems," *Journal of Peace Research,* XIV (No. 1, 1977), 23–40.

[51] Richard Garwin, "Anti-Submarine Warfare and National Security," *Scientific American,* Vol. 227 (July 1972), 14–25.

America's interest to sacrifice the ability to meet a threat that is not likely to materialize in order to reassure the Russians that we are not menacing their retaliatory capability. When both sides rely on ICBM's, one side's missiles can attack the other's, and so the state cannot be indifferent to the other's building program. But because one side's SLBM's do not menace the other's, each side can build as many as it wants and the other need not respond. Each side's decision on the size of its force depends on technical questions, its judgment about how much destruction is enough to deter, and the amount of insurance it is willing to pay for—and these considerations are independent of the size of the other's strategic force. Thus the crucial nexus in the arms race is severed.

Here two objections not only can be raised but have been, by those who feel that even if American second-strike capability is in no danger, the United States must respond to a Soviet buildup. First, the relative numbers of missiles and warheads may be used as an index of each side's power and will. Even if there is no military need to increase American arms as the Russians increase theirs, a failure to respond may lead third parties to think that the U.S. has abandoned the competition with the U.S.S.R. and is no longer willing to pay the price of world leadership. Furthermore, if either side believes that nuclear "superiority" matters, then, through the bargaining logic, it will matter. The side with "superiority" will be more likely to stand firm in a confrontation if it thinks its "stronger" military position helps it, or if it thinks that the other thinks its own "weaker" military position is a handicap. To allow the other side to have more SLBM's—even if one's own second-strike capability is unimpaired—will give the other an advantage that can be translated into political gains.

The second objection is that superiority *does* matter, and not only because of mistaken beliefs. If nuclear weapons are used in an all-or-none fashion, then all that is needed is second-strike capability. But limited, gradual, and controlled strikes are possible. If the other side has superiority, it can reduce the state's forces by a slow-motion war of attrition. For the state to strike at the other's cities would invite retaliation; for it to reply with a limited counterforce attack would further deplete its supply of missiles. Alternatively, the other could employ demonstration attacks—such as taking out an isolated military base or exploding a warhead high over a city—in order to demonstrate its resolve. In either of these scenarios, the state will suffer unless it matches the other's arms posture.[52]

These two objections, if valid, mean that even with SLBM's one

---

[52] The latter scenario, however, does not require that the state closely match the number of missiles the other deploys.

cannot distinguish offensive from defensive strategic nuclear weapons. Compellence may be more difficult than deterrence,[53] but if decision makers believe that numbers of missiles or of warheads influence outcomes, or if these weapons can be used in limited manner, then the posture and policy that would be needed for self-protection is similar to that useful for aggression. If the second objection has merit, security would require the ability to hit selected targets on the other side, enough ammunition to wage a controlled counterforce war, and the willingness to absorb limited countervalue strikes. Secretary Schlesinger was correct in arguing that this capability would not constitute a first-strike capability. But because the "Schlesinger Doctrine" could be used not only to cope with a parallel Russian policy, but also to support an American attempt to change the status quo, the new American stance would decrease Russian security. Even if the U.S.S.R. were reassured that the present U.S. Government lacked the desire or courage to do this, there could be no guarantee that future governments would not use the new instruments for expansion. Once we move away from the simple idea that nuclear weapons can only be used for all-out strikes, half the advantage of having both sides rely on a sea-based force would disappear because of the lack of an offensive-defensive differentiation. To the extent that military policy affects political relations, it would be harder for the United States and the Soviet Union to cooperate even if both supported the status quo.

Although a full exploration of these questions is beyond the scope of this paper, it should be noted that the objections rest on decision makers' beliefs—beliefs, furthermore, that can be strongly influenced by American policy and American statements. The perceptions of third nations of whether the details of the nuclear balance affect political conflicts—and, to a lesser extent, Russian beliefs about whether superiority is meaningful—are largely derived from the American strategic debate. If most American spokesmen were to take the position that a secure second-strike capability was sufficient and that increments over that (short of a first-strike capability) would only be a waste of money, it is doubtful whether America's allies or the neutrals would judge the superpowers' useful military might or political will by the size of their stockpiles. Although the Russians stress war-fighting ability, they have not contended that marginal increases in strategic forces bring political gains; any attempt to do so could be rendered less effective by an American assertion that this is

---

[53] Thomas Schelling, *Arms and Influence* (New Haven: Yale University Press 1966), 69–78. Schelling's arguments are not entirely convincing, however. For further discussion, see Jervis, "Deterrence Theory Re-Visited," Working Paper No. 14, UCLA Program in Arms Control and International Security.

nonsense. The bargaining advantages of possessing nuclear "superiority" work best when both sides acknowledge them. If the "weaker" side convinces the other that it does not believe there is any meaningful difference in strength, then the "stronger" side cannot safely stand firm because there is no increased chance that the other will back down.

This kind of argument applies at least as strongly to the second objection. Neither side can employ limited nuclear options unless it is quite confident that the other accepts the rules of the game. For if the other believes that nuclear war cannot be controlled, it will either refrain from responding—which would be fine—or launch all-out retaliation. Although a state might be ready to engage in limited nuclear war without acknowledging this possibility—and indeed, that would be a reasonable policy for the United States—it is not likely that the other would have sufficient faith in that prospect to initiate limited strikes unless the state had openly avowed its willingness to fight this kind of war. So the United States, by patiently and consistently explaining that it considers such ideas to be mad and that any nuclear wars will inevitably get out of control, could gain a large measure of protection against the danger that the Soviet Union might seek to employ a "Schlesinger Doctrine" against an America that lacked the military ability or political will to respond in kind. Such a position is made more convincing by the inherent implausibility of the arguments for the possibility of a limited nuclear war.

In summary, as long as states believe that all that is needed is second-strike capability, then the differentiation between offensive and defensive forces that is provided by reliance on SLBM's allows each side to increase its security without menacing the other, permits some inferences about intentions to be drawn from military posture, and removes the main incentive for status-quo powers to engage in arms races.

IV. FOUR WORLDS

The two variables we have been discussing—whether the offense or the defense has the advantage, and whether offensive postures can be distinguished from defensive ones—can be combined to yield four possible worlds.

	OFFENSE HAS THE ADVANTAGE	DEFENSE HAS THE ADVANTAGE
OFFENSIVE POSTURE NOT DISTINGUISHABLE FROM DEFENSIVE ONE	1 Doubly dangerous	2 Security dilemma, but security requirements may be compatible.
OFFENSIVE POSTURE DISTINGUISHABLE FROM DEFENSIVE ONE	3 No security dilemma, but aggression possible. Status-quo states can follow different policy than aggressors. Warning given.	4 Doubly stable

The first world is the worst for status-quo states. There is no way to get security without menacing others, and security through defense is terribly difficult to obtain. Because offensive and defensive postures are the same, status-quo states acquire the same kind of arms that are sought by aggressors. And because the offense has the advantage over the defense, attacking is the best route to protecting what you have; status-quo states will therefore behave like aggressors. The situation will be unstable. Arms races are likely. Incentives to strike first will turn crises into wars. Decisive victories and conquests will be common. States will grow and shrink rapidly, and it will be hard for any state to maintain its size and influence without trying to increase them. Cooperation among status-quo powers will be extremely hard to achieve.

There are no cases that totally fit this picture, but it bears more than a passing resemblance to Europe before World War I. Britain and Germany, although in many respects natural allies, ended up as enemies. Of course much of the explanation lies in Germany's ill-chosen policy. And from the perspective of our theory, the powers' ability to avoid war in a series of earlier crises cannot be easily explained. Nevertheless, much of the behavior in this period was the product of technology and beliefs that magnified the security dilemma. Decision makers thought that the offense had a big advantage and saw little difference between offensive and defensive military postures. The era was characterized by arms races. And once war seemed likely, mobilization races created powerful incentives to strike first.

In the nuclear era, the first world would be one in which each side relied on vulnerable weapons that were aimed at similar forces and each side understood the situation. In this case, the incentives to strike first would be very high—so high that status-quo powers as well as aggressors would be sorely tempted to pre-empt. And since the forces could be used to change the status-quo as well as to preserve it, there would be no way for both sides to increase their security simultaneously. Now the familiar logic of deterrence leads both sides to see the dangers in this world. Indeed, the new understanding of this situation was one reason why vulnerable bombers and missiles were replaced. Ironically, the 1950's would have been more hazardous if the decision makers had been aware of the dangers of their posture and had therefore felt greater pressure to strike first. This situation could be recreated if both sides were to rely on MIRVed ICBM's.

In the second world, the security dilemma operates because offensive and defensive postures cannot be distinguished; but it does not operate as strongly as in the first world because the defense has the advantage, and so an increment in one side's strength increases its security more than it decreases the other's. So, if both sides have reasonable subjective security requirements, are of roughly equal power, and the variables discussed earlier are favorable, it is quite likely that status-quo states can adopt compatible security policies. Although a state will not be able to judge the other's intentions from the kinds of weapons it procures, the level of arms spending will give important evidence. Of course a state that seeks a high level of arms might be not an aggressor but merely an insecure state, which if conciliated will reduce its arms, and if confronted will reply in kind. To assume that the apparently excessive level of arms indicates aggressiveness could therefore lead to a response that would deepen the dilemma and create needless conflict. But empathy and skillful statesmanship can reduce this danger. Furthermore, the advantageous position of the defense means that a status-quo state can often maintain a high degree of security with a level of arms lower than that of its expected adversary. Such a state demonstrates that it lacks the ability or desire to alter the status-quo, at least at the present time. The strength of the defense also allows states to react slowly and with restraint when they fear that others are menacing them. So, although status-quo powers will to some extent be threatening to others, that extent will be limited.

This world is the one that comes closest to matching most periods in history. Attacking is usually harder than defending because of the strength of fortifications and obstacles. But purely defensive postures are rarely possible because fortifications are usually supplemented by armies and mobile guns which can support an attack. In the nuclear era, this world would be one in which both sides relied on relatively invulnerable ICBM's and believed that limited nuclear war was impossible. Assuming no MIRV's, it would take more than one attacking missile to destroy one of the adversary's. Pre-emption is therefore unattractive. If both sides have large inventories, they can ignore all but drastic increases on the other side. A world of either ICBM's or SLBM's in which both sides adopted the "Schlesinger Doctrine" would probably fit in this category too. The means of preserving the status quo would also be the means of changing it, as we discussed earlier. And the defense usually would have the advantage, because compellence is more difficult than deterrence. Although a state might succeed in changing the status-quo on issues that matter much more to it than to others, status-quo powers could deter major provocations under most circumstances.

In the third world there may be no security dilemma, but there are security problems. Because states can procure defensive systems that do not threaten others, the dilemma need not operate. But because the offense has the advantage, aggression is possible, and perhaps easy. If the offense has enough of an advantage, even a status-quo state may take the initiative rather than risk being attacked and defeated. If the offense has less of an advantage, stability and cooperation are likely because the status-quo states will procure defensive forces. They need not react to others who are similarly armed, but can wait for the warning they would receive if others started to deploy offensive weapons. But each state will have to watch the others carefully, and there is room for false suspicions. The costliness of the defense and the allure of the offense can lead to unnecessary mistrust, hostility, and war, unless some of the variables discussed earlier are operating to restrain defection.

A hypothetical nuclear world that would fit this description would be one in which both sides relied on SLBM's, but in which ASW techniques were very effective. Offense and defense would be different, but the former would have the advantage. This situation is not likely to occur; but if it did, a status-quo state could show its lack of desire to exploit the other by refraining from threatening its submarines. The desire to have more protecting you than merely the other side's fear of retaliation is a strong one, however, and a state that knows that it would not expand even if its cities were safe is likely to believe that the other would not feel threatened by its ASW program. It is easy to see how such a world could become unstable, and how spirals of tensions and conflict could develop.

The fourth world is doubly safe. The differentiation between offensive and defensive systems permits a way out of the security dilemma; the advantage of the defense disposes of the problems discussed in the previous paragraphs. There is no reason for a status-quo power to be tempted to procure offensive forces, and aggressors give notice of their intentions by the posture they adopt. Indeed, if the advantage of the defense is great enough, there are no security problems. The loss of the ultimate form of the power to alter the status quo would allow greater scope for the exercise of nonmilitary means and probably would tend to freeze the distribution of values.

This world would have existed in the first decade of the 20th century if the decision makers had understood the available technology. In that case, the European powers would have followed different policies both in the long run and in the summer of 1914. Even Germany, facing powerful enemies on both sides, could have made herself secure by developing strong defenses. France could also have made her frontier almost impregnable. Furthermore, when crises arose, no one would have had incentives to strike first. There would have been no competitive mobilization races reducing the time available for negotiations.

In the nuclear era, this world would be one in which the superpowers relied on SLBM's, ASW technology was not up to its task, and limited nuclear options were not taken seriously. We have discussed this situation earlier; here we need only add that, even if our analysis is correct and even if the policies and postures of both sides were to move in this direction, the problem of violence below the nuclear threshold would remain. On issues other than defense of the homeland, there would still be security dilemmas and security problems. But the world would nevertheless be safer than it has usually been.

Massive Retaliation

JOHN FOSTER DULLES

. . . As a loyal member of the United Nations, we had responded with force to repel the Communist aggression in Korea. And when that effort exposed our military weakness, we rebuilt rapidly our military establishment, and we helped to build quickly new strength in Western Europe.

KOREA

These were the acts of a nation which saw the danger of Soviet communism; which realized that its own safety was tied up with that of others; and which was capable of responding boldly and promptly to emergencies. These are precious values to be acclaimed. And also, we can pay tribute to the congressional bipartisanship which puts politics second and the nation first.

But we need to recall that what we did was in the main emergency action, imposed on us by our enemies.

Let me illustrate.

We did not send our Army into Korea because we judged, in advance, that it was sound military strategy to commit our Army to fight land battles in Asia. Our decision had been to pull out of Korea. It was a Soviet-inspired decision that pulled us back.

We did not decide in advance that it was wise to grant billions annually as foreign economic aid. We adopted that policy in response to the Communist efforts to sabotage the free economies of Western Europe.

We did not build up our military establishments at a rate which involved huge budget deficits, a depreciating currency and a feverish economy because this seemed, in advance, to be good policy. Indeed, we decided otherwise until the Soviet military threat was clearly revealed. . . .

. . . It is necessary also to say that emergency measures—however good for the emergency—do not necessarily make good permanent policies. Emergency policies are costly, they are superficial and they

Excerpts from a speech delivered before the Council on Foreign Relations, New York City, January 12, 1954.

imply that the enemy has the initiative. They cannot be depended upon to serve our long-time interests.

Now this "long time" factor is of critical importance.

SOVIET PLANS

The Soviet Communists are planning for what they call "an entire historical era," and we should do the same. They seek through many types of maneuvers gradually to divide and weaken the free nations by over-extending them in efforts which, as Lenin put it, are "beyond their strength, so that they come to practical bankruptcy." Then, said Lenin, "our victory is assured." Then, said Stalin, will be "the moment for the decisive blow."

In the face of such a strategy, our own measures cannot be judged adequate merely because they ward off an immediate danger. That, of course, needs to be done. But it is also essential to do this without exhausting ourselves.

And when the Eisenhower Administration applied this test, we felt that some transformations were needed.

It is not sound military strategy permanently to commit United States land forces to Asia to a degree that gives us no strategic reserves.

It is not sound economics to support permanently other countries; nor is it good foreign policy, for in the long run, that creates as much ill will as good.

It is not sound to become permanently committed to military expenditures so vast that they lead to what Lenin called "practical bankruptcy."

Change was imperative to assure the stamina needed for permanent security. But also it was imperative that change should be accompanied by understanding of what were our true purposes. There are some who wanted and expected sudden and spectacular change. That could not be. That kind of change would have created a panic among our friends, and our enemies might have miscalculated and misunderstood our real purposes and have assumed that we were prepared to tolerate their aggression.

So while we had to change also we had to change carefully.

We can, I believe, make a good report in these respects.

NATIONAL SECURITY

Take first the matter of national security. We need allies and we need collective security. And our purpose is to have them, but to have them on a basis which is more effective and on a basis which is less costly. How do we do this? The way to do this is to place more reliance upon community deterrent power, and less dependence upon local defensive power.

This is accepted practice so far as our local communities are concerned. We keep locks on the doors of our homes; but we do not have armed guards in every home. We rely principally on a community security system so well equipped to catch and punish any who break in and steal that, in fact, would-be aggressors are generally deterred. That is the modern way of getting maximum protection at bearable cost.

INTERNATIONAL SECURITY

What the Eisenhower Administration seeks is a similar international security system. We want for ourselves and for others a maximum deterrent at bearable cost.

Local defense will always be important. But there is no local defense which alone will contain the mighty land power of the Communist world. Local defense must be reinforced by the further deterrent of massive retaliatory power.

A potential aggressor must know that he cannot always prescribe the battle conditions that suit him. Otherwise, for example, a potential aggressor who is glutted with manpower might be tempted to attack in confidence that resistance would be confined to manpower. He might be tempted to attack in places where his superiority was decisive.

The way to deter aggression is . . .

MORE SECURITY, LESS COST

. . . To depend primarily upon a great capacity to retaliate instantly by means and at places of our choosing. . . . Now the Department of Defense and the Joint Chiefs of Staff can shape our military establishment to fit what is our policy instead of having to try to be ready to meet the enemy's many choices. And that permits of a selection of military means instead of a multiplication of means. And as a result it is now possible to get, and to share, more security at less cost.

Now let us see how this concept has been practically applied to foreign policy, taking first the Far East. In Korea this Administration effected a major transformation. The fighting has been stopped on honorable terms.

That was possible because the aggressor, already thrown back to and behind his place of beginning, was faced with the possibility that the fighting might, to his own great peril, soon spread beyond the limits and the methods which he had selected.

The cruel toll of American youth, and the nonproductive expenditure of many billions has been stopped. Also our armed forces are no longer committed to the Asian mainland. We can begin to create a strategic reserve which greatly improves our defensive posture.

This change gives added authority to the warning of the members of the United Nations which fought in Korea that if the Communists renewed the aggression, the United Nations' response would not necessarily be confined to Korea.

I have said, in relation to Indo-China, that if there were open Red Chinese aggression there, that would have "grave consequences which might not be confined to Indo-China."

I expressed last month the intention of the United States to maintain its position in Okinawa. This is needed to ensure adequate striking power to implement our new collective security concept.

All this is summed up in President Eisenhower's important statement of Dec. 26. He announced the progressive reduction of the United States ground forces in Korea. And in doing so, he pointed out that United States military forces in the Far East will now feature "highly mobile naval, air and amphibious units"; and he said that in this way, despite some withdrawal of land forces, the United States will have a capacity to oppose aggression "with even greater effect than heretofore."

The bringing home of our land forces also provides a most eloquent rebuttal to the Communist charges of "Western imperialism" in Asia.

EUROPEAN SECURITY

Let us turn now to Europe. . . .

Last April, when we went to the meeting of the NATO Council, the United States put forward a new concept which is now known as that of the "long haul." That meant a steady development of defensive strength at a rate that will preserve and not exhaust the economic strength of our allies and ourselves. This defensive strength would be reinforced by the striking power of strategic air based upon internationally agreed positions.

At this April meeting our ideas met with some skepticism. But when we went back as we did last month, December, we found that there had come about general acceptance of this "long haul" concept, and recognition that it better served the probable needs than an effort to create full defensive land strength at a ruinous price. . . .

FOREIGN AID

Turning now to foreign aid we see that new collective security concepts reduce nonproductive military expenses of our allies to a point where it is desirable and practicable also to reduce economic aid. There was need of a more self-respecting relationship, and that, indeed, is what our allies wanted. Trade, broader markets and a flow of investments are far more healthy than intergovernmental grants-in-aid.

There are still some strategic spots where local governments cannot maintain adequate armed forces without some financial help from us. In these cases we take the judgment of our military advisers as to how to proceed in the common interest. For example, we have contributed largely, ungrudgingly, and I hope constructively, to help to end aggression and advance freedom in Indo-China.

We do not, of course, claim to have found some magic formula that insures against all forms of Communist successes. It is normal that at some times at some places there may be setbacks to the cause of freedom. What we do expect to insure is that any setbacks will only be temporary and local because they will leave unimpaired those free world assets which in the long run will prevail.

If we can deter such aggression as would mean general war, and that is our confident resolve, then we can let time and fundamentals work for us. Under these conditions we do not need self-imposed policies which sap our strength.

Mutual Deterrence

NIKITA S. KHRUSHCHEV

While visiting the USA we became convinced that the most farsighted statesmen, businessmen, representatives of the American intelligentsia —not to speak of workers and farmers—desire not a continuation of the armament race, not a further increase in nervous tension, but calm and peace.

After the launching of the Soviet artificial satellites and cosmic rockets which demonstrated the possibilities of modern technology, the fact that the USA is now by no means less vulnerable in the military sense than any other country has firmly entered the mind of the American people.

I believe that nobody will suspect me of the intention of intimidating anybody by such words. No, this is the actual state of affairs, and

Excerpt of an address to the Supreme Soviet, January 14, 1960 it is evaluated in this way not only by us but also by Western statesmen of the USA herself. . . .

We cannot as yet give up completely the production of nuclear arms. Such decisions must be the result of an agreement among countries possessing nuclear arms.

Our state has at its disposal powerful rocket equipment. The air force and navy have lost their previous importance in view of the modern development of military equipment. This type of arms is not being reduced but replaced.

Almost the whole of the air force is being replaced by rocket equipment. We have by now cut down sharply and it seems will continue to cut down and even discontinue the manufacture of bombers and other obsolete machinery.

In the navy, the submarine fleet assumes great importance, whilst abovewater ships can no longer play the part they did in the past.

In our country, the armed forces have been to a considerable extent transferred to rocket and nuclear arms. These arms are being perfected and will continue to be perfected until the time they are banned.

The proposed reduction will in no way reduce the firepower of our armed forces, and this is the main point.

I am emphasizing once more that we already possess so many nuclear weapons, both atomic and hydrogen, and the necessary rockets for sending these weapons to the territory of a potential aggressor, that should any madman launch an attack on our state or on other Socialist states we would be able literally to wipe the country or countries which attack us off the face of the earth.

The Central Committee of the Communist Party and the Soviet Government can inform you, Comrade Deputies, that, though the weapons we have now are formidable weapons indeed, the weapon we have today in the hatching stage is even more perfect and more formidable.

The weapon, which is being developed and is, as they say, in the portfolio of our scientists and designers, is a fantastic weapon.

The following question arises, however, inevitably: if the possibility is not excluded that some capitalist countries will draw level with us in the field of contemporary armament, will they not, possibly, show perfidy and attack us first in order to make use of the factor of the unexpectedness of attack with such a formidable weapon as the rocket-atomic one and thus have an advantage to achieve victory?

No. Contemporary means of waging war do not give any country such advantage.

The "No-Cities" Doctrine

ROBERT S. MC NAMARA

. . . What I want to talk to you about here today are some of the concrete problems of maintaining a free community in the world today. I want to talk to you particularly about the problems of the community that bind together the United States and the countries of Western Europe. . . .

Today, NATO is involved in a number of controversies, which must be resolved by achieving a consensus within the organization in order to preserve its strength and unity. . . .

It has been argued that the very success of Western European economic development reduces Europe's need to rely on the U.S. to share in its defenses.

It has been argued that the increasing vulnerability of the U.S. to nuclear attack makes us less willing as a partner in the defense of Europe, and hence less effective in deterring such an attack.

It has been argued that nuclear capabilities are alone relevant in the face of the growing nuclear threat, and that independent national nuclear forces are sufficient to protect the nations of Europe.

I believe that all of these arguments are mistaken. . . . In our view, the effect of the new factors in the situation, both economic and military, has been to increase the interdependence of national security interests on both sides of the Atlantic, and to enhance the need for the closest coordination of our efforts.

A central military issue facing NATO today is the role of nuclear strategy. Four facts seem to us to dominate consideration of that role. All of them point in the direction of increased integration to achieve our common defense. First, the Alliance has over-all nuclear strength adequate to any challenge confronting it. Second, this strength not only minimizes the likelihood of major nuclear war, but it makes possible a strategy designed to preserve the fabric of our societies if war should occur. Third, damage to the civil societies of the Alliance resulting from nuclear warfare could be very grave. Fourth, improved non-nuclear forces, well within Alliance resources, could enhance deterrence of any aggressive moves short of direct, all-out attack on Western Europe.

Excerpts from a speech delivered at the Commencement Exercises, University of Michigan, Ann Arbor, Michigan, June 16, 1962.

Let us look at the situation today. First, given the current balance of nuclear power, which we confidently expect to maintain in the years ahead, a surprise nuclear attack is simply not a rational act for any enemy. Nor would it be rational for an enemy to take the initiative in the use of nuclear weapons as an outgrowth of a limited engagement in Europe or elsewhere. I think we are entitled to conclude that either of these actions has been made highly unlikely.

Second, and equally important, the mere fact that no nation could rationally take steps leading to a nuclear war does not guarantee that a nuclear war cannot take place. Not only do nations sometimes act in ways that are hard to explain on a rational basis, but even when acting in a "rational" way they sometimes, indeed disturbingly often, act on the basis of misunderstandings of the true facts of a situation. They misjudge the way others will react, and the way others will interpret what they are doing. We must hope, indeed I think we have good reason to hope, that all sides will understand this danger, and will refrain from steps that even raise the possibility of such a mutually disastrous misunderstanding. We have taken unilateral steps to reduce the likelihood of such an occurrence. . . .

For our part, we feel and our NATO allies must frame our strategy with this terrible contingency, however remote, in mind. Simply ignoring the problem is not going to make it go away.

The U.S. has come to the conclusion that to the extent feasible, basic military strategy in a possible general nuclear war should be approached in much the same way that more conventional military operations have been regarded in the past. That is to say, principal military objectives, in the event of a nuclear war stemming from a major attack on the Alliance, should be the destruction of the enemy's military forces, not of his civilian population.

The very strength and nature of the Alliance forces make it possible for us to retain, even in the face of a massive surprise attack, sufficient reserve striking power to destroy an enemy society if driven to it. In other words, we are giving a possible opponent the strongest imaginable incentive to refrain from striking our own cities.

The strength that makes these contributions to deterrence and to the hope of deterring attack upon civil societies even in wartime does not come cheap. . . .

. . . Relatively weak national nuclear forces with enemy cities as their targets are not likely to be sufficient to perform even the function of deterrence. If they are small, and perhaps vulnerable on the ground or in the air, or inaccurate, a major antagonist can take a variety of measures to counter them. Indeed, if a major antagonist came to believe there was a substantial likelihood of it being used independently, this force would be inviting a pre-emptive first strike against it. In the event of war, the use of such a force against the cities of a major nuclear power would be tantamount to suicide, whereas its employment against significant military targets would have a negligible effect on the outcome of the conflict. Meanwhile, the creation of a single additional national nuclear force encourages the proliferation of nuclear power with all of its attendant dangers.

In short, then, limited nuclear capabilities, operating independently, are dangerous, expensive, prone to obsolescence, and lacking in credibility as a deterrent. Clearly, the United States nuclear contribution to the Alliance is neither obsolete nor dispensable.

At the same time, the general strategy I have summarized magnifies the importance of unity of planning, concentration of executive authority, and central direction. There must not be competing and conflicting strategies to meet the contingency of nuclear war. We are convinced that a general nuclear war target system is indivisible, and if, despite all our efforts, nuclear war should occur, our best hope lies in conducting a centrally controlled campaign against all of the enemy's vital nuclear capabilities, while retaining reserve forces, all centrally controlled.

We know that the same forces which are targeted on ourselves are also targeted on our allies. Our own strategic retaliatory forces are prepared to respond against these forces, wherever they are and whatever their targets. This mission is assigned not only in fulfillment of our treaty commitments but also because the character of nuclear war compels it. More specifically, the U.S. is as much concerned with that portion of Soviet nuclear striking power that can reach Western Europe as with the portion that also can reach the United States. In short, we have undertaken the nuclear defense of NATO on a global basis. . . .

Limited Nuclear Options

JAMES SCHLESINGER

THE NEED FOR OPTIONS

President Nixon underlined the drawbacks to sole reliance on assured destruction in 1970 when he asked:

From Report of the Secretary of Defense to Congress on the FY 1975 budget and the FY 1975-79 defense program, March 4, 1974, pp. 35-41.

"Should a President, in the event of a nuclear attack, be left with the single option of ordering the mass destruction of enemy civilians, in the face of the certainty that it would be followed by the mass slaughter of Americans? Should the concept of assured destruction be narrowly defined and should it be the only measure of our ability to deter the variety of threats we may face?"

The questions are not new. They have arisen many times during the nuclear era, and a number of efforts have been made to answer them. We actually added several response options to our contingency plans in 1961 and undertook the retargeting necessary for them. However, they all involved large numbers of weapons. In addition, we publicly adopted to some degree the philosophies of counterforce and damage-limiting. Although differences existed between those two concepts as then formulated, particularly in their diverging assumptions about cities as likely targets of attack, both had a number of features in common.

—Each required the maintenance of a capability to destroy urban-industrial targets, but as a reserve to deter attacks on U.S. and allied cities rather than as the main instrument of retaliation.

—Both recognized that contingencies other than a massive surprise attack on the United States might arise and should be deterred; both argued that the ability and willingness to attack military targets were prerequisites to deterrence.

—Each stressed that a major objective, in the event that deterrence should fail, would be to avoid to the extent possible causing collateral damage in the USSR, and to limit damage to the societies of the United States and its allies.

—Neither contained a clear-cut vision of how a nuclear war might end, or what role the strategic forces would play in their termination.

—Both were considered by critics to be open-ended in their require-ment for forces, very threatening to the retaliatory capabilities of the USSR, and therefore dangerously stimulating to the arms race and the chances of pre-emptive war.

—The military tasks that each involved, whether offensive counter-force or defensive damage-limiting, became increasingly costly, complex, and difficult as Soviet strategic forces grew in size, diversity, and survivability.

Of the two concepts, damage-limiting was the more demanding and costly because it required both active and passive defenses as well as a counterforce capability to attack hard targets and other strategic delivery systems. Added to this was the assumption (at least for planning purposes) that an enemy would divide his initial attack between our cities and our retaliatory forces, or switch his fire to our cities at some later stage in the attack. Whatever the realism of that assumption, it placed an enormous burden on our active and passive defenses—and particularly on anti-ballistic missile (ABM) systems—for the limitation of damage.

With the ratification of the ABM treaty in 1972, and the limitation it imposes on both the United States and the Soviet Union to construct no more than two widely separated ABM sites (with no more than 100 interceptors at each), an essential building-block in the entire damage-limiting concept has now been removed. As I shall discuss later, the treaty has also brought into question the utility of large, dedicated anti-bomber defenses, since without a defense against missiles, it is clear that an active defense against bombers has little value in protecting our cities. The salient point, however, is that the ABM treaty has effectively removed the concept of defensive damage limitation (at least as it was defined in the 1960s) from the contention as a major strategic option.

Does all of this mean that we have no choice but to rely solely on the threat of destroying cities? Does it even matter if we do? What is wrong, in the final analysis, with staking everything on this massive deterrent and pressing ahead with a further limitation of these devastating arsenals?

No one who has thought much about these questions disagrees with the need, as a minimum, to maintain a conservatively designed reserve for the ultimate threat of large-scale destruction. Even more, if we could all be guaranteed that this threat would prove fully credible (to friend and foe alike) across the relevant range of contingencies—and that deterrence would never be severely tested or fail—we might also agree that nothing more in the way of options would ever be needed. The difficulty is that no such guarantee can be given. There are several reasons why any assurance on this score is impossible.

Since we ourselves find it difficult to believe that we would actually implement the threat of assured destruction in response to a limited attack on military targets that caused relatively few civilian casualties, there can be no certainty that, in a crisis, prospective opponents would be deterred from testing our resolve. Allied concern about the credibility of this particular threat has been evident for more than a decade. In any event, the actuality of such a response would be utter folly except where our own or allied cities were attacked.

Today, such a massive retaliation against cities, in response to anything less than an all-out attack on the U.S. and its cities, appears less and less credible. Yet . . . deterrence can fail in many ways. What we need is a series of measured responses to aggression which bear some relation to the provocation, have prospects of terminating hostilities before general nuclear war breaks out, and leave some possibility for restoring deterrence. It has been this problem of not having sufficient options between massive response and doing nothing, as the Soviets built up their strategic forces, that has prompted the President's concerns and those of our Allies.

Threats against allied forces, to the extent that they could be deterred by the prospect of nuclear retaliation, demand both more limited responses than destroying cities and advanced planning tailored to such lesser responses. Nuclear threats to our strategic forces, whether limited or large-scale, might well call for an option to respond in kind against the attacker's military forces. In other words, to be credible, and hence effective over the range of possible contingencies, deterrence must rest on many options and on a spectrum of capabilities (within the constraints of SALT) to support these options. Certainly such complex matters as response options cannot be left hanging until a crisis. They must be thought through beforehand. Moreover, appropriate sensors to assist in determining the nature of the attack, and adequately responsive command-control arrangements, must also be available. And a venturesome opponent must know that we have all of these capabilities.

Flexibility of response is also essential because, despite our best efforts, we cannot guarantee that deterrence will never fail; nor can we forecast the situations that would cause it to fail. Accidents and unauthorized acts could occur, especially if nuclear proliferation should increase. Conventional conflicts could escalate into nuclear exchanges; indeed, some observers believe that this is precisely what would happen should a major war break out in Europe. Ill-informed or cornered and desperate leaders might challenge us to a nuclear test of wills. We cannot even totally preclude the massive surprise attack on our forces which we use to test the design of our second-strike forces, although I regard the probability of such an attack as close to zero under existing conditions. To the extent that we have selective response options—smaller and more precisely focused than in the past—we should be able to deter such challenges. But if deterrence fails, we may be able to bring all but the largest nuclear conflicts to a rapid conclusion before cities are struck. Damage may thus be limited and further escalation avoided.

I should point out in this connection that the critics of options cannot have the argument both ways. If the nuclear balance is no longer delicate and if substantial force asymmetries are quite tolerable, then the kinds of changes I have been discussing here will neither perturb the balance nor stimulate an arms race. If, on the other hand, asymmetries do matter (despite the existence of some highly survivable forces), then the critics themselves should consider seriously what responses we should make to the major programs that the Soviets currently have underway to exploit their advantages in numbers of missiles and payload. Whichever argument the critics prefer, they should recognize that:

—inertia is hardly an appropriate policy for the United States in these vital areas;

—we have had some large-scale pre-planned options other than attacking cities for many years, despite the rhetoric of assured destruction;

—adding more selective, relatively small-scale options is not necessarily synonymous with adding forces, even though we may wish to change their mix and improve our command, control, and communications.

It is worth stressing at this point . . . that targets for nuclear weapons may include not only cities and silos, but also airfields, many other types of military installations, and a variety of other important assets that are not necessarily collocated with urban populations. We already have a long list of such possible targets; now we are grouping them into operational plans which would be more responsive to the range of challenges that might face us. To the extent necessary, we are retargeting our forces accordingly.

Which among these options we might choose in a crisis would depend on the nature of any enemy's attack and on his objectives. Many types of targets can be pre-programmed as options—cities, other targets of value, military installations of many different kinds, soft strategic targets, hard strategic targets. A number of so-called counterforce targets, such as airfields, are quite soft and can be destroyed without pinpoint accuracy. The fact that we are able to knock out these targets—counterforce though it may be—does not appear to be the subject of much concern.

In some circumstances, however, a set of hard targets might be the most appropriate objective for our retaliation, and this I realize is a subject fraught with great emotion. Even so, several points about it need to be made.

—The destruction of a hardened target is not simply a function of accuracy; it results from the combined effects of accuracy, nuclear yield, and the number of warheads applied to the target.

—Both the United States and the Soviet Union already have the necessary combinations of accuracy, yield, and numbers in their missile forces to provide them with some hard-target-kill capability, but it is not a particularly efficient capability.

—Neither the United States nor the Soviet Union now has a disarming first strike capability, nor are they in any position to acquire such a capability in the foreseeable future, since each side has large numbers of strategic offensive systems that remain untargetable by the other side. Moreover, the ABM Treaty forecloses a defense against missiles. As I have already noted in public: "The

Soviets, under the Interim Offensive Agreement, are allowed 62 submarines and 950 SLBM launchers. In addition, they have many other nuclear forces. Any reasonable calculation would demonstrate, I believe, that it is not possible for us even to begin to eliminate the city-destruction potential embodied in their ICBMs, let alone their SLBM force."

The moral of all this is that we should not single out accuracy as some sort of unilateral or key culprit in the hard-target-kill controversy. To the extent that we want to minimize unintended civilian damage from attacks on even soft targets, as I believe we should, we will want to emphasize high accuracy, low yields, and airburst weapons.

To enhance deterrence, we may also want a more efficient hard-target-kill capability than we now possess: both to threaten specialized sets of targets (possibly of concern to allies) with a greater economy of force, and to make it clear to a potential enemy that he cannot proceed with impunity to jeoparize our own system of hard targets.

Thus, the real issue is how much hard-target-kill capability we need, rather than the development of new combinations of accuracy and yield per se. Resolution of the quantitative issue, as I will discuss later, depends directly on the further evolution of the Soviet strategic offensive forces and on progress in the current phase of the Strategic Arms Limitation Talks. . . .

With a reserve capability for threatening urban-industrial targets, with offensive systems capable of increased flexibility and discrimination in targeting, and with concomitant improvements in sensors, surveillance, and command-control, we could implement response options that cause far less civilian damage than would now be the case. For those who consider such changes potentially destabilizing because of their fear that the options might be used, let me emphasize that without substantially more of an effort in other directions than we have any intention of proposing, there is simply no possibility of reducing civilian damage from a large-scale nuclear exchange sufficiently to make it a tempting prospect for any sane leader. But that is not what we are talking about here. At the present time, we are acquiring selective and discriminating options that are intended to deter another power from exercising any form of nuclear pressure. Simultaneously . . . we and our allies are improving our general purpose forces precisely so as to raise the threshold against the use of any nuclear forces.

The Countervailing Strategy

HAROLD BROWN

A significant achievement in 1980 was the codification of our evolving strategic doctrine, in the form of Presidential Directive No. 59. In my Report last year, I discussed the objectives and the principal elements of this countervailing strategy, and in August 1980, after P.D. 59 had been signed by President Carter, I elaborated it in some detail in a major policy address. Because of its importance, however, the countervailing strategy warrants special attention in this Report as well.

Two basic points should underlie any discussion of the counter-vailing strategy. *The first is that, because it is a strategy of deterrence, the countervailing strategy is designed with the Soviets in mind.* Not only must we have the forces, doctrine, and will to retaliate if attacked, we must convince the Soviets, *in advance,* that we do. Because it is designed to deter the Soviets, our strategic doctrine must take account of what we know about Soviet perspectives on these issues, for, by definition, deterrence requires shaping Soviet assessments about the risks of war—assessments they will make using their models, not ours. We must confront these views and take them into account in our planning. We may, and we do, think our models are more accurate, but theirs are the reality deterrence drives us to consider.

Several Soviet perspectives are relevant to the formulation of our deterrent strategy. First, Soviet military doctrine appears to contemplate the possibility of a relatively prolonged nuclear war. Second, there is evidence that they regard military forces as the obvious first targets in a nuclear exchange, not general industrial and economic capacity. Third, the Soviet leadership clearly places a high value on preservation of the regime and on the survival and continued effectiveness of the instruments of state power and control—a value at least as high as that they place on any losses to the general population, short of those involved in a general nuclear war. Fourth, in some contexts, certain elements of Soviet leadership seem to consider Soviet victory in a nuclear war to be at least a theoretical possibility.

From Report of the Secretary of Defense to the Congress on the FY 1982 Budget, FY 1983 Authorization Request and FY 1982–1986 Defense Programs, pp. 38–43. January 19, 1981.

All this does not mean that the Soviets are unaware of the destruction a nuclear war would bring to the Soviet Union; in fact, they are explicit on that point. Nor does this mean that we cannot deter, for clearly we can and we do.

The second basic point is that, because the world is constantly changing, our strategy evolves slowly, almost continually, over time to adapt to changes in U.S. technology and military capabilites, as well as Soviet technology, military capabilities, and strategic doctrine. A strategic doctrine that served well when the United States had only a few dozen nuclear weapons and the Soviets none would hardly serve as well unchanged in a world in which we have about 9,000 strategic warheads and they have about 7,000. As the strategic balance has shifted from overhwelming U.S. superiority to essential equivalence, and as ICBM accuracies have steadily improved to the point that hard target kill probabilities are quite high, our doctrine must adapt itself to these new realities.

This does not mean that the objective of our doctrine changes; on the contrary, deterrence remains, as it always has been, our basic goal. Our countervailing strategy today is a natural evolution of the conceptual foundations built over a generation by men like Robert McNamara and James Schlesinger.

The United States has never—at least since nuclear weapons were available in significant numbers—had a strategic doctrine based simply and solely on reflexive, massive attacks on Soviet cities and populations. Previous administrations, going back almost 20 years, recognized the inadequacy as a deterrent of a targeting doctrine that would give us too narrow a range of options. Although for programming purposes, strategic forces were sometimes measured in terms of ability to strike a set of industrial targets, we have always planned both more selectively (for options limiting urban-industrial damage) and more comprehensively (for a wide range of civilian and military targets). The unquestioned Soviet attainment of strategic parity has put the final nail in the coffin of what we long knew was dead—the notion that we could adequately deter the Soviets solely by threatening massive retaliaton against their cities. . . .

Our countervailing strategy—designed to provide effective deterrence—tells the world that no potential adversary of the United States could ever conclude that the fruits of his aggression would be worth his own costs. This is true whatever the level of conflict contemplated. To the Soviet Union, our strategy makes clear that no course of aggression by them that led to use of nuclear weapons, on any scale of attack and at any stage of conflict, could lead to victory, however they may define victory. Besides our power to devastate the full target system of the USSR, the United States would have the option for more selective, lesser retaliatory attacks that would exact a prohibitively high price from the things the Soviet leadership prizes most—political and military control, nuclear and conventional military force, and the economic base needed to sustain a war.

Thus, the countervailing strategy is designed to be fully consistent with NATO's strategy of flexible response by providing options for appropriate response to aggression at whatever level it might occur. The essence of the countervailing strategy is to convince the Soviets that they will be successfully opposed at any level of aggression they choose, and that no plausible outcome at any level of conflict could represent "success" for them by any reasonable definition of success.

Five basic elements of our force employment policy serve to achieve the objectives of the countervailing strategy.

A. *Flexibility*

Our planning must provide a continuum of options, ranging from use of small numbers of strategic and/or theater nuclear weapons aimed at narrowly defined targets, to employment of large portions of our nuclear forces against a broad spectrum of targets. In addition to pre-planned targeting options, we are developing an ability to design other employment plans—in particular, smaller scale plans—on short notice in response to changing circumstances.

In theory, such flexibility also enhances the possibility of being able to control escalation of what begins as a limited nuclear exchange. I want to emphasize once again two points I have made repeatedly and publicly. First, I remain highly skeptical that escalation of a limited nuclear exchange can be controlled, or that it can be stopped short of an all-out, massive exchange. Second, even given that belief, I am convinced that we must do everything we can to make such escalation control possible, that opting out of this effort and consciously resigning ourselves to the inevitability of such escalation is a serious abdication of the awesome responsibilities nuclear weapons, and the unbelievable damage their uncontrolled use would create, thrust upon us. Having said that, let me proceed to the second element, which is escalation control.

B. *Escalation Control*

Plans for the controlled use of nuclear weapons, along with other appropriate military and political actions, should enable us to provide leverage for a negotiated termination of the fighting. At an early stage in the conflict, we must convince the enemy that further escalation will not result in achievement of his objectives, that it will not mean "success," but rather additional costs. To do this, we must leave the enemy with sufficient highly valued military, economic, and political resources still surviving but still clearly at risk, so that he has a strong incentive to seek an end to the conflict.

C. *Survivability and Endurance*

The key to escalation control is the survivability and endurance of our nuclear forces and the supporting communications, command and control, and intelligence (C³I) capabilities. The supporting C³I is critical to effective deterrence, and we have begun to pay considerably more attention to these issues than in the past. We must ensure that the United States is not placed in a "use or lose" situation, one that might lead to unwarranted escalation of the conflict. That is a central reason why, while the Soviets cannot ignore our *capability* to launch our retaliatory forces before an attack reaches its targets, we cannot afford to rely on "launch on warning" as the long-term solution to ICBM vulnerability. . . . Survivability and endurance are essential prerequisites to an ability to adapt the employment of nuclear forces to the entire range of potentially rapidly changing and perhaps unanticipated situations and to tailor them for the appropriate responses in those situations. And, without adequate survivability and endurance, it would be impossible for us to keep substantial forces in reserve.

D. *Targeting Objectives*

In order to meet our requirements for flexibility and escalation control, we must have the ability to destroy elements of four general categories of Soviet targets.

1. *Strategic Nuclear Forces*

The Soviet Union should entertain no illusion that by attacking our strategic nuclear forces, it could significantly reduce the damage it would suffer. Nonetheless, the state of the strategic balance after an initial exchange—measured both in absolute terms and in relation to the balance prior to the exchange—could be an important factor in the decision by one side to initiate a nuclear exchange. Thus, it is important—for the sake of deterrence—to be able to deny to the potential aggressor a fundamental and favorable shift in the strategic balance as a result of a nuclear exchange.

2. *Other Military Forces*

"Counterforce" covers much more than central strategic systems. We have for many years planned options to destroy the full range of Soviet (and, as appropriate, non-Soviet Warsaw Pact) military power, conventional as well as nuclear. Because the Soviets may define victory in part in terms of the overall post-war military balance, we will give special attention, in implementing the counter-vailing strategy, to more effective and more flexible targeting of the full range of military capabilities, so as to strengthen deterrence.

3. *Leadership and Control*

We must, and we do, include options to target organs of Soviet political and military leadership and control. As I indicated earlier, the regime constituted by these centers is valued highly by the Soviet leadership. A clear U.S. ability to destroy them poses a marked challenge to the essence of the Soviet system and thus contributes to deterrence. At the same time, of course, we recognize the role that a surviving supreme command could and would play in the termination of hostilities, and can envisage many scenarios in which destruction of them would be inadvisable and contrary to our own best interests. Perhaps the obvious is worth emphasizing: possession of a capability is not tantamount to exercising it.

4. *Industrial and Economic Base*

The countervailing strategy by no means implies that we do not—or no longer—recognize the ultimate deterrent effect of being able to threaten the full Soviet target structure, including the industrial and economic base. These targets are highly valued by the Soviets, and we must ensure that the potential loss of them is an ever-present factor in the Soviet calculus regarding nuclear war. Let me also emphasize that while, as a matter of policy, we do not target civilian population *per se*, heavy civilian fatalities and other casualties would inevitably occur in attacking the Soviet industrial and economic base, which is collocated with the Soviet urban population. I should add that Soviet civilian casualties would also be large in more focused attacks (not unlike the U.S. civilian casualty estimates cited earlier for Soviet attacks on our ICBM silos); indeed, they could be described as limited only in the sense that they would be significantly less than those resulting from an all-out attack.

E. *Reserve Forces*

Our planning must provide for the designation and employment of adequate, survivable, and enduring reserve forces and the supporting C^3I systems both during and after a protracted conflict. At a minimum, we will preserve such a dedicated force of strategic weapon systems.

Because there has been considerable misunderstanding and misinterpretation of the countervailing strategy and of P.D. 59, it is worth restating what the countervailing strategy is *not*.

—It is *not* a new strategic doctrine; it is *not* a radical departure from U.S. strategic policy over the past decade or so. It *is* a refinement, a re-codification of previous statements of our strategic policy. It *is* the same essential strategic doctrine, restated more clearly and related more directly to current and prospective conditions and capabilities—U.S. and Soviet.

—It does *not* assume, or assert, that we can "win" a limited nuclear war, nor does it pretend or intend to enable us to do so. It *does* seek to convince the Soviets that they could not win such a war, and thus to deter them from starting one.

—It does *not* even assume, or assert, that a nuclear war could remain limited. I have made clear my view that such a prospect is highly unlikely. It *does,* however, prepare us to respond to a limited Soviet nuclear attack in ways other than automatic, immediate, massive retaliation.

—It does *not* assume that a nuclear war will in fact be protracted over many weeks or even months. It *does,* however, take into account evidence of Soviet thinking along those lines, in order to convince them that such a course, whatever its probability, could not lead to Soviet victory.

—It does *not* call for substituting primarily military for primarily civilian targets. It *does* recognize the importance of military and civilian targets. It does provide for increasing the number and variety of options available to the President, covering the full range of military and civilian targets, so that he can respond appropriately and effectively to any kind of an attack, at any level.

—It is *not* inconsistent with future progress in arms control. In fact, it *does* emphasize many features—survivability, crisis stability, deterrence—that are among the core objectives of arms control. It does *not* require larger strategic arsenals; it *does* demand more flexibility and better control over strategic nuclear forces, whatever their size.

—Lastly, it is *not* a first strike strategy. Nothing in the policy contemplates that nuclear war can be a deliberate instrument for achieving our national security goals, because it cannot be. The premise, the objective, the core of our strategic doctrine remains unchanged—deterrence. The countervailing strategy, by specifying what we would do in response to any level of Soviet attack, serves to deter any such attack in the first place.

The Impossibility of
Limited Nuclear War

LEONID BREZHNEV

Q. Can a nuclear war be considered winnable?

A. Western political and military writers contend that Soviet military doctrine is based exclusively on the belief that a world nuclear war can be won. But that is a simplistic and distorted view of our approach. In fact, the Soviet Union holds that nuclear war would be a universal disaster and that it would most probably mean the end of civilization. It may lead to the destruction of all humankind. There may be no victor in such a war, and it can solve no political problems. As Leonid Brezhnev pointed out in his reply to a Pravda correspondent on 21 October 1981: "Anyone who starts a nuclear war in the hope of winning it has thereby decided to commit suicide. Whatever strength the attacker may have and whatever method of starting a nuclear war he may choose, he will not achieve his aims. Retaliation is unavoidable. That is our essential point of view."

AVERTING WAR BY ALL MEANS

Soviet people are not thinking in terms of winning a nuclear war but of averting such a war by all means. They take into account the changing relevance of armed forces as an instrument of politics. Here is how Leonid Brezhnev put it: "By and large, it is probably safe to say that people are gradually coming to understand that none of the problems in the world can be solved from positions of strength, by any sabre-rattling." (Speech in Alma-Ata, 29 August 1980.) Armed force, and doubly so nuclear force, is acquiring new functions. In this sense, we see eye to eye with Rear Adm. Gene LaRocque, director of the U.S. Center for Defense Information, who says neither side could eventually consider itself a victor in the event of a major nuclear war between the U.S.S.R. and the U.S.A. More than a hundred million people would perish on either side, and up to three-quarters of the two countries' economic potentials would be destroyed.

From *The New York Times,* Saturday, November 21, 1981, Leonid Brezhnev, "Excerpts from a Soviet Booklet on Nuclear War" *The Threat to Europe.*

'LIMITED NUCLEAR WAR'

The same applies to the idea of a "limited nuclear war" in Europe or elsewhere as conceived in U.S. Presidential Directive 59 of 25 July 1980. One might discourse on "limited nuclear war" in theory only, but on the practical plane it is nothing less than unrealistic.

Q. In the West one hears now and then that Soviet military doctrine is of an aggressively offensive nature, considers a first strike possible and includes plans for a sudden, blitzkrieg-style invasion of Western Europe. Is this true?

A. That is another popular theme in Western military and political propaganda. They use a very simple ruse to adduce that Soviet doctrine is aggressively offensive. They do so by quoting from works of Soviet military theorists devoted not to doctrine or military policy but to particular aspects of combat, such as tactics in the battlefield. These quotes are passed off as Soviet doctrine, though that is a deliberately incorrect and specious approach. It gives not the slightest idea of Soviet doctrine, which is defensive but, of course, necessarily envisages the training of soldiers for various actions in the field of battle.

Soviet military doctrine is of a purely defensive nature. "We never had and never will have any strategic doctrine other than a defensive one," says the declaration of the Warsaw Treaty states of 15 May 1980. It does not admit of either a first or pre-emptive strike or of any "lightning" invasion of Western Europe. In so doing it follows definite political, ethical and military principles. There is no aggressive element in Soviet military doctrine because the Soviet Union has no political, economic, social or military aims in Europe or anywhere else that it intends to secure by armed force.

Q. Why then do Soviet theoretical works on military strategy of, say, the early 60's refer to offensive action, to building up a military advantage? Doesn't this prove that Soviet military strategy reposes on these principles even today?

A. No, it proves no such thing. Soviet military strategy is neither immutable nor everlasting. It changes with the changing world. The same happens in the United States, where the strategy of flexible response and thereupon that of realistic deterrence replaced a doctrine of massive retaliation. Soviet theoretical works of the early 60's reflected the views of their time. And it was a time when the United States commanded a considerable nuclear-missile advantage, when it threatened the Soviet Union with massive nuclear strikes and declared that a nuclear war against the U.S.S.R. was winnable.

EMERGENCE OF DÉTENTE

The equilibrium of strategic forces that shaped up between the U.S.S.R. and the U.S.A. compelled the latter to accept détente, which made considerable headway in the 70's and slackened the war danger.

Technological advances and growth of nuclear weapons stockpiles had made nuclear war altogether senseless. Soviet military doctrine, which has always reposed on the principle of retaliatory, that is, defensive, action, says nothing at all in the new conditions of the 70's and early 80's of nuclear war being winnable and, more, lays the accent still more emphatically than before on preventing it, on maintaining the military equilibrium and on lowering the level of military confrontation by means of military détente. "There is no task that we intend to accomplish by armed force," Leonid Brezhnev said in an interview to Vorwärts, the weekly of the Social Democratic Party of Germany.

Q. It is said that the numerical strength of the Soviet armed forces is far greater than the country needs for defense. Is that true?

A. The strength of the Soviet armed forces is not greater than needed for defense. It matches the defensive needs. To see this you must consider at least two pertinent factors: the regional strength balances and the geostrategic factor.

SPECIAL SOVIET SITUATION

The Soviet Union's strategic situation compels it, for purposes of defense, to insure not only a general equilibrium of strength between it and the U.S.A., and between the Warsaw Treaty countries and NATO, but also a regional equilibrium in separate theaters, each with its own military specifics. To begin with, the strength of the armed forces of the Soviet Union and its allies must match the area of the territory they defend, the overall length of frontiers and the nature of the potential dangers. No other country in the world has anything even remotely equal or similar to these factors. The armies of the Warsaw Treaty countries have a territory of 23,500,000 square kilometers to defend, out of which 22,500,000 square kilometers are Soviet territory. This is more than the area of the United States, Europe and China combined. The NATO armies have only 2 million square kilometers, or one-eleventh of that area, to defend.

Faced in the West by the NATO bloc, which includes three nuclear powers, the Soviet Union is simultaneously exposed to danger in the east from two American Pacific nuclear fleets and from China, with its growing nuclear potential and the world's most numerous army. Furthermore, the deployment of U.S. Naval nuclear forces in the northern sector of the Indian Ocean within reach of southern regions of the Soviet Union combines with the string of U.S. military bases stretching from the Mediterranean across the Middle East to Pakistan and countries in Southeast Asia. In effect, the Soviet Union is compelled to reckon with the likelihood of a blockade being put up around it. This is being made increasingly apparent, among other things, by the growing political and military cooperation between the United States and China.

AN AMERICAN ADVANTAGE

Further, it ought to be borne in mind that by virtue of its favorable geographical situation, the United States can insure the defense of its own national frontiers by a minimal force. The Soviet Union, on the other hand, is compelled to guarantee proper balance and dependable defense by distributing its forces along the entire length of its borders and, moreover, insuring a rough equilibrium in the world ocean where it is exposed to growing dangers from the U.S. nuclear Navy. Lastly, we ought to remember that the United States can add freely to its troop strength in Europe and Asia by moving reserves and weaponry stationed in its national territory, where they are not pinned down by anyone and in no way hemmed in. In this sense, the Soviet Union would be in a far less favorable position in the event of a conflict.

It is therefore completely wrong to compare the aggregate strength of the Soviet armed forces to the strength of NATO troops in Europe, as this is often done in the West, and to overlook the radical distinctions in the geostrategic position of the U.S.S.R. and the U.S.A., the Warsaw Treaty organization and NATO. It is clear that the more complicated global geostrategic situation of the Soviet Union makes its position in the European theater less favorable than that of the United States. This is proof enough that Soviet troop strength balances with the real defensive needs of the country as a whole and does not exceed these needs.

Q. Isn't the military balance steadily tipping in favor of the Soviet Union? This can't help creating alarm in the West.

A. During the first roughly 20 years after the war, the United States had a strategic nuclear advantage over the U.S.S.R. At the turn of the 70's, the defensive efforts of the Soviet Union ended this superiority. Since then, there has been military-strategic equilibrium.

COMMENTS OF AMERICANS

This is acknowledged by the Soviet Union and by Western statesmen as well.

President Carter, for example, said on 25 April 1979 that the strategic forces of the United States and the Soviet Union today are essentially equivalent. The same was said on 5 April 1979 by Harold Brown, who acknowledged that despite the Russian military achievements, the Soviet Union has no military superiority in the nuclear field and that today there is a strategic balance; the United States, he said, is not likely to be strategically behind in 1985.

Part II
Case Studies in the Twentieth Century Use of Force

The ten studies in Part II are taken from the twentieth century and are arranged in chronological order. The cases under the heading "The Great Power Era" deal with the use of force amongst the great powers prior to 1945. Those under the heading "The Superpower Era" examine instances in which the superpowers were involved in using either conventional forces or nuclear weapons (or nuclear threats). All of the studies illustrate the general principles explained in Part I. The cases deal with different types of military technologies, ranging from chemical to nuclear weapons, and treat the use of military force in both wartime and peacetime. In all of the examples, military power was essential to the successful pursuit of national goals, or was thought to be so. Each of these selections either demonstrates a specific way of using military power—in an offensive, defensive, or deterrent fashion—or identifies the factors that restrained states in their use of force.

Stephen Van Evera looks at how belief in the virtue of the offensive affected the great powers' foreign policies in the decades before World War I and how it caused the July 1914 crisis to spiral out of control. Edward L. Katzenbach, Jr., describes the innumerable rationalizations used to extend the life of the horse cavalry well into the twentieth century and, in doing so, shows that military organizations may strongly resist technological change. Frederic J. Brown shows why restraint prevailed in the use of chemical weapons in World War I and II, contrary to the expectations of the time. Sir George Sansom explains why the Japanese decided to launch what they considered to be a preventive war against the United States and indicated why their strategic calculations were faulty.

Louis Morton discusses the reasons why the United States used the atomic bomb against Japan. Morton H. Halperin details the evolution of a system of mutual restraints in the American and Chinese use of force during the Korean War and speculates on why the two countries accepted the restraints. Albert and Roberta Wohlstetter explain the reasons why the Soviet Union put missiles into Cuba in September of 1962 and why it took them out in October and November of the same year. John Lewis Gaddis tests the strategy of flexible response in its application to Vietnam by the Kennedy and Johnson administrations and finds it wanting. Barry M. Blechman and Douglas M. Hart show why the Nixon Administration felt it necessary to make veiled nuclear threats against the Soviet Union during the 1973 Middle East War and ask whether the threats prevented the Russians from sending troops to aid Egypt against Israel. Finally, Raymond L. Garthoff examines why the Soviet Union became embroiled in its own Vietnam by invading Afghanistan in December of 1979.

The Cult of the Offensive
and World War I

STEPHEN VAN EVERA

During the decades before the First World War a phenomenon which may be called a "cult of the offensive" swept through Europe. Militaries glorified the offensive and adopted offensive military doctrines, while civilian elites and publics assumed that the offense had the advantage in warfare, and that offensive solutions to security problems were the most effective.

This article will argue that the cult of the offensive was a principal cause of the First World War, creating or magnifying many of the dangers which historians blame for causing the July crisis and rendering it uncontrollable. The following section will first outline the growth of the cult of the offensive in Europe in the years before the war, and then sketch the consequences which international relations theory suggests should follow from it. The second section will outline consequences which the cult produced in 1914, and the final section will suggest conclusions and implications for current American policy.

THE CULT OF THE OFFENSIVE AND INTERNATIONAL
RELATIONS THEORY

The Growth of the Cult

The gulf between myth and the realities of warfare has never been greater than in the years before World War I. Despite the large and growing advantage which defenders gained against attackers as a result of the invention of rifled and repeating small arms, the machine gun, barbed wire, and the development of railroads, Europeans increasingly believed that attackers would hold the advantage on the battlefield, and that wars would be short and "decisive"—a

From "The Cult of the Offensive and the Origins of the First World War" by Stephen Van Evera, *International Security*, Summer 1984 (Vol. 9, No. 1) pp. 58–107. © 1984 by the President and Fellows of Harvard College and of the Massachusetts Institute of Technology. Reprinted by permission of MIT Press, Cambridge, Massachusetts, and the copyright holders. Portions of the text have been omitted; all referential and some explanatory footnotes have also been omitted.

I would like to thank Jack Snyder, Richard Ned Lebow, Barry Posen, Marc Trachtenberg, and Stephen Walt for their thoughtful comments on earlier drafts of this paper.

"brief storm," in the words of the German Chancellor, Bethmann Hollweg. They largely overlooked the lessons of the American Civil War, the Russo–Turkish War of 1877–78, the Boer War, and the Russo-Japanese War, which had demonstrated the power of the new defensive technologies. Instead, Europeans embraced a set of political and military myths which obscured both the defender's advantages and the obstacles an aggressor would confront. The mindset helped to mold the offensive military doctrines which every European power adopted during the period 1892–1913.

In Germany, the military glorified the offense in strident terms, and inculcated German society with similar views. General Alfred von Schlieffen, author of the 1914 German war plan, declared that "Attack is the best defense," while the popular publicist Friedrich von Bernhardi proclaimed that "the offensive mode of action is by far superior to the defensive mode," and that "the superiority of offensive warfare under modern conditions is greater than formerly." German Chief of Staff General Helmuth von Moltke also endorsed "the principle that the offensive is the best defense," while General August von Keim, founder of the Army League, argued that "Germany ought to be armed for attack," since "the offensive is the only way of insuring victory." These assumptions guided the Schlieffen Plan, which envisaged rapid and decisive attacks on Belgium, France, and Russia.

In France, the army became "Obsessed with the virtues of the offensive," in the words of B. H. Liddell Hart, an obsession which also spread to French civilians. The French army, declared Chief of Staff Joffre, "no longer knows any other law than the offensive. . . . Any other conception ought to be rejected as contrary to the very nature of war," while the President of the French Republic, Clément Fallières, announced that "The offensive alone is suited to the temperament of French soldiers. . . . We are determined to march straight against the enemy without hesitation." . . . French military doctrine reflected these offensive biases. In Marshall Foch's words, the French army adopted "a single formula for success, a single combat doctrine, namely, the decisive power of offensive action undertaken with the resolute determination to march on the enemy, reach and destroy him."

Other European states displayed milder symptoms of the same virus. The British military resolutely rejected defensive strategies despite their experience in the Boer War which demonstrated the power of entrenched defenders against exposed attackers. General W. G. Knox wrote, "The defensive is never an acceptable role to the Briton, and he makes little or no study of it," and General R. C. B. Haking argued that the offensive "will win as sure as there is a sun in the heavens." The Russian Minister of War, General V.

A. Sukhomlinov, observed that Russia's enemies were directing their armies "towards guaranteeing the possibility of dealing rapid and decisive blows. . . . We also must follow this example." Even in Belgium the offensive found proponents: under the influence of French ideas, some Belgian officers favored an offensive strategy, proposing the remarkable argument that "To ensure against our being ignored it was essential that we should attack," and declaring that "We must hit them where it hurts."

Mythical or mystical arguments obscured the technical dominion of the defense, giving this faith in the offense aspects of a cult, or a mystique, as Marshall Joffre remarked in his memoirs. . . . British and French officers suggested that superior morale on the attacking side could overcome superior defensive firepower, and that this superiority in morale could be achieved simply by assuming the role of attacker, since offense was a morale-building activity. One French officer contended that "the offensive doubles the energy of the troops" and "concentrates the thoughts of the commander on a single objective," while British officers declared that "Modern [war] conditions have enormously increased the value of moral quality," and "the moral attributes [are] the primary causes of all great success." In short, mind would prevail over matter; morale would triumph over machine guns.

Europeans also tended to discount the power of political factors which would favor defenders. Many Germans believed that "bandwagoning" with a powerful state rather than "balancing" against it was the guiding principle in international alliance-formation. Aggressors would gather momentum as they gained power, because opponents would be intimidated into acquiescence and neutrals would rally to the stronger side. Such thinking led German Chancellor Bethmann Hollweg to hope that "Germany's growing strength . . . might force England to realize that [the balance of power] principle had become untenable and impracticable and to opt for a peaceful settlement with Germany," and German Secretary of State Gottlieb von Jagow to forecast British neutrality in a future European war: "We have not built our fleet in vain," and "people in England will seriously ask themselves whether it will be just that simple and without danger to play the role of France's guardian angel against us." German leaders also thought they might frighten Belgium into surrender: during the July crisis Moltke was "counting on the possibility of being able to come to an understanding [with Belgium] when the Belgian Government realizes the seriousness of the situation." This ill-founded belief in bandwagoning reinforced the general belief that conquest was relatively easy.

The belief in easy conquest eventually pervaded public images of international politics, manifesting itself most prominently in the widespread application of Darwinist notions to international affairs. In this image, states competed in a decisive struggle for survival which weeded out the weak and ended in the triumph of stronger states and races—an image which assumed a powerful offense. . . . This Darwinist foreign policy thought reflected and rested upon the implicit assumption that the offense was strong, since "grow or die" dynamics would be impeded in a defense-dominant world where growth could be stopped and death prevented by self-defense.

Consequences of Offense-Dominance

Recent theoretical writing in international relations emphasizes the dangers that arise when the offense is strong relative to the defense. If the theory outlined in these writings is valid, it follows that the cult of the offensive was a reason for the outbreak of the war.

Five major dangers relevant to the 1914 case may develop when the offense is strong, according to this recent writing. First, states adopt more aggressive foreign policies, both to exploit new opportunities and to avert new dangers which appear when the offense is strong. Expansion is more tempting, because the cost of aggression declines when the offense has the advantage. States are also driven to expand by the need to control assets and create the conditions they require to secure themselves against aggressors, because security becomes a scarcer asset. Alliances widen and tighten as states grow more dependent on one another for security, a circumstance which fosters the spreading of local conflicts. Moreover, each state is more likely to be menaced by aggressive neighbors who are governed by the same logic, creating an even more competitive atmosphere and giving states further reason to seek security in alliances and expansion.

Second, the size of the advantage accruing to the side mobilizing or striking first increases, raising the risk of preemptive war.* When

---

* In a "preemptive" war, either side gains by moving first; hence, one side moves to exploit the advantage of moving first, or to prevent the other side from doing so. By contrast, in a "preventive" war, one side foresees an adverse shift in the balance of power, and attacks to avoid a more difficult fight later.

"Moving first" in a preemptive war can consist of striking first *or mobilizing* first, if mobilization sets in train events which cause war, as in 1914. Thus a war is preemptive if statesmen attack because they believe that it pays to strike first; or if they mobilize because they believe that it pays to mobilize first, even if they do not also believe that it pays to strike first, if mobilizations open "windows" which spur attacks for "preventive" reasons, or if they produce other effects which cause war. Under such circumstances war is caused by preemptive actions which are not acts of war, but which are their equivalent since they produce conditions which cause war.

A preemptive war could also involve an attack by one side and mobilization by the other—for instance, one side might mobilize to forestall an attack, or might attack to forestall a mobilization, as the Germans apparently attacked Liège to forestall Belgian preparations to defend it (see below). Thus four classes of preemp-

the offense is strong, smaller shifts in ratios of forces between states create greater shifts in their relative capacity to conquer territory. As a result states have greater incentive to mobilize first or strike first, if they can change the force ratio in their favor by doing so. This incentive leads states to mobilize or attack to seize the initiative or deny it to adversaries, and to conceal plans, demands, and grievances to avoid setting off such a strike by their enemies, with deleterious effects on diplomacy.

Third, "windows" of opportunity and vulnerability open wider, forcing faster diplomacy and raising the risk of preventive war. Since smaller shifts in force ratios have larger effects on relative capacity to conquer territory, smaller prospective shifts in force ratios cause greater hope and alarm, open bigger windows of opportunity and vulnerability, and enhance the attractiveness of exploiting a window by launching a preventive attack.

Fourth, states adopt more competitive styles of diplomacy—brinkmanship and presenting opponents with *faits accomplis,* for instance—since the gains promised by such tactics can more easily justify the risks they entail. At the same time, however, the risks of adopting such strategies also increase, because they tend to threaten the vital interests of other states more directly. Because the security of states is more precarious and more tightly interdependent, threatening actions force stronger and faster reactions, and the political ripple effects of *faits accomplis* are larger and harder to control.

Fifth, states enforce tighter political and military secrecy, since national security is threatened more directly if enemies win the contest for information. As with all security assets, the marginal utility of information is magnified when the offense is strong; hence states compete harder to gain the advantage and avoid the disadvantage of disclosure, leading states to conceal their political and military planning and decision-making more carefully.

The following section suggests that many of the proximate causes of the war of 1914 represent various guises of these consequences of offense-dominance: either they were generated or exacerbated by the assumption that the offense was strong, or their effects were

---

tion are possible: an attack to forestall an attack, an attack to forestall a mobilization, a mobilization to forestall an attack, or a mobilization to forestall a mobilization (such as the Russian mobilizations in 1914).

The size of the incentive to preempt is a function of three factors: the degree of secrecy with which each side could mobilize its forces or mount an attack; the change in the ratio of forces which a secret mobilization or attack would produce; and the size and value of the additional territory which this changed ratio would allow the attacker to conquer or defend. If secret action is impossible, or if it would not change force ratios in favor of the side moving first, or if changes in force ratios would not change relative ability to conquer territory, then there is no first-strike or first-mobilization advantage. Otherwise, states have some inducement to move first.

rendered more dangerous by this assumption. These causes include: German and Austrian expansionism; the belief that the side which mobilized or struck first would have the advantage; the German and Austrian belief that they faced "windows of vulnerability"; the nature and inflexibility of the Russian and German war plans and the tight nature of the European alliance system, both of which spread the war from the Balkans to the rest of Europe; the imperative that "mobilization meant war" for Germany; the failure of Britain to take effective measures to deter Germany; the uncommon number of blunders and mistakes committed by statesmen during the July crisis; and the ability of the Central powers to evade blame for the war. Without the cult of the offensive these problems probably would have been less acute, and their effects would have posed smaller risks. Thus the cult of the offensive was a mainspring driving many of the mechanisms which brought about the First World War.

THE CULT OF THE OFFENSIVE AND THE CAUSES OF THE WAR

German Expansion and Entente Resistance

Before 1914 Germany sought a wider sphere of influence or empire, and the war grew largely from the political collision between expansionist Germany and a resistant Europe. Germans differed on whether their empire should be formal or informal, whether they should seek it in Europe or overseas, and whether they should try to acquire it peacefully or by violence, but a broad consensus favored expansion of some kind. The logic behind this expansionism, in turn, rested on two widespread beliefs which reflected the cult of the offensive: first, that German security required a wider empire; and second, that such an empire was readily attainable, either by coercion or conquest. Thus German expansionism reflected the assumption that conquest would be easy both for Germany and for its enemies . . . and most German officers and civilians believed they could win a spectacular, decisive victory if they struck at the right moment.

Bandwagon logic fed hopes that British and Belgian opposition to German expansion could be overcome. . . . Victory, moreover, would be decisive and final. . . . The presumed power of the offense made empire appear both feasible and necessary. Had Germans recognized the real power of the defense, the notion of gaining wider empire would have lost both its urgency and its plausibility.

Security was not Germany's only concern, nor was it always a genuine one. In Germany, as elsewhere, security sometimes served as a pretext for expansion undertaken for other reasons. Thus proponents of the "social imperialism" theory of German expansion note that German elites endorsed imperialism, often using security arguments, partly to strengthen their domestic political and social position. Likewise, spokesmen for the German military establishment exaggerated the threat to Germany and the benefits of empire for organizationally self-serving reasons. Indeed, members of the German elite sometimes privately acknowledged that Germany was under less threat than the public was being told. For example, the Secretary of State in the Foreign Office, Kiderlen-Wächter, admitted, "If we do not conjure up a war into being, no one else certainly will do so," since "The Republican government of France is certainly peace-minded. The British do not want war. They will never give cause for it. . . ."

Nevertheless, the German public believed that German security was precarious, and security arguments formed the core of the public case for expansion. Moreover, these arguments proved persuasive, and the chauvinist public climate which they created enabled the elite to pursue expansion, whatever elite motivation might actually have been. . . . The same mixture of insecurity and perceived opportunity stiffened resistance to German expansion and fuelled a milder expansionism elsewhere in Europe, intensifying the conflict between Germany and its neighbors. In France the nationalist revival and French endorsement of a firm Russian policy in the Balkans were inspired partly by a growing fear of the German threat after 1911, partly by an associated concern that Austrian expansion in the Balkans could shift the European balance of power in favor of the Central Powers and thereby threaten French security, and partly by belief that a war could create opportunities for French expansion. . . .

Russian policy in the Balkans was driven both by fear that Austrian expansion could threaten Russian security and by hopes that Russia could destroy its enemies if war developed under the right conditions. Sazonov saw a German–Austrian Balkan program to "deliver the Slavonic East, bound hand and foot, into the power of Austria–Hungary," followed by the German seizure of Constantinople, which would gravely threaten Russian security by placing all of Southern Russia at the mercy of German power. Eventually a "German Khalifate" would be established, "extending from the banks of the Rhine to the mouth of the Tigris and Euphrates," which would reduce "Russia to a pitiful dependence upon the arbitrary will of the Central Powers." At the same time some Russians believed these threats could be addressed by offensive action: Russian leaders spoke of the day when "the moment for the downfall of Austria–Hungary arrives," and the occasion when "The Austro-Hungarian ulcer, which today is not yet so ripe as the Turkish, may be cut up." Russian military officers contended that "the Austrian army represents a serious force. . . . But on the occasion of the first great defeats all of this multi-national and artificially united mass ought to disintegrate."

In short, the belief that conquest was easy and security scarce was an important source of German–Entente conflict. Without it, both sides could have adopted less aggressive and more accommodative policies.

The Incentive to Preempt

American strategists have long assumed that World War I was a preemptive war, but they have not clarified whether or how this was true. Hence two questions should be resolved to assess the consequences of the cult of the offensive: did the states of Europe perceive an incentive to move first in 1914, which helped spur them to mobilize or attack? If so, did the cult of the offensive help to give rise to this perception?

The question of whether the war was preemptive reduces to the question of why five principal actions in the July crisis were taken. These actions are: the Russian preliminary mobilization ordered on July 25–26; the partial Russian mobilization against Austria–Hungary ordered on July 29; the Russian full mobilization ordered on July 30; French preliminary mobilization measures ordered during July 25–30; and the German attack on the Belgian fortress at Liège at the beginning of the war. The war was preemptive if Russia and France mobilized preemptively, since these mobilizations spurred German and Austrian mobilization, opening windows which helped cause war. Thus while the mobilizations were not acts of war, they caused effects which caused war. The war was also preemptive if Germany struck Liège preemptively, since the imperative to strike Liège was one reason why "mobilization meant war" to Germany.

The motives for these acts cannot be determined with finality; testimony by the actors is spotty and other direct evidence is scarce. Instead, motives must be surmised from preexisting beliefs, deduced from circumstances, and inferred from clues which may by themselves be inconclusive. However, three pieces of evidence suggest that important preemptive incentives existed, and helped to shape conduct. First, most European leaders apparently believed that mobilization by either side which was not answered within a very few days, or even hours, could affect the outcome of the war. This judgment is reflected both in the length of time which officials assumed would constitute a militarily significant delay between mobilization and offsetting counter-mobilization, and in the severity of the consequences which they assumed would follow if they mobilized later than their opponents.

Second, many officials apparently assumed that significant mobilization measures and preparations to attack could be kept secret for a brief but significant period. Since most officials also believed that a brief unanswered mobilization could be decisive, they concluded that the side which mobilized first would have the upper hand. Third, governments carried out some of their mobilization measures in secrecy, suggesting that they believed secret measures were feasible and worthwhile.

THE PERCEIVED SIGNIFICANCE OF SHORT DELAYS. Before and during the July crisis European leaders used language suggesting that they believed a lead in ordering mobilization of roughly one to three days would be significant. In Austria, General Conrad believed that "every day was of far-reaching importance," since "any delay might leave the [Austrian] forces now assembling in Galicia open to being struck by the full weight of a Russian offensive in the midst of their deployment." In France, Marshall Joffre warned the French cabinet that "any delay of twenty-four hours in calling up our reservists" once German preparations began would cost France "ten to twelve miles for each day of delay; in other words, the initial abandonment of much of our territory." In Britain, one official believed that France "cannot possibly delay her own mobilization for even the fraction of a day" once Germany began to mobilize. In Germany, one analyst wrote that "A delay of a single day . . . can scarcely ever be rectified." Likewise Moltke, on receiving reports of preparations in France and Russia during the July crisis, warned that "the military situation is becoming from day to day more unfavorable for us," and would "lead to fateful consequences for us" if Germany did not respond. . . .

Germans also placed a high value on gaining the initiative at Liège, since Liège controlled a vital Belgian railroad junction, and German forces could not seize Liège with its tunnels and bridges intact unless they surprised the Belgians. As Moltke wrote before the war, the advance through Belgium "will hardly be possible unless Liège is in our hands . . . the possession of Liège is the *sine qua non* of our advance." But seizing Liège would require "meticulous preparation and surprise" and "is only possible if the attack is made at once, before the areas between the forts are fortified," "immediately" after the declaration of war. In short, the entire German war plan would be ruined if Germany allowed Belgium to prepare the defense of Liège.

This belief that brief unanswered preparations and actions could be decisive reflected the implicit assumption that the offense had the advantage. Late mobilization would cost Germany control of East and West Prussia only if Russian offensive power were strong, and German defensive power were weak; mobilizing late could only be a "crime against the safety" of Germany if numerically superior enemies could destroy it; lateness could only confront Russia with "certain catastrophe" or leave it in danger of "losing before we have time to unsheath our sword" if Germany could develop a powerful offensive with the material advantage it would gain by preparing first; and lateness could only condemn France to "irreparable inferiority" if small material inferiority translated into large territorial losses. Had statesmen understood that in reality the defense had the advantage, they also would have known that the possession of the initiative could not be decisive, and could have conceded it more easily.

WAS SECRET PREPARATION BELIEVED FEASIBLE? The belief that delay could be fatal would have created no impulse to go first had European leaders believed that they could detect and offset their opponents' preparations immediately. However, many officials believed that secret action for a short time was possible. Russian officials apparently lacked confidence in their own ability to detect German or Austrian mobilization, and their decisions to mobilize seem to have been motivated partly by the desire to forestall surprise preparation by their adversaries. Sazonov reportedly requested full mobilization on July 30 partly from fear that otherwise Germany would "gain time to complete her preparations in secret." Sazonov offers confirmation in his memoirs, explaining that he had advised mobilization believing that "The perfection of the German military organization made it possible by means of personal notices to the reservists to accomplish a great part of the work quietly." Germany could then "complete the mobilization in a very short time. This circumstance gave a tremendous advantage to Germany, but we could counteract it to a certain extent by taking measures for our own mobilization in good time."

Similar reasoning contributed to the Russian decision to mobilize against Austria on July 29. Sazonov explains that the mobilization was undertaken in part "so as to avoid the danger of being taken unawares by the Austrian preparations." Moreover, recent experience had fuelled Russian fears of an Austrian surprise: during the Balkan crisis of 1912, the Russian army had been horrified to discover that Austria had secretly mobilized in Galicia, without detection by Russian intelligence; and this experience resolved the Russian command not to be caught napping again. In one observer's opinion, "the experience of 1912 . . . was not without influence as regards Russia's unwillingness to put off her mobilization in the July days of 1914." Top Russian officials also apparently believed that Russia could itself mobilize secretly, and some historians ascribe the Russian decision to mobilize partly to this erroneous belief. . . .

Like their Russian counterparts, top French officials also apparently feared that Germany might mobilize in secret, which spurred the French to their own measures. Thus during the July crisis General Joffre spoke of "the concealments [of mobilization] which are possible in Germany," and referred to "information from excellent sources [which] led us to fear that on the Russian front a sort of secret mobilization was taking place [in Germany]." In his memoirs, Joffre quotes a German military planning document acquired by the French government before the July crisis, which he apparently took to indicate German capabilities, and which suggested that Germany could take "quiet measures . . . in preparation for mobilization," including "a discreet assembly of complementary personnel and materiel" which would "assure us advantages very difficult for other armies to realize in the same degree." . . .

To sum up, then, French policymakers feared that Germany could mobilize secretly; Russians feared secret mobilization by Germany or Austria, and hoped Russian mobilization could be secret; while Central Powers planners saw less possibility for preemptive mobilization by either side, but hoped to mount a surprise attack on Belgium.*

DID STATESMEN ACT SECRETLY? During the July crisis European statesmen sometimes informed their opponents before they took military measures, but on other occasions they acted secretly, suggesting that they believed the initiative was both attainable and worth attaining, and indicating that the desire to seize the initiative may have entered into their decisions to mobilize. German leaders warned the French of their preliminary measures taken on July 29, and their pre-mobilization and mobilization measures taken on July 31; and they openly warned the Russians on July 29 that they would mobilize if Russia conducted a partial mobilization. Russia openly warned Austria on July 27 that it would mobilize if Austria crossed the Serbian frontier, and then on July 28 and July 29 openly announced to Germany and Austria its partial mobilization of July 29, and France delayed full mobilization until after Germany had taken the onus on itself by issuing ultimata to Russia and France. However, Russia, France, and Germany tried to conceal four of the five major preemptive actions of the crisis: the Russians hid both their preliminary measures of July 25–26 and their general mobilization of July 30, the French attempted to conceal their preliminary mobilization measures of July 25–29, and the Germans took great care to conceal their planned *coup de main* against Liège. Thus

* During the July crisis, adversaries actually detected signs of most major secret mobilization activity in roughly 6–18 hours, and took responsive decisions in 1–2 days. Accordingly, the maximum "first mobilization advantage" which a state could gain by forestalling an adversary who otherwise would have begun mobilizing first was roughly 2–4 days.

states sometimes conceded the initiative, but sought it at critical junctures.

Overall, evidence suggests that European leaders saw some advantage to moving first in 1914: the lags which they believed significant lay in the same range as the lags they believed they could gain or forestall by mobilizing first. These perceptions probably helped spur French and Russian decisions to mobilize, which in turn helped set in train the German mobilization, which in turn meant war partly because the Germans were determined to preempt Liège. Hence the war was in some modest measure preemptive.

If so, the cult of the offensive bears some responsibility. Without it, statesmen would not have thought that secret mobilization or preemptive attack could be decisive. The cult was not the sole cause of the perceived incentive to preempt; rather, three causes acted together, the others being the belief that mobilization could briefly be conducted secretly, and the systems of reserve manpower mobilization which enabled armies to multiply their strength in two weeks. The cult had its effect by magnifying the importance of these other factors in the minds of statesmen, which magnified the incentive to preempt which these factors caused them to perceive. The danger that Germany might gain time to complete preparations in secret could only alarm France and Russia if Germany could follow up these preparations with an effective offensive; otherwise, early secret mobilization could *not* give "a tremendous advantage" to Germany, and such a prospect would not require a forestalling response. Sazonov could have been tempted to mobilize secretly only if early Russian mobilization would forestall important German gains, or could provide important gains for Russia, as could only have happened if the offense were powerful.

"Windows" and Preventive War

Germany and Austria pursued bellicose policies in 1914 partly to shut the looming "windows" of vulnerability which they envisioned lying ahead, and partly to exploit the brief window of opportunity which they thought the summer crisis opened. This window logic, in turn, grew partly from the cult of the offensive, since it depended upon the implicit assumption that the offense was strong. The shifts in the relative sizes of armies, economies, and alliances which fascinated and frightened statesmen in 1914 could have cast such a long shadow only in a world where material advantage promised decisive results in warfare, as it could only in an offense-dominant world.

The official communications of German leaders are filled with warnings that German power was in relative decline, and that Germany was doomed unless it took drastic action—such as provoking and winning a great crisis which would shatter the Entente, or directly instigating a "great liquidation" (as one general put it). German officials repeatedly warned that Russian military power would expand rapidly between 1914 and 1917, as Russia carried out its 1913–1914 Great Program, and that in the long run Russian power would further outstrip German power because Russian resources were greater. In German eyes this threat forced Germany to act. Secretary of State Jagow summarized a view common in Germany in a telegram to one of his ambassadors just before the July crisis broke:

> Russia will be ready to fight in a few years. Then she will crush us by the number of her soldiers; then she will have built her Baltic fleet and her strategic railways. Our group in the meantime will have become steadily weaker. . . . I do not desire a preventive war, but if the conflict should offer itself, we ought not to shirk it.

. . . During the war, Chancellor Bethmann Hollweg confessed that the "window" argument had driven German policy in 1914: "Lord yes, in a certain sense it was a preventive war," motivated by "the constant threat of attack, the greater likelihood of its inevitability in the future, and by the military's claim: today war is still possible without defeat, but not in two years!"

Window logic was especially prevalent among the German military officers, many of whom openly argued for preventive war during the years before the July crisis. . . . After the war Jagow recalled a conversation with Moltke in May 1914, in which Moltke had spelled out his reasoning:

> In two–three years Russia would have completed her armaments. The military superiority of our enemies would then be so great that he did not know how we could overcome them. Today we would still be a match for them. In his opinion there was no alternative to making preventive war in order to defeat the enemy while we still had a chance of victory. The Chief of General Staff therefore proposed that I should conduct a policy with the aim of provoking a war in the near future.

. . . German leaders also saw a tactical window of opportunity in the political constellation of July 1914, encouraging them to shut their strategic window of vulnerability. In German eyes, the Sarajevo assassination created favorable conditions for a confrontation, since it guaranteed that Austria would join Germany against Russia and France (as it might not if war broke out over a colonial conflict or a dispute in Western Europe), and it provided the Central powers with a plausible excuse, which raised hopes that Britain might remain neutral. . . .

Whether the Germans were aggressive or restrained depended on whether at a given moment they thought windows were open or closed. Germany courted war on the Balkan question after Sarajevo because window logic led German leaders to conclude that war could not be much worse than peace, and might even be better, if Germany could provoke the right war under the right conditions against the right opponents. German leaders probably preferred the status quo to a world war against the entire Entente, but evidence suggests that they also preferred a continental war against France and Russia to the status quo—as long as Austria joined the war, and as long as they could also find a suitable pretext which they could use to persuade the German public that Germany fought for a just cause. This, in turn, required that Germany engineer a war which engaged Austrian interests, and in which Germany could cast itself as the attacked, in order to involve the Austrian army, to persuade Britain to remain neutral, and to win German public support. These window considerations help explain both the German decision to force the Balkan crisis to a head and German efforts to defuse the crisis after it realized that it had failed to gain British neutrality. The German peace efforts after July 29 probably represent a belated effort to reverse course after it became clear that the July crisis was not such an opportune war window after all.

Window logic also helped to persuade Austria to play the provocateur for Germany. Like their German counterparts, many Austrian officials believed that the relative strength of the central powers was declining, and saw in Sarajevo a rare opportunity to halt this decline by force. . . . the Austrian foreign ministry reportedly believed that, "if Russia would not permit the localization of the conflict with Serbia, the present moment was more favorable for a reckoning than a later one would be." . . .

Thus the First World War was in part a "preventive" war, launched by the Central powers in the belief that they were saving themselves from a worse fate in later years. The cult of the offensive bears some responsibility for that belief, for in a defense-dominated world the windows which underlie the logic of preventive war are shrunken in size, as the balance of power grows less elastic to the relative sizes of armies and economies; and windows cannot be shut as easily by military action. Only in a world taken by the cult of the offensive could the window logic which governed German and Austrian conduct have proved so persuasive: Germans could only have feared that an unchecked Russia could eventually "crush us by the numbers of her soldiers," or have seen a "singularly favorable situation" in 1914 which could be "exploited by military action" if material superiority would endow the German and Russian armies with the ability to conduct decisive offensive operations against one another. Moltke claimed he saw "no alternative to making preventive war," but had he believed that the defense dominated, better alternatives would have been obvious. . . .

The Scope and Inflexibility of Mobilization Plans

The spreading of World War I outward from the Balkans is often ascribed to the scope of rigidity of the Russian and German plans for mobilization, which required that Russia must also mobilize armies against Germany when it mobilized against Austria–Hungary, and that Germany also attack France and Belgium if it fought Russia. Barbara Tuchman writes that Europe was swept into war by "the pull of military schedules," and recalls Moltke's famous answer when the Kaiser asked if the German armies could be mobilized to the East: "Your Majesty, it cannot be done. The deployment of millions cannot be improvised. If Your Majesty insists on leading the whole army to the East it will not be an army ready for battle but a disorganized mob of armed men with no arrangements for supply." . . .

The scope and character of these plans in turn reflected the assumption that the offense was strong. In an offense-dominant world Russia would have been prudent to mobilize against Germany if it mobilized against Austria–Hungary; and Germany probably would have been prudent to attack Belgium and France at the start of any Russo–German war. Thus the troublesome railroad schedules of 1914 reflected the offense dominant world in which the schedulers believed they lived. Had they known that the defense was powerful, they would have been drawn towards flexible plans for limited deployment on single frontiers; and had such planning prevailed, the war might have been confined to Eastern Europe or the Balkans.

Moreover, the "inflexibility" of the war plans may have reflected the same offensive assumptions which determined their shape. Russian and German soldiers understandably developed only options which they believed prudent to exercise, while omitting plans which they believed would be dangerous to implement. These judgments in turn reflected their own and their adversaries' offensive ideas. Options were few because these offensive ideas seemed to narrow the range of prudent choice.

Lastly, the assumption of offense-dominance gave preset plans greater influence over the conduct of the July crisis, by raising the cost of improvisation if statesmen insisted on adjusting plans at the last minute. Russian statesmen were told that an improvised partial mobilization would place Russia in an "extremely dangerous situation," and German civilians were warned against improvisation in similar terms. This in turn reflected the size of the "windows" which improvised partial mobilizations would open for the adversary on the frontier which the partial mobilization left unguarded, which in turn reflected the assumption that the offense was strong (since if defenses were strong a bungled mobilization would create less opportunity for others to exploit). Thus the cult of the offensive gave planners greater power to bind statesmen to the plans they had prepared.

RUSSIAN MOBILIZATION PLANS. On July 28, 1914, Russian leaders announced that partial Russian mobilization against Austria would be ordered on July 29. They took this step to address threats emanating from Austria, acting partly to lend emphasis to their warnings to Austria that Russia would fight if Serbia were invaded, partly to offset Austrian mobilization against Serbia, and partly to offset or forestall Austrian mobilization measures which they believed were taking place or which they feared might eventually take place against Russia in Galicia. However, after this announcement was made, Russian military officers advised their civilian superiors that no plans for partial mobilization existed, that such a mobilization would be a "pure improvisation," as General Denikin later wrote, and that sowing confusion in the Russian railway timetables would impede Russia's ability to mobilize later on its northern frontier. . . . Thus Russian leaders were forced to choose between full mobilization or complete retreat, choosing full mobilization on July 30.

The cult of the offensive set the stage for this decision by buttressing Russian military calculations that full mobilization was safer than partial. We have little direct evidence explaining why Russian officers had prepared no plan for partial mobilization, but we can deduce their reasoning from their opinions on related subjects. These suggest that Russian officers believed that Germany would attack Russia if Russia fought Austria, and that the side mobilizing first would have the upper hand in a Russo–German war (as I have outlined above). Accordingly, it followed logically that Russia should launch any war with Austria by preempting Germany.

Russian leaders had three principal reasons to fear that Germany would not stand aside in an Austro–Russian conflict. First, the Russians were aware of the international Social Darwinism then sweeping Germany, and the expansionist attitude toward Russia which this worldview engendered. . . . Second, the Russians were aware of German alarm about windows and the talk of preventive war which this alarm engendered in Germany. Accordingly, Russian leaders expected that Germany might seize the excuse offered by a Balkan war to mount a preventive strike against Russia, especially since a war arising from the Balkans was a "best case" scenario for Germany, involving Austria on the side of Germany as it did. Thus General Yanushkevich explained Russia's decision to mobilize against Germany in 1914: "We knew well that Germany was ready for war, that she was longing for it at that moment, because our big armaments program was not yet completed . . . and because our war potential was not as great as it might be." Accordingly, Russia had to expect war with Germany: "We knew that war was inevitable, not only against Austria, but also against Germany. For this reason partial mobilization against Austria alone, which would have left our front towards Germany open . . . might have brought about a disaster, a terrible disaster." In short, Russia had to strike to preempt a German preventive strike against Russia.

Third, the Russians knew that the Germans believed that German and Austrian security were closely linked. Germany would therefore feel compelled to intervene in any Austro–Russian war, because a Russian victory against Austria would threaten German safety. German leaders had widely advertised this intention: for instance, Bethmann Hollweg had warned the Reichstag in 1912 that if the Austrians "while asserting their interests should against all expectations be attacked by a third party, then we would have to come resolutely to their aid. And then we would fight for the maintenance of our own position in Europe and in defense of our future and security." And in fact this was precisely what happened in 1914: Germany apparently decided to attack on learning of Russian *partial* mobilization, before Russian full mobilization was known in Germany. This suggests that the role of "inflexible" Russian plans in causing the war is overblown—Russian full mobilization was sufficient but not necessary to cause the war; but it also helps explain why these plans were drawn as they were, and supports the view that some of the logic behind them was correct, given the German state of mind with which Russia had to contend.

In sum, Russians had to fear that expansionist, preventive, and alliance concerns might induce Germany to attack, which in turn reflected the German assumption that the offense was strong. The Russian belief that it paid to mobilize first reflected the effects of the same assumption in Russia. Had Europe known that the defense dominated, Russians would have had less reason to fear that an Austro–Russian war would spark a German attack, since the logic of expansionism and preventive war would presumably have been weaker in Germany, and Germany could more easily have tolerated some reduction in Austrian power without feeling that German safety was also threatened. At the same time, Russian soldiers would presumably have been slower to assume that they could improve their position in a Russo–German war by mobilizing preemptively. In short, the logic of general mobilization in Russia largely reflected and depended upon conclusions deduced from the cult of the offensive, or from its various manifestations. Without the cult of the offensive, a partial southern mobilization would have been the better option for Russia.

It also seems probable that the same logic helped persuade the Russian General Staff to eschew planning for a partial mobilization. If circumstances argued against a partial mobilization, they also argued against planning for one, since this would raise the risk that Russian civilians might actually implement the plan. This interpretation fits with suggestions that Russian officers exaggerated the difficulties of partial mobilization in their representations to Russian civilians. If Russian soldiers left a partial mobilization option undeveloped because they believed that it would be dangerous to exercise, it follows that they also would emphasize the difficulty of improvising a southern option, since they also opposed it on other grounds.

GERMAN MOBILIZATION PLANS. The Schlieffen Plan was a disastrous scheme which only approached success because the French war plan was equally foolish: had the French army stood on the defensive instead of lunging into Alsace–Lorraine, it would have smashed the German army at the French frontier. Yet General Schlieffen's plan was a sensible response to the offense-dominant world imagined by many Germans. The plan was flawed because it grew from a fundamentally flawed image of warfare.

In retrospect, Germany should have retained the later war plan of the elder Moltke (Chief of Staff from 1857 to 1888), who would have conducted a limited offensive in the east against Russia while standing on the defensive in the west. However, several considerations pushed German planners instead toward Schlieffen's grandiose scheme, which envisioned a quick victory against Belgium and France, followed by an offensive against Russia.

First, German planners assumed that France would attack Germany if Germany fought Russia, leaving Germany no option for a one-front war. By tying down German troops in Poland, an eastern war would create a yawning window of opportunity for France to recover its lost territories, and a decisive German victory over Russia would threaten French security by leaving France to face Germany alone. For these reasons they believed that France would be both too tempted and too threatened to stand aside. . . .

Second, German planners assumed that "window" considerations required a German offensive against either France or Russia at the outset of any war against the Entente. German armies could mobilize faster than the combined entente armies; hence, the ratio of forces would most favor Germany at the beginning of the war. Therefore, Germany would do best to force an early decision, which in turn required that it assume the offensive, since otherwise its enemies would play a waiting game. As one observer explained,

Germany "has the speed and Russia has the numbers, and the safety of the German Empire forbade that Germany should allow Russia time to bring up masses of troops from all parts of her wide dominions." Germans believed that the window created by these differential mobilization rates was big, in turn, because they believed that both Germany and its enemies could mount a decisive offensive against the other with a small margin of superiority. If Germany struck at the right time, it could win easily—Germans hoped for victory in several weeks, as noted above—while if it waited it was doomed by Entente numerical superiority, which German defenses would be too weak to resist.

Third, German planners believed that an offensive against France would net them more than an offensive against Russia, which explains the western bias of the Schlieffen Plan. France could be attacked more easily than Russia, because French forces and resources lay within closer reach of German power; hence, as Moltke wrote before the war, "A speedy decision may be hoped for [against France], while an offensive against Russia would be an interminable affair." Moreover, France was the more dangerous opponent not to attack, because it could take the offensive against Germany more quickly than Russia, and could threaten more important German territories if Germany left its frontier unguarded. Thus Moltke explained that they struck westward because "Germany could not afford to expose herself to the danger of attack by strong French forces in the direction of the Lower Rhine," and Alfred von Wegerer wrote later that the German strike was compelled by the need to protect the German industrial region from French attack. In German eyes these considerations made it too dangerous to stand on the defensive in the West in hopes that war with France could be avoided.

Finally, German planners believed that Britain would not have time to bring decisive power to bear on the continent before the German army overran France. Accordingly, they discounted the British opposition which their attack on France and Belgium would elicit: Schlieffen declared that if the British army landed, it would be "securely billeted" at Antwerp or "arrested" by the German armies, while Moltke said he hoped that it would land so that the German army "could take care of it." In accordance with their "bandwagon" worldview, German leaders also hoped that German power might cow Britain into neutrality; or that Britain might hesitate before entering the war, and then might quit in discouragement once the French were beaten—Schlieffen expected that, "If the battle [in France] goes in favor of the Germans, the English are likely to abandon their enterprise as hopeless"—which led them to further discount the extra political costs of attacking westward.

Given these four assumptions, an attack westward, even one through Belgium which provoked British intervention, was the most sensible thing for Germany to do. Each assumption, in turn, was a manifestation of the belief that the offense was strong. Thus while the Schlieffen Plan has been widely criticized for its political and military naiveté, it would have been a prudent plan had Germans actually lived in the offense-dominant world they imagined. Under these circumstances quick mobilization would have in fact given them a chance to win a decisive victory during their window of opportunity, and if they had failed to exploit this window by attacking, they would eventually have lost; the risk of standing on the defense in the West in hopes that France would not fight would have been too great; and the invasion of France and Belgium would have been worth the price, because British power probably could not have affected the outcome of the war.

Thus the belief in the power of the offense was the linchpin which held Schlieffen's logic together, and the main criticisms which can be levelled at the German war plan flow from the falsehood of this belief. German interests would have been better served by a limited, flexible, east-only plan which conformed to the defensive realities of 1914. Moreover, had Germany adopted such a plan, the First World War might well have been confined to Eastern Europe, never becoming a world war.

"Mobilization Means War"

"Mobilization meant war" in 1914 because mobilization meant war to Germany: the German war plan mandated that special units of the German standing army would attack Belgium and Luxemburg immediately after mobilization was ordered, and long before it was completed. (In fact Germany invaded Luxemburg on August 1, the same day on which it ordered full mobilization.) Thus Germany had no pure "mobilization" plan, but rather had a "mobilization and attack" plan under which mobilizing and attacking would be undertaken simultaneously. As a result, Europe would cascade into war if any European state mobilized in a manner which eventually forced German mobilization.

This melding of mobilization and attack in Germany reflected two decisions to which I have already alluded. First, Germans believed that they would lose their chance for victory and create a grave danger for themselves if they gave the Entente time to mobilize its superior numbers. In German eyes, German defenses would be too weak to defeat this superiority. . . . Second, the German war plan depended on the quick seizure of Liège. Germany could only secure Liège quickly if German troops arrived before Belgium prepared its defense, and this in turn depended on achieving surprise against

Belgium. Accordingly, German military planners enshrouded the planned Liège attack in such dark secrecy that Bethmann Hollweg, Admiral Tirpitz, and possibly even the Kaiser were unaware of it. They also felt compelled to strike as soon as mobilization was authorized, both because Belgium would strengthen the defenses of Liège as a normal part of the Belgian mobilization which German mobilization would engender, and because otherwise Belgium eventually might divine German intentions towards Liège and focus upon preparing its defense and destroying the critical bridges and tunnels which it controlled.

Both of these decisions in turn reflected German faith in the power of the offense, and were not appropriate to a defense-dominant world. Had Germans recognized the actual power of the defense, they might have recognized that neither Germany nor its enemies could win decisively even by exploiting a fleeting material advantage, and decided instead to mobilize without attacking. The tactical windows that drove Germany to strike in 1914 were a mirage, as events demonstrated during 1914–1918, and Germans would have known this in advance had they understood the power of the defense. Likewise, the Liège *coup de main* was an artifact of Schlieffen's offensive plan; if the Germans had stuck with the elder Moltke's plan, they could have abandoned both the Liège attack and the compulsion to strike quickly which it helped to engender.

Brinkmanship and Faits Accomplis

Two *faits accomplis* by the Central powers set the stage for the outbreak of the war: the Austrian ultimatum to Serbia on July 23, and the Austrian declaration of war against Serbia on July 28. The Central powers also planned to follow these with a third *fait accompli*, by quickly smashing Serbia on the battlefield before the Entente could intervene. These plans and actions reflected the German strategy for the crisis: "*fait accompli* and then friendly towards the Entente, the shock can be endured," as Kurt Riezler had summarized.

This *fait accompli* strategy deprived German leaders of warning that their actions would plunge Germany into a world war, by depriving the Entente of the chance to warn Germany that it would respond if Austria attacked Serbia. It also deprived diplomats of the chance to resolve the Austro–Serbian dispute in a manner acceptable to Russia. Whether this affected the outcome of the crisis depends on German intentions—if Germany sought a pretext for a world war, then this missed opportunity had no importance, but if it preferred the status quo to world war, as I believe it narrowly did, then the decision to adopt *fait accompli* tactics was a crucial step on the road to war. Had Germany not done so, it might have recognized where its policies led before it took irrevocable steps, and have drawn back.

The influence of the cult of the offensive is seen both in the German adoption of this *fait accompli* strategy and in the disastrous scope of the results which followed in its train. Some Germans, such as Kurt Riezler, apparently favored brinkmanship and *fait accompli* diplomacy as a means of peaceful expansion. Others probably saw it as a means to provoke a continental war. In either case it reflected a German willingness to trade peace for territory, which reflected German expansionism—which in turn reflected security concerns fuelled by the cult of the offensive. Even those who saw *faits accomplis* as tools of peaceful imperialism recognized their risks, believing that necessity justified the risk. . . . *Faits accomplis* were dangerous tools whose adoption reflected the dangerous circumstances which Germans believed they faced.

The cult of the offensive also stiffened the resistance of the Entente to the Austro–German *fait accompli,* by magnifying the dangers they believed it posed to their own security. Thus Russian leaders believed that Russian security would be directly jeopardized if Austria crushed Serbia, because they valued the power which Serbia added to their alliance, and because they feared a domino effect, running to Constantinople and beyond, if Serbia were overrun. Sazonov believed that Serbian and Bulgarian military power was a vital Russian resource, "five hundred thousand bayonets to guard the Balkans" which "would bar the road forever to German penetration, Austrian invasion." If this asset were lost, Russia's defense of its own territories would be jeopardized by the German approach to Constantinople: Sazonov warned the Czar, "First Serbia would be gobbled up; then will come Bulgaria's turn, and then we shall have her on the Black Sea." This would be "the death-warrant of Russia" since in such an event "the whole of southern Russia would be subject to [Germany]."

Similar views could be found in France. During the July crisis one French observer warned that French and Serbian security were closely intertwined, and the demise of Serbia would directly threaten French security:

> To do away with Serbia means to double the strength which Austria can send against Russia: to double Austro–Hungarian resistance to the Russian Army means to enable Germany to send some more army corps against France. For every Serbian soldier killed by a bullet on the Morava one more Prussian soldier can be sent to the Moselle. . . . It is for us to grasp this truth and draw the consequences from it before disaster overtakes Serbia.

These considerations helped spur the Russian and French decisions to begin military preparations on July 25, which set in train a further sequence of events: German preliminary preparations, which were detected and exaggerated by French and Russian officials, spurring them on to further measures, which helped spur the Germans to their decision to mobilize on July 30. The effects of the original *fait accompli* rippled outward in ever-wider circles, because the reactions of each state perturbed the safety of others—forcing them to react or preempt, and ultimately forcing Germany to launch a world war which even it preferred to avoid.

Had Europe known that, in reality, the defense dominated, these dynamics might have been dampened: the compulsion to resort to *faits accomplis*, the scope of the dangers they raised for others, and the rippling effects engendered by others' reactions all would have been lessened. States still might have acted as they did, but they would have been less pressured in this direction.

Problems of Alliances: Unconditionality and Ambiguity

Two aspects of the European alliance system fostered the outbreak of World War I and helped spread the war. First, both alliances had an unconditional, offensive character—allies supported one another unreservedly, regardless of whether their behavior was defensive or provocative. As a result a local war would tend to spread throughout Europe. And second, German leaders were not convinced that Britain would fight as an Entente member, which encouraged Germany to confront the Entente. In both cases the cult of the offensive contributed to the problem.

UNCONDITIONAL ("TIGHT") ALLIANCES. Many scholars contend that the mere existence of the Triple Alliance and the Triple Entente caused and spread the war. . . . But the problem with the alliances of 1914 lay less with their existence than with their nature. A network of defensive alliances, such as Bismarck's alliances of the 1880s, would have lowered the risk of war by facing aggressors with many enemies, and by making status quo powers secure in the knowledge that they had many allies. Wars also would have tended to remain localized, because the allies of an aggressor would have stood aside from any war that aggressor had provoked. Thus the unconditional nature of alliances rather than their mere existence was the true source of their danger in 1914.

The Austro–German alliance was offensive chiefly and simply because its members had compatible aggressive aims. Moreover, German and Russian mobilization plans left their neighbors no choice but to behave as allies by putting them all under threat of attack. But the Entente also operated more unconditionally, or "tightly," because Britain and France failed to restrain Russia from undertaking mobilization measures during the July crisis. This was a failure in alliance diplomacy, which in turn reflected constraints imposed upon the Western allies by the offensive assumptions and preparations with which they had to work.

First, they were hamstrung by the offensive nature of Russian military doctrine, which left them unable to demand that Russia confine itself to defensive preparations. All Russian preparations were inherently offensive, because Russian war plans were offensive. This put Russia's allies in an "all or nothing" situation—either they could demand that Russia stand unprepared, or they could consent to provocative preparations. Thus the British ambassador to St. Petersburg warned that Britain faced a painful decision, to "choose between giving Russia our active support or renouncing her friendship." Had Russia confined itself to preparing its own defense, it would have sacrificed its Balkan interests by leaving Austria free to attack Serbia, and this it would have been very reluctant to do. However, the British government was probably willing to sacrifice Russia's Balkan interests to preserve peace; what Britain was unable to do was to frame a request to Russia which would achieve this, because there was no obvious class of defensive activity that it could demand. . . .

Second, Britain and France were constrained by their dependence upon the strength and unity of the Entente for their own security, which limited their ability to make demands on Russia. Because they feared they might fracture the Entente if they pressed Russia too hard, they tempered their demands to preserve the alliance. Thus Poincaré wrote later that France had been forced to reconcile its efforts to restrain Russia with the need to preserve the Franco–Russian alliance, "the break up of which would leave us in isolation at the mercy of our rivals." Likewise Winston Churchill recalled that "the one thing [the Entente states] would not do was repudiate each other. To do this might avert the war for the time being. It would leave each of them to face the next crisis alone. They did not dare to separate." These fears were probably over-drawn, since Russia had no other option than alliance with the other Entente states, but apparently they affected French and British behavior. This in turn reflected the assumption in France and Britain that the security of the Entente members was closely interdependent. French leaders felt forced in their own interests to aid Russia if Russia embroiled itself with Germany, because French security depended on the maintenance of Russian power. This in turn undermined the French ability to credibly threaten to discipline a provocative Russia. . . .

Third, British leaders were unaware that German mobilization meant war, hence that peace required Britain to restrain Russia from mobilizing first, as well as attacking. As a result, they took a more relaxed view of Russian mobilization than they otherwise might, while frittering away their energies on schemes to preserve peace which assumed that war could be averted even after the mobilizations began. This British ignorance reflected German failure to explain clearly to the Entente that mobilization did indeed mean war—German leaders had many opportunities during the July crisis to make this plain, but did not do so. We can only guess why Germany was silent, but German desire to avoid throwing a spotlight on the Liège operation probably played a part, leading German soldiers to conceal the plan from German civilians, which led German civilians to conceal the political implications of the plan from the rest of Europe. Thus preemptive planning threw a shroud of secrecy over military matters, which obscured the mechanism that would unleash the war and rendered British statesmen less able to wield British power effectively for peace by obscuring what it was that Britain had to do.

Lastly, the nature of German war plans empowered Russia to involve France, and probably Britain also, in war, since Germany would be likely to start any eastern war by attacking westward, as Russian planners were aware. Hence France and Britain would probably have to fight for Russia even if they preferred to stand aside, because German planners assumed that France would fight eventually and planned accordingly, and the plans they drew would threaten vital British interests. We have no direct evidence that Russian policies were emboldened by these considerations, but it would be surprising if they never occurred to Russian leaders.

These dynamics reflected the general tendency of alliances toward tightness and offensiveness in an offense-dominant world. Had Europe known that the defense had the advantage, the British and French could have more easily afforded to discipline Russia in the interest of peace, and this might have affected Russian calculations. Had Russia had a defensive military strategy, its allies could more easily and legitimately have asked it to confine itself to defensive preparations. Had British leaders better understood German war plans, they might have known to focus their efforts on preventing Russian mobilization. And had German plans been different, Russian leaders would have been more uncertain that Germany would entangle the Western powers in eastern wars, and perhaps proceeded more cautiously.

The importance of the failure of the Western powers to restrain Russia can be exaggerated, since Russia was not the chief provocateur in the July crisis. Moreover, too much can be made of factors which hamstrung French restraint of Russia, since French desire to prevent war was tepid at best, so French inaction probably owed as much to indifference as inability. Nevertheless, Russian mobilization was an important step toward a war which Britain, if not France, urgently wanted to prevent; hence, to that extent, the alliance dynamics which allowed it helped bring on the war.

THE AMBIGUITY OF BRITISH POLICY. The British government is often accused of causing the war by failing to warn Germany that Britain would fight. Thus Albertini concludes that "to act as Grey did was to allow the catastrophe to happen," and Germans themselves later argued that the British had led them on, the Kaiser complaining of "the grossest deception" by the British.

The British government indeed failed to convey a clear threat to the Germans until after the crisis was out of control, and the Germans apparently were misled by this. Jagow declared on July 26 that "we are sure of England's neutrality," while during the war the Kaiser wailed, "If only someone had told me beforehand that England would take up arms against us!" However, this failure was not entirely the fault of British leaders; it also reflected their circumstances. First, they apparently felt hamstrung by the lack of a defensive policy option. Grey voiced fear that if he stood too firmly with France and Russia, they would grow too demanding, while Germany would feel threatened, and "Such a menace would but stiffen her attitude."

Second, British leaders were unaware of the nature of the German policy to which they were forced to react until very late, which left them little time in which to choose and explain their response. Lulled by the Austro–German *fait accompli* strategy, they were unaware until July 23 that a crisis was upon them. . . . They also were apparently unaware that a continental war would begin with a complete German conquest of Belgium, thanks to the dark secrecy surrounding the Liège operation. Britain doubtless would have joined the war even if Germany had not invaded Belgium, but the Belgian invasion provoked a powerful emotional response in Britain which spurred a quick decision on August 4. This reaction suggests that the British decision would have been clearer to the British, hence to the Germans, had the nature of the German operation been known in advance.

Thus the British failure to warn Germany was due as much to German secrecy as to British indecision. Albertini's condemnation of Grey seems unfair: governments cannot easily take national decisions for war in less than a week in response to an uncertain provocation. The ambiguity of British policy should be recognized as an artifact of the secret styles of the Central powers, which reflected the competitive politics and preemptive military doctrines of the times. . . .

CONCLUSION

The cult of the offensive was a major underlying cause of the war of 1914, feeding or magnifying a wide range of secondary dangers which helped pull the world to war. The causes of the war are often catalogued as an unrelated grab-bag of misfortunes which unluckily arose at the same time; but many shared a common source in the cult of the offensive, and should be recognized as its symptoms and artifacts rather than as isolated phenomena.

The consequences of the cult of the offensive are illuminated by imagining the politics of 1914 had European leaders recognized the actual power of the defense. German expansionists then would have met stronger arguments that empire was needless and impossible, and Germany could have more easily let the Russian military buildup run its course, knowing that German defenses could still withstand Russian attack. All European states would have been less tempted to mobilize first, and each could have tolerated more preparations by adversaries before mobilizing themselves, so the spiral of mobilization and counter-mobilization would have operated more slowly, if at all. If armies mobilized, they might have rushed to defend their own trenches and fortifications, instead of crossing frontiers, divorcing mobilization from war. Mobilizations could more easily have been confined to single frontiers, localizing the crisis. Britain could more easily have warned the Germans and restrained the Russians, and all statesmen could more easily have recovered and reversed mistakes made in haste or on false information. Thus the logic that led Germany to provoke the 1914 crisis would have been undermined, and the chain reaction by which the war spread outward from the Balkans would have been very improbable. In all likelihood, the Austro–Serbian conflict would have been a minor and soon-forgotten disturbance on the periphery of European politics. . . .

The Horse Cavalry
in the Twentieth Century

EDWARD L. KATZENBACH, JR.

THE PROBLEM

Lag-time, that lapsed period between innovation and a successful institutional or social response to it, is probably on the increase in military matters. Moreover, as the tempo of technological change continues to quicken, it is likely that lag-time will increase as well. . . .

Of course, at first there would seem to be a paradox here. As weapons systems have become more complex, the lead-time needed to bring them from the drawing board to the assembly line has become markedly longer. On the basis of the longer lead-time one might hypothesize that the institutional lag might lessen inasmuch as prior planning would seem eminently more possible. It might even be surmised that the institutional response might be made to coincide with the operational readiness of new weapons. To date, however, military institutions have not been able to use this lead-time effectively because real change has so outdistanced anticipated change. Moreover, there is not the urgency that there should be in the military to make major institutional adjustments in the face of the challenge of new weapons systems, if for no other reason than that the problem of testing is so difficult. . . . It is quite impossible to *prove* that minor adjustments in a traditional pattern of organization and doctrine will not suffice to absorb technological innovations of genuine magnitude.

Furthermore the absence of any final testing mechanism of the military's institutional adequacy short of war has tended to keep the pace of change to a creep in time of peace, and, conversely, has whipped it into a gallop in time of war. The military history of the past half century is studded with institutions which have managed to dodge the challenge of the obvious. . . . The most curious of all was the Horse Cavalry which maintained a capacity for survival that borders on the miraculous. The war horse survived a series of

From Public Policy, 1958, pp. 120–149. Copyright © 1958 by John Wiley & Sons, Inc. Reprinted by permission of John Wiley & Sons, Inc. Portions of the text and some footnotes have been omitted.

challenges each of which was quite as great as those which today's weapons systems present to today's traditional concepts. . . . It continued to live out an expensive and decorous existence with splendor and some spirit straight into an age which thought it a memory. . . .

The horse cavalry has had to review its role in war four times since the end of the nineteenth century in the face of four great changes in the science of war: the development of repeating automatic and semi-automatic weapons, the introduction of gasoline and diesel-fueled engines, the invention of the air-borne weapon, and the coming of the nuclear battlefield. Each new challenge to the horse has been, of necessity, seriously considered. Each has demanded a review of doctrine, a change in role and mission. And in each review there have been, of necessity, assumptions made as to the relevance of experience to some pattern of future war . . . [for] the paradox of military planning is that it must be reasonably precise as to quite imprecise future contingencies.

THE WEAPONS PROBLEM

By the year 1900, or thereabouts, the clip-fed breech-loading repeating rifle was in the hands of the troops of all the major powers. . . . Self-firing automatic weapons were also on the assembly lines of the world's armament makers. Hiram Maxim had registered the last of a famous series of machine gun patents in 1885. By the time (1904–1905) of the Russo-Japanese War the guns of Maxim and Hotchkiss were in national arsenals everywhere, or almost everywhere, for the expense of new weapons was rapidly shrinking the ranks of those powers which could be considered "great." At roughly the same time it had been found that the use of glycerine in the recoil mechanism of artillery pieces enabled these to remain aimed after being fired. This in turn meant that the artillery piece itself became a rapid fire (20 rounds per minute) weapon. . . . Firepower, in short, had a new meaning.

For the elite of the armies of the world, the cavalry, each of these developments would seem to have been nothing short of disaster. For that proud and beautiful animal, the horse, has a thin skin and a high silhouette, and its maximum rate of speed on the attack is only 30 m.p.h. Especially in conjunction with barbed wire, automatically manufactured since 1874 and in military use at the end of the century, it is difficult to imagine a target more susceptible to rapid fire.

The cavalry had always considered itself to have a variety of missions. The cavalry was the good eye of the infantry. It was taught to collect, and if necessary to fight for information about the enemy. The cavalry protected friendly, and harried enemy flanks and rear. It covered any necessary withdrawal. It was used in pursuit of defeated enemy. And above and beyond all else, the cavalry was used to charge the faltering, the weary, or the unwary, to deliver the *coup de grâce* with the *arme blanche:* with cold steel, with saber or lance, to "crown victory" as the proud phrase went.

It was clear that the introduction of the automatic and the semi-automatic weapon would make some cavalry missions more difficult. But there was no doubt in any cavalryman's mind, and there was little doubt in the minds of most others, that most cavalry missions would have to continue simply because there was no viable substitute. The horse was transport, and the horse was mobility. A group of horsemen could cover a hundred miles in twenty-four hours with a load of around 225–250 pounds. The beast was reasonably amphibious; at least it could swim rivers. To scout, to patrol, to cover flank, rear and withdrawal, to raid—these missions remained untouched.

There remained, however, one really great problem area. Did automatic fire relegate the horse to a transport role or should it still be considered as part of a weapons system? At the time the problem was never stated quite this simply. Indeed it was never stated simply at all, but in essence this was the issue from roughly the end of the Boer War until World War I. The reason why the question so divided men was this: Cavalry as an arm was an integrated weapon made up of horse, man and cold steel fighting as one. If horses were to be considered simply as transportation, and if man and horse were to be separated for the fire fight, then the cavalry as an arm would no longer exist. Only mounted infantry would remain.[1]

On the issue of the relationship between horse and man hung a number of subsidiary issues. Should the horseman be armed with the new automatic weapons? If so, he would have to be dismounted in action, for the horse, as differentiated from the elephant, is a most unsatisfactory gun platform. Yet to deprive cavalry of the new weapons would be to deprive the weapons of mobility. And if the horse could no longer be used to charge the new guns, then of what possible use was honed steel, e.g., lance and sword, even if one took into serious account the last ditch defense of it, to wit that it was "always loaded"? Finally, and here one comes to the most burning question in any issue of military policy—the effect of change on morale. If the cavalry were deprived of its cold steel, would it lose that fine edge of morale, that élan without which of course it would not be "cavalry," no matter what its mission?

There should have been some way to learn through experience just what could and could not be done with the cavalry with and

---

[1] Perhaps this will be better understood if a modern analogy is cited—the substitution of missile for manned aircraft, for example.

against the new weapons. There were, after all, two wars of some importance during the period under consideration—the Boer War (1898–1901) and the Russo-Japanese (1904–1905). In both, cavalry and repeating and automatic weapons were used. Each fall, moreover, there were great maneuvers in each country of Europe. Present at each were foreign observers with, at least by modern standards, a free run of the field of action. Why was it then that there could be no final decisions on these matters?

The answer lies in the number of variables. For instance, before the problem of the cavalry armament could even be tackled, the difficult question had to be answered as to what the rapid-fire weapons could do and should be doing.

. . . For each demonstrable fact there was an awkwardly intangible "if" which could neither be properly accounted for nor possibly forgotten. If into the balance of judgment concerning the machine gun was thrown the urgent problem of its resupply and its vulnerability to long-range artillery fire, then a rational conclusion might be reached that the weapon was primarily defensive in character and should be dug into the earth, into a well sandbagged bunker, there to pour forth its withering fire into an attacking force. Yet if, on the other hand, it was concluded that the withering fire of the weapon made it ideal to use on the surprise target, the target of opportunity on the enemy flank, then the weapon became offensive. If an offensive weapon, then the machine gun could well be designated a cavalry weapon. If defensive, then was it not an infantry, or even an artillery weapon? Of course this initial decision was a serious one for it might well determine the future of the weapon. Once assigned to an organization, a branch or arm of a service, it was at least likely that the weapon's development would be stunted except in line with the mission of the unit to which it was assigned.

Within the military staff of all nations the machine gun raised many more problems than it solved—as can be expected of any new weapons system. These problems were, furthermore, broadly intellectual rather than narrowly technical. Indeed the mechanical improvement of a given weapons system is usually less urgent and almost always less baffling than deciding a proper and fitting target for it, and then solving the galaxy of problems of organization and control which hinge on this basic decision. . . .

So in the period between 1900 and 1914 the immediate problem was to conceptualize the mission or missions of the machine gun and the tactics of the new clip-fed, bolt-action rifle and the automatic gun. The second problem was to decide the future tactics and armament of cavalry in view of the concept arrived at. What actually happened was that the new was absorbed into old organizational and tactical concepts, and nothing of the old was rejected. The reasoning from country to country may, however, be of lasting interest. The matter of the cavalry *charge* provides an excellent focal point.

THE CHARGE

It is hard to see where there was room for claim and counterclaim in so substantive an issue as this—the charge of a wave of horsemen, gaily colored (except in the United States), helmets shining, plumes flying, sabers drawn or lances at the ready. Surely a comprehensive and conclusive study of the charge and its role, if any, in modern war was not outside the bounds of logical possibility. Yet just as it was impossible in the 1930s to analyze the role of the battleship in the air age and is now impossible to assess the relationship between the naval aircraft carrier and the nuclear bomber, so it was impossible to evaluate the charge—and for much the same reasons.

The reasons why the charge was continued varied from one country to another. But basically it was continued because the cavalry liked it. In virtually all countries the cavalry was a club, an exclusive one, made up at the officer level of those who could afford to ride when young, hunt, dress and play polo when older. The impression that one absorbs from contemporary cavalry reviews, from the pictures, the social columns, the interests expressed in the less than serious articles, together with the portrait of the cavalry-man in the contemporary novel, is of a group of men who were at once hard-riding, hard-drinking, and hard-headed. Its leadership was derived from the countryside rather than from the city. The cavalry was the home of tradition, the seat of romance, the haven of the well-connected. New York City's Squadron A, the proud majors in the Prussian Cavalry Reserve, the French Horse Breeders' Association, all had a built-in loyalty to the cavalry, and if the Chief of Cavalry said that the charge was still feasible, he had important backing. So it was that in Europe the charge was still considered not only feasible, but a future way of war.

American cavalrymen, however, thought that European cavalry had much to learn. And in many respects the U.S. "Red Necks" were quite the most realistic of the world's cavalries in the period just prior to World War I. To be sure, they retained the saber charge, executing it with the same straight saber, a thrust weapon, used by the Canadian cavalry. But in the years just before World War I until just after World War II the U.S. Cavalry preferred to practice the charge with the Colt semi-automatic .45 pistol. (The pistol charge was never actually used in battle. The last battle charge of the U.S. Cavalry seems to have been in the Philippines during the insurrection of 1901.) Of course it might be argued that to put a .45 in the hands of a man on a horse was simply to mount the inaccurate on the unstable, but given the argument that the essence of the charge was its psychological impact, the sound of the .45 might have had an effect comparable to the sight of saber or lance.

But what the U.S. Cavalry did have that the others did not was a genuine appreciation of the importance of dismounted action. It is this which is given the more elaborate treatment in the regulations, and it is this that the trooper really expected to be the rule in combat. But was this the result of a thoughtful analysis of the new weapons or something else?

Certainly the articles in the *Journal of the U.S. Cavalry Association* are the most sophisticated in regard to the new repeating arms and their impact on cavalry. In the years just after the turn of the century the great argument in U.S. Cavalry circles was whether or not the saber should be retained at all. But it seems to have been generally admitted that while "Mounted charges may yet be used on rare occasions when the enemy is demoralized, out of ammunition, or completely taken by surprise . . . ," nonetheless "for cavalry to make a mounted charge against enemy troops who are dismounted and armed with the present magazine gun, would be to seek disaster." The corollary that ". . . the trooper must bear in mind that in fighting his carbine is his main reliance"[2] was also accepted.

Were it not that certain European cavalry groups were at the time tending to reject the thesis to which the U.S. subscribed, there would be nothing in any way remarkable about the U.S. position, so patently obvious and right does it seem in retrospect. Yet in the early nineteen hundreds U.S. doctrine was different, and hence needs a word of explanation.

The U.S. cavalryman had a tradition quite different from that of any of the Europeans. He had always done the bulk of his fighting on his feet. Therefore there was no break in tradition for him to recognize the revolution in firepower for the great change it was. Cavalry during the Civil War most frequently fought dismounted, although clashes between cavalry were fought with the sword, and in the wars against the Indians cavalrymen also dismounted to fight with the aimed accurate fire quite unattainable on horseback. Horses were considered transportation, and the ground was considered a respectable substance on which to fight a battle. U.S. cavalrymen did not feel morally obligated to die on a horse—which European cavalrymen did. In short, the U.S. Cavalry reacted to the new firepower as it did because its history and its tradition made it quite natural for it to do so. In Europe the cavalry history of the U.S. Civil War was scarcely known until the very late nineteen

    [2] "Comment and Criticism," *Journal of the U.S. Cavalry Association (JUSCA)*, Vol. 13, No. 48, April 1903, pp. 720, 721.

hundreds, and hence the relevance of that war to cavalry problems was largely overlooked. Or given European experience and tradition, would a study of the Civil War have made any real difference?

Of all the cavalry arms of the world that which seems in retrospect to have been the furthest behind the times was that of the German Empire. The German Cavalry had adopted the lance for all ninety-three of its cavalry regiments in 1890 instead, as was true in the mid-nineteenth century, of having only one in four so armed. The lance was, of course, much more than a shaft of wood taller than a man, one tipped with steel and pennant decked: a lance was a state of mind. And it was a reminder that those who carried it still believed that the cavalry really was an arm to be reckoned with. . . .

Why was it that such serious students of war as the Germans are reputed to have been were in general quite so oblivious to the impact of the new firepower? There seem to have been several reasons. The first and most important was the attitude of Emperor William II towards cavalry. A young U.S. Cavalry lieutenant who witnessed German maneuvers in the fall of 1903 was frankly appalled by it. He noted the total lack of realism in the great rolling charges of the cavalry against both rifle and artillery. And he noted too the fact that the Kaiser was so proud of his cavalry that his umpires, knowing their place, pronounced the charges successful!! In Germany, in short, the well-known penchant of the Emperor for the charge undoubtedly did much to insulate the Germans from any serious thought of change.

There was, however, another reason as well. Even after seeing machine guns fired in the late 1880s, the German General Staff refused to take them seriously. Their reason lay in their mis-reading of their own experience with the *mitrailleuses* during the war of 1870–71 when these were badly misused. The fact that past experience happened to be irrelevant did not make it any less important, however, and it was not until 1908 that the machine gun was given the serious attention in Germany that it so obviously deserved. Even then it was only the infantry that recognized the importance of the new automatic weapons. Cavalry units, although armed with them, did not take them very seriously. German cavalry went trotting off to war in 1914, pennons flying from their lances, just as units of French infantry went off to war in red trousers, and for much the same reason: psychological effect. For the real effect of cavalry was, when on the charge, a psychological one, and was generally admitted as such. It was the role of the charge to break the enemy's will, and what could do this more effectively than a charge by lancers? The same argument was used by those who wanted to keep the infantry in red pants. They advanced the proposition that the sense of belonging was the essence of group spirit, and group spirit in turn was the touchstone of the will to fight, the ingredient that won battles. They added the corollary that nothing gave units the sense of oneness that did red trousers, and that therefore camouflaged material would actually sabotage national security. . . .

So tradition, personal predilection, and misinterpreted past experience kept the cavalry charge alive in Germany. The experience of the British after the Boer War likewise suggests how difficult it is to test the relevance of one's own experience in war.

THE RELEVANCE OF EXPERIENCE

From the end of the Boer War to the beginning of World War I the great debate in the British Cavalry, as in other countries, dealt with the retention of the lance and the charge. The arguments put forward for their retention inevitably raise the question of whether faith was not interfering with reason. . . .

A U.S. Cavalry officer noted on a trip to Aldershot in 1903 that "Every change is made entirely with reference to the Boer War and the Boer country, as though future wars would be fought under the same conditions."[3] But what this observer should also have noted was that there was a wide division of opinion as to just what that war proved, and how genuinely relevant it really was. . . .

Like other modern wars the Boer War was made up of a series of actions no one of which was decisive. The Boers, fine shots and fine horsemen, used their horses as transportation. In effect they fought as mounted infantry, employing the mobility of the horse in combination with the aimed firepower of infantry. They possessed all the advantages of great space and a friendly and embattled population, and the British were hard put to it to bring them to terms. But these were virtually the only points on which there was any agreement whatsoever. What did the facts mean, if anything?

Two of Great Britain's best known military figures, Lord Roberts, the British Chief of Staff, and Field-Marshal Sir John D. P. French, Cavalry Commander in Africa and, in 1914, Commander-in-Chief of the British Expeditionary Forces, led two factions within the army whose views of the future of cavalry were in direct opposition.

The Right Honorable Field-Marshal Earl Roberts placed the *imprimatur* of his authority on a book called *War and the Arme Blanche* by one Erskine Childers. In his introduction to this book Lord Roberts set forth his basic beliefs. . . . Lord Roberts believed simply that the "main lesson" to be learned from the Boer War and the Russo-Japanese War was that "knee to knee, close order charg-

[3] Frank R. McCoy, "Notes of the German Maneuvers," *JUSCA*, Vol. 14, No. 49, January 1904, pp. 30, 31.

ing is practically a thing of the past." He qualified his opinion somewhat. "There may be, there probably will be, mounted attacks, preferably in open order against Cavalry caught unawares, or against broken Infantry," he wrote. But even these mounted attacks, he said, should be carried out with the rifle, rather than with steel.[4] These ideas he actually wrote into the British regulations, *Cavalry Training,* in 1904.

. . . The general argument, as one can imagine, was first that lances and sabers were not killing men in war, and second, that infantry and mounted infantry were killing, when dismounted, cavalrymen. Three wars, the U.S. Civil War, the Boer War, and the Russo-Japanese War, were cited as proof of the contention. In retrospect this point of view hardly needs explanation. It seems quite obvious to think that the armaments which took the warrior off his feet and put him on his belly would by the same token take him off his charger and put him on the ground.

For a time Lord Roberts was Commander-in-Chief of the British Army, and his views were thus imposed for a brief moment on the generals. What this meant in effect was that the lance disappeared in Britain between 1903 and 1906. But Lord Roberts proved unpopular, and as is the way with unpopular leaders, he was eased gently out of office in quite short order, to become a disturbing shadow amongst their eminences in the House of Lords. And the lance came back into use in 1906 to remain for better than two decades— until 1927, to be precise.

Sir John French, an officer whom one of the most distinguished of Great Britain's War Secretaries, Lord Haldane, called "a real soldier of the modern type"[5] was an old Hussar. He had entered the army through the Militia and had thus avoided Sandhurst and the mental training this would have involved. For Sir John the experience of the Boer War was disturbing only because a number of his colleagues had been disturbed by it. As he thought over this experience, his final assessment as of the very eve of World War I was that "It passes comprehension that some critics in England should gravely assure us that the war in South Africa should be our chief source of inspiration and guidance, and that it was not normal."[6]

The Field-Marshal's reasoning was very simple. First, he said, "The composition and tactics of the Boer forces were as dissimilar from those of European armies as possible," and he added that "Such tactics in Europe would lead to the disruption and disbandment of any army that attempted them."[7] Second, he noted that in

[4] Erskine Childers, *War and the Arme Blanche* (London, 1910). With an introduction by the Right Hon. Field-Marshal Earl Roberts, V.C., K.G., p. xii.

[5] Richard Burdon Halden, *An Autobiography* (London, 1929), p. 295.

[6] General Friedrich von Bernhardi, *Cavalry* (New York, 1914), with a preface by Field-Marshal Sir J. D. P. French, p. 9.

[7] *Ibid.,* p. 9.

South Africa both unlimited space and the objective of complete submission of the enemy made it a most unusual war. Third, he maintained that the British had not at the time developed proper means for remounting the cavalry with trained horses. But to say this is really to say nothing at all. It is only by uncovering Sir John's basic premises that there is really any possibility of understanding his view of his own experience.

Perhaps Sir John summarized his own thinking best when he wrote sometime during the course of 1908 that "The Boers did all that could be expected of Mounted Infantry, but were powerless to crown victory as only the dash of Cavalry can do."[8] It was the "dash of Cavalry" of which Sir John was thinking. There is ample evidence to document the point. If cold steel were thrown away as "useless lumber," he wrote, ". . . we should invert the role of cavalry, turn it into a defensive arm, and make it a prey to the first foreign cavalry that it meets, for good cavalry can always compel a dismounted force of mounted riflemen to mount and ride away, and when such riflemen are caught on their horses they have power neither of offence nor of defence and are lost."[9] Based on this analysis of the effect of rapid fire on mounted cavalry action, he deduced that the proper role of cavalry was first to fight the battlefield's greatest threat, i.e., the enemy cavalry. "The successful cavalry fight confers upon the victor command of the ground."[10] This, he said, was a job for cold steel. Only when the enemy cavalry was out of action did he think that the cavalry would rely more on the rifle than on steel—which is not to say that he ruled "out as impossible, or even unlikely, attacks by great bodies of mounted men against other arms on the battlefield."[11]

So it was that Sir John and his followers decided that the experience of recent wars was irrelevant. The Boer War was not relevant because it had not been fought in Europe and because the Boers had not been armed with steel as were cavalries in Europe. The war in Manchuria between the Russians and the Japanese was irrelevant not only because it had not been fought in Europe, but also because the cavalry used there had been badly mounted, rode indifferently, and, above all, were poorly trained, i.e., in dismounted principles. "They were," wrote Sir John, "devoid of real Cavalry training, they thought of nothing but of getting off their horses and shooting. . . ."[12] From one principle, note, Sir John never deviated: *Unless the enemy cavalry was defeated, the cavalry could not carry out its*

[8] From his introduction to the English edition of Lt. Gen. Friedrich von Bernhardi, *Cavalry in Future Wars* (London, 1909), p. x.
[9] Bernhardi, *Cavalry, op. cit.,* p. 11.
[10] *Ibid.,* p. 13.
[11] *Ibid.,* p. 15. See also A. P. Ryan, *Mutiny at the Curragh* (London, 1956), pp. 97–100 for a further elaboration of Sir John's views.
[12] Bernhardi, *Cavalry in Future Wars, op. cit.* p. xxiii.

other responsibilities. And there was a corollary of this, to wit: *"Only cavalry can defeat cavalry,"* cavalry being defined of course as "a body of horsemen armed with steel."

Sir John, however wrong he may have been in his estimate of the firepower revolution of his day, made one point of real consequence when he insisted that the cavalry should keep its mind on a war likely to be fought—which a war in Manchuria, the United States, or South Africa was not. To talk about wars which are likely seems eminently sensible, although there are times when the unlikely ones are given rather more attention than they warrant depending on what set of premises are in search of some wider acceptance. To cite a recent example, the war in Korea in 1950–1952 provided what seemed to the U.S. Air Force to be irrelevant experience because bombers were not effectively used. To the U.S. Navy and Marine Corps, on the other hand, it seemed very relevant indeed because Korea was a peninsula admirably suited to the projection of naval power. To the U.S. Army it presented a whole new way of thinking: that limited war involving ground troops might well be the way of the future despite and because of the horrors of nuclear exchange.

THE LIMITS OF A WEAPONS SYSTEM EVALUATION

But even if history in terms of recent war experience seemed irrelevant for one reason or another to the problem of the charge, it is hard to believe that war is a science so limited that means could not be found to test in practice the effectiveness of the charge, that a conclusive study could not be made of charges made in a variety of patterns, in different formations, and with different weapons against simulated "enemy formations." But the simple truth is that nothing is more difficult to test than a weapon's effectiveness. . . .

There is a grievously large number of intellectual stumbling blocks in first setting up and then later evaluating any test experience. For example, during the summer of 1936[13] the U.S. Infantry maneuvered against the U.S. Cavalry at Fort Benning, Georgia. As the problem started, the cavalry rode and the infantry trucked to the given maneuver area. The motor vehicles being rather faster than the horses the infantry had ample time to get into position first. This proved a most frightening advantage. The infantry, well camouflaged, waited with some excitement while the cavalry were allowed to pass concealed forward infantry units. Only when the advance units of cavalry hit the main units of infantry did the infantry's stratagem become apparent. It was at that moment that the infantrymen rose shouting from entrenched positions waving bed sheets. The horses thought their Day of Judgment had arrived

---

[13] The story is from eye-witness reports and there is a date problem.

as ghosts rose over the battlefield, and what followed is best left to the imagination.

To infantrymen the maneuver proved conclusively that trucks gave the infantry a mobility with which the cavalry could not hope to compete and that when minus multicolored uniforms and not drawn up in drill formation, the infantry made unsatisfactory cavalry targets. Yet to the cavalrymen—and this raised a furor that still stays in men's minds—the whole exercise only proved that infantrymen were practical jokers. The problem, that is to say, of "proving out" doctrine in the field of maneuver is distressingly difficult.

Essentially the problem lies in one's estimate of that appalling obscurity, "the nature of man." The cavalryman knows, as he charges "the enemy designate," that if this were really the enemy, he would be quite too frightened to fire accurately. And he knows this because it is part of a credo without which he would never be induced to charge in the first place. Therefore the "effect of fire" becomes a subjective instead of an objective judgment, mitigated by one's belief in a concatenation of other effects—of surprise, of fear, of the use of the defilade. So while all will call for more realism in testing, getting a consensus as to what "realism" is, more frequently than not, quite outside the realm of possibility.

FACTORS IN INSTITUTIONAL SURVIVAL

The role of history. On the morrow of victory after World War I, a member of the House of Commons rose to criticize the Secretary of War, Mr. Winston Churchill. He noted that the cavalry was at "practically the same figure as before the war, and yet if I should have thought anything had been proved by the War, it was that cavalry was less useful (than) we had previously thought it was going to be."[14]

Shortly thereafter, in 1930 to be precise, there appeared a history of the French Cavalry in the World War by a Professor of Tactics at l'École Militaire et d'Application du Génie, a most prolific writer by the name of Capitaine F. Gazin. The next to the last paragraph reads as follows:

> Today, really more than yesterday, if the cavalry is to have power and flexibility, following along with technical progress, it must have horses with better blood lines, cadres filled with burning faith, and above all well trained troops conscious of the heavy weight of past glory.[15]

There would seem to be no reasonable doubt but that in the minds of the doughboy, the *poilu* or Tommy Atkins, the day of the

[14] *125 H.C. Deb. 25*, pp. 1366 ff.
[15] F. Gazin, *La Cavalerie dans la Guerre Mondiale* (Paris, 1930), p. 325.

horse was over. The cavalryman had been called a number of things during the war, "Pigsticker," the "Rocking Horseman," etc., which indicated what the infantry thought of his contribution. But to the cavalryman himself the cavalry was not dead, and the history of the Great War was never written really in meaningful terms. To him the role of the horseman in the victory became swollen with the yeast of time. Indeed, in cavalry historiography, the role of the horse in World War I was most emphasized at that moment in time when the cavalry was most threatened in army reorganization plans, between 1934 and 1939.

The cavalry had been used in the First World War. The Germans used it extensively on that last stronghold of the cavalryman, the eastern frontier. The British and French used it extensively in 1914 during the retreat from Le Mans during late August and early September. Indeed the largest item of export from Great Britain to its forces on the Continent for the war as a whole was horse fodder. . . . For the most part the cavalry fought dismounted, but it did fight mounted as well. It did charge machine guns. In one case the Canadians charged a group of German machine guns, and came out unscathed, so great was the surprise achieved when the horsemen charged, blades bared. And it was used mounted as late as 1918. Indeed this claim has been made for its work at that time—by a cavalryman: "It may or may not be true to say that we (the allies) should have defeated the Germans just the same in the autumn of 1918, even without our cavalry. But it is certainly true that, had it not been for that same cavalry, there would have been no autumn advance at all for the Germans would have defeated us in the spring."[16]

But the campaign which did more to save the horse cavalry than any other was not fought in Europe at all. It was fought on the sands of Palestine, at Gaza, at Beersheba, at Jerusalem, and it was fought in part, and indeed in large part, with the lance. It was as dashingly romantic as anything that happened during that singularly drab war, and strong drink it was to the cavalry. In a sense, it kept the cavalry going for another quarter century. There was irony in this for the most eager of the cavalrymen, men of the stamp of Sir John French, had for a decade defended the cavalry regulations on the basis of the forecast of their utility for the big war on the continent, only to have the cavalry successfully used only on the periphery of the great battlefields.

So experience, that most revered of teachers, continued to couch the "lessons" of war in a certain studied ambiguity. The horse

---

[16] Lt. Col. T. Preston, "Cavalry in France," *Cavalry Journal* (British), No. 26 (1936), p. 19.

retained that place in warfare which it had had for a thousand years—in the minds of its military riders.

Mission justification for the future, 1920–1940. On the eve of World War II the General Officers of the U.S. Army were, next to those of Poland, Rumania and possibly the USSR, most convinced of the continuing utility of the horse. The French had four divisions of mixed horse and mechanized cavalry. The Germans had a debated number of horses and mechanized cavalry, for use largely as reconnaissance. The British were converting from oats to oil as rapidly as possible.

A number of problems immediately present themselves. A first very general question must be asked of the cavalrymen themselves: What did they consider their mission to be in the period between 1920 and roughly 1935 when the development of both plane and tank had reached the stage at which their future development could be foreseen with some clarity, and at which therefore some reasonable readjustment of forces to the fact of their existence could be expected? How can one account for those great differences in thinking between the responsible staffs of the larger nations during the years between 1935 and the outbreak of war in 1939? . . .

The basic argument of the cavalrymen in their journals and in their manuals in the period between the great wars was an absolutely sound one. They argued in essence that new weapons obviated only those with like characteristics. They argued that while a better tank scrapped a worse one, the tank as a weapons system could not replace the horse until such time as it could perform all the missions of a horse. Whether these missions were worthwhile was seldom considered.

Many of the arguments which cavalrymen of all nations advanced to substantiate their claims as to their future role in war will be recognized by any student of recent military history as a version of what one can only describe as standardized clap-trap. One was the argument that, since most of the world was roadless, "To base our transportation needs solely upon conditions existent in the comparatively tiny proportion of the earth's surface containing roads . . . is putting too many eggs in the same basket."[17] This will be recognized as a cavalry variant on the navy contention that "since the world is 60 per cent water . . . ," and the air contention that "since air surrounds the earth and the shortest distance between two points. . . ." Another argument familiar to all military historians came up again and again in the journals. This one was to the effect that mechanical aids and auxiliaries end by neutralizing each other, an argument which in its most outrageous form had the anti-tank

[17] Major Malcolm Wheeler-Nicholson, *Modern Cavalry* (New York, 1922), p. vii.

weapon returning the battlefield to the horse.[18] "It is quite within the bounds of possibility that an infantry anti-tank weapon may be produced which will make tanks useless as weapons of attack," wrote one enthusiast[19] in a vein not unlike that used by airmen against seamen at roughly the same moment in time. The difficulty of supplying tanks was brought up as the supply problem is brought up as a limitation on each new weapons system.[20] And, of course, the essentially experimental nature of tanks—"as yet untried" is the term—raised its head perennially and everywhere.

But there were other problems and more serious ones. If the tank could be made to replace the cavalry on the charge, did that mean that the tank could take over all the other cavalry missions: reconnaissance, raids, flank protection in rough country? Could the plane be made to supplement the tank in such a way that the two used in combination could effectuate a complete substitution for the horse? Or would some kind of combination of horse and tank, and plane and tank be a future necessity? And if this were so with whom would the control lie, with tankmen or horsemen or pilots? And finally if this was a problem of phasing out the horse, what factors should govern the timing of this phasing?

These questions do not seem to have been asked with any precision largely perhaps because they edged too closely on the emotion-packed matter of prestige, on the one hand, and on an essentially insoluble organization problem on the other. Naturally armor wanted maximum independence as do those who service and fire any weapon. The tankman wanted a command of his own, just as the machinegunner wanted his own battalion, the artillery its own regiment, the horse cavalry its own division and the airman his own service. And this is logical for in a decentralized structure growth is faster as imagination is given a freer rein. But the difficulty is that, war being all of one cloth, each weapon component also wishes to control elements of the others. And this is why the sparks flew between arms in the period between the World Wars, and before the First and after the Second. Where, as in Germany and Great Britain, armor was given its independence, it thrived. Where, as in the United States and Poland, the Cavalry (Horse) remained in control, tank doctrine never grew roots. But where, as in France, mechanized and horse were joined together in what at first blush seemed to be a happy marriage, a unity was forced which was pitifully inadequate from every standpoint.

[18] Anonymous, "Oil and Oats," *Cavalry Journal* (British), Vol. 28, No. 107, Jan. 1938, p. 31; Col. Sir Hereward Wake, "The Infantry Anti-Tank Weapon," *Army Quarterly*, Vol. 17, No. 2, Jan. 1929.

[19] Wake, *op. cit.*, p. 349.

[20] Lt. F. A. S. Clark, "Some Further Problems of Mechanical Warfare," *Army Quarterly*, Vol. 6, No. 2, July 1923, p. 379.

For the man on the horse there was much greater difficulty in understanding the tank than in understanding the rapid fire weapon. Perhaps this could be expected since tank and horse were competitors for the same missions. Certainly the limpid eye and high spirit of the one and the crass impersonal power of the other was enough to render partisans of the one quite helpless when it came to understanding the military views of the other, quite as helpless indeed as the seabased fighter is to understand the landbased or the airbased and their view of world geography.

Practicality and the concept of the balanced force. One finds the horse cavalryman making the same points over and over again. He stressed the tanks' need for spare parts, without taking into consideration that one of the greatest difficulties of the cavalry was that horses do not have spare parts. He stressed the lack of mobility of the tank along mountain trails without mention of the appalling problem of getting horses overseas—they have a tendency to pneumonia, together with a soft breast which becomes raw and infected with the roll and pitch of the ship. Whereas the point was occasionally made that the Lord took care of the resupply of horses—i.e., that while factories could be bombed out, sex could not—no mention was ever made that in wartime as in peace it still took four or five years to produce each animal. And, finally, although the horse was claimed to have certain immunities to gas warfare, the peculiar problems of getting gas masks on the poor beasts were omitted.

Yet whether partisans were ankle deep in the sands of prejudice or not, there were certain aspects of the relationship between horses and planes, and horses and tanks which were so obvious that they could hardly be missed. However low and slow it flew, the plane would not be a substitute for a still lower and still slower man on a horse. And the plane could not penetrate forests and neither, within limits, could tanks. So there was, and indeed there still is, a gap between what the horse can do and what the plane and tank can do. But admitting the gap, there still remained the most vexing problem of all, to wit whether that gap was worth filling and if so how. And this was something which each general staff decided somewhat differently and for itself.

The U.S. Cavalry was, in retrospect, as retrogressive in 1940 as it had been progressive in the years before World War I. It had never crossed the sea during World War I due to transportation difficulties, and spent its war chasing Mexicans. But it shared every confidence that its future role would be everything that it had not been in the recent past. As of 1940 it labored under the most embarrassing of illusions. The U.S. Cavalry believed that it had modernized itself. And it defended its horse cavalry on the sacred ground of "balanced force." "Each arm has powers and limitations," explained Major General John K. Herr, Chief of Cavalry, before the Subcommittee on Military Affairs of the House Committee on Appropriations on March 11, 1940. "The proper combination is that which arranges the whole so that the powers of each offset the limitations of the others." It was because the Poles did not have that balance that they were, said General Herr, overrun by the Germans.

> Judging from Spain, had Poland's cavalry possessed modern armament in every respect and been united in one big cavalry command with adequate mechanized forces included, and supported by adequate aviation, the German light and mechanized forces might have been defeated.

Then General Herr went on to add these words of comfort:

> Mechanized cavalry is valuable and an important adjunct but is not the main part of the cavalry and cannot be. Our cavalry is not the medieval cavalry of popular imagination but is cavalry which is modernized and keeping pace with all developments.[21]

Yet it certainly does not seem that the U.S. cavalry was "keeping pace with all developments." Putting horses in trucks to give them mobility (this was the so-called "portée cavalry"), and adding inadequate anti-tank batteries can hardly be called modernizing. Is there any reasonable explanation for the illusion?

Concepts of modernization. One cannot help but be impressed with the intellectual isolation in which the U.S. armed forces operated in the 1930's. *The Journal of the U.S. Cavalry Association* paid almost no attention to mechanization throughout the period. Compared to the military periodicals on the continent, the U.S. journal seems curiously antiquated. And because there was so little critical thinking going on within the service, it is not surprising that there was virtually no thinking going on in Army ordnance either, for ordnance, after all, works on a demand basis and if there is no demand, there is likely to be no new hardware. In the United States there was in short no intellectual challenge.

Not only were there no pressures to change cavalry thinking from inside the arm, there were no pressures from outside either. United States industry was never anxious to sell to the services during the depression years or before. They were no more willing to put money into military research and development than were the services or the Congress. The few Secretaries of War who can be considered adequate were interested in the managerial aspects of their office

---

[21] The text of General Herr's testimony before Congress may be found reprinted in *JUSCA*, Vol. 49, No. 3, May–June 1940. See p. 206. . . .

and not in matters which they considered "purely military." And finally there was a not inconsiderable pressure for the *status quo* in the Congress. The U.S. had some ten millions of horses, and government spending in this direction, little though it was, was a chief source of revenue to all the many horse breeders, hay growers, and saddlemakers.

In Great Britain, the situation was markedly different. Although the British had their branch journals,—the tankers founded their own in 1937—they also had great advantage in having two journals which were more generally read. The first was the *Army Quarterly* which published on all topics of concern to the army as a whole, and the other was *The Journal of the Royal United Service Institution* which crossed service lines. Into these journals there poured articles from a singularly able, and remarkably prolific and dedicated group of publicists of whom J. F. C. Fuller and Captain Basil H. Liddell Hart are simply the best known. Officers in the British Empire were simply unable to escape, as were U.S. officers, from challenge. Thus from 1936 onwards there was an increasingly strong movement in favor of conversion to oil. Furthermore this was helped rather than hindered by the stand taken by many in Parliament. For Parliament was at least conscious of *The Times* military correspondent, Liddell Hart, and the battle he was waging for mechanized warfare, a form of warfare which would, so he thought, limit and shorten future wars by making them more rapid, hence shorter and cheaper than the war of the trenches. To be sure there were those who, like Admiral of the Fleet Sir Roger Keyes, took a position against the reduction of cavalry. But they were in the minority. Most felt that the Household Cavalry and two mounted regiments still left in Egypt in 1939 were probably two too many. . . .

After World War II the French, as is the wont of democracies, held an inquiry into the military disasters of some five years before. But the questions which were put to the generals and the questions which they wanted to answer were all in terms of why they had not understood and appreciated the role of the tank and the plane. Never does the question seem to have been asked in the converse, i.e., why was the horse thought to have been so useful circa 1939? It would have been interesting to know too what thinking had been done as to the circumstances under which Cavalry divisions, offensive forces, were to be used in conjunction with the Maginot Line, a defensive ideal. Perhaps they were to have been used in the second phase of the struggle in a counter-offensive after the enemy had partially defeated himself by throwing his troops against the defensive fires of the Line. . . .

However, the overall development of French cavalry thinking between the wars is plain enough. What they did was to absorb the new machines of war into old doctrine. Instead of allowing the characteristics of new weapons to create new doctrine, the French General Staff simply gave them missions to fulfill that were within the old framework. Thus tanks were made subordinate and supporting weapons to the infantry, and subordinate and supporting weapons to the cavalry. In a sense the French achieved what General Herr of the U.S. Cavalry wanted to achieve, except that the French did look forward to complete mechanization at some future date, which Herr did not. And the *Revue de Cavalerie,* a strange hodgepodge of oats, history and oil, reflects that point of view.

The German experience was somewhat different again. Whereas the French looked back to the stalemate at Verdun, the great achievement of defensive weapons, the Germans looked back to the great offensives of 1918 and to the very near miss of the Schlieffen plan in 1914. Particularly in the case of the younger officers the great objective was regaining the lost means of offensive. A defeated army, the Germans were in a position to start once more from the beginning. To be sure there was a very difficult period of struggle with German horse cavalrymen, but those in Germany with an interest in tanks had an advantage which those in the democracies did not. They had the interest of the Chief of State. When Hitler saw Panzer units in action, he said repeatedly, "That's what I need! That's what I want to have!"[22] To Hitler they were the keystone in a concept of total war.

The *Revue de Cavalerie* stopped publication during the war and never appeared again. The British *Cavalry Journal* disappeared forever as well. Only the *Journal of the U.S. Cavalry Association* continued to appear. Its heroes were the horse-drawn artillery which landed on Guadalcanal, the animals flown over the Burma "Hump" into China, the U.S. units which were remounted on Italian Cavalry horses in Italy and German horses in Germany; the great heroes were the only real cavalry left—the Cossacks. Duly noted was how greatly needed were horse cavalry during the battles in Normandy and elsewhere.

In his closing chapter of *He's in the Cavalry Now,* Brig. Gen. Rufus S. Ramey, a former commander of the U.S. Cavalry School, concluded in 1944, "Currently we are organizing and training adequate mechanized horse cavalry for field employment."[23] His was the final testament. The last old Army mule, except for the West Point Mascot, was retired in 1956. The horse cavalry had been disbanded five years before.

New Item. In 1956 the Belgian General Staff suggested that for

---

[22] General Heinz Guderian, *Panzer Leader* (New York, 1952), p. 30.
[23] Brig. Gen. Rufus S. Ramey, *He's in the Cavalry Now* (New York, 1944), p. 190. There were 60,170 animals in the U.S. Forces on December 31, 1943.

the kind of dispersed war which low yield atomic weapons necessarily create, the horse, which in Europe could be independent of depots, should be reintroduced into the weapons system.[24]

CONCLUSION

The military profession, dealing as it does with life and death, should be utterly realistic, ruthless in discarding the old for the new, forward-thinking in the adoption of new means of violence. But equally needed is a romanticism which, while perhaps stultifying realistic thought, gives a man that belief in the value of the weapons system he is operating that is so necessary to his willingness to use it in battle. Whether a man rides a horse, a plane or a battleship into war, he cannot be expected to operate without faith in his weapons system. But faith breeds distrust of change. Furthermore there is need for discipline, for hierarchy, for standardization within the military structure. These things create pressures for conformity, and conformity too is the enemy of change. Nor is there generally the pressure for the adoption of the new that is found in other walks of life. There is no profit motive, and the challenge of actual practice, in the ultimate sense of war, is very intermittent. Finally, change is expensive, and some part of the civilian population has to agree that the change is worth the expense before it can take place. What factors then make for change in situations short of war?

Surely the greatest instigation of new weapons development has in the past come from civilian interest plus industrial pressure. The civilian governors get the weapons system *they* want. Hitler gets his tanks, the French public their line of forts. When society shows an interest in things military, weapons are adopted—apparently in great part because of the appeal they make to a set of social values and economic necessities. The abolition of the horse cavalry came about first in those countries which could not afford to raise the horses and in which there were those with a hungry intellectual interest in the ways of war. When there was no interest in the military, as in the United States, there was no pressure to change and the professional was given tacit leave to romanticize an untenable situation. Thus the U.S. Horse Cavalry remained a sort of monument to public irresponsibility in this, the most mechanized nation on earth.

[24] "Belgians Hit U.S. Concept of Atomic War," *Christian Science Monitor,* August 25, 1956.

Chemical Warfare:
A Study in Restraints

FREDERIC J. BROWN

. . . [World War I] was [a] war without limits—the brains and muscle of modern industrial nations applied without restriction to the art
of war. In the minds of expert and layman alike, World War I was
about to pass a threshold into new levels of violence when it ended. It
was the mind that could speculate not the eye that had seen which
would project World War I as it could have been in 1919.

MILITARY PERSPECTIVES

Speculation would play a significant role in determining the future
of gas warfare; however, there were more substantial factual inputs
that would influence subsequent decision-makers—the lessons learned
from the experiences of World War I.

Tactical characteristics. The tactical military lessons were mixed, a
potpourri of individual or unit experiences extremely difficult to
evaluate in the aggregate in order to rate gas as "effective" or "nonef-
fective." More important to military analysts than an imprecise
evaluation of effectiveness were the characteristics of poison gas as
observed on the battlefield. By November 1918, it was apparent that
chemical warfare had three central characteristics: it was an extremely
versatile weapon, tractable to almost any tactical situation; the logistic
requirements complicated the battlefield enormously; and its employment demanded unprecedented sophistication of individual and unit
training.

The tactical versatility of gas was derived from the diverse properties of the gases employed. Gas could be persistent or nonpersistent
over a wide range of lethality—from an extremely toxic cyanic compound to a nonlethal, harassing tear or sneezing gas. The effect of the
gas could be immediate or delayed for several hours.

These properties gave chemical warfare a role in the offensive or
defensive, in mobile or position warfare. A lethal, nonpersistent agent
could be placed on enemy positions just before attack and it would be

From *Chemical Warfare: A Study in Restraints* by Frederic J. Brown, pp. 32–48 and
290–298. Copyright © 1968 by Princeton University Press. Reprinted by permission.
Portions of the text and some footnotes have been deleted.

dissipated before friendly troops arrived. A persistent agent such as mustard could be placed to protect a flank during an attack, to deny an area to the enemy, or as a very effective barrage in front of a defensive position. Such flexibility applied, of course, to all belligerents, provided that each could support the logistic requirements of gas warfare.

The logistic demands were enormous. Gas substituted for nothing. Its requirements were an additional load to an already overloaded battlefield. To be effective, a high concentration of gas had to be maintained over the enemy position. The Germans found that 12,000 kilograms of Green Cross [nonpersistent] shells were necessary to gas an area one kilometer square. Similar consumption figures were experienced by other belligerents.[1]

Graver problems were presented to both logisticians and tacticians by the requirements for individual and collective protection in a toxic environment. In addition to the other stresses and dangers of war, the very air the soldier breathed and the harmless inanimate objects he touched had become potential weapons against him. The range of problems posed was infinite: How would the soldier eat, drink, sleep, perform bodily functions, use his weapon, give and receive commands; how would he protect horses, pigeons, and watch dogs; how would he know when his immediate area was contaminated? By November 1918, many of these issues had been broached but they had not been solved. The battlefield had experienced a quantum jump in sophistication; it had become too "complicated."

Nothing indicated the spectrum of new problems better than the gas mask. A highly personal symbol of gas warfare, it was awkward, heavy to carry, and uncomfortable to wear. An officer in the 3rd Division, AEF, described it:

> The mask is safe but it is the most uncomfortable thing I ever experienced. If . . . [anyone wants to] know how a gas mask feels, let him seize his nose with a pair of fire tongs, bury his face in a hot feather pillow, then seize a gas pipe with his teeth and breathe through it for a few hours while he performs routine duties. It is safe, but like the deadly poison which forced its invention, it is not sane.[2]

It was not just that the mask was uncomfortable. The survival of the individual was determined by the quality of the mask. Either it worked

---

[1] . . . High ammunition expenditure rates were not unique to gas; however, gas required a special infrastructure—meteorological stations, special purpose units with specialized training, etc.—that was not required for conventional warfare.

[2] R. Cochrane, *Gas Warfare in World War I*, 20 Studies (Army Chemical Center: Chemical Corps Historical Office, 1957-1960), Study 14, p. 34. . . . The mask also reduced vision and muffled the voice—two essential requirements to command on the battlefield. . . .

faultlessly or the soldier died. Life was dependent upon 100 per cent reliability. This unique and disquieting reliance on science and industry, was not the only psychological problem related to wearing the mask. There was the added trauma of divorcement from the external environment. The gas mask "makes the soldier blind and deaf when he enters into material warfare, despoils him of his feed and drink, his nicotine and alcohol, and then makes war a fearful means for the destruction of morale."[3]

As well as indirect psychological effects derived from protective measures, fears of gas warfare produced other reactions. One was a psychoneurosis, "Gas Fright." Soldiers, hearing a report that gas was in the area, would acquire all of the symptoms of gas poisoning although they had not been gassed. Gas could induce severe morale problems among troops already fatigued and dispirited by a difficult tactical situation. The First Army of the AEF was in such a situation facing the Kriemhilde Stellung in October 1918. The history of the 42nd Division commented:

> . . . an important cause of the low morale was the mounting fear of the enemy's use of gas . . . it was largely responsible for creating so great a straggler problem that, as Bullard said, a solid line of MP's back of the fighting front had become necessary to keep the men in the line. The basis of that fear was the gas atmosphere that the enemy maintained over much of the front by his regulated gas fire each day. When it did not cause real casualties, it supported apprehension and panic, and hastened the onset of battle fatigue and gas mask exhaustion.[4]

The combined effects of tactical flexibility, logistical complexity, and adverse psychological response to an alien environment required highly trained units. For front-line troops, instantaneous reaction was required twenty-four hours per day. If the unit was not properly trained, it suffered debilitating casualties.[5]

In summary, chemical warfare was an enigma from the perspective of tactical military employment. If it could be used unilaterally, there was no question that it was effective. Unfortunately, however, it could not be used unilaterally. Once the enemy retaliated, the game did not appear worth the candle. No transitory advantage justified the difficulties of a chemical battlefield. The problems of fighting in an alien

---

[3] Maj. G. Soldan, *Der Mensch und die Schlacht der Zunkuft* (Oldenberg: Verlag Stalling, 1925). . . .

[4] Cochrane, *op. cit.*, Study 17, pp. 40–41. . . .

[5] All armies experienced roughly equivalent gas-casualty rates, dependent upon the training of troops. Casualties at Ypres in 1915 were estimated at over 30 per cent. Later in the year, the gas-casualty rate declined to less than 3 per cent as training improved. Yet the first attack on U.S. troops in 1918 produced over 30 per cent casualties—not a glowing testimonial to U.S. preparations. . . .

environment appeared insoluble. Science and technology might develop an answer but this was a mixed blessing at best.

Science and technology. If it can be said that science and the industrial revolution approached the battlefield in the American Civil War, it can be said to have arrived during World War I. In no other area was this as apparent as chemical warfare. A General could improve upon or detract from the capabilities of the chemical warfare equipment given to him; but the life and death decisions of strategic magnitude were made in laboratories and industrial plants.

Throughout the war there was a scientific race between belligerents. The Germans seized the initiative when they introduced chlorine gas at Ypres in April 1915; six months passed before the Allies could retaliate. In July 1917, the Germans introduced mustard gas; it was June 1918 before the Allies could retaliate in kind,[6] and not until the last month of the war that they had sufficient stocks of mustard gas. This provided a significant advantage to the Germans in the spring-summer offenses of 1918.

Thirty different chemical substances were tested in combat during the war,[7] each of which posed a unique problem for defense. Since no army could afford to find itself in a defenseless position due to a new enemy gas, there were continual efforts at improvement. The British alone issued 7 different masks to their troops—a total of 50 million masks. . . .

The role of science was equal to if not greater than the traditional value of physical courage in determining success on the battlefield. As toxic agents and their methods of delivery became more sophisticated in 1917 and 1918, the necessity for professional-military assimilation of science and technology became more pronounced. It was not a comforting thought to realize that an enemy with a superior technical expertise and industrial capability could introduce a weapon which would overcome one's own superior training and leadership. This was a disturbing reality that the military profession faced in looking back at World War I. Chemical warfare was the most striking example.

A question of honor. However, there was more to disturb the military profession than science and technology. Chemical warfare did not fall within the limits of the honor of the profession. The code of war was unwritten, but it was understood. Essentially based upon the code of chivalry, it had varied as mores changed and as the increasing range of weapons changed the nature of the battlefield. In 1914, it was represented by the Rules of Land Warfare in the Hague Conventions. Violation could be tolerated only through necessity of

---

[6] Due to a brilliant manufacturing feat of the French. The British did not have mustard gas until September 1918.

[7] . . . Over 3,000 substances were investigated for war use.

war and even here the accountability rested with the Head of State.

Two hallmarks of the profession were that war would be limited in its efforts to combatants only, and that the most honorable and heroic way to defeat the enemy was in hand-to-hand combat. In the minds of certain World War I military leaders, gas violated these customs and typified the contemporary degeneration of the profession in the face of unlimited war.

General Peyton March, the Chief of Staff of the United States Army during and after the war, recalled a visit to a hospital in France:

> [The hospital contained] . . . over one hundred French women and children who had been living in their homes in rear of and near the front and who were gassed. The sufferings of these children, particularly, were horrible and produced a profound impression on me. War is cruel at best, but the use of an instrument of death, which once launched, cannot be controlled, and which may decimate noncombatants—women and children—reduces civilization to savagery.[8]

While March was primarily concerned about the gassing of noncombatants, two general officers more closely connected with the initiation at Ypres condemned the effect on troops. General von Deimling, Commanding General of a German Corps at Ypres, commented: "I must confess that the commission for poisoning the enemy just as one poisons rats struck me as it must any straightforward soldier; it was repulsive to me."[9] Lord French, the British Commander in France, expressed the "deepest regret and some surprise" that the German Army claiming to be "the chief exponent of the chivalry of war should have stooped to employ such devices against brave and gallant foes. . . ."[10] Reactions such as these would be reinforced with time as the rationale of wartime necessity faded from view. A sense of guilt for past actions combined with the natural desire to enhance the image of one's profession could make gas an exceedingly unpopular subject for military discussion.

At the end of World War I, the prospects of military acceptance of chemical warfare were unfavorable. On balance, the military characteristics of gas warfare did not justify its use unless the situation ensured unilateral employment. Unless some nation made a significant technological breakthrough in protection, a mutual exchange of gas would create a toxic battle environment causing more problems to

---

    [8] Gen. P. March, *The Nation at War* (Garden City, N.Y.: Doubleday-Doran, 1932), p. 333. This passage was written in 1931, but it was not inconsistent with his immediate postwar attitude.

    [9] Gen. von Deimling, *Reminiscences* (Paris: Montaigne, 1931). . . .

    [10] *The Despatches of Lord French* (London: Chapman and Hull Ltd., 1917), p. 360. In the British Army, the Gas Brigade and gas itself were referred to as "frightfulness. . . ."

be raised than could be solved. Nevertheless, the rewards for a breakthrough would be high. . . .

The question was complicated, however, by the side issues that gas introduced. Gas symbolized the encroachment of science and technology into military decision-making, and became "an affair of honor" to the military profession. If the military continued to view gas from these perspectives, its future would not be promising.

FEARS FOR THE FUTURE—ESCALATION

The issues that gas posed to the military were dwarfed by the problems it presented to the makers of national security policy. The history of the use of toxic agents in World War I made a near perfect model of escalation: escalation of delivery systems, of weapon capabilities, and of targets selected. . . .

By the time of the 1918 offensive, at least 50 per cent of the artillery shells fired by the Germans were gas shells. The last ominous increment to delivery capability was never employed. In 1918, the British contracted for 250 bombing aircraft each with a 7,500-pound bomb load. . . .

The last and most foreboding input to the model of escalation was target selection. The initial use of gas was confined to a military target, but as the war developed and the use of gas increased in intensity, it was impossible to avoid noncombatants. One of the objections to the release of clouds of gas from cylinders was that the size of the cloud produced significant gas concentrations at undesired locations. In discussing this problem, Hanslian referred to effects as far as 20 kilometers behind the front and deaths at a distance of 15 kilometers. There is no indication, however, that the belligerents did not tacitly agree that a certain "spillover" of gas into towns was an inevitable accompaniment to its tactical use in a congested countryside.

The strategic use of gas was an entirely different question. The delivery system could only be by airplane and the implications were truly frightening. The Germans initiated strategic bombing on Christmas Eve 1914—one aircraft with one bomb. The bombing effort gradually escalated to two serious raids on London (June 13, 1917 and July 7, 1917) causing 832 casualties. After the July 7th raid, the English War Cabinet appointed a committee headed by Jan Christian Smuts to study the air defense of the United Kingdom. In its report, this committee gave serious consideration to the "probability" of the Germans using gas to attack London. Thus by the fall of 1917, the Germans had initiated unrestricted city bombing and the British had matched the capability of gas with the potential of the airplane, at least in defensive contingency planning.

By late 1918, the potential of the airplane was becoming real capability. The bomber force would be available in 1919. There was no shortage of toxic agent. The Allies were prepared.[11] As the capability was being gathered, the Allies made plans for the forthcoming air offensive. The order called for unrestricted bombing. In addition to authorizing the use of high explosives, the order provided a ready case for gas bombing.

There is no indication that a decision was ever made to initiate strategic gas bombing. The mere fact that it had quite obviously been seriously considered was enough to complete a rather terrifying model of escalation that would haunt the makers of postwar policy.

During the war there had been two attempts to halt the spiral of escalation. The first was offered by the United States in May 1915—after German initiation at Ypres but before British retaliation at Loos. President Wilson proposed that Germany discontinue submarine warfare against merchant ships and the use of poison gas, while England would terminate the blockade of neutral ports. The offer was refused by both powers.[12]

The other attempt was an appeal against the use of gas by the International Committee of the Red Cross on February 6, 1918. The Red Cross put its finger on the root of the problem when it predicted that the use of gas "threatens to increase to a never foreseen extent."[13] The appeal was rejected by both sides in notes designed more for propaganda effect than for serious negotiation. The atmosphere of distrust could not be overcome despite a mutual interest in terminating gas warfare.

Viewed in retrospect, the image of gas was no more encouraging to the decision-maker than it was to the military professional. The other group whose impressions would influence the future of poison gas was the general public. It will be recalled that the Allies had changed the focus of gas propaganda several times during the war. By 1918, poison gas was being represented as an unwanted but German-introduced feature of the war in which Allied science and technology were proving their superiority.

[11] In the spring of 1918, Colonel Fries suggested to General Pershing that the Allies deliver gas by airplane. As the incident was related by General Harbord, Chief of Staff, AEF, General Pershing refused the idea because the AEF would not initiate and "at that time" the enemy was not using gas against civilian populations, although the situation could change. "While our aviators were not allowed to initiate such warfare, *we were not unprepared to retaliate if it came to that*" (Maj. Gen. J. Harbord, *The American Army in France, 1917–1919* [Boston: Little, Brown, 1936], p. 223 [italics mine]).

[12] E. Franklin, "Chemical Warfare—Its Possibilities and Probabilities," *International Conciliation*, No. 248 (March 1929), p. 57.

[13] Comité International de la Croix-Rouge (CICR), *Documents relatifs à la Guerre Chimique et Aérienne* (Genéve: CICR, 1932), p. 6. Trans. by author.

Under the circumstances, gas was being presented quite rationally, and it apparently was not the subject of any more unfavorable reaction than that directed at all the new weapons of war. The situation could change rapidly, however, if interest groups, including decision-makers and the military, desired to use gas as a *cause célèbre* to promote a particular want.

Only the future would tell. . . .

SUMMARY AND CONCLUSIONS

To advocates of chemical warfare, World War II repeated the pattern of World War I. Toxic agents had been on the verge of acceptance as a major strategic weapons system but then were not employed. In both cases, the war ended before chemical warfare had the opportunity to display its potential. In the former case, realization of the potential effectiveness of gas was impeded due to the unavailability of a delivery system (the long-range bomber) commensurate with the capabilities of the weapon.

The situation was totally different in World War II. The supporting infrastructure required for effective employment had been developed. Non-use resulted from the interaction of a variety of objective and subjective restraints. For the first time since the advent of the nation at arms a major weapon employed in one conflict was not carried forward to be used in a subsequent conflict. Can this be considered a favorable indicator of inhibitions on the employment of nuclear weapons in general war, or is it an accident unlikely to recur?

It is extremely difficult to predict the future employment of nuclear weapons. Nevertheless, I believe that a study of American chemical warfare policy can provide an understanding of the nature of restraints which should prove as valid in the present and future as it has in the past. . . .

Three general areas of restraint have emerged in this study. First, there are those forces which were expected to restrain but which were proven generally ineffective in the heat of war. Second, there is the problem of non-assimilation by the professional military—a significant but little-appreciated subjective inhibition on employment. Last are the agreed components of deterrence—cost, capability, and credibility; this study evaluates their effectiveness as an element of restraint and emphasizes several critical aspects of deterrence developed from the study of chemical warfare.

Overestimation of the influence of public opinion was a serious fallacy of interwar prognostication. In the belief that adverse public sentiment was a major hope of preventing war, the United States actively encouraged anti-gas propaganda in the immediate post-World War I period. During World War II, however, this restraint was ineffective. Without government encouragement, American public attitudes toward the employment of gas shifted from opposition to passive acceptance if not support of initiation. The combination of bitter, costly island invasions in the Pacific Theater, and the identification of the entire enemy population as evil created an environment wherein the primary criterion for weapon use was rapid termination of the conflict rather than the "humanity" of a particular weapon.

Although public opinion per se was not a direct restraint on the use of gas, indirect effects of public attitudes in the interwar period were operative throughout the war. Due in significant measure to its awareness of the abhorrence with which the public viewed gas during the twenties and thirties, the Army never seriously pressed for gas warfare readiness; an Army desiring integration into the mainstream of American life would not burnish its image by meaningful support of a weapon so distasteful to the public. Public opinion, therefore, contributed to the nation's low state of readiness for chemical warfare at the outbreak of war.

Public opinion also had an impact on the decision-making elite of World War II. Profoundly influenced by the anti-gas propaganda, President Roosevelt would not even consider the possibilities of American initiation or preparation beyond the minimum amount required for retaliation. Anti-gas propaganda conditioned the attitudes of other leaders, both military and civilian, as well. Chemical warfare was consistently associated with a normative qualifying expression. State Department as well as JCS* papers on chemical warfare referred to "this inhuman method of warfare" or "this particularly inhuman form of warfare."

The other great hope of opponents of gas warfare lay in the creation of legal restraints, which turned out to have no greater direct effect than had public opinion. No power considered any treaty restriction or limiting declaration of a belligerent to be more than a statement of intent, which could be violated if the exigencies of unlimited war required.

The legal restraint was moderately effective; but in an unanticipated sense. The numerous interwar attempts to codify prohibition served to focus public and elite group attention on the problems and prospects of chemical warfare. Due to extensive conferences, specific national decisions had to be made on chemical warfare policy at times when national capability and popular sentiment created environments of unreality. Particularly in the United States, ratification of the chemical warfare prohibition of the Washington Conference established a questionable precedent for future negotiation and made it exceedingly difficult to promote actual chemical warfare readiness.

---

* [*Editors' note:* Joint Chiefs of Staff.]

A comparable effect developed in Germany. Readiness was impeded by the legal prohibition of Versailles and the Geneva Protocol; in addition, there were the specific arms control measures of the Peace Treaty. The Germans lost ten years in the international race to develop more effective chemical warfare weapons, and this hiatus provoked a serious "crisis of confidence." Ironically, the Germans made the major offensive chemical warfare breakthrough of the interwar period—nerve agents—yet forfeited the advantage by presuming that the Allies had made a similar advance. Thus, a former legal restraint helped indirectly to negate a major technological breakthrough.

Similar to the case with public attitudes, the legal restraint gained its limited effectiveness in an indirect and unanticipated manner. Based upon this experience, it would appear that the primary value of the legal restraint rests in its tendency to reinforce other existing restraints. Treaty prohibition, though imperfect, reinforced both public and military dislike and fear of chemical warfare and provided a ready excuse for lack of substantive preparation. Any legal restraint derived from custom or a general principle of law prohibiting weapons causing unnecessary suffering—if such exists and can be applied—should be even more effective, in that each would represent a more universal consensus of expert and lay attitudes.

Acceptance of a weapon within the military establishment is a prerequisite to employment. Influenced by the counter-propaganda writings of articulate military proponents of chemical warfare, most civilians assumed that the military accepted and was eager to employ chemical weapons. This assumption was false. Aside from those military leaders institutionally committed to toxic agents, the military establishment as a whole was opposed to their use. As an area weapon developed by scientists to strike insidiously and from afar, gas did not accord with the honor of the profession. In addition, the immense logistical and training burden unique to gas warfare required greater battlefield effect than could be attained with other weapons in order to justify resort to such a high-cost weapon. It could not be proven that the use of gas would provide any quantum jump in probability of battlefield success, particularly when the enemy could be expected to retaliate in kind. With major financial restraints imposed throughout the Depression, no national military establishment was inclined to emphasize weapons of doubtful effectiveness when Artillery, Infantry, and the Air Force were faced with acute shortages in conventional weapons.

Since gas warfare was not assimilated into the military establishment of any major power, its use was precluded in World War II. Without professional support for meaningful gas warfare readiness, no nation was prepared to employ toxic agents when it entered the war. For the Axis Powers, during the successful first half of the war, there was no incentive to commit the resources required for increased chemical warfare preparedness when other weapons of proven utility were in constant demand. The same logic, albeit reversed in its time sequence, applied to the Allied Powers.

This lack of assimilation was particularly evident in the United States response to the extreme asymmetry of readiness existing between the United States and Japan toward the end of World War II. Despite its awareness that the Japanese could not retaliate, the United States did not employ toxic agents. The central reason for this lay in the general military disinterest in gas which had retarded readiness sufficiently to preclude timely, serious consideration of initiation. Decades of conditioning to a second-strike philosophy prevented such logistic preparedness in the forward areas which could have provided an incentive to striking the first blow.

The implication here is that lack of assimilation is a more fundamental inhibition to initiation than fear of retaliation. No major belligerent in World War II accepted gas warfare. As a result, a defensive aura surrounded the entire area of toxic chemical warfare. Aside from Japan, each nation maintained a credible retaliatory capability, yet the capability was in each case more potential than real. There was never sufficient readiness to provide the incentive for immediate initiation.

Even if any nation had developed a material capability adequate to make initiation feasible, fear of the costs of enemy retaliation would have remained as a restraint sufficient to deter it. Whether the prospective victim actually possessed sufficient retaliatory capability to inflict intolerable levels of punishment is essentially irrelevant. Partially due to poor chemical warfare intelligence on the part of all belligerents, which credited the enemy with a capability commensurate with the assumed diabolical nature of his intentions, each nation saw asymmetrical chemical warfare capabilities as favoring the enemy. When the potential initiator realized his superiority and his invulnerability to direct enemy retaliation, as was the case of the United States, in the last stages of the Pacific War, initiation was deterred by threat of retaliation against an ally, China. In World War II, the restraint of enemy retaliation was magnified in effect by the demands of coalition warfare. The presence of allies that were hostages for the good conduct of the coalition leader increased the stability of mutual deterrence.

These restraints, proven in war, varied considerably from interwar predictions. Neither public opinion nor legal restriction was directly effective; but, on the other hand, lack of assimilation and fear of retaliation proved to be significant restraints. In World War II, the lesson was clear; the loci of decision-making with respect to gas warfare lay within the professional military establishments themselves. Military lack of interest kept the issue of initiation from reaching civilian elite groups.

American experience with toxic agents during World War II revealed several general characteristics of successful deterrence. Readiness to retaliate was communicated through statements of heads of government backed up with overt chemical warfare preparations. The unrestricted nature of war, exemplified by the unlimited bombing policy, gave credibility to the threat to employ toxic agents in response to enemy initiation. No nation doubted that the potential target nation possessed a retaliatory capability sufficient to punish the initiator, directly, or indirectly, through a coalition partner, and general military dislike of toxic agents was sufficient to restrain any inclination to develop a possible disarming first-strike capability.

Each belligerent saw escalation of toxic agent employment as an inevitable effect of initiation. Once World War II began, there does not appear to have been any serious consideration of initiation solely for tactical success. It was tacitly assumed that any use of gas would immediately escalate to the strategic level and, therefore, that any initiation should itself be at the strategic level. Essentially the same logic applied to the choice of chemical agents. It was assumed that there was no effective limiting point between the employment of nonlethal and lethal agents. For this reason, nontoxic chemical agents were not employed in a combat environment.

Based upon Japanese actions, however, the validity of both assumptions is questionable. The Japanese employed nontoxic and toxic agents against the Chinese both before and after United States entry in the war, yet the United States ignored the situation. Due to lack of readiness and unwillingness to employ, the United States preferred to overlook a situation that, in terms of declaratory policy, would have required retaliation. As long as Japanese violation of tacitly agreed limits did not affect a core interest of the United States as defined by decision-makers or by reaction of the general public, there was no automaticity of escalation. The effect of this American response was to diminish the credibility of the American policy which enabled the Japanese to reallocate their chemical warfare readiness resources.[14]

World War II also saw in the United Kingdom and Germany the establishment of the most extensive and costly passive defense systems yet developed. In neither case did civil defense measures act as a destabilizing element in the maintenance of mutual deterrence. Each accepted civil protection as a necessary component of readiness for a nation continuously under the threat of surprise strategic attack. If it had any specific effect, the existence of effective civil defense acted as

---

[14] There is no indication that, despite attendance at interwar international conferences, the Japanese thought that in initiating they were doing anything other than field testing a new weapon. One can only speculate that it was their inexperience with chemical warfare which prevented them from realizing the implications of initiating employment.

a stabilizing element by reducing the expected reward, and thus incentive, for a surprise first strike.

A further element of restraint demonstrated in the Second World War was the impact on decision-making of an irrational leader. Hitler was accepted by the Allied Powers as a national leader likely to make irrational decisions. This image was in itself a stimulant to British preparations for gas warfare and thus indirectly contributed to deterrence. With his back to the wall, Hitler apparently decided to initiate gas warfare, but the inevitability of defeat was so obvious by early 1945 that he had lost authority over his key military subordinates. The result was failure to implement his decision.

This development would suggest that the critical time for one belligerent's initiation of a mass-casualty weapon is during that period when it is becoming obvious that eventual victory is improbable unless a new element is introduced into the war to restore the momentum of the offensive, but before it is obvious to the military establishment that the initiative has passed to the enemy and that eventual defeat is certain. In short, the decision would have to be made before the national leader has, by failure, undermined his power to have such a momentous decision implemented.

It remains one of the ironies of the Second World War that toxic agents, considered sufficiently humane to be used for the execution of convicted prisoners, were not employed in a war which saw the extensive use of another weapon with enormous destructive powers—the atomic bomb. The heritage of World War I was responsible—poison gas was a weapon too technologically demanding and psychologically disquieting to be assimilated by the military profession. It was an unacceptable anachronism, born too early out of a unique marriage of science and war. Added to this primary and most effective restraint of nonassimilation was mutual possession of a credible deterrent force. . . .

Japan's Fatal Blunder

SIR GEORGE SANSOM

In the light of what we know today the decision of the leaders of Japan to make war upon the United States appears as an act of folly, by which they committed themselves to a hopeless struggle against a Power with perhaps ten times their own potential industrial and military strength. But was that decision in fact as reckless as it now seems, or can it be regarded as the taking of a justifiable risk in the circumstances in which it was made?

Perhaps it is too soon to expect a complete answer to this question, but there is already available a good deal of useful information upon which a preliminary judgement can be based. There is, for instance, an interesting series of reports published by the United States Strategic Bombing Survey,* which was conducted (by civilians) primarily for the purpose of ascertaining the degree to which air-power contributed to the defeat of Japan. During this enquiry there was collected a mass of statistical and other information regarding political and economic conditions in Japan prior to and during the war. These studies, together with two volumes of Interrogations compiled by the United States Navy,† include valuable data based upon oral and documentary evidence obtained in Japan in 1945, not long after the surrender, when memories were fresh. It should be understood that the answers elicited by interrogations cannot all be taken at face value. Allowance must be made for certain factors of error. Thus, the "Summaries" of the Bombing Survey, in which general conclusions are drawn, naturally tend to place emphasis on the part played by aircraft in reducing Japan to the point of surrender and, by implication, to underestimate the importance of the general strategic conduct of the war and the particular effectiveness of submarine action on vital Japanese lines of communication by sea. Moreover, the interrogations were not always skillfully conducted and the replies sometimes betray a

Reprinted by permission from *International Affairs*, October 1948, pp. 543–555. One footnote has been omitted.

*[*Editors' note:* United States Strategic Bombing Survey, *Japan's Struggle to End the War* (Washington, D.C.: Government Printing Office, 1946).]

†[*Editors' note:* United States Strategic Bombing Survey, *Interrogations of Japanese Officials,* 2 vols. (Washington, D.C.: Government Printing Office, 1946).]

desire to please the questioners, if not to mislead them. Different and more reliable results might have been obtained from really searching cross-examination by experienced persons. Nevertheless, the documents are extremely interesting and suffice to establish beyond reasonable doubt a number of important facts. The following tentative appraisal draws freely upon information which they contain, though it is supplemented at a few points by knowledge derived by the writer from other sources during a visit to Japan early in 1946.

There is no doubt that Japan was preparing for war at least a decade before 1941, but this does not necessarily mean that she had decided before that year to make war upon the United States or the British Commonwealth. The most that can be safely said is that certain influential army leaders and their civilian supporters contemplated war if the European situation should so develop as to make it feasible and advantageous. There was no concealment of Japan's intention to get ready for war. But during 1940 there was still no agreement in influential circles as to the course which Japan should take in international affairs, or even as to the lines upon which her economy should be further developed and controlled. The full powers which the Government had progressively acquired in preceding years were exercised only partially; a medley of State controls existed side by side with autonomous direction in separate branches of production and trade; and, in general, conflict between the military and the leaders of industry and finance continued unabated and unresolved.

It is sometimes stated by British and American writers that Big Business in Japan—the so-called *Zaibatsu*—co-operated enthusiastically in preparations for war or at least meekly gave way to military pressure. The evidence for this view is poor. On the contrary, during the early part of 1940 the influential Economic Federation of Japan (*Nihon Keizai Remmei*) resisted the Government's plans for industrial expansion, arguing that they were basically unsound. Their opposition was, it is true, based on technical rather than political grounds, but it cannot be said that they co-operated freely with the military leaders in the development of an economy designed for warlike purposes.

In fact, under the Yonai Government, which was in power until July 1940, there were still elements in the Cabinet that favoured a cautious if not a pacific foreign policy, and were inclined to take the side of the industrialists in resisting totalitarian trends. It was at this point that the military used their strongest political weapon. By withdrawing the War Minister, they forced the resignation of the Yonai Cabinet, in which the relatively liberal Mr. Arita was Foreign Minister. The second Konoye Cabinet was then formed, with Tojo, a convinced expansionist, as War Minister. Its announced policy was the development of a highly organized National Defence State and the consolidation of an Asiatic "Co-Prosperity Sphere." This was definitely a war Cabinet, and its immediate purpose was to bring the industrialists to heel. Once the Government reached a firm decision the resistance of the industrialists was sooner or later bound to collapse. The close concentration of industrial power in Japan, having historically been achieved largely under official direction or with official support, had never acquired true independence or substantial political strength. It could struggle against this measure or that, but in matters of high policy it could not successfully challenge the authority of the bureaucracy with which it was so organically related.

In September 1940, Tojo let it be known that national mobilization required an intensified control which was inconsistent with the old liberal economic structure. But still the struggle continued and, surprisingly, the resistance of the industrial and financial leaders, represented by the Economic Federation, increased rather than diminished. The planned economy which was the object of Hoshino and Ohashi—two officials who had gained experience in Manchuria—was fought with some success by members of the *Zaibatsu* who, whatever their views as to war and peace, realized the limitations of the Japanese economy. But they were at length forced to execute plans in which they had little faith.

These facts are cited as showing that as late as 1941, despite long preparation, there was yet no effective centralized control of the Japanese industrial structure; and, quite apart from the conflict between Government and private enterprise, there was another defect in the country's war-making capacity, for the administrative machine, seemingly so efficient in normal times, turned out to be rigid and unmanageable. It was even necessary for Tojo, when he became Prime Minister in 1941, to seek legislation which would compel the various ministries to obey his orders. Such a diagnosis of the radical weaknesses in Japan's governmental structure at a juncture when her national existence was about to be staked upon its efficiency may seem too sweeping, but it could be supported by further evidence. It is sufficient to say here that the subsequent course of events, in both the economic and military spheres, shows that part of the failure of the Japanese economy to meet the demands made upon it in time of war can be traced back to faulty arrangements in time of peace. That governments or individuals should contract bad habits is not surprising, but it is surprising that the rulers of Japan should not have realized how inadequate, even by their own standards, was their country's organization for a war of their own choosing against powerful enemies.

The degree of their economic miscalculations is easy to measure by results. More difficult is an assessment of their political judgement. There can be no doubt that the coalition which began to rule Japan in July 1940 was determined to make use of the European war to further an expansionist policy in Asia and, if possible, to settle the conflict with China on favorable terms. When France was defeated and England appeared to the Japanese to be about to follow her in disaster, the Konoye Government began to feel confident enough to probe the weaknesses of possible antagonists by such measures as flouting British and American interests in China, blackmailing the United Kingdom into closing the Burma Road, pressing the Netherland Indies for economic concessions and moving troops into northern Indo-China. In the summer of 1940 it even looked as if an attack upon British possessions in the Far East was imminent. But action was postponed, partly because the progress of the Battle of Britain raised doubts about the expected collapse of the United Kingdom, but also because the Japanese army and navy wished to complete their armament and to collect further stocks of basic materials. They appear to have decided that, tempting as it was, an attack upon British and Dutch territories alone would be strategically unsound, because it would leave on their flank unimpaired American strength which might intervene at a moment chosen by the United States. They were, moreover, not yet satisfied that they had the whole country with them, for despite their vigorous domestic propaganda there were still dissidents in high places and doubtless also among the people. The distribution of political influence within Japan was traditionally such that any decisive move required much bargaining and persuasion. The firmly established system of checks and balances was customary rather than constitutional, but it had the effect of delaying political action. Even within the ruling coalition there were differences of opinion on the timing and the length of each step taken on the road to war, and there were cautious or conservative elements whose hesitations had to be overcome.

This was the condition reached by the summer of 1941. The extremists continued to strengthen their position step by step, by committing Japan to engagements from which it was difficult if not impossible to withdraw. Perhaps this period was the most crucial in Japanese history, since a vital decision on war or peace is not a simple choice of alternatives at a given moment, but is influenced by the cumulative effect of previous commitments, none of which is separately decisive. The extremists had in July 1941, by a series of gradual manoeuvres, gone far towards creating a situation in which their voice would be dominant. They then took a long step by establishing bases in Southern Indo-China. All available evidence goes to show that they did not expect this move to evoke strong reactions from the United States or the United Kingdom. It was represented as nothing but a strategical development in the war against China, but its implications were perfectly clear. It was the first phase of a projected southward movement. It is interesting to note, from the captured German documents published in January 1948 by the United States Government, that the draft secret protocol of November 1940 to the agreement between the U.S.S.R. and the Tripartite Powers states that "Japan declares that her territorial aspirations centre in the area of Eastern Asia to the south of the Island Empire of Japan."[1] The sharp counter-measures of the United States and the United Kingdom came as a surprise to the extremists and threw the moderates into confusion, though they must have had some warning from the Japanese Embassy in Washington. The situation is well described in the Summary Report of the United States Bombing Survey, as follows:

> Though the conservative wing of the ruling coalition had endorsed each move of its coalition partners, it hoped at each stage that the current step would not be the breaking-point leading to war. It arranged and concluded the Tripartite Pact (September 1940) and hoped that the Western Powers would be sufficiently impressed with the might and solidarity of the Axis to understand the futility of further resistance. It approved of the Indo-China adventure, assuming that Japan would get away with this act of aggression as easily as with previous ones.

But while the freezing of Japanese assets and the embargo upon the export of strategic materials to Japan imposed by the Western Powers shocked the conservatives and frightened the moderates, they had already gone too far in their acquiescence. They could not now suggest any course but negotiations with the United States, and over the terms of these negotiations they could exercise no control, since the power of final decision had already passed into the hands of the extremists. All they could now hope for was that the extremists would make enough concessions to satisfy the United States, and this was a vain hope, because to make any effective concessions would be to admit that the whole of Japanese policy since 1931 had been a blunder, for which the military party and its civilian allies were responsible. The Army's prestige would never recover from such a blow. War was inevitable. The only question now was what kind of war.

Such in broad outline was the political background of the decision to go to war. It remains to consider on what grounds the military

---

[1] J. Sontag and J. S. Beddie, eds., Declaration 3, Draft Secret Protocol No. 1, *Nazi Soviet Relations*, 1939–40 (U.S.A. Department of State, 1948), p. 257.

leaders of Japan based their judgement that Japan could successfully challenge the United States and the British Commonwealth. It cannot be assumed that they blindly led their country into war with no prospect of success. Theirs was a considered policy, attended by calculated risks. Examined in retrospect it proves to have been based upon mistaken assumptions, and executed with insufficient skill and foresight; but it was not, as conceived, irrational. It must also be remembered that the economic sanctions imposed upon Japan in 1941 were such as to make war appear a reasonable, if dangerous, alternative.

The planners who decided that the risk of war could be taken were not blind to the frightful disparity between their own strength and that of their enemies. They counted upon certain favourable circumstances to balance their own deficiencies. Late in the summer of 1941 they were convinced that Germany would be victorious and that within a few months, Russia having been defeated, the United States and the United Kingdom would be obliged to accept supremacy of Germany in Europe. This outlook, though it promised them membership of a successful alliance, was in one respect not entirely pleasing to them, since they felt some distrust of their Axis partners, which the Germans in Japan by their arrogant behavior did nothing to diminish. Some Japanese expansionists therefore felt that their plans might be upset by a premature settlement of the European conflict, which would leave them without any spoils of war in the Pacific; and this fear probably, though not certainly, was an additional motive for the rapid seizure of territories in Asia from which they could derive supplies of oil and rubber, and strategic bargaining power. As they saw the position, those objectives—stepping stones to further expansion—could be attained by a short and restricted campaign. They would engage in hostilities in the Pacific for a strictly limited purpose. First they would conquer an area enclosed within a perimeter including Burma, Malaya, Sumatra, Java, Northern New Guinea, the Bismarck Archipelago, the Gilbert and Marshall Islands, Wake and the Kuriles. This, they calculated, could be achieved in a few months if American sea and air power could be weakened by surprise attacks upon Pearl Harbor and the Philippines. The United States, preoccupied with the European situation, would be unable to take the offensive before Japan had accomplished the necessary strengthening of the perimeter and established forward air and sea bases. Once firmly entrenched on that perimeter they could obtain from the occupied areas what they required to sustain and expand their deficient economy—oil, rubber, bauxite, metals, food. Thus supplied, they could wage defensive warfare which, it was supposed, would within a year or two weaken the American purpose and so lead to a compromise peace. Negotiation would leave to Japan a substantial portion of her gains and a dominant position in Eastern Asia.

This was not at that time a strategy which could be condemned out of hand as unrealistic. It could be regarded, and presented to the Japanese people, as a reasonable and honourable alternative to submitting to sanctions. It aroused misgivings in some circles in Japan, and even its proponents knew that it would throw a great strain upon Japan's capacity; but they counted upon the shock of rapid conquests, and upon the fighting qualities of their soldiers and sailors. Certainly in the first few months of the war nothing happened to make them revise their opinions. Their successes were greater and easier than they had foreseen.

So encouraged were they by their achievement that they began to consider an extension of their perimeter. They planned an advance into the Solomons and Port Moresby, to be followed by a further advance into New Caledonia, Samoa, and the Fijis, the capture of Midway and the occupation of the Aleutians. It was here that they made their first cardinal blunder, for . . . "by stretching and overextending her line of advance, Japan was committed to an expensive and exacting supply problem. She delayed the fortification of the perimeter originally decided upon, jeopardised her economic program for exploiting the resources of the area already captured and laid herself open to early counter-attack in far advanced and, as yet, weak positions."[2]

This blunder in execution also laid bare certain weaknesses in the original conceptions of the Japanese planners. Perhaps the most important of these was their misjudgement of the temper of the United States, for the attack on Pearl Harbor had a stimulating psychological effect upon the American people which in military importance far outweighed the losses sustained at Pearl Harbor. The Japanese army had persuaded the Japanese people that the democratic states were materialistic, irresolute, incapable of matching the unique Japanese spirit. They had argued, not without some plausibility, that the United States had for a decade or more shown a strong aversion to protecting its interests in the Far East by warlike measures, despite repeated provocation. They inferred that those interests were not regarded as of vital importance and that consequently in the long run a spirit of compromise would prevail. They seem to have been deceived by their own propaganda, for even after their initial reverses in the first half of 1942 at Midway and towards the end of the year at Guadalcanal, they appear still to have supposed that they could fight the war on their own terms. They did not yet realize that their original plan of restricted warfare, which

---

[2] United States Strategic Bombing Survey, Summary Report, *Pacific War* (Washington, United States Government Printing Office, 1946), p. 4.

could be sustained for a limited period by their 1941 economy was no longer feasible.

It was not until 1943 that they had fully grasped the fact that they could no longer dictate the scale or location of hostilities, but were involved in total war in which the initiative had already passed to the American forces. That they made this mistake is indicated by their failure to carry out complete economic mobilization until 1943. An index of the gross national product (computed by the United States Bombing Survey with the assistance of Japanese experts) shows a rise from 100 in 1940 to only 101 in 1941 and 102 in 1942. It was not until 1943 that a substantial increase was gained by a production drive which raised the figure to 113 for 1943 and 124 for 1944. This was the peak of Japanese production, and it was reached by forcing an ever-growing proportion of the total economy into direct war purposes, while straining the civilian population almost to breaking point. It was a remarkable performance, but it was too little and too late. No effort was made to carry out a coherent plan of overall expansion of the Japanese economy, perhaps because a balanced development was impossible in view of its previous distortion. Even if the foregoing explanation of the delay in carrying out full economic mobilization errs in placing too much emphasis upon a tardy appreciation of the strategic position, it is clear that the Japanese tradition of government depending upon slow and cautious compromise was ill-adapted for times of emergency that demanded bold decision and quick performance.

The subsequent course of the Pacific war needs no detailed recital here. It is enough to say that although the Japanese made after 1942 immense military and economic efforts to meet conditions for which they had not originally planned, both were insufficient to stem the tide which began to flow against them. Nearly all their calculations had gone wrong. The British Isles were not invaded, the Soviet Union did not collapse, the United States showed not the least disposition to compromise, but began to plan the outright defeat of Japan. The prospect of a negotiated peace vanished. Plans to draw upon the occupied territories for essential materials could not be executed, because submarine and air attacks upon Japanese shipping prevented not only the carriage of needed supplies to Japan, but also the full support of Japanese forces in the field. Japanese commanders have testified that only 20 per cent of the supplies dispatched to Guadalcanal reached their destination, and that of 30,000 troops landed, 10,000 died of starvation or disease and 10,000 were evacuated early in 1943 in a debilitated condition. Though Japanese troops everywhere fought stubbornly and well, inflicting heavy losses upon their opponents, by the opening months of 1943 not only had the Japanese advance been stopped, but their overall strategic plan had been upset. This was the result of an overwhelming superiority of American power, and it revealed a basic error in the initial premises of that plan. It had been supposed that the perimeter could be held indefinitely, but American experience showed after the engagements of 1942 that it was not necessary to reduce the whole perimeter. The widely spread Japanese positions were dependent upon supply by sea, and it was necessary to destroy them only at points selected by the American command. So long as attacks upon Japanese shipping were maintained, other points could be by-passed as a general advance was begun towards bases within striking distance of Japan.

It was after the evacuation of Guadalcanal, in February 1943, that thoughtful Japanese began to suspect that their prospects of victory had disappeared, while those who knew all the facts saw that the situation was desperate. It is surprising that, to quote the words of Hoshino, Chief Secretary of the Tojo Cabinet, "the real Japanese war economy only began after Guadalcanal." Perhaps even more surprising is the confusion which is revealed in the direction both of the war economy and the national strategy after that date. Full credit must be given to the Japanese people for their efforts to restore and develop their war potential after 1942, but their leaders seem never to have reached a clear and comprehensive view of their country's situation. Some rough estimates of national strength were compiled before the war. They were tentative and incomplete, and perhaps this was in the circumstances unavoidable.

But it is strange that, so far as is known, a full re-appraisal in the light of the new conditions was not attempted until September 1943. This was made not by the Government for its own purposes, but by Takagi, an officer of the Naval General Staff, at the request of Admiral Yonai, who had been out of office since his Cabinet fell in 1940. This influential statesman, when asked in 1945 what he considered the turning point of the war replied: "To be very frank, I think the turning point was the start. I felt from the very beginning that there was no chance of success." Takagi's report strengthened Admiral Yonai's fears that the prosecution of the war by the Tojo Government was unsatisfactory. It confirmed his judgement that Japan should seek a compromise peace before she suffered a crushing defeat. Yonai was not alone in this feeling. It was shared by certain influential persons outside the Government and a number of naval officers. They had indeed good reason for their anxiety. The circumstances beyond Japan's control were grave enough—the growing shortages of materials, losses of aircraft, warships and merchant vessels, and the certainty of long-range air attacks upon the centres of production at home. And, added to these, was growing confusion within Japan.

Nominally, by 1943 the Japanese Government had achieved full control of all national organs and activities, but Japan had evidently not become a solid authoritarian state. Animosity between Army and Navy was such that the submarine service resented the diversion of its vessels from combatant functions to army transport duties, and towards the end of the war the Army began to build submarines for its own use and declined naval advice. Army and Navy details, it is said, would fight outside factories for supplies designated for one or the other service. Ginjiro Fujihara, an industrial magnate who at a critical juncture became director of aircraft production, even alleged (no doubt untruthfully) that army and navy rivalry was responsible for keeping down the total output by about 50 per cent. In addition to their inter-service quarrels, the armed forces displayed hostility towards civilian organs. The director of the General Mobilization Bureau testified on interrogation that they would never disclose their stocks or discuss their requirements with him, would not submit demands through the appropriate ministry and thus thwarted all attempts at co-ordination of supply. Control bodies set up by the Government for key materials tried to enforce a system of priorities, but the Army and Navy would help themselves to supplies without troubling to obtain priority-certificates. Civilian manufacturing firms were, it is reported, obliged to resort to black market transactions in order to secure material or machines. It is of course easy to exaggerate the extent and importance of such abuses, which are common enough in all countries at war; but it is clear that there was a serious lack of harmony between the two fighting services. Admiral Toyoda (Commander-in-Chief Combined Fleet, and later Chief of Naval General Staff) said upon interrogation: "There was not full understanding and agreement between Army and Navy prior to and during the war." This discord he ascribed to the great political power of the Army, which the Navy did not share. It showed itself, he thought, not so much in operational matters as in the division of supplies. But General Yamashita, the Japanese commander in the Philippines, was only apprised of the intended naval strike on Leyte Gulf in a *written* communication from Tokyo which was two weeks on the way and reached him on the day of the operation.

Uneasy relations between Army and Navy were paralleled by quarrels between civilian organs. It is remarkable that, despite their reputed gift for careful and strict organization, the Japanese authorities were not in practice able to exercise their unlimited powers of control. Under a surface appearance of national unity, old divisions of opinions, old patterns of influence, persisted with very little change. It is perhaps comforting to discover that what appears to be a solid monolithic state can hide grave structural weaknesses behind a forbidding exterior.

By July 1944, the invasion of Saipan had succeeded and Tojo's Cabinet had collapsed. The strenuous efforts made to raise production in Japan had led to a considerable increase in capacity, yet by late in the summer output had begun to decline because shipping losses had cut down essential imports. National morale was still high but by the autumn of 1944 Japan was on the verge of economic collapse, and that was before the heavy strategical bombing of the home islands. Tojo was succeeded as Prime Minister by Koiso, a retired general, whose Government set up a Supreme War Direction Council intended ostensibly to strengthen national defence, but in fact obliged to consider ways of terminating the war. The story of the steps by which most of its members at length reached a decision in favour of surrender is a long and complicated one. Not much progress was made at first, but certain members of the Cabinet were cautiously working for peace and carrying on discussions with senior statesmen who, though out of office, retained great personal influence. High naval officers were predominant among the service men who favoured attempts to secure a negotiated peace, while the Army command still thought in terms of prolonged resistance, hoping that they could inflict such losses upon an invading force that a compromise could be secured, which would leave to Japan something better than the prospect of unconditional surrender. The peace party was growing in confidence, but only slowly, and was hampered by the fear that, since the Japanese people were still ignorant of the true state of affairs, a premature move might bring about internal chaos.

Meanwhile, with the loss of the Philippines and the intensification of bombing, which affected both military targets and urban populations, the situation became more and more desperate in the eyes of the peace party, less and less hopeful in the eyes of the last-ditchers. But it seems that there was little prospect of obtaining the agreement of any substantial portion of the Army leaders so long as Germany continued to resist. It was not until April 8, 1945 that the Koiso Government fell and was succeeded by a Cabinet under Admiral Suzuki, whose mission was to bring the war to an end, though publicly both Government and people were still committed to a continued resistance. Progress towards peace was still slow, for nobody would come out with an open declaration that the war was lost. Early in May, however—shortly after the end of the European war—the balance began to turn in favour of peace. Appraisals of the economic situation showed that the country was utterly incapable of continuing effective resistance, and there were even some signs of a decline in public morale. Still no specific proposals for ending the war were made, though on June 6 the Supreme War Council definitely stated to the Emperor that it was necessary to bring it to an end. On June 20, the Emperor summoned the Council, and showed himself in favour of positive steps, including an approach to the Soviet Union with a request for mediation. Discussions with Russia made no progress, the Soviet Government temporized and the Japanese ambassador in Moscow reported that in his opinion there was no alternative to unconditional surrender.

Time went by, and still no firm decision had been reached when the Potsdam Declaration was issued on July 26, 1945. The Prime Minister, the Foreign Minister and the Navy Minister (Yonai) were in favour of accepting its terms, the War Minister and the Chiefs of Staff were opposed. It is interesting to note, as illustrating the nature of the opposition, that Toyoda had not approved of the War from the beginning, yet was unable to agree to unconditional surrender, which he thought dishonourable. A strong military group still held out for resistance to invasion. Differences of opinion continued until August 9, 1945, by which time an atomic bomb had been dropped on Hiroshima (August 6) and the Soviet Union had declared war upon Japan (August 9). After repeated meetings on August 9, just before midnight the Inner Cabinet appealed to the Emperor for a final expression of his wish and the Emperor declared in favour of peace. There were further cabinet discussions as to the interpretation of the Potsdam terms, but they were finally accepted on August 14. This was more than twelve months after the fall of the Tojo Government, and four months after the formation of the Suzuki Cabinet, which was certainly intended to bring an end to hostilities. It may well be asked why, in the light of Japan's inability, so manifest after the end of 1944, to carry the war to a successful conclusion, the discussion was prolonged well into 1945, while her factories and her houses were being destroyed, her warships sunk and her armies cut off from their homes? The answer is not clear, but it seems as if the delay was something dictated by the nature of Japanese institutions. The slow process by which an apparently unanimous will to war was created before 1941 had to be repeated in reverse before a will to peace could be announced.

The fact that the decision to accept the Potsdam terms was reached soon after the explosion of the atomic bomb and the Russian declaration of war has been interpreted as showing that the bomb and the Russian action were what produced Japan's surrender. This is a view which it is difficult to accept. It might be correct to say that these two menacing events accelerated a decision which was being reached by slow and devious processes characteristic of Japanese political life. But it cannot be truthfully said that any one single cause brought about the surrender; at the same time there is good reason for thinking that, even had no atomic bombing attacks been delivered, the disintegration of Japan's economic life, under sustained blockade and continued aerial and naval bombardment, would within a few months—perhaps weeks—after June 1945 have brought about unconditional surrender, even without the need for invasion. But all this is in the realm of conjecture, and not even the participants themselves can say with certainty what course the debates in the War Council would have taken in hypothetical conditions. Even if we were today certain that it was not the atomic bomb which caused the surrender, it would not follow that the decision to use the bomb was wrong. That decision was necessarily taken in the light of such sure knowledge as was then at the disposal of our Governments; and although intelligence reports on conditions in Japan were remarkably good, that knowledge was not sufficient to justify abstaining from the use of a weapon which might end the war quickly, and save the lives of thousands of allied prisoners, possibly hundreds of thousands of allied soldiers, to say nothing of great numbers of enemy soldiers and civilians. Discussion of the rights and wrongs of the use of the atomic bomb at Hiroshima frequently confuses two separate issues. If the question is whether it was immoral to use such a destructive weapon, then one must bring into consideration incendiary raids, such as that of the night of March 9, 1945, which killed probably 100,000 people and destroyed over 250,000 homes, in circumstances of appalling terror. If the question is whether the use of the atomic bomb was strategically unnecessary or (in the light of subsequent history) politically mistaken, then moral considerations are irrelevant so long as the right of a belligerent to attack civilian targets is admitted. There cannot by any rational standard of morals be a valid distinction between methods of killing civilians in which one is right and the other is wrong because it is quicker and more effective.

The Decision to Use
the Atomic Bomb

LOUIS MORTON

It is now more than ten years since the atomic bomb exploded over Hiroshima and revealed to the world in one blinding flash of light the start of the atomic age. As the meaning of this explosion and the nature of the force unleashed became apparent, a chorus of voices rose in protest against the decision that had opened the Pandora's box of atomic warfare.

The justification for using the atomic bomb was that it had ended the war, or at least ended it sooner and thereby saved countless American—and Japanese—lives. But had it? Had not Japan already been defeated and was she not already on the verge of surrender? What circumstances, it was asked, justified the fateful decision that "blasted the web of history and, like the discovery of fire, severed past from present"?[1]

The first authoritative explanation of how and why it was decided to use the bomb came in February 1947 from Henry L. Stimson, wartime Secretary of War and the man who more than any other was responsible for advising the President.[2] This explanation did not answer all the questions or still the critics. During the years that have followed others have revealed their part in the decision and in the events shaping it. These explanations have not ended the controversy, but they have brought to light additional facts bearing on the decision to use the bomb. With this information and with the perspective of ten years, it may be profitable to look again at the decision that opened the age of atomic warfare.

Reprinted by special permission from *Foreign Affairs*, January 1957, pp. 334–353. Copyright © 1956 by the Council on Foreign Relations, Inc., New York. Some footnotes have been omitted.

[1] James Phinney Baxter, 3rd, *Scientists Against Time* (Boston: Little, Brown, 1946), p. 419.

[2] Henry L. Stimson, "The Decision to Use the Atomic Bomb," *Harper's*, February 1947. The article is reproduced with additional comments in Henry L. Stimson and McGeorge Bundy, *On Active Service in Peace and War* (New York: Harper, 1948), chapter 13, and in *Bulletin of the Atomic Scientists*, February 1947.

THE INTERIM COMMITTEE

The epic story of the development of the atomic bomb is by now well known. It began in 1939 when a small group of eminent scientists in this country called to the attention of the United States Government the vast potentialities of atomic energy for military purposes and warned that the Germans were already carrying on experiments in this field. The program initiated in October of that year with a very modest appropriation and later expanded into the two-billion-dollar Manhattan Project had only one purpose—to harness the energy of the atom in a chain reaction to produce a bomb that could be carried by aircraft if possible, and to produce it before the Germans could.[3] That such a bomb, if produced, would be used, no responsible official even questioned. "At no time from 1941 to 1945," declared Mr. Stimson, "did I ever hear it suggested by the President, or by another responsible member of the Government, that atomic energy should not be used in the war." And Dr. J. Robert Oppenheimer recalled in 1954 that "we always assumed if they [atomic bombs] were needed, they would be used."[4]

So long as the success of the project remained in doubt there seems to have been little or no discussion of the effects of an atomic weapon or the circumstances under which it would be used. "During the early days of the project," one scientist recalled, "we spent little time thinking about the possible effects of the bomb we were trying to make"[5] It was a "neck-and-neck race with the Germans," the outcome of which might well determine who would be the victor in World War II. But as Germany approached defeat and as the effort to produce an atomic bomb offered increasing promise of successs, those few men who knew what was being done and who appreciated the enormous implications of atomic energy became more and more concerned. Most of this concern came from the scientists in the Metallurgical Laboratory at Chicago, where by early 1945 small groups began to question the advisability of using the weapon they were trying so hard to build. It was almost as if they hoped the bomb would not work after it was completed.

On the military side, the realization that a bomb would probably be ready for testing in the summer of 1945 led to concrete planning for the use of the new weapon, on the assumption that the bomb when

---

[3] The one exception was the Navy's work in the field of atomic energy as a source of power for naval vessels. *Hearings Before the Special Committee on Atomic Energy*, Senate, 79th Cong., 1st Sess., S.R. 179, pt. 3, pp. 364–389, testimony of Dr. Ross Gunn.

[4] Stimson, *Harper's*, p. 98; U.S. Atomic Energy Commission, *Transcript of Hearings Before Personnel Security Board in the Matter of Dr. J. Robert Oppenheimer, 12 April–6 May 1954* (Washington: G.P.O., 1954), p. 33.

[5] *Senate Hearings*, pt. 2, p. 302, testimony of Dr. John A. Simpson.

completed would work. By the end of 1944 a list of possible targets in Japan had been selected and a B-29 squadron was trained for the specific job of delivering the bomb. It was also necessary to inform certain commanders in the Pacific about the project, and on December 30, 1944, Major-General Leslie R. Groves, head of the Manhattan District, recommended that this be done.[6]

Even at this stage of development no one could estimate accurately when the bomb would be ready or guarantee that, when ready, it would work. It is perhaps for this reason—and because of the complete secrecy surrounding the project—that the possibility of an atomic weapon never entered into the deliberations of the strategic planners. It was, said Admiral William Leahy, "the best kept secret of the entire war" and only a handful of the top civilian and military officials in Washington knew about the bomb.[7] As a matter of fact, one bright brigadier-general who innocently suggested that the Army might do well to look into the possibilities of atomic energy suddenly found himself the object of the most intensive investigation. So secret was the project, says John J. McCloy, that when he raised the subject at a White House meeting of the Joint Chiefs of Staff in June 1945 it "caused a sense of shock, even among that select group."[8]

It was not until March 1945 that it became possible to predict with certainty that the bomb would be completed in time for testing in July. On March 15, Mr. Stimson discussed the project for the last time with President Roosevelt, but their conversation dealt mainly with the effects of the use of the bomb, not with the question of whether it ought to be used. Even at this late date, there does not seem to have been any doubt at the highest levels that the bomb would be used against Japan if it would help bring the war to an early end. But on lower levels, and especially among the scientists at the Chicago laboratory, there was considerable reservation about the advisability of using the bomb.

After President Roosevelt's death, it fell to Stimson to brief the new President about the atomic weapon. At a White House meeting on April 25, he outlined the history and status of the program and predicted that "within four months we shall in all probability have completed the most terrible weapon ever known in human history."[9] This meeting, like Stimson's last meeting with Roosevelt, dealt largely

---

[6] "Memo, Groves for CofS, 30 Dec. 1944 sub: Atomic Fission Bombs," printed in *Foreign Relations of the United States: The Conferences at Malta-Yalta, 1945* (Washington: G.P.O., 1955). . . .

[7] Admiral William D. Leahy, *I Was There* (New York: Whittlesey House, 1950), p. 434.

[8] John J. McCloy, *The Challenge to American Foreign Policy* (Cambridge: Harvard University Press, 1953), p. 42. See also . . . James F. Byrnes, *Speaking Frankly* (New York: Harper, 1947), p. 257.

[9] Stimson's memorandum of this meeting is printed in *Harper's*, pp. 99–100.

with the political and diplomatic consequences of the use of such a weapon rather than with the timing and manner of employment, the circumstances under which it would be used, or whether it would be used at all. The answers to these questions depended on factors not yet known. But Stimson recommended, and the President approved, the appointment of a special committee to consider them.

This special committee, known as the Interim Committee, played a vital role in the decision to use the bomb. Secretary Stimson was chairman, and George L. Harrison, President of the New York Life Insurance Company and special consultant in the Secretary's office, took the chair when he was absent. James F. Byrnes, who held no official position at the time, was President Truman's personal representative. Other members were Ralph A. Bard, Under Secretary of the Navy, William L. Clayton, Assistant Secretary of State, and Drs. Vannevar Bush, Karl T. Compton and James B. Conant. Generals Marshall and Groves attended at least one and possibly more of the meetings of the committee.

The work of the Interim Committee, in Stimson's words, "ranged over the whole field of atomic energy, in its political, military, and scientific aspects."[10] During the first meeting the scientific members reviewed for their colleagues the development of the Manhattan Project and described vividly the destructive power of the atomic bomb. They made it clear also that there was no known defense against this kind of attack. Another day was spent with the engineers and industrialists who had designed and built the huge plants at Oak Ridge and Hanford. Of particular concern to the committee was the question of how long it would take another country, particularly the Soviet Union, to produce an atomic bomb. "Much of the discussion," recalled Dr. Oppenheimer, who attended the meeting of June 1 as a member of a scientific panel, "revolved around the question raised by Secretary Stimson as to whether there was any hope at all of using this development to get less barbarous [sic] relations with the Russians."[11]

The work of the Interim Committee was completed June 1, 1945, when it submitted its report to the President, recommending unanimously that:

1. The bomb should be used against Japan as soon as possible.

2. It should be used against a military target surrounded by other buildings.

---

[10] Stimson, *Harper's*, p. 100.
[11] *Oppenheimer Hearings*, pp. 34, 257, testimony of Dr. Oppenheimer and Dr. Compton; Byrnes, *op. cit.*, pp. 260–261; Stimson, *Harper's*, pp. 100–101.

3. It should be used without prior warning of the nature of the weapon.

(One member, Ralph A. Bard, later dissented from this portion of the committee's recommendation.)

"The conclusions of the Committee," wrote Stimson, "were similar to my own, although I reached mine independently. I felt that to extract a genuine surrender from the Emperor and his military advisers, they must be administered a tremendous shock which would carry convincing proof of our power to destroy the empire. Such an effective shock would save many times the number of lives, both American and Japanese, than it would cost."[12]

Among the scientists working on the Manhattan Project were many who did not agree. To them, the "wave of horror and repulsion" that might follow the sudden use of an atomic bomb would more than outweigh its military advantages. "It may be very difficult," they declared, "to persuade the world that a nation which was capable of secretly preparing and suddenly releasing a new weapon, as indiscriminate as the rocket bomb and a thousand times more destructive, is to be trusted in its proclaimed desire of having such weapons abolished by international agreement."[13] The procedure these scientists recommended was, first, to demonstrate the new weapon "before the eyes of representatives of all the United Nations on the desert or a barren island," and then to issue "a preliminary ultimatum" to Japan. If this ultimatum was rejected, and "if the sanction of the United Nations (and of public opinion at home) were obtained," then and only then, said the scientists, should the United States consider using the bomb. "This may sound fantastic," they said, "but in nuclear weapons we have something entirely new in order of magnitude of destructive power, and if we want to capitalize fully on the advantage their possession gives us, we must use new and imaginative methods."[14]

These views, which were forwarded to the Secretary of War on June 11, 1945, were strongly supported by 64 of the scientists in the Chicago Metallurgical Laboratory in a petition sent directly to the President. At about the same time, at the request of Dr. Arthur H. Compton, a poll was taken of the views of more than 150 scientists at the Chicago Laboratory. Five alternatives ranging from all-out use of

---

[12] Stimson, *Harper's*, p. 101. The same idea is expressed by Sir Winston Churchill, *Triumph and Tragedy* (Cambridge: Houghton, 1953), pp. 638–639.

[13] "Report of the Committee on Social and Political Implications," signed by Professor James Franck of the University of Chicago and submitted to the Secretary of War, June 11, 1945, *Bulletin of Atomic Scientists*, May 1, 1946, p. 3.

[14] *Ibid.*, pp. 3–4.

the bomb to "keeping the existence of the bomb a secret" were presented. Of those polled, about two-thirds voted for a preliminary demonstration, either on a military objective or an uninhabited locality; the rest were split on all-out use and no use at all.[15]

These views, and presumably others, were referred by Secretary Stimson to a distinguished Scientific Panel consisting of Drs. Arthur H. Compton, Enrico Fermi, E. O. Lawrence and J. Robert Oppenheimer, all nuclear physicists of the first rank. "We didn't know beans about the military situation," Oppenheimer later said. "We didn't know whether they [the Japanese] could be caused to surrender by other means or whether the invasion [of Japan] was really inevitable. . . . We thought the two overriding considerations were the saving of lives in the war and the effect of our actions on the stability of the postwar world."[16] On June 16 the panel reported that it had studied carefully the proposals made by the scientists but could see no practical way of ending the war by a technical demonstration. Almost regretfully, it seemed, the four members of the panel concluded that there was "no acceptable alternative to direct military use."[17] "Nothing would have been more damaging to our effort," wrote Stimson, ". . . than a warning or demonstration followed by a dud and this was a real possibility." With this went the fear, expressed by Byrnes, that if the Japanese were warned that an atomic bomb would be exploded over a military target in Japan as a demonstration, "they might bring our boys who were prisoners of war to that area."[18] Furthermore, only two bombs would be available by August, the number General Groves estimated would be needed to end the war; these two would have to obtain the desired effect quickly. And no one yet knew, nor would the scheduled ground test in New Mexico prove, whether a bomb dropped from an airplane would explode.[19]

Nor, for that matter, were all those concerned certain that the bomb would work at all, on the ground or in the air. Of these doubters, the greatest was Admiral Leahy, who until the end remained unconvinced. "This is the biggest fool thing we have ever done," he told Truman after Vannevar Bush had explained to the President how the bomb worked. "The bomb will never go off, and I speak as an expert on explosives."[20]

[15] Ibid., p. 1; Leo Szilard, "A Personal History of the Bomb," in The Atlantic Community Faces the Bomb, University of Chicago Roundtable, No. 601, Sept. 25, 1949, p. 15. See also P. M. S. Blackett, Fear, War, and the Bomb (New York: Whittlesey House, 1949), pp. 114–116.

[16] Oppenheimer Hearings, p. 34.

[17] Quoted in Stimson, Harper's, p. 101. The Scientific Panel was established to advise the Interim Committee and its report was made to that body.

[18] Ibid., Byrnes, p. 261.

[19] Ibid., Oppenheimer Hearings, p. 163, testimony of General Groves.

[20] Harry S. Truman, Year of Decisions (Garden City: Doubleday, 1955), p. 11. Leahy in his memoirs frankly admits this error.

Thus, by mid-June 1945, there was virtual unanimity among the President's civilian advisers on the use of the bomb. The arguments of the opponents had been considered and rejected. So far as is known the President did not solicit the views of the military or naval staffs, nor were they offered.

MILITARY CONSIDERATIONS

The military situation on June 1, 1945, when the Interim Committee submitted its recommendations on the use of the atomic bomb, was distinctly favorable to the Allied cause. Germany had surrendered in May and troops from Europe would soon be available for redeployment in the Pacific. Manila had fallen in February; Iwo Jima was in American hands; and the success of the Okinawa invasion was assured. Air and submarine attacks had virtually cut off Japan from the resources of the Indies, and B-29s from the Marianas were pulverizing Japan's cities and factories. The Pacific Fleet had virtually driven the Imperial Navy from the ocean, and planes of the fast carrier forces were striking Japanese naval bases in the Inland Sea. Clearly, Japan was a defeated nation.

Though defeated in a military sense, Japan showed no disposition to surrender unconditionally. And Japanese troops had demonstrated time and again that they could fight hard and inflict heavy casualties even when the outlook was hopeless. Allied plans in the spring of 1945 took these facts into account and proceeded on the assumption that an invasion of the home islands would be required to achieve at the earliest possible date the unconditional surrender of Japan—the announced objective of the war and the basic assumption of all strategic planning.

Other means of achieving this objective had been considered and, in early June, had not yet been entirely discarded. One of these called for the occupation of a string of bases around Japan in order to increase the intensity of air bombardment. Combined with a tight naval blockade, such a course would, many believed, produce the same results as an invasion and at far less cost of lives. "I was unable to see any justification," Admiral Leahy later wrote, ". . . for an invasion of an already thoroughly defeated Japan. I feared the cost would be enormous in both lives and treasure." Admiral King and other senior naval officers agreed. To them it had always seemed, in King's words, "that the defeat of Japan could be accomplished by sea and air power alone, without the necessity of actual invasion of the Japanese home islands by ground troops."[21]

The main arguments for an invasion of Japan—the plans called for an assault against Kyushu (Olympic) on November 1, 1945, and

---

[21] Leahy, *op. cit.*, pp. 384–385. . . .

against Honshu (Coronet) five months later—are perhaps best summarized by General Douglas MacArthur. Writing to the Chief of Staff on April 20, 1945, he declared that this course was the only one that would permit application of the full power of our combined resources —ground, naval and air—on the decisive objective. Japan, he believed, would probably be more difficult to invade the following year. An invasion of Kyushu at an early date would, moreover, place United States forces in the most favorable position for the decisive assault against Honshu in 1946, and would "continue the offensive methods which have proved so successful in Pacific campaigns."[22] Reliance upon bombing alone, MacArthur asserted, was still an unproved formula for success, as was evidenced by the bomber offensive against Germany. The seizure of a ring of bases around Japan would disperse Allied forces even more than they already were, MacArthur pointed out, and (if an attempt was made to seize positions on the China coast) might very well lead to long drawn-out operations on the Asiatic mainland.

Though the Joint Chiefs had accepted the invasion concept as the basis for preparations, and had issued a directive for the Kyushu assault on May 25, it was well understood that the final decision was yet to be made. By mid-June the time had come for such a decision and during that period the Joint Chiefs reviewed the whole problem of Japanese strategy. Finally, on June 18, at a meeting in the White House, they presented the alternatives to President Truman. Also present (according to the minutes) were Secretaries Stimson and Forrestal and Assistant Secretary of War John J. McCloy.[23]

General Marshall presented the case for invasion and carried his colleagues with him, although both Admirals Leahy and King later declared they did not favor the plan. After considerable discussion of casualties and of the difficulties ahead, President Truman made his decision. Kyushu would be invaded as planned and preparations for the landing were to be pushed through to completion. Preparations for the Honshu assault would continue, but no final decision would be made until preparations had reached the point "beyond which there would not be opportunity for a free choice."[24] The program thus approved by Truman called for:

1. Air bombardment and blockade of Japan from bases in Okinawa, Iwo Jima, the Marianas and the Philippines.

---

[22] This message is reproduced in *The Entry of the Soviet Union Into the War Against Japan: Military Plans, 1941–1945* (Department of Defense Press Release, September 1955), pp. 55–57.

[23] Forrestal says in his *Diaries* that neither he nor Stimson was present, while McCloy's definite recollection is that Stimson was present but Forrestal was not. A summary of this meeting is contained in *The Entry of the Soviet Union . . .*, pp. 77–85. . . .

[24] McCloy, *op. cit.*, p. 41. . . .

2. Assault of Kyushu on November 1, 1945, and intensification of blockade and air bombardment.

3. Invasion of the industrial heart of Japan through the Tokyo Plain in central Honshu, tentative target date March 1, 1946.

During the White House meeting of June 18, there was dicussion of the possibility of ending the war by political means. The President displayed a deep interest in the subject and both Stimson and McCloy emphasized the importance of the "large submerged class in Japan who do not favor the present war and whose full opinion and influence had never yet been felt."[25] There was discussion also of the atomic bomb, since everyone present knew about the bomb and the recommendations of the Interim Committee. The suggestion was made that before the bomb was dropped, the Japanese should be warned that the United States had such a weapon. "Not one of the Chiefs nor the Secretary," recalled Mr. McCloy, "thought well of a bomb warning, an effective argument being that no one could be certain, in spite of the assurances of the scientists, that the 'thing would go off.'"[26]

Though the defeat of the enemy's armed forces in the Japanese homeland was considered a prerequisite to Japan's surrender, it did not follow that Japanese forces elsewhere, especially those on the Asiatic mainland, would surrender also. It was to provide for just this contingency, as well as to pin down those forces during the invasion of the home islands, that the Joint Chiefs had recommended Soviet entry into the war against Japan.

Soviet participation was a goal long pursued by the Americans. Both political and military authorities seem to have been convinced from the start that Soviet assistance, conceived in various ways, would shorten the war and lessen the cost. In October 1943, Marshal Stalin had told Cordell Hull, then in Moscow for a conference, that the Soviet Union would eventually declare war on Japan. At the Tehran Conference in November of that year, Stalin had given the Allies formal notice of this intention and reaffirmed it in October 1944. In February 1945, at the Yalta Conference, Roosevelt and Stalin had agreed on the terms of Soviet participation in the Far Eastern war. Thus, by June 1945, the Americans could look forward to Soviet intervention at a date estimated as three months after the defeat of Germany.

But by the summer of 1945 the Americans had undergone a change of heart. Though the official position of the War Department still held that "Russian entry will have a profound military effect in that almost

[25] *The Entry of the Soviet Union. . .*, p. 83. . . .
[26] McCloy, p. 43. . . .

certainly it will materially shorten the war and thus save American lives,"[27] few responsible American officials were eager for Soviet intervention or as willing to make concessions as they had been at an earlier period. What had once appeared extremely desirable appeared less so now that the war in Europe was over and Japan was virtually defeated. President Truman, one official recalled, stated during a meeting devoted to the question of Soviet policy that agreements with Stalin had up to that time been "a one-way street" and that "he intended thereafter to be firm in his dealings with the Russians."[28] And at the June 18 meeting of the Joint Chiefs of Staff with the President, Admiral King had declared that "regardless of the desirability of the Russians entering the war, they were not indispensable and he did not think we should go so far as to beg them to come in."[29] Though the cost would be greater he had no doubt "we could handle it alone."

The failure of the Soviets to abide by agreements at Yalta had also done much to discourage the American desire for further cooperation with them. But after urging Stalin for three years to declare war on Japan, the United States Government could hardly ask him now to remain neutral. Moreover, there was no way of keeping the Russians out even if there had been a will to do so. In Harriman's view, "Russia would come into the war regardless of what we might do."[30]

A further difficulty was that Allied intelligence still indicated that Soviet intervention would be desirable, if not necessary, for the success of the invasion strategy. In Allied intelligence, Japan was portrayed as a defeated nation whose military leaders were blind to defeat. Though her industries had been seriously crippled by air bombardment and naval blockade and her armed forces were critically deficient in many of the resources of war, Japan was still far from surrender. She had ample reserves of weapons and ammunition and an army of 5,000,000 troops, 2,000,000 of them in the home islands. The latter could be expected to put up a strong resistance to invasion. In the opinion of the intelligence experts, neither blockade nor bombing alone would produce unconditional surrender before the date set for invasion. And the invasion itself, they believed, would be costly and possibly prolonged.[31]

According to these intelligence reports, the Japanese leaders were fully aware of their desperate situation but would continue to fight in the hope of avoiding complete defeat by securing a better bargaining

[27] Letter, Stimson to Grew, May 21, 1945, reproduced . . . in *The Entry of the Soviet Union* . . ., pp. 70–71.
[28] Walter Millis, ed., *The Forrestal Diaries* (New York: Viking, 1951), p. 78.
[29] *The Entry of the Soviet Union* . . ., p. 85. . . .
[30] Statement to Leahy quoted in Leahy, p. 369. . . .
[31] *The Entry of the Soviet Union* . . ., pp. 85–88. . . .

position. Allied war-weariness and disunity, or some miracle, they hoped, would offer them a way out. "The Japanese believe," declared an intelligence estimate of June 30, "... that unconditional surrender would be the equivalent of national extinction, and there are as yet no indications that they are ready to accept such terms."[32] It appeared also to the intelligence experts that Japan might surrender at any time "depending upon the conditions of surrender" the Allies might offer. Clearly these conditions, to have any chance of acceptance, would have to include retention of the imperial system.[33]

How accurate were these estimates? Judging from postwar accounts of Japan, they were very close to the truth. Since the defeat at Saipan, when Tojo had been forced to resign, the strength of the "peace party" had been increasing. In September 1944 the Swedish Minister in Tokyo had been approached unofficially, presumably in the name of Prince Konoye, to sound out the Allies on terms for peace. This overture came to naught, as did another the following March. But the Swedish Minister did learn that those who advocated peace in Japan regarded the Allied demand for unconditional surrender as their greatest obstacle.[34]

The Suzuki Cabinet that came into power in April 1945 had an unspoken mandate from the Emperor to end the war as quickly as possible. But it was faced immediately with another problem when the Soviet Government announced it would not renew the neutrality pact after April 1946. The German surrender in May produced another crisis in the Japanese Government and led, after considerable discussion, to a decision to seek Soviet mediation. But the first approach, made on June 3 to Jacob Malik, the Soviet Ambassador, produced no results. Malik was noncommittal and merely said the problem needed further study. Another overture to Malik later in the month also came to naught.

At the end of June, the Japanese finally approached the Soviet Government directly through Ambassador Sato in Moscow, asking that it mediate with the Allies to bring the Far Eastern war to an end. In a series of messages between Tokyo and Moscow, which the Americans intercepted and decoded, the Japanese Foreign Office

---

[32] G-2 memorandum prepared for ODP and quoted in Ray S. Cline, *United States Army in World War II. The War Department. Washington Command Post: The Operations Division* (Washington: Department of the Army, Office of Military History, 1951), p. 347. . . .

[33] *Ibid.* . . .

[34] Robert J. C. Butow, *Japan's Decision to Surrender* (Stanford: Stanford University Press, 1954), pp. 40, 54–57. Other accounts of the situation in Japan are Toshikazu Kase, *Journey to the Missouri* (New Haven: Yale University Press, 1950); U.S. Strategic Bombing Survey, *Japan's Struggle to End the War* (Washington: G.P.O., 1946); Takushiro Hattori, *Complete History of the Greater East Asia War* (Japan: Masu Shobo Co., 1953), v. 4.

outlined the position of the government and instructed Ambassador Sato to make arrangements for a special envoy from the Emperor who would be empowered to make terms for Soviet mediation. Unconditional surrender, he was told, was completely unacceptable, and time was of the essence. But the Russians, on one pretext and another, delayed their answer until mid-July when Stalin and Molotov left for Potsdam. Thus, the Japanese Government had by then accepted defeat and was seeking desperately for a way out; but it was not willing even at this late date to surrender unconditionally, and would accept no terms that did not include the preservation of the imperial system.

Allied intelligence thus had estimated the situation in Japan correctly. Allied invasion strategy had been reexamined and confirmed in mid-June, and the date for the invasion fixed. The desirability of Soviet assistance had been confirmed also and plans for her entry into the war during August could now be made. No decision had been reached on the use of the atomic bomb, but the President's advisers had recommended it. The decision was the President's and he faced it squarely. But before he could make it he would want to know whether the measures already concerted would produce unconditional surrender at the earliest moment and at the lowest cost. If they could not, then he would have to decide whether circumstances warranted employment of a bomb that Stimson had already labeled as "the most terrible weapon ever known in human history."

THE DECISION

Though responsibility for the decision to use the atomic bomb was the President's, he exercised it only after careful study of the recommendations of his senior advisers. Chief among these was the Secretary of War, under whose broad supervision the Manhattan Project had been placed. Already deeply concerned over the cost of the projected invasion, the political effects of Soviet intervention and the potential consequences of the use of the atomic bomb, Stimson sought a course that would avoid all these evils. The difficulty, as he saw it, lay in the requirement for unconditional surrender. It was a phrase that might make the Japanese desperate and lead to a long and unnecessary campaign of attrition that would be extremely costly to both sides. But there was no way of getting around the term; it was firmly rooted in Allied war aims and its renunciation was certain to lead to charges of appeasement.

But if this difficulty could be overcome, would the Japanese respond if terms were offered? The intelligence experts thought so, and the radio intercepts from Tokyo to Moscow bore them out. So far as the Army was concerned there was much to be gained by such a course. Not only might it reduce the enormous cost of the war, but it would also make possible a settlement in the Western Pacific "before too many of our allies are committed there and have made substantial contributions towards the defeat of Japan."[35] In the view of the War Department these aims justified "any concessions which might be attractive to the Japanese, so long as our realistic aims for peace in the Pacific are not adversely affected."[36]

The problem was to formulate terms that would meet these conditions. There was considerable discussion of this problem in Washington in the spring of 1945 by officials in the Department of State and in the War and Navy Departments. Joseph C. Grew, Acting Secretary of State, proposed to the President late in May that he issue a proclamation urging the Japanese to surrender and assuring them that they could keep the Emperor. Though Truman did not act on the suggestion, he thought it "a sound idea" and told Grew to discuss it with his cabinet colleagues and the Joint Chiefs. On June 18, Grew was back with the report that these groups favored the idea, but that there were differences on the timing.

Grew's ideas, as well as those of others concerned, were summarized by Stimson in a long and carefully considered memorandum to the President on July 2. Representing the most informed military and political estimate of the situation at this time, this memorandum constitutes a state paper of the first importance. If any one document can be said to provide the basis for the President's warning to Japan and his final decision to use the atomic bomb, this is it.

The gist of Stimson's argument was that the most promising alternative to the long and costly struggle certain to follow invasion was to warn the Japanese "of what is to come" and to give them an opportunity to surrender. There was, he thought, enough of a chance that such a course would work to make the effort worthwhile. Japan no longer had any allies, her navy was virtually destroyed and she was increasingly vulnerable to air attack and naval blockade. Against her were arrayed the increasingly powerful forces of the Allies, with their "inexhaustible and untouched industrial resources." In these circumstances, Stimson believed the Japanese people would be susceptible to reason if properly approached. "Japan," he pointed out, "is not a nation composed of mad fanatics of an entirely different mentality from ours. On the contrary, she has within the past century shown herself to possess extremely intelligent people. . . ." But any attempt, Stimson added, "to exterminate her armies and her population by gunfire or other means will tend to produce a fusion of race solidity and antipathy. . . ."

---

[35] OPD Compilation for the Potsdam Conference, quoted in Cline, *op. cit.*, p. 345.
[36] Ibid., pp. 345–346.

A warning to Japan, Stimson contended, should be carefully timed. It should come before the actual invasion, before destruction had reduced the Japanese "to fanatical despair" and, if the Soviet Union had already entered the war, before Russian attack had progressed so far.[37] It should also emphasize, Stimson believed, the inevitability and completeness of the destruction ahead and the determination of the Allies to strip Japan of her conquests and to destroy the influence of the military clique. It should be a strong warning and should leave no doubt in Japanese minds that they would have to surrender unconditionally and submit to Allied occupation.

The warning, as Stimson envisaged it, had a double character. While promising destruction and devastation, it was also to hold out hope to the Japanese if they heeded its message. In his memorandum, therefore, Stimson stressed the positive features of the warning and recommended that it include a disavowal of any intention to destroy the Japanese nation or to occupy the country permanently. Once Japan's military clique had been removed from power and her capacity to wage war destroyed, it was Stimson's belief that the Allies should withdraw and resume normal trade relations with the new and peaceful Japanese Government. "I personally think," he declared, "that if in saying this we should add that we do not exclude a constitutional monarchy under her present dynasty, it would substantially add to the chance of acceptance."

Not once in the course of this lengthy memorandum was mention made of the atomic bomb. There was no need to do so. Everyone concerned understood clearly that the bomb was the instrument that would destroy Japan and impress on the Japanese Government the hopelessness of any course but surrender. As Stimson expressed it, the atomic bomb was "the best possible sanction," the single weapon that would convince the Japanese "of our power to destroy the empire."[38]

Though Stimson considered a warning combined with an offer of terms and backed up by the sanction of the atomic bomb as the most promising means of inducing surrender at any early date, there were other courses that some thought might produce the same result. One was the continuation and intensification of air bombardment coupled with surface and underwater blockade. This course had already been considered and rejected as insufficient to produce surrender, though its advocates were by no means convinced that this decision was a wise one. And Stimson himself later justified the use of the bomb on the

[37] In his diary, under the date June 19, Stimson wrote: "The last-chance warning . . . must be given before an actual landing of the ground forces in Japan, and fortunately the plans provide for enough time to bring in the sanctions to our warning in the shape of heavy ordinary bombing attack and an attack of S-1 [the atomic bomb]." Stimson and Bundy, p. 624.

[38] Stimson, *Harper's*, pp. 101, 104.

ground that by November 1 conventional bombardment would have caused greater destruction than the bomb. This apparent contradiction is explained by the fact that the atomic bomb was considered to have a psychological effect entirely apart from the damage wrought.[39]

Nor did Stimson, in his memorandum, consider the effect of the Soviet Union's entry into the war. By itself, this action could not be counted on to force Japan to capitulate, but combined with bombardment and blockade it might do so. At least that was the view of Brigadier-General George A. Lincoln, one of the Army's top planners, who wrote in June that "probably it will take Russian entry into the war, coupled with a landing, or imminent threat of landing, on Japan proper by us, to convince them [the Japanese] of the hopelessness of their position."[40] Why, therefore, was it not possible to issue the warning prior to a Soviet declaration of war against Japan and rely on that event, together with an intensified air bombardment, to produce the desired result? If together they could not secure Japan's surrender, would there not still be time to use the bomb before the scheduled invasion of Kyushu in November?

No final answer to this question is possible with the evidence at hand. But one cannot ignore the fact that some responsible officials feared the political consequences of Soviet intervention and hoped that ultimately it would prove unnecessary. This feeling may unconsciously have made the atom bomb solution more attractive than it might otherwise have been. Some officials may have believed, too, that the bomb could be used as a powerful deterrent to Soviet expansion in Europe, where the Red tide had successfully engulfed Rumania, Bulgaria, Jugoslavia, Czechoslovakia and Hungary. In an interview with three of the top scientists in the Manhattan Project early in June, Mr. Byrnes did not, according to Leo Szilard, argue that the bomb was needed to defeat Japan, but rather that it should be dropped to "make Russia more manageable in Europe."[41]

It has been asserted also that the desire to justify the expenditure of the two billion dollars spent on the Manhattan Project may have disposed some favorably toward the use of the bomb. Already questions had been asked in Congress, and the end of the war would almost certainly bring on a full-scale investigation. What more striking justification of the Manhattan Project than a new weapon that had ended the war in one sudden blow and saved countless American lives? "It was my reaction," wrote Admiral Leahy, "that the scientists and others wanted to make this test because of the vast sums that

[39] *Ibid.*, p. 105.
[40] Quoted in Cline, p. 344.
[41] Szilard, *op. cit.,* pp. 14–15.

had been spent on the project. Truman knew that, and so did other people involved."[42]

This explanation hardly does credit to those involved in the Manhattan Project and not even P. M. S. Blackett, one of the severest critics of the decision to use the bomb, accepted it. "The wit of man," he declared, "could hardly devise a theory of the dropping of the bomb, both more insulting to the American people, or more likely to lead to an energetically pursued Soviet defense policy."[43]

But even if the need to justify these huge expenditures is discounted —and certainly by itself it could not have produced the decision—the question still remains whether those who held in their hands a weapon thought capable of ending the war in one stroke could justify withholding that weapon. Would they not be open to criticism for failing to use every means at their disposal to defeat the enemy as quickly as possible, thereby saving many American lives?

And even at that time there were some who believed that the new weapon would ultimately prove the most effective deterrent to war yet produced. How better to outlaw war forever than to demonstrate the tremendous destructive power of this weapon by using it against an actual target?

By early 1945 the stage had been set for the final decision. Stimson's memorandum had been approved in principle and on July 4 the British had given their consent to the use of the bomb against Japan. It remained only to decide on the terms and timing of the warning. This was the situation when the Potsdam Conference opened on July 17, one day after the bomb had been successfully exploded in a spectacular demonstration at Alamogordo, New Mexico. The atomic bomb was a reality and when the news reached Potsdam there was great excitement among those who were let in on the secret. Instead of the prospect of long and bitter months of fighting the Japanese, there was now a vision, "fair and bright indeed it seemed" to Churchill, "of the end of the whole war in one or two violent shocks."[44]

President Truman's first action was to call together his chief advisers—Byrnes, Stimson, Leahy, Marshall, King and Arnold. "I asked for their opinion whether the bomb should be used," he later wrote. The consensus was that it should.[45] Here at last was the miracle to end the war and solve all the perplexing problems posed by the necessity for invasion. But because no one could tell what effect the bomb might have "physically or psychologically," it was decided to

---

[42] Leahy, p. 441.
[43] Blackett, *op. cit.*, p. 138.
[44] Churchill, *op. cit.*, p. 638.
[45] . . . Truman, *op. cit.*, p. 415. General Eisenhower was at Potsdam and his advice, Truman says, was asked. The various participants differ in their recollections of this meeting. . . .

proceed with the military plans for the invasion.

No one at this time, or later in the conference, raised the question of whether the Japanese should be informed of the existence of the bomb. That question, it will be recalled, had been discussed by the Scientific Panel on June 16 and at the White House meeting with the JCS, the service Secretaries and Mr. McCloy on June 18. For a variety of reasons, including uncertainty as to whether the bomb would work, it had then been decided that the Japanese should not be warned of the existence of the new weapon. The successful explosion of the first bomb on July 17 did not apparently outweigh the reasons advanced earlier for keeping the bomb a secret, and evidently none of the men involved thought the question needed to be reviewed. The Japanese would learn of the atomic bomb only when it was dropped on them.

The secrecy that had shrouded the development of the atomic bomb was torn aside briefly at Potsdam, but with no visible effect. On July 24, on the advice of his chief advisers, Truman informed Marshal Stalin "casually" that the Americans had "a new weapon of unusual destructive force." "The Russian Premier," he recalled, "showed no special interest. All he said was that he was glad to hear it and hoped we would make 'good use of it against the Japanese.'"[46] One cannot but wonder whether the Marshal was preoccupied at the moment or simulating a lack of interest.

On the military side, the Potsdam Conference developed nothing new. The plans already made were noted and approved. Even at this late stage the question of the bomb was divorced entirely from military plans and the final report of the conference accepted as the main effort the invasion of the Japanese home islands. November 15, 1946, was accepted as the planning date for the end of the war against Japan.

During the conference, Stalin told Truman about the Japanese overtures—information that the Americans already had. The Marshal spoke of the matter also to Churchill, who discussed it with Truman, suggesting cautiously that some offer be made to Japan. "Mr. Stimson, General Marshall, and the President," he later wrote, "were evidently searching their hearts, and we had no need to press them. We knew of course that the Japanese were ready to give up all conquests made in the war." That same night, after dining with Stalin and Truman, the Prime Minister wrote that the Russians intended to attack Japan soon after August 8—perhaps within two weeks after that date.[47] Truman presumably received the same information, confirming Harry Hopkin's report of his conversation with Stalin in Moscow in May.

[46] Truman, p. 416. . . .
[47] Truman, p. 396; Churchill, p. 642. See also Byrnes, p. 205; Leahy, p. 420.

All that remained now was to warn Japan and give her an opportunity to surrender. In this matter Stimson's and Grew's views, as outlined in the memorandum of July 2, were accepted, but apparently on the advice of the former Secretary of State Cordell Hull it was decided to omit any reference to the Emperor. Hull's view, solicited by Byrnes before his departure for Potsdam, was that the proposal smacked of appeasement and "seemed to guarantee continuance not only of the Emperor but also of the feudal privileges of a ruling caste." And should the Japanese reject the warning, the proposal to retain the imperial system might well encourage resistance and have "terrible political repercussions" in the United States. For these reasons he recommended that no statement about the Emperor be made until "the climax of Allied bombing and Russia's entry into the war."[48] Thus, the final terms offered to the Japanese in the Potsdam Declaration on July 26 made no mention of the Emperor or of the imperial system. Neither did the declaration contain any reference to the atom bomb but simply warned the Japanese of the consequences of continued resistance. Only those already familiar with the weapon could have read the references to inevitable and complete destruction as a warning of atomic warfare.

The receipt of the Potsdam Declaration in Japan led to frantic meetings to decide what should be done. It was finally decided not to reject the note but to await the results of the Soviet overture. At this point, the military insisted that the government make some statement to the people, and on July 28 Premier Suzuki declared to the press that Japan would ignore the declaration, a statement that was interpreted by the Allies as a rejection.

To the Americans the rejection of the Potsdam Declaration confirmed the view that the military was still in control of Japan and that only a decisive act of violence could remove them. The instrument for such action lay at hand in the atomic bomb; events now seemed to justify its use. But in the hope that the Japanese might still change their minds, Truman held off orders on the use of the bomb for a few days. Only silence came from Tokyo, for the Japanese were waiting for a reply from the Soviet Government, which would not come until the return of Stalin and Molotov from Potsdam on August 6. Prophetically, Foreign Minister Tojo wrote Sato on August 2, the day the Potsdam Conference ended, that he could not afford to lose a single day in his efforts to conclude arrangements with the Russians "if we were to end the war before the assault on our mainland."[49] By that time, President Truman had already decided on the use of the bomb.

[48] *Memoirs of Cordell Hull* (New York: Macmillan, 1948), v. 2, p. 1593.
[49] Kase, *op. cit.*, p. 222.

Preparations for dropping the two atomic bombs produced thus far had been under way for some time. The components of the bombs had been sent by cruiser to Tinian in May and the fissionable material was flown out in mid-July. The B-29s and crews were ready and trained, standing by for orders, which would come through the Commanding General, U. S. Army Strategic Air Forces in the Pacific, General Spaatz. Detailed arrangements and schedules were completed and all that was necessary was to issue orders.

At General Arnold's insistence, the responsibility for selecting the particular target and fixing the exact date and hour of the attack was assigned to the field commander, General Spaatz. In orders issued on July 25 and approved by Stimson and Marshall, Spaatz was ordered to drop the "first special bomb as soon as weather will permit visual bombing after about 3 August 1945 on one of the targets: Hiroshima, Kokura, Niigata, and Nagasaki." He was instructed also to deliver a copy of this order personally to MacArthur and Nimitz. Weather was the critical factor because the bomb had to be dropped by visual means, and Spaatz delegated to his chief of staff, Major-General Curtis E. LeMay, the job of deciding when the weather was right for this most important mission.

From the dating of the order to General Spaatz it has been argued that President Truman was certain the warning would be rejected and had fixed the date for the bombing of Hiroshima even before the issuance of the Potsdam Declaration. But such an argument ignores the military necessities. For operational reasons, the orders had to be issued in sufficient time "to set the military wheels in motion." In a sense, therefore, the decision was made on July 25. It would stand unless the President changed his mind. "I had made the decision," wrote Truman in 1955. "I also instructed Stimson that the order would stand unless I notified him that the Japanese reply to our ultimatum was acceptable."[50] The rejection by the Japanese of the Potsdam Declaration confirmed the orders Spaaz had already received.

THE JAPANESE SURRENDER

On Tinian and Guam, preparations for dropping the bomb had been completed by August 3. The original plan was to carry out the operation on August 4, but General LeMay deferred the attack because of bad weather over the target. On August 5 the forecasts were favorable and he gave the word to proceed with the mission the following day. At 0245 on August 6, the bomb-carrying plane was airborne. Six and a half hours later the bomb was released over Hiroshima, Japan's eighth largest city, to explode 50 seconds later at a height of about 2,000 feet. The age of atomic warfare had opened.

[50] Truman, pp. 420–421.

Aboard the cruiser *Augusta* on his way back to the United States, President Truman received the news by radio. That same day a previously prepared release from Washington announced to the world that an atomic bomb had been dropped on Hiroshima and warned the Japanese that if they did not surrender they could expect "a rain of ruin from the air, the like of which has never been seen on this earth."[51]

On August 7, Ambassador Sato in Moscow received word at last that Molotov would see him the next afternoon. At the appointed hour he arrived at the Kremlin, full of hope that he would receive a favorable reply to the Japanese proposal for Soviet mediation with the Allies to end the war. Instead, he was handed the Soviet declaration of war, effective on August 9, Thus, three months to the day after Germany's surrender, Marshal Stalin had lived up to his promise to the Allies.

Meanwhile, President Truman had authorized the use of the second bomb—the last then available. The objective was Kokura, the date August 9. But the plane carrying the bomb failed to make its run over the primary target and hit the secondary target, Nagasaki, instead. The next day Japan sued for peace.

The close sequence of events between August 6 and 10, combined with the fact that the bomb was dropped almost three months before the scheduled invasion of Kyushu and while the Japanese were trying desperately to get out of the war, has suggested to some that the bombing of Hiroshima had a deeper purpose than the desire to end the war quickly. This purpose, it is claimed, was nothing less than a desire to forestall Soviet intervention into the Far Eastern war. Else why this necessity for speed? Certainly nothing in the military situation seemed to call for such hasty action. But if the purpose was to forestall Soviet intervention, then there was every reason for speed. And even if the Russians could not be kept out of the war, at least they would be prevented from making more than a token contribution to victory over Japan. In this sense it may be argued that the bomb proved a success, for the war ended with the United States in full control of Japan.

This theory leaves several matters unexplained. In the first place, the Americans did not know the exact date on which the Soviet Union would declare war but believed it would be within a week or two of August 8. If they had wished to forestall a Soviet declaration of war, then they could reasonably have been expected to act sooner than they did. Such close timing left little if any margin for error. Secondly, had the United States desired above everything else to keep the Russians out, it could have responded to one of several unofficial Japanese overtures, or made the Potsdam Declaration more attractive to Japan. Certainly the failure to put a time limit on the declaration suggests

[51] The statement is published in *The New York Times*, August 7, 1945. . . .

that speed was not of the essence in American calculations. Finally, the date and time of the bombing were left to Generals Spaatz and LeMay, who certainly had no way of knowing Soviet intentions. Bad weather or any other untoward incident could have delayed the attack a week or more.

There is reason to believe that the Russians at the last moved more quickly than they had intended. In his conversations with Harry Hopkins in May 1945 and at Potsdam, Marshal Stalin had linked Soviet entry with negotiations then in progress with Chinese representatives in Moscow. When these were completed, he had said, he would act. On August 8 these negotiations were still in progress.

Did the atomic bomb accomplish its purpose? Was it, in fact, as Stimson said, "the best possible sanction" after Japan rejected the Potsdam Declaration? The sequence of events argues strongly that it was, for bombs were dropped on the 6th and 9th, and on the 10th Japan surrendered. But in the excitement over the announcement of the first use of an atomic bomb and then of Japan's surrender, many overlooked the significance of the Soviet Union's entry into the war on the 9th. The first bomb had produced consternation and confusion among the leaders of Japan, but no disposition to surrender. The Soviet declaration of war, though not entirely unexpected, was a devastating blow and, by removing all hope of Soviet mediation, gave the advocates of peace their first opportunity to come boldly out into the open. When Premier Suzuki arrived at the palace on the morning of the 9th, he was told that the Emperor believed Japan's only course now was to accept the Potsdam Declaration. The militarists could and did minimize the effects of the bomb, but they could not evade the obvious consequences of Soviet intervention, which ended all hope of dividing their enemies and securing softer peace terms.

In this atmosphere, the leaders of Japan held a series of meetings on August 9, but were unable to come to agreement. In the morning came word of the fate of Nagasaki. This additional disaster failed to resolve the issues between the military and those who advocated surrender. Finally the Emperor took the unprecedented step of calling an Imperial Conference, which lasted until 3 o'clock the next morning. When it, too, failed to produce agreement the Emperor told his ministers that he wished the war brought to an end. The constitutional significance of this action is difficult for Westerners to comprehend, but it resolved the crisis and produced in the cabinet a formal decision to accept the Potsdam Declaration, provided it did not prejudice the position of the Emperor.

What finally forced the Japanese to surrender? Was it air bombardment, naval power, the atomic bomb or Soviet entry? The United States Strategic Bombing Survey concluded that Japan would have surrendered by the end of the year, without invasion and without the atomic bomb. Other equally informed opinion maintained that it was the atomic bomb that forced Japan to surrender. "Without its use," Dr. Karl T. Compton asserted, "the war would have continued for many months."[52] Admiral Nimitz believed firmly that the decisive factor was "the complete impunity with which the Pacific Fleet pounded Japan," and General Arnold claimed it was air bombardment that had brought Japan to the verge of collapse.[53] But Major-General Claire Chennault, wartime air commander in China, maintained that Soviet entry into the Far Eastern war brought about the surrender of Japan and would have done so "even if no atomic bombs had been dropped."[54]

It would be a fruitless task to weigh accurately the relative importance of all the factors leading to the Japanese surrender. There is no doubt that Japan had been defeated by the summer of 1945, if not earlier. But defeat did not mean that the military clique had given up; the Army intended to fight on and had made elaborate preparations for the defense of the homeland. Whether air bombardment and naval blockade or the threat of invasion would have produced an early surrender and averted the heavy losses almost certain to accompany the actual landings in Japan is a moot question. Certainly they had a profound effect on the Japanese position. It is equally impossible to assert categorically that the atomic bomb alone or Soviet intervention alone was the decisive factor in bringing the war to an end. All that can be said on the available evidence is that Japan was defeated in the military sense by August 1945 and that the bombing of Hiroshima, followed by the Soviet Union's declaration of war and then the bombing of Nagasaki and the threat of still further bombing, acted as catalytic agents to produce the Japanese decision to surrender. Together they created so extreme a crisis that the Emperor himself, in an unprecedented move, took matters into his own hands and ordered his ministers to surrender. Whether any other set of circumstances would have resolved the crisis and produced the final decision to surrender is a question history cannot yet answer.

[52] Compton, "If the Atomic Bomb Had Not Been Dropped," *Atlantic Monthly*, December, 1946, p. 54.
[53] H. H. Arnold, *Global Mission* (New York: Harper, 1949), p. 598. . . .
[54] *The New York Times*, August 15, 1945. . . .

The Korean War

MORTON H. HALPERIN

FOREIGN-POLICY OBJECTIVES

Prior to the outbreak of the Korean War, the United States believed that a major objective of the Soviet Union was to expand the area under its control. Thus, in responding to the North Korean attack— which had not been anticipated—American objectives were developed in the framework of the belief that the attack was part of a general plan for expansion and perhaps a prelude to general war. The United States sought to prevent the success of this Communist attempt to expand by the use of force in the belief that allowing the Soviets to succeed in Korea would encourage aggression elsewhere. General Omar Bradley expressed this purpose at the MacArthur hearings in describing Korea as "a preventive limited war aimed at avoiding World War III."[1] President Harry Truman later described his objectives in intervening in the Korean War in similar terms:

> Communism was acting in Korea just as Hitler, Mussolini, and the Japanese had acted ten, fifteen, and twenty years earlier. I felt certain that if South Korea was allowed to fall Communist leaders would be emboldened to override nations closer to our own shores. If the Communists were permitted to force their way into the Republic of Korea without opposition from the free world, no small nation would have the courage to resist threats and aggression by stronger Communist neighbors. If this was allowed to go unchallenged it would mean a third world war, just as similar incidents had brought on the second world war.[2]

The defense of Korea was partly motivated by the feeling that the action was necessary to convince the West Europeans that the United States would come to their aid. The Administration was wary of committing its military power, thereby leaving itself exposed to Soviet

From *Limited War in the Nuclear Age* by Morton H. Halperin, pp. 39–58. Reprinted by permission of the author. Some footnotes have been omitted.

[1] Hearings before the Committee on Armed Services and the Committee on Foreign Relations, *Military Situation in the Far East*, U.S. Senate, 82nd Congress, 1st Session, 1951, five parts, p. 154.

[2] Harry S. Truman, *Memoirs,* Vol. II: *Years of Trial and Hope.* Garden City, N.Y.: Doubleday & Co., 1956, p. 333.

aggression in Europe. During the latter stages of the Korean War, in fact, the major American buildup occurred in Europe and not in the Far East. The Administration was also aware of the danger of splitting the NATO alliance in a dispute over Far Eastern policy. A major objective throughout the war was to prevent adverse repercussions in Europe while using the episode to strengthen NATO and build up its military capability. America's NATO allies, particularly the British, constantly applied pressure on the United States to prevent expansion of the war and to bring it swiftly to a conclusion. Following an almost inadvertent reference by President Truman at a press conference to the possibility of using atomic weapons, British Prime Minister Clement Attlee flew to the United States to confer with Truman and to propose the seeking of a cease fire in Korea to be followed by the admission of Communist China to the United Nations. Partly because the defense effort in Korea was carried on under UN auspices, the United States felt obliged constantly to consult its allies on policy and was influenced by their continuous efforts to halt the expansion of the war and to bring about its conclusion.

Soviet objectives were more closely related to the situation in the Far East. The Soviets were interested in the capture of South Korea for its own sake and probably expected a relatively quick and easy North Korean victory. In addition, the Soviets probably hoped to prevent Japan's alignment with the Western powers. Allen Whiting has suggested the nature of the Soviet Far Eastern objective:

> In view of the multiple pressures directed at Japanese foreign policy, the Communist leaders may have conceived the Korean War as serving ends beyond the immediate control of the peninsula. Military victories in Taiwan and Korea could be heralded as ushering in the Communist era in Asia, and as demonstrating the impotence of America's "puppets," Chiang Kai-shek and Syngman Rhee. The resultant effect upon Japan might swing opportunistic groups behind existing neutralist opposition to Yoshida and prevent his supporting American policy.[3]

This interpretation of Soviet strategy in the Korean War was offered by John Foster Dulles right after the North Korean attack. Dulles, who was at the time the State Department planner for the Japanese Peace Treaty, suggested that the Korean attack may have been motivated in part by a desire to block American efforts to make Japan a full member of the free world. He conjectured also that the attack may have been ordered because the Communists could not tolerate the "hopeful, attractive Asiatic experiment in democracy" that was under way in South Korea.[4]

---

[3] Allen S. Whiting, *China Crosses the Yalu: The Decision to Enter the Korean War.* (New York: Macmillan Co., 1960), p. 37.

[4] *New York Times,* July 2, 1950.

The Chinese objectives in entering the Korean War were also based on general political considerations, but of a defensive nature. According to Whiting the Chinese also hoped to influence the course of United States-Japanese relations. Moreover they were worried about the loss of prestige they would suffer if they allowed the Western "imperialists" to march unhindered to their borders. And they were perhaps most concerned with the beneficial effects of United Nations success in Korea on the many opponents of the Communist regime still active and on Taiwan. Whiting concluded:

> In sum, it was not the particular problems of safeguarding electric-power supplies in North Korea or the industrial base in Manchuria that aroused Peking to military action. Instead, the final step seems to have been prompted in part by general concern over the range of opportunities within China that might be exploited by a determined, powerful enemy on China's doorstep. At the least, a military response might deter the enemy from further adventures. At the most, it might succeed in inflicting sufficient damage to force the enemy to compromise his objectives and to accede to some of Peking's demands. Contrary to some belief, the Chinese Communist leadership did not enter the Korean War either full of self-assertive confidence or for primarily expansionist goals.[5]

The Chinese apparently entered the war with the aim of saving at least some of North Korea. Their minimal objective was to preserve the identity of Communist North Korea rather than its total territorial integrity.

In an effort to secure the political effects discussed, American battlefield objectives and war-termination conditions underwent considerable fluctuation during the course of the war. When the United States first intervened, its objective was simply to restore peace and the South Korean border. Very early in the war and after the Chinese intervention, the United States considered a total withdrawal from Korea.[6] Later its battlefield objective expanded to include the unification of Korea. But in the end, the United States accepted a truce line which closely approximated the *status quo ante*. As Richard Neustadt has pointed out, Truman's original decision to seek the unification of Korea failed to take into account the political-effects objectives that the United States was pursuing, and in the end the recognition of this forced the abandonment of the unification effort.

> Had the unification of Korea been Truman's dearest object, its announcement as a war aim would have been another matter. But it was among the least of the objectives on his mind. In July and August 1950, in

⁵ Whiting, *op. cit.*, p. 159.
⁶ Courtney Whitney, *MacArthur: His Rendezvous with History*. New York: Alfred A. Knopf, 1956, pp. 429–431, 438.

December after Chinese intervention, in his struggles with MacArthur, and thereafter through his last two years of office, his behavior leaves no doubt about the many things he wanted more than that. He wanted to affirm that the UN was not a League of Nations, that aggression would be met with counterforce, that "police actions" were well worth their cost, that the "lesson of the 1930's" had been learned. He wanted to avoid "the wrong war, in the wrong place, at the wrong time," as General Bradley put it—and any "War," if possible. He wanted NATO strengthened fast, both militarily and psychologically. He wanted the United States rearmed without inflation, and prepared, thereafter, to sustain a level of expenditure for military forces and for foreign aid far higher than had seemed achievable before Korea.[7]

Once the Soviets recognized that they could not easily secure their objective of demonstrating American weakness and unwillingness to use force, they seemed to have abandoned the battlefield objective of capturing all of Korea. They may have been willing to accept an end to the war with part or perhaps even all of North Korea in Western hands, and ultimately settled for a virtual restoration of the *status quo ante*.

RISK OF CENTRAL WAR

The Korean War was fought before the era of intercontinental ballistic missiles and fusion weapons. Thus, while both sides could have expanded the war quickly and decisively, there was not the danger that now exists of a sudden unleashing of nuclear missiles which within an hour could destroy a large part of both the United States and the Soviet Union.

Even without this threat of a mutually devastating strategic exchange, the danger of a world war was nevertheless present, and both sides seem to have been determined to prevent its occurrence. Truman has reported that the major American aim in Korea was to prevent a third world war. The Russian decision to remain out of the war seemed to be partly motivated by a fear of igniting a global war. In this situation where neither side could gain a decisive advantage by going first, both sides seemed to recognize that, no matter who started the global war, both would suffer major losses. Though the United States could have attacked the Soviet Union with its very limited stockpile of atomic weapons, it probably could not have presented a Soviet ground attack in Western Europe which might have resulted in Communist domination of the European continent. The Soviets had almost no capacity to attack the United States and could not have prevented an American attack on the Soviet Union. Though both sides avoided forcing the other into starting a global war, neither was

⁷ Richard E. Neustadt, *Presidential Power: The Politics of Leadership.* New York: John Wiley and Sons, 1960, p. 126.

constantly concerned with the possibility of "preemption" by its adversary.

The United States, however, was concerned that the Korean War should not lead it to expend those military capabilities which were considered an important deterrent to general war. In Korea the United States was employing the troops and the matériel which it felt were necessary to deter general war. At the MacArthur hearings, Air Force General Vandenburg rejected a senator's suggestion that the United States should commit a major part of the American Air Force to the Korean War effort. He argued instead that the United States must get a cease fire

> without endangering that one potential that we have which has kept the peace so far, which the United States Air Force; which, if utilized in a manner to do what you are suggesting, would [sic], because of attrition and because the size of the Air Force is such and the size of the air force industry is such that we could not still be that deterrent to [general] war which we are today.[8]

Soviet action during the war, including the failure to commit combat forces, suggests that they shared with the United States the desire to avoid a global war.

IMAGES OF THE ROLE OF FORCE

The North Korean attack on South Korea suggested the willingness of the Communists to seek a limited objective by a limited use of force. The Soviets probably intended to seize South Korea with the use of North Korean forces and then to halt their military operations. When the United States intervened, they recognized their miscalculation of American intentions, but proceeded on the assumption that American intervention need not lead to world war. The attack into South Korea, moreover, seems to have been motivated by the Soviet compulsion to fill power vacuums. In view of the specific United States declaration that South Korea was outside its defense perimeter, the Soviets reasonably could have counted on a quick and easy victory by the North Koreans. But, while Communist conduct during the war reflected a doctrine that included the limited use of military force and limited objectives, neither the Chinese nor the Russians seemed to have any idea of the optimum methods of communicating intentions and capabilities to the other side in the course of such a war.

American images of the role of force, on the other hand, seem to have been much less hospitable to the limitation of warfare. It would appear that the United States had not foreseen the possibility of Soviet

[8] *Military Situation in the Far East, op. cit.,* p. 1385.

military action in South Korea or any other local area unconnected with a general Soviet military offensive. The result was the American decision not to prepare for the defense of South Korea in view of the low estimate of its value in a general war. Thus the decision of June 1950 to defend South Korea was not based on a reestimate of South Korea's military importance, but on recognition that something had occurred for which American military doctrine had not been prepared. In making its policy decisions throughout the war, the United States was operating without any general theoretical notions of the nature of local war in the atomic age, and its decisions were probably affected by the lack of such theory.

Each side's image of the other's intentions influenced its decisions. The Soviets clearly underestimated the likelihood of American intervention. In the Soviet view American action in withdrawing its troops from Korea and the American declarations that it would defend South Korea only as part of its United Nations obligations had meant that the United States would not in fact defend South Korea. The Soviets failed to anticipate the partly moral and partly political American reaction to aggression. They were insensitive to the importance that the United States would attach to repelling "illegal" aggression, as opposed to less clear-cut violations of international law.

The American decision to intervene in Korea and the subsequent decisions were also based on and influenced by estimates of Soviet intentions.[9] In assessing the motives of the North Korean attack, American policy makers gave consideration and, to some extent, credence to five different interpretations, as follows:

1. The "diversionary move" interpretation. In view of the number of other areas, particularly Western Europe, that appeared more militarily significant than South Korea, the North Korean attack was seen as a diversionary move, aimed to draw American resources away from the areas where they were most important. Truman reports that he shared this view in part and was determined not to leave Europe vulnerable to Soviet aggression.

2. The "soft-spot probing" interpretation. By this image of Soviet doctrine, the Soviet compulsion to fill power vacuums had led to the attack on South Korea which had been abandoned by the United States and which was clearly incapable of defending itself.

3. The "testing" interpretation. This was the view that seemed to influence most Truman's image of the North Korean attack. It recalled the progress of Hitler's aggressive moves and asserted that the

    [9] This discussion of the American image of Soviet doctrine is based on Alexander L. George, "American Policy-Making and the North Korean Aggression," *World Politics,* VII (January 1955), pp. 209–232.

North Korean attack should be seen as a prelude to attacks in other areas if that aggression were allowed to succeed. This view differed from the "soft-spot probing" interpretation in its assumption that the Communists' success in Korea would encourage them to attempt aggression in the other areas where Western defense capabilities were far stronger. In short the purpose of the Korean attack was to probe the firmness of Western intentions, and not simply to fill a power vacuum.

4. The "demonstration" interpretation. By this interpretation, the Soviets were mainly concerned with demonstrating their own strength and American weakness in order to promote, on a long-term basis, important shifts in political allegiance throughout the world.

5. The "Soviet-Far-East-strategy" interpretation. This interpretation put emphasis on the idea, already discussed, that the Soviets hoped to prevent the entrance of Japan into the Western camp and to pave the way for further Communist expansion in the Far East.

. . . The inclination of American policy makers toward the "testing" interpretation of Soviet doctrine—in which the Korean attack was equated with Hitler's early expansionist moves—may have reinforced the likelihood that the United States would intervene in Korea. If the "soft-spot probing" interpretation of Soviet conduct had been accepted instead, the United States might have been more prone to cede South Korea while taking steps to prevent the existence of power vacuums elsewhere. The belief that successful aggression would embolden the Soviets made the defense of South Korea seem crucial.

DOMESTIC POLITICAL PRESSURES

During the Korean War the Truman administration continued to pursue its domestic political goals. Despite the war there was politics-as-usual on both sides of the political fence. The President was constantly concerned with promoting his Fair Deal program, consolidating the position of the Democratic Party, strengthening his northern and western liberal support in Congress, and calming the political crises raised by such men as Senator Joseph McCarthy. Nor was the Administration immune to criticism from the Republican Party, which felt that it was possible, necessary, and desirable to attack the Administration's conduct as well as to question the basic concept of limiting war.

After the MacArthur hearings, a Republican minority report declared:

> We believe that a policy of victory must be announced to the American people in order to restore unity and confidence. It is too much to expect

that our people will accept a limited war. Our policy must be to win. Our strategy must be devised to bring about decisive victory.[10]

These few sentences suggest a number of important assumptions about the nature of wartime politics. The first is the notion that the unity of the American people can be achieved only with a declaration that victory is the goal. A further implication is that, after such a declaration, the method of achieving a battlefield victory becomes a "military" problem that is beyond the realm of partisan domestic politics. On the other hand, once the government admits that there are other political considerations that affect and moderate the goal of a strictly military victory, then, according to this Republican statement, it is legitimate to criticize the particular policy adopted. Unity will come only when the country is asked to back an absolute goal. If there is no such goal, then the opposition has a duty to examine and critically appraise the war effort.

Congress, as a whole, also felt itself free to criticize. The hearings into the firing of General Douglas MacArthur were striking in that they required the Administration, *during the war,* to justify its conduct and to explain what it hoped to accomplish in the war and how the war was being conducted, as well as to explicate a host of particulars which must have been of as much interest to the Communists as they were to the senators across the table. Actually the Chinese and the Russians. However, the senators' questions at hearings provided a unique and invaluable opportunity for the Administration to communicate what it wanted to communicate to this hearing did not have that motivation. Congress forced the Administration to discuss its strategy and objectives during the war without any apparent consideration of the effect this would have on the American war effort.

The quotation from the report of the Republican senators also reflects the then still strong American opposition to fighting a local war. The Senators stated flatly that the American people would not accept a strategy of limiting war, and indicated their rejection of the strategy as well. The implication is that during a local war the American government will be subjected to attacks from the political opposition, from Congress, and from public citizens on two grounds: the legitimacy of fighting such a war and the particular strategy employed in the war.

The general public seems to have shared the Republican senators' dissatisfaction with the course of the Korean War, at least in its later stages. On the other hand, the public apparently approved the decision of the Eisenhower administration to end the war short of victory as it had approved the initial decision to intervene. The public's

---

[10] *Military Situation in the Far East, op. cit.,* p. 3590.

frustration with the continuing war probably added to the margin of Eisenhower's victory in 1952; his ending the war enhanced the Republican image as the party of peace and increased the Eisenhower plurality in 1956. The Korean War does not seem to have had a major or lasting impact on popular political attitudes.[11] In this respect, American political leaders seem to have overestimated the effect of the war on the voting public. Korea is taken as demonstrating—as to some extent it did—that extended local wars which cannot be decisively won are not popular with the American public. Leading the United States into a major local war or expanding the war without securing a clear victory is likely to be perceived as a political liability; ending a war on almost any terms may be a political asset.

All these domestic pressures undoubtedly influenced the manner in which the Truman administration conducted its Korean operations, both by hampering its freedom of action and by increasing the costs of various actions.

ATOMIC WEAPONS

The most dramatic limit on the Korean War was that neither side used its atomic weapons. According to Brodie there were four reasons why these weapons were not used by the United States:[12]

1. The Joint Chiefs of Staff and civilian policy makers continued to feel that the war in Korea was basically a Soviet feint. There was, therefore, a strong case for conserving the then relatively limited stockpile of atomic weapons for the principal war which, they thought, would come in Europe. Their fear was not that the employment of nuclear weapons would lead to an expansion of the war and a Soviet attack on Europe, but rather that Korea was deliberately designed as a decoy to get the United States to exhaust its nuclear stockpile and conventional military resources so that the Soviets could later attack with impunity in Europe. It was the desire, then, to save resources and not the fear of provoking the enemy that was one of the main causes of the American decision not to use nuclear weapons in Korea.

2. American policy was also affected by the reports of local Air Force commanders that there were no suitable targets for atomic weapons in Korea. While the impact of this view was considerable, it apparently reflected an uninformed attitude about the possible uses of atomic weapons. Commanders in the field came to think, for example, that atomic bombs were of little use against bridges, a belief which Brodie explained as follows:

---

[11] Angus Campbell et. al., *The American Voter*. New York: John Wiley and Sons, 1960, pp. 49, 50, 527, 546, 555.

[12] Bernard Brodie, *Strategy in the Missile Age*. Princeton, N.J.: Princeton University Press, 1959.

This odd idea probably resulted from a mis-reading of the results at Hiroshima and Nagasaki. Some bridges were indeed badly damaged at those places and some were not, but for the latter it was generally forgotten that a bridge only 270 feet from ground zero at Hiroshima was actually 2,100 feet from the point of explosion, and also that it received its blast effect from above rather than from the side.[13]

Nuclear weapons were still relatively new and had not been extensively tested, and it is probable that commanders in the field were too busy to search out potential targets for nuclear weapons.

3. American allies, particularly the British, were strongly and emotionally opposed to the use of atomic weapons in the Korean War. This pressure from allies strengthened America's own anxieties and moral doubts about again using these weapons.

4. A subsidiary reason for the failure to use atomic weapons in the Korean War was the fear of the retaliatory employment by the Soviets of the few atomic weapons in their possession against Pusan or Japan, despite the American near monopoly of these weapons. Brodie doubts, however, whether this fear played a conscious part in the relevant decisions.

The first two motives just discussed will not be important in the future. The American stockpile of tactical nuclear weapons is now so great that military commanders may urge their use precisely because they are a nonscarce military resource, and certainly no argument can be made that they should not be used because they are scarce. Military officers now have a much better understanding of the capabilities of nuclear weapons, which, moreover, now come in much smaller packages. Thus it will be clear to military commanders that there would be suitable targets for their use in any conceivable future major limited war. While we can expect continued pressure from our allies against the use of nuclear weapons, certain allies might advocate their use in some situations. There will, however, be other international political pressures—for example, from the uncommitted or neutral states—against nuclear weapons, and the possibility of a Soviet nuclear response will be a much more important determinant of the decision.

We know much less about the details of the Russian decision not to use atomic weapons in Korea. The Russians seemed determined not to supply any matériel to the forces fighting in Korea which could clearly be labeled as having been supplied by them after the war began. This would certainly be the case with atomic weapons.[14] In addition, the

---

[13] *Ibid.,* p. 319n.
[14] It was also true, however, of the MIGs which the Soviets supplied probably with Russian pilots.

Soviet stockpile of such weapons was so small that its use in a localized military encounter might have seemed wasteful.

The limit observed by both sides seems not to have resulted from an attempt—or even an awareness of the need—to bargain with the enemy. However the Soviets were probably more restrained than the United States by the fear that the initiation of nuclear attacks would be met by a response in kind.[15]

The Chinese Communists seem genuinely to have feared the possibility of the American use of atomic weapons when they intervened in the Korean War. According to Whiting the Chinese felt that a nuclear response was a real possibility; intervention was considered risky and every effort was made to delay it and to minimize its consequences. The extent of this Chinese concern was reflected both in its shelter-building program and in domestic Chinese Communist propaganda. But Peking was reassured by the three-week testing period of relatively small Chinese intervention which revealed that United States aircraft, though authorized to bomb the Korean ends of the Yalu bridges, were forbidden to venture into Chinese territory.

The background of the limit on the use of atomic weapons in the Korean War, then, suggests a failure of both sides to understand what the other side was likely to do and what the other side's fears and goals were. It also suggests that, to a large extent, the determination of limits is based on considerations other than those that result from the battlefield interaction. Some of the other limiting points established in the war reveal the same pattern.

CHINESE INTERVENTION

One of the major expansions of the Korean War was the decision of the United Nations Command to cross the thirty-eighth parallel. This decision was based partly on the military consideration that one could not stand by and allow the enemy forces to regroup for renewed attack just beyond the border, but also on political grounds—when the battlefield conditions changed in its favor, the United States decided to pursue the unification of Korea by military means. In crossing the parallel the United States was aware of the risk that it might trigger Chinese Communist intervention, and tried by reassuring statements to prevent it. But it apparently underestimated the Chinese reaction and, at the same time, failed to develop a concurrent strategy which, by retaliatory threats or other sanctions, could succeed in preventing Chinese intervention. As Whiting has suggested the threat to use atomic weapons on the Chinese mainland if the Chinese intervened

---

[15] However, if the use of atomic weapons had been confined to the Korean theater—that is, if the decision to use these weapons was not coupled with a decision to expand the war in some other way—it is not clear who would have gained from an atomic exchange.

might have been a much more effective deterrent than the attempt to reassure them that a march to the border did not presage an attack on mainland China.[16] The threat to use atomic weapons would have involved major political costs for the United States, and the American government might not have threatened to launch an atomic attack even if it had recognized that the threat might be effective. Had the Administration been aware of the fact that the fear of greater expansion might have deterred Chinese intervention, an alternative course might have been to threaten to expand the war to China with conventional weapons. But even this was not done. In fact, a decision was made before the intervention that Chinese intervention would not lead to conventional bombing beyond the Yalu. MacArthur reportedly believed that this decision had been leaked to the Chinese.[17]

In choosing, instead, to inform the Chinese of its limited objectives, the United States also considered it important to reassure the Chinese that their hydroelectric plants would not be jeopardized by a march up to the Yalu. But, as Whiting has pointed out:

> It was widely believed in Western circles that a determining factor in Chinese Communist concern over North Korea was the reliance of Manchurian industry upon power supplies across the border as well as along the Yalu River. This belief prompted explicit reassurances from Western spokesmen, both in Washington and at Lake Success, concerning "China's legitimate interests" near the frontier. Yet we have seen that Peking ignored this issue completely in its domestic as well as its foreign communications. The absence of propaganda about the protection of the hydroelectric installations, despite the need to maximize popular response to mobilization of "volunteers," suggests that this consideration played little if any role in motivating Chinese Communist intervention.[18]

In its advance through North Korea, then, the United Nations Command was attempting to communicate two points to the Chinese Communists: first, that it was prepared to go up to but not beyond the Yalu; and second, that it was prepared to respect China's legitimate interests in the northern regions of North Korea. The United States sought, therefore, to establish its limited objectives: that United Nations forces would take all North Korea, that the North Korean government would cease to exist, but China's legitimate industrial interests would be protected. An effort was made to assure the Chinese that the capture of North Korea would not be used as a springboard for an attack into China. The United States assumed that the limits

---

[16] Whiting, op. cit., p. 162. Panikkar, the Indian ambassador in Peking, reported that the Chinese expected an atomic attack, but were nonetheless prepared to intervene.

[17] Whitney, op. cit., pp. 455–456.

[18] Whiting, op. cit., pp. 151–152.

were ones that the Chinese were interested in, and that these limits would serve to keep the Chinese out of the war. But Chinese interests were different and could only be satisfied by different boundary conditions to the war.

Neustadt argues that the Chinese were not in any way affected by the announcement of the United Nations' aim to destroy the North Korean government.

> To judge from what the Chinese said, and later did, Peking's concern was with MacArthur's military progress, never mind its foreign policy objective. Chinese concern was not confined to anything so simple as a buffer zone along the border; an entity called North Korea, not the border, was at stake (perhaps in roughly the same sense that South Korea, under reverse circumstances, was for Washington). Even had the UN promised restoration of an independent North once all resistance ceased—which, naturally, no one proposed—I know of nothing to suggest that Peking would have withheld intervention. The communist world does not take kindly, it appears, to the dismantling of a member state's facilities for governance: the party and the army. MacArthur's military progress threatened both, no matter what came after. In short, the military risks and diplomatic dangers usually associated with MacArthur's march across the parallel existed independent of the words used in the UN resolution. MacArthur's march was authorized before the words were seen, much less approved, at Lake Success.[19]

Washington was apparently convinced even in retrospect that its declarations did not influence the Chinese decision to enter the war and that no other declaratory policy could have altered the Chinese decision. American policy makers concluded that once the decision was made to cross the thirty-eighth parallel, nothing could be done to affect the Chinese decision. In fact, the State Department reportedly argued in December of 1950 that the Chinese decision to intervene was made prior to the crossing of the thirty-eighth parallel. In one sense, at least, this conclusion may be wrong: the Chinese position might have been altered by threats to expand the war with the use of atomic weapons against China. Moreover it is by no means certain that the Chinese were concerned with the preservation of the total territorial integrity of North Korea. As Whiting suggests an American commitment to advance only part way up the peninsula—that is, to permit the maintenance of the North Korean government in some part of its territory—might have been sufficient to deter the Chinese entrance into the war.

---

[19] Neustadt, *op. cit.,* p. 125.

Neither before nor during the first three months of war [Whiting wrote] did the degree of interest in Pyongyang evinced by Peking warrant acceptance at face value of its concern for a "just" peace, based upon the *status quo ante bellum*.

This is not to say that the Chinese Communist leadership was prepared to accept with equanimity the total defeat of North Korea. As a minimal goal, intervention must have been attempted to preserve an entity identifiable as the DPRK, and to prevent unification of all Korea under U.N. supervision. The late date of Chinese Communist entry into the war suggests that it was the political importance of the North Korean government, rather than its territorial integrity, that was at stake. Although intervention was officially predicated upon U.N. crossing of the thirty-eighth parallel, no Chinese People's Volunteers and Democratic People's Republic of Korea defense lines were established during the August-October period, not even to protect Pyongyang. To Peking, a "just" Korean peace was not an end in itself but rather a means towards fulfilling other related goals of policy.[20]

Thus, even after the crossing of the thirty-eighth parallel, Chinese intervention might have been prevented had the United States acted differently. Although trying to impose limits on expansion, the United States failed to grasp adequately either the reasons that the Chinese felt intervention was necessary or the threats that might have deterred their intervention. Both sides expanded the war, the United Nations by crossing the thirty-eighth parallel and the Chinese by entering the war. Each side failed to convey to the other the kind of counteraction to be expected which might have deterred expansion. China attempted to prevent the crossing of the thirty-eighth parallel by declaring her intention to intervene, but this intention, relayed by the Indian ambassador, was not taken seriously by the United Nations Command. The United Nations sought to prevent the Chinese entrance, not be threatening a further expansion but by attempting to satisfy the Chinese security interests that, it was assumed, might lead her to enter the war.

PORTS AND TROOPS

Despite the fact that United States planes, taking off from airfields in South Korea and Japan and from aircraft carriers, consistently bombed targets in North Korea, the Communists engaged in almost no bombing south of the thirty-eighth parallel. This was one of the major asymmetries of the war both from a legalistic point of view and in terms of interfering with the military operations of the enemy. Both sides apparently devoted considerable attention to the question of what targets to attack, and a variety of motives affected the relevant decisions.

[20] Whiting, *op. cit.*, pp. 155–156.

The American decision to bomb targets in North Korea was made prior to the commitment of American ground troops in June 1950. A month later permission was given to bomb industrial targets in North Korea, but the use of incendiary bombs was not allowed because of the civil damage that would have resulted. The Air Force was not authorized to bomb areas close to the Soviet and Chinese borders. Rashin was the single industrial center within the forbidden area and it was the only industrial target in North Korea which was not destroyed by mid-September when an end to strategic bombing was ordered by the Joint Chiefs. Not until June 1952 were attacks on the hydroelectric plants in North Korea authorized; within two weeks almost 90 percent of the North Korea power capacity was destroyed.[21]

American attacks on targets in North Korea steadily expanded. The attacks were aimed at affecting the immediate military situation. The restraints observed had several motives: (1) to avoid extensive civilian destruction considered undesirable on both humanitarian and propaganda grounds; (2) to avoid a spillover of the war into China or the Soviet Union (the spillover into China prior to her entry into the war probably did not have a major impact on Chinese policy, but the incursion did create propaganda and political difficulties); (3) to avoid damaging, in the case of the hydroelectric plants, targets considered vital to the Chinese so as to avoid their entrance into the war, presumably in retaliation.

The Communists exercised far greater restraint on their air forces. Except for a few night "heckling" attacks from small biplanes in the spring of 1951 no air attacks were made on any targets in South Korea. The Communist restraint was not the result of the absence of inviting military targets. The port of Pusan was an extremely inviting target for bombardment and mining. It was the key to the American logistic effort and frequently was lighted up all night. American logistic convoys and troops in the field also could have been hampered by air attacks. A number of factors seem to have influenced the Communist decision not to respond in kind to United Nations air attacks on North Korea:

1. The Communists might have believed that it would have been very difficult, if not impossible, for the United Nations to continue its operations in Korea if Pusan came under heavy attack, and that, once the United Nations committed itself to the defense of South Korea, it was no longer in a position to accept complete withdrawal. Therefore, if attacks on logistic lines made impossible the continued conduct of an effective ground war in Korea, the United States might have been forced to engage in strategic strikes against the Chinese, if not the

   [21] Robert Frank Futrell, *The United States Air Force in Korea 1950–1953*. New York: Duell, Sloan and Pearce, 1961, pp. 449–452.

Russian, homeland.[22] If the Communists found this supposition credible, they may have concluded that, once their initial grab for South Korea failed, they could not afford to do anything that would lead to their complete control over South Korea.[23] They may have recognized that American confinement of the war to the Korean peninsula was dependent on her ability to fight there effectively.

2. In order to avoid attacks on Chinese air bases just north of the Yalu, Red airmen were not allowed to attack United Nations positions from these bases. Although the Communists were permitting the United States the sanctuary of bases in Japan and on aircraft carriers, they apparently were afraid that they would not be granted a similar sanctuary for bombing operations. United States planes managed to keep the North Korean airfields out of commission almost continuously throughout the war. Thus, given that the Chinese limited the use of their fields to staging operations and to fighter planes, the Communists were incapable of bombing operations.

3. There is some evidence to suggest that Soviet pilots constituted a significant part of the "Chinese" air force during the Korean War.[24] If this is true the explanation for target restraint may have been the desire to avoid the capture of Soviet airmen. This proof of direct Soviet involvement in the war would at the least have been politically damaging and, from a Soviet point of view, might have created an intolerable risk of American retaliation.

By the end of the war the United States was exercising almost no target restraint in North Korea and the Communists were doing no bombing in South Korea. Each side was guided by a complex series of motives and incentives. However, despite the asymmetry of the actions, there is nothing to suggest that either side treated its decisions on targeting as being closely related to, affected by, or likely to affect, the opponent's decisions on these questions.

EXPANSION AND LIMITATION

Decisions on expanding the United Nations operations resulted from the rejecting or approving of the field commanders' proposals by the Joint Chiefs of Staff or civilian officials. In some cases, particularly on the question of using atomic weapons, the military never

[22] The United States had secured British concurrence to bomb bases in China in the event of heavy air attacks from Chinese bases on United Nations troops (*H. C. Debs.*, 5th Series, CDXCVI, 970, Feb. 26, 1952) and this was probably communicated to the Chinese. However, Truman reported that he was convinced that Russia would come in if Manchurian bases were bombed.

[23] This thesis implies that the Chinese would not have driven the United Nations forces off the Korean peninsula by ground action even if they had the capability. There is no evidence to substantiate or invalidate this point.

[24] Futrell, *op. cit.*, pp. 370, 651–652.

made the request, and so, in some sense, no decision was made. On three occasions General MacArthur was refused his requests: to employ Chinese Nationalist troops, to impose a naval blockade on China, and to bomb bases and supply lines in China. But a number of MacArthur's requests for permission to expand the war were approved. These included the commitment of American ground forces, the Inchon offensive, and the crossing of the thirty-eighth parallel.

President Truman states that the National Security Council recommended the consideration of three factors relevant to the decision of whether to go on the offensive: action by the Soviet Union and the Chinese Communists, the views of friendly members of the United Nations, and the risk of general war.[25] These and other decisions were also influenced by American doctrine as well as by domestic political pressures. The balancing of the factors varied from decision to decision, but all played a role in the major decisions to limit or expand the war.

Much less is known about the Communist decision-making process or the factors which influenced their decisions to limit or expand the war. The initial decision to keep the Chinese out of the war seems to have been based largely on domestic conditions in China, particularly the desire of the Chinese to implement their program of economic growth and development, and their desire to avoid military entanglements at a time when they had not yet consolidated their hold over their own country.[26] The reasons for the Russians' abstention from open intervention in the war are less clear. The Soviets were determined not to do anything that directly labeled them as participants; they did not publicize the participation of any Russian "volunteers" in the war, nor provide any atomic capability, although they did supply large amounts of conventional military equipment. One likely explanation is the Russian fear that intervention would lead to general war. The United States had the capability of inflicting great destruction on the Soviet homeland with its stock of atomic weapons, while the Soviets had no capability of directly attacking the United States, although they might have been able to capture a large part of Western Europe with ground forces. Thus the Soviets, aware of their inferior strategic position, were probably determined to keep out of the war and to provide no excuse for a direct American attack on the Soviet Union.

Each side apparently made its decisions to limit the war for different reasons and with minimal attention to the battlefield interaction. In addition the two sides observed very different limits. What the United States did in North Korea was quite different from what the

---

[25] Truman, *op. cit.,* p. 359.
[26] It was probably based also on the belief that the United States would not intervene and that the North Korean army would capture all of South Korea. . . .

Communists did in South Korea, but the Chinese used a much greater percentage of their gross national product than the United States did. Nevertheless, while the United States used naval vessels and airplanes to bomb troops and airfields within Korea, the Communists did not. The United States engaged in logistical interdiction; the Communists did not. Each side, then, observed its own series of limits and restraints only in some very general way related to, and dependent on, the limits of the other side.

At least a few of the limits were symmetrical. Both sides restricted their military operations almost entirely to Korea, and neither used nuclear weapons. There was lack of symmetry in that all the military targets in North Korea were attacked but most in South Korea were not. The United States attacked the Chinese points of entry—the Yalu bridges; but the Chinese did not attack the United States' points of entry—the ports. Both sides observed a number of what Schelling has called "legalistic" limitations.[27] The United Nations carefully observed both the Chinese and Russian borders and tried to avoid crossing them inadvertently. There was symmetry in the absence of official declaration of war. The United Nations troops participated in the war in a "police action" capacity, and none of the countries involved, including the United States, declared war. The Chinese used "volunteers," and the Russians supplied equipment and presumably technicians, but little manpower for the battle.

In some cases the limits represented a recognition of the battlefield interaction. But the origin of many of the limits observed, and part of the explanation for others, lay not within the dynamics of the war itself, but within the domestic and international context in which the war was fought.

---

[27] Thomas C. Schelling, *Nuclear Weapons and Limited War*. RAND P-1620, Feb. 20, 1959, p. 1.

Controlling the Risks in Cuba

ALBERT AND ROBERTA WOHLSTETTER

The environment in which smaller powers face large ones, has, it is clear, changed drastically. The intensive development of nuclear and other modern weapons, the vast expansion of communications linking remote parts of the world have on the one hand increased the level of violence possible in a world conflict, and on the other seem to have made minor and local violence a world-wide public concern. It is not easy, however, to trace the implications of this changed environment. Public light on local violence does not pass with equal speed in both directions through the Iron and Bamboo Curtains. Though one striking movement of our time has been the multiplication of realigned, non-aligend and partly aligned nations and their use of many international forums, shifting modes of rivalry and co-operation continue to be dominated by the two principal centres of force: a many-centered East against a not-very-completely allied West. Overwhelming nuclear capabilities, in spite of the many hopeful or ominous predictions of rapid diffusion during the last twenty years, and in spite of the search for independence by the United Kingdom, France, China, and possibly others, still are concentrated in the United States and the Soviet Union.

How does the threat of great power violence increase the risks for the smaller powers? And how might the smaller powers affect the nuclear risks? In a contest between the great powers does the very size of their weapons of destruction inhibit, as it is said, any use of force? What is the role of non-nuclear force? And what are the uses of great power bases on foreign soil?

It is much easier to ask these questions than to answer them; and too much to hope that an analysis of the crisis over the Russian bases in Cuba can provide the answers. However a look at this crisis may illuminate a little the issues and so at least help make the questions more precise. All of the questions at any rate were raised in Cuba. There the two big powers and a small one were engaged in a three-cornered partial conflict (and partial co-operation); and nuclear weapons and their

From *Controlling the Risks in Cuba* (Adelphi Paper No. 7, April 1965), pp. 3–24. Reprinted by permission of the authors. Some footnotes have been omitted.

future, if not immediate, launching from these Russian bases outside the Soviet Union were at the very heart of the matter. It is frequently said that we were very close to nuclear war, that Russia and the United States played a desperate game of "Chicken," with the risks nearly out of control. Threats and warnings were signalled, and not always understood. And we now hear that the resolution of the crisis will affect all future risk-taking, that the crisis was a "turning point."

It is perhaps worth one more look then at this much inspected event, to see how some of the standard sayings about constraints and risks in the use of force apply. What were the interests and what were the dangers in the various policy alternatives open to each of the three powers directly engaged? And how did they affect allies less directly engaged?

THE VIEW FROM CUBA

From the standpoint of Cuba the basing of nuclear weapons there had some clear values. Mr. Theodore Draper,[1] an acute analyst of the development of Castro's Cuba, suggested rather early that Cuba may have invited the Russians to put their bombardment missiles there. Castro himself has fluctuated between attributing the idea to the Cubans and to the Russians. On our count, out of some half a dozen major mentions, the score is about even.[2] Whoever got the idea first, strategic bases in Cuba would have had their uses for Castro as well as for Khrushchev. For one thing there was the prestige; modern weapons impress neighbours and can raise the political status of the country which harbours them, especially if the neighbours are misinformed or uninformed. The prestige, to be sure, is precarious, as the United Kingdom, in spite of its great scientific competence, has found, first with *Blue Streak*, then with *Skybolt*, and now with the recently aired difficulties in the *Valiant* and TSR-2 programmes. However, in the less developed countries and even in secondary industrial powers, arms may be valued more for their flourish than their actual power. It seems that the sheer magnitude of the capabilities of the United States and the Soviet Union has outclassed the nuclear potential of others in ways that were quite unexpected by those who predicted nuclear weapons would be equalizers on the world scene. Yet France and China would scarcely agree, and a less developed country like Cuba might place a sizeable symbolic value on being only the host to nuclear installations.

---

[1] Interview, 6 December, 1962.

[2] Claude Julien, *Le Monde,* 22 and 23 March, 1963; followed by Castro's denial to *Prensa Latina,* 23 March, 1963; Jean Daniel, "Unofficial Envoy: An Historic Report from Two Capitals," *The New Republic,* 14 December, 1963, pp. 15–20; Herbert Matthews, "Return to Cuba," *Hispanic American Report,* Special Issue, January, 1964, p. 16; Juanita Castro, Speech to the World Affairs Council, Los Angeles, 8 February, 1965.

For another thing, the symbol had its important domestic uses. Within Cuba the presence of these bases, while essentially alien and forbidden to Cuban citizens, reinforced and confirmed Castro's defiance of the Northern colossus, made more persuasive his warnings of an American invasion, and distracted attention from gathering difficulties at home. These difficulties had been political as well as economic. 1962 had witnessed an open break in March between Castro and the old guard Communists, followed by a purging and reorganization of Cuba's single political party.[3] A severe drop (the first of several) in the sugar harvest from the preceding year (from 6.8 to 4.8 million tons) was among the early results of an ill-conceived attempt to diversify agriculture quickly at the expense of Cuban comparative advantage. Troubles had also begun to plague the industrial programme. The Cuban planners had left out of their plans the provision of raw materials for the factories they ordered, and were discovering to their dismay that in many cases it cost as much to import the raw materials as to buy the finished products abroad. An extraordinarily rapid collectivizing and statification of farms and even small commercial and manufacturing enterprises, at a pace unequalled in Russia, Asia, or middle Europe, had begun to affect production incentives and to require a large increase in managerial skills; meanwhile Cuba had been losing professionals through emigration. As these internal threats to the Revolution appeared, distraction may have been welcome.

In any case the move had international relevance for the future of Castro's variety of Communism, particularly in Latin America. The missile installation was seen by the Cubans as a great and unprecedented gesture of protection and solidarity by the most powerful country in the Communist world. Inevitably some of this power might be expected to rub off on Castro. By increasing his prestige, it could be expected to serve as an aid in his programme for spreading insurgency throughout Latin America. And it suggested that, like Castro's own communism, successful coups on the same model might be protected against counter-revolution and external attack. One of Castro's explanations for accepting Moscow's offer of long-range missiles could also support this interpretation. It was, he said, "not in order to assure our own defence, but foremost in order to reinforce Socialism on the international plane."[4]

---

[3] The ORI (Integrated Revolutionary Organization), now PURS, a fusion of the Cuban Communist Party and Castro's own 26 July Organization.

[4] Claude Julien, *Le Monde*, 22 March, 1963, reporting an interview which took place in January of that year. Castro repudiated some statements of this interview, but in view of Julien's reputation as an accurate journalist and some of the confirmable details of the setting and circumstances, there is much to suggest this account is authentic. The role of long-range missiles in his insurgency programme has been confirmed by his sister, Juanita Castro, in a talk 8 February, 1965, to the World Affairs Council, Los Angeles.

Speeches in September and early October, 1962, by Cuban communist leaders hammered at the theme, "Cuba is not alone," and Castro's public expressions of thanks to the Soviet Union were emotional to an extreme. Read today, with our present knowledge of the timing of arrangements to install the rockets, these pre-crisis speeches seem to contain implied threats of rocket fire against the United States in case of an invasion, and an identification of Cuba's fate with the final catastrophe. *Goetterdaemmerung*. Castro explained on 20 April, 1963, the second anniversay of Playa Giron, "When the missiles were installed here, it was no longer a problem of six or seven divisions, it was . . . a problem (for the United States) of having to confront the risk of a thermonuclear war." In a recent interview with Barnard L. Collier he made this more explicit. "The missiles were very logical to us. We were running the danger of conventional war . . . The conventional war would be most dangerous to us. We would be destroyed alone."[5]

Cuba was not alone in another sense, because the missile bases supplied hostages. They were a visible symbol that Russia was "contracting in," just as their withdrawal, Castro feared, might make it easier for the United States to underestimate the Soviet Union's solidarity with Cuba. Castro's statement to Collier suggests that the rationalization he had given earlier to the French reporter, Jean Daniel, for accepting missiles hardly represented his actual motives and estimates. To Daniel he had implied that if Russia extended only conventional military aid, the United States would not be deterred from invading, even though Russia would, in spite of American doubts, actually retaliate with thermonuclear weapons and so touch off world war;[6] Russian nuclear missiles in Cuba, however, would deter a US invasion and therefore prevent nuclear war altogether. To Collier, on the other hand, Castro made clear that he himself did not believe the Soviet Union would retaliate with nuclear weapons in the event of US conventional attack, and that if Cuba were to go down he would prefer that it be destroyed not alone, but on a grand scale along with a good deal of the rest of the world. As he said, "For us the danger of a conventional war and a world war were the same, the destruction of Cuba."[7]

[5] *New York Herald Tribune,* 17 August, 1964.

[6] According to Daniel's account of Castro's beliefs (*The New Republic,* 14 December, 1963, p. 18), Russia "recognized that if conventional military aid was the extent of their assistance, the United States might not hesitate to instigate an invasion, in which case Russia would retaliate and this would eventually touch off a world war." Russia therefore decided to install the missiles, and Castro accepted them as a matter of "honour." The passage just quoted was omitted from the *New York Times* version of the interview, but appears in the original in *L'Express,* 6 December, 1963.

[7] *New York Herald Tribune,* 17 August, 1964.

The presence of the missiles meant that the Soviet Union was more obviously engaged—in Castro's phrase, "highly compromised"—in the fate of Cuba. Though not, as it turned out, irretrievably; not at any rate when Russia was caught in the process of installation. If a substantial number of missiles had been installed and made operational before discovery, forcing withdrawal might have been somewhat harder. The quarantine of missiles and ground support equipment on their way to Cuba would, of course, no longer have been open to the United States. Something less focussed on the actual process of installing missiles would therefore have been necessary; perhaps a more general blockade or a still broader and more violent measure. Moreover, though this is arguable, it might have been somewhat more difficult psychologically for the Russians to withdraw immediately after the installation of the missiles than during the process. Perhaps this difficulty would have faded rapidly with time; after some years, surely withdrawal would again be easier. In any case, Chairman Khrushchev was caught *in flagrante*, in a difficult position to maintain.

In the event of conflict between the United States and Cuba, a considerable number of Russian missiles and bombers, at least twenty odd thousand Russian troops[8] and, still more, Russian prestige would have been put in jeopardy. To avoid Russian casualties in some of the attacks that might have been made at the end of October (for example, the non-nuclear bombing of Cuban bases manned by Russian forces) there would have had to be extreme selectivity in the American attack, or evacuation by the Russians on receipt of explicit warning; or some combination of the two. Russian forces in Cuba then, like American forces in Europe, though to a very much lesser extent, would have been hostage to the Cubans in the event of an attack by the United States. This point should not be pushed too far or regarded simply in formal terms. The United States forces which are hostage in Europe number now perhaps 350,000 men and many of their dependents. By comparison, a Russian force of 20 odd thousand, is a token. Nonetheless, a distinctly visible token. As Castro puts it today, "The Soviet Union is seriously compromised in the world with Cuba. That is important. It is like the US in Berlin."[9] But he observes that the "compromising" was even more serious with the surface-to-surface missiles in Cuba.

It was not simply the presence of Soviet troops in Cuba, but their manning and guarding of the long-range rockets that seems to have

---

[8] The estimate by President Kennedy in January, 1963, was 16,000 to 17,000 in Cuba, after a withdrawal of 4,500. 25 January, 1963, Press Conference, as reported in the *New York Times,* 26 January, 1963. The official American figure for the crisis period has stayed around 22,000. Castro now claims the number was much larger.

[9] Interview with Barnard Collier, *New York Herald Tribune,* 19 August, 1964.

faced the United States with a dilemma in October 1962. If the United States undertook some hostile action against Cuba, would it dare leave these lethal weapons alone? Would it not have to destroy them? And would this not bring Russia's intercontinental missiles down on the United States?

The line of argument suggested by these questions without a doubt is plausible. However, it persuades mainly by its vagueness. The precise circumstances and nature of the United States action and the risks to the Russians of their own alternative responses need to be specified, and these are only some of the things which would require examination. We shall not assess how the risks would have looked in connection with the various actions open to the United States, if the installations had been completed. We shall ask: What were the risks involved in the actions taken by the United States and In alternatives it considered during the process of the missile installation by the Russians? Much has been said about this, but how close *were* we to the brink?

Whether or not the Russians might have used their medium and intermediate range missiles located in Cuba or their intercontinental missiles based at home in retaliation against an attack on Cuba, desperate action by the Cubans themselves was another matter. Could the Cubans have used the Russian's missiles based in Cuba? If the surface-to-surface missiles had been in their charge, they may well have been more tempted than the Russians to use them. At least the threat to use these missiles against the United States in any of a number of circumstances might from the standpoint of the Cubans have had a considerable appeal. For one thing, the Cubans know less about the consequences of nuclear exchange: these are sobering, as Chairman Khrushchev used to keep telling Chairman Mao; and there is no reason to suspect that Khrushchev's successors—or ultimately Mao's—would be less sober. (Familiarity breeds respect.) For another, we are told, the Cuban Communists and the Russian ones are rather different. We even had some hints from Chairman Khrushchev on this subject. The Cubans are Southerners, impulsive, romantic revolutionaries; and they would put their own fate (or at least that of the current Cuban government) at stake in an American attack or an American-supported resistance. The Russians are Northern and more controlled (though there are those embarrassing nineteenth century Dostoievskian Russians); they are disciplined Bolsheviks (whose character was formed in conscious contrast to such Dostoievskian Russians); and for all of their twenty odd thousand, clearly much less intimately engaged in Cuba.

Whatever faith we attach to these contrasting characterizations, we have some actual observations on the contrasting behaviour of Chairman Khrushchev and the Cuban Communists. Or more exactly, we can at the very least contrast how the Russians behaved in the crisis and how the Cubans say they would have behaved. In the clutch the Chairman was eminently cautious and controlled about the triggering of Russian missiles in Cuba. The Cubans on the other hand suggested considerably more abandon. Che Guevara apparently had a beady eye on New York, and said later that he would have pulled New York down with Cuba. "If the rockets had remained, we would have used them all and directed them against the very heart of the United States, including New York, in our defence against aggression. But we haven't got them, so we shall fight with what we've got. In the face of an aggressor like the United States, there can be no solution other than to fight to the death, inflicting the maximum damage on the enemy." [10]

This sort of threat might be compared with that posed by a small nuclear power, according to General Pierre Gallois and other enthusiasts for the spread of nuclear weapons. In the writings of these theorists the precise service performed by nuclear weapons for the small powers is seldom very clear. If one of the two major powers planned a nuclear first strike against a small nuclear power, such as Cuba might have become, or for that matter, a secondary industrial power like France, the small power's arsenal might not offer much of a deterrent. To deter a first strike, a nuclear force must be able to survive it. And a second strike capability is a more complicated matter than enthusiasts for diffusion have understood.

However, sometimes the use of nuclear weapons by a small power is contemplated as response to lesser attacks by the great power: a massive retaliation theory, in short, with the smaller power appearing in the role of miniature massive retaliationist. Such nuclear retaliation against a non-nuclear move by a great power would of course be suicidal. The small power is not likely to have a genuine second strike capability against Russia or the United States; if these countries are careful, it is still less likely to have a "preclusive" first strike capability, that is, an ability to prevent the great nuclear power from retaliating. From a responsible leader of a smaller power, then, the threat of a miniature massive retaliation might not be very convincing. It is not clear that Guevara, for example, who has a reputation for disciplined intelligence, would be as abandoned in fact as he claims in retrospect. After all, Chairman Khrushchev tried to sound rather reckless in advance of the crisis. In mid-September of 1962 he called the attention of the governments of the world and world opinion to "the provocations which might plunge the world into the disaster of a universal world war with the use of thermonuclear weapons. . . ." "Bellicose reactionary elements of the United States have long since been conducting in the United States Congress and in the American press an unbridled

---

[10] Interview, 28 November, 1962, with a Longon *Daily Worker* correspondent, reported in the *Los Angeles Times,* 11 December, 1962.

propaganda campaign against the Cuban Republic, calling for an attack on Cuba, an attack on Soviet ships carrying the necessary commodities and food to the Cuban people, in one word, calling for war." ". . . One cannot now attack Cuba and expect that the aggressor will be free from punishment for this attack. If this attack is made, this will be the beginning of war."[11] In short, interception of Russian ships carrying arms to Cuba would mean the start of World War III.

On the other hand, some leaders in small countries have earned a reputation for recklessness. Guevara's uncompromising speed in nationalizing industry, and immediate full implementation of what he regards as communist principles, have an element of ruthlessness and lack of realism which is not the same as recklessness but which should make us thoughtful. And it may be that Castro himself could convince us with a suicidal threat. The *Venceremos* ("We shall win") with which all Cuban letters now are signed might be hollow, but Castro might just mean the *Patria o Muerte* ("Fatherland or Death") which precedes it.[12] He has had a long personal history of near suicidal defiance of big forces; his casual and disastrous assault on the Moncada barracks on 26 July, 1953; his landing on the *Gramma* in Oriente in 1956, announced in advance to Batista, calamitous not only to most of his companions but to the inhabitants who expected him two days earlier; to say nothing of some hair-raising student escapades. *Frente a Todos* ("Against Everybody") has been his slogan.[13] One can understand that more than the traditional guerrilla doctrine of protecting the leader might have influenced Fidel's subordinates to keep him home in the headquarters of the Sierra Maestra when they went out on a raid. When he was in charge, casualties were prohibitive. His own life has been charmed, but not that of his followers. It should give any prospective father figure—or even a brother figure, Russian or otherwise—considerable pause.[14]

[11] *New York Times,* 12 September, 1962. (Soviet Government Statement released by *Tass.*)

[12] He describes the Cubans manning the surface-to-air missiles today in precisely these terms. They are "disciplined and fatherland-or-death types" (Speech, 21 January, 1965). If he had surface-to-surface missiles, he might very well man them with the same "types" and, at the least, almost certainly so describe them.

[13] *Frente a Todos* is the title Fidel gave to his reply in Mexico in 1955 to charges against him of corruption and usurpation of power by the Ortodoxo Party and other groups fighting Batista in Cuba.

[14] Fidel's actual father had trouble. When Fidel was 13 years old he organized a strike of sugar workers against his father, and later when he was 18, his mother reports in a biography written with one of Castro's sisters, that she permitted him to call his father an exploiter and a landlord, one of "those who abuse the powers they wrench from the people with deceitful promises." While the father reacted in rage, Fidel apparently still expected (and received) his financial support even after his marriage, demanded $1,000 to buy weapons for the Moncada attack, left the house finally with $100. Castro's vilification and attack of big forces may have aimed at a continued dependence rather than an absolute break in relations. The United States turned out to be a less tolerant father, withdrawing economic support, intending damage, and even inflicting some, when Castro carried on too long, too noisily, too roughly.

Castro in charge of nuclear rockets might be convincingly reckless.[15] It is precisely this case which would appear to be intolerable to both of the two opposing great powers. It is clear that a persisting threat by Cuba to use nuclear weapons in response to unspecified or vaguely specified non-nuclear moves by the United States would be very hard for the US to bear. But it would also raise grave problems for the Soviet Union. Russia would have every motive to preclude or stop such a threat or, if this were not possible, to separate herself as clearly as could be from the threatener.

From the standpoint of the Cuban people a miniature massive-retaliation policy would place them in double jeopardy. It would raise the stakes and conjure up the possibility of nuclear destruction either before or after a Cuban move. However, the hazards to Cubans were increased considerably by the presence even of Russian-controlled missiles.

The issue of Russian control is raised very acutely by the nightmare vision of Cuba pulling Russia down along with New York. No doubt with exactly this in mind Mr. Khrushchev made every attempt to assure Mr. Kennedy that there was nothing whatsoever to worry about from those romantic Cubans. Good, solid, stolid, sensible Russians were guarding the safety catches on the missiles in Cuba: "The means which are located on Cuba now, about which you are talking and which as you say concern you, are in the hands of the Soviet officers. That is why any possibility of accidental usage of those means, which might cause harm to the United States, is excluded."[16] During the crisis as well as earlier, Chairman Khrushchev indicated that he subscribed to the analysis of the Cubans as temperamental Southerners. "The Cubans are very volatile people, Mr. Khrushchev said, and all of the sophisticated hardware provided for their defence was entirely under the control of Soviet officers . . . and it would never be fired except on his orders as Commander in Chief of all of the armed forces of the Soviet Union."[17]

Of course this raises some interesting questions. How sure could Khrushchev be? What about the use of force by Castro to jump Big Brother *(Frente a Todos)*? Mightn't he try to get hold of Russian nuclear weapons for use against the United States and so ultimately to ensure the engagement of Russia? (To say nothing of the rather grandiose plans he has expressed for spreading his revolution beyond the

---

[15] Some European analyses of the crisis suggest that Castro and the Cubans differed from Khrushchev in that the Cubans do not believe in nuclear threats in response to less than nuclear attack. The claim cannot survive an examination of Castro's and Guevara's speeches. Such suicidal nuclear threats were not only contemplated by Castro, but might be more persuasive issuing from him than from Khrushchev.

[16] 27 October, 1962, message to President Kennedy, published 28 October, 1962, *New York Times.*

[17] Interview with W. E. Knox, American industrialist, *New York Times* Magazine, 18 November, 1962, "Close Up of Khrushchev During a Crisis," described as taking place "a little more than three weeks ago."

Andes.) That, we may surmise, was what a good many of those 22,000 Russian troops were there to prevent: they were there to see that the weapons and in particular the war heads, if they were on the island, would be totally inoperable when seized. Newspaper reports have made clear that the Russian bases were heavily guarded and the Cubans, with the possible exception of a few of the elite, never got near the weapons.

But could these Russian forces be relied on? We know that the Russian troops in the satellites wavered during the revolts in Eastern Europe in the 1950s. The Russians have since rotated their security forces more frequently. However, seeing to it that nuclear weapons would not fall into the hands of irresponsible Cuban users is a much simpler job than preventing sympathetic collusion between rebels and an occupying force. It requires only a very small elite force whose loyalty could be relied on. And the loyalty of even a random sample of Russians might be trusted here: letting Cubans get hold of these weapons would mean placing all of Russia and a good deal else in jeopardy. In any case, there are more sophisticated methods of assurance available. The United States, on 5 July, 1962, announced that it was initiating a programme to install electronic locks (the Permissive Action Link) on its weapons to protect them against unauthorized use. These locks would require release from a central source, possibly very distant. Analogous remote keys conceivably could be held in Moscow itself. And while there is no public evidence whatsoever of mechanical or electronic devices so used in the Soviet Union, a tight political control seems most probable, given the structure of Soviet society; physical possession of these potent weapons would be dangerous in the hands of a dissident internal faction. The interests of the larger powers clearly coincide in preventing unauthorized firings by their own citizens. And both want to keep the keys out of the desperate hands of a smaller power. In the event it was the interests of the major powers that dominated.

So far we have treated the crisis mainly from the viewpoint of the small power. How did these missile bases figure in the calculations of the big powers?

THE VIEW FROM THE SOVIET UNION

Much ink has been spilled over whether the Soviet move into Cuba had a purely political significance for the Russians, or whether Soviet bases in Cuba had also a military worth to them. But Soviet objectives can be both political and military; these purposes are not separate, and neither the political nor military is very simple or pure. If the "purely political" is somewhat nebulous, the "purely military," a kind of art-for-art's sake, has no meaning at all.

The leaders of the Soviet Union in any case, when they address the communist world, have never made the separation. In fact, the shift in the balance of forces, which according to Mr. Khrushchev had come drastically to favour the Socialist countries, was clearly linked in his pronouncements to the development of Soviet military power, and was accompanied by a drum fire of rocket threats against the United States, and all of the countries in which the United States bases its military forces. And this supposed shift in military power is not unrelated to a vision of a future, totally communist world, whether this be single or many-centred. Many American and British writers recently have assured us that the Soviet Union is a *status quo* power, a "have" or satisfied power. This is all very well, but Chairman Khrushchev did not seem to know it. The *status quo* he was looking for seemed to be, as he had told it to Walter Lippmann, the *status quo post* rather than *ante* a major transformation. And there is no evidence that Khrushchev's successors look on the matter more comfortably for the West. To say that they would prefer this to be a peaceful transformation and indeed believe that it may well be, does not exclude latent military power as a major element in the expected transformation. Otherwise one would have to count every acquiescence to a threat of force as a peaceful change. Latent or actual communist military force monitored the early take-overs in Eastern Europe at the end of the war and prevented a reversal of the revolutions in 1953 and 1956. The possibility of its use defined the rules of behaviour both for internal opposition and outside aid. The possible use or threat to use military force is an operative element in many political transformations. In any case, it is apparent that the military build-up in Cuba had a considerable number of entwined political-military functions.

First it should be recalled that the introduction of strategic bombardment vehicles, MRBMs, IRBMs, and IL 28s capped a vast piling up, started considerably earlier, of active defences and ground forces which could be used to defend Cuba against internal as well as external attack, and the building of a base in Cuba which could serve as a centre of weapons transfer and material aid to insurgency in Latin America. From the standpoint of the Soviet Union the purposes of such a build-up partially coincide with some of the Cuban interests we have sketched. The important split between the Russians and the Red Chinese is not accurately represented as an ideological contrast between the foreswearing of any use of revolutionary violence by the Russians and its reckless advocacy by the Chinese. There are of course important differences in national interests. But the Chinese are considerably less reckless and the Russians more flexible and opportunistic than the conventional picture suggests.

Specifically for the Russians, the military build-up was in part a reaffirmation of the relationship between Russia and Cuba, a healing of wounds after the rift in March, 1962, that had resulted in the flight of Escalante, the old line Communist Party bureaucrat. It was a visible demonstration to those who were unaligned or falling out of line that for a small power to line up with the Soviet Union even near the centre of American power was safe, that a changeover to communism would not be reversed and that the power of the Soviet Union was committed as safeguard against any threat of reversal. More than this, by successfully defying the United States, forcing it to accept this major move into Cuba, the Soviet Union could powerfully influence the expectations of the rest of the world, most obviously those of the Latin Americans, but also those expectations and hopes that affect the outcome in Berlin and in more remote regions of Southeast and Southern Asia. And the expectations affected were specifically about relative strength and the will to use that strength. The large-scale Russian introduction of nuclear bombardment vehicles would have appeared also directly to answer the persuasive official American analyses of US superiority published in 1961 and 1962. The tendencies toward division within the communist world only reinforced some of these purposes. For the move was a Soviet blow in competition with the Chinese for leadership of the Socialist countries, and for leading the way in transforming the uncommitted world—and eventually that part of the world now committed to what they regard as the wrong side.

We have been discussing functions objectively served rather than Soviet conscious motivation, which must necessarily remain obscure. If, for example, the move had been successful, if the Soviet Union had gone before the United Nations to defend it, and the United States had acquiesced in the accomplished fact, it might have served any or all of the preceding military-political functions. On the other hand, if the success had been less complete, if the United States had not acquiesced, Soviet withdrawal might then have exacted as a price American withdrawal from some of its military bases on the territory of allies. The tentative skirmishing in the Khrushchev-Kennedy correspondence on the Turkish-Cuban base swap indicated one line of Soviet interest. But elimination of military bases is a directly military as well as political fact. This has been somewhat obscured, because the significance of overseas bases themselves for the 1960s has been understood only in a rather cloudy and sometimes quite erroneous fashion in the current Western discussions. How about the Cuban bombardment bases themselves? Some commentators have stated in rather unqualified fashion that they had essentially no military worth.[18]

[18] See, for example, *The New Republic*, 3 November, 1962, pp. 3ff; *The Reporter*, 22 November, 1962, pp. 21ff; *The Bulletin of the Atomic Scientists*, Vol. 19 (February, 1963), pp. 8ff.

Perhaps the first thing to be said is that it is not very sensible to talk with great confidence on these subjects. Responsible judgement here is difficult even with complete access to privileged information. The classified data are uncertain, the public data still more so, and few of the commentators have looked carefully at the quantitative implications of even the public data. Many who doubted the Russians would install bombardment vehicles in Cuba simply took at face value Chairman Khrushchev's statement that such weapons would add nothing to the capabilities provided by their intercontinental rockets. And then when it was clear that Khrushchev had gambled a great deal on precisely such installations, they persisted in dismissing their military significance. As we have already suggested, such bases have a variety of functions, but Khrushchev's gamble should at least have raised some doubts in the minds of those who dismiss their strategic value out of hand.

Part of the confusion comes from the fact that the military value of these Russian installations was not likely to consist in their efficiency as an addition to the Russian deterrent to American nuclear attack. Because of their proximity, their known position, and their lack of shelter, warning, or protected reliable communications, they would not have been hard to eliminate in an opening blow, nor would they have severely complicated an attack by a large reliable missile force;[19] and so they were not likely to be an economic way to increase a Russian second strike capability. The more likely strategic value concerned their significance for a possible Russian preclusive first-strike, as weapons that, in case of need during a grave crisis of escalation, would help to blunt an American retaliation. Resolution of such an issue would involve a detailed analysis of the entire complex mechanism of American retaliation, as it existed in 1962, including not merely the vehicles (that is, the missiles and aircraft), their physical disposition, their protection and degree of readiness, but also the system for commanding and controlling their response and penetrating enemy defences. For good reason, data on this subject are not publicly available. And overall statements on capability by public officials necessarily must be designed not simply to convey information to the public, important though that is, but also to limit information to the enemy and to affect his estimates favourably to ourselves. A resolution of this complex issue cannot therefore be made one way or the other. Even the much simpler partial question, the comparative vulnerability of our bombardment vehicles to distant as distinct from close, land-based attack, is necessarily shrouded with secrecy.

[19] During the 1950s the belief was widespread that even very vulnerable unprotected bases, if widely separated, would present insuperable co-ordination problems for a missile attack. . . .

Recognition of these limitations on analysis is the beginning of wisdom.

Take the partial problem of protecting the vehicles against the initial blow, from far-off or near-by. This is a quantitative matter demanding more than the standard caution. The probability that a vehicle will survive depends among other things on the number of attacking vehicles, their reliability, their average aiming accuracy, the kiloton yield of their nuclear warheads, and the degree of resistance of the vehicles under attack. This dependence moreover is not simply linear. The number of weapons, for example, required to destroy a vehicle sheltered to a sufficient degree will within relevant limits vary as the square of the average aiming accuracy. That is, double the inaccuracy and four times the number of attacking vehicles are required; triple the inaccuracy and nearly ten times the number of attackers are needed. Requirements are sensitive also to yield and degree of resistance, though less so. Changes in requirement are something less than proportionate to changes in yield or resistance: they vary as the two-thirds power: if a shelter is 8 or 27 times harder, the number of attackers required for a given probability of destruction would increase by factors of 4 or 9 respectively. But the average inaccuracy, for example, of even our own weapons can only be uncertainly estimated with complete access to classified tests. Our estimates of the performance of Russian weapons must be still more uncertain. Estimates are in any case not public and are frequently misrepresented with great confidence in the press. Moreover they change rather rapidly. A careful reading of the public press will confirm that the publicly stated average inaccuracies of bombardment missiles have decreased in the last few years by very large amounts; public estimates have been divided by at least five. Yet a factor of 3 reduction in inaccuracy can lower requirements to destroy hard targets by a factor of 9; a factor of 5 reduction, by 25. Even estimates of the number of vehicles of various types in the Russian force, we know from experience, have been in error. And the errors have not always been in one direction. The Cuban example illustrates some of the uncertainties. Here in a small area close by, under the most intense and continuous air reconnaissance, we counted some 30 missiles; and the Russians removed 42.[20] These comments suggest the limits of our own discussion.

The point to be made then is that some of these sensitive performance characteristics for the offensive vary with distance and improve significantly with close proximity: the important parameter of guidance accuracy, for example. Reliability is another performance

---

[20] ". . . we never knew how many missiles were brought into Cuba. The Soviets said there were 42. We have counted 42 going out. We saw fewer than 42." Roswell L. Gilpatric, 11 November, 1962. ABC's Issues and Answers, telecast.

characteristic which can improve with the simplified missiles possible at close range. A typically blithe argument assessing the military worth of Cuban bases states that while accuracy is improved in the shorter ranges, on the other hand bomb yields are necessarily smaller. Unfortunately, as we have indicated, changes in accuracy affect requirements much more sensitively than changes in yield. And, what is more, there is no law of nature suggesting that a missile payload declines at shorter ranges. For a given thrust, other things being equal, the opposite is true. It is possible to throw larger payloads at shorter distances. All of this is relevant for an exclusive choice between distant and close-in attack.

However, the second point to be noted is that *in the short run* this was not the choice open to the Russians. In the long run they could choose to build intercontinental missiles and base them in Russia, say, or spend an equal amount of resources for missiles based in Cuba. But in the years 1962 and 1963 the Russian bombardment force capable of reaching the United States was sharply limited. The missiles they sent to Cuba were a net addition to this force, since, based in Russia or in one of the European satellites, they could not reach the United States. Moreover the number of MRBMs—48—and the IRBMs—apparently between 24 and 32—which were already installed or on the way[21] was quite sizeable in relation to the public Western and American government estimates of the Russian intercontinental missile force and approximately equalled the Institute of Strategic Studies' estimate of 75 Soviet ICBMs.[22]

Third, our short run need not be so short as to stop in mid-December, 1962—the time the Department of Defence indicated as the operational date for the IRBMs of 2200 nautical mile range. In fact, it appears that the Russians had in addition to the roughly 75 medium and intermediate range missiles shipped to Cuba in 1962 hundreds more that could acquire by location in Cuba the ability to bomb American targets. The ISS estimate suggests a force of MRBMs alone ten times as large as the total number of MRBMs and IRBMs emplaced in Cuba, and beyond this, a growing total force of IRBMs. Further shipments of medium and intermediate range missiles could have been installed in Cuba, if the United States offered no interference, with the same impressive speed that characterized the installation of the first 75. The MRBMs were activated "with the

[21] On the CIA and DOD public accounts, there were 48 MRBMs for which launch positions had been prepared (there were 24 launchers). For the IRBMs, 17 erectors were counted on the way out, with the 17th reckoned by the Americans as a spare. Briefing, 6 February, 1963, by Mr. John Hughes, Special Assistant to General Carroll, reprinted in *Department of Defence Appropriations for* 1964. US Congress, House of Representatives 88th Session, Part I, Washington, DC, 1963.

[22] "The Military Balance," 1962–1963.

passage of hours." (For example, two sets of photographs separated by less than 24 hours, displayed an increase of perhaps 50 per cent in the amount of equipment.[23] There has been almost universal agreement on the logistic efficiency of the Soviet operation.) Such a change in location might have corrected at a stroke what appears to be a great imbalance in the composition of the Russian strategic force: it is heavily weighted towards attacking European theatre targets and by comparison neglects American forces based outside Europe, though these make up the principal retaliatory strength of the alliance.

Fourth, the axis of attack from Cuba outflanked the Ballistic Missile Early Warning System. Unlike submarine launched missiles, of the range estimated to be available to the Soviet Union, these Cuban based missiles would have covered essentially all of the United States, with little or no warning.[24] The co-ordination problems for the Russians are less severe than were suggested by some writers at the time of the crisis, and in fact on the whole before attacking it is easier to communicate at a great distance with land based missiles than with distant submerged submarines.

All of the above is in the short or fairly short run. For a long run in which the Russians were free to spend resources, to build new ICBMs based in Russia or new medium or intermediate range ballistic missiles based in Cuba, the choice this opens up to them cannot be dismissed out of hand. As some of the commentators suggested, the shorter range missiles are cheaper. If they are drastically cheaper for a desired level and type of performance, they would offer the Russians a significantly larger destruction capability for a given budget. Some long run mixture of close and distant basing then might be optimal for a Russian force, providing their decision makers with an improved option in a crisis to strike first.

In sum, Cuba offered to the Russians the means for a very large and immediate expansion of the forces capable of hitting elements of the American retaliatory force based in the United States. Moreover further large increments were readily available. The effect of such a rapid increase in power on the actual military balance could not be lightly dismissed; and the political uses of even an apparent change seemed evident.

---

[23] According to a Defence Department spokesman, 22 October, 1962.

[24] Doubts about this coverage persist in some European and American analyses. They appear to be based on a poorly reasoned uncritically sceptical commentary by Roger Hagan and Bart Bernstein, "The Military Value of Missiles in Cuba," *Council for Correspondence Newsletter,* 22 November, 1962. Hagan and Bernstein relied on newspaper and magazine accounts of intelligence data that themselves confused the MRBMs and IRBMs installed in Cuba with the shorter range T-1 and T-2 and they misread the public statements about the expected operational-date and number of IRBMs.

THE VIEW FROM THE UNITED STATES

The sudden installation of a sizeable number of nuclear bombardment vehicles in Cuba, and the long-term prospects of such a base very near American shores, offered much foundation for sober thought about significant alterations in the military balance. This balance is not a simple one-dimensional matter and neither were the effects of such an installation. However, as we have already indicated, the Russian military build-up touched many problems of defence other than the preservation of a United States second-strike capability in the event of a thermonuclear war. It affected the political and military stability of Cuba and Latin America. And President Kennedy was acutely conscious of the political effects of even the *appearance* of a vast Soviet increase in military power. "The Cuban effort," he commented after the crisis, with Russian deception in mind, "has made it more difficult for us to carry out any successful negotiations, because this was an effort to materially change the balance of power . . . not that [the Soviets] were intending to fire [the missiles] . . . But it would have politically changed the balance of power. It would have appeared to, and appearances contribute to reality."[25]

One of the least understood aspects of the crisis from the standpoint of American as well as Russian interests concerned the role of overseas bases. It was the building of a Russian overseas base of course that prompted the crisis. Our discovery of the installation was preceded by Khrushchev's public deprecation of its utility, his statement that it would add nothing to his long-range rockets based in the Soviet Union. In Western discussion, during the crisis and since, of concessions or disengagements, the possibility of giving up American bases overseas was prominent. The issue was somewhat blurred by the focus on the Turkish-based *Jupiters* whose removal had been planned before the crisis and ironically was delayed by Soviet demand for their removal during the crisis itself. For good reason. Whether or not the *Jupiter* installations were useful, it was apparent that their removal under pressure would be a very different thing from the dismantling of the *Thors* in England, initiated sometime before because they were not worth their keep. (In fact one of the writers of this essay had written a series of critical analyses of the *Thors* and *Jupiters* beginning in 1957; but was clear that October 1962 would have been a poor date for a change.) In any case, the deficiencies of the *Thor* and *Jupiter* bases should not be taken as an example of the general worthlessness or for that matter of the lessening value of overseas bases.

In the West, liberal and conservative opinion sometimes meet on common ground in the depreciation of the role of overseas bases in the

[25] *Washington Post,* 18 December, 1962. The right contrast with mere appearance is not a steady intent to fire, but a contingent choice in future crises.

1960s. Suggestions that modern developments in missilery make them unnecessary might be quoted from the surviving massive retaliationists, but also from *The Liberal Papers*.[26]

Such suggestions are a vast over-simplification of the military implications of current and future states of the art of war. It is true that the deterrent function of some American weapons in a big thermonuclear war was much more dependent on overseas bases when the predominant part of the US force was the short-legged B-47. However, thermonuclear war is not the only problem of national and alliance defence or of the defence of non-aligned powers. US defence programmes have stressed more and more the threat of non-nuclear, conventional and unconventional warfare—moreover, thermonuclear war itself is a lot more complicated than this deprecation of overseas bases suggests.

In brief, overseas bases have vital roles in a possible central war in the 1960s and 1970s—both for deterrence and for limiting damage in case deterrence fails. They do dilute and can dilute even more Soviet offensive preparations by posing the need to set up a *variety* of defensive barriers. They are an important source of continuing information on the enemy. They can be made to complicate the design of his attack —for example, with the extension of the present bomb alarm system. Under several plausible contingencies of outbreak they can help spoil his attack. All this for a thermonuclear war.

But even more obviously today overseas bases have a dominant role in non-nuclear wars. They affect the speed with which the West can react and the cost and size of reaction to aggressions in remote parts of the world. The role of Japan in fighting the Korean war, the movements in May 1962 from various stations to Thailand, and later movements of weapons from Thailand in support of the Indians in their battle with the Chinese all illustrate the continuing importance of overseas bases.

For the Russians also overseas bases in the 1960s and 1970s might conceivably come to have an important role. And this role would have principally to do with non-nuclear internal and external wars. Dr. Guy Pauker suggested a while ago that the massive Russian military aid to Indonesian or other overseas base areas might be the only way Russia has of influencing events in Southeast Asia directly rather than

---

[26] "The United States may find that it will no longer need bases around the periphery of the USSR and Communist China, and that instead, pending effective arms reduction, it should place its chief reliance on long-range missiles to be delivered from its own territory," p. 268, *The Liberal Papers*, ed. James Roosevelt, Anchor Books, Doubleday and Co., Garden City, New York, 1962.

And "The question would then arise whether the security of Japan would be more effectively safeguarded by the use of United States long-range missiles in case of an emergency than by the presence of American troops and/or weapons on Japanese territory." p. 269, *ibid.*

through the agency of its quarrelsome Chinese sometime partner and rival. Whatever the case for the Soviet Union, recent American policy unambiguously requires distant logistic support. The explicit shift in the last four years to stress conventional and unconventional non-nuclear war makes it more necessary than ever, and yet the importance of overseas bases seems to be less and less understood. Perhaps the recent troubles in India and Malaysia, with the demands they may place on British bases east of Suez as well as some American ones, will make their worth more generally appreciated. Less than nuclear contests remote from one or both of the great powers may nevertheless engage their interests in conflict, but such contests are hard to influence without overseas bases.

Our discussion of Cuba suggests that not all the interests of the United States conflict with those of the Soviet Union. Mr. Khrushchev and Mr. Kennedy were both clear about their mutual interest in keeping Castro's finger off a nuclear trigger. On the other hand, the view from the Soviet Union indicates that, in spite of talk about "overriding" interests of both sides in avoiding nuclear war, there are many fundamental points at issue between the great powers. And while there is hardly a doubt that both sides would be worse off in the event of a nuclear war, and that they do and should spend considerable energies and resources in avoiding it, the dubious note in the phrase "overriding interests . . ." is struck by the adjective "overriding." It suggests that the opposing interests are negligible, well understood, and easily resolved or likely to be resolved in the near-term future, if only, we are told, the politicians are sincere.

President Kennedy did not take the Soviet build-up in Cuba as an act unrelated to the future of the world. He related it to Chairman Khrushchev's desire to see the world transformed, to sponsor struggles of liberation, and to revise what the Russians regard as "abnormal" situations, such as West Berlin. In his October 22 speech announcing the Amerian blockade of arms shipments to Cuba, President Kennedy warned that any hostile acts at other points on the globe (he mentioned West Berlin specifically) would meet with equal American determination, and he called upon Mr. Khrushchev to "abandon this course of world domination."

The encounter over this small island, then, on the American view, had to do with the future of the world. However, in this encounter, not only Cuba, but the rest of the aligned and non-aligned world—the OAS, NATO, China, the United Nations—were subordinated to a passive role. The chief actors were the opposing nuclear powers. Castro could obstruct, delay and complicate the resolution of the issue, but in the end he was hardly able to affect it centrally. Members of the OAS and NATO were apprised of the President's decision to institute a quarantine a few hours before it was announced to the public, and the actual signing of the Presidential proclamation of quarantine, was delayed to obtain the formal approval of the OAS members. These friends of the United States without exception rallied to its support and in the week of unrelenting pressure to get the missiles out, their consensus played a part. To assess its importance one should contemplate what might have been the effect of dissent. Can we be sure that a welter of doubts and alternative proposals might not have altered Khrushchev's estimate of the singleness of American resolve? If it had, the crisis might not have ended where it did.

Mr. Khrushchev had worse luck in his dealings with some of his allies. But in the end it was President Kennedy's and Chairman Khrushchev's decisions that determined events. The difficulty in sharing such momentous decisions raises important domestic issues in a democracy, but it has even more obvious problems for allies whose fate may be affected by those decisions.

Nonetheless what transpired was by no means a game of nuclear "Chicken," as the advocates of unilateral disarmament suggest; both President Kennedy and Mr. Khrushchev showed acute consciousness and care about the risks. (Some sober and excellent analysts accept the analogy of "Chicken," but the differences seem to us more significant than the identities. Bertrand Russell, who introduced the parallel in the 1950s as a paradigm of international behaviour today, meant precisely to suggest the recklessness of the statesmen, and the triviality and childishness of what was at issue—a kind of loss of face with the other children in the neighbourhood.) Nor was Cuba a case in which there was no danger of military action. There were possibilities of escalation, of the spread and intensification of violence. The risks of nuclear war are never zero. But the President was aware also of the risks of escalation in *inaction*. Inaction in Cuba would have invited, for example, a spiralling series of actions over Berlin.

From the timing of Mr. Khrushchev's move in Cuba it seems likely that he was conscious of the relation between Cuba and a climax to East-West disagreements over Berlin. President Kennedy at any rate was explicit about the connection. Retreat from a prominent public and formal stand that the United States had taken as recently as mid-September would have invited Mr. Khrushchev to believe that the United States would retreat also in Berlin. (This might also have come to be the belief of the allies of the United States.) However, the risks that Mr. Khrushchev would have undertaken in Berlin are, for a variety of reasons, considerably larger than the risks he undertook in Cuba. The government of the United States had tried to make it clear that if the Soviet Union moved on Berlin or on the Central European front, then NATO in spite of local communist superiority, would throw into the breach a very large conventional force, including perhaps a half dozen American divisions. If these were destroyed or in danger of destruction, it is evident that the risks of an American nuclear response would be raised enormously.

One cliche and over-simple view that seems to have a special appeal in crisis has it that the threat of force or the use of a low level of violence, including even a partial blockade, leads naturally to higher levels of violence. But in Cuba a very rudimentary and limited use of force, reversed the direction, started it down. There was in fact at no time during the crisis any suggestion on the part of President Kennedy and his immediate staff that this was a careless game of bluff, in which they incautiously might let a war get started by chance or unauthorized acts. On the contrary there was every attempt to resist the act of desperation proposed from both the left and the right. "We have been determined," President Kennedy said on 22 October, "not to be diverted from our central concerns by mere irritants, and fanatics." Newspaper accounts during the crisis and a Senate Report published at the end of January, 1963, stressed the extreme concern of the President and his executive committee with even the minute details of actions taken at the lowest levels of government.[27] There was no dearth of management of the crisis.

Some of the statements of President Kennedy and even more those of Chairman Khrushchev may be a little misleading in this respect. In the case of Mr. Khrushchev, up to a certain point he may have wanted to convey an impression of recklessness. When confronted with the threat of having a Russian freighter boarded and searched, he asserted that this "would make talks useless" and bring into action the "forces and laws . . . of war";[28] it would have "irretrievably fatal consequences."[29]

In other words he was indicating to President Kennedy that interception of a freighter would involve thermonuclear massive retaliation, either as a deliberate act of the Russians or because he would not be able to restrain and control his own forces. Not he, but the laws of war would be in charge. After the crisis had receded, moreover, Chairman Khrushchev was anxious to represent his retreat as a statesman's action to save the world from the imminent peril, "the direct threat of world thermonuclear war which arose in the Caribbean area."[30] "If one or the other side had not shown restraint, not done everything needed to avert the outbreak of war, an explosion of irreparable consequences would have followed."[31] He made more than a suggestion

[27] Senator Henry M. Jackson (Democrat, State of Washington), *Los Angeles Times*, 29 January, 1963, and "The Administration of National Security: Basic Issues" for the Committee on Government Operations, 1963.

[28] Message to President Kennedy on 27 October, 1962: "you, in your statement, said that the main aim is not only to come to an agreement [but also to] undertake measures to prevent a confrontation of our ships and thus aggravate the crisis and thus [ignite the fires] of a military conflict in such a confrontation, after which any talks would be already useless as other forces and laws would go into action, the laws of war." *New York Times*, 28 October, 1962.

[29] *Ibid.*

[30] Speech of 12 December, 1962, to the Supreme Soviet, *New York Times*, 13 December, 1962.

[31] *Ibid.*

after the event that the danger of recklessness arose from "the ruling circle of the United States who are rightly called 'madmen.' The madmen insisted and insist now on starting a war as soon as possible against the Soviet Union."[32] Mr. Khrushchev's open and bitter contest with the Chinese and Albanian Communists also required pointed reference to the imminent dangers of thermonuclear war. However, at the peak of the crisis and in fact in the same letter in which he tried for the last time to suggest an inevitable and uncontrollable thermonuclear response to the interception of a Soviet freighter, Chairman Khrushchev made it very plain that he was in careful, thorough and self-conscious charge of the decision on whether or not to respond with nuclear weapons. It was here in fact that he in particular stressed that the Cuban missiles were under his control. And in the following day he emphasized again that "the Soviet government will not allow itself to be provoked."[33] Finally in his *post-mortem* speech to the Supreme Soviet on 12 December, 1962, he indicated that both the Russian and American "sides displayed a sober approach, and took into account that unless such steps were taken that could help overcome the dangerous development of events, a third World War might break out." The madmen in the ruling circle of the United States then were very sober lunatics; and the sober Russians understood that.

Some of President Kennedy's statements in the crisis and after may also have overstated the likelihood of a nuclear exchange. He was appropriately anxious to express the gravity of his concern about such a catastrophe. Theodore Sorensen makes clear that President Kennedy was aware of the pitfalls of public utterance at this time. "His warnings on the presence of Soviet missiles in Cuba had to be sufficiently sombre to enlist support around the world without creating panic here at home."[34] And so on 22 October, 1962, he talked of the world "at the abyss of destruction." In his acceptance of Mr. Khrushchev's retreat on 28 October, 1962, he seemed also to accept the validity of Mr. Khrushchev's earlier threat of uncontrollability. "Developments were approaching a point where events could have become unmanageable." Though control was evident in every one of his moves, President Kennedy's statements did not stress in words that he was in control. It has therefore been possible to misconstrue just what were the risks in the crisis.

The matter is of great importance. The fact that Cuba could be isolated makes a great contrast with the problem in Central Europe. But even on the Central European front American policy differs

[32] *Ibid.*
[33] Message to President Kennedy of 28 October, 1962.
[34] *Decision-Making in the White House,* Columbia University Press, New York, 1963, p. 47.

markedly from that of a dictator who uses a reputation for irresponsibility and apparent willingness to usher in *Goetterdaemmerung* for even minor gains. Threats of uncontrollability should be administered by prescription, against special dangers, and in small doses. Its use except *in extremis* is not compatible with a reputation for being both sane and meaning what one says.

In fact the main risks were of a local, non-nuclear action involving the United States and Russian forces. The possibilities of isolating a limited conflict have seldom been clearer. The situation is very different from Berlin. Remote islands are better than enclaves in satellite territory in this respect. Cuba, surrounded by water rather than East Germans, very distant from the centre of Russian conventional power, did not represent, nor was it contiguous to, any interests that the Soviet Union had dominated for many years. How likely was Chairman Khrushchev to launch missiles at the United States to retrieve a gamble for a quick expansion of this communist foothold in the Western Hemisphere, itself a windfall? Retreat in fact has not even meant the loss of the foothold.

What was threatened was a local non-nuclear action, a measure of very limited violence, only the boarding of ships. On the staircase of ascending steps in the use of force there would have been many landings, many decision points, at which either side could choose between climbing higher or moving down. The United States' nuclear retaliatory force would have made a Soviet missile strike against the United States catastrophic for Russia. But the United States also had an immense local superiority in conventional forces. The Soviet Union clearly would have lost the non-nuclear exchange. Chairman Khrushchev stepped down to avoid a clash of conventional forces in which he would have lost. To avoid this level of loss he would have had irresponsibly to risk very much higher levels.

Some distinguished American analysts tell us that our local superiority in conventional force was an inessential convenience affecting our self-confidence, but not Khrushchev's. Without a deep psychoanalysis of the former Chairman, this would be rather hard to prove or disprove. However, so bald a separation of the determinants of decision on the two sides seems most implausible. Each side strained to affect the anticipations of the other by act as well as word, and its own expectations depended in part on how it read the other's. The American leadership knew that Khrushchev had no basis for confidence in the outcome of any clash with conventional arms in the Caribbean; and a world to lose if he resorted to nuclear weapons.

Inevitably, the question of how nuclear and how conventional arms figured in forcing Khrushchev's withdrawal was much disputed once the crisis had passed, although it is doubtful whether many of the disputants changed their views as a result either of the crisis or the post-crisis debate. Witnesses at the Congressional hearings in the following

spring at any rate interpreted events according to their predisposi-
tions.[35] Those who had held before the crisis that a strategic nuclear
threat can credibly and safely deter all but rather minor border incursions testified that "strategic superiority" was the major factor
forcing Khrushchev's withdrawal. Those who had believed that nuclear
force—in particular a clear-cut second-strike nuclear capability—is
vital, but inadequate as a response to an important range of provocations, took the withdrawal as illustrating "the cutting edge" of the
conventional sword. This single encounter where the United States
had both the capability to dominate in a conventional conflict and
also to inflict overwhelming nuclear damage could not demonstrate
once and for all that conventional superiority will always have a major
utility; still less could it show that it might easily be dispensed with.
Witnesses such as Secretary McNamara who valued and had greatly
increased useable conventional capability in the preceding two years,
were in charge of controlling the risks during the crisis. They deployed
and prepared to use a vast conventional force, including several hundred thousand men poised for invasion. While continuing to deter
nuclear action by the Russians, they prepared a mounting sequence of
threats short of nuclear war. The dispensability of these moves can
only be conjectured. Relying on more desperate threats might have
worked, but would clearly have been a greater gamble.

The relevance to Berlin of the Cuban crisis was, as we have said,
immediately recognized by the President and the other members of the
EXCOM, for a retreat in Cuba would have been evidence of a likely
retreat in Berlin. But our firmness in Cuba cannot conclusively show
the opposite. Some Americans are concerned to play down our conventional superiority in Cuba lest it suggest, illogically to be sure, that
we would be firm *only* where we have conventional superiority. But
for us as for the Russians the stakes as well as the risks are larger in
Berlin.

Not that the risks were small in Cuba. The menace of actual conflict between American and Russian forces even in battle with conventional weapons was emphasized by the long history of debate on the
massive retaliation theory. As General Maxwell Taylor's account
makes clear, much of the doctrinal dispute among the Joint Chiefs
had taken the form of a seemingly scholastic argument over the definition of "general war."[36] "General war" had been defined as a conflict
between the forces of the United States and those of the Soviet Union,
and the definition assumed and made explicit that nuclear weapons

---

[35] *Military Procurement Authorization, Fiscal Year 1964*, Committee on Armed
Services, US Senate, 88th Congress, First Session, 1963, pp. 507, 896 and *passim*, Cf.
also *Hearings on Military Posture*, House Armed Services Committee, 1963.
[36] *The Uncertain Trumpet*, Harper Brothers, New York (1959), 1960, pp. 7ff, 39,
117.

would be used from the outset. The definition was an attempt to enforce by semantics, so to speak, a belief that any hostile contact between American and Russian troops would bring immediate nuclear devastation, and so to discourage such a contact. But in Cuba it was apparent that conventional attack on the Russian missile bases was one of the alternatives contemplated and that therefore the United States was separating the decision to do battle with the Russians from the decision to initiate a nuclear war. Decisions to board Russian ships were even more obviously kept distinct from a nuclear decision.

Chairman Khrushchev was right in his later assertion that the United States and the Soviet Union were both in full control of their nuclear forces.

CONTROL AND AUTOMATIC STAIRS

We stress the point only because, in this respect, some of the American official statements made at the height of the crisis did less than justice to American policy. Any suggestion that the United States could not control its responses even in boarding a Russian freighter, would be bound to raise disturbing questions at home. And under some circumstances it would be self-defeating. If Chairman Khrushchev had thought that American decision makers themselves believed their next move would push events out of control, that they had, in the legal phrase, the last clear chance to avoid nuclear war, he might very well have doubted the desperate move and so have been rather less deterred and less alarmed than the American public and America's allies. He might have found it inconceivable that the American President would deliberately let matters get unmanageable. In fact well before the Cuban crisis the President and Secretary McNamara and Secretary Rusk had declared, and their subordinates had elaborated, a thoughtful doctrine of controlled response, up to and including the conduct of a nuclear war. Yet, as we have mentioned, President Kennedy's statement of 22 October, excellent as it was on the whole, focussed, for understandable reasons, on "the abyss of destruction." And in attempting to get across the essential message of the American nuclear guarantee for neighbours in Latin America, it indicated that "any nuclear missile launched from Cuba against any nation in the Western Hemisphere" would evoke "a *full* retaliatory response upon the Soviet Union" (our italics). This does not sound like a controlled response. The attempt, it appears, was to say that the United States would respond to a missile against its neighbours as it would respond to one against itself. This latter policy would leave open the possibility of controlled reaction. The United States has made clear that a single nuclear missile launched against the United States need not trip an uncontrolled "full" response.

However, it was even more important to make clear, and in American behaviour it was evident, that the United States did not exclude the possibility of control in the non-nuclear spectrum. In fact it insisted upon it. It responded in a carefully limited way to an aggression which involved the installation, but not the firing, of a nuclear weapon. Against such a move the Cuban crisis demonstrated the relevance and the adequacy of the lowest non-nuclear moves in an ascending series of non-nuclear threats and actions: the threat to board and search freighters for military equipment, a single actual boarding of a chartered Lebanese ship, the imposition of a selective economic blockade, a general blockade, the threat or the actual use of bombing with high explosives against strategic missile bases, the threat or actual use of paratroops, and so forth. The later steps in the sequence never had to be more than latent. But one of the reasons the limited American threat worked was that the United States was willing to take the next steps, if necessary, and had the power to do so—to make each next step less profitable for the Soviet Union.

Before the crisis, the alternatives for policy were discussed in terms of a few bare possibilities: a pure American military invasion, a total blockade, or doing nothing. In the crisis it appeared the world was richer in alternatives than had been conceived by extremists of the left or right. There is a good deal between doing nothing and all-out nuclear war, and an appropriate intermediate response could make a nuclear war less rather than more likely. President Kennedy observed that these alternatives became apparent in the course of five days of discussion, that without this time for hammering out alternatives, he might have chosen less wisely and more extremely.[37] The history of this crisis should be an important corrective for the loose assumption that the only time available for decision in the nuclear age is 15 minutes—a magic number supposed to represent the time from radar intercept to impact of an ICBM following a least energy path.

Professor Richard Neustadt, who has written most perceptively about the use, the limits, and the risks of using American presidential power, has taken the Cuban missile confrontation to illustrate the President's extreme awareness of the new dimensions of these risks, of the fact that somewhere in a succession of decisions he may make one that can neither be reversed nor repaired.[38] It has probably always been true that at some time in a sequence of diplomatic acts, warnings of possible military actions, and military acts themselves, statesmen have felt "things in the saddle," events taking over. It then becomes extremely unlikely that adversaries will back away from the contest or its intensification. Even though the new level of violence is likely to leave both of them worse off than *before* the sequence of threats and

[37] *Washington Post*, 18 December, 1962.
[38] *Administration of National Security. Hearings Before the Sub-Committee on National Security Staffing and Operations of the Committee on Government Operations*, United States Senate, 88th Congress, 1st Session. Part I, 1963. p. 76ff.

pre-war manoeuvres had started, nonetheless, there may be some point of no return in the sequence. At that point the outcome may appear to be better than the risk of stopping. The fact that today decisions taken in crisis might precipitate a disaster on a scale without precedent in history is sobering.

There is a sense of course in which any large scale war does enormous, irreparable harm. Population growth and economic recovery after the war replace the lives lost, the wealth annihilated and the suffering, only in a statistical sense that ignores precisely who died and what treasures were destroyed. Some nuclear conflicts might start by miscalculation and end by being quickly brought under control, and conceivably could do less material damage than World War II and I. Nonetheless such a standard is terrible enough and a nuclear war could be enormously worse. This new sense of the possibility of irreparable harm says a good deal about the psychological burden of the Presidency. And not only the Presidency. The Chairman of the CPSU explicitly referred to the "irreparable" consequences of a failure in restraint by either side. It makes clear why neither Nikita Khrushchev nor John Kennedy behaved like the irrational juvenile delinquents who are sometimes presumed to occupy the seats of power today, strapped by their seatbelts in a carefree game of Chicken.

Where the alternative is to be ruled by events with such enormous consequences, the head of a great state is likely to examine his acts of choice in crisis and during it to subdivide these possible acts in ways that make it feasible to continue exercising choice. This sort of behaviour does not fit an increasingly popular and professional picture which has it that political leaders may be thoughtful, responsible and close to reality in between crises, but overreact passionately during the crises themselves. However, there is a good deal of professional evidence as well as common sense opinion to indicate that, as Dewey put it, when any thinking is going on, it is likely to be because there has been some trouble. Routine experience may lead us imperceptibly to ignore a slowly changing or suddenly new reality, but we do sometimes rise to a challenge with heightened alertness and an increased sense of responsibility, especially on matters of great moment. The behaviour of the decision makers in the Cuban crisis at any rate provides a counter example to a good many pessimistic predictions derived from studies by behavioural scientists concerned with reducing international tension.[39]

---

[39] Generalising from 1914, some studies predict that as tensions rise in a crisis, decision makers will tend to decide emotionally rather than by calculation. The range of alternatives they see will narrow and they will be less able to assess the likely consequences of each possible choice. They will see less time before the enemy strikes and this will lead to still greater tension, to a tendency to value early action and dislike delay, to depreciate the dangers of violent action and the rewards of non-violent action, and to

A process of escalation is usually thought of simply as an increase in violence growing out of a limited conflict in which an adversary may act to stave off his loss or an opponent's prospective success. The aspect of "escalators" that inspired its use in this connection, we suspect, is the fact that moving stairways carry a passenger on automatically without any effort of his will. However, as we have suggested there are down-escalators as well as up-escalators, and there are landings between escalators where one can decide to get off or to get on, to go up or down, or to stay there; or take the stairs. Just where automaticity or irreversibility takes over is an uncertain but vital matter, and that is one of the reasons a decision maker may want to take a breath at a landing to consider next steps. It is apparent from President Kennedy's own descriptions of the Cuban crisis as well as Mr. Sorensen's that he gave enormous value to the cautious weighing of alternatives made possible by the interval of almost a week; to the five or six days mentioned for hammering out the first decision. And the decision made was precisely one that left open a variety of choices. Finally the availability of less desperate choices than acquiescence or holocaust had been prepared before the crisis by the deliberate policy of preserving options, developing a force capable of flexible response.

One way in which the overhanging possibility of an irreversible disastrous decision might operate today is to bring on an immobility that, paradoxically, reduces the alternatives to a few extremes. The irreversible sequence might be started then by a desperate act to avoid the loss that looms in the extreme of retreat. But there is more than one way to arrive at a paralysis and gross reduction of choice. The opposite path, proceeding on the perception that commitment is inevitable, can advance commitment to a much earlier stage than necessary in the process of coercion and resisting coercion. This is the danger inherent in threats of massive retaliation. That war can be so massive a disaster tempts us to use the threat of this disaster to paralyse an adversary bent on aggression; but it may end in our own paralysis. The Cuban missile crisis at any rate illustrated an intensive search among alternatives to find a threat that could be executed with a minimal risk, and a slowly ascending sequence of threats which could not be challenged by the Soviet Union without making its position still worse.

---

accept suspicions and fears as facts. There predictions are necessarily somewhat vague. None of them, however, appears to have been borne out by the behavior of decision makers in the missile crisis. See *Content Analysis, a Handbook with Applications for the Study of International Crisis* by Robert C. North, Ole R. Holsti, M. George Zaninovich, and Dina A. Zinnes, Northwestern University Press, 1963, Appendix B, for the hypotheses derived from 1914 and contrast with materials derived from the Cuban crisis and presented by Holsti, North and Brody in *Peace Research Society (International) Papers*, Vol. 2, Oslo, 1965.

There is an important class of situations in which a crisis may be precipitated as the result of an unfounded or exaggerated mutual distrust. These are cases where, in the words of the most brilliant analyst of such reciprocal fears, "people may vaguely think they perceive that the situation is inherently explosive, and respond by exploding."[40] But some of the time guns go off because we do not know they are loaded; grenades explode because we think they are duds; or enemies attack because we are so sure they will not attack that we are unprepared for it. The Cuban missile crisis should remind us of these equally important situations in which an excess of trust or self-confidence causes the trouble, and a sharp awakening to the possibilities of explosion helps bring the trouble under responsible control. Tactics of deception typically attempt to induce trust where it is not warranted. Khruschev and Gromyko during the prelude to the crisis simply lied. And the traditional confidence man feeds on the gullibility and wishfulness of his target. "Never give a sucker an even break" evokes a long history of cases where it is not mutual distrust that is explosive, but fond belief on the one side, a willingness to exploit it on the other, and a violent sense of outrage by the victim at having his innocence exploited. But the victim need not explode. He can carefully signal the danger to his adversary.

The resolution of the missile crisis may be regarded as in the main a brilliant example of a successful communication of a precise and firm intention. However, in some of its aspects, and especially in its generation, the crisis illustrates the possibilities of miscommunication. Under other circumstances, such miscommunication might not have had so fortunate an ending. Moreover, the misunderstandings do not fit one current wishful stereotype: that our troubles stem only from our failure to realize how like us our adversaries really are. Our estimates and those of the Russians, just before the missile confrontation, resembled each other mainly in that they each too easily assumed an identity in modes of thought and valuation. They illustrate rather the difficulty one always has in breaking out of the circle of one's own notion of what is normal in national behaviour.

The missile crisis was precipitated by some poor Russian and American estimates of each other's willingness to take risks. The American leaders did not believe the Russians would be foolhardy enough, in the face of President Kennedy's explicit warning against it, to put into Cuba missiles which were capable of hitting the United States. The Russians on the other hand did not think the Americans would risk a direct confrontation.

The false estimates on both sides did not concern whether the United States had clearly warned the Russians not to put in place in

---

[40] T. C. Schelling, *The Strategy of Conflict,* p. 208.

Cuba surface-to-surface missiles with a significant capability to hit the United States. They had to do with Russian disbelief that the President would act in case they ignored his warning, and an American judgement that the Russians would recognize that the President meant what he said. Yet one curious aftermath of the crisis is a rewriting of history, especially in Europe, that questions not merely whether it was obvious that President Kennedy meant what he explicitly stated in September, but doubts even that he had said it.

The situation is somewhat confused by the interminable wrangle over the distinction between "offensive" and "defensive" weapons. There is of course no sharp distinction between the two and there are many interconnections. An aggressor can defend himself, limit the destruction wreaked against his own territory, among other subtler ways, by using surface-to-surface missiles or bombers to reduce his victim's retaliatory forces before they take off; and once his victim's retaliatory forces are launched on their way, he can use active and passive defences, such as surface-to-air missiles, jet fighters and civil defence to reduce his victim's retaliation further. Moreover, the Cuban surface-to-air missiles and fighters themselves illustrate that active defences can be used to prevent or to impede surveillance and so help to cover the build-up of a force of surface-to-surface missiles and manned bombers. Even the direct use of fighter aircraft or short-range missiles with the help of torpedo boats would provide some minimal capability to hit American coastal targets. All of this ignores still subtler interconnections between the threats or the use of "offensive" or "defensive" weapons.

However, the distinction the President made between offensive and defensive weapons served the purpose of warning well enough, because he made very clear what weapons he had in mind as "offensive." On 4 September he said, ". . . the Soviets have provided the Cuban government with a number of anti-aircraft defence missiles with a slant range of 25 miles which are similar to early models of our Nike. . . . There is no evidence . . . of the presence of offensive ground-to-ground missiles; or of other significant offensive capability either in Cuban hands or under Soviet direction and guidance. Were it to be otherwise, the gravest issues would arise."

In other words the President drew a line with a broad and hairy brush between offensive and defensive weapons in general, but he clearly classed Russian medium and intermediate range surface-to-surface missiles in the offensive category. Emplacing them in Cuba would be strategic trespass. Moreover, the Russians understood him. Their government authorized *Tass* to state on 11 September ". . . there is no need for the Soviet Union to shift its weapons . . . to any other country, for instance Cuba . . . the Soviet Union has rockets so powerful to carry . . . nuclear warheads that there is no need to search for sites for them beyond the boundaries of the Soviet Union . . . the Soviet Union has the capability from its own territory to render assistance to any peace-loving state and not only to Cuba.'' The President knew that the message had been understood. He believed it would be respected. It was this last conviction, supported by Soviet reassurances, ''both public and private, in September, that proved illusory in the following month. In President Kennedy's words,

> I don't think that we expected that he (Khrushchev) would put the missiles in Cuba, because it would have seemed such an imprudent action for him to take, as it was later proved. Now, he obviously must have thought that he could do it in secret and that the United States would accept it. So that he did not judge our intentions accurately.

The Americans assumed in short that the Russians understood that Americans are tolerant but cannot be pushed beyond a certain point, especially when that point has been clearly and publicly announced. But just how imprudent is was for the Russians to put missiles in Cuba depended on whether the Americans were willing to force a showdown. So the American estimate that the Russians would not emplace the missiles depended on an American judgement about how the Russians thought Americans would act. Moreover, there is no doubt that President Kennedy's judgement of the American character was right. His own behaviour, with its brief explosion of anger at Gromyko's continuing deception, and the bitter repetition in the 22 October speech ''That statement was false'' was in a long tradition of sharp moral reactions at confidence betrayed. In more controlled form, it repeated the indignation of acting Secretary Polk and President Wilson at the decoded German message showing that while the German foreign minister had been talking peace he had plotted to encourage a Mexican attack on the United States. Or the fury of Secretary Hull and President Roosevelt at the Japanese representatives Kurusu and Nomura at the time of Pearl Harbour.

On the other hand, to the Russians surely President Kennedy's response was an extraordinary over-reaction. Chairman Khrushchev had enunciated and withdrawn a succession of ultimata on Berlin beginning in 1958, and done so with distinct disappointment, but with comparative equanimity. He could hardly have understood either the enormous importance conferred by domestic party debate (with the Bay of Pigs disaster in the background) on the specific line the President had drawn between offensive and defensive weapons, or the great to-do over the deception. (Khrushchev's experience with cases in which Americans themselves had used deception might have suggested the accompanying sense of guilt and half-heartedness with which this is done. The American response to the shooting down of the U2 piloted by Powers in 1960 forms an interesting cultural contrast with the indignant denial by the Soviet government in the United Nations of actions revealed by the detailed reconnaissance photos of the missiles in Cuba.) Each side in short tended to project its own psychology or certain stereotypes about the behaviour of the other. The Russians acted on the assumption that the Americans were so driven by domestic politics as to be unlikely to react in any decisive way; or that they would act like Russians.

In the period of withdrawing the missiles, once again, Americans tended to project American behaviour on to the Russians. Just as they had exaggerated the Russian estimate of risks and underestimated Russian daring, they now overestimated Russian reluctance to withdraw after a nice try. But here too Russian behaviour is very different from American. The prospect of humiliation was of enormous importance to President Kennedy. It did not have quite the same importance for Khrushchev. Serious students of Russian behaviour with such different approaches as George Kennan and Nathan Leites have long observed that "the Kremlin has no compunction about retreating in the face of superior force."[41] After the withdrawal, many journalists recalled Brest-Litovsk and Lenin's phrase about the good revolutionary being willing to crawl in the mud. But that recollection was much rarer in the actual week of quarantine and crisis. By December, 1962, Khrushchev himself was referring to Lenin's "sensible" and "temporary" concession. The Albanian dogmatists who criticized the withdrawal of missiles, he claimed, were sliding down Trotsky's path of unyielding infantilism at Brest. But the missile withdrawal was not even a temporary retreat, much less a capitulation. The concessions, Khrushchev said, were "mutual."[42]

Such cultural contrasts are of course a matter of degree; but nonetheless real. Ruth Benedict's *The Chrysanthemum and the Sword* offers a brilliant analysis of Japanese feelings toward retreat and humiliation—as far exceeding in depth and range American emotions on the subject. And there are limits to Bolshevik tolerance in withdrawal.

INTERESTS AND INFLUENCE OF THE
TWO PRINCIPALS AND THEIR ALLIES

This retrospect of the interests and policy alternatives open to the three powers in the crisis indicates the need for refining some of the

---

[41] George Kennan, *American Diplomacy*, 1900–1950, p. 112. See also Nathan Leites, *Study of Bolshevism*, Chapter 19, and his recent "Kremlin Thoughts: Yielding, Provoking, Rebuffing, Retreating." RM 3618–ISA, the RAND Corporation, May, 1963, pp. 24ff.

[42] Speech, 12 December, 1962.

questions with which we started. When we say that in the nuclear age force is no longer an instrument of policy, it is not clear whether this is description or exhortation. In fact a blockade, it was generally agreed in September, 1962, was an act of war. Attitudes and definitions changed in October. This is a delicate matter of semantics. The American interdiction of ships carrying arms to Cuba was called a "quarantine." Nonetheless it was an act of force. And threats of higher levels of violence were implicit at every stage in the developing crisis. The questions at issue directly affected Soviet, Cuban, and United States military power.

The availability of nuclear weapons to the great powers had a double aspect. The weapons imposed the need for great responsibility and careful, very conscious control over the limited encounters that took place. On the other hand the use of lower levels of violence in such encounters is in a certain sense encouraged by the knowledge that a decision to escalate to nuclear weapons would be irrational and inappropriate for either of the participants and, for the prudent men in control, uncharacteristically irrational. And prudent antagonists can co-operate to insulate nuclear weapons from less prudent third parties. These encounters were rather clearly isolable from a decision to use nuclear weapons. Each of the nuclear powers took the time and had the information to see that the initiation of nuclear weapons would badly worsen its own position.

American nuclear power immobilized Russian nuclear power. And American local superiority in non-nuclear force together with a demonstrated willingness to use it discouraged further destabilizing moves. The familiar saying that overwhelming nuclear force simply disables its possessor from using any force at all is a rather shallow paradox. Nevertheless thermonuclear weapons clearly suit only the gravest purposes. And while small nations are less able to affect events than big ones, they do have an effect. There are serious limits to the control even a great nuclear power has over its non-nuclear allies. This applies more obviously to relations between the United States and its allies than it does to Russia's relations with its friends. Even allies whose defence and economy depend almost wholly on the United States are, as the headlines continually remind us, far from being its puppets. A variety of South Korean and South Vietnamese regimes in the last few years has made this point vivid. And the point is much more obvious for allies that are themselves great nations.

But in this crisis at any rate a small communist power was the object of contention between its protector and its adversary and could not decisively affect the outcome. It had some capability for mischief, but even this was limited. Close and receding allies of the Soviet Union and the United States as well as the non-aligned countries could do little more than endorse or criticize after the fact. In the climactic encounter it was the United States and the Soviet Union who determined events.

The loneliness of the President's decision in such a crisis raises essential problems for allies, whose fates might be affected by it. They have an interest in sharing and influencing the decision. But also in seeing to it that the decision can be made—in avoiding paralysis. This is an essential dilemma of nuclear control. In some sense the problem is quite as acute from the standpoint of American citizen as it is from that of a Briton, or an Italian, or a Frenchman, or a citizen of any of the NATO or OAS countries. In the five or six days in which the course of quarantine was selected, only an extremely small number of people (the President himself suggested a maximum of 15) had any share in the choice.

In spite of the very just allied as well as domestic concern, this is not the sort of problem that can be neatly "solved." It can be softened somewhat, and essentially the same methods can widen both allied and domestic participation. The crises themselves and the time for decision in crises are, we have suggested, likely to occupy a good deal longer interval than the magic 15 minutes frequently referred to when nuclear dangers are in mind. The small group concerned with the actual management of the crisis conceivably could then include a few high level allied political figures. It is notable that in the missile crisis, while allies were not notified of the American quarantine until the day before its public announcement, the decision itself undertook a very minimal use of force, leaving many decision points still open in the future conduct of the affair.

More important, one can prepare for a variety of contingencies in advance of crises; one can determine what might be done, if they occur. In fact, the quadripartite planning for Berlin at the very least strongly influenced President Kennedy and his immediate associates, predisposed them to the consideration of firm but carefully measured responses to any local action, and also made them more highly conscious of the world-wide repercussions inherent in many such "local" crises.

Unfortunately, however, acute perception of the importance of far off points in space tends to be highly localized in time—to be mostly limited, in fact to times of crisis.[43] The problem of sharing contingency

---

[43] There was a strand of European opinion that seized on the Americans' firm response to Cuba as somehow a verification of the thesis that United States interests are also highly localized; it would act strongly in its own interests, when threatened close to home, but not in Europe, not, for example, in Berlin. We may leave aside the rather curious inference from the fact of positive reaction to a strong provocation close to home—to the conclusion that there would be no reaction to a more distant challenge. However, a careful scrutiny of the American response to Cuba would suggest that far from showing that the United States would not defend Berlin, the defence of Cuba from the very first revelation of the Soviet move was recognized to be a vital part of the defence of Berlin, and the fate of Berlin was prominent in the contingency planning.

planning is complicated by the fact that allies are notoriously
ambivalent about distant troubles. Before the crisis itself, they are
likely to feel that the remote problem is not very important from their
point of view; they may believe either that the chances of disaster are
small; or that the disaster will be local. They are almost sure to feel
their resources are limited and they have troubles "of their own." Indeed America's troubles with Cuba tended to be deprecated by its
allies as something of an American obsession. The United States on
the other hand naturally often felt that its allies underestimated the
depth and complexity of the threat of communism in Latin America,
and its possible ultimate worldwide importance.

NATO collaboration in shaping policy for future crises is not easy
for crises in the NATO treaty area. It is a good deal harder for any of
the multiplicity of crises that, arising outside the NATO periphery,
may ultimately be of concern to NATO. Nonetheless it seems that, for
those allies that feel a concern, rather more contingency planning in
common, formal or informal, bilateral or multilateral, could be done.

The interests of Latin American governments and people in the
outcome of the missile crisis was most obvious. It was the first time
that these countries had come directly in the shadow of a nuclear war.
And the discovery of the missiles and their forced withdrawal in a
dangerous crisis had a large emotional impact. While some of the concern was directed against the United States, on the whole Castro lost
ground. By pulling Latin America into the centre of a confrontation
between the two principal nuclear powers, he appeared to an increased
number of Latin Americans to be dangerously irresponsible. Even
Goulart's Brazil and Mexico, which had opposed OAS concert against
Castro, backed the President's blockade; and there is no doubt that
such effects lasted long beyond the crisis. The losses Castro suffered
contrast with his exalted hopes before the crisis that Russian missiles
in Cuba would fortify his prestige and influence in Latin America. But
they do not show that his hopes were unfounded; just that he had
gambled. Smaller countries may feel a great deal of ambivalence
about the acquisition of nuclear weapons by their neighbors. So the
mingled fear, pride, respect, and distrust inspired in Asia today by the
first Chinese nuclear test. The main trouble with Castro's gamble
from his standpoint was that it failed; at least for the time.

Finally a note of caution: it is easy to read too much into events,
even those of outstanding importance. Once the crisis had passed,
perhaps inevitably it was greeted as the herald of a new era—a testing
and final stabilization of "the balance" of nuclear power between the
Soviet Union and the United States, an essential elimination of the
danger of nuclear war for the foreseeable future. Especially in Europe
the notion seems widespread that the Cuban missile crisis represented
a "turning point." But such an interpretation should be suspect in
particular when advanced by those who before the missile crisis had

felt the era of effortless stability and already arrived, and then during the crisis swung to the opposite extreme of panic in exaggerating the likelihood of war. In fact the "balance" is too vaguely defined, too complex and too changeable for any such assurance. The hazards of change are political as well as technical and military. It would be a mistake to regard the Soviet's emplacement of missiles in Cuba as something like a crucial experiment deliberately conducted by the Russians and establishing for them definitely once and for all that the West is determined to resist any changes in the balance—however the "balance" is defined. Khrushchev himself quickly rejected Lord Home's hopeful declaration that the Russians, sobered by their recent experience in Cuba, might from that time revise their international role.

The Western show of determination in the missile crisis had its effects. Perhaps, as has been said, it made easier the conclusion of the test ban. Perhaps it contributed to the ultimate fall of Khrushchev. At least it provided both Khrushchev's foreign and domestic rivals with a sequence of two misdeeds to cite—"adventurism" followed by "capitulationism."[44] In spite of the ready vocabulary of abuse available to describe the sequence, such an apparently opportune advance followed by a prudent withdrawal in the face of superior force is entirely consistent with a marxist canon of behaviour, which fixes no time-table for communist expansion. The effects of the Western determination, however, in the long run are uncertain and are hardly likely to be definitive. It is most implausible to suppose that this one major Communist failure will foreclose all future significant attempts, should opportunities arise, to make further advance.

The world has changed then; but not completely. It is surely no simpler now than it was before. There are many possible dangers to the West other than a precisely timed world conspiracy of a perfectly unified, permanently hostile communist camp. Some have to do with intense communist rivalries and the great variety of "communisms" today. Even an abating hostility impels caution, so long as the change is uncertain, intermittent and slow. The transformation of the whole world need hardly be at stake, only substantial parts of it. Castro is no Tito, nor a satellite, nor an immediate military threat, nor simply a minor nuisance, but a persistent source and model for insurgency and terror in the hemisphere.

Inevitably, one extreme reading of the missile crisis took it as proving that Communists in a showdown will always retreat, that we need only face them in the future with the alternative of nuclear disaster for them to abandon any use of force to transform the world. This simple view fortunately is not very influential. Yet, if it is dangerously

---

[44] Statement by the People's Government of China of 1 September, 1963.

implausible to suppose that a few future military confrontations are capable of having this happy result, it is at least equally implausible to hold that a single encounter has already had it.

Implementing Flexible Response: Vietnam as a Test Case

JOHN LEWIS GADDIS

In order to discuss the implementation of "flexible response," it is necessary to make a choice. One can examine in overview a series of events in which that strategy manifested itself: the Bay of Pigs, Laos, Berlin, the Cuban missile crisis, the Dominican Republic. Or, one can focus in detail on the event that because of its duration, divisiveness, and cost, overshadowed them all: the war in Vietnam. There are two good reasons for choosing the second approach. First, American policy in Southeast Asia reflected in microcosm virtually all of the elements of "flexible response" as applied in practice. Second, Kennedy, Johnson, and their advisers regarded Vietnam as a fair test of that strategy: it had been Eisenhower's inability to deal with that and comparable problems that had produced the "flexible response" critique in the first place; if the strategy could not be made to work in Vietnam, then there would be serious grounds upon which to question its applicability elsewhere. American leaders took on this test fully aware of the potential difficulties, but at the same time fully confident of their ability to surmount them through a strategy designed to meet just that kind of situation.

To say that their confidence was misplaced is to understate: rarely have accomplishments turned out so totally at variance with intended objectives. The war did not save South Vietnam, it did not deter future

From *Strategies of Containment: A Critical Appraisal of Postwar American National Security Policy* by John Lewis Gaddis. Copyright © 1982 by Oxford University Press, Inc. Reprinted by permission.

aggression, it did not enhance the credibility of United States commitments elsewhere in the world, it did not prevent recriminations at home. It is too easy to blame these disparities on deficiencies in the postwar national security decision-making structure, substantial though those may have been. There has been, as we have seen, no single or consistent approach to containment; to indict all manifestations of that strategy is only to be vague. Nor is it helpful to ascribe the failure in Vietnam to the shift in leadership at the White House after November 22, 1963, however strikingly the personalities of Kennedy and Johnson may have differed. For the fact is that Johnson followed the stategy of "flexible response" faithfully in Vietnam, perhaps more so than Kennedy himself would have done.

The American defeat there rather grew out of assumptions derived quite logically from that strategy: that the defense of Southeast Asia was crucial to the maintenance of world order; that force could be applied in Vietnam with precision and discrimination; that means existed accurately to evaluate performance; and that the effects would be to enhance American power, prestige, and credibility in the world. These assumptions in turn reflected a curiously myopic preoccupation with process—a disproportionate fascination with means at the expense of ends—with the result that a strategy designed to produce a precise correspondence between intentions and accomplishments in fact produced just the opposite.

I

Officials of the Kennedy and Johnson administrations liked to insist that their policies in Vietnam were consistent with the overall direction of American foreign policy since 1947: that conflict, they maintained, was but another in a long series of steps taken to demonstrate that aggression did not pay. "The challenge that we face today in Southeast Asia," Johnson argued, "is the same challenge that we have faced with courage and that we have met with strength in Greece and Turkey, in Berlin and Korea, in Lebanon and in Cuba." The "great lesson of this generation" was that "wherever we have stood firm, aggression has ultimately been halted."[1] To question the need for a similar commitment to South Vietnam, these statements implied, was to dispute the very assumptions that had sustained the strategy of containment from its beginnings.

[1] Johnson remarks at Syracuse University, August 5, 1964, *JPP:1963-4*, p. 930; Johnson remarks to members of Congressional committees, May 4, 1965, *JPP: 1965*, p. 487. See also Rostow to Kennedy, August 17, 1961, Kennedy Papers, NSC File, Box 231, "Southeast Asia—General"; McNamara statement, "United States Policy in Vietnam," March 26, 1964, *DSB*, (April 13, 1964), p. 566; Johnson address at Johns Hopkins University, April 7, 1965, *JPP: 1965*, p. 395; Johnson remarks to National Rural Electric Cooperative Association, July 14, 1965, *ibid.*, p. 751; Johnson press conference statement, July 28, 1965, *ibid.*, pp. 794-95.

In fact, though, a gradual shift had taken place in those assumptions over the years. Kennan, it will be recalled, had stressed distinctions between vital and peripheral interests, between varieties of threats to them, and between levels of feasible response given available means; the Kennedy and Johnson administrations made no such distinctions. Kennan had sought to maintain the global balance of power by applying a combination of political, economic, military, and psychological leverage in carefully selected pivotal areas; Johnson by 1965 was relying almost exclusively on the use of military force in a theater chosen by adversaries. Kennan had hoped to harness forces of nationalism, even where communist, to contain the expanding power and influence of the Soviet Union; Johnson sought to oppose communism, even where nationalist, for the purpose of preserving American credibility in the world. And, in a final ironic twist, Johnson and later Nixon came to rely with plaintive consistency on the assistance of the Soviet Union; the original target of containment, to extricate the United States from the tangle in which its own strategy had ensnared it.

One might explain these remarkable mutations as the result of obtuseness, short-sightedness, or even absent-mindedness, but there is no evidence these qualities played any more prominent role during the Kennedy-Johnson years than is normally the case. What was distinctive about those administrations, though, was their commitment to symmetrical response, and it is here that one must look to account for an evolution of strategic thinking all the more striking for the fact that those carrying it off seemed unaware that it had occurred.

It had been, of course, NSC-68 that had shifted perceptions of threat from the Soviet Union to the international communist movement; that document had also provided a rationale for expanding means and, as a consequence, interests. Eisenhower had rejected the analysis of means set forward in NSC-68, but not its assessment of threats or interests; for this reason he had been willing to extend an ambiguous commitment to the defense of South Vietnam through the SEATO treaty,* an initiative consistent with his administration's concern to achieve maximum deterrence at minimum cost. Expense was

---

*The SEATO treaty, signed September 8, 1954, provided that in case of "armed attack" against any of the signatories or against states or territories which the signatories "by unanimous agreement may hereafter designate," they would "in that event act to meet the common danger in accordance with [their] constitutional processes." In the event of a threat "other than by armed attack" or "by any fact or situation which might endanger the peace of the area," the signatories would "consult immediately in order to agree on the measures which should be taken for the common defense." South Vietnam was not a signatory to the treaty, but a protocol attached to it did extend its provisions to cover "the States of Cambodia and Laos and the free territory under the jurisdiction of the State of Vietnam," (*American Foreign Policy, 1950–1955: Basic Documents* [Washington: 1957], pp. 913–14, 916.)

of less concern to Kennedy who, confronted with an upsurge of Viet Cong insurgency, reverted to NSC-68's concept of expandable means but coupled it with a determination to honor Eisenhower's commitment, even though it had been extended largely as a substitute for means. At the same time, Kennedy was determined to lower the risks of escalation or humiliation that earlier strategy had run; this resolve led, in time, to the deployment of American ground forces, first as "advisers" to the South Vietnamese, then, under Johnson, as full-fledged combatants.[2]

But what, precisely, was the United States interest in Vietnam? Why was the balance of power at stake there? Walt Rostow had warned in his 1962 "BSNP" draft that "major losses of territory or of resources would make it harder for the U.S. to create the kind of world environment it desires, . . . generate defeatism among governments and peoples in the non-Communist world, or give rise to frustrations at home." But when pressed to explain why the "loss" of such a small and distant country would produce these drastic consequences, Washington officials generally cited the SEATO treaty obligation, which, if not honored, would raise doubts about American commitments elsewhere in the world. "The integrity of the U.S. commitment is the principal pillar of peace throughout the world," Rusk wrote in 1965. "If that commitment becomes unreliable, the communist world would draw conclusions that would lead to our ruin and almost certainly to a catastrophic war."

This was curious reasoning. It required justifying the American commitment to South Vietnam as essential to the maintenance of global stability, but then portraying that stability as endangered by the very vulnerability of Washington's commitment. It involved both deterring aggression and being held hostage to it. The confusion, it would appear, stemmed from the failure of both the Kennedy and Johnson administrations to articulate independently derived conceptions of interest in Southeast Asis; instead, they tended to view the American stake there as determined exclusively by threats and obligations. The security of the United States, indeed of the entire non-communist world, was thought to be imperiled wherever communist challenges came up against American guarantees. Vietnam might be insignificant in itself, but as a point of intersection between threat and commitment, it was everything.

Nothing in this argument required the threat to be centrally directed, or even coordinated with communist activities elsewhere. There were, to be sure, frequent references early in the war to the

² Rostow draft, "Basic National Security Policy," March 26, 1962, p. 9; Rusk memorandum, July 1, 1965, *Pentagon Papers*, IV, 23. See also Rusk and McNamara to Kennedy, November 11, 1961, *ibid.*, II, 111; Johnson remarks to members of Congressional committees, May 4, 1965, *JPP: 1965*, p. 486; and Rostow to McNamara, May 2, 1966, Johnson Papers, NSF Agency File, Boxes 11-12, "Defense Department Vol. III."

Sino-Soviet plan for "world domination,"[3] but these became less common as evidence of the Moscow-Peking split became irrefutable. Rationales then shifted to the containment of China, but only briefly; by early 1965 the predominant concern, as Under-Secretary of Defense John McNaughton put it, was simply "to avoid a humiliating US defeat (to our reputation as a guarantor)."[4] Communism need not pose a coordinated threat to the world balance of power, then, but because victories for communism at the expense of the United States, even if uncoordinated, could result in humiliation, the challenge to global stability was no less real. The only difference was that it was now Washington's fear of retreat that linked these threats together, not the internal discipline and control of international communism itself.

Nor did the American commitment in question need to have been prudent. There was a definite sense within the Kennedy administration that Eisenhower had overextended the United States in Southeast Asia: Rostow, as has been seen would have preferred a less formal alliance structure based on offshore strongpoints;[5] Robert Komer, one of his assistants, privately described SEATO in 1961 as a "millstone" directed against non-existent dangers of overt aggression. Nonetheless, Rostow wrote Kennedy later that year: "Surely we are hooked in Viet-Nam; surely we shall honor our . . . SEATO commitment." The problem, simply, was that the dangers of disengagement seemed at each stage to outweigh the costs of pressing on. "The reasons why we went into Vietnam . . . are now largely academic," McNaughton wrote in 1966. "At each decision point we have gambled; at each point, to avoid the damage to our effectiveness of defaulting on our commitment, we have upped the ante. We have not defaulted, and the ante (and commitment) is now very high."[6]

[3] See, for example, the Joint Chiefs of Staff to McNamara, January 13, 1962, *Pentagon Papers*, II, 664; Roger Hilsman address, Tampa, Florida, June 14, 1963, *DSB*, XIX (July 8, 1963), 44; Johnson remarks at the National Cathedral School, Washington, June 1, 1965, *JPP: 1965*, p. 600.

[4] McNaughton memorandum, "Proposed Course, of Action re Vietnam," March 24, 1965, *Pentagon Papers*, III, 695. See also Michael Forrestal to William P. Bundy, November 4, 1964, *ibid.*, p. 592. For further official perceptions of lack of coordination in the international communist movement, see Thomas L. Hughes to Hilsman, April 20, 1963, Kennedy Papers NSC Files, Box 314, Folder 6; Hilsman to Rusk, July 31, 1963, *ibid.*, Folder 10; Johnson to Lodge, March 20, 1964, *Pentagon Papers*, III, 511; Bundy to Johnson, October 21, 1964, Johnson Papers, National Security Files—NSC Staff, Box 2, "Memos for the President, vol. 7"; Rostow to Rusk, December 16, 1964, *ibid.*, NSF Country Files—Vietnam, Box 11, "Memos, Vol. XXIII."

[5] See above, p. 223.

[6] Komer memorandum, "A Doctrine of Deterrence for SEA—The Conceptual Framework," May 9, 1961, Kennedy Papers, NSC Files, Box 231, "Southeast Asia—General"; Rostow to Kennedy, August 17, 1961, *ibid.;* McNaughton memorandum, January 18, 1966, *Pentagon Papers*, IV, 47. See also Rostow's draft, "Basic National Security Policy," March 26, 1962, pp. 141–44, and Arthur Schlesinger's account of Kennedy's conversation with Khrushchev at Vienna in June 1961, in *A Thousand Days*, p. 368.

There was a distinct self-reinforcing tendency in all of this. The more the administration defended its Vietnam policies in terms of safeguarding credibility, the more American credibility seemed to depend upon the success of those policies. "To leave Viet-Nam to its fate would shake . . . confidence . . . in the value of an American commitment and in the value of America's word," Johnson proclaimed in April 1965. And again, in May: "There are a hundred other little nations . . . watching what happens. . . . If South Viet-Nam can be gobbled up, the same thing can happen to them." And still again, in July: "If we are driven from the field in Viet-Nam, then no nation can ever again have the same confidence in . . . American protection."[7] Perceptions in international relations are only in part the product of what people believe; they arise as well from what nations claim. Given the frequency and intensity of these and other comparable pronouncements, it is hardly surprising that they were taken seriously, both at home and abroad. And yet the irony is that the administration made them to stave off pressures for withdrawal that could lead to humiliation; their effect, though, was to widen the very gap between promise and performance from which humiliation springs.

But why this extreme fear of humiliation in the first place? Partly, one suspects, because it might suggest weakness to adversaries: "lessons" of Munich, after all, were still very much alive. Vietnam had also become something of a matter of personal pride: "we have not lost a single nation to communism since 1959," Johnson liked to boast.[8] But a deeper concern, oddly enough, may have been not so much what the world might think as what the United States might do. There was, within both the Kennedy and Johnson administrations, a strange dread of American irrationality—of the unpredictable and uncontrollable reactions that might ensue if the United States was perceived to have "lost" Vietnam. Rusk and McNamara had warned as early as 1961 that such a development "would stimulate bitter domestic controversies in the United States and would be seized upon by extreme elements to divide the country and harass the Administration." Rostow's "BSNP" draft even raised the possibility that "the U.S. might rashly initiate war" if confronted by a major defeat.[9] Johnson may well have entertained the strongest fears of all: "I knew that if we let Communist aggression succeed in taking over South Vietnam," he later recalled,

[7] Johnson Johns Hopkins address, April 7, 1965, *JPP: 1965,* p. 395; Johnson remarks to members of Congressional committees, May 4, 1965, *ibid.,* p. 491; Johnson press conference statement, July 28, 1965, *ibid.,* p. 794.

[8] Johnson remarks in Hartford, Connecticut, September 28, 1964, *JPP: 1964.* See also Johnson's remarks in Detroit, Michigan, September 7, 1964, *ibid.,* p. 1050; and May, *"Lessons" of the Past,* especially pp. 112–14.

[9] Rusk and McNamara to Kennedy, November 11, 1961, *Pentagon Papers,* II, 111; Rostow draft, "Basic National Security Policy," March 26, 1962, p. 9. See also William P. Bundy to McNaughton, November 26, 1964, *Pentagon Papers,* III, 658.

there would follow in this country an endless national debate—a mean and destructive debate—that would shatter my Presidency, kill my administration, and damage our democracy. I knew that Harry Truman and Dean Acheson had lost their effectiveness from the day that the Communists took over in China. I believed that the loss of China had played a large role in the rise of Joe McCarthy. And I knew that all these problems, taken together, were chickenshit compared with what might happen if we lost Vietnam.[10]

The ultimate danger, then, was what the United States might do to itself if it failed to meet obligations it itself had established.

Shortly after the Johnson administration left office, William Whitworth, a writer for the *New Yorker,* sought to interview several of the former President's advisers on the underlying geopolitical rationale for the Vietnam War. The only one who would see him was Eugene V. Rostow, Walt Rostow's older brother, who had served as Under-Secretary of State for Political Affairs from 1966 to 1969. The ensuing discussion took on a revealing circularity. Asked why American security depended upon the defense of Southeast Asia, Rostow emphasized the need to maintain a "balance of power" in the world. But when queried as to why it had been necessary to do that, Rostow fell back upon a classic "flexible response" argument: the need to be able to handle, without resort to nuclear weapons, problems such as Vietnam. Whitworth found this puzzling: "We have the balance in order to deal with the problem, and we have to deal with the problem in order to preserve the balance. The theory is eating its own tail." "Well, in a sense, you're right," Rostow replied. "All I can say is that it has always been very dangerous for people when a potentially hostile power establishes hegemony. I can't particularize how that potential hegemony would be exercised, but I would prefer, even at considerable cost, to prevent the risk."[11]

This spectacle of theories eating tails was no rare thing in Vietnam: the expansion of means to honor a commitment made as a substitute for means; the justification of that commitment in terms of a balance of power made shaky by its very existence; the defense, in the interests of credibility, of policies destructive of credibility; the search, ultimately, for domestic consensus by means that destroyed that consensus—all of these reflect the failure of "flexible response" strategy to proceed in an orderly manner through the stages of identifying interests, perceiving threats, and selecting appropriate responses. Instead, both threats and responses became interests in themselves, with

---

[10] Quoted in Doris Kearns, *Lyndon Johnson and the American Dream* (New York: 1976), pp. 252–53. See also Lyndon B. Johnson, *The Vantage Point: Perspectives of the Presidency,* 1963–1969 (New York: 1971), pp. 151–52.

[11] William Whitworth, *Naive Questions About War and Peace* (New York; 1970), pp. 105–6, 124.

the result that the United States either ignored or forgot what it had set out to do in Vietnam at just the moment it was resolving, with unprecedented determination, to do it.

II

A second prominent feature of "flexible response" as applied in Vietnam was the belief in "calibration," or "fine tuning"—that by being able to move up or down a range of precisely calculated actions, the United States could deter limited aggression without either extreme escalation or humiliation. "Our military forces must be . . . used in a measured, limited, controlled and deliberate way, as an instrument to carry out our foreign policy," one of McNamara's assistants wrote in late 1964. "Never must military operations become an end in themselves." Johnson made the same point some months later: he would not heed, he insisted, "those who urge us to use our great power in a reckless or casual manner. . . . We will do what must be done. And we will do only what must be done."[12] And yet, since this strategy in the end produced *both* escalation *and* humiliation, it would appear to have contained, as did official thinking on the balance of power, certain deficiencies.

Deterrence, ideally, should involve expressing determination without actually having to exhibit it. John Foster Dulles had attempted this delicate maneuver by threatening to use nuclear weapons to discourage aggression at all levels—an approach that at least had the merit of separating the projection of resolve from its actual demonstration, so long as skill, or luck, held out. Lacking the previous administration's self-confidence in such matters, convinced as well of the ineffectiveness of that strategy in limited war situations, Kennedy and his advisers had ruled out nuclear threats in areas like Southeast Asia, but not the need to manifest American firmness there. "We must produce quickly a course of action which convinces the other side we are dead serious," Rostow had warned Kennedy in August 1961. "What the U.S. does or fails to do," Maxwell Taylor added a few months later, "will be decisive to the end result."[13] The difficulty was that, short of embracing Dulles's strategy, all conceivable projections of resolve seemed to require, in one form or another, actual demonstrations of it.

---

[12] Joseph Califano draft presidential statement, December 2, 1964, enclosed in Califano to Bundy, December 3, 1964, Johnson Papers, NSF—Agency Files, Box 11–12, "Defense Department, Volume I"; Johnson message to Congress on Vietnam appropriations, May 4, 1965, *JPP: 1965*, p. 497. See also *JPP: 1963-64*, pp. 372, 1174; *JPP: 1965*, p. 489.

[13] Rostow to Kennedy, August 17, 1961, Kennedy Papers, NCS Files, Box 231, "Southeast Asia—General"; Taylor to Kennedy, October 24, 1961, *Pentagon Papers* , II, 88.

This did not bother the Joint Chiefs of Staff, who, as early as May 1961, had recommended the dispatch of United States troops to South Vietnam "to provide a visible deterrent to potential North Vietnamese and/or Chinese Communist action," and to "indicate the firmness of our intent to all Asian nations." An old Vietnam hand, Brigadier General Edward Lansdale, explained the rationale as follows:

> US *combat* forces, even in relatively small units, are the symbol of our national power. If an enemy engages one of our combat units, he is fully aware that he automatically has engaged the entire power of the US. This symbol of real national strength, employed wisely in Germany, Greece, and the Formosa Straits in a manner not unlike that contemplated for Thailand and Vietnam, has "kept the peace." When the mission of such US force is properly announced and followed immediately by a firm action, recent history teaches that the effect is just the reverse of "escalation" and that our action obtains world support outside the [Sino-Soviet] Bloc.

"[T]he point of installing token U.S. forces before the event," Robert Komer added, "is to signal our intentions to the other fellow, and thus hopefully avoid having to face up to the commitment of substantial US forces after a fracas has developed." It was true that the United States might "end up with something approaching another Korea, but I think the best way of avoiding this is to move fast now before the war spreads to the extent that a Korean type commitment is required.[14]* This theory that immediate small-scale involvement could make massive long-term involvement unnecessary formed the basis of recommendations by Maxwell Taylor and Walt Rostow for the introduction of some 8,000 U.S. combat troops into South Vietnam in November 1961. "In our view," Taylor wrote the President, nothing is more calculated to sober the enemy and to discourage escalation . . . than the knowledge that the United States has prepared itself soundly to deal with aggression at any level."[15]

---

[14] Joint Chiefs of Staff to Gilpatric, May 10, 1961, *Pentagon Papers*, II, 49; Lansdale to Gilpatric, May 10, 1961, Kennedy Papers, NSC Files, Box 231, "Southeast Asia—General"; Komer to Rostow, August 2, 1961, *ibid.;* Komer to Bundy, October 31, 1961, *ibid.* See also Komer memorandum, "A Doctrine of Deterrence for SEA—The Conceptual Framework," May 9, 1961, *ibid.*

*"I'm no happier than anyone about getting involved in another squalid, secondary theatre in Asia. But we'll end up doing so sooner or later anyway because we won't be willing to accept another defeat. If so, the real question is not whether but how soon and how much!" (Komer to Bundy, October 31, 1961, Kennedy Papers, NSC Files, Box 231, "Southeast Asia—General.")

[15] Taylor to Kennedy, November 3, 1961, *Pentagon Papers*, II, 654. See also, on the Taylor-Rostow report, *ibid.*, II, 73–120; Rostow, *The Diffusion of Power*, pp. 270–71, 274–79; and Maxwell Taylor, *Swords and Ploughshares* (New York: 1972), pp. 225–48.

But Kennedy had long been skeptical about the wisdom of sending American forces to fight in Southeast Asia: he had reminded his advisers the previous July of "the reluctance of the American people and of many distinguished military leaders to see any direct involvement of U.S. troops in that part of the world. . . . [N]othing would be worse than an unsuccessful intervention in this area." State Department assessments reinforced this view:

> We do not think the presence of US troops would serve to deter infiltrations short of overt armed intervention. There is not much reason for supposing the Communists would think our troops would be much more successful against guerrilla operations in South Viet-Nam than French troops were in North Viet-Nam. Counter-guerrilla operations require highly selective application of force; selection requires discrimination; and alien troops simply lack the bases for discriminating between friend and foe, except by the direction in which they shoot.

If the South Vietnamese themselves were not willing to make a "serious national effort," Dean Rusk warned in November, then it was "difficult to see how [a] handful [of] American troops can have [a] decisive influence." Persuaded by these arguments, concerned as well about priorities elsewhere (notably Berlin) and the risk of upsetting negotiations then in progress on Laos, Kennedy deferred implementing the Taylor-Rostow recommendation for combat troops. It would have been "like taking a drink," he explained to Arthur Schlesinger. "The effect wears off, and you have to take another."[16]

It is important to note, though, that Kennedy's decision against sending combat troops to Vietnam was not a rejection of "calibration" —just the opposite. The full Taylor-Rostow recommendations, he thought, would have constituted too abrupt an escalation of pressure; he preferred, instead, a more gradual approach, involving an increase of American economic and military aid to Saigon, together with the introduction of U.S. "advisers." Nothing in this procedure precluded the dispatch of ground troops at a later date if that should become necessary. Nor were there illusions as to the impact of these decisions on American credibility: "We are fully cognizant," the State Department cabled Saigon, "of [the] extent to which [these] decisions if implemented . . . will sharply increase the commitment of our prestige struggle to save SVN."[17] Kennedy's actions reflected doubts only

[16] Bundy memorandum, Kennedy meeting with advisers, July 28, 1961, Kennedy Papers, NSC Files, Box 231, "Southeast Asia—General"; Policy Planning Council memorandum, "Security in Southeast Asia," July 27, 1961, enclosed in McGhee to Rostow, July 28, 1961, *ibid.;* Rusk to State Department, November 1, 1961, *Pentagon Papers,* II, 105; Schlesinger, A *Thousand Days,* p. 547.

[17] Rusk to Nolting, November 14, 1961, *Pentagon Papers,* II, 119.

about the appropriate level of response necessary to demonstrate American resolve, not about the importance of making that demonstration in the first place.

"Calibration" during the next two years took the form primarily of efforts to transform South Vietnam into a sufficiently self-reliant anticommunist bastion so that no direct commitment of United States forces would be necessary. The goal, according to Roger Hilsman, was to devise "an integrated and systematic military-political-economic strategic counterinsurgency concept," to orient Saigon's military and security forces "increasingly toward counter-guerrilla or unconventional warfare tactics," to "broaden the effective participation of Vietnamese Government officials in the formulation and execution of government policy," and to "identify the populace with the Vietnamese Government's struggle against the Viet Cong."[18] All of this required several delicate balancing acts: moderating President Ngo Dinh Diem's autocratic control enough to win popular support for his government without at the same time weakening it to the point that it could not resist Viet Cong pressures; providing the assistance necessary for Diem to survive without discrediting him as an American puppet; taking care, simultaneously, to see that Washington's interest in Diem's survival did not allow him to make a puppet out of the United States. In the end, the line proved too fine to walk: frustrated by Diem's repression of Buddhist critics, fearful of a secret deal between his government and North Vietnam, Kennedy in August 1963 authorized a carefully orchestrated effort—in itself an example of "calibration"—to overthrow him.[19] As it happened, though, Washington was able to control neither the timing nor the manner of Diem's removal, nor had it given much thought to what would replace him; the effect was that the very instability Kennedy had feared dominated politics in Saigon for the next three years.

The resulting Viet Cong gains led the Johnson administration by the end of 1964 to approve what Kennedy had rejected—a combat role for the United States in Vietnam. Even so, though, the principle of "calibration" would still apply; there would be no sharp, all-out application of force. Rather, the plan, in Johnson's words, was for military pressures against North Vietnam "progressively mounting in scope and intensity for the purpose of convincing the leaders of the DRV that it is to their interest to cease to aid the Viet Cong and to respect the independence and security of South Vietnam." This "slow squeeze" strategy contemplated action strong enough to end the existing deteriorating situation, but not so violent as to knit the North

[18] Hilsman to Harriman, June 18, 1962, *Pentagon Papers,* II, 673.

[19] See, for example, Hilsman's elaborate "Action Plan" for South Vietnam, undated, Kennedy Papers, NSC File, Box 317, "Meetings on Vietnam"; also, the *Pentagon Papers,* II, 201–76.

Vietnamese people more closely together, provoke Chinese Communist intervention, arouse world opinion, or preclude opportunities for an eventual negotiated settlement. The objective, Bundy noted on the eve of the first air strikes against the North in February 1965, was "to keep before Hanoi the carrot of our desisting as well as the stick of continued pressure. . . . Once such a policy is put into force, we shall be able to speak in Vietnam on many topics and in many ways, with growing force and effectiveness."[20]*

The bombing campaign against North Vietnam was intended to be the most carefully calibrated military operation in recent history. Great significance was attached to not crossing certain geographic "thresholds" for fear of bringing in the Chinese, as had happened in Korea, to avoiding civilian casualties that might intensify opposition to the war within the United States and elsewhere, and to combining the bombing with various inducements, especially periodic bombing pauses and offers of economic aid, to bring Hanoi to the conference table. Target selection was done in Washington, often in the White House itself, with the President at times personally monitoring the outcome of particular missions. Extraordinary precision was demanded of pilots—one 1966 order specified that piers at Haiphong could be hit only if no tankers were berthed at them, that vessels firing on American planes could be struck only if they were "clearly North Vietnamese," and that no attacks were to be launched on Sunday.[21] Even with such restrictions, though, the scale and intensity of the bombing progressively mounted, from 25,000 sorties** and 63,000 tons of bombs dropped in 1965 to 108,000 sorties and 226,000 tons in 1967, from missions directed initially at military bases in the southern "panhandle" of North Vietnam to infiltration routes, transportation facilities, and petroleum storage areas throughout the country, ultimately to factories and power plants in the Hanoi-Haiphong complex itself.[22] And none of it produced discernible progress toward

---

[20] Johnson to Taylor, December 3, 1964, Johnson Papers, NSC Staff Files, Box 2, "Memos for the President, Vol. 7"; Bundy memorandum, "A Policy of Sustained Reprisal," February 7, 1965, *Pentagon Papers*, III, 690; Bundy to Johnson, February 7, 1965, *ibid.*, p. 311. See also Kearns, *Johnson and the American Dream*, pp. 264–65. For the evolution of the "slow squeeze" option, see the *Pentagon Papers*, III, 206–51, 587–683.

*Eugene Rostow argued that Johnson's "bold but prudent action in Vietnam had posed two things: that we would risk bombs over New York in order to protect Saigon, and that Moscow would not bomb New York to protect Hanoi. This was an event and a demonstration of capital importance, which should greatly fortify our system of alliances, and weaken that of our enemies." (Rostow memorandum, April 10, 1965, enclosed in Bill Moyers to Bundy, April 13, 1965, Johnson Papers, NSF Country Files: Vietnam, Box 16, "Memos—Vol. XXXII.")

[21] JSC to CINCPAC, June 22, 1966, *Pentagon Papers*, IV, 105–6.

**A sortie is one flight by one plane.

[22] George C. Herring, *America's Longest War: The United States and Vietnam, 1950–1975* (New York: 1979), p. 147.

what it was supposed to accomplish: a tapering off of infiltration into South Vietnam, and movement toward negotiations. Meanwhile, pressures had been building for the introduction of ground troops. Bundy had recommended this option as early as May 1964: the idea, he wrote Johnson, would be one of "marrying Americans to Vietnamese at every level, both civilian and military . . . to provide what [Saigon] has repeatedly asked for: the tall American at every point of stress and strain." "I do not at all think it is a repetition of Korea," he added in August. "It seems to me at least possible that a couple of brigade-size units put in to do specific jobs . . . might be good medicine everywhere." Rostow agreed, pointing out that such troops could usefully serve as bargaining chips in any future negotiations, and by February 1965 Rusk too had endorsed the idea, along with the bombing, as a way to send "a signal to Hanoi and Peiping that they themselves cannot hope to succeed without a substantial escalation on their part, with all the risks they would have to face."[23] The decisive argument in the end, though, proved to be General William Westmoreland's assertion that troops were needed to guard the air base at Da Nang from which some of the strikes against the north were being launched, a claim almost certainly advanced with a view to securing presidential authorization of a combat mission whose scope could then be widened far beyond the limited purposes for which it was made.[24] This "entering wedge" worked, and by early April 1965 Johnson had approved a combat role for United States forces in Vietnam. The pattern of escalation quickly went beyond Bundy's two brigades: from an initial deployment of 3,500 Marines at Da Nang, U.S. troop strength rose to 184,000 by the end of 1965, 385,000 by the end of 1966, and 486,000 by the end of 1967.[25] Nor, as the Tet offensive of early 1968 seemed to show, was there convincing evidence that those troops had come any closer to accomplishing their mission than had the bombing campaign.

What strikes one in retrospect about the strategy of calibrated escalation is the extent to which, as so often happened in Vietnam, the effects produced were precisely opposite from those intended. The objective of applying incremental pressures beginning in 1961 had been

---

[23] Bundy to Johnson, May 22 and August 31, 1965, Johnson Papers, NSF-NSC Staff Files, Box 1, "Memos for the President, Vol. 4," and Box 2, "Memos for the President, Vol. 6"; Rostow to McNamara, November 16, 1964, *Pentagon Papers,* III, 632; Rusk memorandum, "Viet-Nam," February 23, 1965, Johnson Papers, NSF Country File: Vietnam, Box 14, "Memos, Vol. XXIX."

[24] See, on this point, Guenter Lewy, *America in Vietnam* (New York: 1978), pp. 42–46; Robert L. Gallucci, *Neither Peace Nor Honor: The Politics of the American Military in Viet-Nam* (Baltimore: 1976), pp. 111–12; and the analysis in the *Pentagon Papers,* III, 429–33.

[25] Figures on troop strength are from Herbert Y. Schandler, *The Unmaking of a President: Lyndon Johnson and Vietnam* (Princeton, 1977), p. 352.

to avoid a massive American military involvement: token commitments, it was thought, would demonstrate resolve, thereby obviating the necessity for larger commitments later. The theory was not unlike that of vaccination, in that exposure to minimum risk was expected to provide immunities against more serious dangers. Another analogy, used at the time, was that of a plate-glass window, insufficiently strong in itself to keep out a thief, but capable of producing such conspicuous consequences if shattered as to discourage attempts from being made in the first place. Getting involved, in short, was the best way to avoid getting involved: "I deeply believe," Rostow had written in August of that year, "that the way to save Southeast Asia and to minimize the chance of deep U.S. military involvement there is for the President to make a bold decision very soon."[26]

Bold decisions were made (admittedly not in as bold a manner as Rostow had wanted), but the effect was hardly to minimize American involvement. United States manpower, resources, and prestige were far more deeply committed by 1968 than even "worst case" scenarios seven years earlier had indicated. McNamara had estimated in November 1961 that in the unlikely event that *both* North Vietnam and Communist China overtly intervened in the war, Washington might have to send six divisions, or 205,000 men. Peking did not intervene, Hanoi kept its own participation below the level of overt acknowledgment, but still the United States had more than doubled McNamara's prediction as to "the ultimate possible extent of our military commitment."[27] Calibrated pressures as a deterrent obviously had not worked.

One reason for this was a persistent lack of clarity as to who, or what, was being deterred. Impressed by Khrushchev's "wars of national liberation" speech, the Kennedy administration had at first located the roots of Viet Cong insurgency in Moscow: Rostow in 1961 had even advocated an early form of "linkage," making it clear to the Kremlin that no progress toward détente could take place while guerilla activity continued in Southeast Asia.[28]* By 1964, though,

---

[26] Rostow to Robert F. Kennedy, August 18, 1961, Kennedy Papers, NSC Files, Box 231, "Southeast Asia—General." See also Robert Komer, "A Doctrine of Deterrence for SEA—The Conceptual Framework," May 9, 1961, *ibid.*

[27] McNamara to Kennedy, November 8, 1961, *Pentagon Papers*, II, 108.

[28] Rostow to Kennedy, May 11, 1961, Kennedy Papers, NSC Files, Box 231, "Southeast Asia—General."

*Rostow wanted Kennedy to warn Khrushchev at Vienna that if the United States were "drawn deeper and more directly on to the Southeast Asian mainland," this would require a major increase in military spending and difficulties in relations with Moscow because "it is difficult for a democracy simultaneously to gear itself for possible military conflict and also to take the steps necessary to ease tensions and to expand the areas of U.S.-Soviet collaboration." (Rostow to Kennedy, May 11, 1961, Kennedy Papers, NSC Files, Box 231, "Southeast Asia—General.") There is no evidence that Kennedy actually raised this point with Khrushchev at Vienna—perhaps he realized that the Soviet leader might welcome rather than regret an American distraction in Southeast Asia.

Peking, not Moscow, had come to be seen as the culprit: the objective of American policy, National Security Council staff member Michael Forrestal argued late that year, should be to "delay China's swallowing up Southeast Asia until (a) she develops better table manners and (b) the food is somewhat more indigestible." The absence of official relations precluded opportunities for diplomatic "linkage" with Peking, however, and Johnson's advisers, remembering miscalculations during the Korean War, were extremely cautious about applying military pressure in any form. "China is there on the border with 700 million men," Johnson noted; "we could get tied down in a land war in Asia very quickly if we sought to throw our weight around."[29]

The alternative, it would appear, was direct pressure against Hanoi, but things were not quite that simple. John McNaughton in September 1964 identified at least four separate "audiences" aside from Moscow and Peking that the United States would have to influence: "the Communists (who must feel strong pressures), the South Vietnamese (whose morale must be buoyed), our allies (who must trust us as 'underwriters'), and the US public (which must support our risk-taking with US lives and prestige)." The difficulty, of course, was that actions directed at one "audience" might affect others in undesirable ways. Too sharp an escalation aimed at Hanoi risked alienating public opinion in the United States (especially during an election year), and elsewhere in the world, not to mention the danger of Chinese intervention. Moreover, such action would accomplish little as long as instability continued to reign in Saigon, as it had since the overthrow of Diem late in 1963. On the other hand, though, further restraint could only accelerate deterioration of the military situation in the South; it also conveyed the appearance of weakness and indecisiveness, not only in Hanoi and among American allies in Asia, but in Saigon itself, where the resulting low morale produced still more instability. The need, McNaughton argued, was for action taken "with special care—signaling to the DRV that initiatives are being taken, to the GVN that we are behaving energetically . . . , and to the US public that we are behaving with good purpose and restraint."[30]

[29] Forrestal to William P. Bundy, Novermber 23, 1964, *Pentagon Papers,* III, 644; Johnson remarks at the University of Akron, October 21, 1964, *JPP: 1964,* p. 1391. See also *ibid.,* pp. 1164–65.

[30] McNaughton draft, "Plan of Action for South Vietnam," September 3, 1964, *Pentagon Papers,* III, 559. See also Taylor to Rusk, August 18, 1964, *ibid.,* pp. 545–48; Bundy memorandum, meeting with Johnson, September 9, 1964, Johnson Papers, NSF-NSC Staff Files, Box 2, "Memos for the President, Vol. 6"; William H. Sullivan to William P. Bundy, November 6, 1964, *Pentagon Papers,* III, 594; Rostow to Rusk, November 23, 1964, *ibid.,* pp. 645–46; Taylor briefing of November 27, 1964, *ibid.,* pp. 671–72; William P. Bundy memorandum, November 28, 1964, *ibid.,* p. 676; Bundy memorandum, December 28, 1964, Johnson Papers, NSF—NSC Staff Files, Box 2, "Memos for the President, Vol. 7"; Bundy to Johnson, January 27, 1965, *ibid.* See also Leslie H. Gelb and Richard Betts, *The Irony of Vietnam: The System Worked* (Washington, D.C.: 1979), pp. 12–13.

But "calibration" implies a single target: where several exist, in a constantly shifting but interrelated pattern, the attainment of a precise correspondence between intentions and consequences becomes no easy matter.*

A second problem flowed directly from the first. By eschewing anything other than gradual escalation, matched carefully to the level of enemy provocation, the Johnson administration was in effect relinquishing the initiative to the other side. This was, of course, a standard military criticism of White House policy: the argument was that if only restraints on air and ground action could be lifted, the war could be ended rapidly.[31]† Given the subsequently demonstrated ability of the North Vietnamese and Viet Cong to hold out for years under much heavier pressures, the claim, in retrospect, seems unconvincing. Still, there was one valid element in the military's argument. Theorists of international relations have suggested that deterrence is more likely to work when a potential aggressor is unsure of his ability to control the risks involved in the action he is contemplating. If that confidence exists, deterrence will probably be ineffective.[32] This idea of cultivating uncertainty in the minds of adversaries had been central to Dulles's strategy of "retaliation"—with what effects it is impossible to say, given the difficulty of trying to prove what deterrence deterred. But uncertainty did not carry over into the strategy of "calibration." To proclaim that one intends to do only what is necessary to counter aggression and no more is, after all, to yield control over one's actions to those undertaking the aggression. Washington officials may have had the illusion that they were making decisions on Vietnam force deployments during the Johnson years, but in fact those choices were

---

*McNamara succinctly summarized the problem of impressing multiple "audiences" in a July 1965 memorandum to Johnson: "Our object in Vietnam is to create conditions for a favorable outcome by demonstrating to the VC/DRV that the odds are against their winning. We want to create these conditions, if possible, without causing the war to expand into one with China or the Soviet Union and in a way which preserves support of the American people and, hopefully, of our allies and friends." (McNamara to Johnson, July 20, 1965, Johnson Papers, NSF Country File: Vietnam, Box 74, "1965 Troop Decision.")

[31] See, for example, the Joint Chiefs of Staff to McNamara, January 22, 1964, *Pentagon Papers*, III, 497-98; also Gallucci, *Neighter Peace Nor Honor*, pp. 38-39

†Perhaps the most pungent expression of this idea came from General Thomas S. Power, Strategic Air Force Commander, who told a Pentagon audience in 1964 that "the task of the military in war was to kill human beings and destroy man-made objects," and to do it "in the quickest way possible." It had been "the moralists who don't want to kill" that had given "Hitler his start and got us into the mess in Cuba and Viet-Nam." The "computer types who were making defense policy don't know their ass from a hole in the ground." (Summary, Power briefing, April 28, 1964, Johnson Papers, NSF Agency File, Box 11-12, "Defense Dept. Vol. I")

[32] George and Smoke, *Deterrence in American Foreign Policy*, p. 529.

being made, as a consequence of the administration's own strategy, in Hanoi.[33]

The alternative, of course, was some kind of negotiated settlement with North Vietnam, an option the administration was careful never to rule out. "[We] should strike to hurt but not to destroy," Bundy noted in May 1964, "for the purpose of changing the North Vietnamese decision on intervention in the South." Taylor seconded the point some months later: "it is well to remind ourselves that 'too much' in this matter of coercing Hanoi may be as bad as 'too little.' At some point, we will need a relatively cooperative leadership in Hanoi willing to wind up the VC insurgency on terms satisfactory to us and our SVN allies."[34] But Johnson and his advisers were wary of a "neutralist" solution for South Vietnam along the lines of the shaky 1962 truce in Laos—perhaps with good reason, given the speed with which Hanoi violated the agreements eventually reached at Paris in 1973. The preferred option was to achieve successes on the battlefield, and then approach North Vietnam: "After, *but only after*, we have established [a] clear pattern [of] pressure hurting DRV and leaving no doubts in South Vietnam of our own resolve, we could . . . accept [a] conference broadened to include [the] Vietnam issue," the State Department cabled Saigon in August 1964; such negotiations, if they did occur, would have to bring "Hanoi (and Peiping) eventually [to] accept idea of getting out."[35] This familiar but elusive position of "negotiation from strength" had two difficulties: it contained no safeguards against attempts by Hanoi to bolster its own negotiating position, or against the progressively deeper American involvement the strategy of "calibration" was supposed to prevent.

Finally, the strategy of "calibration" broke down because it failed to ensure that force, once applied, would be used as a precise and discriminating instrument of policy. It provided no safeguards against the subordination of strategic interests to those of the organizations implementing the strategy. Large bureaucracies all too often develop their own institutional momentum: "standard operating procedures" can make an organization impervious either to instructions from above or feedback from below.[36] One strength of McNamara's

[33] See, on this point, Alain Enthoven to Clark Clifford, March 20, 1968, in Enthoven and Smith, *How Much Is Enough*, pp. 298–99; and Schandler, *The Unmaking of a President*, pp. 31–42, 46.

[34] Bundy to Johnson, May 22, 1964, Johnson Papers, NSF-NSC Staff File, Box 1, "Memos for the President, Vol. I"; Taylor to State Department, November 3, 1964, *Pentagon Papers*, III, 591. See also Taylor to State Department, August 18, 1964, *ibid.*, pp. 546–47.

[35] Rusk to Lodge, August 14, 1964, *ibid.*, II, 330. See also William P. Bundy's first draft of this cable, *ibid.*, III, 526.

[36] See, on this point, Graham T. Allison, *Essence of Decision: Explaining the Cuban Missile Crisis* (Boston: 1971), pp. 83, 89.

reforms in the Pentagon had been the extent to which he had overcome this problem in dealing with the military on nuclear and budgetary matters. No such successes, however, occurred in Vietnam. Instead, once American forces were committed, Washington seemed to lose control, leaving the military with a degree of autonomy surprising in an administration that had prided itself on having reduced military authority over the conduct of national security affairs.[37]

The generalization may seem out of place applied to a war whose soldiers complained regularly about civilian-imposed constraints, but the military's grievances in this regard should be treated with skepticism. It is true that during the early period of American involvement, there were significant restrictions on the nature and scope of U.S. military activity, but as time went on without the desired enemy response, these gradually dropped away. By August of 1967, for example, the White House had authorized for bombing some 95 percent of the North Vietnamese targets requested by the Joint Chiefs of Staff. Moreover, the Air Force's perceived institutional interests were allowed to influence the conduct of the air war in important ways. Despite its obvious (and widely appreciated) inapplicability to guerilla warfare, the Air Force insisted successfully on a campaign of strategic bombing in North Vietnam, and even on the use of B-52's, designed originally to deliver nuclear weapons against Soviet targets, to hit suspected Viet Cong emplacements in the south. Similarly, it relied heavily on high-performance jet aircraft for other bombing missions in the south, despite studies indicating that slower propeller-driven models would have been three times as accurate, from five to thirteen times less costly, but with roughly the same loss ratio.[38] It was, in retrospect, an adaptation of ends to fit preferred means, rather than the other way around.

The tendency was even more obvious with regard to the ground war. Like most of his army colleagues, General Westmoreland had little sympathy for or understanding of the irregular warfare concepts that had been popular during the early Kennedy administration: the function of infantry, he insisted, was to seek out, pursue, and destroy enemy forces. As a consequence, he never seriously considered the strategy of holding and securing territory recommended by most counterinsurgency theorists, and implemented with considerable success by the Marines in the area around Da Nang in 1965 and 1966.[39] Instead he chose to emphasize largescale "search and destroy" operations, designed to wear the enemy down through sheer attrition. These

[37] Gelb and Betts, *The Irony of Vietnam,* pp. 239–40; Lewy, *America in Vietnam,* pp. 114–16

[38] Gallucci, *Neither Peace Nor Honor,* pp. 73–80; Lewy, *America in Vietnam,* p. 98.

[39] Gallucci, *Neither Peace Nor Honor,* pp. 114–15, 119–20; Lewy, *America in Vietnam,* pp. 43, 51, 117.

not only disrupted efforts at pacification and provided the enemy with sufficient advance warning to escape; they also frequently forced the Americans to destroy villages in order to reach Viet Cong troops and arms caches located deliberately within those villages. Random "harassment and interdiction" fire against "suspected" but unobserved enemy targets did little to convince inhabitants of the regions affected that their security would be enhanced by supporting Saigon. The Westmoreland strategy even involved, in some instances, the deliberate creation of refugees as a means of securing the countryside, as complete a reversal as can be imagined from the original objectives the American commitment in South Vietnam had been intended to serve.[40]

It was left to the Navy, though, to come up with the most striking example of weapons ill-suited to tasks by retrieving from mothballs the U.S.S. *New Jersey*, the world's last functioning battleship, for the purpose of shelling the jungle in a manner reminiscent of nothing so much as an incident in Joseph Conrad's "Heart of Darkness":

> Once, I remember, we came upon a man-of-war anchored off the coast. There wasn't even a shed there, and she was shelling the bush. It appears the French had one of their wars going on thereabouts. . . . In the empty immensity of earth, sky, and water, there she was, incomprehensible, firing into a continent. Pop, would go one of the six-inch guns; a small flame would dart and vanish, a little white smoke would disappear, a tiny projectile would give a feeble screech—and nothing happened. Nothing could happen. There was a touch of insanity in the proceeding, a sense of lugubrious drollery in the sight; and it was not dissipated by somebody on board assuring me earnestly there was a camp of natives—he called them enemies—hidden out of sight somewhere.[41]

It was all a remarkable departure from the injunctions to do just enough, but no more than was necessary, with which the United States had entered the conflict in Vietnam.

"[T]he central object of U.S. military policy is to create an environment of stability in a nuclear age," Rostow wrote in 1966; "this requires as never before that military policy be the servant of political purposes and be woven intimately into civil policy." To be sure, this had been the objective all along of the "calibration" strategy: it reflected the immense confidence in the ability to "manage" crises and control bureaucracies that was characteristic of "flexible response," the concern to integrate force and rationality, to find some

---

[40] *Ibid.,* pp. 52, 65, 99–101, 106, 108–14; 118–19; Frances FitzGerald, *Fire in the Lake: The Vietnamese and the Americans in Vietnam* (Boston: 1972), pp. 344–45.
[41] Joseph Conrad, *Heart of Darkness,* edited by Robert Kimbrough (New York: 1971), p. 14.

middle ground between the insanity of nuclear war and the humiliation of appeasement. But it was also a curiously self-centered strategy, vague as to the objects to be deterred, heedless of the extent to which adversaries determined its nature and pace, parochial in its assumption that those adversaries shared its own preoccupations and priorities, blind to the extent to which the indiscriminate use of force had come to replace the measured precision of the original concept. "Despite its violence and difficulties, our commitment to see it through in Vietnam is essentially a stabilizing factor in the world," Rostow had insisted, no doubt with complete sincerity and the best of intentions.[42] But when sincerity and good intentions come to depend upon myopic self-absorption, then the price can be high indeed.

III

One of the curious things about the breakdown of "calibration" was official Washington's chronic inability to detect the fact that it had failed. Gaps between objectives sought and results produced widened with only infrequent attempts to call attention to what was happening; those warnings that were advanced produced few discernible responses. This pattern suggests yet another deficiency in "flexible response" theory as applied in Vietnam: a persistent inability to monitor performance, an absence of mechanisms for ensuring that correspondence between the intent of one's actions and their actual consequences that is essential for an effective strategy.

That such lapses should have occurred is puzzling, given the great emphasis both Kennedy and Johnson placed on management techniques designed to achieve precise adaptations of resources to objectives. Exponents of "systems analysis" have explained that their ideas were not applied in Vietnam until it was too late to avoid involvement, but that, once put to use, they quickly revealed the futility of the existing strategy.[43] This view is correct, but narrow. It is true that the Systems Analysis Office in the Pentagon did not begin making independent evaluations of the war until 1966. But, in a larger sense, the Kennedy-Johnson management techniques had been present all along, in the form of both administrations' confidence that they could control bureaucracies with precision, use force with discrimination, weigh costs against benefits, and relate short-term tactics to long-term objectives. The inability to monitor performance, demonstrated so vividly in the failure of "calibration," suggests difficulties in applying these methods, but not their absence.

One reason these methods broke down in Vietnam was their heavy reliance on easily manipulated statistical indices as measurements of

---

[42] Rostow to McNamara, May 2, 1966, Johnson Papers, NSF Agency File, Boxes 11–12, "Defense Department Vol. III." See also Rostow's 1962 draft "Basic National Security Policy," p. 38.

[43] Enthoven and Smith, *How Much Is Enough,* pp. 270–71.

"progress" in the war. Here the primary responsibility rests with McNamara, who insisted on applying to that complex situation the same emphasis on quantification that had served him so well in the more familiar worlds of big business and the Pentagon.[44]* The difficulty, of course, was that the voluminous calculations McNamara insisted on were no better than the accuracy of the statistics that went into them in the first place: there were few if any safeguards against distortion. *"Ah, les statistiques!"* Roger Hilsman reports one South Vietnamese general as having exclaimed. "Your Secretary of Defense loves statistics. We Vietnamese can give him all he wants. If you want them to go up, they will go up. If you want them to go down, they will go down."[45] Or, in the succinct parlance of a later generation of computer specialists, "garbage in, garbage out."

The problem manifested itself first with regard to South Vietnamese performance following the introduction of United States advisers in 1961. The very presence of the Americans, it had been thought, would make possible more accurate monitoring of the situation,[46] but in fact the opposite occurred. The advisers depended on information furnished them by Diem's officers, many of whom combined a desire to please their powerful ally with a reluctance to risk their own necks in battle. The result was a deliberate inflation of statistical indices, the extent of which became clear only after the fall of Diem in November 1963. Of some 8,600 "strategic hamlets" Diem claimed to have constructed, it turned out that only about 20 percent existed in completed form. A high percentage of military operations initiated by Saigon—possibly as many as one third—were launched in areas where the Viet Cong were known *not* to be. One district chief had listed all twenty-four hamlets in his district as secure when in fact he controlled only three. "[T]he situation has been deteriorating . . . to a far greater extent than we had realized," McNamara acknowledged ruefully, "because of our undue dependence on distorted Vietnamese reporting."[47]**

---

[44] See David Halberstam's evocative portrait of McNamara in *The Best and the Brightest,* pp. 215–50.

*McNamara "has been trying to think of ways of dealing with this problem [Vietnam] for so long that he has gone a little stale," Bundy wrote to Johnson in June 1964. "Also, in a curious way, he has rather mechanized the problem so that he misses some of its real political flavor." (Bundy to Johnson, June 6, 1964, Johnson Papers, NSF—NSC Staff File, Box 2, "Memos for the President, Vol. 5.")

[45] Hilsman, *To Move a Nation,* p.523.

[46] See, on this point, the *Pentagon Papers,* II, 410–11.

[47] McNamara to Johnson, December 21, 1963, *ibid.,* III, 494. See also John McCone to McNamara, December 21, 1963, *ibid.,* p. 32; and Johnson, *The Vantage Point,* p. 63. The examples of distorted South Vietnamese reporting are from Hilsman, *To Move a Nation,* pp. 522–23.

**The difficulties, of course, did not end in 1963. The number of "Viet Cong" turned in under the Third Party Inducement Program, which provided monetary rewards for indentifying "defectors" willing to rally to Saigon's cause, rose from 17,836 in 1968 to

Not all such misrepresentations came from the South Vietnamese, though. Anxious to meet Washington's expectations of success, General Paul D. Harkins, commander of U.S. advisers in Vietnam, systematically ignored or suppressed reports from his own subordinates questioning Saigon's optimistic assessments of the war. As a result, Taylor and McNamara could report with conviction as late as October 1963 that "the tactics and techniques employed by the Vietnamese under U.S. monitorship are sound and give promise of ultimate victory."[48] Evidence that the situation was not in fact that rosy did occasionally surface, whether from the rare official visitor who managed to evade Harkins's packaged briefings and carefully guided tours, or from the more fequent published reporting of skeptical American correspondents in Saigon, among them Neil Sheehan and David Halberstam. But although Kennedy worried about these discrepancies, he at no point gave up primary reliance on official channels as a means of monitoring progress in the war; Johnson, if anything, depended on them more heavily.[49] It has been suggested that the accuracy of information tends to decline as the level of its classification rises, if for no other reason than that opportunities for independent verification are diminished thereby.[50] The proposition may not be universally applicable, but that the White House would have been better off reading Halberstam than Harkins seems beyond dispute.

These problems did not disappear with the onset of active American military involvement in Vietnam. The most notorious example, of course, was the use of enemy "body counts" as the chief indicator of "progress" in the ground war. The argument has been made that in such a conflict, where conventional indices—territory taken, distances covered, cities occupied—meant little, emphasis on these kinds of macabre statistics was unavoidable.[51]* That may be,

47,088 in 1969, at which point it was discovered that many of the alleged "defectors" were not Viet Cong at all, but South Vietnamese who had made a deal with friends to report them, and then split the reward. (Lewy, *America in Vietnam,* pp. 91–92.)

[48] Taylor and McNamara to Kennedy, October 2, 1963, *Pentagon Papers,* II, 187. See also Halberstam, *The Best and the Brightest,* pp. 200–205.

[49] Bundy memorandum, Kennedy meeting with Taylor and McNamara, September 23, 1963, Kennedy Papers, NSC Files, Box 200. "Vietnam Memos & Misc." See also Hilsman, *To Move a Nation* pp. 446–47, 502–4.

[50] Gallucci, *Neither Peace Nor Honor,* pp. 132–35; Gelb and Betts, *The Irony of Vietnam,* pp. 304–5. See also Roberta Wohlstetter, *Pearl Harbor: Warning and Decision* (Stanford: 1962), pp. 122–24.

[51] Dave Richard Palmer, *Summons of the Trumpet: U.S.-Vietnam in Perspective* (San Rafael, Cal.: 1978), pp. 119–20.

*The body count phenomenon even extended, at times, to digging up bodies for counting from freshly dug graves. (Lewy, *America in Vietnam,* p. 80.)

but what seems odd is the importance accorded them, given their widely acknowledged inaccuracy. Contemporary evaluations identified a margin of error of from 30 to 100 percent in these statistics, partly as the result of double or triple counting, partly because of the difficulty of distinguishing combatants from non-combatants, partly because of pressure from field commanders for higher and higher levels of "performance." [52] A more reliable index of success in the war was available—the number of North Vietnamese-Viet Cong weapons captured—but this was never given the significance of the body counts, probably because the figures were much less impressive. "It is possible that our attrition estimates substantially overstate actual VC/NVA losses," McNamara admitted in 1966. "For example, the VC/NVA apparently lose only about one-sixth as many weapons as people, suggesting the possibility that many of the killed are unarmed porters or bystanders." [53]

Similar statistical inflation occurred in the air war as well. Despite its acknowledged unreliability in an age of high-performance jet aircraft, pilot instead of photographic reconnaissance was generally used to measure the effectiveness of bombing in the North, presumably because damage claims tended to be higher. Photographic confirmation, when requested, was often not for the purpose of verifying pilot reports but to boost "sortie rates." Allocations of fuel and ordnance depended on these rates; they inevitably became an object of competition between the Air Force and the Navy, both of which shared the task of bombing North Vietnam. The results were predictable: a preference for aircraft with small bomb-load capacities which necessitated more frequent missions; the expenditure of bombs on marginal or already destroyed targets; even, during periods of munitions shortages, the flying of sorties without bombs. As one Air Force colonel put it: "bombs or no bombs, you've got to have more Air Force over the target than Navy." [54]

A second reason for the failure to monitor performance was a persistent tendency to disregard discouraging intelligence. It is a myth that the United States stumbled blindly into the Vietnam War. At every stage in the long process of escalation informed estimates were available which accurately (and pessimistically) predicted the outcome.* As early as November 1961, for example, the CIA was

---

[52] Lewy, *America in Vietnam,* pp. 78–82; Enthoven and Smith, *How Much Is Enough,* pp. 295–96.

[53] McNamara to Johnson, November 17, 1966, *Pentagon Papers,* IV, 371.

[54] Quoted in Gallucci, *Neither Peace Nor Honor,* p. 84; see also *ibid.,* pp. 80–85; Gelb and Betts, *The Irony of Vietnam,* pp. 309–10.

*"The information I received [on Vietnam] was more complete and balanced than anyone outside the mainstream of official reporting could possibly realize." (Johnson, *The Vantage Point,* p. 64.)

forecasting that North Vietnam would be able to match, through increased infiltration, any U.S. troop commitment to South Vietnam, and that bombing the North would not significantly impede that process. Two-and-a-half years later, a series of war games in which several key officials of the Johnson administration took part produced precisely the same conclusion.[55] Despite his own enthusiasm for this alternative in 1961 and 1964, Maxwell Taylor by 1965 was strongly opposing the introduction of ground combat forces on the grounds that a "white-faced soldier armed, equipped and trained as he is [is] not [a] suitable guerrilla fighter for Asian forests and jungles." Clark Clifford, Johnson's long-time personal friend and future Defense Secretary, was warning in May 1965 that Vietnam "could be a quagmire. It could turn into an open end commitment on our part that would take more and more ground troops, without a realistic hope of ultimate victory." George Ball, in a series of eloquent dissents from official policy, stressed that "a deep commitment of United States forces in a land war in South Viet-Nam would be a catastrophic error. If there ever was an occasion for a tactical withdrawal, this is it." Even William P. Bundy, one of the original architects of "calibration," had concluded by June of 1965 that any level of commitment beyond 70,000 to 100,000 troops would pass "a point of sharply diminishing returns and adverse consequences."[56]

"There are no signs that we have throttled the inflow of supplies for the VC," McNamara acknowledged after five months of bombing. "Nor have our air attacks on North Vietnam produced tangible evidence of willingness on the part of Hanoi to come to the conference table in a reasonable mood." And even if military successes on the ground could be achieved, there was no guarantee that these would not simply "drive the VC back into the trees" from which they could launch attacks at some future date. "[I]t is not obvious," the Secretary of Defense admitted, "how we will be able to disengage our forces from Vietnam." And yet, despite this gloomy appraisal, McNamara recommended a continuation of the bombing and an increase in troop strength from 75,000 to 175,000–200,000 men. Early in 1966, on the basis of no more encouraging signs of progress in ground or air operations, he endorsed a new troop ceiling of 400,000

[55] Special National Intelligence Estimate 10-4-61. November 5, 1961, *Pentagon Papers,* II, 107; Robert H. Johnson to William P. Bundy, March 31, 1965, Johnson Papers, NSF Country Files: Vietnam, Box 16, "Memos Vol. XXXII." See also Gelb and Betts, *The Irony of Vietnam,* pp. 25–26; Halberstam, *The Best and the Brightest,* pp. 460–62; and Johnson, *The Vantage Point,* pp. 147–49.

[56] Taylor to State Department, February 22, 1965, *Pentagon Papers,* III, 419; Clifford to Johnson, May 17, 1965, Johnson Papers, NSF Country Files: Vietnam, Box 74, "1965 Troop Decision"; Ball memorandum, "Cutting Our Losses in South Viet-Nam," June 28, 1965, *ibid.,* Box 18, "Memos (B) Vol. XXV"; William P. Bundy memorandum, "Holding On in South Vietnam," June 30, 1965, *ibid.*

men, acknowledging at the same time that the North Vietnamese and Viet Cong could probably match those increases. It might be possible, he thought, eventually to contain the enemy with 600,000 men, but that would risk bringing in the Chinese Communists. "It follows, therefore, that the odds are about even that, even with the recommended deployments, we will be faced in early 1967 with a military stand-off at a much higher level, with pacification hardly underway and with the requirement for the deployment of still more U.S. forces."[57]

McNamara's perserverance in the face of pessimism was not atypical—indeed, the Defense Secretary allowed the second sentiment to overwhelm the first sooner than most officials did. Westmoreland, in December 1965, for example, admitted that "notwithstanding the heavy pressures on their transportaion system in the past 9 months, they [the North Vietnamese] have demonstrated an ability to deploy forces into South Vietnam at a greater rate than we are deploying U.S. forces." Nevertheless, "our only hope of a major impact on the ability of the DRV to support the war in Vietnam is continuous air attack . . . from the Chinese border to South Vietnam." The CIA, whose assessments of the consequences of escalation had been especially discouraging, acknowledged in March 1966 that the bombing so far had been ineffective, but then recommended more of it, with fewer restraints. Later that year, in a comment characteristic of the resolute optimism of Johnson administration officials, Robert Komer argued that "by themselves, none of our Vietnam programs offer high confidence of a successful outcome. . . . Cumulatively, however, they *can* produce enough of a *bandwagon psychology* among the southerners to lead to such results by end-1967 or sometime in 1968. At any rate, do we have a better alternative?"[58]

The problem, as Komer suggested, was that however unpromising the prospects of continued escalation, the alternatives seemed even worse. Withdrawal would constitute humiliation, with all that implied for the maintenance of world order. Negotiations prior to establishing a "position of strength" could only lead to appeasement. Continuation of the status quo would not work because the status quo was too delicate. Public opinion remained solidly behind escalation until 1968; indeed, Johnson saw himself as applying the brake, not the accelerator.[59] As a result, there developed a curious mixture of gloom

[57] McNamara to Johnson, July 20, 1965, Johnson Papers, NSF Country File: Vietnam, Box 74, "1965 Troop Decision"; McNamara to Johnson, January 24, 1966, *Pentagon Papers,* IV, 49-51.

[58] Westmoreland cable, December 27, 1965, *Pentagon Papers,* IV, 39. The CIA and Komer reports are discussed in *ibid.,* pp. 71-71, 389-91. (Emphases in orginal.)

[59] Gelb and Betts, *The Irony of Vietnam,* pp. 159-60. See also Johnson, *The Vantage Point,* p. 147; and Kearns, *Lyndon Johnson and the American Dream,* p. 282.

and optimism: things were bad, they were likely to get worse before they got better, but since the alternatives to the existing strategy appeared even more forbidding, there seemed to be little choice but to "press on."

What has not been satisfactorily explained, though, is how the Johnson administration came to define its options so narrowly. In retrospect, quite a lot—negotiations on Hanoi's terms, a gradual relinquishment of responsibility for the war to the South Vietnamese, even a phased withdrawal in the anticipation of an eventual North Vietnamese-Viet Cong victory—would have been preferable to the strategy actually followed, which produced those same results but at vastly greater costs than if they had been sought in the mid-1960's. As George Kennan told the Senate Foreign Relations Committee in 1966, "there is more respect to be won in the opinion of this world by a resolute and courageous liquidation of unsound positions than by the most stubborn pursuit of extravagant and unpromising objectives."[60] But Johnson and his advisers could never bring themselves to consider "heretical" options, despite abundant evidence that their strategy was not working. Their hesitancy suggests still another reason for the failure to monitor performance in Vietnam: an absence of mechanisms for forcing the consideration of unpalatable but necessary alternatives.

Several explanations have been advanced to account for this lapse. It has been argued that there was a premium on "toughness" during the Kennedy-Johnson years; that advocates of a compromise settlement bore a far heavier burden of proof than did supporters of escalation.[61] But this view fails to explain Johnson's tenacious search for a negotiated settlement with Hanoi, carried on not just for the purpose of defusing opposition to the war at home but also in the genuine hope of finding a way out consistent with American credibility.[62] It has been pointed out that Johnson's circle of close advisers narrowed as critics of the war proliferated, and that this limited the Chief Executive's exposure to dissenting points of view.[63] But the President did keep on and listen to "house heretics" like George Ball; more significantly, he paid close attention to McNamara's growing doubts about the war in 1966 and 1967, but still refused to change the strategy.[64] It has recently been suggested that the whole national security decision-making system was at fault: the system "worked" in that it produced the results it had been "programmed" to produce, given prevailing assumptions about containment and the balance of

[60] Senate Committee on Foreign Relations, Hearings, *Supplemental Foreign Assistance Fiscal Year 1966—Vietnam* (Washington: 1966), pp. 335–36.

[61] Richard. J. Barnet, *Roots of War* (Baltimore: 1972), pp. 109–15.

[62] See the list of American peace initiatives and Hanoi's responses in Appendix A to Johnson, *The Vantage Point*, pp. 579–89.

[63] Gallucci, *Neither Peace Nor Honor*, pp. 132–34.

[64] See Johnson's personally drafted memorandum on McNamara's recommendations, December 18, 1967, in Johnson, *The Vantage Point*, pp. 600–601.

power since 1945; the error was in the "programming."⁶⁵ But this argument oversimplifies variations in perceptions of interests and threats over the years: while it is true that all postwar administrations have committed themselves to the general objective of containment, they have differed significantly over what was to be contained, and over the means available to do it.

It is this problem of perceived means that best explains the Johnson administration's inability to come up with alternatives in Vietnam. The mechanism that has most often forced the consideration of unpalatable options in the postwar years has been budgetary: when one knows one has only limited resources to work with, then distinctions between what is vital and peripheral, between the feasible and unfeasible, come more easily, if not less painfully. The Eisenhower administration found this out in 1954, when it decided that the "unacceptable" prospect of a communist North Vietnam was in fact preferable to the more costly alternative of direct U.S. military involvement. But, as has been seen, budgetary concerns carried little weight during the Kennedy and Johnson administrations. The theory of "flexible response" implied unlimited means and, hence, little incentive to make hard choices among distasteful alternatives.

Kennedy did from time to time emphasize the existence of limits beyond which Washington could not go in aiding other countries. "[T]he United States is neither omnipotent or omniscient," he pointed out in 1961: "we are only 6 percent of the world's population . . . we cannot right every wrong or reverse each adversary." It has been argued that the abortive 1963 plan for a phased withdrawal of American advisers from South Vietnam reflected Kennedy's sense that the limits of feasible involvement in that country were approaching.⁶⁶ But there is no conclusive evidence that Kennedy, on fiscal grounds, was considering a diminished American role there; certainly Johnson did not do so. The new President dutifully stressed the need for economy during his first months in office, but more for the purpose of enhancing his reputation with the business community than from any great concern about the limits of American power in the world scene.⁶⁷ And, as the Vietnam crisis intensified, so too did the conviction of Johnson and his advisers that the United States could afford whatever it would take to prevail there.

"[L]et no one doubt for a moment," Johnson proclaimed in August 1964, "that we have the resources and we have the will to

---

⁶⁵ Gelb and Betts, *The Irony of Vietnam*, pp. 2-3.

⁶⁶ Kennedy address at the University of Washington, November 16, 1961, *KPP: 1961*, p. 726. See also *ibid.*, pp. 340-41, 359; *KPP: 1963*, pp. 659-60, 735; and the *Pentagon Papers*, II, 161.

⁶⁷ *JPP: 1963-64*, pp. 44, 89, 122, 150.

follow this course as long as it may take." In a White House meeting the following month, Rusk pointed out that it had cost $50,000 per guerilla to suppress the insurgency in Greece in the late 1940's; in Vietnam "it would be worth any amount to win." Johnson agreed, emphasizing the need for all to understand "that it was not necessary to spare the horses." "Our assets, as I see them, are sufficient to see this thing through if we enter the exercise with adequate determination to succeed," Rostow wrote in November 1964; "at this stage in history we are the greatest power in the world—if we behave like it." Five months later, as direct American military involvement in Vietnam was beginning, McNamara informed the Joint Chiefs of Staff and the service secretaries that "there is an unlimited appropriation available for the financing of aid to Vietnam. Under no circumstances is a lack of money to stand in the way of aid to that nation." There were always costs in meeting "commitments of honor," Rusk commented in August of that year. "But I would suggest, if we look at the history of the last 30 or 40 years, that the costs of *not* meeting your obligations are far greater than those of meeting your obligations."[68]

"The world's most affluent society can surely afford to spend whatever must be spent for its freedom and security," Johnson told the Congress early in 1965. This assumption of virtually unlimited resources goes far toward explaining the persistence of what was acknowledged to be a costly and inefficient strategy: the idea was that if the United States could simply stay the course, regardless of the expense, it would prevail. "I see no choice," the President added, later that year, "but to continue the course we are on, filled as it is with peril and uncertainty and cost in both money and lives." It might take "months or years or decades," but whatever troops General Westmoreland required would be sent "as requested." "Wastefully, expensively, but nonetheless indisputably, we are winning the war in the South," Robert Komer concluded late in 1966. "Few of our programs—civil or military—are very efficient, but we are grinding the enemy down by sheer weight and mass." Westmoreland agreed. "We'll just go on bleeding them until Hanoi wakes up to the fact that they have bled their country to the point of national disaster for generations. Then they will have to reassess their position."[69]

[68] Johnson remarks to American Bar Association meeting, New York, August 12, 1964, *ibid.,* p. 953; Bundy memorandum, Johnson conference with advisers, September 9, 1964, Johnson Papers, NSF—NSC Files, Box 2, "Memos for the President, Vol. 6"; Rostow to Rusk, November 23, 1964, *Pentagon Papers,* III, 647; McNamara to the Joint Chiefs of Staff and service secretaries, March 1, 1965, *ibid.,* p. 94; Rusk CBS-TV interview, August 9, 1965, *DSB,* LIII (August 30, 1965), 344. (Emphasis in original.)
[69] Johnson report to Congress on national defense, January 18, 1965, *JPP: 1965,* p. 69; Johnson remarks to members of Congressional delegations, May 4, 1965, *ibid.,* p. 487; Johnson press conference, July 28, 1965, *ibid.,* pp. 795, 799; Komer memorandum, date not given, *Pentagon Papers,* II, 575; Westmoreland statement to press, April 14, 1967, quoted in Lewy, *America in Vietnam,* p. 73.

But McNamara's "systems analysis" specialists had reached the conclusion, by 1966, that it might take generations to bring the North Vietnamese to that point. Their studies showed, for example, that although enemy attacks tended to produce significant enemy casualties, operations launched by U.S. and South Vietnamese forces produced few if any. This suggested that despite the massive American military presence in the south, the North Vietnamese and Viet Cong still retained the initiative, and hence could control their losses. Other studies indicated that while bombing raids against North Vietnam had increased four times between 1965 and 1968, they had not significantly impaired Hanoi's ability to supply its forces in the south: enemy attacks there had increased on the average five times, and in places eight times, during the same period. The bombing was estimated to have done some $600 million worth of damage in the north, but at a cost in lost aircraft alone of $6 billion. Sixty-five percent of the bombs and artillery rounds expended in Vietnam were being used against unobserved targets, at a cost of around $2 billion a year. Such strikes, the analysts concluded, probably killed about 100 North Vietnamese or Viet Cong in 1966, but in the process provided 27,000 tons of dud bombs and shells which the enemy could use to make booby traps, which that same year accounted for 1,000 American deaths. But most devastating of all, the systems analysts demonstrated in 1968 that despite the presence of 500,000 American troops, despite the expenditure of more bomb tonnage than the United States had dropped in all of World War II, despite estimated enemy casualties of up to 140,000 men in 1967, the North Vietnamese could continue to funnel at least 200,000 men a year into South Vietnam indefinitely. As one analyst wrote, "the notion that we can 'win' this war by driving the VC/NVA from the country or by inflicting an unacceptable rate of casualties on them is false."[70]

Only the last of these studies had any noticeable impact outside the Office of the Secretary of Defense, though: persuasive though they were, there was little incentive, in an administration confident that it could sustain the costs of the war indefinitely, to pay any attention to them.[71] It was not until Johnson personally became convinced that the costs of further escalation would outweigh conceivable benefits that the discipline of stringency could begin to take hold. That did not happen until after the Tet offensive of February 1968, when the President received Westmoreland's request for an additional 206,000 troops, a figure that could not have been met without calling up Reserves and without major domestic and international economic dislocations.*

[70] Enthoven and Smith, *How Much Is Enough,* pp. 290–306.

[71] *Ibid.,* pp. 292–93.

*Curiously, Westmoreland's request was apparently prompted by the Chairman of the Joint Chiefs of Staff, General Earle G. Wheeler, as a means of forcing the reluctant Johnson to call up the Reserves. (Schandler, *The Unmaking of a President,* pp. 116, 138.)

Johnson had always regarded these as limits beyond which he would not go, not on the basis of rigorous statistical analysis, but rather from the gut political instinct that if he passed those points, public support for the war would quickly deteriorate.[72] In the end, then, the Johnson administration based its ultimate calculation of costs and benefits on criteria no more sophisticated than those employed by Eisenhower prior to 1961, or by Truman prior to 1950. The techniques of systems analysis, which had been designed to avoid the need for such arbitrary judgments, in fact only deferred but did not eliminate them.

Several circumstances discouraged the objective evaluation of performance in Vietnam. The military's relative autonomy gave it a large degree of control over the statistical indices used to measure "progress" in the war; this, combined with the organizationally driven compulsion to demonstrate success and the traditional reluctance of civilians in wartime to challenge military authority, made it difficult to verify charges of ineffectiveness.[73] Such accurate intelligence as did get through tended to be disregarded because the alternative courses of action thereby indicated seemed worse than the option of "pressing on." And the perception of unlimited means made perseverance even in the face of unpromising signals seem feasible: far from widening alternatives, the abundance of means, and the consequent lack of incentives to make hard decisions, actually narrowed them. As a result, the postwar administration most sensitive to the need to monitor its own performance found itself ensnared inextricably in a war it did not understand, could not win, but would not leave.

IV

But effectiveness in strategy requires not only the ability to identify interests and threats, calibrate responses, and monitor implementation; it also demands a sense of proportion, an awareness of how commitments in one sphere compare with, and can distract attention and resources away from, obligations elsewhere. Johnson and his subordinates thought they had this larger perspective: Vietnam, they repeatedly insisted, was important not just in itself, but as a symbol of American resolve throughout the world.* The line between a symbol and a fixation is a fine one, though; once it is crossed, perspectives

---

[72] Schandler, *The Unmaking of a President*, pp. 39, 56, 100–102, 228–29, 290–92. See also Johnson, *The Vantage Point*, pp. 149, 317–19, 406–7.

[73] See, on this point, Gallucci, *Neither Peace Nor War*, pp. 128–30.

*"The idea that we are here simply because the Vietnamese want us to be here . . . ; that we have no national interest in being here ourselves; and that if some of them don't

narrow, often unconsciously, with the result that means employed can become inappropriate to, even destructive of, ends envisaged. This narrowing of perspective, this loss of proportion, this failure to detect the extent to which short-term means can corrupt long-term ends, was the fourth and perhaps most lasting deficiency of "flexible response" as applied in Vietnam.

The tendency appeared vividly in South Vietnam itself, where the administration failed to anticipate the sheer strain several hundred thousand U.S. troops would place on the social and economic structure of that country. Despite American efforts to keep it down, the cost of living in the cities rose by at least 170 percent between 1965 and 1967, just as Westmoreland's "search and destroy" operations were swelling their populations with refugees. Corruption, of course, had always been present in Vietnam, but the proliferation of television sets, motorcycles, watches, refrigerators, and loose cash that accompanied the Americans greatly intensified it. "[T]he vast influx of American dollars," one observer recalls, "had almost as much influence . . . as the bombing had on the countryside":

> It turned the society of Saigon inside out. . . . In the new economy a prostitute earned more than a GVN minister, a secretary working for USAID more than a full colonel, a taxi owner who spoke a few words of English more than a university professor. . . . The old rich of Saigon had opposed the Communists as a threat to their position in society; they found that the Americans took away that position in a much quicker and more decisive fashion—and with it, what was left of the underpinning of Vietnamese values.

A similar phenomenon spread to rural areas as well: "Around the American bases from An Khe to Nha Trang, Cu Chi, and Chu Lai, there had grown up entire towns made of packing cases and waste tin . . . entire towns advertising Schlitz, Coca-Cola, or Pepsi Cola . . . towns with exactly three kinds of industry—the taking in of American laundry, the selling of American cold drinks to American soldiers, and prostitution for the benefit of the Americans."[74]

---

want us to stay, we ought to get out is to me fallacious," Ambassador Henry Cabot Lodge cabled from Saigon in 1966. "In fact, I doubt whether we would have the moral right to make the commitment we have made here solely as a matter of charity towards the Vietnamese and without the existence of a strong United States interest. . . . Some day we may have to decide how much it is worth to us to deny Viet-Nam to Hanoi and Peking—regardless of what the Vietnamese may think." (Lodge to State Department, May 23, 1966, *Pentagon Papers,* IV, 99–100.)

[74] FitzGerald, *Fire in the Lake,* pp. 315–16, 349, 352–53.

The effect of this overbearing presence was to erode South Vietnam's capacity for self-reliance, the very quality the Americans had sought to strengthen in the first place. To be sure, Washington never succeeded in controlling its clients in all respects: the very profligacy of the U.S. investment in South Vietnam made occasional threats to cut it off less than credible. "The harsh truth is," one report noted early in 1968, "that given a showdown situation or an intolerable divergence between GVN and US methods, the US advisor will lose." But recalcitrance is not the same thing as independence. The same report noted that "[t]he Vietnamese in the street is firmly convinced that the US totally dominates the GVN and dictates exactly what course shall be followed."[75] And Vietnamese at the military or governmental level, while certainly not puppets, while clearly resentful at the extent to which the Americans had come to dominate their culture, were at the same time terrified at the prospect that the Americans might one day leave.[76] The result was an ambiguous but deep dependency, the extent of which became clear only after the United States did at last withdraw from the war, in 1973.

It is hard to say, in retrospect, what the cross-over point would have been between the level of outside aid necessary to sustain South Vietnam against its enemies and the amount beyond which self-reliance would have been impaired. Perhaps there was no such point; perhaps South Vietnam never had the capacity to stand on its own. What is clear, though, is that Washington made few efforts to find out. The American buildup took place almost totally without regard to the destructive impact it was having on the society it was supposed to defend. "It became necessary to destroy the town, to save it," an Air Force major explained, following the bombing of a Mekong delta village occupied by Viet Cong after the Tet offensive in 1968.[77] The comment could be applied to the whole American experience in Vietnam, and to the dilemma of disproportionate means which the strategy of "flexible response," despite its original emphasis on matching response to offense, never seemed able to resolve.

Securing South Vietnam's independence had not been the only reason for the American presence in that country, though: there had also been a determination to show potential aggressors elsewhere that aggression would not pay. "To withdraw from one battlefield means only to prepare for the next," Johnson argued. "We must say in southeast Asia—as we did in Europe—. . . . 'Hitherto shalt thou

---

[75] MACCORDS report on Bien Hoa province for period ending December 31, 1967, *Pentagon Papers*, II, 406.
[76] FitzGerald, *Fire in the Lake*, p. 357.
[77] Quoted in Alexander Kendrick, *The Wound Within: America in the Vietnam Years, 1945-1974* (Boston: 1974), p. 251.

come, but no further.' ''[78] Interestingly, administration officials did not consider success in South Vietnam as necessarily a requirement in communicating that message. However things turned out there, John McNaughton reflected in 1964, it was "essential . . . that [the] US emerge as a 'good doctor.' We must have kept promises, been tough, taken risks, gotten bloodied, and hurt the enemy very badly." Sustained reprisals against the north might not work, McGeorge Bundy acknowledged early in 1965—the chances of success, he thought, were between 25 and 75 percent. But "even if it fails, the policy will be worth it. At a minimum it will damp down the charge that we did not do all we could. . . . Beyond that, a reprisal policy . . . will set a higher price for the future upon all adventures of guerrilla warfare."[79] The important thing, in projecting resolve, was to make a commitment; failure, while both possible and undesirable, would not be as bad as not having acted in the first place.

And yet, the signal actually communicated was very different. The inability of the steadily growing American commitment to halt North Vietnamese infiltration or Viet Cong attacks—a pattern made painfully evident by the 1968 Tet offensive—seemed only to demonstrate the irrelevancy of the kind of power the United States could bring to bear in such situations: technology, in this respect, may well have been more of a hindrance than a help in Vietnam.[80] The war also confirmed Mao Tse-tung's theory that relatively primitive forces could prevail against more sophisticated adversaries if they had both patience and will, qualities Ho Chi Minh perceived more accurately than Johnson to be lacking in the American attitude toward Vietnam.[81] Finally, Washington's commitment in that country had grown to the point, by 1968, that the United States would have been hard-pressed to respond anywhere else in the world had a comparable crisis developed.[82] What was demonstrated in Vietnam, then, was not so much the costs of committing aggression as of resisting it. . . .

[78] Johnson address at Johns Hopkins University, April 7, 1965, *JPP: 1965,* p. 395.

[79] McNaughton draft memorandum, "Aims and Options in Southeast Asia," October 13, 1964, *Pentagon Papers,* III, 582; Bundy memorandum, "A Policy of Sustained Reprisal," February 7, 1965, *ibid.,* p. 314.

[80] See, on this point, Lewy, *America in Vietnam,* pp. 60, 96, 175, 181–82, 207, 306, 437–38.

[81] See especially "On Protracted War," in the *Selected Military Writings of Mao Tse-tung* (Peking: 1967), pp. 210–19.

[82] Johnson, *The Vantage Point,* p. 389. See also Schandler, *The Unmaking of a President,* pp. 109, 171.

Nuclear Weapons and The 1973 Middle
East Crisis

BARRY M. BLECHMAN and
DOUGLAS M. HART

Ever since the Eisenhower Administration's policy of massive retaliation failed to stem either the tide of left leaning nationalist revolutions in the third world or continuing Soviet pressures on Central
Europe, mainstream American opinion has tended to view the
potential of nuclear weapons to support U.S. foreign policy rather
skeptically. Because of the tremendous risks associated with the
use of nuclear weapons, most observers agree, a threat of nuclear
war is credible only in certain situations—those in which the nation's most important interests are evidently at stake. As such,
nuclear weapons can serve only narrow and distinct purposes. The
threat of nuclear retaliation, of course, serves to deter attacks on,
or coercion of, the United States itself. Also, it is widely believed
that this nuclear umbrella can be extended to those few nations,
primarily the industrialized democracies, for which—for reasons of
history and ethnic, cultural, economic, and political affinities—an
American threat to risk nuclear holocaust on their behalf may be
credible. Beyond that, however, since the late 1950s few have been
willing to argue publicly that other important political or military
purposes can or should be served by the nation's nuclear arsenal.

There is reason to question whether this common perspective on
the utility of nuclear weapons is complete, however. There is a
minority view which maintains that nuclear weapons (that is, the
threat of nuclear war which they imply) actually have served the
nation's policymakers more often and in more ways than are generally recognized. (Interestingly, this view is held by some on both
the extreme right and the extreme left of the American political
spectrum.) Indeed, there is at least some reason to believe that U.S.
decisionmakers have turned to nuclear threats in support of policy

From "The Political Utility of Nuclear Weapons" by Barry M. Blechman and
Douglas M. Hart, *International Security*, Summer 1982 (Vol. 7, No. 1) pp. 132–156.
© 1982 by the President and Fellows of Harvard College and of the Massachusetts
Institute of Technology. Reprinted by permission of MIT Press, Cambridge, Massachusetts and the copyright holders. Portions of the text have been omitted; all
referential and some explanatory footnotes have also been omitted.

in more than 20 specific incidents. Upon closer investigation, many of these incidents prove to be inadvertent, or misunderstood, or simply false; yet, there is some core number of cases—roughly one-half dozen—for which it can be documented that the nation's leaders consciously employed nuclear threats, or at least deliberately drew attention to the risk of nuclear war, as a means of bolstering American policy.

Most of these incidents took place in the 1950s, but the 1960s and 1970s have not been devoid of them. The most recent took place early in 1980, when the credibility of President Carter's commitment to defend the Persian Gulf came into question, and there was reason to believe that the Soviet Union was preparing to move into Iran. Within ten days of the President's statement, U.S. officials made clear nuclear threats on three separate occasions in a desperate attempt to put a real sanction behind the President's words. . . .

Perhaps the most relevant of the past nuclear threats took place during the Arab-Israeli War in October 1973. For the first time when both had mature and robust strategic nuclear forces, there was a serious threat of military conflict between the United States and the Soviet Union. By 1973, both superpowers had deployed nuclear forces that, on paper at least, seemed likely to be able to survive a first strike and retaliate with devastating force against the attacker. According to Western theories of nuclear deterrence, theories upon which we have staked our survival, such a balance of strategic capabilities should have inclined both sides to avoid any move that might have precipitated escalation and led to a greater risk of confrontation and nuclear war. In short, the balance of strategic nuclear forces should have led to stable political relations. This did not prove to be the case, however; in October 1973 both the United States and the Soviet Union took military steps in the Middle East of some significance. Moreover, for the first time since the Cuban missile crisis in October 1962, U.S. policymakers perceived a need to manipulate the risk of nuclear war overtly with the objective of influencing Soviet behavior.

Why was this done? What was expected to be accomplished? And how? To answer these questions, we interviewed several of the five principal participants in the Washington Special Action Group (WSAG)—the forum for crisis management during the Nixon Administration—and additional members of their senior staffs.[1] These

---

[1] Participants in the WSAG included Secretary of State Henry A. Kissinger, Secretary of Defense James R. Schlesinger, Director of Central Intelligence William E. Colby, the President's Deputy National Security Advisor General Brent Scowcroft, and Chairman of the Joint Chiefs of Staff Admiral Thomas Moorer; President Nixon took no part in the WSAG's deliberations. The ground rules governing our interviews preclude direct quotations.

interviews, and supplementary material found in published sources, can make an important contribution to the current debate on the utility of nuclear weapons in the conduct of American foreign policy.

THE CRISIS

The superpower confrontation in 1973 lasted less than 48 hours, beginning early in the morning of October 24th. There was no time for extensive deliberations, for the formulation of sophisticated policy options, for debate. Decision-makers were occupied almost entirely with keeping abreast of a rapidly changing situation and formulating necessarily *ad hoc* reactions to unfolding events. Given the capabilities of modern communications and control systems, this compression of decision-making time is likely to characterize most future crises and will have to be a fundamental consideration in crisis management.

As the Washington Special Action Group met on the morning of October 24th, fighting between Israel and Egypt continued in the Middle East, despite two UN Security Council cease-fire resolutions in as many days. By this time Israel had repulsed the Syrian and Egyptian incursions which started the war and at considerable cost had begun to move deep into Arab territory. A cease-fire had been declared and was holding on the Syrian front, but fighting continued on the west bank of the Suez Canal, where Israeli forces had trapped an entire Egyptian army. Although the United States put considerable pressure on Israel to abide by the cease-fire, it was clear that American concerns were not decisive. At a minimum, the Israelis seemed determined to retain the encircled Egyptian Third Army as a bargaining chip in any future disengagement talks. Israeli policy-makers might also have contemplated destroying the Third Army as a "lesson" to any future would-be aggressors. Despite contrary orders from Cairo, the commander of the Third Army persisted in attempts to break out of the trap his forces were in, but succeeded only in giving Israel an excuse for continuing operations against the beleaguered units. Israeli troops refused to allow UN observers to reach the surrounded Egyptian divisions. And in Tel Aviv, General Chaim Herzog stated that the Third Army's only option was "surrender with honor."

KISSINGER AND THE DOUBLE-CROSS RISK

The extent to which Israel's belligerent attitude may have resulted from deliberate or inadvertent signals from Henry Kissinger is uncertain. Kissinger flew to Moscow and agreed with the Russians to seek a cease-fire on October 20th. Two days later he was in Israel. He spent three and a half hours closeted with Prime Minister Golda

Meir and members of her cabinet trying to persuade them to accept the cease-fire terms he had negotiated with the Soviets. Mrs. Meir and her "kitchen cabinet" were quite unhappy, to say the least, with the deal. In effect, the Israelis were being asked to forgo destruction of the Third Army in return for the promise of face-to-face talks with the Egyptians "aimed at establishing a just and durable peace in the Middle East." To add insult to injury, the terms of the deal had been delivered with the instructions that no changes, substantive or semantic, could be made in the language of the agreement.

Accounts of Kissinger's performance in Israel vary. Some observers claim that the Secretary encouraged Israel to believe that the twelve-hour deadline for implementation of the cease-fire, stated in the agreement, was actually flexible. The Israelis reportedly interpreted this statement as a sign that Washington was prepared to allow them to complete the encirclement of the Third Army. Another version holds that Kissinger pressed Mrs. Meir and her advisers for an immediate cease-fire and strict adherence to the terms of the agreement. According to this view, Kissinger repeatedly stressed that both the United States and the Soviet Union opposed the destruction of the Egyptian Third Army.

Exactly what the Secretary of State told Mrs. Meir on the 22nd, however, is not nearly as important as the results of the meeting. Kissinger left Israel believing that the end of the war was near and that with careful diplomacy in the weeks ahead the situation could be defused. The Israelis, on the other hand, thought that they had some time left to fulfill their military objectives. And the Soviets thought that Kissinger had taken them to the cleaners. By the time the Secretary's plane had returned to Washington on the 23rd, the tactical situation had deteriorated; Israel seemed to be ignoring the cease-fire. A hotline message from Brezhnev to Nixon late on October 23rd, the eve of the crisis, confirmed that Moscow felt betrayed:

> . . . the words were hard and cold, he urged that the U.S. move decisively to stop the violations. He curtly implied that we might even have colluded in Israel's action.

This feeling of betrayal seems to have been central in determining Moscow's subsequent behavior. Kissinger himself apparently empathized. Upon learning that Israel had completed surrounding the Third Army after the cease-fire deadline, he is reported to have exclaimed, "My God, the Russians will think I double-crossed them. And in their shoes, who wouldn't?"

SOVIET PREPARATIONS FOR INTERVENTION

The Soviets moved decisively to rectify the situation. By October 24th, signs of Soviet preparations for military intervention in Egypt had become a source of serious concern. All seven Soviet airborne divisions were then on alert; three had been placed on alert as early as October 11, the rest in the early morning hours of the 24th. An airborne command post had been established in Southern Russia and Soviet Air Force units were also on alert. Together these forces represented some 40,000 combat troops. According to some reports, preparations for imminent departures were visible at several bases used by the airborne divisions. Indeed, one source reports that one of the seven divisions had been moved from its base outside Moscow to an airfield near Belgrade the week before. On the 17th of October, a unit of 30 *Antonov* transports (the same squadron that spearheaded the invasion of Czechoslovakia in 1968) was said also to have been moved to Belgrade.

In addition, seven Soviet amphibious assault vessels, some possibly with naval infantrymen on board, and two helicopter carriers were deployed in the Mediterranean. The Soviet Mediterranean fleet itself numbered some 85 ships, a figure that Bernard and Marvin Kalb refer to as "unprecedented."

There was also a nuclear specter in the midst of the Soviet naval activity. U.S. intelligence had been tracking a Russian ship carrying radioactive materials since it had entered the Mediterranean via the Bosporus on the 22nd. Our interviewees confirmed that the U.S. intelligence community was quite positive that there was nuclear material aboard the ship, even though the reason for the radioactivity could not be defined. When the ship docked at Port Said on the 25th, there was some speculation that it was transporting warheads for a brigade of Soviet SCUD missiles previously deployed near Cairo. This rumor was never confirmed, and the radioactive emissions could have come from naval weapons with nuclear warheads or from something else. Still, these reports about the movement of nuclear materials on the Soviet ship heightened concern among the members of the WSAG that a Soviet intervention was imminent and introduced a new dimension to the crisis.

Early in the morning of the 24th, an apparent standdown in Soviet airlift of weapons and supplies to Egypt and Syria had been welcomed as a sign that Moscow was prepared to move in concert with the United States to limit arms transfers to the belligerents. But by noon, this pause appeared more ominous. A large portion of the Soviet airlift fleet could not be located by U.S. intelligence systems, electronic intercepts indicated that Soviet flight plans for the next day were being changed, and certain "communications nets'' showed a surge in activity, indicating that a major change in Soviet operations would be expected soon.

THE UN RESOLUTION AND THE SUPERPOWER TANGLE

In the afternoon of the 24th, events began to accelerate even more dangerously. At 3:00 p.m., amid signs of increasing panic in Cairo, President Sadat appealed to the United States and the Soviet Union to impose a joint peacekeeping force between Egyptian and Israeli units. At the UN, a group of nonaligned countries began to circulate informally a draft Security Council resolution calling on the superpowers to separate the combatants. Around 7:00 p.m., Soviet Ambassador Dobrynin informed Kissinger that their UN Ambassador had orders to support such a proposal. About this same time, President Nixon's reply to Sadat's public appeal for joint intervention was received in Cairo. The note, drafted by Kissinger, rejected the proposed joint intervention and stressed the risks of superpower involvement.

> Should the two great nuclear powers be called upon to provide forces, it would introduce an extremely dangerous potential for great-power rivalry in the area.

Perhaps Kissinger hoped that this blunt refusal would reach the Politburo in time to head off the coming showdown. But a phone call to Dobrynin about fifteen minutes later dashed whatever hopes might have existed for containing events at this juncture. The Soviet Ambassador informed the Secretary that the USSR might not wait for the nonaligned proposal in the UN; it might introduce a similar motion itself. Kissinger warned Dobrynin that the situation was becoming very dangerous: "I urged him not to push us to the extreme. We would not accept Soviet troops in any guise. Dobrynin replied that in Moscow, 'they have become so angry, they want troops.' "

Around 9:00 p.m., a message from Brezhnev arrived blaming the Israelis for continued fighting on the west bank of the Suez Canal. This note, however, appears to have been only a preamble to a second Brezhnev message, delivered over the telephone by Dobrynin to Kissinger a half-hour later. The second note is the key to the crisis. . . . Henry Kissinger recently claimed it constituted "one of the most serious challenges to an American President." Senator Fulbright referred to the text as "urgent." Senator Jackson called it "brutal, rough." Publicly, the President described the message as "very firm," and added that it left very little to the imagination. The British Ambassador to the United States at the time was also impressed with the toughness of the language. The note reportedly blamed Israel once again for violating the cease-fire resolutions and called on the United States to send forces in conjunction with the Soviet Union to Egypt. In the crucial passage, Brezhnev warned that if the U.S. was unwilling to participate in such a joint undertaking, the Soviets would be forced to consider unilateral action. Kissinger assembled a team of Kremlinologists to examine the two Soviet messages. These experts found the second communication "totally different" and more threatening than the first. At 11:00 p.m. on October 24th, the Secretary of State again convened the Washington Special Action Group. All the individuals interviewed for this article agree as to the essence of the situation they faced at that time. All evidence pointed to serious preparations by the Soviets for an intervention in Egypt in the very near future— within 24 hours. Brezhnev's second note, a continuing increase in traffic on relevant communications nets, the nuclear specter alluded to previously, and growing evidence of the actual loading of transport aircraft at Soviet airborne division bases led the group to request presidential authority to place U.S. forces on a higher level of alert. As one participant put it, "They [the Soviets] had the capability, they had the motive, and the assets (i.e., transport aircraft) had disappeared from our screens." If the United States had not reacted to these military preparations, all participants agree, it would have been imprudent in the extreme. The only question concerns the form that the reaction took.

THE UNSPOKEN MESSAGE: THE AMERICAN MILITARY ALERT

Nixon gave his concurrence to the alert and the Chairman of the Joint Chiefs of Staff ordered the alert status of U.S. forces advanced to DEFCON III[2] around midnight. By 2:00 a.m., the alert status of all major U.S. commands had been advanced, including the Strategic Air Command—the component charged with nuclear missions. In a key action, fifty to sixty B-52 strategic bombers—a long-standing symbol and central component of U.S. nuclear capabilities—were moved from their base on Guam to the United States. Aerial refueling tankers assigned to the Strategic Air Command were dispersed to a larger number of bases and began non-routine operations. Marginal changes also were made in the status of U.S. strategic submarines and land-based intercontinental missiles. Finally, the aircraft carrier *John F. Kennedy* was dispatched toward the Mediterranean from just west of the Straits of Gibraltar, and the

---

[2] There are five defense readiness conditions (DEFCONs), of which DEFCON 1 indicates a state of war. Although parts of the strategic forces, such as the Strategic Air Command and parts of the Polaris and Poseidon fleets are regularly kept at DEFCON III, the measures taken in the early morning hours of October 25th moved all forces up one level of readiness.

82nd Airborne Division (about 15,000 troops) was told to be ready to move by 6:00 a.m.

The intent was that these military actions themselves would carry the message to the Soviets. There was no public announcement of the alert and, despite Dobrynin's request for an "immediate" reply to Brezhnev's second note, there were no private communications with the Soviets until 5:00 a.m. In a move calculated to show the Administration's displeasure with the Soviets' implied threat and to raise their apprehension about U.S. plans, Kissinger refused any contact with Dobrynin despite the latter's repeated requests, by telephone, for a response. Kissinger and others believed that it would be helpful if the initial signals of the American response picked up by the Kremlin were the indicators of U.S. military activity intercepted by Soviet intelligence systems. The unusual coolness in the Kissinger-Dobrynin relationship also was deliberate and was meant to show the Administration's displeasure with Brezhnev's last message. When a written response finally was given to Dobrynin at 5:40 a.m. on the 25th, it was passed to the Ambassador by Brent Scowcroft, Kissinger's deputy—again, an unusual and deliberate move. The whole manner with which these early morning exchanges were held were meant to show that, even so far as personal relationships were concerned, as long as the Soviets' threat of intervention remained valid, it could no longer be "business-as-usual."

The text of the message delivered to Dobrynin reflected the Administration's concern and contained hints of the potentially serious military confrontation threatened by U.S. military forces:

> Mr. General Secretary:
> I have carefully studied your important message of this evening. I agree with you that our understanding to act jointly for peace is one of the highest value and that we should implement that understanding in this complex situation.
> I must tell you, however, that your proposal for a particular kind of joint action, that of sending Soviet and American military contingents to Egypt, is not appropriate in the present circumstances.
> We have no information which would indicate that the cease-fire is now being violated on any significant scale. . . .
> In these circumstances, *we must view your suggestion of unilateral action as a matter of gravest concern, involving incalculable consequences.*
> It is clear that the forces necessary to impose the cease-fire terms on the two sides would be massive and would require closest coordination so as to avoid bloodshed. This is not clearly infeasible, but it is not appropriate to the situation.
> It would be understood that this is an extraordinary and temporary step, solely for the purpose of providing adequate information concern-

ing compliance by both sides with the terms of the cease-fire. If this is what you mean by contingents, we will consider it.
Mr. General Secretary, in the spirit of our agreements [i.e., the 1973 Agreement on the Prevention of Nuclear War] this is the time for acting not unilaterally, but in harmony and with cool heads. *I believe my proposal is consonant with the letter and spirit of our understandings* and would ensure a prompt implementation of the cease-fire. . . .
You must know, however, that we could in no event accept unilateral action. . . . As I stated above, such action would produce *incalculable consequences* which would be in the interest of neither of our countries and which would end all we have striven so hard to achieve.

Nuclear threats or even allusions to nuclear weapons were absent from the note, save for the oblique reference to the 1973 agreement on preventing nuclear war in the penultimate paragraph. References to matters "of the gravest concern" and repeated use of the phrase "incalculable consequences," however, could only be taken as hints of the possibility of nuclear war if the situation were not contained quickly.

Cleverly, the note also contained a face-saving gesture for Moscow, by permitting the introduction of a small number of observers. This gave Brezhnev a way out of the crisis and eventually resulted in the dispatch of 70 Soviet "representatives" to monitor the cease-fire.

More importantly, the United States sought to placate Soviet concerns by simultaneously reining in its recalcitrant ally. Shortly after the alert was in place, Kissinger informed Israeli Ambassador Simcha Dinitz of Soviet preparations for an intervention and of the U.S. response. His purpose was to impress Jerusalem with the gravity of the situation and the imminent danger of catastrophe should Israel force the Soviets' hand by annihilating the Third Army. Clearly, the Secretary of State hoped to convince Israel to spare the Egyptian unit by demonstrating that further hostilities would have far more than a regional impact. In short, the U.S. adopted a dual approach. On the one hand, it stood tough in the face of the threatened Soviet intervention. On the other hand, more privately, it tried to alter the conditions that had led to the Soviet threat to begin with.

Among the reasons why the Washington Special Action Group selected the alert as the most appropriate response to the threat of Soviet intervention was the group's belief that this type of move would send a clear and immediate signal to the Soviets without engendering a serious public debate in the United States, at least during the crisis itself. This expectation proved to be naive, however, and eventually harmed the Administration's political position at home.

By the 7:00 a.m. news on the 25th, the alert was the lead story in all national media. Most Americans awoke on that Saturday to TV footage of U.S. preparations for war—soldiers returning from leave, B-52s taking off and landing, war ships preparing to go to sea. As the public had gone to sleep unaware of the Soviet preparations for intervention in the Middle East, the reasons for this U.S. military activity were unclear. In the political atmosphere that had resulted from, first, years of increasingly strained efforts to present a favorable picture of the war in Vietnam and, second, the revelations of Presidential misdeeds associated with Watergate, the U.S. military activity was viewed, if not cynically, at least skeptically. Indeed, by the time the Special Action Group reconvened in the morning of October 25th, its primary task was to prove that the crisis was real and not an outrageous attempt to distract attention from Watergate.

The burden of proof then fell on Secretary Kissinger, who had previously scheduled a press conference for noon of the 25th. Perhaps for this reason—to emphasize the gravity of the situation for domestic purposes—but also perhaps to reinforce the message of nuclear danger which already had been communicated to the Soviets by word and deed—the Secretary chose to stress the nuclear aspects of the crisis. In an opening statement during which he departed from a prepared text, glared at the cameras, and intoned in his most ominous voice, Dr. Kissinger dealt extensively with the dangers of superpower confrontations:

> The United States and the Soviet Union are, of course, ideological and to some extent political adversaries. But the United States and the Soviet Union also have a very special responsibility.
> We possess, each of us, nuclear arsenals capable of annihilating humanity. We, both of us, have a special duty to see to it that confrontations are kept within bounds that do not threaten civilized life.
> Both of us, sooner or later, will have to come to realize that the issues that divide the world today, and foreseeable issues, do not justify the unparalleled catastrophe that a nuclear war would represent.

The Secretary returned to the theme of the horrendous consequences of nuclear conflict at several points during the question period (". . . humanity cannot stand the eternal conflicts of those who have the capacity to destroy."). The performance was quite impressive and—regardless of its effect on the American press—delivered a clear message to the Soviet Union.

The crisis ended within hours. In the early afternoon of the 25th, the Soviet Ambassador to the UN, acting on new instructions, stopped his efforts to secure the inclusion of U.S. and Soviet troops in the UN peacekeeping force. The dispatch of an international force excluding both Soviet and U.S. troops was ratified by the

Security Council soon afterwards. Coincidentally, Israeli military activity also ceased. . . . Also around this time, a message arrived from Brezhnev taking advantage of the conciliatory gesture contained in the U.S. note, informing the United States that the Soviet Union was sending a small number of observers to monitor Israeli compliance with the cease-fire.

Participants' memories of when the crisis ended in fact, if not formally, differ, however. Some maintain that it was clear early in the morning of the 25th that the U.S. had achieved its objective. One Soviet aircraft touched down at the Cairo West airfield in the early morning hours, but returned home almost immediately. It was as if this aircraft, containing the lead element of the interventionary force, had been caught en route when the Kremlin decided the risk was too great and reversed course. Other signs that Soviet military forces were returning to normal activities soon followed. If this analysis is accurate, Kissinger's statements at the press conference alluding to nuclear risks could only have been intended to be sure these favorable developments were continued and to emphasize how grave the situation had been for domestic purposes. Others, however, maintain that it was not clear at the time of the press conference that the crisis had been resolved successfully. If so, then Kissinger's remarks were intended primarily to draw a line for the Kremlin, to indicate in the strongest terms that the U.S. was not prepared to tolerate unilateral Soviet intervention in the Middle East and that it was prepared to undertake very grave risks to prevent it.

Communications, or signals, intelligence not only provided the most important warnings that the Soviet Union was preparing to intervene in Egypt in October 1973, but also was the major medium chosen by the United States to transmit the threat designed to thwart the possibility of such a move. Yet the inability of even key participants to identify a distinct end to the crisis illustrates the vagaries of confrontations in which nations communicate primarily through this netherworld of the technology of eavesdropping. As Secretary of Defense Schlesinger stated on October 26th, it was easier to determine when the Soviets had gone on alert than when they had reduced their level of readiness.

ANALYSIS

If the 1973 crisis is to help analysts to understand the potential future role of nuclear weapons, or nuclear threats, in American policy, it is essential to deduce the answers to two crucial questions: Why did American decision-makers decide to stress the nuclear dimension of the crisis? And what were the consequences of this decision?

Reasons for the decision to advance the state of alert of American military forces itself are fairly clear. There was sufficient evidence to believe that a Soviet intervention was likely. There was agreement that such a move left unopposed would have had a major adverse impact, not only on the American position in the Middle East but, given then-recent history (particularly in Southeast Asia), on the U.S. position worldwide. Individuals present at the WSAG meetings agree that the shift to DEFCON III was seen as a clear, unambiguous, and prompt way to convey the gravity with which the United States viewed the situation and of its intent to combat any Soviet move, if necessary, with military force. Most to the point, the alert had the benefit that it would be detected virtually immediately by Soviet intelligence systems through the changes it would cause in U.S. military communications patterns, while it was expected these signals would be relatively invisible to most of the world for some period of time.

At the same time, the alert had the added benefit that, as one participant put it, ". . . [it was] not so desperate a signal as to get the two nations past the point of no return." As such, particularly when combined with the "out" left to the Soviets in the telegraphed response to Brezhnev's message, it allowed both nations sufficient· maneuvering room so that they would be able to defuse the situation before things got too far out of hand.

Another participant explained that the alert fit closely with Kissinger's approach to crisis management. Rather than matching Soviet actions "tit for tat," the Secretary believed, it was necessary to do something more dramatic, something which would get the attention of Soviet decision-makers because it was several times more alarming than their own action. The point, he stressed, was to do something unmistakably above the noise level, something that would make unambiguously plain how seriously the United States viewed the situation and, thus, how grave were the risks of not reaching accommodation.

It was this reasoning which led to inclusion of the nuclear dimension in the American response. A conventional response would not have been sufficient to quickly and forcefully make clear the U.S. position. The war in the Middle East had been going on for several weeks and, as a result, U.S. and Soviet conventional military capabilities had already been enhanced. The U.S. Sixth Fleet in the Mediterranean had already been beefed up, U.S. airlift aircraft were already heavily engaged, U.S. equipment in Europe had already been tapped for use in the Middle East. Given the perceived imminence of the Soviet intervention, and given these previous military preparations, only escalation to the nuclear level, symbolically of course, was seen as dramatic and threatening enough to make absolutely clear the gravity with which the United States perceived the situation and its determination to do whatever was necessary to stop it. It should be noted that this view is not unanimous. Others, even among the participants, believe that the nuclear aspects of the crisis were unimportant. Much of the activity involving strategic forces, they argue, occurred inadvertently; the orders were given for the alert and, virtually automatically, all components of the armed forces advanced their readiness for war, including SAC. As for the shift of B-52s from Guam to the United States, the most visible and clearly deliberate move involving nuclear forces, this, it is argued, was simply the Defense Department's taking advantage of the crisis to carry out a long-sought shift of military assets for reasons of economy. Secretary of Defense Schlesinger had sought permission to make such a move for some time, it is noted, but was denied authorization because the State Department feared the political consequences of further reductions in U.S. military forces in the Pacific. When the crisis erupted, it is said, the Defense Department saw a new opportunity to justify a move.

Those who hold to this view assert that none of the key participants in the crisis took the possibility of nuclear war seriously. That is likely to be the case; nonetheless, it does not detract from the role played by the *risk of* nuclear war in resolving the crisis, nor the perception by at least some American decision-makers that emphasizing these dangers could help to achieve the U.S. objective. To appreciate this, it is important to understand the character of the threat made by the United States. American decisionmakers were not threatening to unleash nuclear war, to launch its nuclear-armed missiles and bombers at the USSR if Soviet troops landed in Egypt; something much more subtle was involved.

Changes in the alert status, disposition, and activity patterns of U.S. nuclear forces, as well as the hints in Nixon's response to Brezhnev and the much clearer statements in Kissinger's press conference, served both to stress the dangers of confrontation and to emphasize the stake which the United States perceived in the situation. In effect, these actions constituted manipulation of the risk of nuclear war; they both drew attention to the ultimate dangers of confrontation and advanced U.S. preparations to fight a nuclear conflict. As such, they carried a clear message. In effect, the U.S. actions said to Soviet decision-makers: "If you persist in your current activity, if you actually go ahead and land forces in Egypt, you will initiate an interactive process between our armed forces whose end results are not clear, but which could be devastating. Moreover, the United States feels so strongly about this issue that it is prepared to participate in this escalatory process until our objectives are achieved. The United States is prepared to continue escalating the confrontation up to and including a central nuclear exchange between us, even though we understand that the consequences of such an interaction potentially are 'incalculable.' '' In short, in its nuclear moves and statements, the United States was demonstrating and making credible the vital stake it perceived in the situation. It indicated that it understood what might result from confrontation, but that it was prepared to carry on in any event. And it posed the choice to the Soviets of cutting short the crisis before the escalatory process went too far, or continuing in awareness that the risks could grow to terrifying proportions.

INFLUENCING FRIENDS AND DETERRING ADVERSARIES

The U.S. actions served one additional purpose as well. They camouflaged the fact, and thus made it politically acceptable, that although the United States had achieved its objective—halting the threatened Soviet intervention—the ostensible Soviet objective in contemplating the intervention also had been achieved: Israeli actions against the encircled Egyptian Third Army were halted. The central difficulty throughout the crisis was the need to influence the behavior of an adversary and the behavior of an ally at the same time. If the United States simply had countered the Soviet threat, and done nothing about Israeli efforts to dismember the Egyptian army, Sadat's regime would have been imperiled and the chances for a negotiated settlement in the Middle East destroyed. Moreover, had Washington put its forces on alert without pressing Israel to comply with the cease-fire, Russian suspicions of a double-cross would have been confirmed and the situation could easily have gotten out of control. On the other hand, the United States could have attempted to halt the Israelis while ignoring the Soviet threat, on the assumption that such a course of action would remove the cause of Moscow's displeasure. However, this would have set a dangerous precedent for future crisis by signalling to the Soviets that coercive threats could be invoked without fear of reciprocal counter-threats.

DOMESTIC AND THIRD PARTY AUDIENCES

It is irrelevant that the survival of the Third Army (and thereby Sadat's regime) was also in the United States' and Israel's long-term interests. . . . Politically, the U.S. could not be seen to be stopping the Israelis in response to Soviet pressures. Use of the word "politically" here refers to both domestic politics and to the consequences of such an action for political relations between the United States and a number of nations. For example, the 1973 War marked one of the most divisive moments in the history of NATO. The oil embargo, which began on October 18, created an atmosphere of panic and disunity in Western Europe. Deliveries of arms purchases made by Israel in several European countries months before the outbreak of hostilities were held up, and the U.S. resupply effort was denied various forms of support by many NATO allies. Emotions were running high. Any sign of U.S. weakness *vis à vis* the Soviet Union during this tense period, Kissinger and others feared, could have permanently crippled the alliance. . . .

THE AFTERMATH OF CRISIS

Finally, the alert gave the United States added leverage in its relations with Israel immediately following the crisis. Although they halted offensive military operations against the Third Army on October 25, the Israelis were reluctant to grant passage to convoys carrying food, water, and medical supplies to the trapped unit. On the afternoon of the 26th, Kissinger made another *démarche* to Dinitz. The crisis had demonstrated quite dramatically how seriously both superpowers viewed the current situation, he said, and it could be a harbinger of future disaster if "humanitarian convoys" were not allowed to reach the Third Army. Kissinger skillfully portrayed the Israelis as holding the key to regional and world stability. The following day Jerusalem bowed to American pressure and agreed to allow the convoys to reach the Egyptian troops.

The import of the U.S. manipulation of the risk of nuclear war was not lost on the Russians. Initially, the Soviets were taciturn about the crisis. Following Kissinger's press conference, *Tass* merely noted the new cease-fire and the dispatch of 7,000 peace-keeping troops to the battle zone. On the following day, however, Brezhnev delivered a polemical address in which he accused "some NATO countries" of formulating an "absurd" response in the wake of "fantastic speculation" as to Soviet intentions. This line became the standard Soviet public interpretation of the events of October 24th and 25th.

According to one member of Kissinger's senior staff, however, the Soviets took a very different tack in private conversations. He noted that the Soviets never tried to belabor their American interlocutor with protests that the United States had misinterpreted their actions, or that it had overreacted. Such contrasting behavior, our interviewee believes, confirms that the Soviets were seriously contemplating an intervention and that they understood the seriousness of the American signals sent by the nuclear threat.

Given, then, that the United States did deliberately draw attention to the risk of nuclear war in October 1973 and that this message was received clearly by the Soviets, what was its effect? How important was the nuclear alert? The answer to this question, of course, is unknown and unknowable short of public testimony by Leonid Brezhnev and other Soviet decision-makers. And even then, one could not be certain that their answers were honest nor their memories clear. Moreover, as was the case with the American participants in the crisis, it may be that the perceptions of those Soviets that were involved would differ—that different individuals would stress different aspects of the U.S. response as decisive.

1962/1973: ANALOGIES TO THE CUBAN MISSILE CRISIS

This question mirrors a more well-known debate over the importance of nuclear forces to the U.S. success in the 1962 Cuban missile crisis. Many observers of that earlier confrontation, perhaps most, conclude that the Soviet Union withdrew its missiles from Cuba in that incident because the United States had overwhelming nuclear superiority. Faced with the certainty that they would "lose" if the situation escalated to a central nuclear exchange, those holding to this viewpoint argue, the USSR decided to terminate the confrontation early. Many others, however, including each of President Kennedy's three senior advisors during the crisis (Secretary of State Dean Rusk, Secretary of Defense Robert McNamara, and National Security Advisor McGeorge Bundy), argue that the decisive factor was U.S. naval superiority in the Atlantic and Caribbean and the huge buildup of conventional forces in the Southeastern United States in preparation for an invasion. According to these individuals, even though the United States had a clear-cut advantage in long-range nuclear forces, a threat to go to nuclear war if the missiles were not removed would not have been credible because no president could have deliberately taken a move that would have resulted in even the few million casualties that would have been expected in 1962. While a threat of nuclear retaliation against the Soviet Union if missiles were launched from Cuba *was* made, this was a deterrent threat, aimed at forestalling the Soviets from shifting the focus of the confrontation elsewhere, particularly to Berlin. The effective compellent mechanism—that which brought about the withdrawal of Soviet missiles—it is argued, was the demonstration of conventional military capabilities.

Our analysis of the 1973 confrontation sheds some light on this debate; it demonstrates that both views are incorrect, or perhaps that both are partially correct.

It is clear that, on October 24, 1973, the Soviets had made all the preparations necessary for them to intervene in Egypt within 24 hours. All of the members of the WSAG believed that the possibility of intervention was serious enough to require a decisive American response. Yet the Soviets chose not to, finding a way, instead, of ending the confrontation and, thus, of appearing to yield to American pressures.[3] Why? The Soviet Union clearly did not back down because the United States had an edge in strategic weaponry and could "win" a nuclear exchange. There was a rough balance of strategic forces between the superpowers in the early 1970s. Neither side possessed the capability for a disarming first strike, and each would have expected to suffer devastating retaliation if it launched nuclear war. On the other hand, it is hard to believe that the alert of U.S. conventional forces, at least in terms of the specific military threat implied by that move, was decisive either. It was probably unclear to both sides which nation would have come out ahead in a naval battle in the Mediterranean or in a contest between their respective interventionary forces in Egypt itself. Indeed, our interviewees noted that there was no time to even contemplate what military steps would have been taken if the alert had failed to dissuade the Soviets from their proposed course.

DEMONSTRATING INTEREST, CAPABILITY, AND WILL

The Soviets chose not to land troops in Egypt because of more fundamental considerations. The United States was able to convince Soviet leaders that strategic parity, an uncertain conventional balance, and domestic problems notwithstanding, the President was willing to risk war with the USSR to block the contemplated Soviet action. This resolve was made credible by three related and mutually reinforcing components of the American response.

First, there was the historical context in which the October 1973 crisis took place. This component is at once the most important and least tangible. For more than 20 years, statements by U.S. decision-makers had made clear the importance which they attached to stability in the Middle East. Moreover, on literally dozens of occasions, the United States had acted in specific situations to ensure that the *status quo* in the Middle East was not changed by force. At times these actions included the deployment of American military forces. Some of these actions stemmed from the long-standing commitment to Israel, but it went well beyond that. Throughout the 1950s, 1960s, and into the 1970s, U.S. armed forces and diplomacy had been used to counter threats to Middle Eastern stability, whether in an Arab-Israeli or intra-Arab context, and whether the threat was posed by local powers, the Soviet Union, or even—on one occasion—by NATO allies. Given this history, the U.S. threat to risk war in order to prevent Soviet intervention in the Middle East sounded genuine; it fit the historic pattern of U.S. behavior

---

[3] Soviet achievement of their tactical objective—final Israeli acceptance of the cease-fire—was a factor, but irrelevant to considerations of the political consequences of the superpower confrontation.

and reflected long-standing American perceptions of its vital interests.

Second, there were the actions taken involving conventional U.S. forces. Apart from their direct effects on U.S. military preparedness, indicators of preparations for the use of conventional forces, such as the alert of the 82nd airborne division, communicated American resolve and seriousness to Soviet decision-makers. It signalled that the United States was contemplating realistic and feasible moves in this early stage of the crisis, and that a number of credible options would be available to the American president if the Soviet intervention took place. Moreover, the conventional alert added credibility to the nuclear threat. It indicated that steps would be taken that would begin and facilitate the escalatory process. It showed that the United States would not have to choose between accepting the Soviet *fait accompli* and initiating nuclear war, in which case, Soviet leaders would reason, the nuclear decision would be unlikely. Rather, American decision-makers would have to choose only between accepting the Soviet intervention and a military action whose worst immediate consequences were calculable. It made the U.S. position and the risk to escalation to nuclear war seem credible.

Third, there was the nuclear threat itself. But it is essential to keep in mind the character of the threat. It was not to unleash nuclear war, but to get involved in the situation militarily and to pursue an escalatory process despite awareness that its potential consequences were incalculable. The nuclear threat, in short, served to make clear just how importantly the United States viewed the stakes in the situation and the ultimate cost which could be suffered by the Soviet Union if it initiated a process of military interaction. . . .

LESSONS

It is always difficult and sometimes misleading to derive lessons from the past. Yet, it has been demonstrated on numerous occasions that statesmen can ignore history only at their peril. Nuclear weapons and the threats they imply can be used, at times, to help protect American interests in difficult situations. Raising the risk of nuclear war obviously is not without its dangers, however. The 1973 crisis can tell us something about both the ways in which nuclear threats can be used to support policy, and the dangers of turning to such desperate tactics.

Today and into the foreseeable future, as in 1973, both the United States and the Soviet Union maintain sizable forces of nuclear-armed missiles and bombers capable of withstanding an attack and retaliating with tremendous destruction against the military forces, economy, and population of the attacker. Under such circumstances, a statesman cannot actually threaten nuclear war more credibly than to draw attention to the fact that a process has been set in motion which, unless stopped, could lead to nuclear war. Such deliberate manipulation of the opponent's assessment of the likelihood of a nuclear exchange can be used to define, and to make clear to the opponent, that one perceives a vital stake in the situation. For such an attempt to define a vital stake in a situation to be credible, however, circumstances must be appropriate. The nation making the nuclear statement must have an evidently vital interest in the situation, such as its geostrategic location or its economic value. And there must be some historical continuity to its interest there. For the United States to manipulate the risk of nuclear war to compel the withdrawal of Cuban forces from Angola would be as inappropriate and ineffective as would Soviet nuclear threats in defense of the Sandinista regime in Nicaragua. Only in certain places and very special circumstances might attempts to manipulate the risk of nuclear war be credible. For the United States, these probably include military contingencies involving Europe, Japan, and Korea, for which a willingness to make first use of nuclear weapons has long been articulated policy. Elsewhere, such U.S. threats probably would only be credible in the Middle East (including the Persian Gulf), and only when taken in response to Soviet, not local, actions. For the Soviet Union, military challenges to its position in Eastern Europe would no doubt trigger credible threats of nuclear war, as would a serious military confrontation with China in Central Asia. In all other places, Soviet nuclear threats would only be credible in the context of direct military confrontation with the United States and, even then, would depend on the circumstances which had precipitated the conflict to begin with.

This view of the character of nuclear threats in an age of substantial nuclear retaliatory capabilities on both sides also suggests that within fairly permissive boundaries, the effectiveness of nuclear threats may not be influenced by the *aggregate* strategic balance. The threat is not so much to go deliberately to nuclear war as it is to participate and persevere in an escalatory process, even though it might *result* in nuclear war. Accordingly, the credibility of the threat would not, from a first approximation, be influenced by calculations of just how badly off each side would be if the escalation ran its course, presuming, of course, that both sides had maintained substantial forces. Its credibility would depend on the ability of the nation making the threat to demonstrate convincingly that it perceived such vital interests at stake that it was even prepared to fight a nuclear war, if that became necessary.

On the other hand, this analysis emphasizes the vital importance of maintaining adequate conventional military forces. For one, in those situations in which the nation's non-nuclear military capabilities are obviously dominant, there is no need for nuclear threats, and thus no need either to run the risks implied by such actions. It would, moreover, be unwise to tarnish this potentially crucial instrument of foreign policy by overuse. But even in more ambiguous situations, adequate conventional forces are necessary to make credible the message contained in nuclear threats. The risk of nuclear war can only be emphasized credibly when one can demonstrate how the initial stages of the escalatory process might take place.

What would have happened if Soviet forces had attempted to land in Egypt despite the U.S. nuclear alert is difficult to say; the risks, though, were tremendous. Say, for example, that coincident with its alert, the United States had not been able to persuade Israel to refrain from attacking the beleaguered Egyptian Third Army—and, as a result, that the Soviet Union had felt compelled, despite its awareness of the dangers, to intervene. What then?

In an optimistic scenario, Soviet airborne forces would have been deployed so as to defend Cairo and the Egyptian heartland in a gesture of greater political than military import, thus avoiding actual conflict with Israeli forces. In response, the United States could have made a comparable deployment of American troops in Israel, well away from the battle area, and the crisis could have been resolved at that point.

But what if the Soviets had decided to intervene in a more direct way in the war? Or what if the Israelis, fearing that such a direct intervention might occur, chose to attack Soviet transports as they entered the war zone? (Note that Israeli aircraft deliberately provoked a battle with Soviet aircraft in 1970, when Soviet air defense units were deployed in Egypt.) Or what if the Soviets, believing that the United States would interfere with Soviet transports during their vulnerable landing period, chose to attack the U.S. Sixth Fleet preemptively, perhaps along with Israeli Air Force facilities? What then? Where would the conflict have ended? Moreover, given that the United States already had introduced the possibility, perhaps likelihood, that the confrontation would escalate to the nuclear level, would not the Soviets have chosen to initiate the use of nuclear weapons, thus gaining whatever advantage might reside in the side that strikes first?

Speculation like this is open-ended. But it serves to illustrate that once the threshold of active military involvement is crossed, finding a stopping point becomes far from easy. By raising the specter of nuclear war at the onset of the confrontation, the United States made more difficult the termination of any escalatory process which might have ensued short of the use of nuclear weapons. Of course, this is precisely what made the nuclear threat so effective. The two go hand in hand; one cannot have the ostensible benefit of a nuclear threat without running its risks. Good reason to turn to nuclear threats only in the most desperate situations.

Finally, we might view the October 1973 crisis in the broader perspective of relations between each of the superpowers and their clients in the third world, and the consequences of those ties for U.S.-Soviet relations. In the 1973 incident, first Egypt and then Israel, through actions of their own, actions which their patrons were powerless to prevent, brought the United States and the Soviet Union to the edge of catastrophe. Evidence that the Soviet Union did not support President Sadat's decision to go to war is persuasive. Similarly, there is no question that the United States sought to prevent an all-out Israeli military victory so as to facilitate a longer-lasting political settlement and to enhance the U.S. position in the Middle East. Yet, the two ostensibly dependent nations dominated the situation. Egypt began the war; Israel continued to act against the Third Army in the face of U.S. protests. The result was the Soviet-American confrontation. . . .

The Soviet Invasion of Afghanistan

RAYMOND L. GARTHOFF

How did the Soviet leaders perceive the events of April 1978 through December 1979? What were their intentions in seeking to influence and to respond to developments in and affecting Afghanistan? While the Soviet leaders were quick to welcome the April 1978 military coup and the subsequent assumption of power by the People's Democratic Party of Afghanistan, they were cautious in their evaluation of the new regime. While welcoming a new putative candidate for the socialist camp, they were wary both of the stability and depth of commitment of the Afghan communists to Soviet-style "real socialism" and of their ability to maintain power and to formulate and carry out a policy attuned to the country. The Soviets were unsure that Afghanistan was ready for socialism and that the undisciplined team of Taraki, Karmal, Amin, and their associates were tried or true Marxist-Leninists. The April 1978 coup was unexpected and was viewed by the Soviets with trepidation and concern. A failed socialist revolution would be worse than none at all.

The Soviet leaders were pleased to see an end to Daoud's shift toward a pro-Western slant of nonalignment but would probably have preferred to see him change rather than leave the scene. When he was ousted, they would probably have preferred a more conservative liberal who would return to the Daoud line of 1973–74, offering apprenticeship in power for PDPA members as Daoud had provided to the Parcham in 1973–75.

Soviet concerns were soon borne out, as the PDPA descended into internecine personal struggles and purges. Karmal and his Parcham faction were frozen out within a few months. Taraki was too detached from reality, blithely assuming that radical and fast-moving changes could be made. He was also too indulgent and dependent on the more practical and efficient, but ambitious and uncontrollable, Amin. The Soviet leaders were alarmed by the growing alienation of the Afghan people as the Taraki-Amin regime pushed its radical reforms with excessive zeal. Nonetheless, by

From *Detente and Confrontation: American-Soviet Relations from Nixon to Reagan,* pp. 915–937. Published by the Brookings Institution, 1985. Reprinted by permission of the publisher. Portions of the text and all footnotes have been omitted.

December 1978 they were willing to conclude a treaty of friendship that considerably raised the Soviet commitment to the new regime. Even then the Soviet leaders declined to consider the PDPA a communist party, or the People's Republic of Afghanistan a member of the socialist community (except for one ambiguous reference in May 1979).

As noted earlier, the uprising in Herat (and bloody massacre of Soviet advisers and their families) in March 1979 had jarred the Soviet leaders into their first real consideration of the possibility of a more direct military role. From their standpoint this shift would not necessarily involve Soviet military operations in the country, although if it did, they would be in *support* of the Taraki-Amin government. Nonetheless, the Soviet leaders were well aware of the potential costs and liabilities of directly committing Soviet military forces beyond advisers and specialists such as helicopter pilots. But the security situation in the country continued to deteriorate throughout the year.

In the late spring and summer of 1979 the Soviets launched the effort outlined earlier to build a political solution to the problem of security and stability. The approach called for cooler and more careful action by the Afghan leadership, a broadening of the leadership of the party and the government (curtailing, and if possible reversing, the purge of the Parcham wing of the party and also bringing in nonparty, apolitical bureaucrats), broadening public support by less radical programs, and attempting to crush those insurgents who would not desist.

Safronchuk, the emissary sent by Moscow to press this political program, was well aware that the alternative (and fallback) was to seek a military solution with more active Soviet assistance and, if necessary, the introduction of Soviet troops. Soon after his arrival in late June, Safronchuk acknowledged in a remarkably frank conversation with Amstutz, the American chargé, that if Soviet troops were brought in (to help deal with the insurgency), it would have bad repercussions internationally and internally in Afghanistan. He also agreed with the American's observation that Soviet troops would have a difficult time in the rugged terrain of the country. When Amstutz expressed the hope that Afghanistan would not become an area of confrontation between the United States and the Soviet Union, Safronchuk said, "I agree with you completely." He also agreed when warned that if the Soviets did bring troops into the country, it "would very much complicate and harm Soviet-American relations." Safronchuk could hardly have been expected to say the opposite. But if he had really believed then that Soviet troops would or even might be required in Afghanistan, it is highly unlikely that he would have done more than deny that such action was planned, while leaving the possibility open in the future. He certainly did not need to volunteer, as he did, that "it would be bad policy in terms of internal Afghan affairs." Safronchuk also noted that Lenin had declared that "every revolution must defend itself."

Safronchuk was not the only frank and forthright official from the Soviet bloc in Kabul. As noted earlier, the East German ambassador, Schweisau, a few weeks later confirmed that Safronchuk had been sent to find a political solution, and to bring about a "radical change" in the leadership as well as broaden the base for support at all levels. Ambassador Schweisau himself brought up the question of possible Soviet military intervention in an extraordinary conversation with Amstutz on July 18, in which he also said that Amin had to be removed. He noted the speculation in the Kabul diplomatic community that the Soviets might eventually have to intervene militarily. "Were they to do so," he said, "it would solve one problem but create another." It could eliminate the present (Amin) government, but the "entire Afghan nation" would turn against the Soviet Union, just as they turned on the British invaders in the nineteenth century.

These evaluations of the consequences of a Soviet military intervention were realistic and prescient. They strongly suggest that at least the Soviet representatives in Kabul recognized the hazards of direct intervention. Beyond that, the fact that these sentiments were voiced further suggests that Moscow at that time had considered a possible direct military role but that it was deemed too costly and clearly less advantageous than internal political manipulation of the leadership and a broader Afghan political program in the country. A political solution incorporating these elements would obviate the need for direct Soviet military intervention.

It also seems clear that at that point there was little concern over possible *American* intervention. The frank Soviet (and undoubtedly Soviet-authorized East German) acknowledgments to the U.S. chargé d'affaires of Soviet dissatisfaction with and desire to remove Amin could only have been intended to prepare the United States to understand and accept the need for that change in the interests of stabilizing the internal situation in Afghanistan. If there had been real concern then over American ties with Amin (let alone the 1980 charge that Amin had long been a CIA agent), it is inconceivable that Safronchuk and Schweisau would have disclosed Soviet desire and intentions to remove Amin. The American chargé concluded that the Soviet leaders intended these statements by Safronchuk and Schweisau "to send us a signal . . . that they are unhappy with the Amin regime, that they are trying to arrange a change, and (I am speculating here) are hoping this will not have a negative impact on us." In addition, the two Soviet bloc officials calculated that if direct intervention or the introduction of Soviet troops became necessary, the U.S. government would know that the Soviets had tried to use political means and had turned to military means only as a last resort.

The Soviet attempt to engineer the removal of Amin and effect a Khalq-Parcham reconciliation under Taraki, and ultimately the whole possibility of a political solution, collapsed. Not only did Taraki fail to remove Amin, but the abortive assassination left Amin in firm control—and highly suspicious and hostile—even though still dependent on Soviet assistance. And the Taraki centrists and reconciliationists were imprisoned or in sanctuary in the Soviet embassy.

From mid-September to late November the Soviet leaders considered the new situation and possible courses of action. From mid-September to mid-October General Pavlovsky and his team assessed the military requirements not only to deal with the insurgency but also, if necessary, to support the removal of Amin by force. Because of his direct involvement in falsely assuring Amin's safety on September 16, and his responsibility for the sanctuary given Watanjar and the other former Taraki cabinet ministers, Ambassador Puzanov had to be recalled in response to Amin's demand. But Safronchuk remained.

The Soviet policy deliberation in the fall of 1979 involved a complete strategic reappraisal. Amin was now seen not merely as a burden or obstacle to needed policy corrections; he was seen as an enemy. The Soviet advisers, now several thousand in all, were not only assets but also potential hostages. Some had been wiped out in the Afghan army mutinies of Herat in March and Jalalabad in August, and all were potentially at risk to Amin. Soviet advisers and a pro-Soviet (and possibly long-time KGB collaborator) secret police chief, Assadullah Sarwari, had been unable to stem events in September—and Sarwari was now a fugitive secretly holed up in the Soviet embassy in Kabul. The Soviets had the dubious benefit of the expert advice of the Parcham and Tarakite émigrés and fugitives—some of whom had, for example, since 1967 been accusing Amin of being a CIA agent. Earlier known events took on a newly ominous meaning. Amin, for example, had met with a shadowy Afghan with American citizenship, Zia Nassery, in late 1978—and Zia subsequently met with two of the leading Islamic rebel groups. In November and December 1979 Amin was reportedly in contact with Gulbuddin Hekmatyar, the leader of Hizb-i-Islami, one of the main Islamic resistance groups.

The Soviets saw Amin's increasingly desperate attempts to establish contact with President Zia of Pakistan in November and December as further confirmation of their suspicions that he was unreliable on socialism and desired to break away from the Soviet Union. They saw not merely a desire by Amin to reduce dependence on the Soviet Union, but also a strong indication that Amin wanted to emulate President Sadat of Egypt by sending the Soviet advisers home and realigning Afghanistan with the United States, Pakistan, and China.

In addition, the Soviet leaders may even have begun to nurse suspicions of direct ties between Amin and the United States. As in other respects, the Soviet reevaluation in the fall of 1979 may have led them to be more concerned than they had been with respect to Amin's earlier residence in the United States and current contacts. On the whole, Soviet concerns were probably addressed primarily toward potential moves by Amin and the Americans, rather than at existing contacts, but they were nevertheless real concerns.

In their own assessments earlier in the year the Soviet leaders had understood that the growing armed resistance sprang from general dissatisfaction by the Afghan populace, even after the Soviet press began in March 1979 to explain away this phenomenon by blaming foreign intrigue and external support for the counterrevolutionary insurgency. By the fall of 1979 two things had changed: first, there *was* increasing foreign assistance, and second, the changed context meant a possible alignment of resistance forces, foreign interests—and Amin.

Very little has appeared in published sources on the foreign assistance to the Afghan insurgents in the period prior to the Soviet military intervention in late December 1979. While Soviet and Afghan claims must be heavily discounted, they have some foundation. The Soviets may well have believed there was more outside assistance than was in fact the case, particularly as they (and the Afghan regime) were loath to accept that indigenous popular discontent was rising.

One probable source of external, albeit limited and covert, military assistance that included training as well as arms was China. Indeed, the Chinese may have given assistance to Tadzhik guerrillas in Badakhshan and to Kazakh guerrillas in the Wakhan Corridor adjoining China even before the 1978 coup. On the other hand, before the Soviet intervention in late 1979 the Chinese refrained from participating in the limited support given by Muslim countries through Pakistan, and even requested that Pakistan not permit Chinese arms it had received to be sent to the insurgents in Afghanistan. Nonetheless, Soviet suspicion of the Chinese role remained high. Suspicion had also been raised by the completion of the Karakorum Road in 1979 (nominally in 1978), which provided overland access from China to Pakistan near the Wakhan Corridor of eastern Afghanistan.

By mid-1979 Libya was providing financial assistance to Islamic insurgents in Afghanistan, despite Soviet-Libyan ties. Iran under Khomeini also provided assistance to Afghans who fled there and used Iran as a base to mount forays into Afghanistan. Saudi Arabia, Egypt, and Pakistan—all American proxies in Moscow's eyes— were the principal outside sources of support to the insurgents before the Soviet intervention. (This support has been confirmed by secret American diplomatic messages seized in the takeover of the American embassy in Tehran.)

There is also an intriguing implication in cryptic references by Brzezinski in his memoir that the United States supported the Saudi, Egyptian and Pakistani aid to the insurgents during 1979. He states that in April 1979 he "pushed a decision through the SCC [Special Coordinating Committee] to be more sympathetic to those Afghans who were determined to preserve their country's independence." The decision was supported by Vice President Mondale against "rather timid opposition" from the State Department. And by September, after the Amin coup, Brzezinski also personally "consulted with the Saudis and the Egyptians regarding the fighting in Afghanistan." Later an investigative reporter stated that the CIA covertly began providing field hospitals and communications equipment to the Afghan resistance from Pakistan in November 1979. It is not clear, however, whether the United States provided any direct assistance to the Afghan resistance before the Soviet intervention. Substantial military assistance was later provided, as discussed below, but before January 1980 any such aid was minimal.

External military assistance was thus not a serious factor in the situation prior to the Soviet decision to intervene. Its significance as a political factor and perceived threat in Soviet calculations is, however, another matter that it is more difficult to judge. At the least it contributed to Soviet fears of the desire and readiness of the United States, supported by Muslim allies and coordinated with the separate assistance of the Chinese, to attempt to influence the situation in Afghanistan.

The real Soviet fear was that Amin was neither reliable as a partner nor subject to Soviet guidance, and at the same time was ineffective in controlling the growing resistance. In desperation Amin might turn to the United States as Egyptian President Sadat and Somali General Siad had done. Alternatively, he would likely be swept away by a popular Islamic nationalist movement. In either case the Soviet Union would lose all its cumulative investment in Afghanistan—strategic, political, ideological, and economic. And in either case there was a substantial risk that the United States might to some degree displace the Soviet Union in Afghanistan, acquiring new strategic assets and coming closer to completing a geostrategic encirclement of the Soviet Union, ranging in the west from Norway through Turkey and in the east from Alaska through Japan and China to Pakistan. Politically and ideologically, the loss of socialist Afghanistan on the very border of the Soviet Union itself could not be accepted with the same equanimity as was, for example, the overthrow of Salvador Allende in distant Chile. Afghanistan, which had never been aligned with the West, was, after all, in the Soviet backyard. And the Soviet Union, immediately adjacent, was in a position to intervene readily.

The world, including the United States, had accepted the coming to power of the PDPA after the April 1978 coup and its subsequent more open identification with communism and closer alignment with the Soviet Union. Any Soviet measures to ensure continued communist rule in Afghanistan would but represent consolidation of the established status quo with respect to international geopolitics.

To be sure, since the spring of 1979 some American officials had publicly and privately warned the Soviets of vague, unspecified, adverse consequences for Soviet-American relations of a direct Soviet military intervention. But those warnings had become routine and had recently been shown to mean very little. By October the Soviet leaders could look back on the experience of the Cuba brigade incident, with the odd alarmist warnings by the United States that the continued presence of a Soviet brigade in Cuba was unacceptable, followed by acceptance of the status quo. Throughout the year the Americans had also been warning the Soviets not to use bases in Vietnam but then had acquiesced in their use. The Americans had also been warning the Soviet Union against any intervention in Iran, which it was not contemplating (and where it recognized that the United States, as well as the Soviet Union, had real interests). But in Afghanistan the Soviet Union saw vital interests of its own, and by contrast the United States had no substantial interests. The latter had even curtailed sharply its modest remaining economic aid and declined to send a new ambassador to Kabul after the tragic death of Ambassador Dubs.

What were the Soviet interests in Afghanistan? For one, the two have a common 2,500-kilometer border adjoining the Muslim Central Asian republics of the USSR, which are populated by people of the same ethnic background as those in northern Afghanistan. While Soviet vulnerability from and concern over its own Muslim populations should not be exaggerated, this was one factor in Moscow's thinking. In 1978 there had been a Tadzhik riot against Russians in Dushanbe, just north of Afghanistan. After the Soviet intervention the KGB chief in Muslim Soviet Azerbaidzhan, Major General Zia Yusif-zade, publicly linked the situation in Afghanistan (and Iran) with alleged American intelligence efforts to exploit Islam in the Muslim republics of the USSR. And a deputy prime minister of the

Soviet Republic of Kirgiziya was retired after having stated too bluntly that the Soviet Union had helped combat a locust plague in nearby Afghanistan "that could have spread to us." (It can only be wondered what happened to the hapless editor of a Soviet Uzbek-language literary journal who, after visiting Afghanistan, published in October 1979 a Khalq-inspired account of the Afghan revolution that pictured Amin as a hero and Karmal as an untrustworthy villain.) In 1980 the prime minister of the Soviet Republic of Kirgiziya met an even more drastic end—he was assassinated. After the unsurprising failure of a Soviet-sponsored international Islamic conference in Tashkent in 1980, three of the four Soviet Muslim *muftis* were dismissed. But difficulties or vulnerabilities within Soviet Central Asia, while adding to Soviet concerns, were not central to the decision to intervene.

That decision was the result of cumulative developments and evolving considerations. The unexpected emergence of Amin as the leader and the removal of Taraki and other counterweights from the Afghan leadership, and Amin's demonstrated independence and hostility, compelled the Soviet leaders to consider how to deal with a nominally friendly socialist country headed by an opportunistic and hostile leader, and whether and how to remove that leader.

The rapidly deteriorating security situation in Afghanistan also compelled a search for more effective measures. One option was to reinforce the Afghan army by the direct introduction of Soviet military forces. The Soviet political, and probably military, establishments had resisted this action. The awareness of its heavy risks and costs so readily acknowledged by Safronchuk and Schweisau in June and July were widely shared. But while it was then an easy choice in Moscow to pursue internal political means to change the Afghan leadership and policy, by October that option was exhausted. General Pavlovsky, who returned from Afghanistan on October 22, must have reported that the situation was deteriorating rapidly and that a decision must be reached soon either to pull out the Soviet military advisers and let the regime under, or to bolster the Afghan army with a large-scale Soviet military presence as well as increased direct Soviet military support. Continuation of the current policy had no prospect of success and very real risks of a disastrous collapse. It has been speculated that the Soviet military advocated intervention, but there is no direct information to that effect. It is possible that the military had reservations about becoming directly involved in a long counterinsurgency campaign. But as the political calculation moved toward the necessity intervention, the military would have become more inclined to think of ways to meet that challenge.

The two principal problems merged as the Soviets considered a military solution: Amin would be removed, and a new broadened leadership with more enlightened policies could build a broadened popular constituency and thus reduce support for the insurgents, and, braced by the presence of the Soviet army as well as by a new political climate, the Afghan army would be invigorated to carry out the necessary counterinsurgency campaign. The insurgents would lose popular support at the same time that they came under more effective military pressure.

While direct information is lacking, it may be surmised that some questioned whether this scenario was realistic. But there were powerful sources of support for it, not least the political-ideological presumption that if properly led the Afghan people would be *bound* to favor a progressive, socialist order rather than a semifeudal backward one. Moreover, the risks of inaction seemed at least as great as the risks of action.

The strongest argument for intervention (even if a less rational basis for believing it would work) was the absence of an acceptable alternative. The alternative envisaged was seeing a budding socialist Afghanistan succumb either to defection or disintegration. Amin was seen as unscrupulous, unreliable, and hostile, and it was believed that if he retained power, he would eliminate Soviet sympathizers while preparing to reverse alliances. If he did not retain power, a fundamentalist religious-nationalist anti-Soviet regime would probably succeed him. Either of these cases threatened to provide opportunities for the United States and China—increasingly seen as acting in collusion—to inject their own presence and influence.

The Soviet decision to intervene thus rested on a reluctant conclusion that failure to do so would imperil its many long-standing investments in Afghanistan—political, military, economic, and, since 1978, ideological—and their prestige as well.

But even more was involved than retrieving major Soviet interests that were sliding toward loss. The fundamental consideration in the Soviet decision was the need to defend its security interests. For all the rhetoric on aiding a threatened socialist country, the Soviet leaders have been very clear on the issue of security. Brezhnev, in his major statement two weeks after the Soviet intervention, said the Soviet action had been necessary because there had been "a real threat that Afghanistan would lose its independence and be turned into an imperialist military bridgehead on our southern border. . . . To have done otherwise would have meant to watch passively the origination on our southern border of a seat of serious danger to the security of the Soviet state." Reporting to the Central Committee plenum six months later, he reiterated that "*the point* is that the plans to draw Afghanistan into the orbit of imperialist policy and to create a threat to our country from the south have collapsed." The Central Committee resolution at that plenum, in appraising the intervention, claimed that it had prevented the establishment of "a pro-imperialist bridgehead of military aggression on the southern borders of the USSR."

The Soviet leaders decided to intervene militarily in Afghanistan not because they were unwilling to keep it as a buffer, but precisely because they saw no other way to ensure that it would remain a buffer. Intervention was not the next in a series of moves to increase Soviet influence, as in Angola, Ethiopia, and South Yemen, nor the first in a new series involving escalation to direct use of Soviet military power in the third world. It was seen as the only solution to a specific situation on their border that was threatening Soviet security. Clearly, there are some circumstances in which the Soviet Union is prepared to use its armed forces when that is considered essential to ensure its security.

Distinctly secondary, although often tied to the articulation of defending Soviet national security, was the rationale of aiding an endangered progressive or socialist regime. Again, in Brezhnev's key speech in January 1980, immediately following his reference to the threat to the Soviet southern border, came a revealing sentence: "In other words, the time had come when we could no longer fail to respond to the request of the government of friendly Afghanistan." He continued, "To have acted otherwise would have meant leaving Afghanistan prey to imperialism, allowing the forces of aggression to repeat in that country what they had succeeded in doing for example in Chile, where the people's freedom was drowned in blood." That sentence was followed by one cited earlier that "to have acted otherwise would have meant to watch passively the origination on our southern border of a seat of serious danger to the security of the Soviet state."

Western commentary devoted considerable attention to the Soviet move into Afghanistan as an extension of the Brezhnev Doctrine that justified intervention to prevent the overthrow of a socialist regime by internal revolt or subversion. It was the first direct use of Soviet military forces to restore a pro-Soviet regime other than in Warsaw Pact countries (the previous cases being Hungary in 1956 and Czechoslovakia in 1968). The Brezhnev Doctrine, however, was above all the articulation of a rationale for Soviet action in cases where Soviet security needs were perceived as justifying direct action. In other words, it is a rationale to legitimize such action where it is deemed warranted. But it is not a mandate that the Soviets intervene where action is not considered necessary, prudent, and feasible. For example, the Soviet leaders did not feel impelled to undertake quixotic application of the Brezhnev Doctrine in Chile in 1973 or Grenada in 1983 (or to block adverse peaceful change in Jamaica in 1981), where the capacity to do so was lacking. Nor did it act in Poland in 1956, or 1970, or 1980–81, where other measures were feasible and clearly deemed preferable; nor in Yugoslavia in 1948 or any later time, nor—even within the Warsaw Pact—in Romania or Albania. Nor would the Soviets feel obliged to respond militarily in the event of a threat or actual change in rule in Nicaragua or Angola or Ethiopia or South Yemen. Soviet decisions on direct intervention are made on the basis of national security requirements, including political but not ideological ones. The governing considerations are interests, costs, and risks, not doctrine.

It is true that one Soviet justification was its internationalist duty. Shortly after the intervention in Afghanistan an editorial in a Soviet journal declared that "at critical moments solidarity with a victorious revolution calls not only for moral support but also for material assistance including, under definite circumstances, military assistance." It continued, "To deny support to the Afghan revolution, to leave it face to face with the forces of international reaction and aggression, would have been to doom it to defeat, which would have been a serious blow to the entire Communist and national liberation movement." Even then, the discussion went on to justify Soviet action "in the given instance" with a security argument—failure to do so would "make ever more dangerous" international tension in the region. It should also be noted that while expressing support for "the Afghan revolution," Soviet leaders continued to characterize Afghanistan as having only a "socialist orientation" and as "nonaligned," while reaffirming that "the revolutionary process in Afghanistan is irreversible."

A collapse of the Amin regime (even though in Soviet eyes Amin was no longer truly socialist) would have meant a defeat for real socialism or communism in the eyes of the world. This belief was a contributory factor in the Soviet decision. That collapse would have reflected badly on the image of an upward and forward revolutionary movement of history, as any setback does, but also more directly on the Soviet ability to support and defend its own satellites and friends. The December 1978 treaty had raised the Soviet commitment of its prestige. But this consideration alone would probably not have been sufficient and was ancillary to Soviet security interests.

In the case of Afghanistan, the risks of direct confrontation were correctly recognized to be nil, while the political costs were probably recognized to be considerable (although still underestimated). But the strength of the Soviet security interest was overriding. Considerations of a negative impact on Soviet relations with the United States and Western Europe, and on Soviet relations with countries of the third world (especially Muslim countries), were not only secondary but were almost certainly considered in terms of how to cushion expected reactions, rather than as factors that weighed in the basic decision on whether to intervene.

Even if the Soviet leaders had known at the time what they later learned about Western and world reactions, they almost certainly would have made the same decision. Nor would alternative feasible threatened punitive responses by the West have carried greater weight. The decision to intervene was not motivated, or even influenced, by perceptions of American weakness, vacillation, or distraction. Vacillation in Washington over the handling of the Soviet brigade in Cuba may well have devalued the significance of American "warnings," but beyond that, if anything, it merely reflected that each superpower is especially sensitive to events in its backyard. The fact that the United States did not react more strongly to the Iranian seizure of the embassy and hostages was not yet clear in November 1979 when the decision was made. Indeed, it is possible that the Soviet leaders believed the United States was planning to launch a military attack on Iran. While that consideration might have been expected to mitigate somewhat the world reaction to a Soviet move in Afghanistan parallel in time, and to distract American attention, the Soviets nonetheless sought through public and private warnings to prevent such American action. If the question of possible American action in Iran had any substantial influence on the Soviet decision, it would have been to reinforce the need to act before the United States became more directly committed in Southwest Asia.

Considerations of American military weakness and of a changed strategic military balance between the two superpowers did not enter the picture. It was obvious in Moscow that the United States could not and would not counterintervene militarily in Afghanistan, under any administration and regardless of the strategic balance. Indeed, had the events in and affecting Afghanistan that occurred in 1978–79 taken place in 1968–69, or 1958–59, the Soviet reaction and decision would probably have been the same.

The Soviet leaders did not see their decision to intervene militarily as an opportune option but as a security imperative; not as an opportunity for expansion but as a reluctant necessity to hold on; not as something they were free to do but as something they were regrettably bound to do. It was a decision forced by events, not an opportunity created by them.

This difference is significant. For example, American moves that are designed to show muscle and a readiness to stand up to the Soviets, measures that could usefully influence the Soviet leaders against seizing opportunities, work in the opposite way when the Soviets see the need for defensive actions, required to stave off a perceived threat or to bolster themselves against it. The Soviet leaders could not afford to let themselves be deterred from defending their own borders. Insofar as the Soviet decision was influenced by their views of the American strategic posture, it was affected not by any perception of American weakness, but by heightened concern over the American buildup of its strength, particularly the Indian Ocean fleet, the quest for new bases in the area, and the development of security ties with China.

Subsequent American actions tended to confirm to the Soviet leaders that they needed to secure Afghanistan. They perceived the Carter Doctrine, intended to deter Soviet advances in the Persian Gulf area, quite differently, particularly because they had never intended to move on the Gulf. Soviet claims of American and Chinese designs on Afghanistan seemed to be confirmed by the coordination of assistance to the Afghan resistance, and more generally by the establishment of a quasi alliance marked by Secretary of Defense Brown's visit to China in January 1980, a visit planned and announced before the Soviet intervention. When American intelligence collection facilities were set up in China in 1980 to monitor strategic missile tests in the central Soviet Union, making up for the major stations lost in Iran, the Soviets felt vindicated in their earlier suspicion that the United States had had designs on Afghanistan for that very purpose.

As many Western observers have noted, American-Soviet relations were already at a low point at the time the Soviet leaders decided to intervene militarily in Afghanistan. The Soviets saw little to lose from any worsening of relations that their action in Afghanistan might provoke. The SALT II Treaty was in trouble; NATO was clearly going to decide to install new missiles in Europe; and the United States was playing the China card to the limit. And there was little under way in prospective areas of cooperation that Washington could curtail if it chose to react. In addition, the Soviet leaders almost certainly underestimated the American reaction.

It would not be correct to draw a conclusion (as some have done) that the Soviet leaders gave priority to Afghanistan over détente. The Soviet leaders, as U.S. and other leaders would do in similar circumstances, gave priority to addressing a perceived threat to their security in Afghanistan, even if it should have costs in terms of the already deteriorated relations with the United States (and the West more generally). It was certainly not seen as a choice between expansionism and détente.

The final Soviet decision was made only in late November, with the decision presented to the Central Committee on November 27. After that date a variety of military preparations were undertaken, as well as a number of preparatory actions in Afghanistan, as noted earlier. The presentation to the Central Committee and discussion are not available, but the decision probably came as a surprise to most members and a shock to some. Brezhnev later stated frankly, "It was no simple decision for us to send Soviet military contingents to Afghanistan." Indeed, as another political spokesman put it, it was in fact "a very difficult decision." In his report to the Central Committee plenum the next June, Brezhnev said, "We had no choice but to send troops. And events have confirmed that this was the only correct decision." And in a candid explanation of Soviet policymaking, Dmitry Polyansky, a former member of the Politburo, mentioned the decision on Afghanistan as an illustration of collective decisionmaking: "Decisions are made collectively, and in no case is a decision made individually. Questions are carefully discussed, but final decisions are made with unanimity. The decision on the dispatch of Soviet troops to Afghanistan was made in accordance with this practice. . . . The debate on this question was not easy. But the final decision was adopted with unanimous approval."

While direct evidence of the Soviet decisionmaking on intervention in Afghanistan is thin, in this case there is no reason to doubt these Soviet statements about its difficult nature. Similarly, although the positions individual leaders may have taken can only be inferred or speculated on, as is true of the arguments advanced by various institutions, it seems quite likely that there were both reservations and final agreement by the leaders as a group. Those most concerned with the international repercussions, such as Gromyko and Suslov, may well have been concerned over the adverse effects in various foreign countries and in the world communist movement— but they were also aware of the need to save the Soviet foreign political investment in Afghanistan. The military no doubt smarted over the Soviet casualties and reverses suffered by the army they had been training, and were highly reluctant to suffer the defeat of withdrawal, but they may have recognized at least the possibility that there would be a long and inconclusive campaign. While the Soviet army could gain useful direct combat experience, the campaign could also be debilitating and drain resources needed for meeting other military requirements. Overall, the Soviet leaders saw the overriding consideration as avoiding a serious political, ideological, and strategic setback that not only would weaken the Soviet security buffer, but could lead to a serious new threat by permitting one or another degree of American and Chinese presence directly at the weakest Soviet border area.

The compelling nature of the motivation to defend Soviet national security probably contributed to the underestimation of the costs and negative consequences of the decision. As the scenario of action was being developed, the sequence of planned events and desired outcomes tended to become a given, and possible failures tended to be obscured. Moreover, the decision in November was not the actual denouement in December. A quiet removal of Amin (for which there were undoubtedly several plans, not initially including the one finally resorted to) and his replacement by Karmal and a reconciliation coalition (including not only Parcham leaders but also Khalq associates of Taraki, as well as the relatively popular military men such as General Qader and Colonel Watanjar) would have as much legitimacy as Amin ever had. Karmal, after all, had been the other vice president along with Amin under Taraki in May 1978, and General Qadar was a familiar figure from precommunist days. For such a new government to call for a greater Soviet troop presence in the country would probably provoke some criticism abroad but would not even appear to be an invasion. General Paputin's suicide (or other untimely demise) after the failure to bring about a more smooth removal of Amin in mid-December could not, however, make amends for this critical snag in implementing the plans.

Taraki and even Amin may well have asked earlier for more direct Soviet military assistance, including the dispatch of Soviet troops, as the Soviets subsequently claimed. But the Soviet leaders were certainly disingenuous in citing these requests for Soviet troops as justification for their intervention in December. It may be indicative that Amin made no known complaint, and certainly no public one, when the Soviet Union brought in airborne troop units from December 8 to 25. If the Soviet leaders had in fact received earlier Afghan pleas to send in troops, they evidently chose not to meet them then. This course of events strongly suggests that they were not looking for an opportunity to station their troops in Afghanistan until it became necessary to shore up a regime responsive to Soviet direction. Central Committee official Vadim Zagladin was not being coy when he remarked that "moving troops into the territory of another country is always a difficult matter" requiring careful consideration of "all aspects and interrelationships" of such a measure.

Once the Soviet troops had been introduced in sizable numbers, as the commander of the Turkestan Military District, General Yury Maksimov stated, the Soviet expectation soon after the event was that "the presence of our troops will permit the stabilization of the situation in Afghanistan, will allow the democratic forces to consolidate and the gains of the revolution to be secured, and will permit cooling the ardor of those who initiated military adventures." While this estimate was woefully erroneous, it is not hard to see how Soviet military and political leaders would have been able to convince themselves of this sequence once they had bitten the bullet and decided to take the step.

Moreover, as the Soviet leaders were reaching their decision, they saw no easier alternative. To withdraw and permit the Amin regime to turn to the West or to collapse would but substitute certain great costs and risks for what otherwise remained only possible ones. Things had gone too far for that option in terms of commitment of Soviet prestige, and in any case the strategic consequences of permitting a power vacuum to develop on their border were too great. Continuation of the course pursued since May 1978 was also no longer a real alternative. Earlier attempts to advise and persuade the Afghani had not succeeded, nor had attempts to bring about a more moderate and responsive leadership. In addition, Amin was increasingly considered likely to turn to the West and perhaps to strike a deal with some of the insurgents. Finally, the several thousand Soviet advisers were only an asset up to a point; they could also become hostages to Amin. The slaughter of Soviet military advisers in Herat and Jalalabad by mutinous Afghan army units was a real, if not primary, consideration to the Soviet military leaders in particular. Amin might be able to place large numbers hostage in a showdown unless he were quickly neutralized. He could even call for an Afghan *jihad* against Soviet invaders. Similarly, the possibility or even probability that Amin would execute the imprisoned Afghan communist leaders and perhaps carry out a wide blood purge was another factor calling for early and decisive action.

These factors, while not basic to the Soviet decision, did add urgency and help sustain the decision to press ahead, despite setbacks such as the failure to eliminate Amin in mid-December and to install Karmal first and have him request Soviet troops before they had to be dispatched. Amin's frantic efforts to establish contact with President Zia of Pakistan in December, even if his precise purpose was unclear, were another reason for urgency. In short, in November and increasingly throughout December the Soviet leaders saw a need to act quickly before Amin took any of a number of possible preemptive actions, both within Afghanistan and internationally: denunciation of the 1978 Soviet-Afghan treaty, taking hostage or expelling the Soviet advisers, entering into a concordat with the Islamic revolutionaries, executing the imprisoned Afghan communists and military leaders, even appealing to the United States for military assistance. In light of those possible hazards, the effective elimination of Amin and simultaneous installation of Karmal and introduction of Soviet troops seemed necessary, prudent, and at acceptable cost.

While it is highly unlikely that the Soviet Union (or the United States) ever considers foreign policy decisions directly in terms of compatibility with the Basic Principles of détente agreed upon in

1972, the Soviet leaders undoubtedly considered their action in Afghanistan as consistent with those principles. It was, as they saw it, a defensive measure to sustain the stability of the status quo by preventing Afghanistan from plunging into chaos and falling under hostile external influences. It was intended to preserve, not upset, an existing geopolitical balance. But even if that were not the case, the Soviets saw the Basic Principles as reflecting an implicit acceptance by each of the two powers of the vital interests of the other. And Afghanistan had never been in the American security system. Since April 1978 it had gravitated into the Soviet orbit, and the Soviet Union had the right to ensure that Afghanistan did not become hostile to its interests. The situation was, in the Soviet view, comparable to that involving American interests in the Dominican Republic, where the United States had intervened directly in 1965 without an invitation from a previously recognized government. And before departing, the United States established a responsive government. Soviet commentators did not publicly use that comparison because they did not want to admit that the Soviet Union also resorted to imperialist-style military interventions. But in speaking to foreign audiences they did draw a parallel to the American removals of Ngo Dinh Diem in Vietnam and Allende in Chile. Moreover, the Soviets had warned the United States months earlier that it might become necessary to remove Amin, and they had tried to accomplish that by less extreme political means. The Soviets' perception thus led them to distort their own expectations of the American reaction, which they preferred to hope would be a limited, transient objection for the record. They even believed that such a preposterous allegation as Amin's being a CIA agent would be understood as popular propaganda. It was meant to signify that objectively, if not consciously, Amin was capable of serving American interests by pulling Afghanistan away from the Soviet Union (and by giving socialism a bad name in Afghanistan and the world). At the very least, the American leaders should certainly understand that the Soviet action was limited to Afghanistan.

The Soviet leaders had understood the U.S. warnings, including President Carter's raising the matter at the summit meeting in June 1979, as an attempt to intimidate them from taking measures to defend and retain their position of influence in their primary security zone. After Amin's coup in September they no longer tried to communicate with the U.S. government on this matter. In part the reason was the greater risk that Amin might turn to the United States, in part an understanding that the United States could never directly acquiesce, and in part a belief that the United States was behaving in increasingly unpredictable and unreasonable ways, notably with respect to the Soviet brigade in Cuba. But the most basic reason was that the Soviet leaders conceived of the whole problem as an internal one within a sphere of predominant Soviet security interest and they therefore could not visualize that the U.S. reaction could be keyed to a perceived Soviet challenge to the West and its vital interests.

Part III
Recent Perspectives On The Use Of Force

With the loss of numerical strategic superiority in the middle 1970s, Americans worried ever more about the credibility of strategic deterrence, about ballistic missile defense at home and conventional defense in Europe, about America's ability to project power abroad to uphold its interests, about the desirability and achievability of arms control with the Russians, and about the stability of the world as gradually more countries acquire nuclear weapons. The selections in Part III address these issues.

In the first section, Paul H. Nitze argues that if the Soviet Union acquired nuclear superiority, it might believe that after a first strike against the United States, an American President would be self-deterred from retaliating. Colin Gray argues that the United States needs a nuclear warfighting capability if its policy of extended deterrence is to have credibility. Robert J. Art distinguishes between the political and military uses of nuclear forces and argues for a nuclear strategy that is neither a minimal deterrent nor victory seeking. Robert Jervis explains why escalation dominance is not achievable for nuclear states and why potential military conflicts between them must be seen as competitions in risk taking. Zbgniew Brzezinski and his two associates argue that a space-based defense against ballistic missiles can stabilize American-Russian relations, and Charles L. Glaser argues that it cannot.

In the second section, John J. Mearsheimer assesses the conventional balance of forces between the NATO Alliance and the Warsaw Pact and concludes that, under likely conditions, NATO can stave off a conventional attack by Warsaw Pact forces. Samuel P. Huntington argues that, with the declining credibility of nuclear threats, NATO can best deter a Russian attack by adopting a strategy that relies on what he calls conventional retaliation by carrying the war into Eastern Europe. McGeorge Bundy and his three American associates argue against our long-standing policy of using nuclear weapons in Europe should NATO be unable to contain a conventional attack by the Soviet Union, a policy of first use that Karl Kaiser and his three German associates strongly support.

In the third section, Ernst B. Haas calls for a retreat from indiscriminate containment of communist expansion and sets forth the conditions under which the United States should selectively engage the Soviet Union. Samuel P. Huntington offers an expansive view of America's interests and the military forces needed to attain them. Joshua M. Epstein criticizes the logic of the strategy of "horizontal escalation" and its attendant expensive requirements. Kenneth N. Waltz concludes that a tripwire, not a warfighting, strategy best serves American interests in the Persian Gulf. Linton F. Brooks and John J. Mearsheimer analyze the pros and cons of the "Maritime Strategy," a strategy that calls for an expansive and expensive American navy and for its early offensive use.

In the fourth section, Bernard Brodie asks what the sensible political, military, and economic objectives of arms control are. Samuel P. Huntington undertakes an historical comparison of arms races to determine whether quantitative or qualitative races are the more unstable. In surveying the American-Russian experience with nuclear arms control since the early 1960s, Thomas C. Schelling concludes that things have gone awry since 1972 because of a misplaced emphasis on numbers rather than on stability.

In the last section, Waltz questions the conventional wisdom about nuclear proliferation by arguing that the measured spread of nuclear forces may increase the chances of peace and promote international stability. Lewis Dunn strongly contests this view.

Deterring Our Deterrent

PAUL NITZE

During much of Henry Kissinger's dominance over U.S. foreign policy, détente with the Soviet Union was the centerpiece of that policy. U.S. military strength was viewed as necessary to make détente work, rather than to make possible actual defense of ourselves or our allies against Soviet military pressure; Kissinger said that war with the Soviet Union was unthinkable.

This view was supported by the proposition that any war between the Soviet Union and ourselves would be nuclear and would inevitably result in hundreds of millions of casualties on both sides. This, in turn, implied that it makes little difference, within limitations of the type contemplated by the Vladivostok accord, whether the Soviet side comes to have more or bigger offensive warheads, the degree to which they improve their weapons technology, the extent of the asymmetrically better Soviet defenses (both active and passive), or whether one side or the other strikes first, provided only that we maintain strategic offensive forces for retaliation approximately as numerous and powerful as those we now have and have programmed for the future.

No more serious question faces us than whether these propositions are true or false.

To assess their probable truth or falsity, three sets of considerations are pertinent: One has to do with the interaction of policy and military strategy; the second concerns the various methods of assessing relative capabilities; the third relates to the interaction between the perceived strategic balance and foreign policy, including détente.

POLICY AND MILITARY STRATEGY

Twenty years ago, I wrote the following:

A strong case can be made that no rational body of men would initiate a general atomic war unless they believed that the power of their initial attack and its immediate effects on the enemy would be so great as to

"Deterring our Deterrent" by Paul H. Nitze, reprinted with permission from *Foreign Policy* #25 (Winter 1976–77). Copyright © 1976 by the Carnegie Endowment for International Peace.

assure that the subsequent phases of the war would be substantially one-sided. In order to achieve such a one-sided result, the attacking side (either Russia in an initial attack, or the West in response to an aggression by Russia or China which could be met only by general war) would logically concentrate the full power of its initial atomic attack on the military—primarily the retaliatory—capabilities of the other side. The attacker's object would be to destroy, in the initial blow, a large proportion of the base structure from which the defender must launch his retaliatory action (including the planes or missiles on the bases and the submarines and carriers which might support the main retaliatory action). The attacker would attempt to destroy a sufficiently large proportion of this base structure to reduce the power of the defender's retaliatory action to a level which the attacker's own defense system could contain. If he should succeed in this attempt he will have assured that the remaining phases of the war will be substantially one-sided. . . . The side which has lost effective control of the intercontinental air spaces will face a truly agonizing decision. It may still have the capability of destroying a few of the enemy's cities. But the damage it could inflict would be indecisive and out of all proportion to the annihilation which its own cities could expect to receive in return.[1]

Today some of the phrases in that passage seem out of date, but I believe the central points remain valid, particularly those which emphasize that the objective of military strategy under the circumstance of actual conflict would be to bring the war to an end under conditions less disastrous than other possible outcomes.

A much more succinct and elliptical formulation appeared in the November 1975 issue of *Communist of the Armed Forces*, the leading Soviet military publication:

The premise of Marxism-Leninism on war as a continuation of policy by military means remains true in an atmosphere of fundamental changes in military matters. The attempt of certain bourgeois ideologists to prove that nuclear missile weapons leave war outside the framework of policy and that nuclear war moves beyond the control of policy, ceases to be an instrument of policy and does not constitute its continuation is theoretically incorrect and politically reactionary.

Implicit in this statement is the view that a war involving nuclear missiles should and can be an extension of policy. A suicidal war would not be an extension of policy; therefore Soviet military forces should not be limited in capability to that sufficient to assure mutual destruction. The force requirements for meeting the criterion of making war an extension of policy for one's own side are reasonably obvious, and include the following:

1. A powerful counterforce capability—one sufficient to reduce

---

[1] Paul H. Nitze, "Atoms, Strategy and Policy," *Foreign Affairs*, January 1956.

the enemy's offensive and defensive capabilities significantly and progressively below one's own;

2. Forces sufficiently hardened, dispersed, mobile, or defended as to make a possible counterforce response by the other side disadvantageous—that is, such that a counterforce response would only serve to weaken the relative position of the responder by using up a far higher percentage of his surviving forces than the percentage of the attacker's reserve forces he could hope to destroy;

3. Sufficient survivable reserve forces, whether or not there were such a counterforce response, to hold the enemy's population and industry disproportionately at risk;

4. Active and passive defense measures, including civil defense and hardened and dispersed command and control facilities, sufficient to ensure survival and control even if the enemy response to the initial counterforce attack were an immediate retaliatory strike on one's population and industry;

5. The means and the determination not to let the other side get in the first blow—i.e., to pre-empt if necessary.

An examination of the Soviet strategic nuclear program and their military doctrinal literature indicates that they are indeed attempting to achieve capabilities consistent with fulfilling all five requirements. One cannot, of course, prove or disprove judgments as to Soviet reasoning. But the programs begun about 1962 and continued at a high level of effort since that time seem to reflect a fundamental state of mind on the Soviet side that contains no doubt as to the desirability of a force which can meet this set of criteria.

ASSESSING NUCLEAR CAPABILITIES

That the Soviets are making rapid and significant progress in their strategic force programs is clear. But to assess the degree of Soviet progress in achieving these goals, to determine the truth or falsity of the judgments implied by Kissinger's policy statements, and to decide whether and to what extent U.S. strategic programs should be augmented or modified, the U.S. and Soviet relative nuclear capabilities must be assessed in detail and in a pertinent manner. Furthermore, it is important to illuminate the questions, how much is enough for the Soviet side to believe that a nuclear war could, for them, be an extension of policy through military means, and how much is enough for us to deny them that possibility.

There are three distinctly different ways, increasing in depth and sophistication . . . to measure relative capabilities and crisis stability. These are:

1. That which each side has *before* a strike;

2. That surviving to the United States and that remaining to the Soviet side *after an initial counterforce strike* by the Soviets;

3. That remaining to each side *after an exchange* in which the Soviet side attacks U.S. forces and the United States responds by reducing Soviet reserved forces to the greatest useful extent.

The first method involves so-called "static" indicators. It does not assess how these capabilities might react upon each other in an actual exchange. It tends not to differentiate between those capabilities useful in a counterforce role and those useful in holding the other side's population and industry hostage.

The second method, being the first step in a dynamic analysis, is more sophisticated. It reflects the counterforce capabilities of those weapons used in the initial counterforce strike, but does not distinguish between the counterforce and the countervalue capabilities of the forces remaining to each side after that first step.

The third method, which carries the dynamic analysis a step further, most clearly brings out the stability or potential instability of the relationship by making it possible to assess the relative counterforce capabilities of each side and the countervalue capabilities remaining to each side after a two-sided counterforce exchange in which all useful counterforce targets have been addressed.

The following charts illustrate the results of one such set of analyses. A word about the indices shown in these charts. In comparing the two disparate strategic forces, different indices are more significant in the different methods of analysis. In Figure 1, the most useful static index is the index of equivalent weapons (EW) of a strategic force (perhaps the most sophisticated single index, a measure which accounts for the number and yield of the warheads, the accuracy of those warheads, and the characteristics of the targets against which they might be used). In Figure 3, since the counterforce targets which it was considered useful to address have been addressed, the primary indices of interest are the countervalue ones. These include throw-weight (TW), which is the best overall measure of the countervalue potential of a strategic force;[2] total megatons, which is the best index of aggregate fallout effects; equivalent megatons, which is the best index of aggregate blast damage effects; and numbers of weapons, which is the best index of target coverage.

The calculations reflected in these charts are based on the assumption that U.S. forces would be on a normal alert status when attacked. Strategic warning generated by Soviet implementation of civil defense preparations, or by an evolving crisis situation, would enable the United States to bring additional forces, primarily a portion of the non-alert bomber forces, up to an alert status. Based on optimistic assumptions as to the additional forces that could be

---

[2] "Throw-weight" is a measure of the useful weight of payload that can be propelled to intended distance.

brought up to alert, this could reduce the Soviet advantage after a counterforce exchange (as shown in Figure 3), by 20 per cent in number of warheads and 40 per cent in megatonnage. This result, however, is highly dependent upon the timely deployment of the B-1 force, which has not yet been finally approved. The effect of Soviet implementation of its evacuation program and other aspects of its civil defense program, which such strategic warning would permit, could be significantly more important in limiting its potential civilian casualties than the increase in numbers and megatonnage available to the United States as a result of having had such warning.

Trends shown in these charts by all methods and in all indices move in a direction favorable to the Soviet Union from the mid-1960s through the mid-1980s. Today, after a strategic nuclear counterforce exchange under normal U.S. alert conditions, the Soviet Union would hold superiority in all indices of capability except numbers of warheads, and even that sole remaining U.S. advantage would be gone within two or three years. Neither SALT I nor the projected SALT II agreements (assumed for the analyses shown) have had—or promsie—any discernible effect in arresting the trend toward an increasingly large margin of Soviet superiority. Moreover, the relationship is becoming unstable; the Soviets in coming years will be able to increase their ratio of advantage by attacking U.S. forces (the obverse, however, is not true). This is shown in Figure 4, where methods one and three (before-any-strike, and after-a-counterforce-exchange) are compared for the ratios of throw-

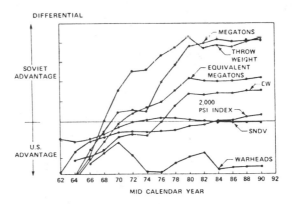

BALANCE OF DEPLOYED FORCES
(Static or preattack levels)

EW: equivalent weapons
SNDV: strategic nuclear delivery vehicles

FIGURE 1.

CAPABILITIES AFTER SOVIET FIRST STRIKE

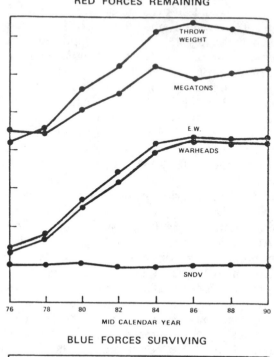

RED FORCES REMAINING

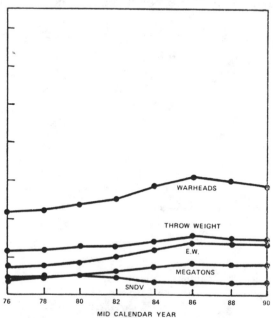

BLUE FORCES SURVIVING

FIGURE 2.

COMPARISON OF ALTERNATIVE INDICES OF CAPABILITY
(After a counter force exchange)

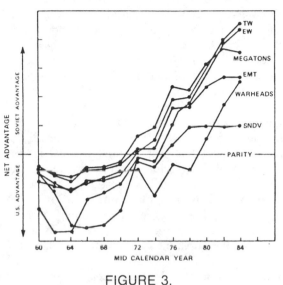

FIGURE 3.

SOVIET—U.S. THROW-WEIGHT RATIOS

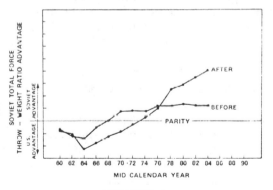

FIGURE 4.

weight. The point at which the curves cross indicates that point at which the Soviets could, by initiating such an exchange as postulated here, increase the ratio of advantage they held before the exchange.

U.S. OPTIONS AND SOVIET CIVIL DEFENSE

Does any of this make any difference? Isn't it true that we could, in the event of a Soviet counterforce attack, forgo a counterforce response and devote all of our surviving forces to an attack on Soviet population and industry? Wouldn't such an attack satisfy Kissinger's estimate of hundreds of millions of casualties on both sides? Isn't deterrence thereby assured?

It is desirable that the Soviet leadership should think so. It is, moreover, possible that a president, in the absence of all other options other than surrender, would make the decision, in the limited time which might be available for him for decision, to launch such a countervalue retaliatory attack. But is it desirable for a future president to be in the position of having no other useful option? Is this the high quality deterrence to which the United States is entitled and strove mightily over post-World War II decades to maintain? And would the Soviet leadership think it must lose hundreds of millions of citizens if the president were to make that decision?

I believe the answer to all these questions is negative.

Let me begin with the last question. The Soviet Union has for many years put emphasis upon the planning, organization, and training of cadres to implement a civil defense program. That program calls for the substantial evacuation of its cities and industrial plants, the sheltering of those who must stay, and the rapid construction of expedient fallout shelters by those who are evacuated and cannot otherwise be protected. In some of their civil defense manuals, the Soviets have estimated that the effective implementation of this program should hold casualties to 3 per cent or 4 per cent of their population. This would be a large number of casualties, but not hundreds of millions, and not a number large enough to keep their society from being able to recover with reasonable speed. This goal may not be achievable; there are many uncertainties. However, it is possible to make some gross approximations of the possible effectiveness of Soviet civil defense.

The most difficult nuclear effect for a dispersed population to defend against is fallout. Fallout is proportional to the megatonnage and the fission fraction of the weapons which are ground burst. The United States has, over the last 15 years, substantially reduced the megatonnage of its weapons in favor of more numerous, smaller yield, more accurate warheads. Today our most survivable force is our Poseidon submarine force at sea; the aggregate megatonnage of its 2,000 or so normally alert reliable warheads is approximately 80 megatons. Because of their relatively low individual yield, it would be best to use them against point targets even in a countervalue attack, and they are most effective when fused for a height of burst optimum for blast damage effects; they would, however, then produce negligible fallout. Against such an attack the stated goal of the Soviet civil defense program might well be achieved.

Our alert bomber force is our next most survivable force. Its aggregate deliverable megatonnage could be 10 times as much as that of our alert SLBM force, but the alert bombers must be launched-on-warning and a prompt decision made as to the targets which they are to hit; otherwise their survivability would be little better than that of the non-alert bombers.

Of course, the Minuteman missiles with a megatonnage roughly equal to that of the alert bomber force could be launched from under attack, but to do so allows only minutes for the decision to be made. Rough computations indicate that if all these forces were used in an all-out and immediate countervalue response to a Soviet counterforce first strike, the estimates in the Soviet civil defense manuals are overoptimistic from the Soviet viewpoint. They are not, however, wholly out of the ball park. The usual assumption that the United States possesses vast population overkill is, in essence, without foundation.

The crucial question is whether a future U.S. president should be left with only the option of deciding within minutes, or at most within two or three hours, to retaliate after a counterforce attack in a manner certain to result not only in military defeat for the United States but in wholly disproportionate and truly irremediable destruction to the American people. I believe not. This would be to make certain that military strategy had completely escaped from the control of policy.

U.S. VS. SOVIET DEFENSE PROBLEMS

Does any of this make any difference short of a nuclear war? The defense problems of the United States and the Soviet Union are quite different. The United States must be able to project its power over many thousands of miles to support allied defense structures on lines close to the concentrations of Soviet power. The Soviet basic defensive task is much simpler; that is, to maintain military preponderance on the exterior lines of its relatively compact land mass. Its only difficult problem is its long and narrow lines of communication to eastern Siberia. There can be little doubt that the Soviet Union has more than adequate military power for this basic defensive task.

For many years, U.S. strategic nuclear preponderance has made it possible to offset Soviet military superiority at the periphery and to deter its offensive employment. It has also made it possible for the United States confidently to use the seas for projection of its supporting power despite the Soviet Union's always very real sea denial capabilities.

An imbalance in favor of the Soviet Union in the strategic nuclear relationship would reverse these factors.

There is a further problem, moreover, in that the Soviet Union has in recent years been paying increasing attention to projectible power, including air mobility, longer-range tactical air capabilities, intermediate-range missiles and projectible sea power. To counter such capabilities in the absence of confidence in the adequacy of our nuclear deterrent, could be difficult and imprudent. Not to counter them could leave us with wholly inadequate tools of policy.

COUNTERFORCE VS. COUNTERVALUE

What bearing does the foregoing analysis have upon the future design of our strategic forces? A clear distinction should be made between counterforce and countervalue aspects of nuclear strategy. Neither can be ignored; both are essential to meaningful deterrence; but the requirements for each are different, distinguishable, and important.

In the past we have failed to appreciate this distinction and have thus fallen between two stools. We have prided ourselves on our advanced technology which has given us superior accuracy, higher yield-to-weight ratios in smaller yield re-entry vehicles (RVs), and leadership in developing multiple independently targeted re-entry vehicles (MIRVs). For political reasons and because of the presumed destabilizing nature of a counterforce capability, we have, however, forgone the accuracy and yield combinations which would give us high single-shot kill capabilities against Soviet silos and other hardened targets. On the other hand, in part to reduce the widespread destruction of a nuclear war, if it were to occur, we have progressively reduced the megatonnage of our force. This megatonnage is now so low that it is possible for the Soviet Union to plan a civil defense program which would make a far smaller percentage of their population hostage to a U.S. countervalue attack, particularly after it has been reduced in capability by an initial Soviet counterforce attack, than our population is to a Soviet countervalue response.

The Soviet leadership appears to be fully conscious of the differing requirements for countervalue and counterforce capabilities. The question has been asked why the Soviets continue to test high megatonnage single RVs on their SS-18s and SS-19s. I believe the answer is that they see the importance of deterring the deterrent; in other words, they wish to be able, after a counterforce attack, to maintain sufficient reserve megatonnage to hold U.S. population and industry hostage in a wholly assymmetrical relationship. Concurrently, the accuracy and yield combinations and numbers of MIRVed RVs they are deploying promise to meet their full requirements for a highly effective counterforce capability and still permit the withholding of a substantial number of missiles carrying large single RVs.

The question at issue is whether we also would be well advised to make a distinction between forces dedicated to a counterforce role and forces reserved for a countervalue role, and, if so, how much is enough in survivable forces for each of these two roles? My view is that we would be well advised to do so and that it is not impossible to find reasonable criteria to determine, within rough limits, how much is enough for each role. I would suggest two sets of criteria.

The first criterion would be to assure that the relationship of the yield, accuracy, survivability, and reliability of the two sides' forces is such that the Soviet side could not hope by initiating a counterforce exchange to improve either the absolute excess in pounds of its throw-weight over ours, or the ratio of its throw-weight to ours. To achieve this, it is necessary that we deploy forces which result in bringing the throw-weight line in Figure 3 closer to the parity line. This requires an increase in Minuteman survivability, through development of a new multiple-aim-point basing mode, an increase in Minuteman throw-weight, through development of the MX missile, and a substantial improvement in the single-shot kill probability of the U.S. RVs against hard targets, through the development and deployment of missiles and RVs with the requisite combination of accuracy, yield, and reliability to give high probability of destroying some 1,500 to 2,000 hard targets.

The second criterion would be to assure that the forces remaining to the United States after a counterforce exchange would be fully adequate to keep the Soviet population hostage to a countervalue attack in the face of the most effective civil defense programs we judge it possible for the Soviet Union to mount. Something of the order of 3,000 deliverable megatons remaining in reserve after a counterforce exchange should satisfy the second criterion.

Rough computations indicate that we should be able to satisfy both criteria if we deploy 500 MX missiles in a multiple-aim-point mode, if we deploy the Trident II missile in an appropriate number of Trident submarines, if we develop their accuracy and reliability to the levels which now seem technologically feasible, and if we proceed with the planned B-1 deployments augmented with strategic cruise missiles. Such developments and deployments will, however, take time. In the meantime, in order to retain sufficient deterrence during the time required to restore a stable balance, urgent attention should be given to determining quick and possible temporary fixes necessary to meet the problem as it is apt to emerge in the late 1970s and early 1980s. These include rapid development and deployment of a mobile transporter-erector-launcher and hardened capsule for Minuteman III, a variety of simplified point defenses of the class suggested by Richard Garwin[3] and others, provision for a potential rapid increase in bomber and SLBM alert rates and testing of reliable and appropriate methods to launch Minuteman from under verified large-scale attack against our silos.

The objective of such short- and long-range programs would not be to give the United States a war-fighting capability; it would be to deny to the Soviet Union the possibility of a successful war-fighting capability. We would thus be acting to maintain a situation in which each side is equally and securely deterred from initiating the use of nuclear weapons against the other or the allies of the other. It is only if, and when, we persuade the Soviet side that there is no reasonable prospect that they can successfully alter that situation that we can expect them seriously to negotiate for long-term agreements assuring stable mutual deterrence at lower and equal levels of strategic nuclear capabilities.

[3] U.S., Congress, Testimony prepared for the Joint Committee on Defense Production, April 28, 1976.

War-Fighting for Deterrence

COLIN S. GRAY

. . . The American public is being informed today, more and more often explicitly, that it has a choice between a policy of nuclear deterrence and a policy of nuclear defense, or nuclear war-fighting. This is a false opposition. The analysis in this article presents a preferred theory of deterrence, and specifies particular kinds of strategic capability as being necessary to provide postural expression for the theory, while also recognizing the relevant uncertainties and judgmental elements.

SCHOOLS OF THOUGHT AND PLANNING TO WIN

. . . There are three principal schools of deterrence theory represented prominently in the current debate over US nuclear-weapons policy. . . . these are: (1) *deterrence* by anticipation of massive societal punishment; (2) *deterrence* by anticipation of being denied victory; and (3) *deterrence* by anticipation of US victory. The distinctive conceptual bases and postural requirements of these three are as different in analysis as they tend to be confused or neglected in public debate. (1) says that the Soviet Union should be deterred if it fears suffering great damage to its economy and society; (2) says that the Soviet Union should be deterred if it fears suffering defeat (on its own, probably distinctively Soviet, terms); while (3) says that the Soviet Union should be deterred if it confronts a United States that has a plausible (in Soviet estimation of US terms) story concerning US victory in nuclear war.

Notwithstanding the ever popular nightmare vision of a World War III that decides the "fate of the earth" in a manner fundamentally unfriendly to human existence, the historical record shows that the nuclear planners of the United States have never intended that deterrent effect upon Soviet minds should function primarily via threats of society-wide punishment. Even the *Broiler, Bushwacker,* and *Halfmoon,* US nuclear-weapon employment plans of 1947–8,

From "War-Fighting for Deterrence" by Colin S. Gray, *Journal of Strategic Studies,* V. 7 (March 1984), pp. 5–29. Copyright by Frank Cass and Co. Reprinted by permission of seventh issue of *Journal of Strategic Studies* published by Frank Cass and Company, Ltd., 11 Gainsborough Rd., London E11, England. Portions of the text and most footnotes have been omitted.

focussed upon "governmental control facilities, industrial centres, petroleum plants and transportation assets, and other elements of the domestic Soviet infrastructure that supported the Soviet forces in the field," and were intended to paralyze the Soviet ability to wage war, rather than to punish Soviet society *per se* for the sins of its rulers.

It is certainly true that because of the co-location of Soviet military, political, and war-supporting industrial assets with major urban areas, and the yield and accuracy characteristics of the US strategic weapons fielded to date, Soviet urban-industrial areas are massively at risk virtually regardless of the shifting emphasis in US nuclear weapons employment policy. . . . The same judgement applies to the United States, even though the US generally has been more careful than has the Soviet Union in isolating its strategic-nuclear assets from civil society. A fairly comprehensive Soviet attack against military targets in the United States would, in practice, probably be indistinguishable from a counter-societal assault.

Proponents of a strategy for victory in nuclear war are not blind to the dangers of the nuclear age, ignorant of the pervasive operation of "friction" in war, or heedless of superordinate political and moral questions. A theory of victory is necessary by definition if the United States is to have a nuclear strategy. If there is no such theory, on what basis can American officials plan for nuclear-weapon employment? Since strategy translates, or rather is intended to translate, means into the achievement of ends, it is deprived of sense if it lacks a theory of success. If nuclear weapons in action can produce only defeat, why would a tolerably rational US government ever have operational resort to them? Also, contrary to assertions by some people, victory is not an apolitical goal. By victory this author means no more and certainly no less than that the United States achieves its political objectives (whatever they may be—and they may be quite modest). In short a theory of victory is necessary if defense planning is to have political integrity. The United States has no business threatening either prompt or delayed apocalypse as the reality of its nuclear strategy. Aside from the major issue of credibility of threat, history and common sense tell us that all systems of international security are accident-prone and miscalculation-prone. Deterrence by defense is an approach to war-prevention and is the approach to war-survival. . . .

It is paradoxical that the United States and the Soviet Union have adopted dominant official attitudes towards nuclear war that virtually reverse what one might expect, given the character of their different political systems. In the United States, where the general public truly is a "player," albeit an occasional and a filtered "player" in nuclear policymaking, the official message—beyond deterrence—is one of despair. In the words of Secretary of Defense Caspar Weinberger: "We, for our part, are under no illusions about the dangers of a nuclear war between the major powers; we believe that neither side could win such a war."

This is not an unreasonable view, but it happens to be profoundly discouraging of effort to penetrate the nuclear veil and to think constructively about the ways in which war, even nuclear war, might be waged for advantage or to preclude disadvantage (why else would one be fighting?), and in which damage at home and to allies might be minimized. Overall, notwithstanding the dominant "war-fighting" theme *(for deterrence)* in recent US policy guidance, the fuel for American policy paralysis in time of acute crisis is provided in ample measure by the continuing official insistence that nuclear war cannot be won and hence, *ergo,* that actual nuclear use must be futile. The Soviet Union, with no need to be concerned about the quantity and quality of domestic public support for its nuclear weapons policies, paradoxically adheres through its actions—though not in its words these days—to the concept of assured survival.

With respect to the political logic behind strategy, the United States should define its strategic nuclear force requirements in such a way as to provide some compensation for the vast asymmetry in political vulnerability to intimidation that obtains to its disadvantage. Roughly equivalent strategic forces, posing roughly equivalent kinds and scales of damage to superpower homelands—were this the case—should be hindered in their ability to provide for stability in deterrence because one party, the United States, would have a visibly fearful populace to act as a brake upon policy, while the other party would not. In short, the asymmetry in political systems could mean that parity in strategic forces may not translate readily into parity in deterrent effect.

It is a fact which has long been accepted that, for the foreseeable future, the most vital of US foreign policy interests around the periphery of Eurasia can be defended, *in extremis,* only by nuclear threats. To assert that the United States should plan to win any nuclear conflict in which it might engage is a statement of planning and human psychological necessity (how could the US plan to lose or draw?), should be a statement of the politically obvious (is the US to issue threats that lack any credibility of prospective operational success?), and almost certainly will be necessary if a very determined Soviet adversary is to be deterred. . . .

The Reagan administration, like the Carter administration before it, is right to stress the need to deter Soviet minds, to persuade them that they will be denied their objectives. But, how can a United States with a defenseless homeland threaten credibly to take the most severe of risks on behalf of others? Only a United States that has a full nuclear campaign story of national survival would be fitted adequately to bear the kind of extended-deterrence burdens that are accepted at present.

Victory or defeat are, of course, both relative and absolute terms. Nobody would prefer to "win" a nuclear war at a price of ten, twenty or more million casualties, compared to the successful deterrence of the events that could produce such a war. Unfortunately, US policy choice will never be framed in that manner. When statesmen take risks in an acute crisis, they do not know, in detail with any degree of confidence, what those risks entail. Most states, at most times, go to war optimistically, if not always euphorically. No one can estimate ahead of time what success in war is worth. Among other complications, what would be the cost of not fighting at all? Or what would be the cost of defeat? Just as armies cannot be motivated to fight for a better standard of living, so the worth—and hence some sense of "acceptable cost"—of victory perennially must be incalculable. All too often the opinion is offered that a victory was not worth the price paid. Unfortunately, or perhaps fortunately in some instances, a state enters and conducts the business of war without knowing what the price will be.

If satisfied powers are not prepared to take risks for peace with security, and if need be to bear some painful damage, then they are likely to enjoy neither peace nor security. Large-scale wars among first-rate opponents for issues deemed vital by them all have always been expensive enterprises. The scale of *potential* destruction in a nuclear war certainly far transcends the possibility of such a war serving political purposes in a bluntly instrumental fashion. Be that as it may, the super and great powers of the world today cannot eschew knowledge of nuclear-weapon technology, and the Western Alliance, for certain, is not at all willing to forgo the deterrent value of nuclear threats. Coming to terms with the enduring facts of the nuclear age should mean more than focussing near-exclusively upon the deterrence of war; it should also mean thinking about, and planning carefully for the conduct of nuclear war—both for the purpose of enhancing credibility of deterrence and in order to be prepared to behave responsibly should deterrence either fail or fail to be relevant.

WAR-FIGHTING DETERRENCE

To assert the deterrent merit of a true war-fighting or classical strategy approach to nuclear policy is not to be blind to the physical realities of the nuclear age. Such an approach recognizes the fact that war, latent as threat or active in policy execution, remains the ultimate regulator and arbiter to the international security system.

. . . For a blend of reasons that are sociological, moral, strategic and political-prudential, the United States has lost confidence in the possibility of winning wars. The United States has been quite remarkably short of visible success in the conduct of military operations since 1945, and this fact—attribute it to what one will—has reinforced an unwillingness, which has been both judgemental and visceral, to think operationally and politically about nuclear war (as opposed to prewar deterrence, on which subject an ocean of ink has been spilt).

In 1815, when asked as to the object of his campaign in Belgium, the Duke of Wellington, a little surprised to be asked such a foolish question, replied, "Why, to beat the French." In the 1980s the US government would appear to be incapable of defining its operational intentions in plain English. The Secretary of Defense, using verbal formulae that almost squirm on the page, informs his readers that

. . . should deterrence fail, our strategy is to *restore peace on favorable terms*. In responding to an enemy attack we must defeat the attack and achieve our national objectives while limiting—to the extent possible and practicable—the scope of the conflict. We would seek to deny the enemy his political and military goals and to counterattack with sufficient strength to terminate hostilities at the lowest possible level of damage to the United States and its allies. [Emphasis in the original]

What does this mean? In 1945 the Allies restored peace "on favorable terms." Beyond signalling a plain intention not to acquiesce in a military defeat, and flagging a very healthy and responsible concern for the damage that the Western side might suffer as a consequence of any excessive zeal in its pursuit of military advantage, this crucial paragraph in the Department of Defense Annual Report for FY 1984 does not say anything very profound. What would constitute "favorable terms"? —restoration of the status quo ante? (What about reparations for wartime damages?) Improvement upon the status quo ante to the point where a Soviet attack would be far less easy to launch in the future?

From the important Western perspective of escalation control and crisis management, there is much to be said in favor of a declaratory policy that promises only to thwart an attack with minimum damage inflicted and suffered. However, as applied deterrence theory, this focus on denial of Soviet victory leaves a great deal to be desired. At the ratified level of theory, its threat to deny victory actually is a contingent promise to limit liability. Whatever the United States in particular and NATO in general might elect to do operationally in the event of war, it is difficult to resist the logic of promoting deterrent effect in peacetime by maximizing (not minimizing) the anxieties that Soviet policy makers and defense planners feel when they contemplate the risks of military adventure.

Among the more troubling thoughts triggered by Weinberger's statement—and the myriad of similar expressions with which senior Western policy makers attempt to tackle the "unthinkable"—is that there may be a fatal (for NATO) mismatch of determination as between a Soviet Union bent upon "victory" and a NATO more or less resolute to avoid defeat. This can be no more than speculation, but it seems more likely than not to this commentator that a NATO focussing narrowly upon the defeat of the Soviet attack at the minimum cost in damage suffered would be a NATO potentially inviting defeat at the hands of an enemy dedicated to complete victory who, ipso facto, would likely be less than very sensitive to the level of damage inflicted *and even suffered at home.* . . .

It is very noticeable that although the Reagan administration has proceeded down the path of a war-fighting theory of deterrence pegged out by its predecessors, generally it has respected the political convention of not talking publicly about planning to win wars. Such silence does damage to the quality of US strategic policy. The stress that is placed upon defeating the enemy's strategy . . . is entirely sensible—provided one does not permit the identified need to defeat attack to foreclose discussion of how one avoids defeat oneself. . . . In order to extend deterrence credibly on behalf of distant allies, the United States needs both to be able to deny victory to the Soviet Union and—no less important—to avoid defeat itself. These requirements add up to a requirement for a capability to win wars.

An apparently valid criticism of this approach to US deterrence problems would be the argument that the United States, as a country wedded fundamentally to essentially defensive objectives in international security matters, should not adopt policy guidance for the direction of war planning that plainly exceeds the scope and intensity of American interests (not to mention American military capabilities). In other words, the United States does not wish to defeat the Soviet Union, *per se;* its ambitions in truth are limited to defeating those aspects of Soviet grand strategy that impinge upon the security of countries whose political integrity are vital interests of the United States. . . .

Notwithstanding the brief aberration in Korea from Inchon to the Yalu in the fall of 1950, the United States will never flex its military muscles in hope of positive gain. In the interest of deterring war, of restoring deterrence during the course of a war, or—truly *in extremis*—in the hope of limiting damage, the United States will threaten, and possibly execute, nuclear strikes against

. . .those types of Soviet targets—including hardened ones such as military command bunkers and facilities, missile silos, nuclear weapons and other storage, and the rest—which the Soviet leaders have given every indication by their actions they value most, and which constitute their tools of control and power.[1]

The nuclear strategy favored by this author is, indeed, bereft of a worthy "positive political object" . . . but that lack, if such it be, stems from the basic political stance of the United States in world affairs, and does not merit the pejorative attention it has been accorded. Fundamentally, as the Carter and Reagan administrations have recognized, the United States has to design its strategy with the negative political object preferably of deterring, but if need be of defeating, what one day may be a very desperate, very determined, and militarily exceedingly competent Soviet Union. Whether the West can defend itself without in the process destroying itself, is a challenge that has moral, political, economic and strategic dimensions. The United States should not, and certainly would not, wage a general war *in order* to destroy the Soviet state and reconstitute the world security order in accordance with American preferences. But the dynamics of conflict . . . might leave the United States with little choice between surrender and the pursuit of a military decision. . . .

The case of confronting directly the issue of defeat avoidance, or damage limitation, virtually makes itself. The countervailing strategy, in an era when a good offense is not the same as a good defense, fails to explain why Soviet strategic forces would not function as a persuasive counterdeterrent. Domestic critics on the political left, of all levels of strategic sophistication, have noticed the gaping hole in the edifice of official strategic nuclear logic that has been reconstructed of recent years. . . .

The United States does not have a theory of, let alone adequate plans for, war. Instead, there is a persuasive theory of prewar deterrence—that reads, at first perusal, as if it were a war-fighting theory—always provided one neglects to probe into the area of credibility (the self-deterrence problem), and there is a somewhat inchoate theory, or set of half-articulated tentative assumptions, of damage limitations in war through reciprocated, or roughly parallel, targeting restraints.

US policy today is adequate, indeed more than adequate, to deter the highly unlikely possibility of a Soviet nuclear assault on urban-industrial America. Also, in addition, there is some good reason to

[1]The President's Commission on Strategic Forces, *Report* (Washington, DC: April 1983), p. 6.

be confident that US policy would not be paralyzed by fear into inaction in the event of a large-scale assault against military targets in the continental United States. . . . No matter how irrational strategically it would be for the United States to retaliate following a Soviet counterforce first strike, as contrasted with the rationality of issuing prewar contingent threats to do just that, this author predicts with high confidence that the US President, indeed virtually any US President, would order a strike back if the physical machinery of command, control and communications permitted. No one can predict with any accuracy just how much damage even a carefully constrained Soviet counterforce first strike might wreak. . . .

One can show, with impressive strategic logic, that even a United States capable of launching under or after attack should find that it is deterred from exercising its deterrent—because of the amount that would remain to be lost. However, this author is firmly convinced that no US President would sit still for 2 to 50 million US prompt fatalities. Regardless of strategic reasoning, the President, or—more likely—his or her successor as NCA, would order a volley to be fired back for the sake of national honor or even just to satisfy the primitive motive of revenge. Millions of dead Americans would constitute a debt of blood to be repaid, inappropriate and even fatal though such repayment might prove to be. More to the point, and of great value for deterrence, it is highly unlikely that Soviet leaders mis-estimate the US proclivity to strike back in anger. Soviet "style" prefers, indeed insists upon, "avoiding dependence on a potential adversary for Soviet security." The idea that the Soviet Union would rest the prospects for survival or damage limitation, in a context where it had a choice, upon the theory (guess) that the United States either would not strike back or would strike back only in a very constrained manner, is a cultural absurdity. Whether or not the kind and level of damage the Soviet Union would anticipate receiving would suffice to deter is another question entirely. Effective deterrence is not only a matter of credibility.

The case for putative military effectiveness in US war planning, therefore, is pertinent even with regard to classes of Soviet actions where a US retaliatory strike would be as certain as the physical machinery of command allowed. The author concedes, if that is the correct term, the point often made by liberal critics of war-fighting deterrence, that the credibility of US retaliation is very high indeed in the event of a Soviet first strike, of any character or quantity, against the American homeland. What is not conceded is that the character of the possible US nuclear strike back prospectively is unimportant for the stability of deterrence.

The heart of the argument for a war-fighting, military effectiveness approach to deterrence pertains not to the relatively easy cases outlined above, wherein the Soviet Union very substantially eases the burden of American decision by initiating intercontinental strategic warfare. Instead, the case for military effectiveness relates most directly to the problems of extended deterrence. The issue is both one of (Soviet) perceptions in peace and crisis time of the credibility of contingent American threats, and of operational plans that a sensibly fearful US President would be likely to implement. The two are, of course, connected intimately if indeterminately. The political truth that gives meaning and purpose to a strategic analysis that otherwise can seem arid and divorced from the statecraft of real life has been very well expressed by Edward Luttwak: "Superpowers, like other institutions known to us, are in the protection business. When they cannot protect clients, they lose influence, not just locally but worldwide."

It is not suggested here that the scale and quality of the extended deterrent duty that burdens the US strategic forces is fixed as by some law of nature. Also, the point needs to be appreciated that extended deterrence, no matter how benign the purpose, can have an unintended, unwelcome and even dangerous effect upon those on whose behalf it is provided. . . .

Western officials and theorists have long wrestled with the tension that exists between the deterrent value of threatening an undifferentiated nuclear war—holocaust probably in a hurry, apocalypse now, Armageddon in an afternoon—and threatening carefully controlled, discrete nuclear actions, with the possibility that the liability to state and society might be limited. The latter may be more credible, but is the prospect insufficiently awesome in Soviet speculative contemplation? Strategic theorists remain in a state of disarray, or healthy contention, on the subject of the policy requirements of a stable deterrent, but defense professionals in and close to the US government, of both political parties, have long endorsed the proposition that SIOP planning and, if need be, execution, must be controlled, flexible, and very attentive indeed to the subject of avoiding unwanted collateral damage. The core of the reasoning of defense professionals has been expressed succinctly by Laurence Martin:

> To regard nuclear war entirely as something too horrible to contemplate and to evolve no strategies more subtle than all-out mutual annihilation would lead towards paralysis in crisis and vulnerability to nuclear blackmail by more stout-hearted or reckless opponents. At most it might lead to a precipitate descent into catastrophe for lack of a better alternative to surrender.

Proportionality . . . plays a significant role in the strategic reasoning of deterrence theorists and practitioners. Threats that manifestly are disproportionately large to the scale of the hypothetical offense are deemed to be incredible and hence ineffective. In addition, should disproportionately damaging action actually be taken, almost certainly one would trigger, if not license, an enemy counterblow on a similar or even larger scale. In short, as a consequence of a large mismatch between values and the means intended for their defense, the United States could find itself defending assets of modest value in a war waged on a highly immodest scale.

NUCLEAR WAR OR NUCLEAR HOLOCAUST?

A true war-fighting doctrine for deterrence, worthy of the ascription, must posit military requirements both for the ability to damage Soviet state power in a manner particularly fearsome in the Soviet perspective, and for the physical protection of essential western values. The war-fighting theory that has dominated the official US defense community since the first days of the Nixon administration, and which has been recorded in the successive milestones of the policy guidance provided by NSDM-242, PD-59 and NSDD-13, has been a severely, indeed fatally, truncated theory. One cannot have a war-fighting approach to war planning unless one adopts a campaign perspective which takes full account of the damage that the enemy could inflict. . . .

Military effectiveness, rather than the punishment of Soviet society, is mandated in US SIOP planning both for reasons of expected deterrent effect and because it offers the best available prospect for the control of nuclear escalation. Churlish though it may be to take note of the fact, it is quite evident that the US government still has not taken full and proper account of the asymmetry in values between the Soviet and US political systems. The US government, reportedly, has directed the Joint Strategic Target Planning Staff (JSTPS) in Omaha to plan attacks against Soviet leadership and military targets, in part with a view to identifying target sets that lend themselves to "firebreak" application for the control of escalation. The US government knows, though it has yet fully to absorb, the fact that the Soviet state regards societal damage in a rather different perspective from the US political system. The great care shown by the US JSTPS to avoid unwanted collateral damage probably is effort wasted—in the Soviet perspective.

In the Soviet view, the worst that the United States can do is to strike at the control structure of the Soviet state and at its more lethal military instruments. In other words, a United States gravely concerned not to "provoke" the Soviet Union onto a path of explosive nuclear escalation probably should not be overly concerned about the policy effects of collateral damage (from Soviet military targets) to Soviet society. The Soviet state, if it is capable of being "provoked," would be provoked by the reality or anticipation of damage to its essential instruments of coercive control, not by collateral damage to civilian society. This may seem to be a point of very modest value, but American readers should be aware of the fact that their JSTPS agonizes over DGZs* and weapons with a view to minimizing the unwanted damage that would be inflicted upon Soviet society at large. It is suggested here, heretical though it may appear, that although the US JSTPS certainly should strain to avoid planning to do more than the least necessary damage to Soviet society, it is improbable that collateral damage to the urban-industrial USSR would trigger any deviant twist to Soviet targeting strategy against the United States. . . .

One may be close to agreement with the deterrence reasoning of the Reagan administration, with its emphasis upon the need to pose technically credible threats to the highest values of the Soviet state, but still be uneasy over the extent to which the US government really understands what it is about. To explain, the US government, for more than ten years, has expressed a need for flexibility and control in nuclear war planning; also, it has expressed fairly extreme aversion to strike plans limited to major Soviet urban areas. What we have here is a classic example of disconnected strategic thought. The US government appears now to believe that:

- maximum Soviet anxiety pertains to threats to the political control structure;
- discrete threats should be posed to Soviet "leadership," nuclear, other military, and war-supporting industry, targets; and
- *somehow*, escalation control for early war termination would be promoted by fairly strict American adherence to a countermilitary targeting campaign.

The obvious fallacy in the above lies in the prospective fact that a Soviet leadership is most unlikely to be moved to targeting restraint by the operation of US JSTPS rules of engagement with regard to collateral civilian damage. In the Soviet perspective, as one part of official US policy reasoning recognizes today, the US will have "done its worst" if it strikes at Soviet leadership and military targets. There are many good theoretical reasons why the United States should write its war plans so as to menace the jugular vein of Soviet imperial power. But American theorists, politicians,

*Editors' note—designated ground zeroes.

officials and outside commentators should recognize the full implications of their recommendations. . . .

The case against a deterrence theory that posits as its sole, or at
least overwhelming, requirement the need for a capability to punish
Soviet society on a near-Carthaginian scale, is both moral and
strategic-pragmatic. In the moral dimension—no matter what good
may be intended (to prevent war from occurring)—this author, in
company with the National Conference of Catholic Bishops, believes it is absolutely wrong either to attack civilian, non-combatant
targets deliberately, or even to threaten such. All things are *not*
permissible. . . .

The strategic-pragmatic case against a societal-punishment theory of deterrence, simply stated, is that at worst it is unlikely to
work, while at best it is a distinctly inferior deterrent. When searching for the meaning of an adequate deterrent, a defense community
has to ask two central questions: what does the enemy find most
deterring? and what would it be in our interest actually to do should
deterrence fail? Theorizing about the value structures of foreign
elites, and about the kinds of risks that they might be prepared to
run in defense of those things that they are believed to hold most
dear, is a notoriously inexact science. As Bernard Brodie once
wrote: ". . . good strategy presumes good anthropology and sociol-
ogy. Some of the greatest military blunders of all time have resulted
from juvenile evaluations in this department." . . .

It makes neither moral nor strategic-pragmatic sense for a United
States seeking to deter a Soviet Union that holds to the view that it
is the duty, if not the pleasure of its citizens to be ready to die for
the state, to prepare war plans that identify the punishment of
society as the allegedly ultimate threat. Attacks against the Soviet
economy in general, or even against those parts of the economy
believed to be essential for recovery, and—necessarily—the co-
located work force, would not help the United States stave off defeat
(let alone contribute to any facsimile of the restoration of "peace on
favorable terms"); they would punish ordinary Russians for the
misdeeds of their state exploiters; and they might trigger a mode of
Soviet targeting response which was calibrated to punish the United
States according to Soviet understanding of American official and
social values. . . .

At some risk of appearing to stretch the meaning of words, the
point should be made that all participants in the contemporary
debate over nuclear strategy, save for outright nuclear pacifists and
possibly for the Catholic Bishops (whose position on what is and is
not permitted is so evasive that one cannot with high confidence
separate out plain confusion from calculated ambiguity), endorse
some form of nuclear war fighting. This has to be true. Anyone who

concedes the need for a nuclear deterrent for the goal of war prevention, logically must also will the means. The means must comprise nuclear forces, detailed plans for their employment, and an honest intention actually to use them in very bad circumstances. Whether one plans to bomb cities or to strike discretely at geographically more or less isolated military facilities, one is—in both cases—planning to fight a nuclear war. . . .

DETERRENCE, JUDGEMENT, AND UNCERTAINTY

It would seem to be virtually self-evident that a country like the United States that has a founding state ideology of commitment to the life, liberty and pursuit of happiness of individual Americans, cannot credibly threaten to initiate an "exchange" of nuclear strikes against essentially civilian targets. As an operational strategy for compellent effect, such an idea affronts American values both in the sense of an absolute ethic (targeting non-combatants is morally wrong) and in the sense of an ethic of consequences (it would license an intolerable Soviet attack upon American society). However, that which is glaringly self-evident to American critics of theories of deterrence by the threat of societal punishment, may be less self-evident to Soviet defense planners. Soviet officials are obliged to define the American working class, objectively, as a (misguided) ally; an obligation which might encourage the paying of some attention to issues of collateral damage. In addition, Soviet officials should reason that the American ruling class and its political puppets have an enormous economic stake in their exploited workers. However, on balance, Soviet ideology should incline Soviet officials to discount the genuineness of the concern for individual life and quality of life that Americans know is a high value of their state and society. In other words, the deterrent leverage believed to be provided by Soviet threats to American urban areas could be considerably less in Soviet than in American estimation.

The absence of strategic defenses for the American homeland reflects, in alternative US judgements, a particular theory of strategic stability, the limitations of the effectiveness of active defense technology, and disbelief in the utility of civil defense. But, in Soviet perspective, the absence of US strategic defenses can be held to reflect a very high degree of confidence in the efficacy of offensive means of damage limitation, or official US disdain for, even disinterest in, prospective civilian casualties. This line of speculation is intended to illustrate how inaccurate US policy science could be with regard to the structure of the nuclear deterrence relationship of the superpowers.

This author believes that the United States should adopt a damage-limiting strategy for war fighting (appropriately so-called), hopefully for stable deterrence. But, it is possible that this strategic logic could be out of tune with a logic informed by Soviet "cultural thoughtways." It should be recalled that among the many elements in the case for strategic defense, a powerful theme is the credibility that such defense should lend to the contingent threats of US strategic offensive action. Plainly, if Soviet officials are misled by their ideology and culture into believing that the US government has a view of the "value" of its citizens functionally approximating their view of the "value" of Soviet citizens, then those officials may wonder (and possibly even tremble) at the absence of US strategic defense. It should follow that Soviet officials are likely to underrate the deterrent leverage that they actually enjoy by courtesy of the threat to American civilians. The more cynical, ruthless and self-interested the Soviet leadership assumes the US government to be, the less damaging is the absence of US strategic defense to the stability of deterrence. . . .

There is an overwhelming strategic-pragmatic case for placing a heavy emphasis upon military effectiveness in US SIOP planning. This analysis has argued that the US government is correct in believing that the stability of deterrence is best assured if Soviet officials understand that, in the most general terms, "the power of the Soviet state" is held at risk by US nuclear forces. More specifically, the US government is correct in translating that "power," for targeting purposes, into "those types of Soviet targets [very largely military assets] . . . which the Soviet leaders have given every indication by their actions they value most, and which constitute their tools of control and power." Not only should plausible threats to such target sets have the most beneficial influence for deterrence, but also it would make some sense for the United States actually to conduct a counter-military campaign in the event that deterrence failed. One can only say "some sense," because a truly vigorous nuclear campaign for damage limitation, comprising on this assessment realization of the ultimate threat to Soviet official values, must be assumed to unleash the full fury of the Soviet strategic war plan against the United States (in the somewhat unlikely event that it had not been unleashed already on a Soviet timetable for war-fighting effect). It is worth noting, as a qualification, that a relatively gradual escalation in the scale and character of US counter-military targeting may serve to trigger Soviet discovery of useful "firebreaks"—meaning that deterrence might be restored. However, one cannot help but notice that a United States bereft of the physical means of balanced offensive-defensive capabilities for the assurance of its national survival probably should hesitate before attacking target sets assessed to lie in the highest category of Soviet official values.

Strong though this author believes the deterrent case to be in favor of a heavily counter-military focus in US nuclear strategy, he wishes neither to overstate that case nor to appear to obscure the extent to which it rests upon judgement. In the process of demolishing the reasoning of MAD . . . advocates both of a genuine (which is to say a true damage-limiting) and of a very incomplete (as with "the countervailing strategy" of PD-59) war-fighting approach to deterrence, have tended to exaggerate the robustness of their argument. In particular, the critics of MAD theory who have not endorsed damage limitation as an essential requirement, appear not to have noticed that their preference, for controlled and flexible targeting of Soviet military and political-control assets, has some of the same crucial weaknesses as does MAD. . . .

The honest advocate of a war-fighting approach to deterrence stability should recognize three very important areas of uncertainty pertaining to his argument. First, even if the highest values of the Soviet state are its "tools of power and control," and—it should be added—the public respect for its power and will to sustain power, the prospective loss of a half or more of its industrial base (and a sizeable fraction of the work force) is not exactly a trivial matter. The Soviet Union may believe, or perhaps hope, that—*in extremis*— it could win a war, and as a consequence, through the expansion of its territorial and hegemonic empire, exploit the rest of the world as a recovery base for a very severely damaged Soviet homeland. Soviet defense planners undoubtedly have to hand very detailed contingency plans for postwar economic recovery. . . . Soviet leaders should be more deterred by the plausible prospect of losing a war as a result of direct Western action against the coercive instruments of the Soviet state and the means of control of those instruments, than by the prospect of suffering industrial damage (which, in time, can be made good), but the difference is relative rather than absolute and cannot be established with any precision. This is a policy matter to be determined only by judgement in the face of very severe uncertainty.

Second, strategic and political logic and military capability may be very different. To argue for the deterrent and, if need be, defensive merit in holding at risk key Soviet military and political assets is one thing; to have confidence that those assets could be destroyed or neutralized may be something else. Many, though certainly far from all, key Soviet military and political targets are super-hard, are mobile or at least movable, while some have yet to be identified with high confidence. A US threat to Soviet leadership and other control targets is not a threat that Soviet officials would be likely to undervalue, but there is and has to be a great deal of uncertainty as to how vulnerable Soviet leaders believe their control structure and military forces to be. No matter how convincing conceptually the deterrent case for threatening such targets, pragmatically one must take account of such factors as location uncertainty, hardness uncertainty, and the inappropriateness of the *extant* US nuclear weapon arsenal for striking at super-hard and at mobile targets. In addition, both superpowers are aware of the large question mark that hangs over the issue of the likelihood of operational availability of space-deployed or of air-breathing reconnaissance assets for target location in wartime. Conceptually, again, one can solve the problem by making provisions for the wartime reconstitution of space assets and of other means of overhead reconnaissance, but in practice one may find that one's reconstitution assets have been degraded or destroyed.

In short, the relative deterrent value of counter-military, as opposed to counter-urban-industrial targeting, could differ as between practice and theory. Possibly, to be realistic, one should not contrast the quality of threat inherent in the prospect of damage to industry as opposed to the control structure and to military targets, in the light of Soviet values. Instead, one should perhaps contrast the deterrent quality of a rather low-confidence threat to many key Soviet control and other military targets (for reason of their hardness, location uncertainty and the technical limitations of US strategic forces), to the deterrent quality of a highly robust threat to lay waste a very large fraction of the industrial base of the Soviet Union.

Third, to revisit briefly an argument advanced already, it is probably a logical error of considerable magnitude to believe that a stress on counter-military targeting could assist greatly in evading the awesome, if not policy-paralyzing, choice between suicide and surrender. Not only would one be assaulting the highest of Soviet values by counter-military targeting, and thereby minimizing if not removing entirely any Soviet incentives to exercise restraint, also one would be licensing a campaign that—if it were to be waged efficiently on both sides—would have to produce a vast amount of civilian damage. Both superpowers have very many military assets co-located with civilian society, while in addition many civilian facilities clearly have military value. Desmond Ball has shown how extensive is the military-civilian interface on the European USSR, while—on the American side—to cite but three examples, consider the implications for civilian damage of the dispersal fields to be used by SAC aircraft (bombers and tankers), the urban locations of the switching stations of the Bell telephone system, and the collateral damage that would be caused by attacks upon power stations (including nuclear power stations) and the national power grid.

The proponents of a war-fighting approach to deterrence stability serve the causes of truth, of sensible defense planning, and of credibility for their arguments when they recognize frankly the force of the three points made above. These points, to repeat, are that there is deterrent value in threatening Soviet industry; that counter-military and counter-control targeting may not be capable of being executed very effectively; and that counter-military and counter-control targeting, even if controlled and flexible in execution, may not serve to enable an American president to evade the surrender or suicide dilemma that lurks in MAD philosophy.

CONCLUSIONS

The uncertainties, soft realms of judgement, and heavy recourse to theory that characterize war-fighting (*inter alia*) concepts of stable deterrence do not serve to rescue the idea of threats of societal punishment for deterrence from the waste dump of policy and intellectual history. What this analysis means is that the United States needs a better theory of war-fighting deterrence, not that the theory should be discarded. The fragilities in the war-fighting approach that is officially authoritative today can be greatly alleviated, if not wholly eliminated, in two ways. First, the United States should begin to construct, step by step, a multi-layered architecture of active and passive strategic defense, so that homeland protection in time of war ceases to depend entirely upon the improbable operation of a process of reciprocated targeting restraint (between two countries with sharply divergent cultures and values). Second, the United States should acquire strategic offensive forces, and essential support systems (*inter alia* for target acquisition, precise navigation, and logistics for sustainability) so that it could do—and keep on doing—what it claims to be necessary in order to fight and prevail in war.

The United States needs a hard-target counterforce capability that enjoys enduring survivability; a National Command Authority that is truly survivable (which is not the case today, or prospectively tomorrow either); survivable and/or reconstitutable overhead surveillance and reconnaissance assets for target identification for controlled and discriminating attack purposes in the course of a war (which also is lacking today); a survivable attack assessment system; and nuclear or conventional warheads so designed, and so navigated that they would pose a truly credible threat to the deep-underground bunker complexes of the Soviet leadership and to other very high-value super-hard targets.

The Case for the "Mad-Plus" Posture*

ROBERT J. ART

Strategists since World War II have divided into two distinct camps in their attempt to wrestle with nuclear strategy—the finite deterrers and the flexible responders. The former are commonly associated with assured destruction, countervalue or countercity targeting, and small nuclear forces; the latter, with war waging, limited nuclear options, counterforce targeting, and large nuclear forces. Finite deterrers have held to the position that what makes nuclear deterrence stable is the threat to destroy the cities of an adversary in a retaliatory blow. Because a second strike countervalue blow is sufficient, nuclear deterrence requires no counterforce capabilities and only a small number of nuclear weapons, as long as a portion of them are invulnerable to a first strike. The threat to devastate a potential attacker's cities, even only a small number of them, is all that is required to dissuade him from attacking. And when both sides have an assured destruction capability, mutual assured destruction, or MAD, obtains and makes nuclear deterrence quite stable. Flexible responders argue that the threat to destroy cities in retaliation, when the adversary can do the same to the retaliator, has lost its credibility for dealing with a wide range of political/military contingencies and, therefore, that a range of options short of countercity blows is required to strengthen deterrence.

The finite deterrent position stresses that, because a nuclear war will likely get quickly out of control and involve massive numbers of explosions, limited nuclear options are superfluous at best and dangerous at worst. They are superfluous because they will have no utility in such an all-out war. They could not prevent cities from

From "Between Assured Destruction and Nuclear Victory: The Case for the 'Mad-Plus' Posture" by Robert J. Art, *Ethics*, V. 95 (April 1985), pp. 497–516. Copyright by the University of Chicago. Reprinted by permission of the University of Chicago Press. Portions of the text have been omitted; all referential and some explanatory footnotes have also been omitted.

* I wish to thank Robert O. Keohane, Susan Okin, and Stephen Van Evera for helpful comments on an earlier draft of this piece. But especially I thank John Mearsheimer for pushing me to think about what I really wanted to say, for forcing me to reconceptualize the first draft and for carefully reading two subsequent drafts.

being devastated and can, therefore, serve no useful military or political purpose. They are dangerous because they foster the belief that nuclear war can be limited and, as a consequence, could make it appear less horrendous and hence more likely. The flexible response position stresses two counterpoints: first, in the era of mutual assured destruction, threats to retaliate massively against an adversary's cities lack sufficient credibility to deter him from undertaking hostile acts against one's allies; second, the threat of a retaliatory countercity blow, if it had to be implemented, would end all hope of quickly limiting and ending such a war short of total devastation to both.

In the last few years, as both the Americans and Russians have developed highly accurate, sophisticated, and ever larger numbers of nuclear forces, the difference between the two traditional camps has widened. The advance of technology and the growth in numbers have widened the gap because the flexible responders want to exploit further the potentialities for greater flexibility, while the finite deterrers fear a lowering of the restraints on nuclear use that the additional exploitation of flexibility could bring.

As a consequence, many finite deterrers no longer argue simply that a small number of nuclear weapons delivered on cities is sufficient for the stability of deterrence. Many now take the position that the *only* utility nuclear weapons possess is to deter the use of other nuclear weapons. Former Secretary of Defense Robert Mc-Namara has forcefully argued this position. . . . Similarly, several flexible responders now argue that nuclear wars can be successfully waged and won and that the best way to deter them and extend the American nuclear umbrella over its allies is to convince the adversary that one can indeed fight and win them. A prominent exponent of this view is Colin Gray.

Thus, finite deterrers may be moving to the view that nuclear weapons have very limited military, and hence almost no political, utility because their initial use makes so little sense. Flexible responders may be turning from war wagers into war winners. The possibilities that have developed over the last ten years for greater flexibility in nuclear use have begun to drive both camps from their respective centers toward the extremes inherent in each.

In my view, both these camps miss the mark. On the one hand, finite deterrers are naive because they do not understand the effects on *statecraft* that the nuclear revolution has produced. Nuclear deterrence dissuades an adversary from taking actions other than simply using his nuclear weapons against another state that may or may not have them. Nuclear deterrence produces restraining effects that are based on the fear of nuclear war, but such effects extend far beyond simply dissuading initial nuclear use. Finite deterrence severely downplays these larger political effects. On the other hand, the flexible responders, when they become obsessed with flexibility and move toward war winning, are also naive because they do not understand the effects on *warfare* that the nuclear revolution has produced. War waging has some specific but quite limited virtues for deterrence, escalation control, and damage limitation. War winning, however, is impossible precisely because of the fact that there is no defense now against all-out nuclear use and probably not for the foreseeable future. A nuclear war could therefore be controlled and won only if one side consciously chose to lose the war, an event as unlikely in the future as it has been rare or nonexistent in the past. It is not necessary to win a nuclear war in order to deter it; one has only to ensure that both are likely to lose it.

There is a reasonable position between these two extremes. It embodies elements of both finite deterrence and flexible response. In what follows, I etch this position out by treating in turn, first, the political effects of nuclear deterrence and, second, the irrelevance for the stability of deterrence of symmetry in counterforce capabilities. I thus will lay the groundwork for a position between these two extremes by analyzing the strengths and weaknesses of the finite deterrent and flexible response positions, respectively, in the next two sections.

In the last section of this article, I conclude that if we think about nuclear strategy politically, we find that there is a viable position between the finite deterrent and flexible response positions that, for lack of a better term, I call the "MAD-plus" posture. It is one that relies heavily on the restraining effects of mutual assured destruction, but that favors some limited war-waging capability for both escalation-signaling and damage-limitation purposes. It favors some limited counterforce (what I later term "weak" counterforce) but not a "robust" counterforce capability that would undermine MAD. The purpose of a weak counterforce capability (which both the Americans and the Russians now have), or, better put, a targeting policy directed at soft military targets, is to avoid initial attacks on cities and thereby limit damage. The MAD-plus posture also favors some investment in command, control, communications, and intelligence (what is referred to as C^3I) to preserve control in any nuclear war that starts out limited precisely for the purpose of keeping the war limited. Some C^3I is necessary in order to maintain control over the nuclear exchanges and thereby buy enough time so that political leaders in both capitols can negotiate quickly to bring the limited war swiftly to an end. In essence, the MAD-plus posture is a hedge: it relies mainly on assured destruction but favors buying some limited options or flexibility for added insurance.

THE POLITICAL EFFECTS OF NUCLEAR DETERRENCE

Nuclear weapons have political consequences that extend far beyond their military effects. Neither the assured destructors nor the flexible responders, however, accept this premise. Because the former argue that the only thing the possession of nuclear weapons does for a state is to prevent another state from using them against it, nuclear weapons dissuade only nuclear use and therefore only a small number are needed. Because the latter argue that a small number of nuclear weapons is sufficient neither to deter a nuclear attack nor to limit damage should one occur, a state needs a large number of them to deter attacks on itself and its allies and to limit damage to both should war occur. For the finite deterrers, only the civilian population of the adversary need be held hostage; for the war wagers, in addition to civilians, the adversary's nuclear weapons, other military forces, command centers, and political control structures must be subject to devastation.

Oddly enough, from the same mistaken premise, they draw opposite conclusions. While the finite deterrers call for fewer of them and the war wagers for more of them, both share a common misunderstanding about the political role of nuclear weapons. Both have grossly underestimated the powerful restraining effects that the possession of nuclear weapons have had on superpower statecraft and on that of the other states that possess them. Nuclear weapons do things other than simply prevent other states from using them. The existence of nuclear weapons not only dissuades nuclear use but also dampens down the likelihood of the use of conventional forces against an adversary that also possesses nuclear weapons or against a close nonnuclear ally of a nuclear state. Nuclear weapons have made a general war, either conventional or nuclear, between the superpowers and their associated clients less likely. Nuclear weapons make a superpower and its associated clients that are involved in a conventional war more careful than they would otherwise be about how they conduct it for fear of going beyond the permissible limits and provoking intervention by the other superpower. The threat of retaliation, the possibility of escalation, the concomitant risk that things could get out of control, and the knowledge that if they do all is lost—it is these four factors that have forced nuclear statesmen to be more cautious than their pre-World-War-II "conventional" predecessors.

Most wars have occurred because someone miscalculated but in a very particular way—either about what the opponent would do, what he could do, or what could be done to him. Stalin may have lost twenty million Russians in World War II, but he certainly did not expect that outcome when he made his deal with Hitler. Hitler may ultimately have been mad, but he was banking on a short war and Allied weakness. Bethmann Hollweg may have sought relief from imperial Germany's political and military encirclement by deliberately launching a Continental war, but he certainly did not seek a world war. In these cases and others, miscalculations occurred because someone was more certain about what would happen than they should have been and than events ultimately warranted.

The nuclear age does not encourage such miscalculations to arise out of such supposed certainties. The threat to both parties that matters could quickly get out of control, together with the horrendous costs that would be imposed on both if they did, has built in a bias in nuclear statecraft toward a degree of caution and restraint that, although it can never eradicate miscalculation, has, nevertheless, minimized it greatly. That is all we can expect. But that is significant. Nuclear weapons have narrowed the range of matters about which statesmen can be certain because they have widened the range of those over which uncertainty reigns. *Ironically, miscalculation has decreased because uncertainty has increased.* It is the potential for loss of control through escalation that has built into nuclear diplomacy a degree of uncertainty about the course of events that is greater than what once obtained. It is not so much the destruction that is assured, but that which *could* occur if matters got out of control, that is the basis for the MAD world in which we live today.

The existence of nuclear weapons has thus introduced a clear and pronounced restraint into the conduct of superpower diplomacy that has affected world politics generally. Wars have continued to occur, certainly; but they have not escalated into a general one between the superpowers. Clearly crises have occurred because risks have been taken by the superpowers. We do not live in a risk-free world. But when excessive risk taking has resulted in crises, the potential for escalation has worked to defuse them. The Cuban missile crisis is a case in point. Khrushchev would clearly not have put offensive missiles into Cuba had he known that Kennedy would have reacted as forcefully as he did. He would not have knowingly and willingly put himself and his nation into the position of being humiliated, as both subsequently were. Once he saw how strong a stance Kennedy took, he backed down. But Kennedy, though insistent on getting the missiles out, also acted with restraint: he started with the least bellicose action to get the missiles out (the blockade) and did all that he could to help Khrushchev save some semblance of face, both done from his awareness of what a single misstep could bring.

The Cuban missile crisis must therefore be seen as the exception that proves the rule. Superpower statesmen have to calculate carefully because the costs of miscalculation are potentially so horrendous. Sometimes they make mistakes. But the last forty years of American-Russian relations have seen only one grievous one. And when one occurs, both nations have acted quickly to rectify it because each has a shared interest in avoiding an all-out confrontation. Each superpower will not cease testing the other, to see what it can get away with. But it will calculate as carefully as it can before it probes because it has to. Thus, nuclear deterrence can work to produce more probing actions but quick retreat if the probe hits steel. Since 1945, the "stability-instability paradox," well known to nuclear strategists, has worked more to dampen down undue risk taking by the superpowers with respect to whether they provoke crises and how they manage them than it has to embolden either to careless adventurism.

Thus, because significant political effects flow from the possession of nuclear weapons, it is wrongheaded to argue either that the only function of nuclear weapons is to deter their use by another, *or* to assert that the capability to wage and win a nuclear war is necessary to deter it. Therefore, Robert McNamara is clearly wrong when he argues that nuclear weapons are "totally useless" except to deter another state from using them. The dampening down of risk-taking behavior in general, not simply initial nuclear use, flows from the existence of nuclear deterrence. So, too, is Colin Gray wrong when he argues that a denial of a Russian victory requires an American one. It is sufficient to demonstrate simply that the Soviet Union could not win a war and could suffer terribly if it persisted, even if the United States also lost it, to deter the Soviet Union. In the nuclear era, one nation does not have to win for the other to lose. Both can lose and therefore decide the risks are not worth taking. Thus, it is the generalized caution imposed on the superpowers by their mutual possession of a retaliatory capability that invalidates the claims of both the finite deterrers and the war wagers.

The fear that things could quickly get out of control, together with the costs involved if they do—these are what work to dissuade nuclear statesmen from taking undue risks. If escalation could be controlled, there would be no risk in escalating. In the nuclear era, it is precisely the potential for the loss of control that is the keystone of restraint and the essence of deterrence. In his final work, *War and Politics,* Bernard Brodie put the case well when he argued:

> We have ample reason to feel now that nuclear weapons do act critically to deter wars between the major powers, and not nuclear wars alone but any wars. That is really a very great gain. We should no doubt be hesitant about relinquishing it even if we could. We should not complain

too much because the guarantee is not ironclad. It is the curious paradox of our time that one of the foremost factors making deterrence really work and work well is the lurking fear that in some massive confrontation crisis it might fail. Under these circumstances one does not tempt fate. If we were absolutely certain that nuclear deterrence would be 100 per cent effective against nuclear attack, then it would cease to have much if any deterrence value against non-nuclear wars, and the arguments of the conventional buildup schools would indeed finally make sense.

In short, what makes nuclear deterrence extend so far is the fear that it might not.

Finally, if nuclear weapons have these political effects, it is because of the destruction they can wreak and the way that they can do it. As Thomas Schelling put it many years ago, "Victory is no longer a prerequisite for hurting the enemy." One can now destroy the enemy without having first vanquished him. Nuclear weapons have therefore separated the power to hurt from the power to defeat, what Schelling called, respectively, "coercive power" and "brute force." Because each superpower has it within its power to absorb a first strike from the other and still retaliate with a large number of warheads, the incentive for striking first is low. Each, therefore, can destroy, but not disarm, the other. What is balanced in the nuclear age is the power to hurt, not the power to disarm. What has ultimately ended all wars, as Schelling reminded us, was not the military defeat of the adversary but the ability to threaten credibly to destroy him after he was defeated militarily unless he surrendered. The outcome of the brute-force exchange had to occur first before the exercise of coercive power to bring surrender could come into play. What nuclear weapons have done is to reverse permanently the traditional sequence of warfare: it is no longer necessary to vanquish the enemy in order to be in the position of threatening to destroy him. The latter can be done now without the former.

This condition, assured destruction, leads to the following three propositions:

First, if you do not have to destroy the other fellow's nuclear forces to devastate him, why bother?

Second, if you cannot destroy the other fellow's capability to devastate you, why try?

Third, great disparities in offensive forces can be safely tolerated when the power to hurt, not the power to disarm, is what is being balanced. The balancing of terror, that is, is not highly sensitive to changes in the quantitative balance of forces as long as the attacker-to-target ratio is greater than one to one. With populations vulnerable, force ratios have less "force" than they once did. From a military standpoint, then, force ratio disparities are not worrisome. Militarily, it is not necessary to match forces; but, I shall argue later, there are political reasons for doing so—for having a rough parity in numbers of offensive forces.

Thus, the virtue of the assured destruction or finite deterrent school is that it reminds us of the fundamental condition of the nuclear era: as long as defense of populations is impossible, matching the adversary in the number of forces he has is not necessary. Its vice is that it is far too restrictive in its view of what nuclear weapons do in fact restrain and deter.

THE IRRELEVANCE OF COUNTERFORCE SYMMETRY

Is the flexible responder's world, with its emphasis on war waging (if not winning) and counterforce targeting better than the finite deterrer's MAD world, with its emphasis on limited forces and countervalue targeting? Is it better to be able to target only cities rather than to be able to knock out military forces? The answer is, it depends on what one means by counterforce, on what types of forces one wishes to knock out. If by a counterforce world we mean one in which any nuclear power possessed a first strike capability against any other nuclear power's nuclear forces, clearly a MAD world is preferable. A true or "fully robust" counterforce world would be one in which all nuclear powers felt that each had an effective disarming capability. In a surprise attack, one adversary could knock out the other's offensive (and potential retaliatory) forces. If we are interested in preventing the use of nuclear weapons, which we should be, the attempt to attain such a capability is insane. As Schelling once put it, "Military technology that puts a premium on haste in a crisis puts a premium on war itself." A counterforce world would encourage speedy decisions, hasty actions, preemptive strategies, grandiose ambitions, aggressive foreign policies, and the like. Clearly a counterforce world lessens the political restraints on the physical use of nuclear force. It is desirable, therefore, that nuclear statesmen continue to feel insecure about defense against nuclear attack and about their own first strike capabilities and secure only about their own and their adversary's retaliatory capabilities.

If a fully robust counterforce world is not desirable, is something short of it, what we might term a "weak" counterforce world, also undesirable? Is a world, that is, in which both sides possess considerable counterforce capabilities, but those still well short of a disarming capability, destabilizing? The answer to this question should be no simply because, no matter how extensive their counterforce capabilities are and no matter how great the asymmetry

between them may be in this regard, neither side would be emboldened to strike first when the other would retain the capability to
retaliate on its cities. Weak counterforce capabilities can and do
exist in a MAD world. But that does not alter the fundamental
condition of mutual vulnerability to which both superpowers are
subject.

In order to develop this argument more fully, I will attack the
position, first developed by Paul Nitze in 1976, that asserts that a
perceived asymmetry in counterforce capability (in Russia's favor)
both weakens deterrence and puts the United States at a disadvantage in crises and intense bargaining situations. His argument received wide currency in the United States and was reflected in the
Carter administration's PD-59 and "countervailing strategy" pronouncements. As explained by then Secretary of Defense Harold
Brown, the countervailing strategy held to the view that, although
the United States did not believe that either nation could prevail
militarily in a nuclear war, nevertheless, for the stability of deterrence and the advantageous resolution of crises, the United States
had to strengthen significantly its own war-waging posture and thus
"countervail" against the Soviet Union.

I begin with Nitze's argument because he stated the asymmetry
position in the most extreme form. In his influential article, he
argued:

> In sum, the ability of U.S. nuclear power to destroy without question
> the bulk of Soviet industry and a large proportion of the Soviet popula-
> tion is by no means as clear as it once was, even if one assumes most of
> U.S. striking power to be available and directed to this end.
>
> A more crucial test, however, is to consider the possible results of a
> large-scale nuclear exchange in which one side sought to destroy as
> much of the other side's striking power as possible, in order to leave
> itself in the strongest possible position after the exchange.

Nitze was concerned about the potential postattack position of
the United States vis-à-vis the Soviet Union. If the Russians could
wipe out most of America's land-based missile forces in a first strike
and if the Americans did not have the same capability to wipe out
most of Russia's land-based missiles in a first strike, then the Soviet
leaders might be tempted to launch an attack on America's land
forces, but they would more likely be emboldened to take risks that
they otherwise would not because they would be acting from a
supposedly superior position. In short, argued Nitze, asymmetries
in counterforce capabilities, even if MAD still obtained, could be
destabilizing and produce a more dangerous world for the United
States. Brown's countervailing strategy picked up this line of reasoning when it argued:

The Soviet Union should entertain no illusion that by attacking our strategic nuclear forces, it could significantly reduce the damage it would suffer. Nonetheless, the state of the strategic balance after an initial exchange—measured both in absolute terms and in relation to the balance prior to the exchange—could be an important factor in the decision by one side to initiate a nuclear exchange. Thus, it is important—for the sake of deterrence—to be able to deny to the potential aggressor a fundamental and favorable shift in the strategic balance as a result of a nuclear exchange.

Why, however, would asymmetries in counterforce capabilities be destabilizing if neither side had a robust or truly disarming counterforce capability? Why would the Russians attack land-based missiles when they could not get at the sea-based ones? Did the fact that the latter were invulnerable to a disarming attack not make the former, in effect, invulnerable also? The crux of Nitze's and presumably Brown's worry was this: the United States would be "self-deterred" from retaliating against Russian cities once it had suffered a massive strike against its land-based forces. It would not hit back at Russian cities because that would cause a retaliatory Russian strike against American cities. The United States would be left in the same position many argued it once was in the fifties with its policy of massive retaliation: shoot off everything or do nothing. After its disarming blow against the land-based forces then, the Soviet Union would be in a position to intimidate the United States. In order to remedy this potential for "self-deterrence," the United States had to develop counterforce capabilities symmetrical to what the Soviet Union already had. America had, in short, to develop more of a war-waging capability in order to bolster deterrence.

The Nitze scenario and variants on it—and especially his call for the United States to develop a more formidable war-waging capability—received firm support from President Reagan's Commission on Strategic Forces in its April 1983 report:

In order to deter such Soviet threats we must be able to put at risk those types of Soviet targets—including hardened ones such as military command bunkers and facilities, missile silos, nuclear weapons and other storage, and the rest—which the Soviet leaders have given every indication by their actions they value most, and which constitute their tools of control and power.

Effective deterrence of any Soviet temptation to threaten or launch a massive conventional or limited nuclear war thus requires us to have a comparable ability to destroy Soviet military targets, hardened and otherwise. . . . A one-sided strategic condition in which the Soviet Union could effectively destroy the whole range of strategic targets in the United States, but we could not effectively destroy a similar range of targets in the Soviet Union, would be extremely unstable over the long run.

. . . We must have a credible capability for controlled, prompt, limited attacks on hard targets ourselves. This capability casts a shadow over the calculus of Soviet risk-taking at any level of confrontation with the West.

Early in the Reagan administration, Secretary of Defense Weinberger's call for the United States to be able to wage a "protracted" nuclear war through to a successful conclusion signified the final step in this line of reasoning. Under the early Reagan, America's policy shifted from countervailing to prevailing, from war waging to war winning. The later Reagan administration backed off from war winning in its subsequent pronouncements, but it continued to invest considerable sums to procure a formidable war-waging capability. But whether it be for war waging or war winning, the rationale has been that because they (the Russians) have it, we need it. Is this the case? Why should symmetry in counterforce capabilities be necessary? Why must we be able to wage a nuclear war as effectively as some argue the Russians can and/or intend in order to deter it or in order to limit damage in it if it should occur? Is symmetry in war-fighting capabilities between the Russians and the Americans necessary for nuclear stability?

My judgment is no. I should like to offer seven reasons why I think the Nitze counterforce scenario, its many variants, and the entire symmetry-in-war-waging argument makes little military, and even less political, sense.

1. If the war wagers and counterforcers can argue that the United States would be deterred from attacking Russian cities in retaliation for a Russian first strike counterforce blow against America's Minuteman force, why can the "MAD men" not argue that, similarly, they would likely be deterred from attacking the Minuteman missiles in the first place because they cannot be certain that we would not retaliate against any, a few, or all of their cities? If self-deterrence works to prevent us from retaliating, would not self-deterrence also work to prevent them from attacking? Why does self-deterrence work only for us and not for them?

2. If neither the United States nor the Soviet Union is prepared to threaten to attack cities, *even if neither would ever want to execute that threat,* then each cannot deter the other, no matter how effective their war-fighting capabilities are. To repeat, what provides restraint is the fear that things will get out of control and that all could be lost—both sides' cities, that is,—if caution is abandoned. The war wagers, however, argue that the Soviet leaders value their machinery and their mechanisms of political control

more than they do their populace. They do not accept the MAD world logic. The conclusion, they assert, is that our threat to devastate their population carries little weight with them.

How, . . . in reality, can that conclusion make any military or political sense? First, a significant percentage of Russian hard targets are located in or near cities so that extensive counterforce attacks would produce civilian casualties that would likely be indistinguishable from purely countervalue attacks. Colin Gray, for example, admits as much when he states: "Not only would one be assaulting the highest of Soviet values by counter-military targeting, and thereby minimizing if not removing entirely any Soviet incentives to exercise restraint, also one would be licensing a campaign that—if it were to be waged efficiently on both sides—would have to produce a vast amount of civilian damage. Both superpowers have very many military assets co-located with civilian society." If extensive counterforce attacks would have much the same results for civilians as would pure population attacks, why do we need to fine tune our forces for hard target kills when we cannot avoid extensive civilian damage in the process? And would that be the best way for the United States to limit damage to its civilians when the Russians know that American leaders value their populace highly? Second, would it not be extremely difficult to convince the Soviet leaders that limited counterforce strikes against military targets so colocated were aimed, not at their populace, but at them (or vice versa)? Is an attack on Moscow (or Washington) meant to be "only" decapitating, the precursor to a rolling or tit-for-tat exchange, or merely a one-time shot to show that we (or they) mean business? How could they (or we) know which was the case?

. . . Finally, either extensive countervalue attacks or extensive counterforce attacks against the Soviet political mechanisms would kill so many Russian civilians that there would be little left to control! Political leaders do not value political control mechanisms per se; they value the power over others that such mechanisms yield. If there is no one left (or very few) to control, what, precisely, can be the point of the machinery for control? Surely mechanisms for control, apart from the objects of control, have little political meaning to those who possess them. Either type of attack, therefore, will eradicate the civilians. And since the leaders need the civilians to control, why go after them the hard way (counterforce) rather than the easy way (countervalue)? If there is logic to this argument, then the Soviet leaders must value their populace as much as American leaders do, even if they do so for different reasons. Thus, even the war wagers' emphasis on control mechanisms leads one inexorably back to populations and to the logic of MAD.

3. . . . What will end the nuclear war as well as prevent it is the threat of wiping out cities. Who has more weapons left over after an extensive brute-force exchange or after a series of small exchanges is irrelevant to the conclusion of the war as long as each party can still devastate the other. Postattack calculations about throw weight ratios, warheads ratios, missile ratios, and the like, make little sense. What has always brought a war to a successful conclusion for one party or a draw for both is the need to settle in order to avoid further or extensive civilian deaths. It is hard to see how disparities in force sizes, however measured, will make any difference to war termination when both will surely retain enough forces to threaten however many cities each still retains intact.

4. The Nitze scenario of an extensive Russian first strike against America's Minuteman force, although theoretically possible, glosses over the real and intractable operational difficulties the Soviet Union would have in executing such an attack. The fratricide problem alone makes the timing of such an attack inordinately complicated. Although no one would advocate such a posture unless there were no choice, the United States could always resort to a launch-on-warning or -on-attack posture. It is difficult to imagine a Communist Party chairman of the Soviet Union imagining that an American president would simply watch the Russian missiles rain down on the United States. Would he not have to calculate that, if he shot at all of America's land-based silos, he might in effect be shooting at empty ones?

5. A massive disarming strike against America's Minuteman force would require something approaching 2,000 separate explosions. Would that be a truly limited and containable strike? Would a decision by the Soviet leaders to launch an attack of such magnitude not be equivalent to a declaration of World War III? Why would they go after America's land-based forces when America's sea-based forces remained intact? Are not land-based systems invulnerable because the sea-based ones are? Given the civilian casualties that an attack of such magnitude would have for the United States, could the Russian leaders seriously think that an American president would leave Russian cities intact? Why would they take such a risk? Why would they feel more emboldened in a crisis when such presumed capability carries such a high risk of an American counterresponse?

6. The United States today already possesses considerable counterforce capabilities and will, shortly, have even more. If these are to be used intelligently, that is, for deterrent purposes, they should be directed in our declaratory posture toward soft, not hard, military targets. If we ever need actually show that we are serious about escalation and if we want to hold our cities and theirs in hostage in

the early phases of a nuclear war, surely limited counterforce attacks against credible, but containable, soft military targets is the least destabilizing counterforce posture available. If they ever were to occur, counterforce attacks should be limited and undertaken, not to disarm or to sever political control, but to demonstrate resolve in a way that still manages to limit the damage done.

7. Most of the above points have been directed to prewar deterrence. Should such a war occur, the best way to limit damage is not to institute extensive and wide-ranging counterforce attacks but, rather, to negotiate to stop the war immediately. The next best way is to limit any exchanges that may occur. The worst way to attempt to stop the war is to engage in massive counterforce exchanges that will heighten the incentives to preempt and that will, in any case, bring horrendous civilian deaths. And the deliberate, extensive targeting of Russian command, communications, control, and intelligence facilities is absurd. We (and they) need someone who is in control and with whom we can negotiate. We and they both require that someone remain in charge to limit the exchanges. In short, damage limitation does not require an extensive counterforce targeting capability. The execution of such a strategy on a large scale would likely produce the very best results that it is intended to prevent—namely, extensive damage.

Beyond all these points lies a final one that renders the attempt to acquire a war-winning posture illusory. If a full-scale nuclear war is inherently uncontrollable, it is wasteful, if not absurd, to try to develop fully the means to control it. Selectivity, protractedness, fine tuning, discrimination—all these are entities not likely to exist or persevere in a protracted nuclear war of any size. Desmond Ball has persuasively shown that command, control, and communications systems are inherently more vulnerable than the strategic forces themselves, for both the Americans and the Russians, and will likely remain so for the foreseeable future. The consequence of this fact is that "the capability to exercise strict control and coordination would inevitably be lost relatively early in a nuclear exchange." Any nuclear war, then, once it begins and if it continues, is likely to get out of hand. As long as that condition obtains, the pursuit of the ability to conduct a fully controlled and sizeable nuclear war is a fool's chase. It is not that we should not take precautions to preserve some options for selectivity and controllability. These are prudent measures. But to believe that matters can, in fact, be controlled and to operate under that assumption is wrong. The probability that things will get quickly out of control remains uncertain enough that gambling it will not is foolhardy. Because that is so, we are driven back to the MAD world of deterrence, almost, that is, but not quite.

THE CASE FOR THE "MAD-PLUS" POSTURE

Is there, then, nothing at all to be said for war waging, even after we have thrown out both war winning and symmetry in counterforce capabilities? Is finite deterrence, with its emphasis on small nuclear forces and countervalue targeting, the only sensible posture to take? Are there valid reasons why it is sensible not to have a nuclear force that is dramatically smaller in size than one's adversary's? Are there valid reasons to have some limited war-waging capabilities? I believe there are valid reasons both to match roughly one's adversary in numbers and to have a limited war-waging capability, though I stress the word "limited." I offer three reasons.

First, what makes military sense in the nuclear age—the absence of a compelling need to match exactly the adversary in the number of nuclear forces he possesses—makes little political sense for the two superpowers because their nuclear forces are used to protect territories other than merely their own. The logic of finite deterrence is impeccable for the restricted case of an attack on a superpower's homeland. (This is often referred to as type 1 deterrence, deterrence of an attack only on one's own territory.) For as long as a percentage of one's forces is invulnerable to a first strike, the adversary's cities can be held hostage to retaliation by a relatively small number of weapons. To deter one superpower from attacking only it directly, therefore, the other superpower needs to have a force merely some fractional size of the former's.

What works for type 1 deterrence, however, has not proved politically feasible for type 2 deterrence. The latter encompasses the difficult problem of "extended deterrence," that is, extending the protection of each superpower's nuclear umbrella over its non-nuclear and small nuclear allies. The political imperatives that are rooted in these type 2 deterrent uses of their nuclear forces have pushed the superpowers to maintain a rough equivalence in the sizes of their forces and sometimes to strive for a superiority, that is, for a disarming or robust counterforce capability. For extended deterrent purposes, like it or not, if one superpower has a force dramatically smaller than the other, it looks weaker to the allies over whom the superpower's nuclear umbrella is being extended. Simply put, America's allies, especially the NATO allies, would feel better with an American superiority, bad with an American inferiority, and can tolerate an American equality with the Soviet Union. For the superpowers who have extended deterrent uses for their nuclear forces, the military logic of finite deterrence for the type 1 case is not sufficient for the political logic of alliance management inherent in the type 2 case, no matter how "illogical" the logic of the extended deterrent world may seem. Political concerns, therefore, dictate that having a small nuclear force when one's superpower adversary has a large one is politically disadvantageous and hence untenable. One of the underpinnings of finite deterrence—that large disparities in force sizes do not matter—does not hold.[1]

Second, finite deterrence has difficulties handling escalation scenarios that involve competitions in risk taking. Although it is true that, strictly speaking, what happens on the battlefield is not central to the outcome of any nuclear war that may begin, it is not totally irrelevant. To see the force of this argument, we must distinguish between how nuclear weapons are initially used and what subsequently happens on the battlefield.

In the nuclear era, it is the case that defeat on the battlefield cannot easily, if at all, be translated into victory in the war simply because the side that has suffered a temporary battlefield loss can always up the ante and go to a higher level of violence if he deems what he is fighting for worth the escalation. Battlefield victories have little meaning if the adversary can still destroy you after suffering them. In the nuclear era, "escalation dominance"—the ability to contain or defeat an adversary at all levels of violence except at the highest (all-out nuclear war)—is not feasible simply because the adversary can suffer defeat at one level and go to the next higher one. It is not the military outcomes of battles that will determine how intensely the war is waged and when it will stop. Rather, it is how much each adversary values what he is fighting for that will determine the scope, scale, and intensity of the conflict. Resolve, not battlefield victory, is the crucial element in any competitive risk-taking situation. Each party has a shared interest in avoiding an escalation to all-out war where they both would be destroyed. Each will be forced to weigh how much he and his adversary value what both are fighting for in order to determine how firm to stand. As has been pointed out many times before, this is the proverbial game of chicken. Ultimately, one side is likely to give way to avoid devastation. It is true, therefore, that when defense of populations is not possible, escalation dominance loses its utility.

---

[1] I do not accept the converse, however: that an American nuclear superiority—a robust or disarming counterforce capability—would "solve" the problems inherent in extended deterrence. First of all, neither superpower would allow the other to acquire such a capability, which makes the issue academic. Second of all, for the NATO alliance at least, even when the United States was perceived by its allies to be ahead, in the fifties and sixties, still they were not satisfied. The United States in its era of nuclear advantage had to take many additional actions *in the theater* (within Western Europe) to assuage its allies, such as permanently stationing 300,000 American troops there. For lack of space, I simply assert this proposition: extended deterrent problems cannot be solved by seeking superiority or advantageous positions with central strategic systems; they must be handled with in-theater solutions. The way to extend deterrence, that is, is to make the territory being protected look sufficiently important to the United States such that its extension of its nuclear umbrella over it looks credible.

What happens on the battlefield, however, can have meaning for structuring the dynamics of competitive risk-taking situations. Battlefield actions are important for what they signal about resolve, not whether they defeat the adversary. How battles are started can affect both the perceptions of resolve and the subsequent dynamics of a competitive risk-taking situation. It is not sufficient to argue, therefore, that escalation involves a competition in risk taking and simply leave matters at that. How, exactly, does one demonstrate resolve if one has to fire one or several nuclear weapons? Are demonstration shots—those that involve explosions in remote areas where there are no military forces and civilians—demonstrations of one's resolve to use nuclear weapons or of one's fear of using them? Is it sufficient simply to fire one off to a place where its military effects are harmless? Or does one need to make a significant military statement by the initial use of one's nuclear forces, *knowing full well that any military gain thereby achieved is only temporary if the adversary decides to reciprocate?* Does it make sense to use such forces initially against the adversary's cities, even if only one small city is destroyed? That may demonstrate resolve all right, but will it not overly provoke the adversary and cause him to return the blow, when in fact the point of one's initial use was to cause him to stop his military action?

These questions are perplexing. The initial use of nuclear weapons in small numbers involves what Schelling once called "threats that leave something to chance." The line between deliberate escalation in order to stop a war and escalation that gets out of control is a fine one, indeed. By definition, escalatory actions that are taken to manipulate risk involve the chance that they will get out of control. If they could not, there would be no risk, escalation could be controlled, and escalation to manipulate risk would turn into escalation dominance. In competitions in risk taking, the effectiveness of escalatory threats lies precisely in the fact that they can get out of control. Because that is the case, one must worry about how to walk the fine line, how to signal the adversary politically, how to get him to stop, and how to avoid provoking him into his own escalation.

There can be no definitive answers to the questions asked above. But surely common sense dictates that soft counterforce targets— divisions, transportation nodes, and the like—make more sense to threaten initially than countervalue ones if one is trying both to signal resolve and yet not overly to provoke one's adversary. And if that be the case, escalatory threats designed to signal politically must have *some* military effect if they are to have a chance of succeeding. Hence, hitting military targets can make great political sense. Thus, a second underpinning of finite deterrence, an exclusive reliance on countervalue targeting, no longer holds.

Third, finally, surely some war-waging capability is desirable for rapid war termination. Finite deterrers provide a partial answer when they argue that the best way to limit damage in any nuclear war that begins small is to stop it as quickly as possible. But, again, it is not sufficient to leave matters there. We must ask what is required of one's forces and command and control facilities for this to happen. In order to limit damage, two requirements have to be met: first, someone must be in command who has the will and desire to terminate the war; second, he must have control over his forces to limit their use. If a nuclear war begins (and ends) as an all-out spasm response by both sides, the matter of control is academic. But if it begins with a severely limited use of nuclear weapons, we must take some precautions to do what we can to maintain control in order to keep use severely limited. This requires soft counterforce targeting and sufficient investment in command, control, and intelligence capabilities such that we can have reasonable confidence that the national command authority can survive for a few limited exchanges of blows.

What is required for damage limitation in the event a limited nuclear war begins, therefore, is some prudent investment in controllability. What is not required, however, is an investment to endure a protracted and extensive nuclear war. That is beyond the pale of feasibility. Nor is it desirable to engage in extensive counterforce exchanges against hardened targets—the adversary's command and control centers and his nuclear forces—for the reasons outlined earlier. What we should procure are war-waging capabilities that are designed to end the war quickly with severely limited nuclear use. What we must avoid are war-waging capabilities that are designed for long endurance and extensive use. If this be so, that some very limited war-waging flexibility is desired, then the third tenet of the assured destruction school—an opposition to flexibility—also is no longer tenable.

There is a final point that needs to be made. In the mid-eighties, we may be on the verge of a race to build effective population defenses. The MAD-plus position clearly does not call for this type of insurance and in fact finds it dangerous. Is a world in which both superpowers have an assured defense of populations preferable to the one in which they do not? Is the BAD world (Both Assured of Defense) better than the MAD-plus world?

There can be no definitive answer to this question, but informed speculation is in order. A MAD-plus world is one in which the leaders of both superpowers know that, if they do not calculate correctly and tread carefully, events could get out of control. In a MAD world, escalation and loss of control are ever-present contingencies, even if they are almost never ever-present occurrences. As argued above, it is this knowledge that makes MAD nuclear statesmen cautious, restrained, and careful calculators. In a BAD world, however, these restraints would be relaxed. If their populations were thought defendable or invulnerable to retaliatory strikes, BAD statesmen would be more likely to take greater risks. As then Secretary of Defense Harold Brown put it in 1979: "I have always been concerned about massive ABM systems because I have always felt there was some possibility that some clever briefer could delude a political decision maker into thinking that they were going to work." The costs of guessing wrong would presumably be less than in a MAD world if the safety net of population defense worked. A MAD world discourages unwarranted risk taking; a BAD world would not. A MAD world balances terror; a BAD world does not. A MAD world has little or no safety net for bad judgment; a BAD world presumably does.

If, however, a BAD world turns out to be one in which a credible population defense is not really feasible and one in which risk taking is not restrained, then the costs would be horrendous. Historically, for every offensive innovation, there developed a defensive response. But in the past, no weapon possessed the speed and destructive power of nuclear weapons. Population defenses require a degree of perfection to be effective that offensive forces do not. They must be held to a higher standard of workability. There is therefore a gross asymmetry between how well nuclear offenses and defenses have to work in order to be effective that tips the balance toward the offense. Even if the population defense is nearly perfect, it is still not perfect and enough missiles will get through to assure population devastation. For the foreseeable future, therefore, the offense will always get through, either ballistically or in some other fashion.

A 100 percent population defense would be nice to have but so, too, would immortality. If a credible population defense is not presently and foreseeably feasible and if neither superpower would, anyway, sit still and permit its offensive forces to be so stymied, is it not better to live in a world in which the risks of using nuclear weapons are thought to be great, not small? Is the best restraint on nuclear weapons use not fear of the uncertainties surrounding their use? And in this "MAD" world of ours, is it not better to purchase a little bit of extra insurance along the lines of the MAD-plus posture described above?

Escalation Dominance and Competition in Risk-Taking

ROBERT JERVIS

IS DETERRENCE WITHOUT DEFENSE POSSIBLE?

. . . Can a country have the means of deterrence without that of defense? For example, in order to deter a Soviet attack in the Persian Gulf, must the West be physically able to block Russian conquest of the area, as many pronouncements on the countervail ing strategy imply? Or, . . . can the United States deter an attack even though its defense capabilities are inadequate? Can the threat to use force be credible when the force will not directly prevent the other side from reaching its goal? . . .

Official doctrine is . . . ambiguous on this point. The issue is, of course, related to the question discussed earlier of the need to deny the Soviets any gains from aggression, so two statements by Secretary Brown will serve here to reveal the position and its problems: "We must ensure that no adversary would see himself better off after a limited exchange than before it. We cannot permit an enemy to believe that he could create any kind of military or psychological asymmetry that he could then exploit to his advantage." "Our countervailing strategy seeks to deny the Soviets victory, and an improved relative balance would appear to be a minimum condition of 'victory.' "

The essential point in considering the meaning and validity of these statements is the simplest one: barring an unforeseen techno logical breakthrough which would repeal the nuclear revolution, neither side will be able to gain a "victory" or even a "military advantage" in the sense of being able to guarantee the protection of its society during a war. If there is a war and cities and other values are spared, the reason will be that the adversary was persuaded to do so, not that he was deprived of the ability to destroy them. The implications of this vulnerability point in two opposing directions. First, if no outcome which leaves a state decimated can be considered a victory, then it is easy to have the ability to deny victory to the other side. (We will return to the crucial question of what makes

From *The Illogic of American Nuclear Strategy* by Robert Jervis, pp. 126–146. Copyright 1984 by Cornell University. Reprinted by permission of publisher, Cornell University Press. Portions of the text have been omitted; all referential and some explanatory footnotes have also been omitted.

a threat to carry out such destruction credible.) Second, if deterrence without defense is a chimera and what is needed is the ability not only to destroy the other, but also to protect oneself, then the goal is beyond either superpower's reach.

If one tries to argue for a middle position—that denying the Russians any military advantage contributes strongly to deterrence and may even be necessary for it—problems abound. Taken literally, Brown's statement means that the United States needs the ability to ensure that the Russians could not believe that a limited nuclear exchange would leave them better off according to some measure of nuclear power than they were before the war—for instance, a better ratio vis-à-vis remaining Western warheads, megatonnage, or hard-target kill ability. To simplify, let us look only at warheads. Brown's position implies that the United States needs something that is impossible in an era of accurate MIRVs and fixed land-based forces. Under these conditions, attacking the other's ICBMs will yield a warhead ratio vis-à-vis the other which is better than the one that existed before the strike. But it is hard to see this as terribly disturbing. As I noted earlier, no one is much concerned over the long-standing vulnerability of submarines in port, which would allow the Soviets to destroy hundreds of American warheads with only a few of their own. . . .

It can be argued that these situations are not dangerous because although the Russians could improve their military position, they could not gain a meaningful advantage over the United States. In other words, what is important is not ensuring that the Russians would not be better off after the strike than before it, but seeing that their post-strike position was not sufficient to permit them to exact concessions. This makes a bit more sense, but still is not entirely clear since it raises in slightly different form the question of what superiority means. Does it mean that the Russians would be able to outlast the United States in a counterforce war of attrition? That the Soviets could destroy enough American warheads so that the United States could not attack large numbers of OMT and leadership targets? (In the latter case, it should be noted, the relevant comparison is not between American and Soviet warheads but between American warheads and Soviet targets.) In either case, military advantage would be useful only if it could be translated into an ability to terminate the war on acceptable terms. These terms would have to include keeping one's society intact, which could be accomplished only by mutual restraint. Why should the Russians believe that the probability of maintaining this restraint would be greater if they were able to gain an advantage in warheads than it would if they were not? . . .

ESCALATION DOMINANCE VERSUS COMPETITION IN RISK-TAKING

The attempt to escape the nuclear revolution by acquiring the capacity for deterrence by denial is misguided. This capability is not necessary to deter the Soviet Union from adventures and would not produce the desired degree of security even if it were achieved. The enormous costs of a nuclear war—and the costs and risks of lower levels of violence—mean that fear and tolerance of punishment are crucial in modern wars and confrontations. To explore this issue more fully and examine the central issue of the dynamics of bargaining and credibility, we should focus on two conflicting views of the role of force: escalation dominance and "competition in risk-taking." By the latter I mean, following Thomas Schelling, that when all-out war will destroy both sides, maneuvering short of that level of violence is very strongly influenced by each side's willingness to run risks. As I will discuss below, this willingness is not closely linked to the military balance, since military advantage cannot protect the state from destruction. Escalation dominance, by contrast, means having military capabilities that can contain or defeat the adversary at all levels of violence with the possible exception of the highest. (The last phrase is needed because it is hard to talk of one side's having an advantage in an unrestrained nuclear war.) Thus Weinberger argues that deterrence of nuclear war requires that "the Soviets recognize that our forces can and will deny them their objectives at whatever level of nuclear conflict they contemplate." Those who stress the importance of this capacity argue that in the hands of an aggressor it is a strong tool for expansion, and in the hands of a defender it greatly eases the task of maintaining the status quo. If the Russians possessed escalation dominance in Europe, they could launch a war in relative safety because no matter what the West did, it would lose. If NATO did not escalate, it would be defeated. Tactical nuclear weapons would not alter the outcome; they would only create more casualties on both sides. Escalation to limited strategic nuclear war would likewise fail because of superior Russian capability on this level also. The West would be in a very weak position, not only having to bear the onus of escalating at each stage, but unable to prevent a Soviet conquest of Europe by doing so. Thus Senator Sam Nunn's conclusion: "Under conditions of strategic parity and theater nuclear inferiority, a NATO nuclear response to nonnuclear Soviet aggression in Europe would be a questionable strategy at best, a self-defeating one at worst."

Equally, if the West were in a position of escalation dominance the Soviets would be stymied. They would not be able to conquer Western Europe at any level of violence, assuming (and, as we will see, this apparently straightforward assumption is problematic) that the West matched the Soviet behavior—that is, used conventional forces against their conventional army, employed tactical nuclear weapons if they did, and responded to their initiation of limited strategic nuclear strikes with similar moves. Nitze has made a similar argument on the strategic level: "If our counterforce capabilities, survivable after an initial Soviet strike, were sufficient to out-match Soviet residual forces, while our other forces were capable of holding Soviet population and industry in reciprocal danger to our own, the quality of deterrence would be high because the Soviets would know we were in a position to implement a credible military strategy in the event deterrence were to fail."

These arguments rest on three beliefs: that what matters most is what is happening on the battlefield; that deterrence without defense is difficult if not impossible; and that the threat to escalate lacks credibility unless a state can defeat the other side on the level of violence it is threatening to move to (otherwise escalation will only raise costs on both sides).

In criticizing this position I will assume that both sides can predict the military impact of moving to a higher level of violence and that these predictions agree. Given the unprecedented nature of the war, the difficulty of assessing the balance, and the differences between the two sides' perspectives, this is a gross oversimplification. In the actual event, neither NATO nor the USSR could be sure that escalation would not reverse their military fortunes. But the simplification is useful because the situation it assumes is the hardest case for my argument to deal with.

The first problem with the logic of escalation dominance is that a state confident of winning at a given level of violence may yet be deterred because it judges the cost of fighting at that level to be excessive. The other side of this coin is that even if defense cannot succeed, the threat to defend can deter if the potential attacker thinks that the status-quo power is sufficiently strongly motivated to be willing to fight for what it knows will be a losing cause. Nuclear weapons have not changed the fact that victory is not worthwhile if the costs entailed are greater than the gains. . . .

Escalation in a Losing Cause

But what credibility is there in the threat to fight what would be a losing battle? Often, quite a bit: such behavior is common—states usually resist conquest. Even if a state knows it will lose if an adversary persists, the reasons for fighting are several. National honor is one. The desire to harm and weaken the enemy is another, often coupled with the hope of earning a place at the conference table if their allies eventually win. Finally, and most important here, if the state can raise the cost of conquest higher than the value the other side will gain in victory, it can make the contest into a game of Chicken. That is, although war will lead to the state's defeat, the adversary will prefer to make concessions rather than fight. So even when it is obvious that war would damage the state more than the adversary, this does not mean the latter can be sure that the former will not fight; the game of Chicken does not have a determinative solution. Furthermore, if the war lasts a considerable length of time, the adversary may reach the breaking point before the defender, realizing that even though it can win, the price will be excessive. The United States withdrew from Vietnam even though no one doubted that victory was possible.

Increasing the Costs to the Other Side

The second and third lines of rebuttal to the escalation-dominance position stress that the focus on the battlefield, which is a form of conventionalization, is misleading. The second counterargument is that in order to raise the cost to its opponent, the side that is losing can move to a higher level of violence even if it does not believe it can win at that level. A state which realizes this can be deterred even if it thinks it can win the war. For example, when Italy invaded Ethiopia, Britain refrained from attacking the Italian navy not because the British could not have prevailed, but because the expected damage to their own navy was seen to outweigh the benefits. Thus it is not correct to claim that a threat to escalate will be credible if and only if it is believed the action will bring a military victory; one must consider the price that both sides would have to pay. . . . the United States might deter a Soviet invasion of Western Europe by threatening to use tactical nuclear weapons even if the Russians believed that they could win such a war. To gain control of Europe at the cost of having much of Eastern Europe and the Red Army destroyed might not be a good bargain.

But why would a state be willing to escalate if doing so would not bring victory? In the case of the American use of tactical nuclear weapons, such escalation would make a great deal of sense if the American decision-makers believed that war could be kept to this level of violence. For in that case the Soviet Union (and the Europeans) would pay most of the price; although the U.S. army in Europe would presumably be destroyed, the American homeland would remain untouched. Even without this added incentive, however, escalation could be a rational choice for the same reasons that fighting in a losing cause would be: national honor, the desire to harm and weaken those who represent abhorred values, and the belief that the other will retreat rather than pay the price which can be exacted for victory.

The third and most important reason why it is incorrect to

concentrate on who can win on the battlefield is that the war may spread even if no one wants it to. The use of force involves a significant but hard-to-measure possibility of mutually undesired escalation. A state unable to win on the battlefield could thus rationally enter into a conflict in the belief that the other side would rather concede than engage in a struggle which could escalate. Similarly, a state with escalation dominance might avoid a confrontation in the knowledge that while it would win a limited war, the risk that the conflict would expand was excessive. The common claim that militarily effective options are needed is not correct. A state can increase the cost to the other side by making limited attacks on the other's society or by taking other actions that increase the chance of undesired escalation.

A state unwilling to wage all-out war in responding to a major provocation could rationally decide to take actions which it believed entailed, say, a 10 percent chance of leading to such a war. (The difficulty of making such an estimate does not effect the basic point.) The threat to do so could be "implementable," to use Schlesinger's term, and the result can be deterrence without the ability to deny the other its objectives. For example, the Russians would be deterred from invading Western Europe even if they enjoyed escalation dominance if they believed that probable Western responses would create an unacceptable risk of world war. Risk, of course, puts pressures on both sides. But a given level of risk may be acceptable to the defender of the status quo and intolerable to an aggressor; the threat to raise the risk to a given level may be credible when made by the former and not credible when made by the latter. The fact that deterrence is usually easier than compellence aids the status-quo power.

Risk-Taking and Military Advantage

What is crucial in this context is that the ability to tolerate and raise the level of risk is not closely tied to military superiority. Because the credibility of the threat to escalate is not determined by the military effectiveness of the action, escalation dominance does not give any state a great advantage. If NATO leaders were willing to tolerate increased destruction and increased risk of all-out war, they could escalate from conventional to tactical nuclear warfare even if they did not expect this action to turn the tide of battle. On the other hand, if they believed escalation could halt the Russian invasion, but only at an intolerable risk of all-out war, their position would be weak. . . .

The links between military power—both local and global—and states' behavior in crisis are thus tenuous. Escalation dominance does not make it safe to stand firm. As Thomas Schelling points out,

"Being able to lose a local war in a dangerous and provocative manner may make the risk . . . outweigh the apparent gains to the other side." Similarly, even "if the tactical advantages are unimpressive, one's purpose in enlarging some limited war may be to confront the enemy with a heightened risk." The exact location of the battle lines and the question whether American troops are pushing back Soviet forces or vice versa matter much less than each side's beliefs about whether the war can be kept limited. This is true not only for warfare in Europe or the Persian Gulf, but also for nuclear counterforce wars. Imagine a situation in which the Russians believed that they could gain advantages, in terms of various measures of residual strategic forces, over the United States in a missile duel. What would they gain thereby? As Warner Schilling has noted, "the strategic debate has focused on numbers of missiles and warheads as if they were living creatures whose survival was of value in their own right, to the near exclusion of any effort to relate these military means to potential differences in the war outcomes among which statesmen might actually be able to discriminate in terms of the values about which they do care." Since a state cannot protect itself by destroying many of the other side's weapons, an advantage in remaining warheads could help it reach an acceptable termination of the war only if its adversary was persuaded or coerced into sparing cities.

This outcome might be the result if both sides waged a purely counterforce war, although even then the destruction would be so great that the costs to the "winner" might well outweigh the gains. But even if the Russians were confident that they would come out ahead in this contest, could they expect that the United States would limit its response to Soviet strategic forces and exhaust its forces while leaving Soviet cities intact? The reply, of course, is that the United States would be restrained by the Soviet threat to respond in kind. But the crucial point is that each side's hold over the other's cities is not affected by who is "ahead" in the counterforce exchange. It is hard to imagine the Russians thinking "that in the aftermath of a Soviet nuclear strike . . . an American president [would] tote up the residual megatonnage or [warheads] of both sides and sue for peace or even surrender if his side came up short."

Now that the state which is losing can do overwhelming damage to the superior power, military superiority even on several levels is not controlling. In discussing the Cuban missile crisis, Bernard Brodie puts the point very well. "The essential question was: How much did the strictly local forces affect the Russians' willingness to open hostilities with us—or, for that matter, our willingness to get into such hostilities with them? And the answer clearly was, little or none—unless both sides had been completely convinced that a quite considerable shooting war could develop on the spot without its substantially widening and incurring extremely grave risk of nuclear weapons being introduced." . . .

Resolve and Threats That Leave Something to Chance

The threat of escalation implicit in the limited use of force acts through two related mechanisms, neither of which is linked to the local military balance. First, the use of force demonstrates a state's resolve, its willingness to run high risks rather than retreat. It provides evidence that the state will continue to fight and even escalate further unless a satisfactory settlement can be arranged. Of course it does not prove this; the state may be bluffing or its resolve may melt in the face of a firm response. But it gives some credibility to its threats. For example, during the Cuban missile crisis it seems that Kennedy's "quest for a means of impressing Khrushchev with his determination was provided . . . by United States naval harassment of . . . Soviet submarines."

The second mechanism involves the threat of unintended as opposed to intended escalation. As Brodie points out, "violence between great opponents is inherently difficult to control." The implications are best discussed by Thomas Schelling, whose formulation I cannot improve upon:

> The idea . . . that a country cannot plausibly threaten to engage in a general war over anything but a mortal assault on itself unless it has an appreciable capacity to blunt the other side's attack seems to depend on the clean-cut notion that war results—or is expected to result—only from a deliberate yes-no decision. But if war tends to result from a process, a dynamic process in which both sides get more and more concerned not to be a slow second in case the war starts, it is not a "credible first strike" that one threatens, but just plain war. The Soviet Union can indeed threaten us with war: they can even threaten us with a war that we eventually start, by threatening to get involved with us in a process that blows up into war. And some of the arguments about "superiority" and "inferiority" seem to imply that one of the two sides, being weaker, must absolutely fear and concede while the other, being stronger, may confidently expect the other to yield. There is undoubtedly a good deal to the notion that the country with the less impressive military capability may be less feared, and the other may run the riskier course in a crisis; other things being equal, one anticipates that the strategically "superior" country has some advantage. But this is a far cry from the notion that the two sides just measure up to each other and one bows before the other's superiority and acknowledges that he was only bluffing. Any situation that scares one side will scare both sides with the danger of a war that neither wants, and both will have to pick their way carefully through the crisis, never quite sure that the other knows how to avoid stumbling over the brink.

Schelling's concept of the threat that leaves something to chance is crucial to understanding this process. This is the threat to do something which could lead to still further escalation even though the state might not want that to occur. Any time military forces are set in motion, there is a danger that things will get out of control. Statesmen cannot be sure that they will; if they could be, then the threat to take initial action would be no more credible than the threat to wage all-out war. But no one can be sure that they will not; the workings of machines and the reaction of humans in time of stress cannot be predicted with high confidence. Morton Halperin has pointed out that there are two kinds of escalation: one that results from an explicit decision to increase the scope, area, or level of violence in a measured fashion and the other that involves an unintended "explosion" and a disastrous leap to all-out war. Willingness to engage in the former implies a belief that the latter is not inevitable, but it also exerts pressures by increasing the chance that the latter will occur.

Because confrontations and the use of violence unleash forces whose results cannot be predicted with confidence, states can deter a wide range of transgressions without making specific threats about what they will do in the event that the other takes the forbidden actions. The deterrent may be effective even if the threat to respond, when viewed as an isolated act, is not. This point is missed by those who hold the frequently expressed view that the American "threat of nuclear response has . . . lost credibility with respect to Western Europe and has virtually none at all as a deterrent to Soviet action in China, Southwest Asia, or Eastern Europe." This claim is probably valid for the contingency that the United States would use nuclear weapons as an immediate response to a Soviet invasion of China or Iran. But the common phrase "the credibility of the American threat" is misleading. The problem the Soviets face is not only that the United States might fulfill any commitments it had made, but also that their action could start a process the end result of which would be disaster. Could the Russians really be confident that a major attack on China would not lead to the involvement of U.S. strategic forces, especially if Chinese and Soviet nuclear weapons were employed? Could they be certain that the use of military force in the Persian Gulf would not lead to a general war?

It is in the wider context of the possible chain of effects which violent change in the status quo could set off that the influence of nuclear weapons must be seen. A state may then be deterred even if it is sure that its adversary's initial response will not be to carry out its threat; states contemplating expansion must be concerned not with how their efforts would begin, but how they would end. If the Russians attacked Europe and NATO resisted, nuclear war could readily result even if the United States did not immediately launch SAC. States cannot carefully calibrate the level of risks that they are running. They cannot be sure how close they are to the brink of war. . . .

Although undesired escalation obviously does not occur all the time, the danger is always present. The room for misunderstanding, the pressure to act before the other side has seized the initiative, the role of unexpected defeats or unanticipated opportunities, all are sufficiently great—and interacting—so that it is rare that decision-makers can confidently predict the end-point of the trajectory which an initial resort to violence starts. . . .

Willingness to Run Risks

Because the threat that leaves something to chance exerts pressure on both sides, it is not an automatic way to protect the status quo. The function of crises, then, is to create risks which, given the existence of mutual vulnerability, will bring pressure to bear on both sides. As Brodie argued soon after the Cuban missile conflict, the fact that states can take actions which create " 'some' risk [of nuclear war] is what makes [crisis bargaining] possible. We rarely have to threaten general war. We threaten instead the next in a series of moves that seems to tend in that direction. The opponent has the choice of making the situation more dangerous, or less so. This is all pretty obvious when stated, but so much of the theorizing . . . about the inapplicability of the nuclear deterrent to the future overlooks this simple fact."

Indeed it is missed by those who stress the importance of escalation dominance. If confrontations and crises can get out of hand and lead to total war, advantages on the battlefield have little significance. They are hard to translate into successful war termination and as long as conflict continues, both sides will be primarily concerned with the danger of all-out war. Thus crises and limited wars involving both superpowers are competitions in risk-taking. A state which has gained battlefield victories but finds the risks implicit in continued fighting intolerable will be likely to make concessions; a state which is losing on the ground but finds this verdict so painful that it is willing to undergo still higher levels of pain and danger is likely to prevail. What is often crucial, then, are each side's judgments of the chances that the conflict will expand, the willingness of each to bear costs and risks, and its perceptions of the other's willingness to do so. . . .

This analysis refutes the basic position of the countervailing strategy put forth by Harold Brown . . .—the importance of maintaining military advantage: the United States "seek(s) to convince the Soviets that they could not win . . . a [limited] war, and thus to deter them from starting one." While this ability probably contributes to deterrence, it is not necessary for it. Being able to do better than the adversary in a limited war does not make it safe to engage in such a conflict. For example, it was fear of unpredictable escalation rather than lack of military options which led the Truman administration to refrain from expanding the Korean conflict to encompass the enemy forces in China. Likewise, the Soviet Union has long been deterred from moving against Berlin not by lack of local superiority, but by fear of escalation, either intended or uncontrolled. . . . It is important to remember that the costs of a conflict include not only the losses incurred at that level of violence, but also the danger of undesired consequences which are not under the complete control of either party. Luckily, decision-makers are less apt to overlook this than are analysts. . . .

Thus it is clear that escalation dominance is not necessary for deterrence. In principle it is not sufficient for deterrence either. A state superior at all levels of violence could decide to allow its adversary to alter the status quo rather than pay the price of a limited conflict and the chance of escalation to mutually unacceptable levels. I cannot think of any important cases which fit this description, however. States do not seem able to use the lever of competition in risk-taking to force others to abandon territory they control or positions of influence they have established.[1]

Soviet Views

Although the Soviets ridicule the notion of using nuclear weapons for political bargaining, they understand the dangers and uses of unintended escalation very well. As Benjamin Lambeth has shown, their writings are full of appreciation for the unpredictability of military ventures. The same attitude was revealed by Khrushchev during the Cuban missile crisis. In his letter to Kennedy which opened the way for an agreement, he said:

> If you have not lost command of yourself and realize clearly what this could lead to, then, Mr. President, you and I should not now pull on the ends of the rope in which you have tied a knot of war, because the harder you and I pull, the tighter this knot will become. And a time may come when this knot is tied so tight that the person who tied it is no longer capable of untying it, and then the knot will have to be cut. What that would mean I need not explain to you, because you yourself understand perfectly what dread forces our two countries possess.

Khrushchev also clearly perceived the role of the limited use of force in this process for he stressed the need "to avert contact of

---

[1] Of course when one state feels much more strongly than another the former can prevail, even in compellence, although it is militarily inferior at all levels. Thus Iceland was able to win the Cod War against England. In many cases, a strong ally will make concessions to a weaker one because the costs are less for it than for its partner and both sides would suffer greatly if relations badly deteriorated.

our ships, and, consequently, a deepening of the crisis, which because of this contact can spark off the fire of military conflict, after which any talks would be superfluous because other forces and other laws would begin to operate—the laws of war." After the crisis, he justified his concessions in terms of the prudence required by "the smell of scorching in the air." So whatever doctrinal differences exist between the United States and the USSR, they do not seem to affect this point. It is possible, of course, that if American leaders argue loudly and persuasively enough that nuclear war can be controlled, the Soviets will lose their fear. This could be particularly dangerous because there is some evidence that the Soviets are willing to engage in provocations when they think they can control the risks and pull back to safety if their probes create a dangerous situation. But at this point the Russians show a healthy skepticism toward the idea that control is easy or even possible.

As long as decision-makers realize that things can get out of hand, crises and the limited use of force will have most of their impact because they generate risks even if neither side explicitly affirms this view. In other words, I am not arguing that the United States is facing a choice between escalation dominance and competition in risk-taking as ways of bringing pressure to bear. Even though it can choose the former as the basis for declaratory and procurement policy, it cannot escape from the fact that in tense situations, decision-makers are going to be preoccupied with the danger of all-out war. Since military advantage cannot control the risk of escalation, the attempt to banish this element cannot succeed no matter what Western policy is.

Similarly, mutual assured destruction exists as a fact, irrespective of policy. No amount of flexibility, no degree of military superiority at levels less than all-out war, can change the fundamental attribute of the nuclear age. Not only can each side destroy the other if it chooses, but that outcome can grow out of conflict even if no one wants it to. Most of the dilemmas of U.S. defense policy stem from the vulnerability of its cities, not from policies which might permit the Soviets marginal military advantages in unlikely and terribly risky contingencies. Once each side can destroy the other, any crisis brings up the possibility of this disastrous outcome. Standing firm, although often necessary, has a significant degree of risk which cannot be much reduced by the development of a wider range of military options. Carrying out actions that are militarily effective does not take one's society out of hostage; what undercuts the credibility of the American threats is not that they cannot deny the Soviets any gain or advantage, but that carrying them out may lead to disaster.

Defense In Space Is Not 'Star Wars'

ZBIGNIEW BRZEZINSKI, ROBERT JASTROW, and MAX M. KAMPELMAN

Faith moves mountains. When it is in eternal religious values, faith is an indispensable strength of the human spirit. When it is directed toward political choices, it is often an excuse for an analytic paralysis.

Regrettably, our national debate over President Reagan's suggestion that the country develop a strategic defense against a Soviet nuclear attack is taking on a theological dimension that has no place in a realistic search for a path out of the world's dilemma. The idea of basing our security on the ability to defend ourselves deserves serious consideration. . . .

For many years, our search for security has been restricted to designing offensive weapons to deter aggression through fear of reprisals. We must not abandon nuclear deterrence until we are convinced that a better means is at hand. But we cannot deny that, for both the Soviet Union and the United States, the costs, insecurities and tensions surrounding this search for newer, more effective and more accurate nuclear missiles produce a profound unease that in itself undermines stability.

The conventional view is that stability in the nuclear age is based on two contradictory pursuits: the acquisition of increasingly efficient nuclear weapons and the negotiation of limits and reductions in such weapons. The United States is diligently pursuing both objectives, but the complexity of arriving at effectual arms control agreements is becoming apparent as more precise and mobile weapons, with multiple warheads, appear on both sides. Unlike ours, moreover, many Soviet missile silos are reloadable, and thus the number of silos does not indicate the number of missiles, further complicating verification.

We must never ignore the reality that the overwhelming majority of the Soviet strategic forces is composed of primarily first-strike weaponry. And given the large numbers of first-strike Soviet SS-17, -18 and -19 land-based missiles, no responsible American leader can make decisions about security needs without acknowledging that a Soviet first strike can become a practical option.

From *New York Times Magazine*, January 27, 1985, pp. 28, 29, 46, 48, 51. Copyright 1985 by The New York Times Company. Reprinted by permission.

The Russians could strike us first by firing the reloadable portion of their nuclear arsenal at our missiles, the Strategic Air Command and nuclear submarine bases, and if the surviving American forces (essentially nuclear submarines) were to respond, the Russians could immediately counter by attacking our cities with missiles from nonreloadable silos and, a few hours later, with whatever of their first-strike reloadable weapons had survived our counterattack. They are set up for launching three salvos to our one.

To us, this catastrophic exchange is unthinkable. But, with the strong probability that the American response would be badly crippled at the outset by a Soviet strike, some Russian leader could someday well consider such a potential cost bearable in the light of the resulting "victory." Furthermore, such an analysis might well anticipate that an American president, knowing that a strike against our cities would inevitably follow our response to a Soviet first strike, might choose to avoid such a catastrophe by making important political concessions. No responsible American president can permit this country to have to live under such a threat, not to speak of the hypothetical danger of having to choose either annihilation or submission to nuclear blackmail. Hence the understandable and continual drive for more effective offensive missiles to provide greater deterrence.

The result is that weapons technology is shaping an increasingly precarious American-Soviet strategic relationship. For this reason, we urge serious consideration be given to whether some form of Strategic Defense Initiative (S.D.I.) might not be stabilizing, enhancing to deterrence and even helpful to arms control. To that end, we address the major issues in strategic defense from three points of view:

(1) The technical: Is a defense against missiles technically and budgetarily feasible?

(2) The strategic: Is a defense against missiles strategically desirable? Does it enhance or diminish stability? Does it enhance or diminish the prospects for arms control and a nuclear-weapons build-down?

(3) The political: What are the political implications of strategic defense for our own country and for our relations with our allies? What are the implications for the larger dimensions of our relationship with the Soviet Union? How do we seek the needed domestic consensus on a viable strategy?

A great deal has been written about the state of missile defense technology. Some experts say the technology sought is unattainable, others that it is merely unattainable in this generation. Yet the promise of the Strategic Defense Initiative is real. Some of the technologies are mature and unexotic. Their deployment around the end of this decade would involve mainly engineering development. Technically, these vital defenses could be in place at this moment were it not for the constraints accepted by the United States in its adherence to the antiballistic missile treaty of 1972.

With development and some additional research, we can now construct and deploy a two-layer or double-screen defense, which can be in place by the early 1990's at a cost we estimate to be somewhere in the neighborhood of $80 billion. A conservative estimate of the effectiveness of each layer would be 70 percent. The combined effectiveness of the two layers would be over 90 percent: Less than one Soviet warhead in 10 would reach its target—more than sufficient to discourage Soviet leaders from any thought of achieving a successful first strike.

The first layer in the two-layer defense system—the "boost-phase" defense—would go into effect as a Soviet first-strike missile, or "booster," carrying multiple warheads rises above the atmosphere at the beginning of its trajectory. This boost-phase defense—based on interception and destruction by nonnuclear projectiles—would depend on satellites for the surveillance of the Soviet missile field and the tracking of missiles as they rise from their silos. These operations could only be carried out from space platforms orbiting over the Soviet Union. Because they are weightless in orbit, such platforms could be protected against attack by heavy armor, on-board weapons and maneuverability.

After the booster has burned out and fallen away, the warheads arc through space on their way to the United States. The second layer of the defense—the terminal defense—comes into play as the warheads descend. Interception would be at considerable altitude, above the atmosphere if possible. This second phase requires further engineering, already under way, because interception above the atmosphere makes it difficult to discriminate between real warheads and decoys. In the interim, interception can take place in the atmosphere, where differences in air drag separate warheads from decoys. In either event, destruction of the warheads would take place at sufficiently high altitudes, above 100,000 feet, so that there would be no ground damage from warheads designed to explode when approached by an intercepting missile.

Of the two layers in the defense, the boost phase is by far the most important. It would prevent the Russians from concentrating their warheads on such high-priority targets as the national-command authority (the chain of command, beginning with the President, for ordering a nuclear strike), key intercontinental-ballistic missile silos or the Trident submarine pens, because they could not predict which booster and which warheads would escape destruction and get through.

This fact is important. Simply a so-called "point defense" of our missile silos, it has been suggested, would be sufficient to restore much of the credibility of our land-based deterrent, now compromised by 6,000 Soviet ICBM warheads. It is particularly necessary to protect the 550 silos containing our Minuteman III ICBM's, of which 300 have the highly precise Mark 12A warheads. These are the only missiles in the possession of the United States with the combination of yield and accuracy required to destroy hardened Soviet military sites and the 1,500 hardened bunkers that would shelter the Soviet leadership. But their very importance to us illustrates the difficulty of a point defense, because the value of the silos to us means they will be among the highest-priority targets in any Soviet first strike. The Russians can overwhelm any point defense we place around those silos, if they wish to do so, by allocating large numbers of warheads to these critical targets. But if we include a boost-phase defense to destroy their warheads at the time of firing, their objective becomes enormously more difficult to accomplish.

The boost-phase defense has still another advantage. It could effectively contend with the menace of the Soviet SS-18's, monster missiles twice the size of the 97.5-ton MX. Each SS-18 carries 10 warheads, but probably could be loaded with up to 30. The Russians could thus add thousands of ICBM warheads to their arsenal at relatively modest cost. With numbers like that, the costs favor the Russians. But a boost-phase defense can eliminate all a missile's warheads at one time—an effective response to the SS-18 problem.

The likely technology for an early use of the boost-phase defense would use "smart" nonnuclear projectiles that home in on the target, using radar or heat waves, and destroy it on impact. The technology is close at hand and need not wait for the availability of the more devastating but less mature technologies of the laser, the neutral particle beam or the electromagnetic rail gun. The interceptor rocket for this early boost-phase defense could be derived from air-defense interceptors that will soon be available, or the technology of antisatellite missiles (ASAT) launched from F-15 aircraft. These rockets could weigh about 500 pounds, the nonnuclear supersonic projectiles about 10 pounds.

Interceptor rockets would be stored in pods on satellites and fired from space. The tracking information needed to aim the rockets would also be acquired from satellites orbiting over the Soviet missile fields. The so-called "space weapons" of strategic defense are indispensable for the crucial boost-phase defense. To eliminate them would destroy the usefulness of the defense.

We estimate that the cost of establishing such a boost-phase defense by the early 1990's would be roughly $45 billion. That price tag includes 100 satellites, each holding 150 interceptors—sufficient to counter a mass Soviet attack from all their 1,400 silos; plus four geosynchronous satellites and 10 low-altitude satellites dedicated to surveillance and tracking; plus the cost of facilities for ground-control communications and battle management.

The technology used for the terminal defense could be a small, nonnuclear homing interceptor with a heat-seeking sensor, which would be launched by a rocket weighing one to two tons and costing a few million dollars each. Interception would take place above the atmosphere, if possible, to give wider "area" protection to the terrain below. These heat-seeking interceptors can be available for deployment in about five years if a decision is reached to follow that course. . . .

The technology for a terminal defense within the atmosphere would be somewhat different, but would probably also depend on heat-seeking missiles. The cost of this terminal layer of defense would be about $15 billion and include $10 billion for 5,000 interceptors, plus $5 billion for 10 aircraft carrying instruments for tracking of the Soviet warheads.

The estimated $60 billion for this two-layer defense is a ball-park figure, of course. However, even with its uncertainties, it is surely an affordable outlay for protecting our country from a nuclear first strike.

To be sure, the above is not an attractive option to those who place all their eggs in the arms control basket and underestimate the immense difficulty of attaining an effective and truly verifiable pact. It is also not appealing to those wedded to the idea that it is best to assure survival by simply maintaining the perilous balance of terror between the United States and the Soviet Union. We favor energetically pursuing arms-control negotiations and seeking to achieve credible deterrence, but these options by themselves are unfortunately not as likely to provide a more secure future as the alternative strategy of mutual security combining defense against missiles with retaliatory offense.

The simplest and most appealing option, quite naturally, is comprehensive arms control. Large reductions in both launchers and warheads, as well as effective restrictions on surreptitious deployment or qualitative improvements, would enhance nuclear stability and produce greater mutual confidence. It would, if properly negotiated and effectively monitored, enhance mutual survival.

How likely is such a future? Some progress in arms control is probably possible, but genuinely effective arms control would require that: (1) there be a restraint imposed on qualitative weapons enhancement; (2) mobile systems, relatively easy to deploy secretly, be subject to some form of direct verification; (3) a method be devised for distinguishing nuclear-armed and nonnuclear cruise missiles, and (4) monitoring arrangements be devised for preventing surreptitious development, testing and deployment of new systems. So far, the Soviet record of compliance with the SALT I and SALT II accords is sufficiently troubling to warrant skepticism regarding the likelihood of implementing any such complex and far-reaching agreement.

Moreover, such an agreement would have to recognize that it is no longer possible to limit space-based systems without imposing a simultaneous limit, along the above lines, on terrestrially deployed systems, which prevent the greater threat to survival. After all, the space-based defenses include no weapons of mass destruction and no nuclear weapons. And it should be some cause for concern to note the Soviet insistence on prohibiting space-based *defensive systems*, the only method now available to inhibit the first-strike use of land-based Soviet offensive systems.

Finally; a comprehensive and genuinely verifiable agreement, limiting both qualitatively and quantitatively the respective strategic forces, on earth and in space, will require a much more felicitous political climate than currently exists. Negotiations may lead to such improvement, but in the setting of intense and profound geopolitical rivalry, how realistic is it to expect in the near future accommodation sufficient to generate the political will essential for a genuine breakthrough in arms-control negotiations? The mere mentions of Afghanistan, Nicaragua, Sakharov and Soviet violations of the humanitarian provisions of the Helsinki Final Act dramatize the depths of the problem. There may be no direct negotiating linkage between these acts of Soviet misconduct and arms control, but their political interaction is evident.

This is why there is currently such an emphasis on maintaining peace via the doctrine of deterrence based on mutual assured destruction, called MAD. But what does this mean in an age when weapons are becoming incredibly precise, mobile and difficult to count? In the absence of a miraculous breakthrough in arms control, the only possible protection within the framework of the deterrence approach is to stockpile more offensive systems. This is in part what we are doing. But how many of such systems will be needed in the likely conditions of the next decade? If Soviet strategic forces continue to grow both quantitatively and qualitatively, our country will have to deploy, at enormous cost, probably no fewer than 1,500 to 2,000 mobile Midgetmen to preserve deterrence. How will they be deployed? Where? And at what cost? And will the Soviet Union and the United States be more or less secure with the deployment of such precise weaponry capable of effective preemption? The Soviet answer is clear: The Russians are busy enhancing the survivability of their leadership and of their key facilities by hardening, dispersal and deception.

This second traditional alternative, mutual assured destruction, cannot be an acceptable, long-run option, although it is a necessary policy in the absence of an alternative, given the dynamics of weapons technology. Thus, a new third option, the Strategy of Mutual Security, must be explored as preferable.The combination of defense against space missiles with retaliatory offense in reserve enhances deterrence.

And it does not compromise stability, even if only the United States were initially to have such a strategic defense. The deployment of the systems described above would not give us absolute protection from Soviet retaliation against a possible first strike by us, a reasonable though misplaced Soviet concern. Furthermore, the Russians know we are not deploying first-strike counterforce systems in sufficient numbers to make a first strike by us feasible. In any case, we can be quite certain that the Russians will also be moving to acquire an enhanced strategic defense, even if they do not accept President Reagan's offer to share ours. Indeed, they are doing so now and have been for some time.

As our strategic space-defense initiative expands incrementally, it should be realistically possible to scale down our offensive forces. Such a transition, first of the United States and eventually of the Soviet Union, into a genuinely defensive posture, with neither side posing a first-strike threat to the other, would not only be stabilizing but it would also be most helpful to the pursuit of more far-reaching arms control agreements. Strategic defense would compensate for the inevitable difficulties of verification and for the absence of genuine trust by permitting some risk-taking in such agreements. This is another reason why strategic defense should not be traded in the forthcoming negotiations in return for promises that can be broken at any time

No significant public policy can be carried out in a democracy without being fully discussed and accepted by the broad polity. Nor can an interested public be expected to resolve disputes among experts as to questions of technical feasibility. The current debate over President Reagan's initiative for a strategic defense program suffers from that conflict among scientists. It is important to clarify this issue.

We can begin a two-tiered strategic defense that would protect command structure as well as our missiles and silos and thus discourage any thoughts by the Soviet military that a first-strike effort would be effective. Some within the scientific community minimize the importance of this technical feasibility and emphasize instead the view that it is scientifically impossible today to provide

a strategic defense that will protect our cities. Such a broad defense
of populations is today not feasible, but it is prudent for our society
to keep in mind the rising tide of technical and scientific advances
so rapidly overwhelming the 20th century.

The "impossible" is a concept we should use with great hesitation. It is foolhardy to predict the timing of innovations. We are
persuaded that the laws of physics do not in any way prevent the
technical requirements of a defensive shield that would protect
populations as well as weapons. A total shield should remain our
ultimate objective, but there is every reason for us to explore
transitional defenses, particularly because the one we have discussed would serve to deter the dangers of a first strike. Defenses
against ballistic missiles can be effective without being "perfect,"
and the technology for this is nearly in hand.

Society must also not forget that ever since the beginning of the
scientific age, the organized scientific community has not had a
particularly good record of predicting developments that were not
part of the common wisdom of the day. In 1926, for example, A. W.
Bickerton, a British scientist, said it was scientifically impossible to
send a rocket to the moon. In the weapons field, United States Adm.
William D. Leahy told President Harry S. Truman in 1945: "That
[atomic] bomb will never go off, and I speak as an expert in
explosives." And Dr. Vannevar Bush, who directed the Government's World War II science effort, said after the war that he
rejected the talk "about a 3,000-mile rocket shot from one continent
to the other carrying an atomic bomb . . . and we can leave that out
of our thinking." In the strategic area, as late as 1965, the capable
Secretary of Defense Robert S. McNamara wrote: "There is no
indication that the Soviets are seeking to develop a strategic force
as large as our own."

Our debate and our discussion, furthermore, must not ignore
what the Russians, who have always understood the need for
defenses, are doing in space. They have spent more on strategic
defensive forces since the anti-ballistic missile (ABM) treaty was
signed in 1972 than on strategic offensive forces. Their antisatellite
program began nearly two decades ago. The Soviet military is now
working aggressively on a nationwide missile-defense system; and it
now appears ready to deploy a system capable of defending the
country not only against aircraft, but also many types of ballistic
missiles. Clearly, the Soviet work in strategic defense has taken
place in spite of ABM treaty provisions. The large radar installation
in central Siberia expressly violates that treaty with us. Yet the
planning for it must have begun many years ago.

The recent Geneva meeting must be considered a major productive result of President Reagan's March 1983 speech announcing

that we would begin developing a strategic defense initiative. We are reminded that in 1967 President Lyndon B. Johnson proposed to Prime Minister Aleksei N. Kosygin a ban on ABM's, which was flatly rejected. In 1969, President Nixon proposed to the Congress that our country begin such an ABM program, because the Russians showed little desire to join us in prohibiting such weapons. Shortly after Congress approved that program, the Russians embraced the idea of an ABM treaty. Had our Government not announced its S.D.I. program, we might still be in the cold storage of the Soviet freeze precipitated by their walking out of the Geneva negotiations.

Arms control has been said to be at a dead end, and the stalemate has reflected an impasse in thought and in conception. Our present policy requires both us and the Soviet Union to rely on a theory of mutual annihilation based on a strategic balance of offensive weapons. The American approach has been to depend on deterrence alone and not on defending ourselves from Soviet offensive weapons, while the Russians have made it clear by their actions that they intend to defend themselves against our missiles. In any event, what is clear is that mankind must find ways of lifting itself out of this balance of terror. Mutual assured destruction must be replaced by mutual assured survival. Our safety cannot depend on our having no defense against missiles. The proper role of government is to protect the country from aggression, not merely avenge it. It is astounding that a President should be faulted for seeking a formula and an approach that will protect us from the continual threats and terrors coming from the volatile vagaries of adventurism and miscalculation.

Even if a perfect defense of our population should be impossible to achieve—and none of us can be certain of that—the leaders of our Government have a responsibility to seek defense alternatives designed to complicate and frustrate aggression by our adversaries. The very injection of doubt into their calculations strengthens the prospect of hesitation and deterrence. It may not be possible to destroy the world's ballistic missiles, but if we can return them to the status of a retaliatory deterrent rather than a pre-emptive strike we will have reduced the need for the existing large arsenal and thereby the threat of war.

The argument has been made that the S.D.I. is politically harmful because our North Atlantic Treaty Organization allies have not received the initiative with any enthusiasm. Their skepticism is an understandable initial reaction. First of all, our allies were taken by surprise by the President's March proposal of a Strategic Defense Initiative. At times, secret discussions are necessary, but doubtless allied cooperation will be forthcoming in direct proportion to timely and honest consultation. Furthermore, European political leaders feel under great pressure from an activist peace movement that emphasizes traditional arms-control negotiations as a major objective. A new approach, which the Russians criticize as hostile, is, therefore, looked upon as troubling, regardless of its merit.

As to the substance of the initiative, coupling our national security interest with that of our allies is a foundation of NATO defense. Any tendency toward decoupling produces great concern on their part. Western European leaders look upon all security proposals with that criterion in mind. Should America technically succeed in providing a shield against missiles, Europeans wonder whether they would then not be left in an exposed position, facing a superior Soviet conventional military force.

The concerns may be understandable, but will diminish with time and discussion. First of all, President Reagan's call for strategic defense brought the Russians back to the Geneva negotiating table. More important, however, it will become increasingly evident to our friends, as some of the confusion about the technology dissipates, that the ability of the United States to protect its missiles immeasurably strengthens our power to deter and thereby serves to protect our allies. Indeed, such a system is expected to be at least as effective against the SS-20's aimed at western Europe as it is against ICBM's. Finally, a development pulling the world away from the precipice of nuclear terror goes far to help create an encouraging atmosphere for dialogue and agreement, a vital prerequisite for peace.

In light of the above, we reach two basic conclusions:

(1) Developing a stabilizing, limited two-tier strategic defense capability is desirable and called for by the likely strategic conditions immediately ahead. Such a deployment would be helpful both in the military and in the political dimensions. It is a proper response to the challenge posed by political uncertainties and the dynamics of weapons development. The two-layered defense described here can be deployed by the early 1990's. Americans will rest easier when that limited defense is in place, for it will mean that the prospect of a Soviet first strike is almost nil.

(2) A three- or four-layer defense, using such advanced technologies as the laser now under investigation in the research phase of the Strategic Defense Initiative, may become a reality by the end of the century. If this research shows an advanced system to be practical, its deployment may well boost the efficiency of our defense to a level so close to perfection as to signal a final end to the era of nuclear ballistic missiles. A research program offering such enormous potential gains in our security must be pursued, in spite of the fact that a successful outcome cannot be assured at this juncture.

The current debate is necessary. There are many questions, technical and political, ahead of us. For the debate to be constructive, however, we must overcome the tendency to politicize it on a partisan basis. Our objectives should be to find a way out of the current maze of world terror. The President's initiative toward that end is a major contribution to arms control and stability. The aim of making nuclear weapons impotent and obsolete should be encouraged and not savaged.

Why Even Good Defenses May Be Bad

CHARLES L. GLASER

Once again, the United States is in the midst of a debate over whether to deploy defenses designed to protect U.S. cities and population from Soviet missile attack. This debate is, most immediately, the result of President Reagan's "star wars" speech, in which he asked the rhetorical question: "wouldn't it be better to save lives than to avenge them?" He offered a future vision of "truly lasting stability" based upon the "ability to counter the awesome Soviet missile threat with measures that are defensive." Just six months later a senior interagency group recommended to the President that the "U.S. embark on early demonstrations of credible ballistic missile defense technologies to its allies and the Soviet Union."

There is, in addition to this most recent catalyst, a deep-seated, enduring reason why the possibility of defending the United States from Soviet nuclear attack is a recurrent issue. Put most simply, it is quite natural for the United States to want to remove itself from a situation in which the Soviet Union has the capability to virtually destroy it. The United States cannot, today, physically prevent the Soviet Union from wreaking such destruction. U.S. security therefore depends upon its ability to deter Soviet nuclear attack. If deterrence works, then the United States will be able to avoid nuclear war with the Soviet Union. Unfortunately, the possibility that deterrence could fail cannot be easily dismissed. Deterrence will have to work for decades and centuries—that is, unless the current situation, in which the United States is vulnerable to Soviet nuclear attack, is dramatically altered. While one cannot specify with confidence the way in which the superpowers' nuclear arsenals

From "Why Even Good Defenses May Be Bad" by Charles L. Glaser, *International Security*, Fall 1984 (Vol. 9, No. 2) pp. 25–56. © 1984 by the President and Fellows of Harvard College and of the Massachusetts Institute of Technology. Reprinted by permission of MIT Press, Cambridge, Massachusetts, and the copyright holders. Portions of the text have been omitted; all referential and some explanatory footnotes have also been omitted.

The author would like to thank Robert Art, Albert Carnesale, Lynn Eden, Michael Nacht, Thomas Schelling, Stephen Van Evera, Stephen Walt, and the members of the Avoiding Nuclear War working group for their helpful comments on earlier drafts of this article.

might come to be used, knowing that deterrence could fail in a variety of ways is sufficient to create a feeling that, given enough time, deterrence will fail. Consequently, as long as the United States remains vulnerable to Soviet nuclear attack, the possibility of nuclear attack will create an interest in defense against it.

The current debate over the deployment of ballistic missile defense (BMD), like the one in the late 1960s, is highly polarized. . . . The vast majority of the debate has pivoted on the technological feasibility of effective BMD. The implicit assumption is that if effective BMD could be developed and deployed, then the United States should pursue the BMD route and the associated change in its nuclear strategy. The principal argument against defenses is that they will not work. Opponents of defense, presumably because they believe that effective defense is infeasible, tend not to examine carefully either the advantages or the disadvantages of effective defense. As a result, examination of a world in which the superpowers have deployed effective defense has been left to the advocates of defense, and a question of fundamental importance continues to be overlooked by the debate:

Could the deployment of effective defenses by both superpowers create a nuclear situation preferable to our current one, in which both countries maintain redundant assured destruction capabilities?

I am using the term "defense" to refer only to area defense, i.e., systems designed to protect cities and other value targets. BMD that would protect the United States by reducing the Soviet Union's ability to inflict damage is an area defense. By contrast, a point defense is designed principally to protect nuclear force capabilities.[1]

By "effective defenses," I have in mind systems that are capable of denying one's adversary an assured destruction capability. Defenses which cannot eliminate assured destruction capabilities are far less interesting because they would not significantly reduce the damage the United States would suffer in an all-out nuclear war.[2]

---

[1] This distinction is important because these two types of defense have fundamentally different strategic implications: a country's area defense, if sufficiently effective, could *reduce* the size of the *adversary's* deterrent threat; a country's point defense, by increasing the size of its offensive force that would survive a counterforce attack, could *increase* the size of the *country's* deterrent threat.

[2] An assured destruction capability is generally understood to be the capability, following a full scale counterforce attack against one's forces, to inflict an extremely high level of damage upon one's adversary. The levels of potential damage which analysts believe assured destruction requires are usually similar to those prescribed by Robert McNamara, U.S. Secretary of Defense from 1960 to 1968. McNamara's criteria for assured destruction, which were influenced by the diminishing marginal damage potential of increasing the size of the U.S. force, required that the United States be able to destroy, in a retaliatory attack, approximately 25 percent of the

Another way, then, of stating the above question is: Could the United States be more secure than it is today if, as a result of mutual deployment of defenses, neither the United States nor the Soviet Union had assured destruction capabilities? My objective in this essay is to analyze this question. . . .

The article focuses on situations in which *both* the United States and the Soviet Union deploy defenses. This case is important because it is the most probable outcome of U.S. deployment of defense. The Soviet Union is extremely likely to deploy defenses in response to a U.S. deployment. There is little reason to assume that in the long run the United States could maintain a technological advantage that enabled only the United States to have effective defense. Furthermore, the case of symmetric deployment is especially interesting due to the intuitive appeal of reducing U.S. vulnerability to attack without creating an advantage that threatens Soviet security.[3]

This analysis of how mutual deployment of effective defense would affect U.S. security proceeds through a number of stages. I identify three features of the nuclear situation that affect the United States' ability to avoid nuclear war with the Soviet Union: 1) the United States' ability to deter premeditated Soviet attack; 2) the

---

Soviet population and 50 percent of Soviet industry. He judged that such a level of destruction would be intolerable to the Soviet Union and, therefore, that the capability to inflict this level of damage would be sufficient to deter deliberate Soviet nuclear attacks on the United States.

A related, but conceptually distinct, interpretation of assured destruction focuses on the relationship between the costs a decision-maker associates with the nuclear attack and the damage that would result from such an attack. Assured destruction in this interpretation requires that the potential damage in one's retaliatory capability should be sufficiently high that increasing the potential damage would not result in significantly higher costs to the adversary. In this article, assured destruction is intended to have this second meaning. Clearly, any evaluation of the costs associated with such unprecedented damage is highly subjective. Many people believe that the United States would have to be able to reduce damage to itself far below the levels specified by McNamara before it could significantly improve the outcome of an all-out war; others believe that any reduction in damage, even if damage remained well above these levels, would be significant. The two different understandings of assured destruction are often not distinguished because McNamara said that an assured destruction capability would be sufficiently large to annihilate one's adversary in retaliation and because analysts tend to assume that costs to one's adversary could not be increased if the adversary could already be annihilated.

The arguments in this article do not depend upon a specific assessment of the level of retaliatory damage required for assured destruction. Instead, the arguments view the level of damage required for assured destruction as an imprecise boundary, above which additional damage does not significantly increase the costs of an attack, and below which reductions in damage would significantly reduce the costs. People disagree on the location of this boundary, but the arguments apply in all cases.

[3] It should not go unmentioned that many of the advocates of BMD favor asymmetric deployment—that is, situations in which the United States can gain a strategic advantage by deploying BMD which is superior to Soviet BMD.

crisis stability of the nuclear situation; and 3) the robustness of the U.S. deterrent to changes in Soviet forces. Next, I compare the probability of nuclear war in defensive and assured destruction situations by examining these three features for both types of nuclear situations. The final stage of the analysis compares U.S. security in defensive and assured destruction situations based upon expected costs. This requires considering the damage that would result if nuclear war occurred as well as the probability of its occurrence.

The conclusion of this analysis is that defensive situations, even those in which defenses were perfect, are *not* clearly preferable to assured destruction situations. . . . The arguments for not dramatically altering the nuclear status quo are much stronger than those that call for U.S. deployment of an area defense.

PERFECT DEFENSE

It is important to begin with an examination of the strategic implications of perfect defenses, however distant they may seem, because that is the goal towards which many advocates of strategic defense, including President Reagan, wish to move. Despite the widespread presumption that perfect defenses are desirable if feasible, there are two major shortcomings of a world of perfect defenses that draw into question whether it would be safer than our current nuclear situation.[4]

First, there could be no guarantee that perfect defenses would remain perfect. The technical challenge of developing and deploying a defense that would make the U.S. invulnerable to nuclear attack is enormous. Such a defense is commonly referred to as "perfect." The difficulty of *maintaining* a perfect defense indefinitely is likely to be far greater than developing it in the first place. Consequently, so-called perfect defenses should not be envisioned as a permanent technological solution to the dangers posed by nuclear weapons. The far more likely course of events is that a world of perfect defenses would decay into a world of imperfect defenses.[5]

[4] The following discussion assumes that both countries would know the effectiveness of both their own defense and the adversary's defense. This is admittedly unrealistic, since there would always be uncertainties about the effectiveness of the defenses, and because the implications of these uncertainties could be significant. The reason for assuming that the effectiveness of the defenses would be known, however, is to focus the examination of perfect defenses on other issues. This assumption of certain information strengthens the arguments for perfect defense and therefore reinforces the best case assumptions used in this analysis. Some of the complications that would likely result from uncertainties about effectiveness are discussed later in this article.

[5] Many advocates of pursuing highly effective defense argue that even if the prospects for effective defense do not look extremely promising today, history suggests that major technological changes should be expected. This argument would, however, apply at least as well to the maintenance of the defensive world they advocate and points to the major problems that would exist in defensive situations.

A nuclear situation in which both superpowers were invulnerable to nuclear attack would be extremely sensitive to even small improvements in the ability of one country's offense to penetrate the adversary's defense. For example, the ability to penetrate the adversary's defense with ten warheads would provide the potential for enormous destruction when compared to no destruction. The country that first acquired even a small capability to penetrate the adversary's defense would have attained an important coercive advantage: nuclear attack could be threatened with impunity since effective retaliation would be impossible given the adversary's inability to penetrate one's own defense. Recognizing that the adversary is likely to acquire a similar capability—that is, that one's defense will not remain impenetrable—could create pressure to reap the benefits of the strategic advantage quickly. This time pressure would be especially strong if one's advantage could be used to prevent the adversary from acquiring the capability to penetrate one's defense.

By contrast, when both superpowers possess redundant assured destruction capabilities, as is the situation today, the addition of tens or hundreds or even thousands of warheads would not significantly change the nuclear situation. As a result, the probability of gaining a strategic advantage is extremely low, especially when both superpowers are aware of and react to changes in the other's nuclear force.

The dangers, in a world of impenetrable defenses, that result from this sensitivity to small offensive improvements would be increased by the strong incentives the superpowers would have to defeat each other's defense. Each country could be expected to make the acquisition of a strategic advantage a priority. Moreover, because there would be no guarantee that perfect defenses would remain perfect, even a country that did not want to acquire an advantage would feel compelled to acquire additional strategic capabilities. Such a country would want to improve its defense to offset anticipated improvements in the adversary's offense. In addition, there would probably be a strong instinct to improve one's offense as well as a hedge against the possibility of not being able to offset, with improvements in one's defense, the adversary's enhanced offense. One's adversary, however, would not be able to know with confidence that these strategic programs were intended only to maintain a situation of equal capability. Consequently, even if both countries preferred to remain in a world of perfect defense, an interactive competition which threatened to reduce the effectiveness of the defenses would be likely to ensue. (Nuclear situations would continue to be sensitive to relatively small changes when the defenses were imperfect. This lack of "robustness" to changes is examined in detail below.)

The second problem with perfect defenses is that they could increase the probability of superpower conventional wars. Today's nuclear forces greatly increase the potential costs of any direct U.S.–Soviet military confrontation. As a result, nuclear weapons increase the risk of starting a conventional war, and therefore contribute to the deterrence of conventional war. Impenetrable defenses would eliminate this contribution. There is disagreement among strategic analysts about which features of the superpowers' extensive survivable strategic arsenals are most critical for deterrence of conventional war. Few, if any, commentators however believe that the existing arsenals do not contribute at all to the deterrence of conventional war. . . .

IMPERFECT DEFENSE AND THE PROBABILITY OF NUCLEAR WAR

Understanding security in a world of perfect defense is relatively easy because as long as the defenses remain impenetrable, there is no possibility of a strategic nuclear war.[6] Assessing security in a nuclear situation in which imperfect defenses have been deployed is more difficult. Since, in this case, the United States would be vulnerable to Soviet strategic nuclear attack, we need to evaluate the United States' ability to reduce the probability of these attacks.

The following analysis considers nuclear situations in which both countries have imperfect defenses, but each is capable of denying the other an assured destruction capability. Implicit in this formulation is a relationship between one country's offensive force and the adversary's defensive force. When defenses are imperfect there will always be, at least in theory, an offense which is sufficiently large to have an assured destruction capability. Therefore, for one country's imperfect defense to deny the adversary an assured destruction capability, either the size of the adversary's offense must be limited or the defense must be able to expand and improve to offset increases in the size of the offense. This analysis does not examine the feasibility of achieving these conditions. It assumes the establishment of a nuclear situation in which neither the United States nor the Soviet Union has assured destruction capabilities.

The probability that the United States will avoid war with the Soviet Union depends upon the following three features of the nuclear situation:

1) *The United States' ability to deter Soviet nuclear attack during periods when war does not appear to be imminent, that is, when there is not a severe crisis.* Deterrence of this type of attack requires that the Soviet Union believe that the net effect of starting

[6] The assertion depends on the assumption made above that both countries know that the defenses are perfect. If defenses were not known to be perfect, although in fact they were, then nuclear attack might be carried out (but would not result in damage) and nuclear threats might be used coercively.

a nuclear war would be negative, that is, that the Soviet Union would be worse off after the war than before it. I will term these "premeditated attacks." Surprise attacks, including the infamous "bolt from the blue," fall within this category.

2) *The crisis stability of the nuclear situation.* In a crisis, one or both superpowers might fear a nuclear attack by the other. If striking first is believed to be preferable to being struck first, and if a country believes the probability that the adversary will strike first is sufficiently high, then launching a first strike would be preferable to taking a chance on being struck first. This type of first strike is commonly termed a "preemptive attack." Unlike the case of premeditated attack, the country launching a preemptive attack would expect to be less well off after the war than before it. The crisis stability of the nuclear situation is a measure of how severe a crisis must be (or how high one's estimate that the adversary will strike first must be) before striking first becomes one's best option.

3) *The robustness of the nuclear situation.* The adequacy of U.S. forces depends not only on their ability to reduce the probability of preemptive and premeditated attacks, but also on how sensitive this ability is to potential changes in the Soviet forces. The more easily the Soviet Union could build forces that either would make a premeditated attack attractive or would significantly increase the incentives for preemptive attack, the greater the probability of a nuclear war. The robustness of the U.S. nuclear force is a measure of the difficulty the Soviet Union would encounter in trying to reduce U.S. security.

These three measures of the quality of the nuclear situation (the United States' ability to deter premeditated attacks, the degree of crisis stability, and the robustness of U.S. forces to change) are frequently used to assess the adequacy of U.S. nuclear forces. What distinguishes the following analysis from standard analyses of the nuclear situation is the assumption that assured destruction capabilities do not exist. Past analyses have asked the question: what capabilities are required to minimize the probability of war? The answers all include the need for an assured destruction capability (or at least a large retaliatory capability). This analysis, by examining the effect on these three measures of the nuclear situation, explores how the elimination of assured destruction capabilities by mutual deployment of defenses would affect the probability of nuclear war.

PREMEDITATED ATTACKS: IS ASSURED DESTRUCTION NECESSARY FOR DETERRENCE?

Consider a nuclear situation in which Soviet defenses could deny the United States an assured destruction capability. In this situation, the most basic and generally accepted U.S. deterrent requirement (that is, possession of an assured destruction capability) would not be satisfied. A natural conclusion is that the U.S. deterrent would be inadequate. This belief fueled opposition to strategic defense during the earlier BMD debate. But closer examination of nuclear situations in which *both* superpowers deploy defenses shows that U.S. deterrent requirements could be satisfied without U.S. possession of an assured destruction capability.

The requirement that the United States have an assured destruction capability implicitly assumes that the Soviet Union can annihilate the United States: the standard argument is that to deter an annihilating attack, the United States should be able to threaten credibly to annihilate the Soviet Union in retaliation. But if the United States could, by deploying defenses, eliminate the Soviet Union's annihilation capability, then deterrence of this attack would not be necessary. Furthermore, it is difficult to imagine any other Soviet actions the deterrence of which requires the United States to threaten the annihilation of the Soviet Union. So, if the Soviet Union did not have the ability to annihilate the United States, then the United States would not need to be able to annihilate the Soviet Union in retaliation. Consequently, a mutual deployment of defenses that eliminated both U.S. and Soviet annihilation capabilities need not result in an inadequate U.S. deterrent. The United States would, of course, still need a nuclear retaliatory capability to deter other Soviet nuclear attacks.

What capability would the United States need to deter attacks against its homeland when defenses had denied the Soviet Union an annihilation capability? Deterrence requires that the United States have the ability following any Soviet attack to inflict costs greater than the benefits the Soviet Union would achieve by attacking. To determine the U.S. retaliatory requirement, we must estimate the value the Soviet leaders would place on attacking the United States. We need to consider why the Soviet Union might attack the United States and what it would hope to gain by doing so. In the most general terms, the Soviet Union could use its nuclear force to damage or weaken the United States and to coerce the United States. The U.S. forces required to deter these actions are examined briefly below.

For all of the concern about attacks against U.S. cities, it is not clear why the Soviet Union would ever launch an all-out counter-value attack. Still, such an attack is not impossible, so we need to estimate the value the Soviet Union might place on attacking U.S. cities. One possible reason for attacking U.S. cities would be to weaken the United States, thereby reducing the U.S. ability to oppose the Soviet Union's pursuit of its foreign policy objectives.

Presumably people believe the Soviet Union is interested in annihilating the United States because this would make it the dominant
world power. The analogy, if U.S. defenses had eliminated the
Soviet ability to annihilate the United States, would be a countervalue attack designed to weaken the United States.

To deter this type of attack, the United States would need a
retaliatory capability that could weaken the Soviet Union as much
as the Soviet countervalue attack could weaken the United States.
A countervalue capability roughly equivalent to the Soviet countervalue capability should be sufficiently large to satisfy this requirement. In fact, this is a very conservative requirement because U.S.
retaliation would not only deny the Soviet Union the desired increase in relative world power, but would also inflict direct costs
by destroying Soviet value targets. Because the Soviet Union
could first attack U.S. forces, and then attack U.S. cities, the
United States should have forces that provide a countervalue
capability essentially equal to the Soviets' both before and after
a Soviet counterforce attack.[7] I will call this an "equal countervalue
capability."

The second way in which the Soviet Union might use its nuclear
capability is to coerce the United States. While the benefits to the
Soviet Union of attacking U.S. cities can be questioned, the potential benefits of coercing the United States are far more obvious. If
the Soviet Union could inflict enormous damage on the United
States and the United States lacked the ability to deter these attacks,
then the Soviet Union might be able to compel the United States to
compromise its security and vital interests.

As in other cases, deterrence would require that the United States
be able to threaten the Soviet Union with expected costs greater
than expected benefits. In the case of coercion, however, the United
States could deny the Soviet Union any benefit simply by refusing
to perform the action the Soviet Union demanded. The costs threatened by the United States need not be greater than the benefits the
Soviet Union hopes to gain through its coercive demand because
any U.S. attack combined with refusal of the Soviet demand would
result in a net Soviet loss. If faced with a coercive threat, the United
States could refuse the Soviet demand and tell the Soviet Union

---

[7] Including in this analysis uncertainty and imperfect information about the level
of vulnerability to countervalue attack would weaken this argument. Redundant
assured destruction capabilities are extremely large by any reasonable evaluation.
There is little opportunity to misjudge this destructive potential, and assessments of
damage are therefore not sensitive to relatively small differences in force size. In
contrast, in a defensive situation in which each country's ability to inflict damage has
been greatly reduced, relative force capabilities would be harder to evaluate, and
uncertainties, misevaluations, and misperceptions would be more likely to result in a
perceived advantage that could result in a failure of deterrence.

that attacks against value targets would be reciprocated. To adopt this strategy, the United States would have to be confident that it could deter the Soviet Union. This would require that the United States believe that the Soviet Union finds the U.S. retaliatory threats credible.

A large disparity in U.S. and Soviet countervalue capabilities could undermine U.S. credibility. So, a reasonable force requirement for denying the Soviet Union the coercive use of its nuclear forces is that the Soviet Union not have an advantage in countervalue capabilities: an advantage should not exist in the deployed forces, nor should the Soviet Union be able to gain a countervalue advantage in surviving forces by launching a counterforce attack. Therefore, U.S. forces which satisfy the equal countervalue requirement should be sufficient to deny the Soviet Union a capability which enables it to coerce the United States.[8]

In summary, a reasonable requirement for deterrence of Soviet attacks on the United States is possession of an equal countervalue capability. Requiring that the United States possess an equal countervalue capability is significantly different from requiring an assured destruction capability. The equal countervalue requirement explicitly couples U.S. and Soviet capabilities to inflict countervalue damage. The equal countervalue requirement could be satisfied by both the United States and the Soviet Union at all levels of vulnerability to attack. In contrast, the assured destruction requirement demands that the United States have a retaliatory force capable of inflicting a specific level of countervalue damage independent of the size of the Soviet ability to inflict damage. According to the equal countervalue requirement, if the United States can reduce the Soviet Union's ability to inflict countervalue damage, then the United States can afford to have its ability to inflict countervalue damage in retaliation reduced. Moreover, improvements in Soviet defenses which reduce the damage the United States could inflict on the Soviet Union could be compensated for by improvements in U.S. defenses. The assured destruction requirement, on the other hand, demands that improvements in Soviet defenses be offset either by an increase in the size of the U.S. offense or by an increase in the ability of the offense to penetrate the Soviet defense.

[8] This does not mean, however, that the Soviet Union would necessarily be unable to coerce the United States. As in a situation of mutual assured destruction capabilities, if the Soviet Union were able to convince the United States that it would carry out a threat to attack U.S. cities, then the Soviet Union might be able to coerce the United States. The U.S. possession of an equal countervalue capability, by making possible a highly credible retaliatory threat comparable to the Soviet threat, would make it difficult for the Soviet Union to make its coercive threat convincing. If the Soviet Union were able to coerce the United States, the key to its success would be greater resolve and willingness to take risks than the United States, and not an advantage in nuclear forces.

CRISIS STABILITY: WHAT WOULD BE THE EFFECT OF DEFENSES?

There is a common belief that defenses capable of eliminating an adversary's assured destruction capability would decrease crisis stability: a country that can protect itself (that is, a country that can deny its adversary a second strike annihilation capability) is more likely to strike preemptively in a crisis. The following analysis explores this proposition and identifies the conditions under which it is correct.

Crisis stability depends upon the decision-maker's incentives to strike preemptively in a crisis, that is, during times when there is reason to believe one's adversary is likely to launch a first strike. The decision to preempt in a crisis would depend upon how the costs of being struck first compare to the costs of being struck second. If the adversary has an assured destruction capability, then there would be little if any incentive for a rational decision-maker to preempt: a preemptive attack could not deny the adversary an annihilating retaliatory capability, so there would be little difference between the costs of being struck first and second. In an assured destruction situation, the vulnerability of the adversary's forces does not create a preemptive incentive. The adversary's force is sufficiently large and survivable that the fraction of the force that would survive a counterforce attack would still be able to inflict the damage required for annihilation.

For the same reason, the adversary would have little incentive to preempt if one's own surviving force would be sufficiently large to annihilate the adversary. Since a leader's decision to preempt would be fueled by anticipation of the adversary's preemption, possession of an assured destruction capability by either country should be sufficient to create a highly crisis-stable nuclear situation.

If one's own defense eliminates the adversary's assured destruction capability *and* if the adversary's retaliatory capability is partially vulnerable, then preemption would reduce the damage from an all-out countervalue attack. As a result, if the decision-maker anticipates a countervalue first strike, then there would be an incentive to preempt.[9] Since without defenses there would be virtually no incentive to preempt (because the adversary could maintain

---

[9] The assumption that decision-makers would anticipate a countervalue strike is implicit in many discussions of crisis stability. It underlies the logic that says if a counterforce attack could reduce the adversary's countervalue potential, then there will be an incentive to strike first. A crisis, however, should provoke fears of a counterforce attack. If we assume the adversary's first strike would be counterforce, then the nuclear situation is far more crisis-stable than if we assume the attack would be countervalue. If we assume that both countries anticipate counterforce first strikes, then the effect of defenses on crisis stability is likely to be minimal. Given this assumption, the incentives to preempt would be small, or nonexistent, with or without defenses.

his assured destruction capability), deploying defenses that eliminate assured destruction capabilities would decrease crisis stability. . . .

Because reducing the degree of offensive force vulnerability would enhance crisis stability, one way to offset the decrease in crisis stability that would result from deploying effective defenses would be to accompany the deployment with programs to reduce offensive force vulnerabilities. One approach for reducing force vulnerability is to protect offensive forces with active defenses. Area defenses, although not designed specifically for this mission, could increase force survivability. In addition, there are many other ways to increase force survivability, including deploying point defenses. If effective area defense were feasible, then defenses that could provide a high degree of force survivability, including survivability of command and control, would also be feasible. In this case, the reduction in crisis stability that would result from deploying effective defenses could be small.

In summary, effective defenses would be likely to decrease crisis stability. It would probably be possible, however, to keep this negative effect of defenses quite small. The source of preemptive incentive is offensive force vulnerability. Therefore, if offensive forces could be made highly survivable, then the effect on crisis stability of defenses that eliminate assured destruction capabilities would be small.

ROBUSTNESS: THE PRIMARY INADEQUACY OF DEFENSIVE SITUATIONS

We do not live in a static world. Consequently, in addition to evaluating U.S. security as if U.S. and Soviet forces could be held constant, we must also examine the effect of possible changes in Soviet forces on U.S. security and the probability of these changes. More specifically, we must evaluate not only the United States' ability to deter premeditated Soviet attack and the degree of crisis stability, but also the probability of changes in Soviet forces that could reduce the United States' ability to deter premeditated attacks or that could reduce crisis stability. The robustness of U.S. forces is a measure of the difficulty the Soviet Union would encounter in trying to reduce U.S. security.[10]

---

[10] Arms race stability is the standard measure of this characteristic of the nuclear situation. I have chosen to use the term "robustness" to avoid the confusion that surrounds the term "arms race stability." Arms race stability brings to mind at least two issues which are related to robustness, but which are conceptually distinct. First, arms race stability is often considered an indicator of the likelihood and/or intensity of arms races that will occur in a specific nuclear situation. Arms races, however, can occur for a variety of reasons which are only peripherally related to the effect of building nuclear forces on the adversary's security. Consequently, arms

All other things being equal, the more easily U.S. security could be jeopardized by changes in Soviet forces, the less desirable the nuclear situation. A nuclear situation which would be highly desirable when the two countries' forces could be held fixed, but which lacks robustness, might not be preferable to one which is less desirable when the forces are held fixed, but which is more robust.

I have already discussed the lack of robustness of nuclear situations in which perfect defenses have been deployed. This section extends that analysis by considering cases in which imperfect defenses have been deployed. The conclusion remains the same: nuclear situations in which defenses significantly reduce the vulnerability of value targets would lack robustness.

The following discussion compares the difficulty the Soviet Union would have undermining U.S. deterrence of premeditated attacks in defensive and in assured destruction situations. It assumes that the requirement for deterrence of premeditated attacks, that is, the equal countervalue requirement, is satisfied in the initial nuclear situation. The United States' deterrence of premeditated attacks could be undermined by two types of changes: improvements in Soviet defenses that reduce the United States' ability to retaliate, and improvements in the penetration capability of Soviet offenses that increase the vulnerability of U.S. value targets to attack.

The robustness of U.S. nuclear forces to these changes depends upon two interdependent factors. The first is the magnitude of the change in potential countervalue damage required so that the Soviet Union would no longer be deterred from launching a premeditated attack. Specifically, how much must the Soviet Union reduce the U.S. countervalue threat to gain a strategic advantage? or how large an increase in Soviet countervalue capability is required to provide a significant advantage? The second factor is the technical difficulty of changing the threat to value targets by this amount. For example, assuming that in a specific nuclear situation the Soviet Union, to gain an advantage, must increase its countervalue capability by 50 warheads, how difficult would it be for the Soviet Union to achieve

---

races can occur in highly robust nuclear situations, as has occurred in our current highly redundant and diversified assured destruction situation.

Second, use of the term "arms race stability" can connote a belief that arms races cause wars. Whether arms races actually cause wars is a theoretical issue on which there is substantial disagreement. But one can assert that the probability of war depends upon the robustness of the nuclear situation without believing that, in general, arms races cause wars. Robustness is a measure of how sensitive a country's security would be to the adversary's buildup of forces. It does not imply that the process of competitive armament itself leads to war. Rather, assuming a force buildup takes place either competitively or unilaterally, a war is more likely when the initial nuclear situation is less robust.

this change? The combination of these two factors determines the overall difficulty of acquiring a strategic advantage.

The discussion of perfect defenses focused on the first factor, the magnitude of the change, and argued that even small changes could have strategic significance. Situations in which imperfect defenses had been deployed would suffer, although less severely, from the same sensitivity. The following example illustrates this observation. Imagine three nuclear situations, one in which both superpowers have impenetrable defenses, one in which each superpower can penetrate the other's defense with ten warheads, and one in which both superpowers have assured destruction capabilities. Now consider how a change in one country's nuclear force that enabled it to penetrate the adversary's defense with ten additional warheads would affect the adversary's security in each situation. The addition of ten warheads of countervalue capability to one country's force would be less significant when added to the nuclear situation in which both countries started with ten penetrating warheads than when added to a situation in which both countries had perfect defenses. The advantage in countervalue capability would be harder to use coercively when the adversary would be able to threaten retaliation against one's own value targets.

In contrast, the addition of ten penetrating warheads to one force when both countries had assured destruction capabilities comprised of thousands of warheads would be far less significant than when added to the nuclear situation in which both countries had ten penetrating warheads. The addition to the mutual assured destruction situation might not even change the country's ability to inflict damage; the addition in the ten warhead situation, while it might be difficult to use coercively, could result in a significant difference in the two countries' ability to inflict damage.

The general conclusion to be drawn from this specific example is that the lower the vulnerability of value targets in a given nuclear situation, the smaller the change in their vulnerability required to gain an advantage. This conclusion can be restated specifically in terms of defenses: the smaller the number of warheads that could penetrate a country's defense, the more sensitive that country's security would be to offensive changes that reduce the effectiveness of its defense.

The second factor affecting robustness, the technical difficulty of changing countervalue capability to gain an advantage, depends upon the type, size, and number of changes required to achieve a strategic advantage. The type of change is determined by whether the status quo is an assured destruction situation or a defensive situation. In assured destruction situations, it is the difficulty of reducing the adversary's offensive threat that affects robustness. In defensive situations, on the other hand, both the difficulty of further reducing the adversary's offensive threat and the difficulty of penetrating the adversary's defense would affect robustness.

Assessing the relative difficulty of penetrating a specific defensive system with an offensive system or of defeating a specific offensive system with a defensive system is beyond the scope of this paper. Moreover, such an assessment would necessarily be highly speculative because effective defensive systems have not yet been developed. Consequently, it is impossible to compare the difficulty of defeating those defensive systems with the difficulty of developing defensive systems to defeat today's offenses or the offenses of the future. One fact that bears upon this issue should, however, be mentioned. Even if defenses were developed that were perfect against currently deployed offenses, experts believe that the task of developing offensive countermeasures to defeat those defenses would be relatively easy. The defensive system would be understood by its adversary, enabling the development of countermeasures designed specifically with the defense in mind. The defense, by contrast, to remain effective, would have to be able to overcome the full range of possible countermeasures. This asymmetry means that defenses may always be at a disadvantage, that is, the development of effective defenses against a competitive threat may always be more difficult than developing offenses that can penetrate defenses.

The size of the change required to gain a strategic advantage affects the technical difficulty of achieving the change. (This is why the two factors affecting robustness are interdependent.) A defense which must reduce the offensive threat by a large amount is harder to build than one that must reduce the same offensive threat by a small amount. Similarly, a new offensive system which must be able to penetrate the adversary's defense with many weapons would be harder to build than one that had to penetrate the same defense with only a few weapons. Even taking into account the likely asymmetry between offense and defense mentioned above, it is not possible to say with certainty whether the changes required to gain an advantage in an assured destruction situation would be easier or harder to achieve than in a defensive situation. As discussed above, however, the size of the requisite change in assured destruction situations is larger than in defensive situations. Due to this difference, gaining an advantage will tend to be more difficult in assured destruction situations than in defensive situations.

The larger the number of changes in a country's forces required to gain an advantage, all else being equal, the harder the advantage will be to obtain. The number of force changes required to achieve an advantage depends upon the diversity of the adversary's forces.

In assured destruction situations, ensuring one's ability to destroy large numbers of the adversary's value targets is the strategic requirement. Diversification of one's offensive force helps to ensure the continuing achievement of this objective by increasing the number of defensive changes that are required before the adversary could eliminate one's assured destruction capability. For example, an offensive force which could annihilate the adversary with either an air-breathing threat or a ballistic missile threat requires that the adversary develop two types of highly effective defense. Obviously, this is a harder task than developing an effective defense against a single threat.

This article has discussed defenses in general, not defenses against specific types of offensive threats. But when we think about the feasibility of defense, it is crucial to keep in mind the potential diversity of offensive threats. If BMD were technologically feasible, but defense against advanced technology bombers or cruise missiles were impossible, then the strategic significance of BMD would be greatly reduced. The technological feasibility of defenses that would reduce vulnerability to attack is determined by the difficulty of defending against all offensive threats.

By contrast, in a nuclear situation in which one's own defenses have significantly reduced the vulnerability of value targets, the strategic requirement is the maintenance of a low level of vulnerability. In this case the adversary's ability to diversify offensive forces makes maintaining low vulnerability more difficult. Each of these offensive threats must be defended against, and the adversary's ability to defeat any of the defenses would be sufficient to make maintenance of low vulnerability impossible. . . .

A lack of robustness would not be so dangerous if the United States and the Soviet Union would not have incentives to try to change the equal countervalue condition of the nuclear situation. If a political environment could be created in which the superpowers chose not to attempt to gain a strategic advantage, then the need to make the nuclear situation resistant to change would be reduced. Moreover, superpower cooperation in structuring the nuclear situation could contribute to the situation's robustness. But, in a world of imperfect defenses, as described for the case of perfect defense, countries would feel tremendous pressure to pursue, or at least to prepare to pursue, capabilities for defeating the adversary's defense. Even in the unlikely event that a highly robust situation could be achieved (which would require making one's defense highly resistant to the adversary's offensive innovations), it would be hard to have high confidence in this robustness: a country could not know with certainty that offensive threats that would undermine the defense could not be developed. This uncertainty could not be overlooked because the change required to gain an advantage would still be small and the adversary's incentive to try to alter the nuclear situation would be obvious.

These conditions would make establishing a political environment in which cooperation was possible far harder under conditions of reduced vulnerability than under assured destruction. And, given our limited success in negotiating strategic arms control treaties when both countries have redundant assured destruction capabilities, there is little reason to be optimistic about the prospects for cooperation. . . .

COULD DEFENSE CREATE A PREFERABLE NUCLEAR SITUATION?

The preceding discussion of imperfect defenses capable of eliminating both superpowers' assured destruction capabilities compared the probability of nuclear war in defensive and assured destruction situations. Specifically, it compared the United States' ability to deter Soviet premeditated attack, the crisis stability, and the robustness of defensive and assured destruction situations. This analysis of the probability of nuclear war is, however, not by itself sufficient to determine in which type of nuclear situation the United States would be more secure. This is because U.S. security depends upon the cost if war were to occur, as well as the probability of war.

Comparison of nuclear situations requires a measure that combines these U.S. security objectives, that is, to minimize the probability of war and to minimize the costs if war occurs.[11] These objectives should be evaluated simultaneously. For example, if a change in the nuclear situation would reduce the damage of a nuclear attack but would also increase the probability of the attack, then the change might not increase U.S. security. Examining only the probability of war or the costs if war were to occur is insufficient to understand the net effect of the change. The correct measure of security is the probability of the war multiplied by the costs if there were a war, which is the expected cost. . . .

Saying that defenses are neither clearly desirable nor clearly undesirable might appear to provide little policy insight. However, although indeterminate, this conclusion differs markedly from the conventional wisdom that effective defenses would be desirable, and weighs heavily against deploying defense to limit U.S. vulnera-

[11] This formulation of objectives assumes that the United States is a strictly status quo power. This may not be entirely accurate, but is a reasonable assumption for this discussion of nuclear weapons policy. A further concern about this formulation is that it does not include the objective of minimizing losses that could result from nuclear coercion. While this is clearly an objective of U.S. policy, the nuclear capabilities required to achieve it closely resemble those required to minimize the probability of nuclear war. Consequently, not explicitly including this objective does not bias the analysis.

bility to attack. Recall that the analysis has considered a best case for defense. Even making these optimistic assumptions, a defensive situation might not be preferable to our current assured destruction situation. More realistic, less optimistic assumptions about defenses result in nuclear situations which would be more dangerous than today's. Advocates of strategic defense are driven by the promise of a world far safer than the current one. If defenses could create such a world, then taking a chance on ending up in one of the more dangerous, and more likely, defensive situations might be justified. But to run great risks and to spend enormous resources in the hope of reaching a nuclear situation that might not be preferable to our current assured destruction situation, and might be worse, make little sense.

The remainder of this section explains how this conclusion follows from the preceding analysis. The analysis first identified three factors that influence the probability that the U.S. will be able to avoid nuclear war with the Soviet Union: 1) the U.S. ability to deter premeditated attacks; 2) the crisis stability of the nuclear situation; and 3) the robustness of the nuclear situation. I then evaluated how the deployment by both superpowers of effective defenses, that is, defenses sufficiently capable to deny the adversary an assured destruction capability, would affect these factors. The findings of this evaluation are:

1) Effective defenses need not undermine deterrence of premeditated attacks. Assured destruction is not necessary for deterrence; an equal countervalue capability (i.e., the possession of a countervalue capability equal to the Soviets' both before and after a Soviet counterforce attack) is sufficient for deterrence of premeditated attacks. The equal countervalue requirement could be satisfied when defenses of any level of effectiveness had been deployed and at all levels of vulnerability of value targets to attack.

2) Crisis stability would be likely to decrease if assured destruction capabilities were eliminated by defense. It might, however, be possible to keep this negative effect of defense quite small. At least in principle, a defensive situation could be made as crisis-stable as an assured destruction situation by deploying invulnerable retaliatory capabilities. While making one's retaliatory capability entirely invulnerable might not be possible, achieving a high level of invulnerability might be possible.

3) The Achilles heel of defensive situations is the tremendous difficulty of maintaining them. Defensive situations, unlike assured destruction situations, would be likely to lack robustness. This means that changes in the adversary's forces that could undermine deterrence of premeditated attack and create incentives for preemptive and preventive attack would be far more likely in defensive

situations. The lack of robustness would likely result in tense superpower relations, making security cooperation extremely difficult. Due to the difficulty of creating robust defensive situations, the probability of nuclear war would be higher than in assured destruction situations.

Overall, then, this evaluation concludes that the probability of nuclear war in defensive situations would be higher than in assured destruction situations. This increase in the probability would not be due primarily to a decrease in the United States' ability to deter premeditated attacks or to maintain crisis stability: if the superpowers could not change their forces, then there might be defensive nuclear situations in which these wars would not be more likely than in assured destruction situations. This constraint, however, is unrealistic. The superpowers would be able to alter the status quo, that is, to change the offensive and defensive forces which are deployed at a given time. Due to the lack of robustness in defensive situations, this competitive armament would be more likely to result in a nuclear war in defensive situations than in assured destruction situations. . . .

ADDITIONAL PROBLEMS WITH STRATEGIC DEFENSE

This examination of strategic defense has analyzed a best case for defense. Effective defense was hypothesized to be technologically and economically feasible. Even with these highly controversial assumptions, the decision to pursue the deployment of defense and to make the associated fundamental shift in nuclear strategy is found to have serious shortcomings. The case for effective defense and for starting to deploy defenses in the foreseeable future is further weakened by a number of factors:

1) *Uncertainty*. The effectiveness of U.S. defenses would be uncertain and small uncertainties would be highly significant. In addition to the uncertainties inherent in the operations of complex systems, the effectiveness of defenses would be uncertain due to the severe limits on testing. The defense could not be tested against a full scale attack or against Soviet offenses. And while estimates could be made of effectiveness against deployed Soviet offenses, there would always be reasonable questions about Soviet penetration aids that could be quickly added to their offensive force.

Small uncertainties would be significant because, with the large offensive forces which are currently deployed, a small difference in the percentage of penetrating weapons would translate into a large difference in destructive potential. The uncertainties involved with a defense which was in fact perfect would be likely to be large enough to leave the United States unsure about whether it was vulnerable to an annihilating attack by the Soviet Union.

The effect of uncertainty would affect U.S. policy in a number of ways. The United States would never feel adequately defended. (Nor would the Soviet Union.) Even without uncertainties, there would always be arguments that the United States needed additional defense to improve its protection against Soviet attacks and as a hedge against Soviet offensive breakthroughs. The strength of these arguments would be greater than those made about the inadequacy of today's offensive forces since defensive capability would start to become redundant only once the defenses were perfect. The existence of uncertainties would be likely to result in unrelenting requests for additional defenses, yet fulfilling these requests would yield little satisfaction and add little to the public's sense of security.

A second effect of uncertainty would be the creation of fears that the Soviet Union had a superior defensive capability. Prudent military analysis could require assessing uncertainties in favor of Soviet defense and against U.S. defense. As a result, if the United States and the Soviet Union had comparable defensive capabilities, U.S. defenses would not provide confidence that the United States was maintaining a strategic nuclear balance and would likely be judged inferior. This conclusion would contribute to the demands for improving defensive capabilities.

2) *Allies.* Any comprehensive analysis of defensive situations must consider the reaction of U.S. allies and the implications for their security. One issue of great importance to them has already been raised, that is, the effect of defenses on the probability of conventional war. If strategic defense were believed to increase the probability of conventional war, then tremendous resistance from the European allies should be anticipated. Conventional wars in Europe are expected to be so costly that they are barely less unacceptable than are nuclear wars to many Europeans. A second concern would focus on the vulnerability of allies to nuclear attack. A policy that drastically reduces the United States' vulnerability to nuclear attack while leaving its European and other allies highly vulnerable cannot look good from their perspective. A third concern would be the effect of defenses on the independent deterrent capabilities of the French and British. A highly effective but imperfect Soviet defense would leave the United States with a modest retaliatory capability, but would probably eliminate the value of these independent European deterrents.

3) *Suitcase bombs.* The ability to defend effectively against ballistic missiles, cruise missiles, and bombers could greatly increase the importance of clandestinely delivered nuclear weapons. Nuclear bombs could be placed on Soviet ships and commercial airplanes, or could be carried into the United States by Soviet agents. These alternative types of delivery are possible today, but are not of great

importance due to the Soviets' large ballistic missile and air-breathing threats.

These alternative forms of delivery would not necessarily render defense useless: the Soviet ability to deliver clandestine weapons in a crisis might be severely limited; hiding weapons before a crisis would be risky unless early detection would be impossible; and the damage from clandestine attacks might be less extensive than is currently possible without defenses. Still, the observation that defense against the delivery systems which are most important today would not eliminate vulnerability to nuclear attack raises basic issues about strategic defense: What threats must the United States be able to defend against? How would a "partial defense," that is, a defense against standard delivery systems, affect the nuclear threat? How would highly effective or perfect defense against standard delivery systems affect the political and military uses of nuclear weapons?

CONCLUSION

Strategic defense and the prospect of being invulnerable to nuclear attack have undeniable appeal. But there is no excuse for being romantic or unrealistic about the nature of a world in which the superpowers have built tens of thousands of nuclear weapons and sophisticated delivery systems, and in which the knowledge about these technologies cannot be destroyed. Strategic defense cannot return us to a pre-nuclear world. Defensive situations have not been studied as carefully or extensively as assured destruction situations. There is, however, no reason to believe defensive situations would be either less complex or easier to manage than assured destruction situations.

The best of worlds in which both superpowers have effective defense would not be so good and might not be preferable to today's redundant assured destruction situation: in all but the case of perfect defense, the U.S. would still depend upon deterrence for its security; the lack of robustness in defensive situations would make them sensitive to small changes in forces and would create strong incentives to pursue threatening improvements in offensive forces; the acquisition of these forces would increase the probability of nuclear war; the probability of large conventional wars between the superpowers and their allies might well increase; and, the threat posed by clandestinely delivered nuclear weapons would be much more significant than today.

Any serious policy for deploying defenses must address the dangers that would result from the difficulty of maintaining the defensive situation. This article has argued that no defensive situation could be highly robust. The most robust defensive situations will require superpower cooperation. This brings to the forefront the issue of U.S.–Soviet relations in a defensive world. Recent statements by the President have suggested that effective defenses would eliminate the need for offensive weapons. This outcome is not impossible, but is extremely unlikely. A more realistic assessment is that deploying defenses would lead to an intense offensive and defensive nuclear weapons competition between the superpowers and to tense, strained relations. We should expect that arms control agreements to limit or reduce offensive nuclear forces would be difficult, if not impossible, to negotiate. Careful thought should be given to whether, in a defensive situation, a cooperative relationship between the superpowers would be possible, and to whether the pressures for confrontation could be kept low. If these would not be possible, and I believe they would not be, then the prospects for improving security by shifting to a world of effective defenses must be judged to be especially gloomy. . . .

Why the Soviets Can't Win Quickly in Europe

JOHN J. MEARSHEIMER

In light of the emergence of strategic parity and NATO's manifest lack of enthusiasm for tactical nuclear weapons, the importance of the balance of conventional forces in Central Europe has increased significantly in the past decade. Regarding that balance, the conventional wisdom is clearly that the Warsaw Pact enjoys an overwhelming advantage. In the event of a conventional war, the Soviets are expected to launch a *blitzkrieg* that will lead to a quick and decisive victory. . . .

The fact of the matter is that the balance of conventional forces is nowhere near as unfavorable as it is so often portrayed to be. In fact, NATO's prospects for thwarting a Soviet offensive are actually quite good. Certainly, NATO does not have the capability to *win* a conventional war on the continent against the Soviets. NATO does have, however, the wherewithal to *deny* the Soviets a quick victory and then to turn the conflict into a lengthy war of attrition, where NATO's advantage in population and GNP would not bode well for the Soviets.

The aim of this article is to examine closely the Soviets' prospects for effecting a *blitzkrieg* against NATO. In analyzing this matter, two closely related issues must be addressed. First, one must determine whether the Soviets have the force structure, the doctrine, and the raw ability to implement this strategy. In other words, do the Soviets, when viewed in isolation, have the capacity to effect a *blitzkrieg?* Secondly, when NATO's defense capabilities and the theater's terrain are considered, what then are the prospects for Soviet success? It may well be that the Soviet military is well-

From "Why the Soviets Can't Win Quickly in Central Europe" by John J. Mearsheimer, *International Security*, Summer 1982 (Vol. 7, No. 1) pp. 121–157. © 1982 by the President and Fellows of Harvard College and of the Massachusetts Institute of Technology. Reprinted by permission of MIT Press, Cambridge, Massachusetts and the copyright holders. Portions of the text and some footnotes have been omitted.

The author wishes to thank the following people for their helpful comments on earlier drafts of this essay: Robert Art, Mary Mearsheimer, Stephen Meyer, Barry Posen, and Jack Snyder.

primed to launch a *blitzkrieg,* but that NATO in turn has the capability to thwart it.

Any assessment of the NATO-Pact balance is dependent on certain assumptions made about the preparatory moves both sides take before the war starts. Among the many that might be considered, three scenarios are most often posited. The first of these is the "standing start" attack, in which the Soviets launch an attack after hardly any mobilization and deliver a knockout blow against an unsuspecting NATO. This is not, however, a likely eventuality. First of all, without significantly improving the readiness of their standing forces, the Soviets would not have the capability to score a decisive victory. Instead, they would have to settle for capturing a portion of West German territory. Such a limited victory is hardly an attractive option. Secondly, for a war in Europe to become a realistic possibility, there would have to be a significant deterioration in East-West relations. Given such a development, it is very likely that both sides will take some steps, however limited, to increase the readiness of their forces. It is difficult to imagine a scenario where an alert Pact catches NATO completely unprepared.

The second scenario is a more realistic and more dangerous one. Here, in the midst of a crisis, NATO detects a Pact mobilization, but does not mobilize its forces for a fear of triggering a Soviet attack. Surely, if NATO fails to respond quickly to a Pact mobilization as posited in this second scenario, the Pact would soon be in a position to inflict a decisive defeat on NATO.

In the third scenario, NATO's mobilization begins immediately after the Pact starts to mobilize. Here, the Pact does not gain an overwhelming force advantage as a result of NATO's failure to mobilize. It is with this third scenario that I shall concern myself in the present essay. The focus will thus be on a conflict in which both sides are alerted and where neither enjoys an advantage as a result of the other's failure to mobilize. . . .

Before directly assessing Soviet prospects for launching a successful *blitzkrieg,* we must examine briefly the balance of forces on the Central Front and the doctrines of the two sides.

THE BALANCE OF FORCES ON THE CENTRAL FRONT

The Pact has 57⅓ divisions located in Central Europe, while NATO has 28⅓, giving the Pact slightly more than a 2:1 advantage in divisions. Comparing numbers of divisions, however, gives a distorted view of the balance, since this measure does not account for the significant differences, both qualitative and quantitative, among each nation's divisions. There are generally two alternative ways of assessing the balance. One is to focus on the manpower on each side, while the other is to compare weaponry.

Manpower

Robert Lucas Fischer, in his 1976 study of the conventional balance in Europe . . . notes that NATO has 414,000 men in its divisions, while the Pact has 564,000. With this measure of divisional manpower, the Soviet advantage shrinks to 1.36:1. Fischer calculates that when overall manpower levels on the Central Front are considered, the Pact's advantage shrinks even further to 1.09:1. This is because NATO has traditionally had more men assigned to combat units which are not organic to divisions. Since the study was issued, the Pact has added approximately 50,000 men, raising the overall advantage in manpower to 1.15:1—hardly an alarming figure. In the British Government's recent *Statement on Defence Estimates, 1981*, the Soviets are given an advantage in overall manpower of 1.2:1. Under the category of "soldiers in fighting units," the Soviets are again given a 1.2:1 advantage. These figures are clear evidence that NATO is not hopelessly outnumbered. Perhaps the most important problem with comparing manpower levels, however, is that it does not account for weaponry.

Weapons

It is not difficult to compare numbers of specific weapons on each side. For example, the Pact has approximately a 2.5:1 advantage in tanks and about a 2.8:1 advantage in artillery. Such comparisons, however, do not take into account qualitative differences within the same category of weapons (i.e., NATO's artillery is significantly better than Pact artillery); nor do they deal with the problem of comparing different categories of weapons (i.e., tanks vs. artillery). To counter this problem, the Defense Department has devised a system of weighing weapons within the same category as well as across different categories. Three principal characteristics of each weapon are considered: mobility, survivability, and firepower. Using this system, the Defense Department weighs all the weaponry in every division on the Central Front and then arrives at a composite figure, known as armored division equivalents (ADEs), for both NATO and the Warsaw Pact. Unfortunately, the number of armored division equivalents on each side is classified. Very importantly, however, the ratio is not. Looking at standing forces, the Pact has a 1.2:1 advantage. Again, it is clear that NATO is not hopelessly outnumbered.

Reinforcement and Mobilization

Now, consider the critical matter of comparative reinforcement capabilities. Although NATO's reinforcement capability is not as great as the Soviets' in an absolute sense, NATO has the potential to keep the overall ratio of forces very close to the pre-mobilization ratio. The notion that the Soviets can rely on some massive second echelon that NATO cannot match is a false one. However, the ratio of forces in any future mobilization will be heavily influenced by the timeliness with which each side starts to mobilize. If NATO begins mobilizing its forces before the Pact does, or simultaneously with the Pact, then the force ratios will remain close to the 1.2:1 (in armored division equivalents) and 1.36:1 (in divisional manpower), the ratios which obtained before mobilization. If NATO starts mobilizing a few days after the Pact, then the balance of forces should approach but not exceed a 2:1 ratio in the very early days of mobilization and then fall to a level close to the pre-mobilization ratios. But once the gap in mobilization starting times reaches seven days (in the Pact's favor), NATO begins to face serious problems, problems which become even more pronounced as the mobilization gap widens further. As noted, the assumption here is that NATO starts mobilizing immediately after the Pact, thus ensuring that the overall force ratios never reach 2:1, and, in fact, remain reasonably close to the pre-mobilization ratios.

Numbers and Strategy: The Critical Connection

. . . The previous analysis of the balance of forces in Europe indicates that the Soviets do not enjoy . . . an overwhelming advantage. They do not have the numerical superiority to simply crush NATO. In a conventional war in Europe, whether or not the Soviets prevail will depend on how they employ their forces against NATO's defenses. In other words, success will be a function of strategy, not overwhelming numbers. This is not to deny that the Soviets would be better served with an overall advantage in armored division equivalents of 1.8:1 rather than, say, 1.2:1. But regardless of which ratio obtains, ultimate success will turn on the issue of strategy. More specifically, success will depend on the Soviets' capability to effect a *blitzkrieg*.

Doctrine

NATO's forces are divided into eight corps sectors which are aligned in layer-cake fashion along the inter-German border (see Figure 1).[1] There are four corps sectors each in Northern Army Group (NORTHAG) and Central Army Group (CENTAG). There are also German and Danish forces located in Schleswig-Holstein, which is adjacent to the northern portion of the Central Front.

NATO's forces are arrayed to support a strategy of forward defense. In other words, to meet a Pact offensive, the forces in each

---

[1] A corps normally controls from 2–3 divisions as well as a number of nondivisional assets. In NATO, corps are comprised of forces from only one nation.

of NATO's corps sectors are deployed very close to the border between the two Germanies. The objective is to meet and thwart an attack right at this boundary. Political as well as military considerations dictate the choice of this strategy. A number of defense analysts in the West, however, argue that NATO's chances of thwarting a Pact attack are negligible as long as NATO employs a forward defense. They claim that the Soviets can mass their forces at points of their choosing along NATO's extended front, achieve overwhelming force ratios, and then blast through NATO's forward defense. It would then be very easy to effect deep strategic penetrations, since NATO has few reserves which could be used to check the Soviets' armored spearheads. . . . The subsequent discussion will address the charge that NATO's strategy of forward defense is fundamentally flawed.

Soviet Blitzkrieg Strategy

How do the Soviets plan to fight a non-nuclear war in Europe? What, in other words, is their doctrine for fighting a conventional war? Western analysts often assume that the Soviets have a neatly packaged doctrine for fighting a conventional war. As will become evident, this is not the case. The assumption here is that they will employ a *blitzkrieg*. This strategy calls for the attacker to concentrate his armored forces at one or more points along the defender's front, pierce that front, and race deep into the defender's rear. The aim is to avoid a broad frontal attack and, instead, to drive a small number of powerful armored columns into the depths of the defense. Although it may be necessary to engage in a set-piece battle to accomplish the initial breakthrough, a high premium is placed on avoiding further battles of this sort and, instead, following the path of least resistance deep into the opponent's rear. Of course, the tank, with its inherent flexibility, is the ideal weapon for implementing such a strategy.

The *blitzkrieg* is predicated upon the assumptions that the defender's army is geared to fighting along a well-established defensive line, and that the defender has a vulnerable communications network located in its rear. This network would be comprised of numerous lines of communication, along which move supplies as well as information, and key nodal points which join these various lines. Destruction of this central nervous system is tantamount to destroying the army. The attacker, therefore, attempts to pierce the defender's front and then drive *deep* into the defender's rear, severing lines of communication and destroying key junctures in the communications network as he proceeds.

Although the Soviets do not use the term *blitzkrieg,* it is clear that they pay serious attention to the question of how to effect a

Figure 1. NATO Corps Sectors West Germany

blitzkrieg against NATO. They continually emphasize the importance of massing large tank forces on narrow fronts, breaking
through NATO's forward defenses, and then racing deep into NA-
TO's rear so as to bring about the rapid collapse of NATO's
forces. . . .

Soviet Prospects for Effecting a Blitzkrieg in Central Europe

By choosing a forward defense strategy, NATO has effectively
determined that a war in Europe will be won or lost along the inter-
German border. It is thus imperative that NATO thwart the Pact in
those initial battles along the border. . . . If the Soviets win those
initial battles and penetrate with large armored forces deep into
NATO's rear, NATO's fate is sealed, since it has neither the reserve
strength necessary to counter such penetrations, nor the strategic
depth which would allow for retreat and the establishment of a new
front.

To determine whether the Soviets can successfully launch a
blitzkrieg against NATO's forward defense, two key questions must
be answered. First, can the Soviets achieve the necessary force
ratios on their main axes of advance so that they can then open
gateways into NATO's rear? In other words, given the deployment
of NATO's forces as well as the terrain, how likely is it that the
Soviets will be able to repeat the German achievement opposite the
Ardennes Forest in 1940? . . .

Second, if the Soviets are able to tear open a hole or two in
NATO's defensive front, will the Soviets be able to exploit those
openings and penetrate into the depths of the NATO defense before
NATO has a chance to shift forces and slow the penetrating spearheads? Effecting a deep strategic penetration in the "fog of war,"
when the defender is doing everything possible to seal off the gaps
in his defense, is difficult and requires a first-rate army. How capable
is the Soviet Army of accomplishing this difficult task? Although it
is not possible to provide definitive answers to these questions,
there is good reason to believe that NATO is capable of thwarting a
Soviet *blitzkrieg* and turning the conflict into a war of attrition.

The Initial Deployment Patterns

When considering Soviet deployment patterns for a conventional
European war, the most basic question is: how will the Soviets
apportion their forces across the front? More specifically, will the
Soviets disperse their forces rather evenly across the front, mounting attacks along numerous axes, or will they concentrate their
forces at one, two, or three points along the inter-German border?
In many of the accounts by Western analysts, it is assumed that a

Soviet offensive will be a multi-pronged one. . . [and] that the Soviets will achieve overwhelming superiority in forces on *each* of these avenues of attack.

It is possible that the Soviets might choose to launch an offensive along multiple axes of advance. This would be consistent with their doctrine for fighting a nuclear war in Europe, where the emphasis is on keeping the attacking forces widely dispersed so that they are not vulnerable to nuclear attacks. However, such a deployment pattern would hardly facilitate employment of a *blitzkrieg*, simply because it would be virtually impossible for the Soviets, given the present overall balance of forces, to achieve overwhelming force ratios on any of the axes. This can be demonstrated by looking at a *hypothetical* but realistic model of the Central Front.

Let us assume that the Pact has 64 armored division equivalents while NATO has 32; in other words, the Pact has a 2:1 force advantage across the front.[2] Furthermore, assume that the Soviets plan to employ a multi-pronged attack, aiming to strike along six main axes. In keeping with the dictates of a forward defense, NATO divides its 32 divisions evenly among its eight corps sectors (see Figure 2). It is usually assumed that to overwhelm the defense, an attacking force needs more than a 3:1 advantage in forces on the main axes of advance; assume, then, in the first instance, that the Soviets decide that they require a 5:1 advantage. They would therefore need 20 divisions per axis, which would allow them only three main axes of advance[3] (see Figure 3). Moreover, they would be quite vulnerable to NATO in the remaining five corps sectors.

If we assume that the Soviets require only a 4:1 advantage on the main axes, they would then need 16 divisions per axis. This would allow them only four main axes; however, they would not have any forces left with which to defend the remaining corps sectors (see Figure 4). If the Soviets were to aim for the projected six axes, they would be able to place approximately ten divisions on each main axis (see Figure 5). This would give them a force ratio on each axis of 2.5:1, which is hardly satisfactory in light of the widely recognized assumption that an attack requires more than a 3:1 advantage

---

[2] It should be emphasized that in light of the balance of standing forces in Central Europe (1.2:1 in terms of armored division equivalents) and the fact that NATO has the capability to match the Pact as it brings in reinforcements, this 2:1 force advantage is a conservative figure. Unless otherwise specified, the unit of measurement in all subsequent discussion of force ratios is armored division equivalents.

[3] This *hypothetical* model is based on the important assumption that the Soviets can only place one main axis in each corps sector. As will become evident in the subsequent discussion, the terrain features along the inter-German border force the attacker to think in terms of a single axis per corps sector. Moreover, in light of the length of the various NATO corps sectors and the length of front the Soviets allot their attacking divisions and armies, it is most likely that the Soviets would locate only one axis in each corps sector.

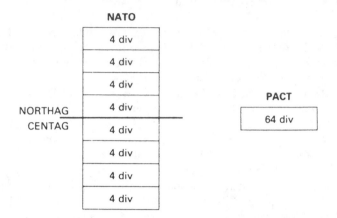

Figure 2. Initial Distribution of NATO Divisions

NATO

| 4 div |
| 4 div |
| 4 div |
| 4 div |
| 4 div |
| 4 div |
| 4 div |
| 4 div |

NORTHAG
CENTAG

PACT

| 64 div |

Figure 3. Distribution of Forces When Soviets Desire 5:1 Advantage

NATO		PACT
4 div	←	20
4 div	←	1
4 div	←	20
4 div	←	1
4 div	←	20
4 div	←	1
4 div	←	1
4 div	←	0

NORTHAG
CENTAG

on each main axis to succeed. Obviously, the more axes you have, the smaller the advantage you achieve on each axis. Finally, the point is reached, in this case with eight main axes of advance, where the distribution of forces on each axis is the same as the overall 2:1 ratio (see Figure 6).

It is apparent from this *hypothetical* model that as long as NATO keeps the overall force ratio under 2:1, it is impossible for the Soviets to have 6–10 axes of advance and at the same time have an overwhelming advantage in forces on each axis (i.e., a ratio of 4:1 or more). They just do not have a great enough overall force advantage to allow them to spread out their forces on numerous widely dispersed axes. The matter of force ratios aside, from

Figure 4. Distribution of Forces When Soviets Desire 4:1 Advantage

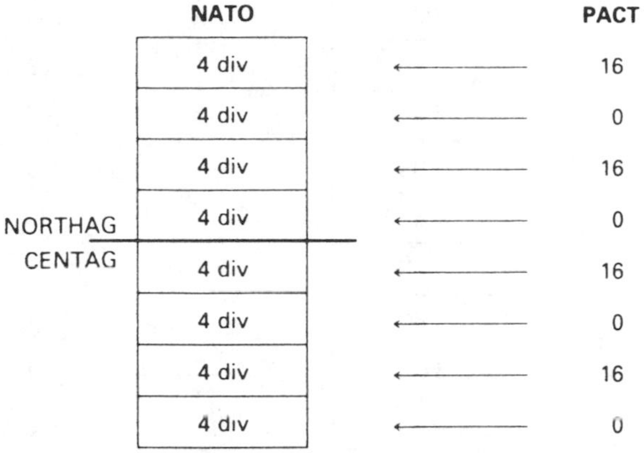

	NATO		PACT
	4 div	←	16
	4 div	←	0
	4 div	←	16
NORTHAG	4 div	←	0
CENTAG	4 div	←	16
	4 div	←	0
	4 div	←	16
	4 div	←	0

Figure 5. Distribution of Forces When Soviets Aim for 6 Main Axes

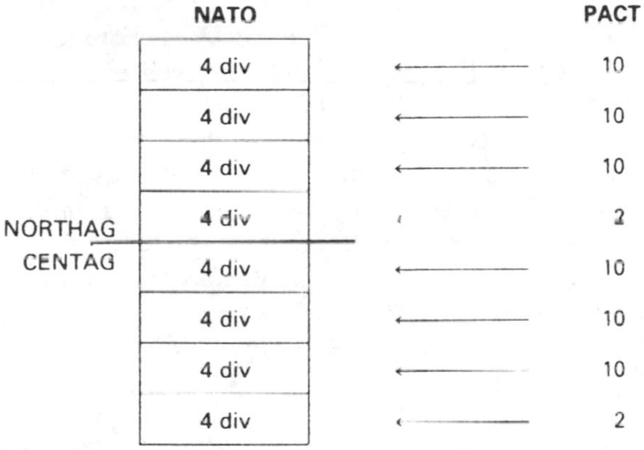

	NATO		PACT
	4 div	←	10
	4 div	←	10
	4 div	←	10
NORTHAG	4 div	←	2
CENTAG	4 div	←	10
	4 div	←	10
	4 div	←	10
	4 div	←	2

NATO's viewpoint, a multi-pronged attack is the most desirable Pact deployment pattern. Then, NATO, whose forces are evenly spread out along a wide front, does not have to concern itself with shifting forces to counter massive concentrations of force by the Pact. From NATO's perspective, a multi-pronged attack results in a propitious meshing of the offensive and defensive deployment patterns.

If the Pact does choose to employ a multi-pronged attack, it will, at best, end up pushing NATO back across a broad front, similar to the way the Soviets pushed the Germans westward across Europe in World War II. This is not a *blitzkrieg,* but a strategy of attrition. If the Soviets hope to defeat NATO with a *blitzkrieg,* they will have

Figure 6. Distribution of Forces When Soviets Aim for 8 Main Axes

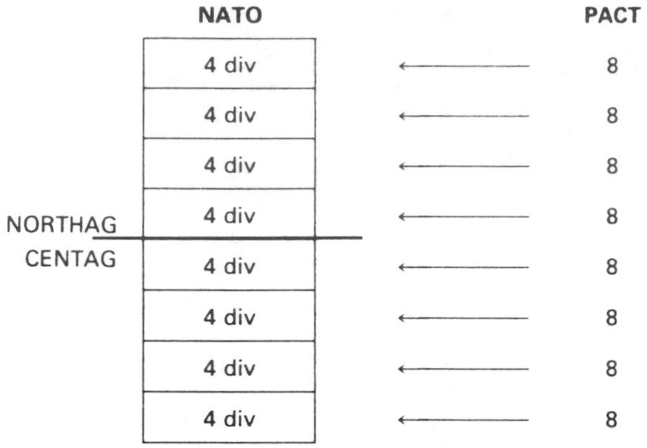

NATO		PACT
4 div	←	8
4 div	←	8
4 div	←	8
NORTHAG 4 div	←	8
CENTAG 4 div	←	8
4 div	←	8
4 div	←	8
4 div	←	8

to concentrate massive amounts of armor on one, two or, at most, three major axes of advance. This raises the obvious questions: where are those axes likely to be? and how well-positioned is NATO to deal with the most likely Pact deployment patterns? More specifically, are NATO's forces positioned so that they can: first, stymie the initial onslaughts on the various potential axes of advance; and secondly, provide the time for NATO to move reinforcements to threatened positions, and, in effect, erase the temporary superiority in forces that the Pact has achieved by massing its forces at specific points? These questions are best answered by closely examining, corps sector by corps sector, both the terrain and the deployment of NATO's forces.

It is most unlikely that the Pact would place a major axis of advance in either the far north or the far south of the NATO front. In the south, this would preclude a major attack against II German Corps, simply because it would not result in a decisive victory. The Allies could afford to lose almost the entire corps sector, reaching back to the French border, and they would still be able to continue the war. Moreover, the mountainous terrain in this part of Germany is not conducive to the movement of large armored forces. In the north, a major offensive against Schleswig-Holstein is unlikely. Although the terrain is not mountainous in this sector there are still enough obstacles (bogs, rivers, urban sprawl around Hamburg) to hinder the movement of a large armored force. Furthermore, a Pact success in this region would not constitute a mortal blow to NATO. The main body of NATO's forces would still be intact and capable of conducting a vigorous defense.

Channeling Forces: The Pact's Axes of Attack in Centag

The Soviets are most likely to locate their main attacks along the front stretching from the I Dutch Corps Sector in the north to the VII American Corps Sector in the south. Let us consider the three key corps sectors in CENTAG (III German, V U.S., and VII U.S.). Generally, the terrain in the CENTAG area is very obstacle-ridden. Besides being a mountainous region, it has numerous rivers and forests. Consequently, there are a small number of natural avenues of attack in CENTAG. Actually, there are three potential axes on which the Soviets are likely to attack.

The most threatening of the three possibilities would be an attack from the Thuringian Bulge through the Fulda Gap, aimed at Frankfurt (see Figure 7). Except for the Fulda River, the terrain on this axis should not greatly hinder the movement of large armored forces. Importantly, the axis cuts across the "wasp-waist" or the narrowest section of Germany. The distance from the inter-German border to Frankfurt is a mere 100 km. Frankfurt, because of its central location in Germany's communications network, would be a most attractive target. Capturing Frankfurt would effectively cut Germany in half, and given the importance of north-south lines of communication, would leave NATO's forces in southern Germany isolated.

The second potential axis of advance is located in the sector covered by the III German Corps. The attacking forces would move through the Göttingen Corridor, just south of the Harz Mountains. The industrialized Ruhr is located due west of Göttingen. Although the terrain on the western half of this axis (between Paderborn and the Ruhr) is suitable for the large-scale employment of tanks, the terrain on the eastern half of the axis, which the attacker must traverse first, is not obstacle-free. There are a number of forests in the region, and the attacking forces would have to cross the Leine River and then the Weser River.

There is a third potential axis of advance in CENTAG, although it is less attractive than the axes which run through the Fulda Gap and the Göttingen Corridor. This axis runs from Bohemia through the area around the city of Hof toward Stuttgart: the Hof Corridor. The terrain that an attacking force would have to traverse there is considerably more obstacle-ridden than the terrain along the other axes. Moreover, Stuttgart is a far less attractive target than either Frankfurt or the Ruhr. Aside from these three axes, there are no attractive alternatives.

NATO's forces in CENTAG should be able to contain a major Soviet attack in this region. There are only a limited number of potential axes of advance, each of which is quite narrow and well defined and each of which NATO is well prepared to defend.

Figure 7. Most Likely Axes of Advance in a Warsaw Pact Attack Against NATO

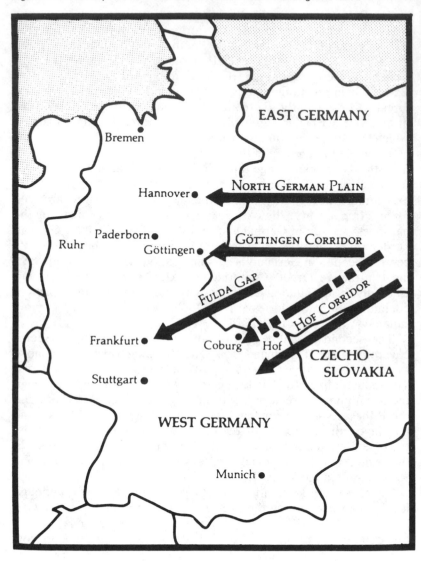

Moreover, NATO has contingency plans to shift forces to combat Soviet efforts designed to achieve overwhelming force ratios at the points of main attack. NATO's prospect of successfully halting a Soviet attack are further strengthened by the terrain, which not only limits the number of potential axes, but also channels the attacking forces across the width of Germany. In other words, the potential axes of advance are rather narrow and do not allow the attacker to spread his forces after the initial breakthrough.[4] In 1940, once the Germans crossed the Meuse River, they came upon the open, rolling plains of northeastern France, which was ideal terrain for armored forces. This would not be the case in CENTAG, where the attacking forces would be canalized by terrain throughout their movement across Germany. This should contribute to NATO's prospects for stopping a Soviet penetration before a decisive blow can be landed.

Another reason for optimism is that the NATO corps sectors in CENTAG are manned by German and American Forces, which are the best in NATO. Furthermore, there are reinforcements in CEN-TAG. The United States has pre-positioned materiel for two divisions in CENTAG's rear. Also, French and Canadian forces (three small French armored divisions and one Canadian brigade) are located in CENTAG and can serve as an operational reserve for this half of NATO's defense.

The North German Plain: Open Road for a Pact Advance?

Now, consider NATO's prospects for containing a Soviet attack directed against NORTHAG. It is widely held that NATO is more vulnerable in this region than in CENTAG. The terrain in NOR-THAG, because it is not mountainous and covered with forests, is generally held to be more favorable to the movement of large armored formations. Frequent reference is made to the suitability of the North German Plain for a *blitzkrieg*. Secondly, there are doubts about whether the Dutch and the Belgians, and even the British, have the capability to withstand a Soviet attack. There is only one German Corps Sector in NORTHAG and there is no U.S. Corps Sector, although pre-positioned materiel for a U.S. Corps, which will serve as an operational reserve for NORTHAG, is being deployed near Bremen. Notwithstanding that NATO is more vulnerable in this region than in CENTAG, the prospects for thwarting a major Soviet attack in NORTHAG are quite good. The terrain is not obstacle-free by any means and, as will become clear, the Belgian

---

[4] It should be noted, however, that the Göttingen Corridor only covers the eastern half of West Germany. (It is approximately 100 km in length.) To the west of Paderborn, the terrain is open and generally well suited for armored warfare.

and Dutch Corps Sectors are not the weak links that they are often said to be.

NORTHAG covers a front of only 225 km while CENTAG defends a front that is more than two times as long (500 km). Appropriately, the corps sectors in NORTHAG are smaller than those in CENTAG. The I Belgian Corps occupies the southernmost and smallest sector in NORTHAG, measuring only 35 km. Approximately one-third of the front is covered by the Harz Mountains, while the terrain throughout the depth of the corps sector is laden with obstacles. Belgium's two divisions, small as they are, are adequate for defending this short front in the initial stages of an attack. Although it is unlikely that the Pact would place a main axis through this corps sector, if it did, forces from the III German Corps, immediately to the south, could be moved north to reinforce the Belgians, and forces from the U.S. Corps in reserve could be moved forward.

The North German Plain, above the Belgian Corps Sector, is covered by the I British and I German Corps. There is widespread agreement that the Pact will place a single main axis against NORTHAG and that that axis will be located on the North German Plain. Although there are no mountains and few forests in this region, there are obstacles in both the German and British Corps Sectors. In the British Corps Sector, there is significant urban sprawl centered on Hannover, which is located in the heart of this corps sector. Armored forces simply will not be able to move rapidly through those urban areas that NATO chooses to defend. Since urbanization continues in this area, it will become increasingly difficult, if not impossible, to avoid large-scale urban fighting in the event of war. There are also a number of rivers in the British sector. The terrain in the I German Corps Sector, on the other hand, is covered, in large part, by the Lüneberger Heath, which is a formidable impediment to the rapid movement of masses of armor. It is for this reason that the North German Plain is usually identified with the British Corps Sector.

The British Army of the Rhine (BAOR) is comprised of four small divisions, a force that is adequate for covering the 70 km corps sector front. There are, however, 13 brigades—or four and one-third formidable divisions—in the I German Corps Sector. Aside from the fact that these German forces are more than adequate for defending their assigned corps sector, they can be rapidly moved to the south to augment the BAOR and, of course, they can also move northward to help the Dutch. This contingent in the I German Corps Sector represents the largest concentration of forces in all of the sectors. Given its central location in NORTHAG as well as the excellent north-south lines of communication in that region, this force is a formidable instrument for thwarting a Pact attack across the North German Plain. Furthermore, there will be an American Corps, part of which is already deployed, in NORTHAG's rear. In sum, NATO *has* the wherewithal to deal with a Pact attack across the North German Plain.

Finally, there is the Dutch Corps Sector, which is manned by two Dutch divisions. Should the Soviets place a main axis through this sector, the Dutch forces, like their British and Belgian counterparts, should be capable of defending their front in the initial stages of the conflict. Then, forces from the adjacent I German Corps can be moved north to assist the Dutch. Moreover, the American Corps will be located directly to the rear of the Dutch Sector. The terrain within the Dutch Corps Sector is not conducive to the rapid movement of armored forces. In addition to the Elbe River, which forms the inter-German border in this sector, a number of other rivers, canals, and bogs are liberally sprinkled throughout this sector. The Lüneberger Heath, which is such a prominent feature in the adjacent I German Corps Sector, extends northward across the Dutch Sector. To add to the woes of the attacker, there is significant urban sprawl around Bremen and Bremerhaven. Finally, even if the attacking forces were able to penetrate through this sector rapidly, it is unlikely that NATO would be mortally wounded. Certainly, NATO would feel the loss of the ports in northern Germany. However, since the attacking forces would exit Germany into the northern part of the Netherlands, NATO would still have access to the most important Belgian and Dutch ports.

Force to Space Ratios

There are a number of additional points concerning Soviet and NATO deployment patterns that merit attention. The discussion has so far focused on the matter of the Pact's achieving overwhelming superiority on specific axes of advance. However, when examining prospects for a breakthrough at the point of main attack, one cannot simply focus on the *balance* of forces. It is also necessary to consider *force-to-space ratios*, or the number of divisions that the defender requires to *hold* a specific sector of territory. If a defender can comfortably hold 100 km with four divisions, then even if the attacker has 24 divisions, that attacker will have to sacrifice a significant number of his 24 divisions before he finally wears the defender down to the point where he can effect a penetration. Obviously, this would be a time-consuming as well as a costly process, during which the defender can bring in reinforcements. There is an important factor which complicates the attacker's task in such a situation: the "crossing the T" phenomenon. Simply put, there is not enough room for the attacker to place all of his 24 divisions at the point of attack. He must therefore locate a portion of his divisions in subsequent echelons behind the attacking forces, where their impact on the battlefield will be minimal while the first echelon is engaged. In essence, the defender is in the enviable position of being able to deal with the attacker's forces on a piecemeal basis. How do these abstract considerations relate to the European Central Front?

It is generally agreed that a brigade can hold a front approximately 7–15 km long. With 7 km, which is obviously the more desirable figure, a brigade should be able to hold its position for an extended period of time before it needs reinforcement. As the figure approaches 15 km, the defender should be able to cope with the initial onslaughts without any problem. However, it will be necessary to bring in reinforcements after a day or so since the attacker's forces will have begun to wear down the defender by then. Since the length of the NORTHAG front is 225 km, if one assumes that each brigade could hold 15 km, then a minimum of 15 brigades would be needed to cover the front. There are actually 30 brigades within the four NORTHAG corps sectors. Given that there are 30 brigades and a 225 km front, this means that each brigade will have to cover 7.5 km, which is extremely close to the most desirable force-to-space ratio for a brigade.

Now, let us assume that NATO deploys its 30 brigades along the NORTHAG front in the traditional "two brigades up, one back" configuration. This would leave 20 brigades to cover 225 km (each brigade would have to cover 11 km), with 10 brigades in immediate reserve. This leaves NATO in very good shape. Two other important points are in order. First, because there are a number of obstacles along the NORTHAG front, NATO would not have to worry about covering every section of the 225 km front. Second, the American Corps in NORTHAG's rear, when fully operational, will provide an additional nine brigades. Also, there are at least six armored infantry brigades in the German Territorial Army that could be assigned to NORTHAG. In short, NORTHAG does not have force-to-space problems.

The length of the CENTAG front is 500 km. Assuming 15 km per brigade, 33 brigades would be required to cover this front. NATO has 33 brigades in the four CENTAG corps sectors, a figure which is hardly alarming in light of the obstacle-ridden terrain along this portion of the NATO front and the fact that the brigades in these corps sectors are the heaviest in NATO and therefore will have the least amount of trouble covering 15 km of front. Furthermore, there are 21 brigades (including the French, but not including the German territorials) available for reinforcement in CENTAG's rear.

"Crossing the T" in Europe

Consider briefly the "crossing the T" phenomenon, which further highlights the problems that the Soviets will have breaking through NATO's forward positions. In one of the U.S. Army's standard scenarios for a major Soviet attack against one of the two U.S. Corps Sectors in CENTAG, a Soviet force of five divisions is pitted against two American divisions. In the opening battle, three Soviet divisions attack across about 40 to 50 km of front against two U.S. divisions. The remaining two Soviet divisions are held in immediate reserve. Thus, in that opening battle the ratio of forces directly engaged is 3:2 in the Pact's favor, not 5:2. (It should be noted that these ratios would be even more favorable to NATO if they were translated into armored division equivalents.) Of course, the key question is: can those three Soviet divisions so weaken the two American divisions that the remaining two Soviet divisions will be able to effect a breakthrough? In this regard, the matter of force-to-space ratios is of crucial importance. Since two divisions, or six brigades, are defending 40–50 km, each of these powerful American brigades will be holding approximately 7 km. Without a doubt, the Soviets would have a great deal of difficulty penetrating that American front.

Now, let us assume that the Soviets start with ten or even fifteen divisions, instead of the five employed in the above scenario. Only a very few of these additional divisions could be placed at the point of main attack, simply because there would be limited room on the front to accommodate them. They would have to be located *behind* the attacking forces, where they would have little impact on the initial battles. Certainly, the forces in each NATO corps sector should be capable of blunting the initial Soviet attack and providing adequate time for NATO to shift forces from other corps sectors and its operational reserves to threatened points along the front.

In sum, given the initial deployment patterns of both NATO and the Pact, it appears that NATO is reasonably well deployed to meet a Soviet *blitzkrieg*. Although both Pact and NATO deployment patterns have been examined, attention has been focused, for the most part, on examining *NATO*'s capability to thwart a *blitzkrieg*. Now let us shift the focus and examine, in detail, *Soviet* capabilities.

SOVIET CAPABILITIES FOR BLITZKRIEG WARFARE

To ascertain whether the Soviet Army has the capacity to effect a *blitzkrieg*, it is necessary to examine that Army on three levels. First, one must consider how the Soviet Army is organized. In other words, are the forces structured to facilitate a *blitzkrieg*? Second, it is necessary to consider doctrine, a subject that has already received some attention. Finally, there is the matter of raw skill. Assuming that the problems with force structure and doctrine are minimal, is the Soviet Army capable of performing the assigned task? There are, of course, no simple answers to these questions. They are nonetheless extremely important questions which have received little serious attention in the West, where it is all too often assumed that the Soviets have only strengths and no weaknesses.

Since almost all the Pact divisions that would be used in a European war are either armored or mechanized infantry, it seems reasonable to assume that the Pact is appropriately organized to launch a *blitzkrieg*. On close inspection, however, there are potential trouble spots in the Pact's force structure. Over the past decade, Soviet divisions have become extremely heavy units. Western analysts pay a great deal of attention to the large and growing number of tanks, infantry fighting vehicles, artillery pieces, rocket launchers, surface-to-air missiles, air defense guns, anti-tank guided missiles (ATGMs), and assorted other weapons that are found in Soviet as well as other Pact divisions. Past a certain point, however, there is an inverse relationship between the mass and the velocity of an attacking force. As the size of the attacking force increases, the logistical problems as well as the command and control problems increase proportionately. Then, it becomes very difficult to move that force rapidly—an *essential* requirement for a *blitzkrieg,* where the attacker is seeking to strike deep into the defender's rear before the defender can shift forces to deal with the penetrating forces. Although the notion is perhaps counterintuitive, bigger divisions are not necessarily better divisions when an attacking force is attempting to effect a *blitzkrieg*.

Consider now the matter of doctrine. As noted earlier, it is not possible to determine exactly how the Soviets plan to fight a conventional war in Europe. This is because the Soviets themselves are not sure; there is presently doctrinal uncertainty in their military circles. Certainly, they continue to emphasize the necessity of rapidly defeating NATO, should a war in Europe break out. The Soviets recognize, however, that it is becoming increasingly difficult to do this, especially because of the proliferation of ATGMs. Moreover, they are well aware of how these organizational problems compound their task. They realize that it will be difficult to effect deep strategic penetrations against prepared defenses. Although there has been a considerable effort to find a solution to this problem, if anything, the Soviets appear to be moving closer to a strategy of attrition. This is reflected in their growing reliance on artillery and dismounted infantry. There is no evidence that the Soviets have made a conscious decision to fight a war of attrition. Instead, it appears that they are being inexorably drawn in this direction by their efforts to neutralize the growing firepower, both ground-based and air-delivered, available to NATO. . . .

Soviet Training and Initiative

Finally, there is the question of whether the Soviet Army has the necessary raw skills. An army that intends to implement a *blitzkrieg* must have a highly flexible command structure as well as officers and NCOs at every level of the chain of command who are capable of exercising initiative. A *blitzkrieg* is not a steamroller: success is ultimately a consequence of able commanders making rapid-fire decisions in the "fog of battle" which enable the attacking forces to make the crucial deep strategic penetrations. Should the Soviets attack NATO, there is a chance that the Soviets will open a hole or holes in the NATO front. Naturally, NATO will try to close those holes and seal off any penetrations as quickly as possible. The key question is: can the Soviets exploit such opportunities before NATO, which is well prepared for such an eventuality, shuts the door? In this battle, the crucial determinant will not be how much firepower the Soviets have amassed for the breakthrough; success will be largely the result of highly skilled officers and NCOs making the decisions that will enable the armored spearheads to outrun NATO's defenses. A *blitzkrieg* depends on split-second timing since opportunity on the battlefield is so fleeting.

There is substantial evidence that Soviet officers and NCOs are sadly lacking in individual initiative and, furthermore, that the Soviet command structure is rigid. . . .

The Soviets are keenly aware of the need for initiative and flexibility, and they go to great lengths to stress the importance of these qualities in their military journals. These are not, however, attributes which can be willed into existence. Their absence is largely the result of powerful historical forces. Fundamental structural change in Soviet society and the Soviet military would be necessary before there would be any significant increase in flexibility and initiative. . . .

Other deficiencies in the Soviet Army cast doubt on the Soviets' capacity to launch a successful *blitzkrieg*. For example, the Soviets have significant problems with training.[5] Overreliance on training aids and simulators is a factor often cited, and there is widespread

---

[5] See Donnelly, "Soviet Soldier," pp. 117–120; Keith A. Dunn, "Soviet Military Weaknesses and Vulnerabilities: A Critique Of The Short War Advocates," memorandum prepared for Strategic Studies Institute, U.S. Army War College, Carlisle Barracks, PA, July 31, 1978, pp. 15–16; Herbert Goldhamer, *Soviet Military Management at the Troop Level*, R-1513-PR (Santa Monica, Calif.: Rand Corporation, May 1974), chapters 2–4; Leon Gouré and Michael J. Deane, "The Soviet Strategic View," *Strategic Review*, Vol. 8, No. 1 (Winter 1980), pp. 84–85; and Karber, "Anti-Tank Debate," p. 108.

feeling that the training process does not satisfactorily approximate actual combat conditions. Training is of special importance for the Soviets since their army is comprised largely of conscripts who serve a mere two years. Moreover, since new conscripts are trained in actual combat units, more than half of the troops in the 19 Soviet divisions in East Germany are soldiers with less than two years of experience. At any one time, a significant number of those troops is either untrained or partially trained. It should also be noted that Soviet soldiers are deficient in map reading, a skill which is of much importance for any army attempting to launch a *blitzkrieg*.[6]

Finally, one must consider the capabilities of the non-Soviet divisions, which comprise approximately half of the Pact's 57⅓ standing divisions. Although the Soviet divisions will certainly perform the critical tasks in any offensive, the non-Soviet divisions will have to play a role in the operation. Otherwise, the size of the offensive would have to be scaled down significantly. One cannot say with any degree of certainty that the East Europeans would be militarily incapable of performing their assigned task or that they would not commit themselves politically to supporting a Soviet-led offensive. The Soviets, however, would have to give serious consideration to the reliability of the East Europeans.[7] If the Soviets indeed pay such careful attention to the lessons of the Great Patriotic War as is widely claimed, they recall what happened opposite Stalingrad in 1942 when the Soviets were able to inflict a stunning defeat on the Germans by ripping through the sectors of the front covered by the Rumanians, the Hungarians, and the Italians.[8]

Although the Soviet Army has important deficiencies, it would still be a formidable opponent in a war in Europe; the Soviet Army is not by any means a hapless giant. Neither, however, is it an army which is well prepared to defeat NATO with a *blitzkrieg*. The shortcomings noted in the foregoing cast extreme doubt on the claim that the Soviets have the capability to launch a *blitzkrieg* with confidence of success. The Soviet Army is definitely not a finely tuned instrument capable of overrunning NATO at a moment's notice. To claim, then, that the Soviets have "adopted and improved the German *blitzkrieg* concept" has a hollow ring. Most importantly,

[6] Dunn, "Soviet Military Weaknesses," pp. 16–17.

[7] See Johnson et al., "The Armies of the Warsaw Pact" and Dale R. Herspring and Ivan Volgyes, "Political Reliability in the Eastern European Warsaw Pact Armies," *Armed Forces and Society*, Vol. 6, No. 2 (Winter 1980), pp. 270–296.

[8] As John Erickson notes, it is very unlikely "that any non-Soviet national force would be alloted an independent operational role on any scale." Erickson, "Soviet Military Capabilities in Europe," *Journal of the Royal United Services Institute*, Vol. 120, No. 1 (March 1975), p. 66. This could lead to problems for the Soviets because it forces them to disperse their own divisions, thus limiting the number available for the principal attacks.

the evidence indicates that the Soviets recognize these shortcomings and their implications for winning a quick victory.

CONCLUSION

Even if one were to discount these weaknesses of the Soviet Army, the task of quickly overrunning NATO's defenses would be a very formidable one. A Pact offensive would have to traverse the obstacle-ridden terrain which covers almost all of Germany and restricts the movement of large armored units. Moreover, there is good reason to believe that NATO has the wherewithal to thwart such an offensive. In short, NATO is in relatively good shape at the conventional level. The conventional wisdom which claims otherwise on this matter is a distortion of reality. . . .

This article highlights how important it is that NATO mobilize its forces immediately after the Pact begins its mobilization. A favorable balance of forces in a crisis will be a function of political as well as military factors. As Richard Betts notes in his very important article on this subject, "Even if intelligence monitoring can ensure warning, it cannot ensure authorization to respond to it."[9] Therefore, it is essential that NATO's political and military leaders carefully consider the various mobilization scenarios that they may face in a crisis. The real danger is that NATO's leaders will not agree to mobilize in a crisis for fear that such a move might provoke a Soviet attack. The risk of pushing the Soviets to preempt can be reduced, however, by avoiding certain provocative moves and by clearly communicating one's intentions to the other side. Nevertheless, the risk of provoking a Soviet attack by initiating NATO mobilization can never be completely erased. That risk, however, must be weighed against the far greater danger that if NATO does not mobilize, the capability to defend against a Pact attack will be lost. Moreover, once the Pact achieves a decisive superiority because of NATO's failure to mobilize, it would be not only difficult, but very dangerous for NATO to attempt to redress the balance with a tardy mobilization. Seeing that process set into motion, the Pact would have a very strong incentive to attack before NATO erased its advantage. In short, it is essential that NATO plan for ways to mobilize that do not provoke a Soviet attack, but, at the same time, ensure that NATO does not lose its present capability to defend itself effectively against a Soviet offensive.

[9] Betts, "Surprise Attack," p. 118.

Conventional Deterrence and
Conventional Retaliation in Europe

SAMUEL P. HUNTINGTON

For a quarter century the slow but continuing trend in NATO
strategy—and in thinking about NATO strategy—has been from
emphasis on nuclear deterrence to emphasis on conventional deterrence. . . . The development of Soviet strategic nuclear capabilities
and, more particularly, the massive deployment by the Soviets of
theater nuclear weapons raised serious questions as to the desirability of NATO's relying overwhelmingly on early use of nuclear
weapons to deter Soviet attack. In the following years, the emphasis
shifted to the need for stronger conventional forces capable of
mounting a forward defense of Germany for a period of time and to
a strategy of flexible response, in which, if deterrence failed and if
conventional defenses did not hold, NATO would have the options
of resorting to tactical, theater, and eventually strategic nuclear
weapons. In 1967 this strategy become official NATO policy in
MC 14/3.

The past several years have seen increasing support for shifting
the deterrent emphasis even further in the conventional direction.
This perceived need derives, of course, from the facts of strategic
parity between the U.S. and the Soviet Union, Soviet achievement
of substantial predominance in theater nuclear forces, and a continued and, in some respects, enhanced Soviet superiority in conventional forces. In these circumstances, in the event of a successful
Soviet conventional advance into Western Europe, how credible
would be the threat of a nuclear response? In the face of Soviet
superiority at that level, why would NATO resort to theater nuclear
weapons, with all the destruction to both sides that would entail?
Even more significantly, why would the United States use or even
threaten to use its strategic nuclear forces, if that would ensure
massive Soviet retaliation against North America? . . . The standard

From "Conventional Deterrence and Conventional Retaliation in Europe" by Samuel
P. Huntington, *International Security*, Winter 1983/84 (Vol. 8, No. 3) pp. 251–275, ©
1984 by the President and Fellows of Harvard College and of the Massachusetts
Institute of Technology. Reprinted by permission of MIT Press, Cambridge, Massachusetts and the copyright holders. Portions of the text and all footnotes have been
omitted.

reassurances of the validity of the American nuclear guarantee, as Henry Kissinger put it in 1979, "cannot be true" and "it is absurd to base the strategy of the West on the credibility of the threat of mutual suicide." . . . The conclusion almost universally drawn from [the] perceived deteriorating credibility of the nuclear deterrent to Soviet conventional attack in Western Europe is the need to strengthen NATO conventional forces. The desirability of doing this is broadly supported by conservative, liberal, and, in Europe, socialist politicians. It has been endorsed in one form or another by a wide variety of military experts and strategists, including General Bernard Rogers, Professor Michael Howard, Senator Sam Nunn, the Union of Concerned Scientists study group, the No First Use "Gang of Four," the American Academy of Arts and Sciences European Security Study, informed Social Democratic Party (SPD) analysts, the Reagan Administration, and, so far as one can gather, those Democratic presidential aspirants who have addressed the issue. The conventional wisdom is, in short, that stronger conventional forces are needed to enhance conventional deterrence and thus compensate for the declining effectiveness of nuclear deterrence.

THE REQUIREMENTS OF CONVENTIONAL DETERRENCE

The conventional wisdom suffers from two significant weaknesses.

First, NATO countries are unlikely to commit the resources necessary to achieve the required strengthening of NATO defenses. . . . After a quarter of a century, deterrence by conventional forces remains appealing, but it also remains an unreality. For understandable reasons, European governments and publics have been unwilling to appropriate the funds and make the sacrifices that would be required to make it effective. This pattern continues. In 1978 the Alliance committed itself to the Long Term Defense Program requiring 3 percent annual increases in defense spending by its member countries. Apart from the United States, however, the members of NATO have . . . generally failed to meet that goal. General Rogers now argues that an effective conventional defense for NATO can be achieved if its members increase their military spending by 4 percent annually. The European Security Study comes to a similar conclusion. But if NATO countries have failed to achieve a sustained 3 percent increase, how realistic is it to talk of 4 percent increases? The attitudes of European publics and governments do not seem to be more favorable to voting larger defense budgets than they have been in the past, and economic conditions for such increases are at present far less propitious. This does not mean that no increases in NATO conventional defense capability will occur. Clearly they will. . . . Thus, while nuclear deterrence of a Soviet conventional attack on Western Europe suffers from a lack of credibility, conventional deterrence of such an attack suffers from a lack of capability.

The second problem with the strengthening-conventional-forces approach is more serious. It concerns not inadequate resources but erroneous, if generally unarticulated, assumptions. It would still be present in some form even if NATO defense spending did increase by 4 percent a year. It is much more salient if that goal is not achieved. It involves the requirements of deterrence.

Military forces can contribute to deterrence in three ways. First, they may deter simply by being in place and thus increasing the uncertainties and potential costs to an aggressor, even though they could not mount an effective defense. Allied forces in Berlin have performed this role for years, and the argument for being able to move airborne forces and Marines rapidly to the Persian Gulf, in the event of a Soviet invasion of Iran, rests on a similar premise. Simply the presence of American forces in Khuzistan might deter the Soviets from moving in on the oil fields. Second, military forces can deter by raising the possibility of a successful defense and hence forcing the aggressor to risk defeat in his effort or to pay additional costs for success. This has been the traditional deterrent role assigned to NATO forces in Germany. Third, military forces can deter by threatening retaliation against assets highly valued by the potential aggressor. This, of course, has been the classic role of strategic nuclear forces. Unlike deterrence by presence or deterrence by defense, however, this form of deterrence is not effective simply because the requisite military capabilities exist; it requires a conscious choice by the defender to retaliate; and hence the aggressor has to calculate not only the defender's capabilities to implement a retaliatory threat but also the credibility of that threat.

One of the striking characteristics of the new conventional wisdom is the extent to which stronger conventional defenses are identified with a stronger conventional deterrent. If only NATO can enhance its military defenses, Soviet aggression will be deterred: this assumption is implicit in most of the arguments for stronger NATO forces and it is at the heart of the report by the European Security Study. . . .

To a limited degree, this assumption is, of course, justified. The stronger NATO forces are, the greater the investment the Soviets would have to make to achieve a given set of goals in Western Europe. Yet the easy identification of deterrence with defense flies in the face of logic and in the face of longstanding traditions in strategic thought. One of the landmark works on this subject (still valuable after twenty years), *Deterrence and Defense* by Glenn Snyder, is, indeed, based on the opposition between defense and deterrence and the extent to which strategies and forces appropriate to serve one goal may not be suited to achievement of the other. In addition, deterrence itself, that is, the effort to influence enemy intentions, may be pursued through both "denial capabilities— typically, conventional ground, sea, and tactical air forces" and "punishment capabilities—typically, strategic nuclear power for either massive or limited retaliation." In the years since Snyder, strategists have generally tended to make the same identification. In the process, concern with the distinction between nuclear and conventional capabilities has tended to obscure the equally important distinction between defensive and retaliatory capabilities. In current NATO planning, nuclear and conventional capabilities can both be used for defensive purposes; only nuclear capabilities can be used for retaliatory purposes. Eliminating or drastically downgrading nuclear forces means eliminating or drastically downgrading the retaliatory component that has always been present in NATO strategy. Those who argue for conventional defense are, in effect, arguing for deterrence without retaliation. This is a fundamental change in NATO strategy, at least as significant in terms of deterrence as the shift from nuclear to conventional forces. For as both logic and experience make clear, a purely denial strategy inherently is a much weaker deterrent than one which combines both denial and retaliation.

For a prospective attacker, the major difference between denial and retaliation concerns the certainty and controllability of the costs he may incur. If faced simply with a denial deterrent, he can estimate how much effort he will have to make and what his probable losses will be in order to defeat the enemy forces and achieve his objective. He can then balance these costs against the gains he will achieve. He may choose zero costs and zero gains; he may decide to limit his gains to what can be achieved by a given level of costs; he may decide to incur whatever costs are necessary to achieve the gains he desires. The choice is his. If, however, he is confronted with a retaliatory deterrent, he may well be able to secure the gains he wants with relatively little effort, but he does not know the total costs he will have to pay, and those costs are in large measure beyond his control. The Soviet general staff can give the Politburo reasonably accurate estimates as to what forces it will require and what losses it will probably suffer to defeat NATO forces in Germany and extend Soviet control to the Rhine. For years, however, it could not predict with any assurance whether U.S. nuclear retaliation to such a move would be directed to battlefield targets, military targets in Eastern Europe and/or the Soviet Union, or industrial and population centers in the Soviet Union. Precisely this uncertainty and absence of control made the threat of retaliation a strong deterrent. If these problems of uncertainty and uncontrollability are eliminated or greatly reduced, the effectiveness of the deterrent is seriously weakened.

The difficulties of relying on deterrence by defensive means have long been emphasized in the strategic field. No defense system—antiaircraft, ABM, or civil defense—deployable now or in the foreseeable future could prevent some nuclear weapons from reaching their targets and causing unprecedented destruction. Hence deterrence of an attack must depend upon the ability to retaliate after absorbing the attack. Much the same is true at the conventional level. In the past, conventional deterrence has usually meant deterrence-by-denial, and the frequency of wars in history suggests that this conventional-denial deterrence was not often effective. . . .

An initial offensive by a strong and determined attacker, particularly if accompanied by surprise, inevitably will score some gains. As Saadia Amiel summed up the lessons of the 1973 Arab-Israeli war and the implications of precision guided munitions (PGMs): "without very clear offensive options, a merely passive or responsive defensive strategy, which is based on firepower and fighting on friendly territory, cannot withstand an offensive strategy of an aggressor who possesses a relatively large, well-prepared standing offensive military force." This is certainly the case in central Europe. Given NATO's current conventional defenses and any likely improvements in them, a Soviet conventional offensive in Europe is, inevitably, going to be at least a partial success. . . . Assume that the Soviet offensive does grind to a halt after Soviet forces have occupied a greater or a lesser portion of West Germany. What then? In theory, the Allies should bring in their reinforcements from North America and put together a counteroffensive to drive the Soviets back. This would, however, be an extraordinarily difficult military and logistical undertaking. Inevitably the pressures would be on all parties to attempt to negotiate a cease-fire and a resolution of the conflict. With their armies ensconced in Hesse, Lower Saxony, and Bavaria and the differing interests of the Allies manifesting themselves, the Soviets would clearly have the upper hand in such negotiations. It takes little imagination to think of the types of appeals the Soviets would make to West German authorities and political groups to accept some degree of demilitarization or neutralization in order to secure Soviet withdrawal and to avoid the replay of World War II in their country.

A Soviet invasion of West Germany that ended with the neutralization and/or demilitarization of all or part of that country would be a tremendous success from the Soviet point of view. It would decisively alter the balance of power in Europe and in the world. Its costs, in terms of losses of men and equipment, would have to be very substantial to outweigh these political, military, and diplomatic gains. In 1939 and in 1941, once they had devised means to neutralize possible Allied retaliation by bomber attacks on cities, Hitler and the Japanese launched their offensives into Poland and southeast Asia expecting, not entirely unreasonably, that their democratic opponents would lack the staying power to deprive them of their initial territorial conquests. In the absence of a credible retaliatory threat against valued Soviet assets, the Allies would be tempting fate to assume that the Soviets would not be tempted to make a comparable move into Western Europe sometime in the next decade or two.

In sum, a substantial increase in NATO conventional forces is unfeasible politically. Even if it could be achieved, it would not compensate for the decline in the credibility of nuclear retaliation as a deterrent. To be effective, deterrence has to move beyond the possibility of defense and include the probability of retaliation. Conventional deterrence requires not just an increase in conventional forces; it also requires a reconstitution of conventional strategy.

THE ROLE OF CONVENTIONAL RETALIATION

The new element required in NATO strategy is conventional retaliation. NATO has four possible means of deterring Soviet aggression: defense with conventional or nuclear forces and retaliation by conventional or nuclear forces. Under MC 14/3, NATO relied on a sequence of three responses, conventional defense, nuclear defense, nuclear retaliation (Figure 1). The decreasing credibility of NATO use of nuclear weapons, however, has loosened the connections between these responses (indicated by the dotted lines in Figure 2). As a result, both nuclear and retaliatory deterrence are weakened. The problem is to restore the latter without resorting to the former. The need, in short, is to add some form of conventional retaliation to NATO strategy (Figure 3). That retaliatory component can best take the form of provision for, in the case of a Soviet attack, a prompt conventional retaliatory offensive into Eastern Europe.

For the threat of retaliation to be an effective deterrent it must (a) be directed against a target that is highly valued by the potential aggressor and (b) have a high degree of probability it will be implemented. It is reasonable to assume that the Soviet elite values, next to the security of the Soviet Union itself, the security of its satellite regimes in Eastern Europe. If the threat of nuclear attacks against the Soviet Union has lost its credibility, the next most effective threat NATO can pose surely is the possibility of a conventional retaliatory offensive directed against the Soviet empire in Eastern Europe. In addition, as Snyder observed, the credibility of the threat of retaliation to "a large-scale Soviet ground attack on Western Europe depends on convincing the enemy that we would gain more by carrying out this threat than we would lose.'' Precisely because this condition is no longer met, the threat of nuclear retaliation has cost its credibility. No such problem arises, however, by the threat of a conventional retaliatory offensive into Eastern Europe.

Figure 1.   Original Flexible Response

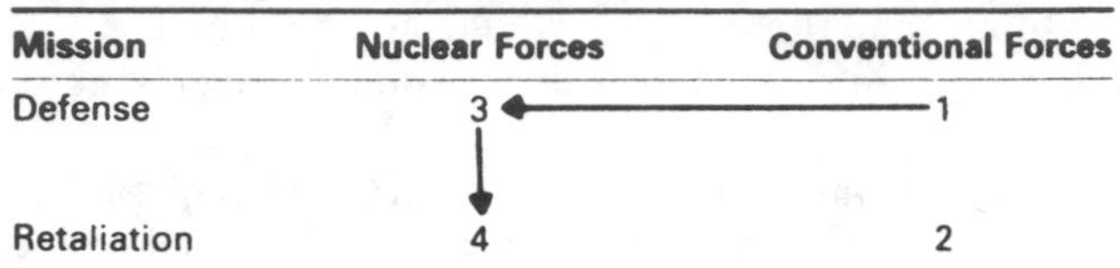

Mission	Nuclear Forces	Conventional Forces
Defense	3 ◄———————————— 1	
Retaliation	4	2

Figure 2.   Deteriorated Flexible Response

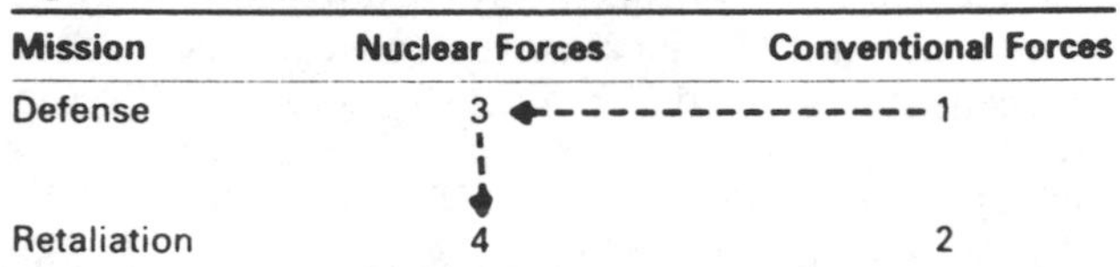

Mission	Nuclear Forces	Conventional Forces
Defense	3 ◄– – – – – – – – – – – – – 1	
Retaliation	4	2

Figure 3.   Reconstituted Flexible Response

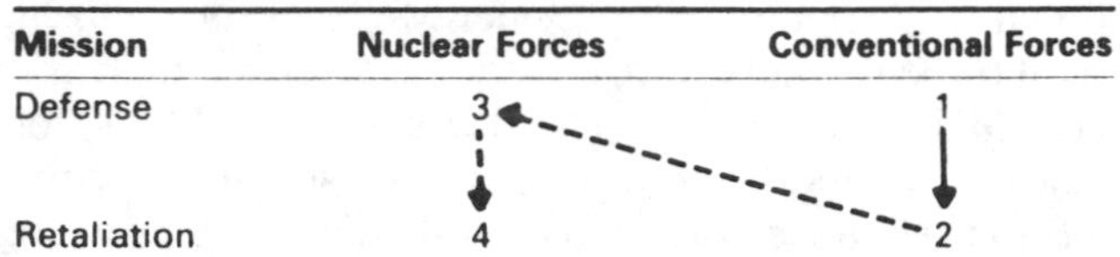

Mission	Nuclear Forces	Conventional Forces
Defense	3 ◄ ╲	1
Retaliation	4	2

Almost every other form of retaliation against conventional attack involves escalation, either vertical, as in NATO doctrine, or, conceivably, horizontal. A conventional offensive into Eastern Europe, in contrast, is retaliation in kind, at the same level and in the same theater as the initial attack. It thus has unimpeachable credibility. Just as the Soviets have to believe that the United States would retaliate in kind against a strategic attack on American cities or a theater nuclear attack on Western Europe, they would also have to believe that the United States and its allies would retaliate in kind against a conventional attack on West Germany. Deterrence without retaliation is weak; retaliation through escalation is risky. Conventional retaliation strengthens the one without risking the other.

Strategy should exploit enemy weaknesses. A deterrent strategy that included provision for conventional retaliation would do this in two ways. First, it would capitalize on the uncertainties and fears that the Soviets have concerning the reliability of their Eastern

European allies, and the uncertainties and fears that the governments of those countries have concerning the reliability of their own peoples. It would put at potential risk the system of controls over Eastern Europe that the Soviets have developed over thirty years and which they consider critical to their own security. The deterrent impact of the threat of conventional retaliation would be further enhanced by prior Allied assurances to Eastern European governments that their countries would not be invaded if they abstained from the conflict and did not cooperate in the Soviet attack on the West. At the very least, such an invitation would create uneasiness, uncertainty, and divisiveness within satellite governments, and hence arouse concerns among the Soviets as to their reliability. In practice, the Allied offensive would have to be accompanied with carefully composed political-psychological warfare appeals to the peoples of Eastern Europe stressing that the Allies were not fighting them but the Soviets and urging them to cooperate with the advancing forces and to rally to the liberation of their countries from Soviet military occupation and political control. A conventional retaliatory strategy is based on the assumption that the West German reserves, territorial army, and populace will put up a more unified, comprehensive, and determined resistance to occupation by Soviet armies than the East German, Czech, Polish, and Hungarian forces and populations will to liberation from Soviet armies. (If this assumption is unwarranted, the foundations of not only a conventional retaliatory strategy but also of NATO would be in question.) Politically speaking, the Soviet Union has more to lose from Allied armies invading Eastern Europe than NATO has to lose from Soviet armies invading Western Europe. The Soviet Union should, consequently, give higher priority to preventing an Allied offensive into Eastern Europe than to pushing a Soviet offensive into Western Europe.

If the satellites did fight, the extent of their participation in a war, it is generally recognized, would depend on the scope and speed of Soviet success in the conflict. So long as the Soviets are moving westward, they are more likely to have complacent and cooperative allies. If, however, they are stalemated or turned back, disaffection is likely to appear within the Warsaw Pact. A prompt Allied offensive into Eastern Europe would stimulate that disaffection at the very start of the conflict. Neither the Soviets nor, more importantly, the satellite governments could view with equanimity West German tanks on the road to Leipzig and Berlin and American divisions heading for Prague and Cracow. From the viewpoint of deterrence, such a prospect would tremendously enhance the undesirability of war for the governments of these satellite countries. Those governments, which provide more than one-third of the Warsaw Pact combat forces on the central front, would lose more than anyone else in such a war and hence would become a puissant lobby urging their Soviet partner not to initiate war.

A conventional offensive into Eastern Europe would thus threaten the Soviets where they are politically weak. It would also be aimed at Soviet military weakness. Both Western observers and Soviet military leaders agree that Soviet officers and NCOs are much better at implementing a carefully detailed plan of attack than they are at adjusting to rapidly changing circumstances. A conventional offensive into Eastern Europe would confront the Soviets with just exactly the situation their doctrine and strategy attempt to avoid: one in which they do not have control of developments and in which they face a high probability of uncertainty and surprise. It would put a premium on flexibility and adaptability, qualities in which the Soviets recognize themselves to be deficient. . . .

A prompt Allied offensive into Eastern Europe would also greatly increase the probability of a protracted war. Soviet planning, however, is in large part directed toward a short-war scenario in which the Soviets score a break-through, occupy a substantial portion of West Germany, and then negotiate a cease-fire from a position of strength. With a retaliatory strategy, Soviet armies might be in West Germany but Allied armies would also be in East Europe, and driving them out would require more time for mobilization and organization of a counteroffensive.

The basic point, moreover, is deterrence. The prospects for the sustained success of the Allied offensive into Eastern Europe do not have to be 100 percent. They simply have to be sufficiently better than zero and to raise sufficient unpleasant uncertainties to increase significantly the potential costs and risks to the Soviets of starting a war.

Current NATO strategy already contemplates the possibility of a counter-offensive. It would occur after the enemy's offensive forces have penetrated NATO territory and then been slowed or brought to a halt and NATO forces have been reinforced. A counteroffensive follows sequentially after the enemy's offensive and is directed to retrieving the initiative and recovering occupied territory. A retaliatory offensive, in contrast, occurs simultaneously with the enemy's offensive. Its primary purpose is not to strike the enemy where he has further advanced, as is usually the case with a counteroffensive; rather it is to attack him in an entirely different sector. It thus would have a very different impact on Soviet force planning. The threat of a counteroffensive will lead the Soviets to make their offensive drive as strong as possible in order to advance as far as they can and do as much damage as they can to NATO's defensive forces and thus to postpone or blunt NATO's counteroffensive possibilities. The threat of a retaliatory offensive, on the other hand, will lead the

Soviets to worry about their defensive capabilities and hence to deploy their forces more evenly across the entire front. A counteroffensive threat, in short, will lead the Soviets to strengthen their offense; a retaliatory offensive threat will lead them to weaken it. . . .

The purpose of a conventional retaliatory option is to deter Soviet attack on Western Europe. The capability to exercise that option, however, could also contribute to the deterrence of Soviet aggressive moves in other parts of the world. At present the Soviets know that they could advance in force into the Persian Gulf area without having to worry about the security of their flank in central Europe. Their position is, in this respect, similar to that of Hitler in the 1930s. Although France had various commitments to Poland and the Little Entente, which presupposed, as DeGaulle argued, an offensively oriented army, it could not in fact pose any deterrent threat against Hitler's moving eastward because it had adopted a purely defensive strategy, symbolized by the Maginot Line. French military strategy left Hitler free to do what he wanted in Eastern Europe. In similar fashion, NATO forces do not now pose even a theoretical restraint on Soviet moves elsewhere. If, however, NATO were prepared to launch a military offensive into Eastern Europe, the Soviets would have to assure themselves as to the adequacy of their defenses there and as to the loyalty of their allies before they could take the offensive against Iran, Pakistan, China, Japan, or any other neighboring state.

The point is sometimes made that NATO is a defensive alliance and that a defensive alliance requires a defensive strategy. This argument has no basis in logic or history. NATO is a defensive alliance politically, which means that its purpose is to protect its members against Soviet attack through deterrence if possible and through defense if necessary. There is, however, no reason why a politically defensive alliance cannot have a militarily offensive strategy. Such a strategy may, indeed, be essential to securing the deterrent purposes of the alliance. For two decades NATO did in fact pursue its purposes primarily through the threat of launching a strategic nuclear offensive against the Soviet Union. If a nuclear offensive is compatible with the defensive purposes of the Alliance, certainly a conventional offensive should be also. . . .

THE MILITARY FEASIBILITY OF CONVENTIONAL RETALIATION

At this point, the reader may well be saying to himself: "Your argument is all wonderful in theory, *but* (a) as you've pointed out, NATO is not meeting its own already-established conventional buildup goals, and (b) the strategy you advocate would require a buildup far larger than anything NATO has contemplated. Conventional retaliation just is not practical.'' The question is: What are the military requirements of a conventional retaliatory offensive? The answer is not as great as one might think.

First, it is necessary to clear away the popular cliché that the offensive requires a three-to-one overall superiority. If this were the case, NATO's problems would be over. Under no circumstances, given the current balance and probable rates of mobilization on each side, could the Warsaw Pact achieve an overall three-to-one superiority over NATO. Most scenarios do not deviate much from Fischer's 1976 estimate that Pact superiority in men in combat units would peak at about 2:1 two weeks after Pact mobilization began, assuming NATO mobilization lagged one week. Unfortunately, however, 3:1 overall superiority is not what is required to attack. It is instead what may be required at the exact point of attack. Achieving that superiority is the product not of overall superiority in numbers but rather of superiority in mobility, concentration of forces, deception, and surprise.

Second, while the Soviets clearly do have a significant conventional superiority in Europe in numerical terms, that superiority is not enough, in itself, to give them a decisive advantage. In 1981, Pact superiority in divisional manpower was roughly 1.36:1, but in terms of overall manpower there was almost equality, with a ratio of 1.09:1. The Pact had many more tanks than NATO, but NATO was better off in attack aircraft. In terms of armored division equivalents (ADEs), perhaps the single most useful measure, the ratio was 1.2:1. Overall the Pact wins the numerical bean count, but it does not have an advantage which would guarantee victory in war. If a high probability currently exists of the Soviets' achieving substantial success in a central European war, that stems as much from their strategy as from their numbers. They are planning to concentrate their forces and use them offensively in the most militarily effective manner possible, while NATO has, for a variety of understandable reasons, been committed to a defensive strategy which almost ensures military defeat.

Third, a force which is inferior in overall strength can still pursue an offensive strategy. History is full of successful examples. The German offensive into France in 1940 and the North Vietnamese offensive in 1975 are two such cases. As U.S. Army FM 100-5 points out, other examples are the Third Army's attack through France in 1944, the U.S. offensive in Korea in 1951, and the Israeli Sinai campaign of 1967. In these cases . . . the attackers succeeded ''by massing unexpectedly where they could achieve a brief local superiority and by preserving their initial advantage through relentless exploitation.''

Obviously, stronger forces are more desirable than weaker ones.

Implementing a strategy that includes conventional retaliation, however, requires more changes in the NATO military mind-set than it does in NATO military forces. For thirty years NATO has thought about conventional warfare exclusively in defensive terms. Fortunately there are signs that this mentality may be changing. SHAPE is developing plans for the deep interdiction of Warsaw Pact second-echelon forces. The aim is to locate Pact follow-on forces through improved intelligence and to attack them with long-range conventional means before they reach the battle zone, while at the same time NATO forces are holding the forward defense line against Pact first-echelon forces. . . . A conventional retaliatory offensive as proposed here is compatible with and would supplement this emphasis on deep interdiction. It would involve NATO operations into the enemy's rear at the operational rather than simply the tactical level. It would employ not just conventional PGMs and missiles but the full range of conventional combined arms, and it would also serve to disrupt enemy logistics and reinforcements. Similarly, a retaliatory offensive is highly compatible with U.S. Army AirLand Battle doctrine, with its emphasis on the initiative, deep attack, and maneuver. . . . There are at least some signs that German military thinking may be moving in a similar direction.

A strategy with an offensive component would better capitalize on the current capabilities of NATO forces in Europe than does a purely defensive strategy. By and large, these forces are heavy forces; two-thirds of the Allied divisions in Germany are armor divisions; most of the rest are mechanized infantry. It is often said, of course, that these forces will enable NATO to have a mobile defense and to launch counteroffensives. That is true, and the same qualities also make them suited for a retaliatory offense. It is a misuse of expensive resources to consign these heavy forces primarily to a defensive role. In addition, NATO's forward defense strategy has always caused problems with respect to how Allied forces in the various sectors could reinforce each other. If the Soviets, for instance, launch their principal attack across the North German plain, what role could the substantial American and German forces in southern Germany play in bringing that advance to a halt? To move those forces laterally, that is parallel to the front, would be a logistical nightmare and could leave Bavaria open to a secondary Soviet attack. Not to move those forces northward, on the other hand, would greatly facilitate the Soviet's overwhelming the NATO forces in the north. The most efficient use of any substantial Allied forces not close to the Soviet attack corridors is to carry the war to the enemy. . . .

In practical terms, what might a retaliatory offensive look like? If the threat of such an offensive is to serve its deterrent purpose, the Soviets must have good reason to believe that an offensive is possible and little knowledge as to exactly where and when it might occur. NATO military planning for such an offensive would have to encompass a variety of alternative scenarios and possible options reflecting:

a. Warsaw Pact deployments and axes of advance;
b. NATO force capabilities and deployments;
c. East European politics, which might dictate withholding or limiting NATO offensive actions.

. . . To give some idea as to what could be involved . . . it might be desirable briefly to elaborate what is undoubtedly the most obvious scenario for both Soviet and NATO planners. Because it is the most obvious scenario, it could also be one which is unlikely to be realized in practice.

Three of the most probable Soviet invasion routes are across the North German plain to Hannover and then northward towards Bremen and Hamburg, through the Göttingen corridor towards the Ruhr, and through the Fulda Gap towards Frankfurt. . . .

The retaliatory offensive could well consist of two prongs. The major thrust would be through the Hof corridor towards Jena and Leipzig. Its primary axis of advance would not be west-east but rather south-north, and hence the problem of river barriers would be minimized. . . . Such an offensive would threaten the most direct Soviet supply routes supporting their forces in the Fulda Gap. The second prong would be launched in a more easterly direction towards Karlovy Vary and Teplice in Czechoslovakia. The immediate Soviet resistance would come from a single division deployed north of Pilsen. If this advance reached the Elbe, it could then either swing north towards Dresden or south towards Prague. The second prong would also help protect the southern and eastern flanks of the main prong.

The Allied forces engaged in these offensive moves would be superior in manpower, tanks, and ADEs to the Soviet forces immediately deployed against them. To the north and east of the 8th Guards Army, however, is the 1st Guards Tank Army. It is . . . designed to make a major contribution to the Soviet offensive into West Germany. If it joined that offensive, however, the Soviets would have to face the possibility of the Allies' overrunning their other forces in the south. If they used the 1st Guards Tank Army to blunt the Allied offensive, they would risk not achieving their breakthrough in the north. The purpose of a retaliatory offensive is to confront them with precisely that sort of dilemma.

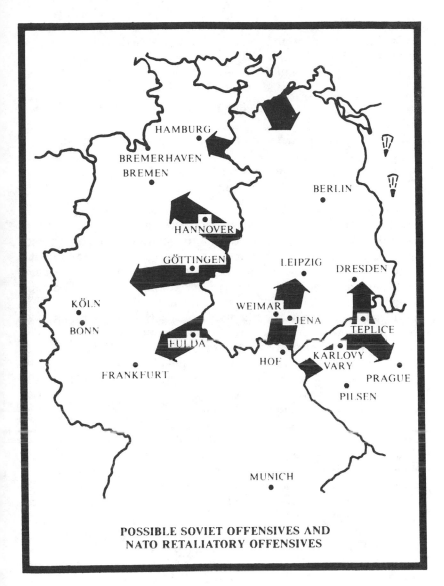

**POSSIBLE SOVIET OFFENSIVES AND
NATO RETALIATORY OFFENSIVES**

Allied military dispositions should supplement political and diplomatic measures in helping to minimize the enthusiasm of satellite
forces for the Soviet cause. The Allied offensive should be directed
at Soviet forces. The thrust into East Germany should be primarily
by German forces and that into Czechoslovakia exclusively by
American ones. . . . The movement of Allied divisions into East
Germany and Czechoslovakia could also be supplemented by the

infiltration by sea and air into Poland and Hungary of specially trained Special Forces units to encourage disaffection and resistance in those countries. . . .

How successful would be a retaliatory offensive such as this? That clearly would depend, among other things, on:

—the size, character, and leadership of the NATO forces commited to the offensive;
—the strength and readiness of the opposing Warsaw Pact forces;
—the degree of surprise NATO achieved; and
—the extent to which non-Soviet Warsaw Pact forces fought vigorously alongside their Soviet allies.

Just how these factors would play out is impossible to predict in advance. At one extreme, it is conceivable although unlikely that NATO forces could sweep north towards the Baltic and join up with amphibious forces in a giant pincer movement cutting East Germany in half and isolating Soviet forces to the west. At the other extreme, they might penetrate only a few kilometers into East Germany and Czechoslovakia. The point is that neither side could know for sure in advance, and that uncertainty is precisely what is required to reinforce deterrence. The Soviets would only know that, if they went to war under these circumstances, they would be putting at risk far more of great value than they would be at present.

Some changes in NATO forces are desirable to enhance the feasibility of a conventional offensive. . . . In addition, . . . it would also be highly desirable to strengthen NATO defensive capabilities through the construction of fortifications and improvement in West German reserves and territorial forces. At present NATO follows a forward defense strategy but lacks forward fortifications. The principal reason for this has been the reluctance of the West German government to create a major fortified line that would give concrete embodiment to a permanent division of Germany. If, however, NATO strategy included provision for the invasion and liberation of at least portions of East Germany, a fortified line along the inter-German border would no longer have the symbolism that the Bonn government fears. The construction of such a line would, of course, make it possible to release additional Allied forces to offensive missions. The same result will also be achieved to the extent that territorial army units play a larger role in area defense.

The special requirements for a conventional offensive capability will obviously compete with other claims on the modest and only slowly growing NATO resources. The central criterion for allocating resources among these competing claims, however, should be the extent to which they contribute to deterrence. . . . A given increase in NATO offensive capabilities . . . will produce a considerably higher return in terms of deterrence than the same investment in defensive capabilities. As a result, this addition to NATO strategy will also lower the total new resources NATO needs to invest to achieve effective deterrence. It could make conventional deterrence not only more credible but also cheaper than it would otherwise be.

THE POLITICS OF CONVENTIONAL RETALIATION

If conventional retaliation is strategically desirable and militarily feasible, the final question is whether it is politically possible. Will the Alliance agree to this amendment to the long-standing strategic doctrines set forth in MC 14/3?

Some may say that this proposal involves a fundamental change in NATO strategy for which it will be difficult if not impossible to mobilize support within the Alliance. In fact, however, incorporation of a conventional retaliatory offensive into NATO's strategy would, in many respects, be less a change in strategy than an effort to prevent a change in strategy. As it is, flexible response is inexorably becoming a dead letter. NATO strategy is changing fundamentally from a multi-pronged flexible response to a single-prong conventional defense. The addition of a conventional retaliatory option would, as the figures on p. 470 indicate, simply restore some element of flexibility to a strategy that is rapidly becoming inflexible. . . . It would adapt flexible response to the conditions of the 1980s. In similar fashion, a retaliatory offensive is not incompatible with the idea of forward defense. The latter is a necessary and appropriate response to German concern that as little of their country as possible become the locus of battle and subject to Soviet occupation. A retaliatory offensive would move at least some of the battle from West Germany to East Germany and Czechoslovakia. It is thus not a substitute for a strategy of flexible response and forward defense, broadly conceived, but rather a fleshing out of that strategy in changed circumstances. It would, in effect, make flexible response more flexible and forward defense more forward. . . .

The strategic environment in the United States is increasingly favorable towards conventional retaliation becoming a NATO option. The other key locus of decision-making is the Federal Republic. One would think that German leaders would endorse a military strategy that, in comparison to the alternatives, promised to produce stronger deterrence at lower cost, to reduce the probability that nuclear weapons would be used in the territory of the Federal Republic, and to shift at least some of the fighting, if war did occur, from the Federal Republic to East Germany and Czechoslovakia. It is hard to see why it might be good politics in West Germany to oppose such a move. If, after the normal debate necessary for policy innovation in any democratic country, the West German government was unwilling to support such a change, the United States would clearly have to reconsider its commitment of forces to a strategy and posture that is doomed to be found wanting. "For deterrence to be credible," as General Rogers has said, "it requires capabilities adequate for successful defense and effective retaliation." Effective retaliation means credible retaliation, and, in today's world, credible retaliation means conventional retaliation. That is the inescapable logic that will drive NATO's strategic choices in this decade.

Nuclear Weapons and the Atlantic Alliance

McGEORGE BUNDY
GEORGE F. KENNAN
ROBERT S. McNAMARA
GERARD SMITH

II

. . . . The disarray that currently besets the nuclear policy and practices of the Alliance is obvious. Governments and their representatives have maintained an appearance of unity as they persist in their support of the two-track decision of December 1979, under which 572 new American missiles of intermediate range are to be placed in Europe unless a satisfactory agreement on the limitation of such weapons can be reached in the negotiations between the United States and the Soviet Union that began last November. But behind this united front there are divisive debates, especially in countries where the new weapons are to be deployed.

The arguments put forward by advocates of these deployments contain troubling variations. The simplest and intuitively the most persuasive claim is that these new weapons are needed as a counter to the Soviet SS-20 missiles; it may be a recognition of the surface attractiveness of this position that underlies President Reagan's striking—but probably not negotiable—proposal that if all the SS-20s are dismantled the planned deployments will be cancelled. Other officials have a quite different argument, that without new and survivable American weapons which can reach Russia from Western Europe there can be no confidence that the strategic forces of the United States will remain committed to the defense of Western Europe; on this argument the new missiles are needed to make it more likely that any war in Europe would bring nuclear warheads on the Soviet Union and thus deter the aggressor in the first place. This argument is logically distinct from any concern about the Soviet SS-20s, and it probably explains the ill-concealed hope of some planners that the Reagan proposal will be rejected. Such varied justifications cast considerable doubt on the real purpose of the proposed deployment.

Reprinted by permission of *Foreign Affairs*, Spring 1982, pp. 753–768. Copyright © 1982 by the Council on Foreign Relations, Inc.

An equally disturbing phenomenon is the gradual shift in the balance of argument that has occurred since the need to address the problem was first asserted in 1977. Then the expression of need was European, and in the first instance German; the emerging parity of long-range strategic systems was asserted to create a need for a balance at less than intercontinental levels. The American interest developed relatively slowly, but because these were to be American missiles, American planners took the lead as the proposal was worked out. It has also served Soviet purposes to concentrate on the American role. A similar focus has been chosen by many leaders in the new movement for nuclear disarmament in Europe. And now there are American voices, some in the executive branch, talking as if European acceptance of these new missiles were some sort of test of European loyalty to the Alliance. Meanwhile some of those in Europe who remain publicly committed to both tracks of the 1979 agreement are clearly hoping that the day of deployment will never arrive. When the very origins of a new proposal become the source of irritated argument among allies—"You started it!"—something is badly wrong in our common understanding.

A still more severe instance of disarray, one which has occurred under both President Carter and President Reagan, relates to the so-called neutron bomb, a weapon designed to meet the threat of Soviet tanks. American military planners, authorized by doctrine to think in terms of early battlefield use of nuclear weapons, naturally want more "up-to-date" weapons than those they have now; it is known that thousands of the aging short-range nuclear weapons now in Europe are hard to use effectively. Yet to a great many Europeans the neutron bomb suggests, however unfairly, that the Americans are preparing to fight a "limited" nuclear war on their soil. Moreover neither weapons designers nor the Pentagon officials they have persuaded seem to have understood the intense and special revulsion that is associated with killing by "enhanced radiation."

All these recent distempers have a deeper cause. They are rooted in the fact that the evolution of essentially equivalent and enormously excessive nuclear weapons systems both in the Soviet Union and in the Atlantic Alliance has aroused new concern about the dangers of all forms of nuclear war. The profusion of these systems, on both sides, has made it more difficult than ever to construct rational plans for any first use of these weapons by anyone.

This problem is more acute than before, but it is not new. Even in the 1950s, a time that is often mistakenly perceived as one of effortless American superiority, the prospect of any actual use of tactical weapons was properly terrifying to Europeans and to more than a few Americans. Military plans for such use remained both deeply secret and highly hypothetical; the coherence of the Alliance was maintained by general neglect of such scenarios, not by sedulous public discussion. In the 1960s there was a prolonged and stressful effort to address the problem of theater-range weapons, but agreement on new forces and plans for their use proved elusive. Eventually the proposal for a multilateral force (MLF) was replaced by the assignment of American Polaris submarines to NATO, and by the creation in Brussels of an inter-allied Nuclear Planning Group. Little else was accomplished. In both decades the Alliance kept itself together more by mutual political confidence than by plausible nuclear war-fighting plans.

Although the first years of the 1970s produced a welcome if oversold détente, complacency soon began to fade. The Nixon Administration, rather quietly, raised the question about the long-run credibility of the American nuclear deterrent that was to be elaborated by Henry Kissinger in 1979 at a meeting in Brussels. Further impetus to both new doctrine and new deployments came during the Ford and Carter Administrations, but each public statement, however careful and qualified, only increased European apprehensions. The purpose of both Administrations was to reinforce deterrence, but the result has been to increase fear of nuclear war, and even of Americans as its possible initiators. Intended as contributions to both rationality and credibility, these excursions into the theory of limited nuclear war have been counterproductive in Europe.

Yet it was not wrong to raise these matters. Questions that were answered largely by silence in the 1950s and 1960s cannot be so handled in the 1980s. The problem was not in the fact that the questions were raised, but in the way they seemed to be answered.

It is time to recognize that no one has ever succeeded in advancing any persuasive reason to believe that any use of nuclear weapons, even on the smallest scale, could reliably be expected to remain limited. Every serious analysis and every military exercise, for over 25 years, has demonstrated that even the most restrained battlefield use would be enormously destructive to civilian life and property. There is no way for anyone to have any confidence that such a nuclear action will not lead to further and more devastating exchanges. Any use of nuclear weapons in Europe, by the Alliance or against it, carries with it a high and inescapable risk of escalation into the general nuclear war which would bring ruin to all and victory to none.

The one clearly definable firebreak against the worldwide disaster of general nuclear war is the one that stands between all other kinds of conflict and any use whatsoever of nuclear weapons. To keep that firebreak wide and strong is in the deepest interest of all mankind.

In retrospect, indeed, it is remarkable that this country has not responded to this reality more quickly. Given the appalling consequences of even the most limited use of nuclear weapons and the total impossibility for both sides of any guarantee against unlimited escalation, there must be the gravest doubt about the wisdom of a policy which asserts the effectiveness of any first use of nuclear weapons by either side. So it seems timely to consider the possibilities, the requirements, the difficulties, and the advantages of a policy of no-first-use.

III

The largest question presented by any proposal for an Allied policy of no-first-use is that of its impact on the effectiveness of NATO's deterrent posture on the central front. In spite of the doubts that are created by any honest look at the probable consequences of resort to a first nuclear strike of any kind, it should be remembered that there were strong reasons for the creation of the American nuclear umbrella over NATO. The original American pledge, expressed in Article 5 of the Treaty, was understood to be a nuclear guarantee. It was extended at a time when only a conventional Soviet threat existed, so a readiness for first use was plainly implied from the beginning. To modify that guarantee now, even in the light of all that has happened since, would be a major change in the assumptions of the Alliance, and no such change should be made without the most careful exploration of its implications.

In such an exploration the role of the Federal Republic of Germany must be central. Americans too easily forget what the people of the Federal Republic never can: that their position is triply exposed in a fashion unique among the large industrial democracies. They do not have nuclear weapons; they share a long common boundary with the Soviet empire; in any conflict on the central front their land would be the first battleground. None of these conditions can be changed, and together they present a formidable challenge.

Having decisively rejected a policy of neutrality, the Federal Republic has necessarily relied on the nuclear protection of the United States, and we Americans should recognize that this relationship is not a favor we are doing our German friends, but the best available solution of a common problem. Both nations believe that the Federal Republic must not have nuclear weapons of its own; both believe that nuclear guarantees *of some sort* are essential; and both believe that only the United States can provide those guarantees in persuasively deterrent peacekeeping form.

The uniqueness of the West German position can be readily demonstrated by comparing it with those of France and the United Kingdom. These two nations have distance, and in one case water, between them and the armies of the Soviet Union; they also have nuclear weapons. While those weapons may contribute something to the common strength of the Alliance, their main role is to underpin a residual national self-reliance, expressed in different ways at different times by different governments, which sets both Britain and France apart from the Federal Republic. They are set apart from the United States too, in that no other nation depends on them to use their nuclear weapons otherwise than in their own ultimate self-defense.

The quite special character of the nuclear relationship between the Federal Republic and the United States is a most powerful reason for defining that relationship with great care. It is rare for one major nation to depend entirely on another for a form of strength that is vital to its survival. It is unprecedented for any nation, however powerful, to pledge itself to a course of action, in defense of another, that might entail its own nuclear devastation. A policy of no-first-use would not and should not imply an abandonment of this extraordinary guarantee—only its redefinition. It would still be necessary to be ready to reply with American nuclear weapons to any nuclear attack on the Federal Republic, and this commitment would in itself be sufficiently demanding to constitute a powerful demonstration that a policy of no-first-use would represent no abandonment of our German ally.

The German right to a voice in this question is not merely a matter of location, or even of dependence on an American nuclear guarantee. The people of the Federal Republic have demonstrated a steadfast dedication to peace, to collective defense, and to domestic political decency. The study here proposed should be responsive to their basic desires. It seems probable that they are like the rest of us in wishing most of all to have no war of any kind, but also to be able to defend the peace by forces that do not require the dreadful choice of nuclear escalation.

IV

While we believe that careful study will lead to a firm conclusion that it is time to move decisively toward a policy of no-first-use, it is obvious that any such policy would require a strengthened confidence in the adequacy of the conventional forces of the Alliance, above all the forces in place on the central front and those available for prompt reinforcement. It seems clear that the nations of the Alliance together can provide whatever forces are needed, and within realistic budgetary constraints, but it is a quite different question whether they can summon the necessary political will. Evidence from the history of the Alliance is mixed. There has been great progress in the conventional defenses of NATO in the 30 years since the 1952 Lisbon communiqué, but there have also been failures to meet force goals all along the way.

In each of the four nations which account for more than 90 percent of NATO's collective defense and a still higher proportion of its strength on the central front, there remain major unresolved political issues that critically affect contributions to conventional deterrence: for example, it can be asked what priority the United Kingdom gives to the British Army of the Rhine, what level of NATO-connected deployment can be accepted by France, what degree of German relative strength is acceptable to the Allies and fair to the Federal Republic itself, and whether we Americans have a durable and effective answer to our military manpower needs in the present all-volunteer active and reserve forces. These are the kinds of questions—and there are many more—that would require review and resolution in the course of reaching any final decision to move to a responsible policy of no-first-use.

There should also be an examination of the ways in which the concept of early use of nuclear weapons may have been built into existing forces, tactics, and general military expectations. To the degree that this has happened, there could be a dangerous gap right now between real capabilities and those which political leaders might wish to have in a time of crisis. Conversely there should be careful study of what a policy of no-first-use would require in those same terms. It seems more than likely that once the military leaders of the Alliance have learned to think and act steadily on this "conventional" assumption, their forces will be better instruments for stability in crises and for general deterrence, as well as for the maintenance of the nuclear firebreak so vital to us all.

No one should underestimate either the difficulty or the importance of the shift in military attitudes implied by a no-first-use policy. Although military commanders are well aware of the terrible dangers in any exchange of nuclear weapons, it is a strong military tradition to maintain that aggressive war, not the use of any one weapon, is the central evil. Many officers will be initially unenthusiastic about any formal policy that puts limits on their recourse to a weapon of apparently decisive power. Yet the basic argument for a no-first-use policy can be stated in strictly military terms: that any other course involves unacceptable risks to the national life that military forces exist to defend. The military officers of the Alliance can be expected to understand the force of this proposition, even if many of them do not initially agree with it. Moreover, there is every reason for confidence that they will loyally accept any policy that has the support of their governments and the peoples behind them, just as they have fully accepted the present arrangements under which the use of nuclear weapons, even in retaliation for a nuclear attack, requires advance and specific approval by the head of government.

An Allied posture of no-first-use would have one special effect that can be set forth in advance: it would draw new attention to the importance of maintaining and improving the specifically American conventional forces in Europe. The principal political difficulty in a policy of no-first-use is that it may be taken in Europe, and especially in the Federal Republic, as evidence of a reduced American interest in the Alliance and in effective overall deterrence. The argument here is exactly the opposite: that such a policy is the best one available for keeping the Alliance united and effective. Nonetheless the psychological realities of the relation between the Federal Republic and United States are such that the only way to prevent corrosive German suspicion of American intentions, under a no-first-use regime, will be for Americans to accept for themselves an appropriate share in any new level of conventional effort that the policy may require.

Yet it would be wrong to make any hasty judgment that those new levels of effort must be excessively high. The subject is complex, and the more so because both technology and politics are changing. Precision-guided munitions, in technology, and the visible weakening of the military solidity of the Warsaw Pact, in politics, are only two examples of changes working to the advantage of the Alliance. Moreover there has been some tendency, over many years, to exaggerate the relative conventional strength of the U.S.S.R. and to underestimate Soviet awareness of the enormous costs and risks of any form of aggression against NATO.

Today there is literally no one who really knows what would be needed. Most of the measures routinely used in both official and private analyses are static and fragmentary. An especially arbitrary, if obviously convenient, measure of progress is that of spending levels. But it is political will, not budgetary pressure, that will be decisive. The value of greater safety from both nuclear and conventional danger is so great that even if careful analysis showed that the necessary conventional posture would require funding larger than the three-percent real increase that has been the common target of recent years, it would be the best bargain ever offered to the members of the Alliance.

Yet there is no need for crash programs, which always bring extra costs. The direction of the Allied effort will be more important than its velocity. The final establishment of a firm policy of no-first-use, in any case, will obviously require time. What is important today is to begin to move in this direction.

V

The concept of renouncing any first use of nuclear weapons should also be tested by careful review of the value of existing

NATO plans for selective and limited use of nuclear weapons. While many scenarios for nuclear war-fighting are nonsensical, it must be recognized that cautious and sober senior officers have found it prudent to ask themselves what alternatives to defeat they could propose to their civilian superiors if a massive conventional Soviet attack seemed about to make a decisive breakthrough. This question has generated contingency plans for battlefield uses of small numbers of nuclear weapons which might prevent that particular disaster. It is hard to see how any such action could be taken without the most enormous risk of rapid and catastrophic escalation, but it is a fair challenge to a policy of no-first-use that it should be accompanied by a level of conventional strength that would make such plans unnecessary.

In the light of this difficulty it would be prudent to consider whether there is any acceptable policy short of no-first-use. One possible example is what might be called "no-*early*-first-use;" such a policy might leave open the option of some limited nuclear action to fend off a final large-scale conventional defeat, and by renunciation of any immediate first use and increased emphasis on conventional capabilities it might be thought to help somewhat in reducing current fears.

But the value of a clear and simple position would be great, especially in its effect on ourselves and our Allies. One trouble with exceptions is that they easily become rules. It seems much better that even the most responsible choice of even the most limited nuclear actions to prevent even the most imminent conventional disaster should be left out of authorized policy. What the Alliance needs most today is not the refinement of its nuclear options, but a clear-cut decision to avoid them as long as others do. . . .

VI

The first possible advantage of a policy of no-first-use is in the management of the nuclear deterrent forces that would still be necessary. Once we escape from the need to plan for a first use that is credible, we can escape also from many of the complex arguments that have led to assertions that all sorts of new nuclear capabilities are necessary to create or restore a capability for something called "escalation dominance"—a capability to fight and "win" a nuclear war at any level. What would be needed, under no-first-use, is a set of capabilities we already have in overflowing measure—capabilities for appropriate retaliation to any kind of Soviet nuclear attack which would leave the Soviet Union in no doubt that it too should adhere to a policy of no-first-use. The Soviet government is already aware of the awful risk inherent in any use of these weapons, and there is no current or prospective Soviet "superiority" that would tempt anyone in Moscow toward nuclear adventurism. (All four of us are wholly unpersuaded by the argument advanced in recent years that the Soviet Union could ever rationally expect to gain from such a wild effort as a massive first strike on land-based American strategic missiles.)

Once it is clear that the only nuclear need of the Alliance is for adequately survivable and varied *second strike* forces, requirements for the modernization of major nuclear systems will become more modest than has been assumed. In particular we can escape from the notion that we must somehow match everything the rocket commanders in the Soviet Union extract from their government. It seems doubtful, also, that under such a policy it would be necessary or desirable to deploy neutron bombs. The savings permitted by more modest programs could go toward meeting the financial costs of our contribution to conventional forces.

It is important to avoid misunderstanding here. In the conditions of the 1980s, and in the absence of agreement on both sides to proceed to very large-scale reductions in nuclear forces, it is clear that large, varied, and survivable nuclear forces will still be necessary for nuclear deterrence. The point is not that we Americans should move unilaterally to some "minimum" force of a few tens or even hundreds of missiles, but rather that once we escape from the pressure to seem willing and able to use these weapons first, we shall find that our requirements are much less massive than is now widely supposed.

A posture of no-first-use should also go far to meet the understandable anxieties that underlie much of the new interest in nuclear disarmament, both in Europe and in our own country. Some of the proposals generated by this new interest may lack practicability for the present. For example, proposals to make "all" of Europe—from Portugal to Poland—a nuclear-free zone do not seem to take full account of the reality that thousands of long-range weapons deep in the Soviet Union will still be able to target Western Europe. But a policy of no-first-use, with its accompaniment of a reduced requirement for new Allied nuclear systems, should allow a considerable reduction in fears of all sorts. Certainly such a new policy would neutralize the highly disruptive argument currently put about in Europe: that plans for theater nuclear modernization reflect an American hope to fight a nuclear war limited to Europe. Such modernization might or might not be needed under a policy of no-first-use; that question, given the size and versatility of other existing and prospective American forces, would be a matter primarily for European decision (as it is today).

An effective policy of no-first-use will also reduce the risk of conventional aggression in Europe. That risk has never been as great as prophets of doom have claimed and has always lain primarily in the possibility that Soviet leaders might think they could achieve some quick and limited gain that would be accepted because no defense or reply could be concerted. That temptation has been much reduced by the Allied conventional deployments achieved in the last 20 years, and it would be reduced still further by the additional shift in the balance of Allied effort that a no-first-use policy would both permit and require. The risk that an adventurist Soviet leader might take the terrible gamble of conventional aggression was greater in the past than it is today, and is greater today than it would be under no-first-use, backed up by an effective conventional defense.

VII

We have been discussing a problem of military policy, but our interest is also political. The principal immediate danger in the current military posture of the Alliance is not that it will lead to large-scale war, conventional or nuclear. The balance of terror, and the caution of both sides, appear strong enough today to prevent such a catastrophe, at least in the absence of some deeply destabilizing political change which might lead to panic or adventurism on either side. But the present unbalanced reliance on nuclear weapons, if long continued, might produce exactly such political change. The events of the last year have shown that differing perceptions of the role of nuclear weapons can lead to destructive recriminations, and when these differences are compounded by understandable disagreements on other matters such as Poland and the Middle East, the possibilities for trouble among Allies are evident.

The political coherence of the Alliance, especially in times of stress, is at least as important as the military strength required to maintain credible deterrence. Indeed the political requirement has, if anything, an even higher priority. Soviet leaders would be most pleased to help the Alliance fall into total disarray, and would much prefer such a development to the inescapable uncertainties of open conflict. Conversely, if consensus is re-established on a military policy that the peoples and governments of the Alliance can believe in, both political will and deterrent credibility will be reinforced. Plenty of hard questions will remain, but both fear and mistrust will be reduced, and they are the most immediate enemies.

There remains one underlying reality which could not be removed by even the most explicit declaratory policy of no-first-use. Even if the nuclear powers of the Alliance should join, with the support of other Allies, in a policy of no-first-use, and even if that decision should lead to a common declaration of such policy by these powers and the Soviet Union, no one on either side could guarantee beyond all possible doubt that if conventional warfare broke out on a large scale there would in fact be no use of nuclear weapons. We could not make that assumption about the Soviet Union, and we must recognize that Soviet leaders could not make it about us. As long as the weapons themselves exist, the possibility of their use will remain.

But this inescapable reality does not undercut the value of a no-first-use policy. That value is first of all for the internal health of the Western Alliance itself. A posture of effective conventional balance and survivable second-strike nuclear strength is vastly better for our own peoples and governments, in a deep sense more civilized, than one that forces the serious contemplation of "limited" nuclear scenarios that are at once terrifying and implausible.

There is strong reason to believe that no-first-use can also help in our relations with the Soviet Union. The Soviet government has repeatedly offered to join the West in declaring such a policy, and while such declarations may have only limited reliability, it would be wrong to disregard the real value to both sides of a jointly declared adherence to this policy. To renounce the first use of nuclear weapons is to accept an enormous burden of responsibility for any later violation. The existence of such a clearly declared common pledge would increase the cost and risk of any sudden use of nuclear weapons by either side and correspondingly reduce the political force of spoken or unspoken threats of such use.

A posture and policy of no-first-use also could help to open the path toward serious reduction of nuclear armaments on both sides. The nuclear decades have shown how hard it is to get agreements that really do constrain these weapons, and no one can say with assurance that any one step can make a decisive difference. But just as a policy of no-first-use should reduce the pressures on our side for massive new nuclear forces, it should help to increase the international incentives for the Soviet Union to show some restraint of its own. It is important not to exaggerate here, and certainly Soviet policies on procurement are not merely delayed mirror-images of ours. Nonetheless there are connections between what is said and what is done even in the Soviet Union, and there are incentives for moderation, even there, that could be strengthened by a jointly declared policy of renouncing first use. At a minimum such a declaration would give both sides additional reason to seek for agreements that would prevent a vastly expensive and potentially destabilizing contest for some kind of strategic advantage in outer space.

Finally, and in sum, we think a policy of no-first-use, especially if shared with the Soviet Union, would bring new hope to everyone in every country whose life is shadowed by the hideous possibility of a third great twentieth-century conflict in Europe—conventional or nuclear. It seems timely and even urgent to begin the careful study of a policy that could help to sweep this threat clean off the board of international affairs. . . .

Nuclear Weapons And
The Preservation Of Peace

KARL KAISER, GEORG LEBER,
ALOIS MERTES
and FRANZ-JOSEF SCHULZE

A RESPONSE TO AN AMERICAN PROPOSAL FOR RENOUNCING THE
FIRST USE OF NUCLEAR WEAPONS

The appropriate strategy for the use of nuclear weapons has been
the subject of discussion since the North Atlantic Alliance was founded.
Open debate on these problems is part of the natural foundations of
an Alliance consisting of democracies which relate to each other as
sovereign partners. It is not the first time in the history of the Alliance
that fears about the danger of nuclear war have caused concern and
anxieties in all member countries, although these are more pronounced
today than before. They must be taken seriously. The questions posed
demand convincing answers, for in a democracy, policy on questions of
peace and war requires constantly renewed legitimization.

When McGeorge Bundy, George F. Kennan, Robert S. McNamara
and Gerard Smith submit a proposal to renounce the first use of nuclear
weapons in Europe,[1] the mere fact that it comes from respected
American personalities with long years of experience in questions of
security policy and the Alliance gives it particular weight. Their reflec-
tions must be taken particularly seriously in a country like the Federal
Republic of Germany which has a special interest in preserving peace,
because in case of war nuclear weapons could first be used on its
territory.

All responsible people must face the issues of the discussion initiated
by the four authors. It is necessary to think through all questions posed
and not to select only those ideas which cater to widespread anxieties.
What matters most is to concentrate not only on the prevention of
nuclear war, but on how to prevent *any* war, conventional war as well.
The decisive criterion in evaluating this proposal—like any new

Reprinted by permission of *Foreign Affairs*, Summer 1982, pp. 1157–1171. Copyright ©
1982 by the Council on Foreign Relations, Inc.
    [1] "Nuclear Weapons and the Atlantic Alliance," published simultaneously in
Europa-Archiv, No. 7, 1982, and *Foreign Affairs*, Spring 1982, pp. 753–768. Page cita-
tions in the body of this article are to *Foreign Affairs*.

proposal—must be: Will it contribute to preserving, into the future, the peace and freedom of the last three decades?

Unfortunately, the current discussion on both sides of the Atlantic about the four authors' proposal has been rendered more difficult by a confusion between the option of the "first use of nuclear weapons and the capability for a "first strike" with nuclear weapons. The authors themselves have unintentionally contributed to this confusion by using both terms. "First use" refers to the first use of a nuclear weapon regardless of its yield and place; even blowing up a bridge with a nuclear weapon in one's own territory would represent a first use. "First strike" refers to a preemptive disarming nuclear strike aimed at eliminating as completely as possible the entire strategic potential of the adversary. A first strike by the Alliance is not a relevant issue; such a strike must remain unthinkable in the future as it is now and has been in the past. The matter for debate should be exclusively the defensive first use of nuclear weapons by the Western Alliance.

II

The current NATO strategy of flexible response is intended to discourage an adversary from using or threatening the use of military force by confronting him with a full spectrum of deterrence and hence with an uncalculable risk. The strategy also aims at improving the tools of crisis management as a means of preventing conflict. The deterrent effect of the doctrine rests on three pillars:

—the political determination of all Alliance members to resist jointly any form of aggression or blackmail;

—the capability of the Alliance to react effectively at every level of aggression; and

—the flexibility to choose between different possible reactions— conventional or nuclear.

The primary goal of this strategy is the prevention of war. To this end it harnesses the revolutionary new and inescapable phenomenon of the nuclear age for its own purposes. Our era has brought humanity not only the curse of the unprecedented destructive power of nuclear weapons but also its twin, the dread of unleashing that power, grounded in the fear of self-destruction. Wherever nuclear weapons are present, war loses its earlier function as a continuation of politics by other means. Even more, the destructive power of these weapons has forced political leaders, especially those of nuclear weapons states, to weigh risks to a degree unknown in history.

The longest period of peace in European history is inconceivable without the war-preventing effect of nuclear weapons. During the same time span more than a hundred wars have taken place in Asia, Africa, and Latin America, where the numbers of dead, wounded and refugees run into the millions.

The continuous increase in the number of nuclear weapons—now comprising many thousands of warheads with ever more refined delivery systems—instills in many people, for understandable reasons, anxieties about the consequences of a war with a destructive power that exceeds the human imagination. But the only new factor here is that more people realize these consequences than in the past. Many political and military leaders were already aware of them when these weapons were developed and the first test results were presented. The fear of the consequences of such a war has to this day fortunately led to a policy which has made an essential contribution to preventing war in Europe—but which at the same time has regrettably stimulated the buildup of arsenals, since neither side wanted to lapse into a position of inferiority.

The strategy of flexible response attempts to counter any attack by the adversary—no matter what the level—in such a way that the aggressor can have no hope of advantage or success by triggering a military conflict, be it conventional or nuclear. The tight and indissoluble coupling of conventional forces and nuclear weapons on the European continent with the strategic potential of the United States confronts the Soviet Union with the incalculable risk that any military conflict between the two Alliances could escalate to a nuclear war. The primary function of nuclear weapons is deterrence in order to prevent aggression and blackmail.

The coupling of conventional and nuclear weapons has rendered war between East and West unwageable and unwinnable up to now. It is the inescapable paradox of this strategy of war prevention that the will to conduct nuclear war must be demonstrated in order to prevent war at all. Yet the ensuing indispensable presence of nuclear weapons and the constantly recalled visions of their possible destructive effect, should they ever be used in a war, make many people anxious.

The case is similar with regard to the limitation of nuclear war: the strategy of massive retaliation was revised because, given the growing potential of destruction, the threat of responding even to low levels of aggression with a massive use of nuclear weapons became increasingly incredible. A threat once rendered incredible would no longer have been able to prevent war in Europe. Thus, in the mid-1960s the Europeans supported the introduction of flexible response, which made the restricted use of nuclear weapons—but also the limitation of any such use—an indispensable part of deterrence aimed at preventing even "small" wars in Europe. Critics of nuclear deterrence today misinterpret this shift in strategy, drawing from it a suspicion of conspiracy between the superpowers to wage a limited nuclear war on European territory and at the expense of the Europeans.

A renunciation of the first use of nuclear weapons would certainly rob the present strategy of war prevention—which is supported by the government and the opposition in the Federal Republic of Germany, as well as by a great majority of the population—of a decisive characteristic. One cannot help concluding that the Soviet Union would thereby be put in a position where it could, once again, calculate its risk and thus be able to wage war in Europe. It would no longer have to fear that nuclear weapons would inflict unacceptable damage to its own territory. We therefore fear that a credible renunciation of the first use of nuclear weapons would, once again, make war more probable.

A decisive weakness of the proposal by the four authors lies in their assertion that a no-first-use policy would render wars less likely, without producing sufficient evidence. Even though the restoration of the conventional balance which they call for (and which will be examined below) increases the conventional risk for the Soviet assault formations, such a policy would liberate the Soviet Union from the decisive nuclear risk—and thereby from the constraint that has kept the Soviet Union, up to now, from using military force, even for limited purposes, against Western Europe. The liberation from nuclear risk would, of course, benefit the United States to the same degree. It must be questioned, therefore, whether renunciation of first use represents a contribution to the "internal health of the Western alliance itself" (p. 66) or whether, instead, a no-first-use policy increases insecurity and fear of ever more probable war.

The argumentation of the four American authors is considerably weakened by their tendency to think in worst-case scenarios. They assume almost fatalistically a total irrationality of state behavior and the impossibility of controlling a supposedly irreversible escalation. We share the authors' opinion that the kind of Soviet adventurism that would undertake a nuclear first strike against the United States can be excluded as a serious possibility. We are also familiar with the recent studies which assert that a limited nuclear war probably becomes more and more difficult to control with increasing escalation. Here we cannot disagree. However, one must at the same time ask under what circumstances a first use of Western nuclear weapons in Europe—should it happen at all—would be probable. This is only thinkable in a situation where a large-scale conventional attack by the Warsaw Pact could no longer be countered by conventional means alone, thus forcing NATO to a limited use of nuclear weapons: small weapons in small quantities, perhaps even only a warning shot. All indications suggest that both sides would be extremely cautious, in order to avoid precisely the dreaded, possibly uncontrollable escalation which some studies rightfully present as a danger, and which the advocates of a no-first-use policy present as a certainty.

III

The Western Alliance is an alliance of equals. Its cohesion is therefore based on the greatest possible realization of the principles of equal risks, equal burdens and equal security. The present NATO strategy reflects this principle. It guarantees that the American military potential with all its components, conventional and nuclear, is included in the defense of Europe. Not only the inhabitants of the Federal Republic of Germany but also American citizens help bear the risks, the conventional as well as the nuclear. The indivisibility of the security of the Alliance as a whole and of its terrritory creates the credibility of deterrence.

The conclusions that can be drawn from the four authors' recommendations with regard to the commitment of the United States to the defense of Europe are profoundly disturbing. To be sure, they assert that no-first-use does not represent an abandonment of the American protective guarantee for Western Europe, but "only its redefinition" (p. 759). Indeed, that would be the case, but in the form of a withdrawal from present commitments of the United States.

The opinion of the four American authors that "the one clearly definable firebreak against the worldwide disaster of general nuclear war is the one that stands between all other kinds of conflict and any use whatsoever of nuclear weapons" (p. 757), amounts to no less than limiting the existing nuclear guarantee of protection by the United States for their non-nuclear Alliance partners to the case of prior use of nuclear weapons by the Soviet Union. Even in the case of a large-scale conventional attack against the entire European NATO territory, the Soviet Union could be certain that its own land would remain a sanctuary as long as it did not itself resort to nuclear weapons. This would apply even more to surprise operations aimed at the quick occupation of parts of Western Europe which are hardly defensible by conventional means.

In such a case, those attacked would have to bear the destruction and devastation of war alone. It is only too understandable that for years the Soviet Union has, therefore, pressed for a joint American-Soviet renunciation of first use of nuclear weapons, on occasion in the guise of global proposals. If the ideas of the authors were to be followed, conventional conflicts in Europe would no longer involve any existential risk for the territory of the Soviet Union and—despite the increased American participation in the conventional defense of Europe suggested by the authors—would be without such risk for the territory of the United States as well.

The authors' suggestion that "even the most responsible choice of even the most limited nuclear actions to prevent even the most imminent conventional disaster should be left out of authorized policy" (p. 762) makes completely clear that a withdrawal of the United States from its previous guarantee is at stake. They thus advise Western

Europe to capitulate should defeat threaten, for example if the Federal Republic were in danger of being overrun conventionally. The American nuclear guarantee would be withdrawn.

The authors assert that the implementation of their astonishing proposal would not be taken in Europe, and especially in the Federal Republic, "as evidence of a reduced American interest in the Alliance and in effective overall deterrence" (p. 761), but that, on the contrary, it would be the best means "for keeping the Alliance united and effective" (p. 761). On this point we beg to differ: the proposed no-first-use policy would destroy the confidence of Europeans and especially of Germans in the European-American Alliance as a community of risk, and would endanger the strategic unity of the Alliance and the security of Western Europe.

IV

Given a renunciation of nuclear first use, the risks of a potential aggressor doubtlessly become more calculable. Moreover, the significance of Soviet conventional superiority would thereby increase dramatically. Conventional war in Europe would once again become possible. It could again become a continuation of politics by other means. Moreover, NATO would face a fundamentally different conventional threat. The elimination of the nuclear risk would free the Warsaw Pact from the necessity to disperse attack forces. As a result NATO would have to produce significantly higher numbers of combat forces than today.

The assertion of the four American authors that there is a tendency to overestimate the conventional strength of the Soviet Union does not correspond to the most recent East-West force comparison undertaken by NATO. They do admit, however, that a no-first-use policy requires stronger conventional forces; in their opinion the Alliance is capable of accomplishing such a buildup within realistic budgets. We believe the authors considerably underestimate the political and financial difficulties which stand in the way of establishing a conventional balance through increased armament by the West. The case would be different if through negotiations a conventional balance could be reached by reductions in Warsaw Pact forces. The authors do not explore this possibility, but the long years of as yet unsuccessful negotiations for mutual and balanced force reductions (MBFR) demonstrate the obstacles on this path.

The establishment of balance through the buildup of Western conventional forces would likewise be extremely difficult. The costs would be of a magnitude that would dramatically exceed the framework of present defense budgets. Suggestions by the authors about possible savings in the nuclear area in case of no-first-use are of little benefit for the non-nuclear weapons states of Europe. (Such savings, incidentally, imply a significant reduction of the Western nuclear arsenal.) In our judgment, the United States and Great Britain would have to introduce the draft, and the European countries would have to extend their period of military service. Because of the necessity for a significantly higher number of military forces, the Federal Republic of Germany would have to accept on its territory large contingents of additional troops, those of the allies and its own: the Federal Republic would be transformed into a large military camp for an indefinite period. Do the four American authors seriously believe that the preconditions for the buildup required by their proposal exist in Western Europe—and the United States?

Even if an approximate conventional balance could be achieved in Europe, two disadvantages to the detriment of Western Europe would remain: first, the Soviet Union has a geographic advantage, it can always quickly change the balance of forces from the relative proximity of its territory; second, there would always be the possibility, not even excluded by the American authors, that, despite no-first-use, conventional war could in an advanced phase degenerate into nuclear war.

Moreover, in commenting skeptically about the idea of a nuclear-free zone, the authors themselves point out that the Soviet Union can move nuclear weapons relatively quickly from deep within its territory into such a zone. If a no-first-use policy is linked with a complete or at least substantial withdrawal of tactical nuclear weapons—and that is apparently meant by the authors—it would, moreover, be easier for the Soviet Union to reach Central Europe with nuclear weapons from its own territory than for the United States.

For Germans and other Europeans whose memory of the catastrophe of conventional war is still alive and on whose densely populated territory both pacts would confront each other with the destructive power of modern armies, the thought of an ever more probable conventional war is terrifying.

To Germans and other Europeans, an ever more probable conventional war is, therefore, no alternative to war prevention through the current strategy, including the option of a first use of nuclear weapons. While the four authors link their proposal with the laudable intention of reducing European anxieties about nuclear war, its implementation could result in anxieties about a more probable conventional war soon replacing anxieties about the much less probable nuclear war. The anti-nuclear protest movement in Europe suspects the United States and the Soviet Union of intending to wage a limited nuclear war on the territory, and at the expense, of the Europeans. Were the movement to apply the logic of its argument to the case of no-first-use, it would naturally arrive at a new suspicion: that a conventional war could now also be waged on European territory and at European expense—particularly since a nuclear risk for the superpowers would no longer exist. All that would then be necessary would be to paint a vivid picture of the terrors of conventional war—once again thinkable—and the insecurity of the Europeans would receive new and dangerous reinforcement.

V

We are grateful for the manner in which the four American authors of a no-first-use proposal have evaluated the particularly exposed position of the Federal Republic of Germany and the special difficulties which ensue for its security policy. It is, however, striking that they do not deal at all with a problem which does not, to be sure, pose itself for a world power like the United States but which the Federal Republic of Germany and all European Alliance partners have to keep in mind: the problem of protecting themselves from political pressure and preserving their free society.

The protection of a free society based on the rule of law is just as important a part of a policy of preserving peace as the prevention of war. War can always be avoided at the price of submission. It is naturally more obvious to Europeans, and in particular to Germans—in their precarious position within a divided country—than to the population of the American superpower that an actual military superiority of the Soviet Union, or a feeling of inferiority in Western Europe, can be exploited to put political pressure on Western Europe.

The feeling of vulnerability to political blackmail, as a result of the constant demonstration of superior military might, would be bound to grow considerably if the nuclear protector of the Atlantic Alliance were to declare—as suggested by the four authors—that it would not use nuclear weapons in case of a conventional attack against Europe. This applies in particular to those exposed areas which even with considerable improvements of conventional forces can only with great difficulty be conventionally defended, or not at all: these include, for example, North Norway, Thrace, and in particular, West Berlin. The protection of these areas lies solely in the incalculability of the American reaction.

The advice of the authors to renounce the use of nuclear weapons even in the face of pending conventional defeat of Western Europe is tantamount to suggesting that "rather Red than dead" would be the only remaining option for those Europeans then still alive. Were such advice to become policy, it would destroy the psychological basis necessary for the will to self-defense. Such counsel would strengthen tendencies in Europe to seek gradual voluntary and timely salvation in preventive "good conduct" and growing subservience vis-à-vis the Soviet Union for fear of war and Soviet superiority. The result would be to restrict the very freedom that the Alliance was founded to protect. . . .

The four American authors hope that a policy of no-first-use could help to clear the way towards a serious reduction of nuclear weapons on both sides. Their further comments on this topic, however, suggest that they themselves do not entertain exaggerated hopes. Indeed, the experience of recent years in the field of tactical nuclear weapons gives little cause for hope that the Soviet side is ready for genuine reductions. Moreover, it is questionable whether the Soviets are ready to renounce their conventional superiority built up at great sacrifice, stubbornly defended during decades and energetically expanded in recent years, at the very moment when such a superiority would be given an increased and decisive importance by a NATO renunciation of first use of nuclear weapons.

We share many of the concerns about the risks of nuclear war. They lead us to conclude that an energetic attempt to reduce the *dependence on an early first use* of nuclear weapons must be undertaken. To be sure, the authors also mention a "no-early-first-use" policy (p. 762) as a possible alternative, but in the last analysis they discard it as a mere variation of nuclear options and therefore call for a clear decision in favor of a renunciation of "any first use of nuclear weapons" (p. 761).

A reduction of dependence on an early use of nuclear weapons should, in the first place, be attempted through mutual, balanced and verifiable reductions of conventional forces by means of East West negotiations which result in an adequate conventional balance. We have pointed out how difficult it would be to restore such a balance by the buildup of Western conventional armament. In our opinion the essential precondition posed by the authors for their suggested renunciation of first use can, therefore, not be fulfilled.

In sum, we consider efforts to raise the nuclear threshold by a strengthening of conventional options to be urgently necessary. The reduction of the dependence on first use, in particular on early first use of nuclear weapons, should be a question of high political priority in our countries.

The Western Alliance has committed itself to a renunciation from the very beginning: the renunciation of the first use of *any* force. The entire military planning, structure and deployment of forces are geared exclusively toward defense. The presence of nuclear weapons has contributed essentially to the success of the Alliance in preventing war and preserving freedom for three decades. We are convinced that a reduction of the dependence on an early use of nuclear weapons would serve this purpose. Under the circumstances of the foreseeable future, however, a renunciation of the option of first use would be contrary to the security interests of Europe and the entire Alliance.

*Selective Engagement with the
Soviet Union*

ERNST B. HAAS

America has sought to understand and come to terms with the
Soviet Union for sixty-six years. We still have no agreed-upon
understanding, and we have yet to come to terms with the Soviet
phenomenon. It is almost a platitude to assert that American policy
toward the Soviets has been both reactive and inconsistent, swinging
from implacable hostility to the desire for mutual accommodation,
and back again. If our Soviet policy were just a piece of our overall
stance toward the world, this might be tolerable. Since the late
1940s, however, our overall posture toward the world has been
largely shaped by our attitudes toward the Soviets; our foreign and
defense policies have been subordinated to our shifting fears, hopes,
and hatreds regarding Moscow's plans.

TOWARD A STRATEGY OF SELECTIVE ENGAGEMENT

I propose a global strategy of "selective engagement" for the
United States. This policy avoids the complete engagement with all
countries and issues that containment strategies have considered
necessary for hemming in the Soviets. It takes for granted that the
expense and risk of containment are greater than the benefits likely
to be obtained. Selective engagement also avoids the assumptions
and implications of détente and entente, because these strategies
are based on the unprovable premise that Soviet intentions are
benign. It argues for doing what is necessary to protect democracy
where it now exists and to work for a future world less likely to be
plagued by war and poverty. It scales down and redefines some
American world order values, recognizing that we cannot, without
risking our own ruin, continue the attempt to mold the world in our
image. Selective engagement aims at the delinking of issues, at
leading us into an international order in which policies are no longer
seen largely as means for containing Communism in general and the

From "On Hedging Our Bets: Selective Engagement with the Soviet Union" by
Ernst B. Haas, in Aaron B. Wildavsky, ed., *Beyond Containment: Alternative
American Politics Toward the Soviet Union,* published by Institute of Contemporary
Studies Press, 1983. Reprinted by permission of the publisher. Portions of the text
have been omitted.

Soviets in particular. Selective engagement is a means for loosening up a system that is too tightly coupled for safety.

This strategy must serve the values we profess. What follows is my subjective ranking of the principles that ought to govern the world in which, realistically, we can expect to live in the next generation. Neither our values nor the world order they imply approximate the utopia of a denuclearized welfare world; the present is not the time for crusades.

The avoidance of war, especially of nuclear war, heads the list. However, an aversion to war does not imply unwillingness to wage it if necessary for self-defense. Nor does it preclude toleration of wars among other nations, preferably at some distance. Second, we should be committed to the enhancement of basic human welfare everywhere, particularly with respect to health, education, housing, and food. Third, we should protect democratic institutions—civil and political rights—in nations where they now exist, while supporting the growth of such institutions in nations where they show promise. Fourth, we should be committed to the protection of the global environment and to the better use of nonrenewable natural resources. Finally, we ought to favor the economic modernization of the underdeveloped countries while also managing the industrial adjustments necessary in the developed countries in order to accommodate the industrial growth of the South. The simultaneous transfer of resources to the developing countries and the protection of existing living standards in the North may call for policies of economic management at variance with our penchant for free markets and unrestricted private enterprise.

My argument for a different strategy toward the Soviet Union is based on certain postulates, or attitudes toward and judgments about our era in history, that go beyond values. I state them baldly here and justify them later in this essay. My prescription for a strategy of selective engagement depends entirely on the persuasiveness of these postulates.

- Because we have no agreed-upon understanding of Soviet plans and motives, we cannot be certain that there is a "Soviet threat." Yet we can no more be certain that there is no such threat.
- The undeniable growth throughout the world of various types of Marxism is not necessarily the same thing as Soviet expansionism. The Soviet Union is not "conquering the Third World."
- However, the future of democracy is very much in doubt in areas lacking the European cultural tradition (with certain exceptions to be explored). Apart from twenty-five or thirty countries, there is no "free world."
- A tightly coupled world is a dangerous world. If all issues on the

global agenda—from nuclear weapons to environmental protection, from human rights to the rights of whales, from Patagonia to Greenland and from Beirut to Bali—hinge on our perception of Moscow's plans, then a crisis anywhere and over anything can trigger a full-scale war. A safer world requires the decoupling of issues.

• In a decoupled world, there is a chance for the survival of democracy even if the overall power of the Soviet Union or of Communism in other countries were to increase. Acceptance of Soviet equality need not mean surrender on the installment plan.

The survival of our values is threatened by two great perils: the presence of a superpower antagonistic to our beliefs and our dependence on weapons that will destroy us if we use them to defend our values. Selective engagement is a bet that we can survive despite these conditions because we are not sure about Soviet motives. But we would hedge the bet by decoupling policies, sacrificing pawns, and reengaging our energies on other issues elsewhere in the world by not betting everything on a containment that relies on nuclear deterrence. . . .

SIX STRATEGIES FOR DEALING WITH THE SOVIET UNION

This essay is dedicated to the proposition that we ought to have a consistent strategy for living in a nuclear world. A strategy that could assure survival as well as the victory of our values would be greatly preferable to the bits of alternating strategies we have followed in the past. In the history of Soviet-American relations we can trace pieces of five separate strategies, each with its own characteristic attitudes and assumptions. A sixth one exists in principle. I label the strategies *rollback, containment, selective containment, détente with rapprochement, entente with mutual appeasement,* and *superpower condominium.*

A strategy of *rolling back* Soviet power and world Communism is associated with implacable ideological opposition to the Marxist world view. It assumes that the global appeal of Marxism can be reversed at an acceptable cost by taking advantage of weakness, dissension, and unrest in the Soviet bloc and among the bloc's Third World allies. Many Americans professed such a commitment in the 1920s, the early 1950s, and again since 1980. Yet the strategy was never fully articulated, let alone implemented. The cost was not considered acceptable, not even in 1956, 1968, and 1982, when the opportunities for doing so seemed most promising, and not even under Republican administrations rhetorically committed to something approximating a rollback. As an overall strategy—as opposed to working for an occasional reversal of alliances in the Third World—rollback does not commend itself in a nuclear era.

Containment was American strategy during the early 1950s. It accepts the existence of the Soviet Union as a fact of history while deploring the implications of that fact. It seeks to freeze the boundaries of the Soviet realm by all appropriate means short of nuclear war, and hopes for the "mellowing" of Communism and of totalitarian institutions as the weaknesses of the system become apparent to its own citizens. The Reagan administration seems to espouse containment in this form and it adds a dose of rollback as well. "Project Democracy" aims to nurture democratic forces in Eastern Europe; by distinguishing policies toward Eastern Europe from the containment of the Soviet Union itself, the Reagan administration seeks to divide the Eastern bloc.

Selective containment moderates the strategy of complete containment by, in effect, sacrificing certain parts of the world because they are considered relatively unimportant to American interests. Selective containment reluctantly tolerates Third World populist-collectivist-totalitarian movements and governments when they do not directly threaten us. While the integrity of defenses and economic health in Western Europe and the Far East continue to be considered of the highest importance, the fate of specific countries in Asia and Africa is considered vital only if their adherence to the Soviet bloc also implies a threat to resources or military access. Whether all or parts of Latin America should be considered within the perimeter of selective containment is a matter of recurrent debate. Selective containment was American strategy from 1956 until 1963, and many advocate it today.

All three strategies imply a set of American beliefs that casts the Soviet Union as the chief enemy of world order. The international system is seen as unstable, polarized, and tightly linked. A setback in one area, or even in such functional fields as trade, money, and technology, is believed to diminish the power of the West in all others. International politics, in this view, is a zero-sum game. Every part of the "free world" is potentially important. All commitments to the "free world" must be honored lest the United States be seen as devoid of will. Negotiations with the Soviets must be conducted to prevent our being duped and to demonstrate American determination to be strong. All conflicts of interest with the Soviet Union are indivisible. In the long run, either the "free world" or Communism must win.

Détente and *entente* both imply a different set of beliefs. These strategies call for active measures designed to defuse confrontations, to transcend the Cold War, and to find means for peaceful coexistence between the two powers. The Soviets become a limited adversary as the international system is seen as multipolar and more stable, and as issues and geographical areas are no longer viewed as one seamless web of conflicting interests. Not all commitments are

then considered equally vital. Third World countries are not necessarily "with us" or "against us." Negotiations with the Soviets
become more businesslike, less designed to display American ma-
chismo. Issues are decoupled and dealt with separately even if they
remain linked in the minds of key strategists. Détente, entente, and
even a superpower condominium aim at the creation of ground rules
for a more peaceful system of international relations.

Détente is not, however, designed to settle all outstanding quarrels or provide for a shared world view among the antagonists. It
does aim at the systematic reduction of tensions that could lead to
war. This requires rapprochement in the sense that timely agreements must be sought about specific grievances that might trigger
war. Détente with rapprochement was America's objective from
1963 until 1976, although we did not abandon selective containment
in Southeast Asia until our defeat in Vietnam. Nor did we forego
the exploitation of targets of opportunity in the Middle East, which
amounted to a rollback of the Soviets in Egypt. Some call the
Nixon-Kissinger strategy of détente with rapprochement a path of
"collaborative competition" because of the continued presence of
zero-sum attitudes.

Yet it was the intent of that strategy to make even selective
containment unnecessary in the long run. Détente was expected to
lead to *entente with mutual appeasement*. The two superpowers
were to recognize their joint stake in a peaceful world and live by a
code of conduct for making it real. Kissinger knew that the competitive element in the détente strategy would not yield to the collaborative aspect unless the Soviets were gradually persuaded that they
could be secure in the existing world order. Hence there had to be
assurances and incentives in order to convince the Soviet leadership
that the status quo could serve their interests, that a classical
balance-of-power system would be preferable to the Soviet penchant
for seeing the world as an unstable "correlation of forces" that
could be made to tilt toward Moscow. These incentives took the
form of a large number of agreements, ranging from trade and
scientific exchange programs to the effort to spell out basic rules of
international conduct to avoid confrontations. Mutual appeasement
implied American acquiescence to some Soviet demands in exchange for similar concessions on their part. Fifty-eight understandings were concluded between 1969 and 1974, over half of all the
Soviet-American agreements made since 1933.

Entente with mutual appeasement was American strategy between 1934 and 1945; it was also the elusive goal of Nixon and
Kissinger. Why did it fail to come to fruition? The answer is that
appeasement was seen as one-sided by each participant. American
leaders increasingly felt that the United States made the concessions

and offered the incentives while the Soviets rearmed, expanded into Africa, and encouraged the Vietnamese. The Soviets apparently felt similarly about American forays into the Middle East and about our unwillingness to agree that aid to national liberation movements is consistent with détente. Successful entente requires *mutual* appeasement; by 1975 even Henry Kissinger had conceded his failure to persuade the Soviets of his vision.

Still another, quite different, strategy is possible: an agreement between the superpowers to split the world into two spheres of interests and to rule it jointly—a *condominium*. The bipolar division of the world would be made final and peace assured by the agreement of the two rulers not to challenge each other's realms. Concommitantly, the two would agree not to permit the emergence of a third bloc or power. Nuclear proliferation in particular would be repressed and controlled, even if that implied the mounting of surgical strikes against a China, an India, or a South Africa. While the possibility of a condominium has sometimes been discussed—it was said to have been proposed by Brezhnev to Nixon in 1972—it constitutes a perennial fear for conservatives in Western Europe and understandably seems to have preoccupied Mao Ze Dong. In any event, the negotiation and management of a condominium would pose formidable problems. The Pope can hardly be expected to draw another line dividing the two realms. Local revolutionary situations would be unlikely to disappear even if a line were drawn, and one would have to imagine complete indifference on the part of the superpowers if intervention were to be avoided. Nuclear proliferation has gone so far as to necessitate a number of massive surgical strikes to make it fade away; it is unlikely that the strikes would be delegated to the Israeli air force even in a condominium arrangement. We had better exclude this strategy from our repertory of options.

The other five strategies remain as possibilities. Should any of them be chosen by us? I do not believe so. Rollback and containment assume that the Soviet Union is inherently expansive; détente and entente are based on the supposition that the Soviets seek to live in peace and equality with us. Yet, as I shall show, we do not know what motivates Soviet policy. Hence it is not safe to choose on the basis of these assumptions and suppositions. All five strategies focus on the Soviet Union as the centerpiece of world politics, as the lodestar of all American concerns. A better strategy cannot confine itself to counting the countries in the democratic and the totalitarian columns and fashioning military policies to protect the democracies. It must integrate all values that we profess, whether they serve democracy and deterrence or not. The fragmented approaches in our past policies fail to meet this criterion because they

confound the Soviet threat with Communism in general. The articulation of a new strategy of *selective engagement* demands that we
think clearly about Soviet motivations, state and rank our own
values, and become conscious about our limitations in realizing
them. Having done so, we must hedge our bets.

WHAT DO THE SOVIETS WANT?

We knew what Hitler wanted, at least after a period of puzzlement
and thrashing around; but after Lenin, Stalin, Khrushchev, and
Brezhnev we still cannot be sure what the Soviets want. . . . The
perennially most popular school of thought in the United States
argues that Soviet conduct is due to an ideological commitment to
establish Communism as a global system by way of the outward
expansion of the Soviet state. I answer that even though there is
evidence that some Soviet leaders do believe in such an ideology,
Soviet conduct has never conformed to the theory sufficiently to
establish it as a valid explanation of policy.

If the argument that the Soviets have an inherent drive toward
aggression were valid, it would be very difficult to account for their
failure to do a number of things. In the following instances the
Soviets had the capability but failed to:

• reassert full control over Romania and Albania;
• insist on domestic and foreign economic policies in Hungary and
  Poland patterned on their own;
• remove Chinese nuclear installations in the 1960s, or escalate
  Sino-Soviet fighting in 1969–70;
• provide fuller support for Vietnam in its war with China;
• prolong American involvement in Vietnam, rather than encouraging negotiations after 1969;
• provide energetic support for Kurdish and/or Azeri secession in
  Iran;
• provide energetic support for socialist governments in Chile and
  Central America;
• provide much more consistent and plentiful nonmilitary support
  for Kwame Nkrumah in Ghana in the 1960s and for Sékou Touré
  in Guinea in the 1970s;
• provide more efficient military support for African groups likely
  to interrupt Western access to key minerals (in Zaire, Niger,
  Zambia, and especially in South Africa);
• take a more flexible negotiating stance toward allies of the United
  States who might be wooed away (Japan especially); and
• take a more flexible negotiating stance in arms control discussions,
  promising to cut back and then cheating instead of taking the
  ceilings seriously.

The Soviet realm has not expanded territorially since 1948, with the exception of the Afghan adventure. Its hegemony in Eastern Europe is weaker today than it was in the aftermath of the Second World War. Soviet influence waxed and waned outside Europe in mirror-image fashion to American influence. But Communism as a mode of government has spread to Africa, Asia, and Latin America, though not necessarily as an expression of a Soviet imperial drive.

There is a more subtle way of making the argument for the inherent aggressiveness of the Soviets. We may safely assume that Soviet pronouncements contain a heavy dose of ex post facto justification and some plain propaganda to legitimate the leadership of the moment. Even after we allow for this, there remains an impressive residue of Soviet concepts that seems to serve as a consistent bedrock of discussion and analysis, such as "the world correlation of forces," "two camps," and "proletarian internationalism." Consistent use of these concepts suggests that the Soviets do have a view of permanent struggle. But since the exact nature of the moment's "world correlation of forces" must always be a subject of debate and judgment, the Soviets can think in terms of gradations, of increments, of advance-and-retreat.

We, on the other hand, are at a disadvantage because we tend to fall back on all-or-nothing categories: conflict or cooperation, peace or war, détente or confrontation. Our reliance on the concept of the "balance of power" is static as contrasted to the Soviets' "world correlation of forces"; our "defense of the free world" is a weak and reactive counterpoise to the dynamic notion of the "two camps," in no small measure because the members of our "camp" are a far more mixed lot than those of the Soviet Union's.

Given this difference between Soviet and American modes of analysis, the subtle version of the aggressiveness thesis argues that the Soviet Union cautiously and prudently expands by skillfully manipulating policy measures that stress both cooperation *and* conflict. In this perspective, détente with rapprochement is a tactic for avoiding confrontations while at the same time facilitating the eventual victory of the Communist camp; détente can never be an end in itself for the Soviets. This explanation cannot easily be proved wrong or right. It may hold for a segment of the Soviet leadership, or for all of it at certain times. The history of détente and its failure is an ambiguous story; it does not dispose of the issue. But even if the subtle explanation were correct, we should not draw the inference that the only proper response is a strategy of containment, total or selective.

The major rival to the argument that the Soviets are motivated to expand holds that the Soviet Union is and wishes to be a superpower, concerned essentially with its own security and survival in a world dominated by the classical security dilemma. Ideology here is not seen as an important determinant of policy. The United States (and China) are considered by the Soviets as threatening, as a serious danger to be warded off. If we were to adopt this view of Soviet conduct, we would expect that policies of rolling back or containing Soviet power would be seen by the Soviets as confirming their fears. Policies of détente and entente, however, would provide reassurance that those fears are wrong. This explanation is popular among those who see the wellsprings of Soviet conduct in internal forces and problems, who believe that by influencing the shape of Soviet economic and social policy we can also mold Soviet foreign behavior.

There are two objections to this view. One is empirical. If the Soviets merely wished to be assured that we recognize them as a superpower with legitimate security interests that entitle them to help manage the world's trouble spots, they would not have to devote great energy to asserting the primacy of the Communist Party of the Soviet Union over other Communist and Marxist movements. They would not have to revile Yugoslavia and China as ideological deviants. Nor would they have to train and arm the Palestine Liberation Organization, the Southwest African People's Organization, Joshua Nkomo, Sékou Touré, or Angola's MPLA. There would be no incentive to ship, via Cuba and Nicaragua, arms and supplies to El Salvador, arm first Somalia and then Ethiopia, and continue to give vociferous verbal support to every self-proclaimed national liberation movement from Puerto Rico to the Philippines. This behavior has been consistent since 1945. It cannot be squared with the notion that Soviet military security dominates policymaking.

The second objection to this explanation is rooted in our tendency to analyze Soviet decision-making as the mirror image of our own. We know how our decisions are made and how our leaders calculate. Hence we think Soviet processes are equally unproblematic. We do not allow for the force of divergent concepts, for belief in strong historical processes, and for the possibility that at some level the idea of historical materialism informs behavior. It is also true that we do not know whether all or only some decisions are so influenced, and whether the concepts are self-correcting at the level of strategic choice as well as for more mundane tactical steps. Our commentators disagree volubly and at length on how such things ought to be interpreted and understood, and how the Soviets reconcile contradictions among their own concepts. Nevertheless, those who believe that "the Soviets are just another superpower" tend not to worry about these conundrums. . . .

These explanations, though popular, represent only the extremes of the possible. There are various mixed explanations that insist that the two extreme theses may be compatible if we consider how the Soviets see the world, instead of being transfixed by our ways of interpreting it. Such mixed perspectives suggest that Soviet policy is both reactive *and* initiatory, alternatively defensive *and* aggressive. They also suggest that, at least under Brezhnev, relations with the United States were to be both cooperative *and* competitive, not one or the other. Everything depends on whether we are talking about arms control, technology transfer, grain sales, emigration, defense budgets, armed assistance to liberation movements, or the situation in the Middle East, Southeast Asia, East Africa, and Central America. Linkages among issues and areas may be explicit in the minds of American leaders; but we should not make the mistake of assuming the acceptance of the same connections in Soviet thinking.

Thus it is possible that Soviet policy in the Middle East is reactive to uncontrollable Arab and Israeli moves, and to the American response to such moves. Yet Soviet policy in Africa and Central America can be initiatory at the same time. The motives of the moment may call for compensating for the failures of Soviet economic planning—implying collaborative moves—while also suggesting that Moscow take advantage of a target of opportunity in Ethiopia or Angola—thus implying conflict. There is no need for the Soviets to opt exclusively for collaboration or conflict as long as the Western response remains open to both. Prudence and restraint can be abandoned when a target of opportunity arises; they can be restored when the American response is overtly and dangerously hostile. Linkage imposed by Washington can be accepted by Moscow when the Soviets reexamine their priorities, at least as long as the structure of economic and technological interdependence remains tenuous. We know that the Soviet leadership is sometimes faction-ridden; we know that there are sharply differing internal priorities. Hence, these commentators say, why assume a uniform and linear form of behavior, or a single mode of thought?

Persuasive as this line of argument undoubtedly is, it does not take us very far in accounting for Soviet behavior. I find it wholly credible that succession crises in the Soviet Union would influence foreign policy, as would shifting domestic priorities and the associated factional struggles. Yet it is a fact that Soviet policy over the long run has been consistently true to its ideology, even if the USSR has been no more militarily aggressive than other major powers in their heydays. These mixed explanations correct overly simple analyses of the mystery without giving us a satisfactory clarification of the mystery itself. They may explain single episodes, but not the historical trajectory of policy. And they are too multifaceted to provide unambiguous explanations of one diagnostically crucial episode: détente in the 1970s.

Détente, and its failure, illustrates our continuing uncertainty about Soviet motivations because it provides ammunition for all the explanations while failing to establish the superiority of any one of them. Did Soviet bad faith cause failure? If so, those who argue that the Soviets merely used détente as a way of catching up and surpassing America may be right. Did American bad faith cause it? If so, then those who argue that bad relations were due to American misunderstanding of Soviet aspirations to secure superpower status have a point. Did mutual misunderstandings about the degree of competition and the extent of collaboration undermine the process? If so, mixed explanations must be brought to bear on the problem.

Unfortunately, we cannot be sure. The two powers did indeed disagree with each other from the start of détente about the issues and areas in which there would be collaboration as opposed to continuing competition—especially with respect to postcolonial struggles in the Third World. Détente, to Western Europe and to Japan, meant permanent collaboration in trade, investment, and arms control; these notions were never equally acceptable to the United States. Linkage of issues aroused expectations in America that were obviously not shared in the Soviet Union. Washington thought that interdependence due to economic ties would increase the Soviet appetite for more butter and fewer guns, thus limiting foreign military activity; the Soviets had quite different plans. They apparently thought that linkage would work toward the loosening of the Western Alliance, and events tended to bear them out. We thought linkage would weaken the Soviet hold on Eastern Europe, but our puny sanctions against Poland and NATO's lackluster response eventually demonstrated the error of our ways. Détente was understood differently in Washington, Moscow, Tokyo, Bonn, and Paris. That much is clear. But what did the Soviets really want: a breathing space for resuming their expansion of influence, or steps toward eventual entente with mutual appeasement? . . .

DOES OUR IGNORANCE OF SOVIET MOTIVES MATTER?

It seems obvious that we cannot choose a strategy for our foreign policy if we cannot fathom the motives of our main adversary. But is this really so? Some commentators argue that our ignorance need not foreclose choice because many of the things the Soviet Union could accomplish should not really matter to us. The importance of this argument cannot be denied. Even though I do not accept the argument that "it doesn't really matter what they want," I concede that a full knowledge of Soviet motives is not necessary because not all aggressive moves must be a matter of concern. Hence, I wish to present the case for a permissible American indifference to Soviet motives.

What follows is a worst-case scenario. I assume the Soviets have concluded that the global correlation of forces gives them the capability safely to embark on a number of enterprises now perceived by Washington as harmful to American interests. After setting forth these enterprises, I ask how their accomplishment would harm the American national interest.

Take war-making capability. Suppose the Soviets develop a workable antiballistic missile (ABM) system and the capability to eliminate American surveillance and communications satellites, thus making even our submarine-based deterrent forces ineffective. Having neutralized our deterrent, they could attack or threaten Western Europe with conventional forces, leading to the dissolution of NATO. The European Common Market would then be integrated with COMECON, though the Western European countries would remain formally sovereign. Having accomplished this, the Soviets then would offer us a nonaggression pact, promising to maintain correct and normal commercial relations and to respect American private property in Europe. Western Europe would become nonaligned and retain a limited capacity for self-defense. NATO would disappear, but in other respects things would remain much the same as before.

What might then happen in other parts of the world? China now would have to make its peace with the Soviet Union, recognizing the finality of its borders in Asia and the moral authority of the CPSU, but domestically it could continue much as before. We assume further that China would not oppose the consolidation of the world socialist system. Japan would now have to choose between maintaining its alliance with the United States and continuing to rely on trade within the Northern Hemisphere in general, or embarking on an independent policy of massive rearmament and penetration in Southeast Asia, or opting for a close partnership with China. Members of the Association of Southeast Asian Nations (ASEAN) would face the same unpleasant choices as Japan, made worse for them by the fact that a united Greater Vietnam would now be fully integrated into a Soviet-led Communist bloc. Eventually, India and Pakistan would also have to bend their policies of official nonalignment; either they would pursue a nuclear arms strategy immediately and seek to distance themselves from the Soviets, or they would be forced to join them.

In Africa, the Soviets would simply continue to support left-leaning governments and movements, especially if they confronted their more conservative neighbors. There would be no need to interfere with European and American purchases of minerals, though the increased Soviet leverage for influencing this trade is obvious. In the Caribbean and Central America the Soviets could then safely continue their current policy of permitting Cuba to support insurgent movements and leftist governments and of seeking closer economic and diplomatic ties with any regime willing to reciprocate. That Mexico, Venezuela, and a number of the Caribbean islands might then seek such ties at the expense of relations with the United States seems obvious. There would almost certainly be an increasing Soviet military presence. And in South America the Soviets might merely exploit such targets of opportunity as presented themselves by virtue of normal domestic unrest without having to go out of their way to establish bases or special access. The Western Hemisphere would gradually cease to be the preserve of the United States.

More dramatic changes would seem to be in store for the Middle East. Lacking a credible nuclear deterrent, the United States would have much more difficulty extending its protective umbrella over Israel than at present, and Israel would seek nuclear capabilities—if the Soviets can be imagined to permit this. More likely, energetic Soviet support for the Arabs would force the kind of settlement on Israel (assuming the Soviets wished to avoid a war) that all Israeli governments have desperately sought to avoid. Arab governments now leaning toward the United States would then face the same unpleasant choices as the countries of Southeast Asia.

Would such developments threaten the United States? While the might of the Soviet Union would eclipse ours, we would not simply disappear from the scene. While Communism would surely expand as a principle of social and economic organization, it would not suddenly engulf all other forms of organized existence. Soviet hegemony would certainly change the world for the worse and trigger changes in our lives we could not easily square with our values. Yet many would prefer such an outcome to a nuclear exchange. Our worst-case scenario is unacceptable only to people who would unequivocally prefer "freedom"—political life as we lead it now—to "peace"—the subordination of that life to the avoidance of massive violence and destruction.

My reasoning here takes for granted that the global political and economic system is tightly coupled—that events in one part of the world have inevitable consequences everywhere else, and that diplomatic and military success or failure engenders a proportionate gain or loss in economic well-being. A major expansion of Soviet influence anywhere is thought to engender a decline in American influence everywhere. Past and present American policies have been predicated on the validity of this assumption. What happens if we take the world to be weakly coupled and the course of action less obviously determined? Scenarios are mindstretchers, not certified descriptions of the future. The strategy of selective engagement I propose rejects several of the assumptions built into the scenario.

I do not believe that the motives imputed to the Soviets are incontrovertibly correct. Nor do I believe that all aspects of international relations are as tightly linked to the preservation of American technological superiority as I have suggested. A fallacious belief in overly tight coupling proved to be one of the reasons for the failure of détente. Trade, investment, human rights, the use of the oceans, and the political future of many parts of the world are far more autonomous from the Soviet-American military balance than was suggested.

For these reasons, tolerating ambiguity about Soviet motives— for which I am arguing—need *not* imply surrender on the installment plan. Our choice need *not* be "freedom" or "peace." In the short run, there is no alternative to maintaining a credible nuclear deterrent. This does require that we guard against Soviet technological breakthroughs of the kind imagined in our scenario and prevent the one-sided obsolescence of our deterrent capability. We also must maintain the present deterrent value of NATO and encourage Japan to upgrade its defenses. On the other hand, a strategy of selective engagement can dispense with the continuous upgrading of our defenses, with the search for ever more expensive technological fixes—provided the Soviet Union can be persuaded to follow the same course. Hence such arms control measures as bilateral freezes are quite consistent with selective engagement.

For the long run, I am persuaded that a stable Soviet-American security relationship cannot be achieved by means of two invulnerable nuclear deterrents in *perpetual* confrontation. But I do believe in maintaining a minimal perimeter of joint defense planning, under which we continue to underwrite the security of the part of the world that matters most to us; this perimeter includes Western Europe, Japan, South Korea, and the Pacific. But why commit ourselves also to maintaining American influence in the Third World, as argued for by devotees of rollback, containment, and even détente? Soviet power in Africa may, or may not, endanger access to natural resources; but it will not pose a military threat to the United States. The same may be said of Vietnamese power in Southeast Asia. The circumstances under which Cuban influence in the Caribbean poses a military threat to us require careful analysis; Marxist victories in Surinam, Grenada, and Nicaragua do not necessarily threaten our way of life. Crudely put, my argument says: who cares what happens in Ethiopia, Laos, or El Salvador? Selective engagement is committed to restraining Soviet power, not Communism everywhere in the Third World.

WHY THE UNITED STATES CAN NO LONGER DOMINATE

When American values and preferences are contrasted with the long list of demands made by other countries, America is properly described as a conservative power, a defender of the status quo. Because we are stronger and richer than other countries, and because the existing world order was shaped in large measure by us, it can come as no surprise that American policy is essentially reactive and defensive. It has much to defend and it must therefore react to challengers, to states that prefer a different order—about 125 of them.

The defense of our values is becoming more costly and more risky. Hence we must define our values modestly, and limit ourselves to what is essential for protecting our own and our allies' freedom while also maintaining peace. And we must do this in full recognition that the world is not going our way.

I am pessimistic about democracy and capitalism as enduring institutions. I want to protect democracy where it has roots; I despair of finding new converts. I fear that free-market economies have served their purposes and will find a hospitable soil neither in the First World nor in the Third. The dominant role of the state in certain Third World nations is a fact. Few people are committed to its demise. In Africa and parts of Asia where the state remains more fiction than fact, the trend is toward building states, not self-reliant voluntary groups and entrepreneurs. Economies free from state regulation have long been a tonic for nostalgia rather than a fact of life in the First World. I find it difficult to believe that the strains of industrial adjustment, of more integrated welfare policies, and of inflation and unemployment will leave more than faint traces of an idealized capitalism in the years ahead. If we wish to serve individual human welfare we must make our peace with these trends. If we wish to create a safer world in which we can coexist with the Soviet Union in relative peace we must so construct our overall foreign policy as to serve these values safely. This task requires the decoupling of the major economic and human rights issues from the Cold War setting. Considering the realities now confronting policies designed to enforce old-fashioned containment, retrenchment is inevitable.

One reality is domestic. The political culture of America is inhospitable to the implementation of any long-range international strategy. General Marshall knew his countrymen when he urged that we wage World War II as rapidly as possible, with overwhelming force, and toward the goal of the enemy's unconditional surrender, because he feared that the country did not have the stomach for a long and indecisive war that might have to end with protracted negotiations. American world order values are conservative as compared with those of the Third World and the Soviets, but that does not mean that American institutions and public opinion are willing to bear the burden of their ideology.

We have become increasingly reluctant to earmark enormous sums for weapons that may never be used and that will not come on line for a decade, though during the height of the Cold War we bore this burden willingly. America, like the rest of the West, is increasingly a culture of economic and social entitlements. Financing entitlements while also rearming poses the classical "guns versus butter" problem. We accepted mass conscription in 1941 without complaining about the infringement of personal freedom, but only after considerable travail—and we disbanded our huge forces rapidly in 1945. Today, even the mild requirement that young men register for a possible draft resulted in 500,000 cases of defiance of the law. The cultural bias favoring individual growth, personal self realization, and the autonomy of small groups militates against the notion of the acceptance of personal sacrifices in the service of national values. A sybaritic and self-indulgent culture is not likely to provide the support for a foreign policy of armed assertion. How can one justify the fine-tuning of the fiscal and manpower policies implied by containment to a public more concerned with private gratification than public welfare?. . .

A still more difficult domestic constraint on the realization of American values is the oft-described swing in the moods of the American public, the condition so feared by Marshall. Our ritualistic and highly personalized presidential election campaigns tend to force these swings into a regular four-year cycle. Consistency and flexibility, as George Kennan complained in 1950 (following David Hume's doubts about the viability of balance-of-power diplomacy), are not to be had in a country whose citizens think in moralistic terms of "either/or." There is no hope for any long-term strategy if the Soviet Union is seen either as a hotbed of Communist conspiracies aiming at world conquest, or as just an insecure newly modernized country eager for reassurance, and if the American public shifts rapidly from one extreme perception to the other. It makes little difference whether the public mood says "get the U.S. out of the UN and the UN out of the U.S." or whether it announces "enlist in the Army, meet exotic people, and kill them." Both sentiments express moralistic extremes common to American culture.

The government that has to cater to both is burdened with some difficult trade-offs. During the 1950s the mood favored harsh confrontational measures against the Soviets. In the 1970s the legacy of the failure of such measures in Vietnam pushed sentiments in the opposite direction. Today, the mood oscillates between the advocacy of nuclear disarmament and the commitment to a new genera-

tion of more deadly and more accurate nuclear weapons, between
"getting the U.S. out of El Salvador" and mounting an intensified
global resistance to Communism.

These are some of the domestic constraints on policy. The picture
abroad offers little reassurance for a consistent long-range strategy.
To repeat the obvious, there are now two superpowers quite capable
of destroying each other in a short war, and much of the world with
them. The Soviet Union insists on being recognized as a world
power, with all this might imply. And the Third World has grown in
power and heterogeneity so as to defy any single and simple policy
of catering to it.

Our allies are no longer our clients. They are willing and able to
assert their individual (and collective) national interests on détente
in Europe, nuclear weapons, arms control, the Middle East, Central
America, and the sale of high-technology items to the Soviet bloc.
Their views of the difficult trade-offs diverge more and more from
ours. During the 1970s the mood favored their preferences on
détente and even entente. It is far from clear that our allies will
continue to reject Soviet demands for full superpower status.

The independence of our allies is caused in no small measure by
the fact that the societies of all industrialized countries show the
same signs of declining national unity as does ours. Wealth engenders self-indulgence, the unwillingness to make personal sacrifices.
In Europe this mood has led to the extremes of the contemporary
unilateral disarmament movement, a movement that prefers faith in
the benign motives of the Soviet Union to a willingness to accept
the logic of nuclear deterrence. The movement sees us, not Moscow,
as the enemies of peace. It seems to prefer life under the shadow of
Soviet hegemony to the continuation of an armed confrontation
along the Elbe River. Given all of this, a return to containment
cannot count on consistent European and Japanese support. Since
going it alone also would imply the growth of a garrison-state
mentality in America, retrenchment is inevitable.

ASPECTS OF SELECTIVE ENGAGEMENT

Selective engagement as an alternative to past strategies must
answer certain perennial questions: When and where should the
expansion of Soviet influence be opposed with military aid and, if
necessary, with counterinsurgency and conventional military operations? When and where should we intervene militarily in the Third
World to prevent the spread of Communism?

I now discuss each of these questions in detail.

Where should we be ready to fight? We should continue our
commitment to the military defense of all democratic countries

against Soviet threats, provided these countries wish to be defended. This commitment also covers threats by allies of the Soviet Union against Third World countries with a democratic tradition. Military action is justified to defend democracy in Western Europe and Japan but also in such countries as Costa Rica, Venezuela, India, Sri Lanka, Israel, and Colombia.

Moreover, military action may also be justified if the Soviet bloc expands into an area containing key commodities that are essential for the economic welfare of the democratic countries. This rule is subject to great abuse. We must be certain that the commodities lost to Soviet control cannot be obtained elsewhere. Soviet penetration of the Middle East oil fields would be a very serious threat to Europe and Japan, though not to us. Soviet control over African copper, chrome, or uranium might or might not be serious, depending on alternative sources of supply. We can reduce the temptation to invoke this justification for war by a timely policy of stockpiling and by the development of alternative materials and sources. Unless these measures are taken the rule can too easily justify an unthinking policy of supporting South Africa, Mobutu's Zaire, or Saudi Arabia's subsidies of the PLO.

In short, the United States need *not* be committed to the military defense of all countries not currently part of the Communist camp. But there is a third contingency that justifies fighting: Soviet penetration of regions so close to the United States as to afford the adversary an opportunity for offensive action. We cannot tolerate the establishment of strong Soviet influence in Canada and Mexico; we must be careful at all times that Soviet power in Cuba remains confined to nonoffensive levels.

How can we prevent the use of this rule from leading to repetitions of the Vietnam tragedy? We must distinguish between spurious and genuine "domino" effects. A genuine domino situation exists when the Soviet Union is able to profit from an indigenous insurgency to assume control over the victorious Marxist government that emerges, then uses this new ally/client as a base for additional subversion in neighboring countries, and finally establishes itself in the area as a military power able to threaten the United States. This did *not* happen in Vietnam. The military hegemony of Hanoi in Indochina does not threaten the military security of the United States, Japan, or Europe. Nor does the expansion of Soviet power in East Africa have such an effect. Normally we should not rely on multilateral agreements for controlling Communist expansion in the Third World on the grounds that such expansion threatens American security. However, we might well encourage multilateral agreements to persuade Third World countries to insure each other and to distance themselves from the Soviets and from us.

The obvious instance of a genuine domino situation is the Caribbean. We may not be threatened by Cubans in Angola and Ethiopia, but Cubans in Nicaragua and Grenada are potentially a different matter. I repeat: the issue here is not the spread of Communism and the replacement of a repressive authoritarian government with a more repressive totalitarian one. The issue is the potential military threat to the United States. There is no domino effect as long as, *but only as long as,* Cuban and Soviet-supported indigenous insurgencies do not lead to the creation of a Soviet-controlled offensive military capability. The Caribbean, then, poses a problem because the success of Marxist insurgencies may endanger the stability of such democracies as Costa Rica, Jamaica, Barbados, and Trinidad, and also lead to the creation of a Soviet military threat.

My reasoning thus leads to these specific rules for selective engagement:

• Do not expect the Soviet Union to abide by spheres-of-interest agreements in the Third World; be prepared to enforce the ones that matter most to American security (as in the Caribbean), and refrain from negotiating others likely to be violated and of secondary concern to us (as in Africa).
• Do not raise symbolic issues critical of the Soviet Union if there is no chance of strong action; do not intervene by deeds in Eastern Europe; and do not make a big issue over Soviet aggression when it does not really hurt American security.
• Do not deny the Soviet Union public recognition as a great power when such recognition entails no substantive cost to us.
• Use conventional forces to oppose Soviet or proxy aggression against the states considered genuinely vital by us.
• Rearm so as to have adequately equipped and sufficiently mobile forces for these missions. This calls for re-equipping conventional forces, *not* equipping our strategic forces with a new generation of missiles or hardening them beyond the needs of MAD-type deterrence.
• Continue arms control negotiations designed to stabilize strategic forces for deterrence and do not seek qualitative improvements not needed for this purpose.
• Continue policies designed to slow down horizontal nuclear proliferation, recognizing that the process cannot be stopped completely.
• Sharply control scientific exchanges with the Soviet Union and the sale of technology and intensify efforts to persuade other NATO members to do the same, until a decline in Soviet defense spending becomes apparent.
• Declare the Caribbean to be a "zone of peace and self-determina-

tion.'' Encourage a consortium led by Mexico, Venezuela, and Colombia to guarantee the confining of insurgencies to the countries of origin by stopping arms transfer and asylum practices for insurgents and by interposing military forces in case of border violations. Support such efforts by adjusting current U.S. military and economic aid practices.

* Approach Cuba and the Soviet Union to spell out the limits of permissible intervention on their part. Intensify pressure on Cuba; reward it for loosening ties with the Soviet Union and for not encouraging insurgencies. Failing such an agreement, intensify naval and air activity to stop Cuban assistance to Marxist regimes and insurgencies.

Should we act to prevent the spread of Communism? Should we support authoritarian governments with diplomacy, military hardware, training, and advisers because they are preferable to totalitarian ones? My way of putting the question assumes that while Communism will spread in the face of our inaction, the power of the Soviet Union need not. I assume that Soviet control over other Marxist states is tenuous, that there are many kinds of Marxism, and that the Soviet model of governance will not necessarily determine the evolution of political life elsewhere even though all successful Marxist regimes begin their programs under totalitarian auspices.

This question leaves us with the most controversial aspect of American policy: what to do in the seventy largely Third World countries whose annual per capita income is less than $1000. Do we protect them from foreign invasion, urge them to respect human rights, make them into democracies, merely cater to their most basic human needs, or give them military and diplomatic aid to defeat indigenous insurgencies? Or do we overthrow their governments when they turn anti-American? Unless we scale down our values, we are committed to encouraging human betterment, to the diffusion of democratic values, to representative democracy and popular participation. Yet of these countries, twelve have Communist regimes, nine are democracies, four are too unstable to permit a classification, and forty-five have single-party authoritarian institutions—some military and some civilian—that are intermittently and haphazardly repressive. We know that these regimes are in no sense committed to our notions of human rights. We know that they rule by coup and countercoup. Despite our efforts to use foreign aid and military assistance for "state-building" and "nation-building," we cannot be optimistic that many of the seventy will soon develop into well-integrated national communities.

Given this situation, American policy has drifted between two poles: aid and intervention designed to strengthen human rights and economic development (under the Kennedy, Johnson, and Carter administrations), or support for local regimes, however repressive they may be, provided they oppose Marxism and are aligned with American positions vis-à-vis the Soviet Union (as under the Nixon, Ford, and Reagan administrations). Either way, there was and is a marked bias in American policy for less toleration of violations of human rights (and a greater tendency to intervene) when the offenses are committed by left-leaning regimes. Either way, our policies were justified by the alleged need to contain Communist and Soviet influence.

I accept the argument that, in principle, authoritarian governments are preferable to totalitarian ones. Both practice repression; neither respects human rights; neither serves democracy. Why then favor one over the other? Authoritarian governments pose less danger to democracy because of their sloppiness, their corruption, and their lack of principled ideology. They are easier to overthrow than totalitarian regimes; they can be and have been transformed into democracies, as illustrated by the modern history of Venezuela, Colombia, and Greece. We have no instance of the transformation of a totalitarian state into something more humane. Totalitarianism—being thorough, ruthless, and imbued with ideological fervor—is not easily displaced. The harm it does to human freedom far exceeds the clumsy repressions of most dictatorships, even though ruthlessness and fanaticism also make possible social and economic improvements often shunned by authoritarian regimes. Authoritarianism, in short, is reversible, but totalitarianism may not be. Hence, if we have to choose, we hedge our bets by supporting authoritarian dictatorships. But why do we have to choose?

We need not support every authoritarian regime that claims to be defending freedom. Support them we must when and if they control countries considered vital for our and our allies' defense or economic welfare. Whether this condition is met can be decided only on a case-by-case basis. Whether a specific insurgency is a response to purely indigenous discontent or whether it is part of a Soviet plan cannot be determined ahead of time. In general, there is no need to take sides and extend any support to an authoritarian government engaged in fighting an insurgency unless it is clear that the defeat of the government will inevitably lead to a military or economic threat to the United States.

Soviet political and military penetration of the Third World is as real as is ours. But how deep and how lasting is it? Egypt, Somalia, Ethiopia, Iraq, and Indonesia have switched sides. Argentina, Angola, Zambia, India, and Iran hedge their bets, sometimes catering to one camp and sometimes to the other. At the moment, Morocco, Zaire, Chile, Colombia, Nigeria, and Saudi Arabia are aligned with

Washington, an alignment buttressed with military understandings, arms sales, commodity purchases, and the willingness to mount an American (or French) military operation when requested. At the moment, Mozambique, Nicaragua, South Yemen, and Ethiopia are tied to Moscow (or Havana, or East Berlin) in much the same ways. So what? Each camp's penetration of these Third World countries remains superficial. Neither camp can prevent defections. Neither Moscow nor Washington can fashion links that cannot be undone. Neither camp dispenses methods of control and penetration that can fundamentally transform Third World societies and cultures without the energetic and active cooperation of the local leadership.

If the Soviets are no better placed than we in asserting effective control over the Third World, we should worry less about "losing" countries. We should recognize that the Third World is diverse and diffuse, subject to nobody's control, and increasingly populated by countries and leaders who are able and willing to follow courses of national development amenable to nobody's tutelage. And we should be willing to decouple our policies toward the Third World from our fixation with Moscow's unfathomable plans. The global system is not as tightly coupled as many leaders believe it to be, but our safety demands that it be loosened even further. Tightly coupled systems—whether in reality or only in the perceptions of decision-makers—are inherently dangerous because the failure of a single part implies the collapse of the whole.

My reasoning leads to the general prescription that we seek to disengage militarily from the Third World. By decoupling from the South in terms of military activity and militarily justified foreign aid, we need to worry less about occasional Soviet forays. We strengthen our position vis-à-vis the Soviets by being able to disregard some of their moves. Moreover, by engaging to deal with the legitimate economic demands of the South, we disengage from confrontation with Moscow because we can then stop thinking in terms of an undifferentiated and seamless Third World about to be preyed upon.

Disengagement of this kind calls for reducing Northern dependence on imports of raw materials essential for military and economic well-being. Bringing about the relative autonomy of the North from Third World commodities implies the need for compensating the South for its loss of export revenues. My specific suggestions are as follows:

- Make another effort to achieve agreement among NATO and Warsaw Pact countries to eliminate or limit the transfer of arms to Third World states. Failing such an agreement, transfer arms only in situations resembling the circumstances under which it would be legitimate for the United States to fight.
- Do not take sides in wars among Third World countries unless one

of the parties occupies a truly crucial position with respect to American strategic needs. There was, for example, no need to support Pakistan in its 1971 war with India. There is good reason to support Egypt and Sudan against Libya in 1983.

• Avoid the formal declarations that proclaim certain areas to be of special military and political concern to the United States (except the Caribbean), such as was done in the Eisenhower, Nixon, and Carter "doctrines."

• Initiate a NATO /OECD (Organization of Economic Cooperation and Development) program of systematic research and development (R&D) aimed at decreasing Western dependence on vital primary commodities from the Third World—notably oil, minerals required for specialty steels, and bauxite.

• As a consequence of the policies of substitution, develop a new approach to Third World exporting countries to compensate them for loss of markets, involving acceptance of those items in the New International Economic Order (NIEO) that deal with technology transfer, multinational corporations, and aid to industrialization.

• Pending success of the R&D program, continue the NATO/OECD program of energetic stockpiling of militarily and industrially vital commodities. Third World opposition to this program should be moderated by generous concessions to a version of the UN's Integrated Program for Commodities.

Selective engagement is a strategy of moderate moods, of not expecting too much, of accepting graciously what cannot be changed without a crusade so bloody as to defy historical experience. It is also a strategy to assure the survival of institutions unique in history, found in few places, and destined to suffer some rude shocks. Hedging one's bets is never as satisfying as indulging one's true desires. But in the face of intractable uncertainty it is certainly safer than gambling with the lives of hundreds of millions.

The Renewal of Strategy

SAMUEL P. HUNTINGTON

CONVENTIONAL DETERRENCE

Conventional forces can contribute to deterrence in three ways. First, by their presence in an area they can increase the uncertainties and the potential costs an aggressor must confront, even if—like the allied troops in Berlin—they could not conceivably mount a successful defense of the area. Second, conventional military forces can deter by raising the possibility of a successful defense and hence forcing the aggressor to risk defeat in his effort or to pay additional costs for success. This has been the traditional deterrent role of the NATO conventional forces in West Germany. Third, conventional military forces can deter by posing the threat of retaliation against the aggressor. This has, of course, been the classic deterrent role of strategic nuclear forces. In principle, there is no reason why conventional military forces cannot do likewise, provided there is something of value to the potential aggressor, like the Soviet empire in Eastern Europe, against which such forces can retaliate. A strategy of conventional retaliation in the form of a prompt offensive into Eastern Europe would help to deter Soviet military action against Western Europe and conceivably also in the second deterrent zone. Posing such a threat is central to a 1980s strategy that emphasizes conventional rather than nuclear deterrence.

A strategy of conventional retaliation would constitute a needed additional corrective to the decline in the credibility of the strategic nuclear deterrent with respect to Europe. It would round out the NATO deterrent with respect to Europe, complementing the decisions on the build-up of NATO conventional strength in the Long Term Defense Program and on theater nuclear force modernization to counter Soviet Backfires and SS-20s. This strategy might require some modest changes in the character, deployment, and levels of NATO forces in Germany, but they would not necessarily be substantial. Implementing a conventional retaliation strategy requires more change in the NATO military mind-set than it does in NATO military forces. Since the beginning, NATO has thought about conventional war almost exclusively in defensive terms. NATO

Reprinted with permission from *Strategic Imperative: New Policies for American Security*, copyright © 1982, Ballinger Publishing Company.

strategy, codified in its present form in MC-14/3, adopted in December 1967, stresses forward defense, flexible response, the NATO triad of conventional, theater nuclear, and strategic nuclear forces, and the eventual restoration of prewar boundaries. It posits, in short, a basically defensive strategy. There is, however, no reason why a defensive alliance should, once war breaks out, be limited to a defensive strategy. For thirty years U.S. nuclear strategy has served a defensive purpose by being offensively oriented. U.S. and NATO conventional strategy in Europe should also have a major offensive component.

Since the beginning of NATO Western planning has assumed that the major battles in a conflict on the central front would be fought in West Germany. As a result, West Germans decry the devastation to which their country would be subjected, even in a purely conventional war. They quite appropriately insist on a forward defense strategy, engaging the Soviets as far as possible from their population centers in Bavaria, the Rhine and Ruhr valleys, and the Hamburg area. Such a strategy, however, means that the allied forces have to be strung out more or less evenly along the entire eastern border of the Federal Republic. At any given point, therefore, they are vulnerable to an overpowering Soviet concentration of offensive forces. The logical extension of the forward defense concept is to move the locus of battle eastward into East Germany and Czechoslovakia. The result would be more effective deterrence and, if deterrence failed, less devastation in West Germany.

Current NATO strategy contemplates the possibility of eventually launching a counteroffensive. A major difference exists, however, between a conventional counteroffensive and a conventional retaliatory offensive. A counteroffensive occurs after the enemy's offensive has been brought to a halt and allied forces have been regrouped and prepared to drive the Warsaw Pact forces out of those portions of Western Europe they have occupied. A conventional retaliatory offensive, like a nuclear retaliatory offensive, would, on the other hand, be launched immediately whether or not the Soviet conventional offensive had been stopped. A counteroffensive, in short, sequentially follows the enemy's offensive; a retaliatory offensive occurs, as far as possible, simultaneously with the enemy's offensive.

This distinction is of fundamental importance in terms of the impact of these two strategies on Soviet military planning. To date the Soviets have been free to concentrate all their planning and forces on offensive moves into West Germany. A Western retaliatory strategy would compel them to reallocate forces and resources to the defense of their satellites and thus to weaken their offensive thrust. Most importantly, it is generally recognized that the extent of satellite participation in a war with NATO will depend upon the scope and speed of Soviet success in the conflict. As long as the Soviets are successful, they are likely to have complacent and cooperative allies. If, however, they are stalemated or turned back, disaffection is likely to appear within the Warsaw Pact. A prompt allied offensive into Eastern Europe would stimulate that disaffection at the very start of the conflict. Neither the Soviets nor, more importantly, the satellite governments could view with equanimity West German tanks on the road to Berlin and Leipzig and American divisions heading for Prague, Budapest, and Warsaw. From the viewpoint of deterrence, such a prospect would tremendously enhance the undesirability of war for the governments of the satellite countries. Those governments, which provide almost half of the Warsaw Pact ground forces on the central front, would lose more than anyone else in such a war and hence would become a puissant lobby urging their Soviet partner not to initiate war. The deterrent impact of a conventional retaliatory strategy on the Soviets could be further enhanced by allied assurances to Eastern European governments that their countries would not be invaded if they opted for neutrality and did not cooperate in the Soviet attack on the West.

Creating the conventional military forces that could, with a high degree of certainty, stop a substantial Soviet invasion of Western Europe appears to be beyond the political will of Western European statesmen and publics. Creating a conventional strategy and military force, however, for a prompt retaliatory invasion of Eastern Europe should not be beyond the ingenuity of Western military planners. For years Western deterrent strategy has assumed that a Soviet nuclear attack on the United States would produce a prompt retaliatory response in kind. Theater nuclear modernization in Europe assumes that Soviet use of theater nuclear weapons against Western Europe must also be met by a prompt retaliation in kind. Surely it is rather anomalous that plans do not exist to respond to a Soviet conventional attack on Western Europe with a prompt retaliatory attack in kind on Eastern Europe. Failure to have the plans and the capability for such action is a major—and potentially dangerous— gap in the overall structure of deterrence.

A strategy of conventional retaliation would help ease NATO's nuclear dilemma in at least two ways. First, as the demonstrations of 1981–82 against Theater Nuclear Force (TNF) modernization indicated, significant elements of public opinion in Western Europe and the United States are deeply concerned about a strategy that relies heavily on nuclear weapons. Shifting the emphasis in alliance strategy from the defensive use of nuclear weapons to the offensive use of conventional forces would moderate this source of opposition to NATO military planning. Second, if aggression does occur, the ability to implement a conventional retaliatory strategy would raise the NATO nuclear threshold and thereby make it more likely that NATO could avoid the "deepening trap" of an increasingly improbable "first nuclear use" that Iklé (1980) warned about. Surely it is politically more credible, militarily more desirable, and morally far more legitimate to have a strategy which, if war occurs, contemplates efforts to liberate Eastern Europe by conventional means rather than early recourse to weapons that make likely the slaughter of countless European, Russian, and, in all probability, American civilians.

Moreover, a conventional retaliatory strategy in Europe is relevant not only to the defense of Western Europe. By forcing the Soviets to face the possibility of a two-front war, it also contributes to second-zone deterrence. The Soviet Union is surrounded both by potentially hostile states and potentially tempting opportunities to exploit its military capabilities for political advantage. Western strategy should capitalize on the former in order to limit the latter; Soviet strategy, just the reverse. A Soviet strategist can only see his country as encircled, and his perception would not be wrong. The classic response for a country in this position is to attempt to use the advantages it offers in terms of interior lines and the opportunities to divorce one area of action from another and thus to concentrate diplomatic attention and military force, if necessary, on one opponent or set of opponents at a time. The Soviet Union has a clear interest in attempting to separate its relations with Japan, China, Southwest Asia, Eastern Europe, Western Europe, and the United States into discrete packages, isolated, insofar as possible, one from the other. The logical corollary and preliminary to Soviet military action in China or the Persian Gulf is the fervent pursuit of detente in Europe; some rapprochement with China is a highly desirable prerequisite to military confrontation in Europe. . . .

The ability to deter Soviet military action against China, Southwest Asia, or Eastern Europe cannot rest primarily on military forces in those areas. It will be many years, perhaps decades, before China is capable of repulsing a Soviet punitive incursion. All the efforts to develop readily deployable U.S. forces for the Persian Gulf cannot remove Soviet geographical advantages or Soviet superiority to any indigenous forces that might oppose them. Nor could any satellite army in Eastern Europe by itself hope to hold the Soviet Army at bay for long. If deterrence is to be reasonably and well assured, consequently, it must rest on the high probability that Soviet military action in any one area will also involve the Soviet Union in military hostilities in other areas. This can only happen if there exists a system of interlocking, reinforcing deterrents and if there is the military capability and strategy to take the offensive against Soviet vital interests in an area other than the one which the Soviets are threatening. . . .

The Japanese are prevented by their constitution, capabilities, and psychology from offensive action, and U.S. air or naval offensive action against the Soviet Union from Japan would be incompatible with the U.S.-Japanese alliance unless it was directly related to an imminent military threat to Japan. China's military forces are and will be for several years capable of only the most limited offensive actions against Siberia or Mongolia. No capabilities, obviously, exist for offensive action from Southwest Asia or Eastern Europe. Only in Western Europe do military forces exist that could pose a significant and credible offensive threat to vital Soviet interests. A conventional retaliatory strategy in central Europe is thus desirable not only to compensate for the eroded credibility of the nuclear deterrent as far as Europe is concerned but also to help meet the new needs to deter Soviet aggression elsewhere.

A conventional retaliatory strategy in Europe would not be a substitute for the deployment of Western forces in the Persian Gulf and Indian Ocean areas or for the modernization of the Chinese armed forces. It would, however, supplement and reinforce these efforts and limit the resources that had to be devoted to them by providing an alternative means of securing an equal amount of deterrence. It is, for instance, in all likelihood politically impossible to deploy Western ground forces in the Persian Gulf area so as to provide deterrence-by-presence. Deterrence-by-defense will be possible under some circumstances, but it will be difficult and expensive; and if the Soviets were free to concentrate their forces on Southwest Asia, they clearly could overrun any force that the Western allies and Japan might deploy in a reasonable amount of time. It consequently makes great sense, as Secretary of Defense Weinberger put it (1981), for the United States, if forced into war, to "be prepared to launch counter-offensives in other regions and try to exploit the aggressor's weaknesses wherever they exist." In 1980 and 1981 the European allies of the United States expressed concern at times about the possible reorientation of American military planning, programs, and money from preparation for a European war to the development of the Rapid Deployment Force and other forces for the projection of American power into the Persian Gulf area (*New York Times* 1981:13). Clearly the United States needs to develop that capability rapidly. The extent of the resources reallocated to that purpose from European defense could be reduced, European worries assuaged, and the security of the Persian Gulf area equally well advanced if NATO adopted a retaliatory strategy in Europe. At present the Soviet Union is free to engage in military adventures in the Persian Gulf without concern about its security along the Elbe even as Hitler in the 1930s could move militarily into Eastern Europe without worrying about his security along the Rhine. A retaliatory strategy in Europe consequently should be particularly appealing to the European allies both because it would move at least some of the fighting eastward if deterrence failed and because it would limit the pressure to reallocate allied military resources from Europe to the Indian Ocean.

A somewhat parallel logic would apply to the deterrence of a Soviet attack on China. The provision of military equipment to China, including some forms of lethal equipment, is appropriate and desirable in terms of strengthening defensive deterrence along the Soviet border. At some point, however, the provision of weapons to China will run into problems of distinguishing between defensive weapons, which could only be used against the only power that might attack China (that is, the Soviet Union), and offensive weapons, which might give the Chinese some capacity for deterrence-by-retaliation against the Soviets but which might also give them the capability to attack Taiwan, to occupy portions of Vietnam, Cambodia, and Laos, and to threaten Thailand and other members of the Association of South East Asian Nations (ASEAN). China itself has recognized its interest in a strong NATO. A NATO strategy of conventional retaliation would reduce the importance of re-arming China beyond a certain point and would contribute to Chinese security by forcing the Soviets again to confront the possibility of a two-front war and potentially disastrous losses in the West if they launched an attack on their enemy in the East.

Finally, with respect to Eastern Europe itself, a NATO conventional retaliatory strategy can provide an additional deterrent to Soviet military action against a satellite government that is attempting to broaden its independence. It would, consequently, encourage satellite governments to see how far they could go in loosening Soviet controls. In 1950 the deployment of American troops to Europe significantly encouraged Tito in his resistance to the Soviets (Windsor 1978). An allied retaliatory strategy could well have a comparable effect in promoting the "Finlandization," if not the "Titoization," of Eastern Europe.

The central need in the containment of Soviet military aggression in the 1980s is thus to see the problem of deterrence as a whole and the ways in which the various geographical and functional components of strategy interlock with each other. It is erroneous to suggest, as some have (Aspin 1976), that the Soviet military build-up on the Chinese frontier does not increase the threat to the West or to believe, as the Chinese never would, that NATO strength and strategy have no relevance to the defense of China. In the 1980s geographical linkage is the essence of deterrence. If it is in the interest of world peace and Western security that the Soviets not go into Iran, China, or Poland, that certainty should be greatly reduced. A defensive posture does not require a purely defensive strategy and, indeed, may be undermined by such a strategy. Neither the United States, nor its major allies, nor China, nor regional powers can produce the conventional military forces to defeat those which the Soviets could mass at whatever place they might be tempted to invade. "It is impossible," as Secretary Dulles said in 1954 (Kaufman 1956:14–15), to match the "potential enemy at all points on a basis of man-for-man, gun-for-gun, and tank-for-tank." This is still the case. In 1954 deterrence could be provided by relying "primarily on our massive mobile retaliatory power which we could use in our discretion against the major sources of aggression at times and places that we chose." This is no longer the case. In the 1980s, allied capacity to launch a conventional retaliatory offensive into Eastern Europe is essential to narrowing the gap between foreign policy and strategy and to insuring against Soviet aggression into either the first or second deterrent zones.

The reasons for NATO putting much greater emphasis on deterrence-by-retaliation seem overwhelming. Yet in some circles there is an apparent reluctance to confront this need, and four arguments are often advanced against a NATO strategy of conventional retaliation.

First, it is argued that NATO military forces are too weak to support an offensive strategy. As we have seen, during the 1970s the conventional and theater nuclear force balances in Europe did shift significantly toward the Warsaw Pact. Every effort should be made to rectify this situation and to reestablish a balance of forces more comparable to that which existed in the mid-1960s. If NATO moves forward with its current plans, the military balance in Europe should be more satisfactory in the later 1980s than it was in the early 1980s. Even the 1982 balance, however, would not preclude NATO from adopting a conventional retaliatory strategy. In the first place, the Pact's advantage on the central front is significant but not necessarily decisive (Mearsheimer 1982). In 1981 the Pact had an advantage in divisional manpower of 1.2–1.36 to 1 and in overall manpower of 1.15–1.2 to 1. The Pact was greatly superior in numbers of tanks, but in terms of armored division equivalents, the Pact advantage was only 1.2 to 1, which could very likely be compensated for by NATO strength in airpower. Unlike the Pact, NATO's air strength is overwhelming in attack planes capable of carrying out the deep interdiction and ground-attack missions necessary to support a ground offensive. The introduction of the Leopard and M-1 tanks will also increase NATO's ground offensive capabilities.

The crucial element in any offensive, moreover, is not the overall military balance between the two sides but rather the military balance at the point of attack. The great advantage of the offensive is that the attacker chooses that point and hence can concentrate his forces there. History is full of successful offensives by forces that lacked numerical superiority, including the German offensive in the West in 1940, the Japanese offensives in Southeast Asia in 1941–42, and the North Vietnamese offensive in 1975 (Stuart 1981). Nothing in the existing balance of forces in central Europe rules out a NATO offensive strategy, and that balance is more likely to become more favorable than less favorable during the course of the decade.

In addition, a NATO offensive strategy would pose serious military problems for the Soviet Union. It would, as we have pointed out, require a reallocation of some Pact forces from offensive to defensive purposes. It would also confront the Soviets with just exactly the situation their doctrine and strategy attempt to avoid: one in which they do not have control of developments and in which they face a high probability of uncertainty and surprise. It would put a premium on flexibility and adaptability, qualities in which the Soviets recognize themselves to be deficient. Furthermore, a prompt allied offensive into Eastern Europe would greatly increase the probability of a protracted war. Soviet planning, however, is in large part directed toward a short-war scenario in which the Soviets score a breakthrough, occupy a substantial portion of West Germany, and then negotiate a cease fire from a position of strength. With a retaliatory strategy, however, Soviet armies might be in West Germany but allied armies would also be in East Europe, and driving them out would require more time for mobilization and organization of a counteroffensive.

The basic point, moreover, is deterrence. The prospects for the sustained success of the allied offensive into Eastern Europe do not have to be 100 percent. They simply have to be sufficiently better than zero and to raise enough unpleasant uncertainties to increase significantly the potential costs and risks to the Soviets of starting a war.

Second, it is at times argued that an allied retaliatory strategy, duplicating in some sense Soviet offensive strategy, would create instability in crises, in which each side would be tempted to strike first. Once implemented, however, this strategy should reduce the probability of crises in which either side seriously considers going to war. At present, assuming a lag of four to seven days in NATO mobilization, it is generally argued that Warsaw Pact numerical superiority would peak seven to twenty-one days after the Pact started mobilizing (Carnegie Endowment 1981). In any crisis, consequently, the Soviets would have substantial incentives to attack during this period before the mobilization and deployment of U.S. and West European reinforcements reduced their advantage. These incentives would decrease if they knew that such an attack would be met by an immediate Eastern European offensive by the on-line NATO forces. Similarly, in the absence of a planned NATO offensive, NATO success would depend entirely on its ability to blunt the Soviet offensive; NATO commanders would, consequently, be under greater incentive to launch preemptive "defensive" tactical air strikes against Soviet troop concentrations than they would be if NATO were itself prepared to launch a prompt retaliatory offensive.

Third, it is argued that instead of capitalizing upon the political weakness of the Soviet empire, a conventional retaliatory strategy would help to solidify the empire by enabling the Soviets to rally Eastern European governments and peoples to the defense of their homelands against Western imperialist aggressors. The Soviets, however, already make every effort to do this and consistently portray NATO as an aggressive alliance. It is not clear that they could say much more than they have been saying if NATO adopted a strategy of conventional retaliation. Again, it must be emphasized that the entire purpose of the strategy is deterrence: to create uncertainty in the minds of Soviet leaders as to what would happen in Eastern Europe. As has been argued, the adoption of this strategy should be accompanied with a clear invitation to Eastern European governments to avoid invasion by opting out of a Soviet-initiated war. At the very least, such an invitation would create uneasiness, uncertainty, and divisiveness within satellite governments, and hence arouse concerns among the Soviets as to their reliability. In practice, the allied offensive would have to be accompanied with carefully composed political-psychological warfare appeals to the peoples of East Europe stressing that the allies were not fighting them but the Soviets, and urging them to cooperate with the advancing forces and to rally to the liberation of their countries from Soviet military occupation and political control. A conventional retaliatory strategy is based on the assumption that the West German reserves, territorial army, and populace will put up a more unified, comprehensive, and determined resistance to Soviet armies than the East German, Czech, Polish, and Hungarian armies and peoples will to the advance of West German forces into East Germany and American forces into elsewhere in Eastern Europe. (If this assumption is unwarranted, the foundations of not only a conventional retaliatory strategy but also of NATO would be in question.)

Finally, the point is made that while a conventional retaliatory strategy may make military and even political sense in terms of the relations between NATO and the Warsaw Pact, opposition to it within NATO would be so great that any effort to adopt it would simply tear the alliance apart. Such is the usual reaction to any new idea, however, and the arguments and need for such a strategy are simply overwhelming. Its adoption would, moreover, reduce the intensity of debate over other NATO issues. Theater nuclear modernization would still be necessary, but adoption of conventional retaliation would clearly help to assuage some of the concerns that underlie the debate over NATO's use of nuclear weapons. As indicated earlier, such a strategy would also ease the tensions involved in allocating forces between the Persian Gulf and Western Europe. A coalition of sixteen democratic countries obviously cannot change its strategy without much soul-searching, discussion, and controversy. The need to strengthen deterrence, however, is compelling; debate on the recasting of NATO strategy to meet the conditions of the 1980s should be delayed no longer. . . .

COPING WITH THIRD WORLD THREATS

The Soviet Union is the principal focus of U.S. strategic planning, and Soviet-American military conflict is more likely in the 1980s than in previous decades. The Soviet Union is not, however, the only conceivable source of threats to American vital interests, and the probability that American forces will engage Soviet forces is still less than the probability of their engaging other forces. Other governments or groups can threaten U.S. vital interests in three ways.

First, they can directly attack particular U.S. interests. A guerrilla force shooting rockets at ships going through the Panama Canal would pose a threat whether or not it had any affiliation with or support from the Soviet Union. An attack by the Iranian government or Islamic fundamentalist insurgents on Saudi oil facilities would pose a comparable threat whether or not those attacks had Soviet backing. The seizure of American embassies, planes, or citizens represents similar, if lower level, action to which the United States has to be prepared to respond militarily. The acquisition of nuclear weapons by a guerrilla group or, in some cases, by a government might also pose a direct challenge to American vital interest.

Second, some governments in the world are partial to the Soviets; others are partial to the West. A significant change in power between these two groups would have implications for U.S. security, even if the Soviet Union itself had not played any significant role in bringing that shift about. Coups d'etat in Saudi Arabia or in other Persian Gulf states or local wars in that area, Southeast Asia, the Middle East, or Africa could engage American interests if they threatened friendly governments.

Third, local conflicts and instability in the Third World can create opportunities for the direct expansion of Soviet or Soviet-proxy military influence and presence. American interests are clearly to minimize these opportunities. At times, however, they will exist; non-military and conventional efforts at deterrence may fail; and the United States may find itself confronted with the need to respond to Soviet-bloc military actions in the Third World.

More specifically, the types of Third World military conflict that might pose threats to U.S. interests in the 1980s include: (1) coups d'etat against friendly governments; (2) insurrections or guerrilla insurgencies against friendly governments; (3) local conflicts in which a friendly government is invaded or in danger of being defeated by a less friendly one; (4) any of the above in which Soviet or Soviet-proxy forces play a significant role.

The United States needs a strategy and the capabilities to deal with threats to its interests that arise from these types of conflicts. Declarations of American interest and deployments of American forces can help deter Soviet intervention and local aggression by regional powers. In some circumstances, they may also be able to reduce the likelihood of coups d'etat against friendly regimes. It is difficult, if not impossible, however, to deter those whom one cannot locate, identify, or be sure exist. The United States, as Steven David has persuasively argued (1982), undoubtedly should be prepared to help friendly governments suppress coups d'etat. The existence of some such U.S. capability—and knowledge of its existence—might have some deterrent effect on coup plotting in friendly countries. But these deterrent effects would be of a highly generalized nature, and the participants in any particular conspiracy or cabal might well have good reason for thinking that such an American capability would not be terribly relevant for their case. Hence a strategy for coping with Third World threats has to be directed to both deterring those challenges that are predictable and responding to those challenges that are not.

While there clearly may be some measure of overlap, the four types of contingencies just mentioned are listed in an order that generally reflects ascending levels of violence. From the 1950s into the 1970s, American strategic attention was largely focused upon the second and third types of contingencies. The Korean War was a clear Contingency Three case; the Vietnam War was a combination of Contingencies Two and Three. In connection with these involvements, American strategists developed theories of limited war and of counterinsurgency. Relatively little attention was paid to strategies for coping either with coups d'etat, which are frequent but seldom serious, or with Soviet military intervention in the Third World which until the mid-1970s was relatively minimal.

Insurrections and local wars remain highly likely in the Third World in the 1980s. Many of these could directly affect major American interests. These could include insurgencies in the Gulf area, in Central America and the Caribbean, and conceivably in South Africa. Local wars that might raise the issue of direct American military intervention to support a friendly government could occur in Southeast Asia (Vietnam versus Thailand), the Persian Gulf (Iran, Iraq, or Yemen versus Saudi Arabia), North Africa (Libya versus Egypt, Tunisia, or the Sudan; Algeria versus Morocco), the Horn of Africa (Ethiopia versus Somalia, Kenya, or the Sudan), and quite possibly elsewhere.

The probability of direct participation by U.S. military forces in either prolonged insurgencies or local wars remains, however, relatively low, except in situations where such conflict might directly affect concrete American interests, such as Saudi oil production. The impact of Vietnam is strongest and most relevant with respect to U.S. military involvement in counterinsurgency situations. The reluctance of any U.S. administration, Congress, and the public to countenance such involvement will undoubtedly remain high for most of the 1980s. The United States may often find it in its interests, as in El Salvador, to provide advice, training, money, and equipment to a friendly government fighting guerrillas. In the absence of a direct threat to concrete American interests or direct and overt involvement of Soviet or Soviet-proxy forces, the United States is not likely to find it militarily necessary, diplomatically desirable, or politically feasible to intervene with U.S. combat forces in such conflicts.

Fewer constraints exist on U.S. military involvement in a local interstate war. Major segments of the American establishment tend automatically to attribute legitimacy to revolutionary movements against Third World governments. They also tend almost automatically to attribute illegitimacy to any direct attack by one state on another across a recognized frontier. Consequently, there is likely to be greater public willingness to help a friendly government respond to an external attack than to an internal attack. In the absence of a simultaneous domestic insurgency or outside great power support, however, local interstate wars in the Third World do not generally lead to quick and decisive outcomes. The limited military capabilities of the combatants are more likely, as in the Iran-Iraq war, to lead to inconclusive stalemates, in which neither party is able to deal a death blow to the other. In this situation, the need for direct U.S. military involvement is also reduced.

During the 1970s the Persian Gulf assumed new importance as far as U.S. security is concerned. During the 1980s the probability of political instability in Saudi Arabia, Kuwait, Bahrein, the United

Arab Emirates, and Oman is very high. Conceivably, a prolonged insurgency, a local interstate war, or direct Soviet military intervention could endanger oil supplies from this region to the United States and its allies. The most likely form of instability, however, is coups d'etat against one or more of these conservative Gulf regimes. The underlying causes of political instability are inherent in the rapid increases in wealth, rising expectations, social dislocation, conflicts between Western and Islamic values, and development of modern armed forces. In Saudi Arabia and the other Gulf states, there are at least four major possible sources of instability. First, conflicts within the established elite (for example, between the Sudairi in Jiluwi factions in Saudi Arabia) could get out of hand, leading to efforts by one group to exclude the other from power. Second, the military and other professional groups produced by modernization could be antagonized by the corruption of the existing regime and by their own failure to share adequately in the riches of oil and hence could attempt to overthrow the existing system through a coup d'etat. Third, Islamic fundamentalist groups (*ulemmas*, traditional tribal and local elites) could react against social and economic change, attempting a coup in order to stop such change. Fourth, Palestinian radical groups, alone or in conjunction with radical modernist or Islamic fundamentalist groups, could promote political upheaval so that less conservative regimes who are actively willing to support their cause against Israel could come into power.

All in all, the likelihood of the existing political elites in the Persian Gulf states surviving this decade is small. Even less likely is the survival of the existing political systems. It is difficult to predict the extent to which coups would bring to power regimes seriously hostile to U.S. interests. It is virtually certain, however, that *any* post-coup regime in a conservative Persian Gulf state will be less sympathetic to U.S. interests concerning oil and the Arab-Israeli dispute and more open to Soviet influence than the current regime in that state. In addition, a successful coup in one Gulf state could well trigger coup attempts in adjoining states. Coping with internal instability in Persian Gulf regimes is, consequently, a top priority for U.S. security policy in the 1980s. An overall strategy for dealing with these contingencies involves four elements.

First and most basic are efforts to conserve energy, to stockpile reserves, and to diversify energy sources so that the dependence of the United States and its allies on oil from this potentially unstable area will be reduced. While such efforts deserved top priority, they probably will not significantly reduce U.S. dependence on Persian Gulf oil before the end of the decade. The dependence of U.S. allies on this oil will continue even longer.

Second, the United States can encourage the existing Gulf regimes to take steps to postpone or reduce the likelihood of a coup. These would include measures to moderate but sustain the pace of economic development; to distribute the fruits of development broadly among key groups in the population; to keep its military happy with money, promotions, and weapons; to divide the military establishment into two or more competing institutions; to limit corruption and distribute it widely; to negotiate the stationing of politically acceptable foreign forces in that country (for instance, Pakistani troops in Saudi Arabia) that could protect the regime; and to develop institutional channels so that those elements of the population which are mobilized through modernization can legitimately participate in politics.

Third, the United States can take measures in tacit cooperation with existing regimes to help them defeat coups if they should occur. In several instances in the recent past, outside assistance has played a significant role in defeating coups. The United States itself has acted to head off or defeat coups in Ethiopia, Venezuela, and elsewhere (David 1982). In a coup, communications play a vital role: the leaders of the coup have to convince the populace and, most importantly, potential supporters in the military and elsewhere that they have successfully deposed the previous regime and established themselves in power. The leader of the regime, on the other hand, has to demonstrate that he is still alive and functioning and able to appeal for support. The United States is fortunate that the Persian Gulf oil states are, indeed, located on the Persian Gulf. To assist in the defeat of coups in these states, the United States should provide radio transmitters and other communications facilities on ships off-shore, which could be used by government leaders to relay messages to their supporters and to appeal to their people. In addition, it would be wise for the United States to maintain a small specially trained, countercoup military force on U.S. ships in the region, equipped with helicopters and VSTOL (vertical short take-off and landing) aircraft, that could in a matter of hours respond to the request of a threatened government for help.

Finally, the United States should position itself so that the damage to its interests is reduced if a coup succeeds. It is in the American interest, consequently, to expand and diversify its relations with the Persian Gulf countries—financially, developmentally, militarily, technologically—so that any successor regime will find it difficult and costly to attack American interests and sever connections with the United States. In addition, while it is difficult to predict who will lead a successor government, it is not so difficult to identify a small number of potential leaders for that government. In contrast to its behavior in Iran, the United States should attempt to develop and maintain friendly contacts with those individuals and groups likely to play leading roles in a successor regime.

The most serious sort of military contingency for the United States in the Third World would be direct Soviet or Soviet-proxy military participation in a coup, insurrection, or local war. The appropriate measures of nonmilitary and conventional deterrence can reduce significantly the probability of such involvement. Nonetheless, it still could happen, particularly in the Persian Gulf area. The likelihood of such intervention would be reduced if the United States were able to deploy ground forces in a deterrence-by-presence posture in the region. Such a deployment, however, would no doubt increase the already high probability of political instability in the region. To counter possible Soviet intervention, the United States needs to strengthen the Rapid Deployment Force authorized by President Carter in 1977, greatly expand and modernize its air and naval transport capabilities, pre-position equipment in the area where possible, maintain a respectable naval presence in the Ara bian Sea, and negotiate agreements for access to local bases in emergencies. Although the Soviets probably could, if they wished, overwhelm local or allied forces in the northern Gulf area, the combination of these measures, plus a revision of NATO strategy to make them worry about their Eastern European flank, could provide fairly persuasive deterrence and then war-fighting capability if deterrence failed.

In the 1980s the United States may still have to come to the help of friendly governments fighting local interstate wars or combatting prolonged insurgencies, as it did in Korea and Vietnam. More than before, however, the United States will likely become involved in the other two contingencies located at opposing ends of the spectrum of violence: countercoup intervention, on the one hand, and counter-intervention against Soviet or proxy military forces, on the other. These two contingencies share one characteristic: they are unlikely to last long. A coup is a matter of hours or days at most. A Soviet military intervention to which the United States responded is also likely to be terminated quickly either because one side or the other has won what it wanted or because both sides react to the dangers of escalation by negotiating a cease-fire or disengagement. Because of their probable short duration, countercoup and counter-Soviet U.S. military intervention in the Third World are also likely to be more politically feasible than U.S. involvement in more prolonged civil and interstate wars. The theorists of limited war in the 1950s and 1960s discussed at length the ways in which war could be limited in terms of goals, targets, geographical areas, and forces and weapons employed. As the experiences of Korea and Vietnam make clear, however, the most significant limit on U.S. military action in a small-scale conflict is the limit of *time* (Huntington 1977). The American public simply will not permit its government to engage in long, drawn-out military actions to defend distant interests and to achieve ambiguous goals. Fortunately, the contingencies the United States is most likely to face during the 1980s are ones which will probably be of short duration. Thus, for both political and military reasons, U.S. strategy in Third World conflicts should be directed toward reacting promptly and achieving a quick decision.

Horizontal Escalation:
Sour Notes of a Recurrent Theme

JOSHUA M. EPSTEIN

INTRODUCTION

The deterrence of Soviet military aggression has been the basis of American national security policy since the Truman Administration. The means proffered to secure containment, however, have changed with each Administration since. But they have all partaken of two archetypal approaches: the symmetrical and the asymmetrical. The historian John Lewis Gaddis has characterized them succinctly:

"Symmetrical response simply means reacting to threats to the balance of power at the same location, time, and level of the original provocation."

"Asymmetrical response involves shifting the location or nature of one's reaction onto terrain better suited to the application of one's strength against adversary weakness."[1]

Following the invasion of Afghanistan, former President Carter committed the United States to the deterrence of further Soviet aggression in the Persian Gulf region. While that deterrent commitment was affirmed intact by the Reagan Administration, the symmetrical thrust of the Carter Doctrine[2] was not; whether one dubs it "horizon-

From *The Use of Force,* Second edition, edited by Robert Art and Kenneth Waltz. Published in 1983 by University Press of America. © by the editors.

Dr. Epstein is a Council on Foreign Relations International Affairs Fellow. This article was written while he was a Post-Doctoral Fellow at Harvard University's Center for International Affairs. While the author bears sole responsibility for all views herein expressed, he wishes to acknowledge the contributions of Barry R. Posen, Steven E. Miller, John Mearsheimer, Robert Art, Kenneth Waltz, and Melissa Healy.

[1] John Lewis Gaddis, "Containment: Its Past and Future," *International Security*, Spring 1981, Vol. 5, No. 4, p. 80. For a thorough analysis of American oscillations between the two approaches, see Gaddis' *Strategies of Containment* (New York: Oxford University Press, 1982).

[2] ". . . an attempt by any outside force to gain control of the Persian Gulf region— will be *repelled* by any means necessary, including military force" (emphasis mine). See 1980 State of the Union Address, U.S. Congress, Senate, Committee on Foreign Relations, "U.S. Security Interests and Policies in Southwest Asia," Hearings before the Subcommittee on Near Eastern and South Asian Affairs, Ninety-Sixth Congress, second session, February–March 1980, p. 350.

tal escalation'' or something else[3], the Reagan Administration's attraction to an asymmetrical conventional strategy for the Persian Gulf was quickly evident.

Shortly after taking office, Reagan Administration strategists reportedly issued guidelines to the military ''to hit the Soviets at their remote and vulnerable outposts in retaliation for any cutoff of Persian Gulf oil.'' In Secretary Weinberger's view, ''our deterrent capability in the Persian Gulf is linked with our ability and willingness to shift or widen the war to other areas.''[4]

One possibility cited at the time was ''to threaten the Soviet brigade in Cuba if Moscow or its surrogates move into the Persian Gulf.'' Direct conventional defense would certainly be attempted ''whatever the odds,'' but the prospects for symmetrical response were accounted as grim ''given the Soviets' inherent geographical advantages and their superior number of available ground forces.''[5]

The same language was carried into the Administration's first Defense Posture Statement a year later.[6] But, in the interim, the strategy seemed to have assumed larger proportions. ''If Soviet forces were to invade the Persian Gulf region, the United States should have the capability to hit back there or in Cuba, Libya, Vietnam, or the Asian land mass of the Soviet Union itself.''[7] The list of remote ''Soviet'' vulnerabilities was longer and the Soviet homeland itself had emerged as a potential target for horizontal escalation. Similarly, the procurement of two additional large-deck nuclear aircraft carrier battlegroups was advocated not merely for their capacity to lash back at Soviet weak points, but, on the contrary, for the alleged ''capability of a 15 carrier 600 ship Navy to fight and win in areas of *highest* Soviet capability''[8] (emphasis mine). But, as ever more challenging horizontal options emerged, the Administration's commitment to direct (symmetrical) defense was reaffirmed: ''whatever the circumstances, we should be prepared to introduce American forces into the region

---

[3] ''geographical escalation'' and ''war-widening strategy'' are other names sometimes used.

[4] George C. Wilson, ''U.S. May Hit Soviet Outposts in Event of Oil Cutoff,'' *The Washington Post*, July 17, 1981, p. 1.

[5] *Ibid.*

[6] For example, ''. . . even if the enemy attacked at only one place, *we* might choose not to restrict ourselves to meeting aggression on its own immediate front. . . . A wartime strategy that confronts the enemy, were he to attack, with the risk of our counteroffensive against his vulnerable points strengthens deterrence and serves the defensive peacetime strategy.'' Caspar W. Weinberger, Secretary of Defense, *Annual Report to the Congress for Fiscal Year 1983* (hereafter referred to as FY 83 Posture Statement), pp. 116, 117.

[7] Leslie H. Gelb, ''Reagan's Military Budget puts Emphasis on a Buildup of U.S. Global Power,'' *The New York Times*, Feb. 7, 1982, pp. Z6, Z7.

[8] John Lehman, Secretary of the Navy, ''America's Growing Need for Seaborne Air Bases,'' *The Wall Street Journal*, March 30, 1982.

should it appear that the security of access to Persian Gulf oil is threatened."[9]

Both direct defense *and* asymmetrical response were apparently embraced; under the latter, not just points of Soviet weakness, but points of extreme Soviet strength as well were contemplated as horizontal targets. This "do everything" quality of the articulated strategy was compounded by the Administration's pointed rejection of planning around any specific set of prototypical (or real) contingencies (e.g., the $1 + 1/2$ or $2 + 1/2$ war sizing devices)[10] and its exhortations to prepare for "prolonged conventional wars simultaneously in several parts of the globe."[11]

Predictably, when the military was called upon to attach a price tag to the strategy, it was whopping: hundreds of billions—by some estimates $750 billion[12]—more than the $1.6 trillion Reagan Five Year Defense Plan. The strategy's requirements were reportedly "so grandiose that the Joint Chiefs of Staff says carrying them out would require 50 percent more troops, fighter planes, and aircraft carriers than are now deployed, along with another Marine amphibious force."[13]

It was against that sobering budgetary backdrop that William Clark, in the National Security Advisor's first major speech, announced, "there is not enough money available to eliminate all the risks overnight."[14] And having thus resurfaced, the budget constraint has since imposed a slackening in the planned pace of American military growth, in turn stimulating a more animated debate on the ranking of defense priorities.

Basic questions remain unresolved, however, concerning the advisability of a "war-widening strategy" *in principle,* particularly about its horizontal counter-offense component. And those underlying questions are not addressed merely by admitting a cutback in the pace of funding; the more basic issue is whether this course, this entire strategic direction, is advisable at all. Moreover, until that issue is settled, the debate on program priorities can only founder.

---

[9] George C. Wilson, "U.S. Defense Paper Cites Gap Between Rhetoric, Intentions," *The Washington Post,* May 27, 1982, p. 1.

[10] *FY 83 Posture Statement,* pp. 115–116. On the $1 + 1/2$ and $2 + 1/2$ war concepts, as peacetime planning devices, see William W. Kaufmann, "The Defense Budget" in Joseph A. Pechman (ed.) *Setting National Priorities, the 1983 Budget* (Washington, D.C.: The Brookings Institution, 1982), p. 81.

[11] "Flood and Leak at the Pentagon," *The New York Times,* Feb. 1, 1982, p. A-14. Richard Halloran, "Needed: A Leader for the Joint Chiefs," *The New York Times,* Feb. 1, 1982.

[12] Robert W. Komer, "Maritime Strategy vs. Coalition Defense," *Foreign Affairs,* Summer 1982, pp. 1128–1129. See also, "Flood and Leak."

[13] George C. Wilson, "U.S. Defense Paper."

[14] *Ibid.*

Recognizing that some—by no means all—within the Administration have "stepped back" to reexamine the strategy's appeal, it may therefore be constructive to raise some of the unanswered questions about "horizontal escalation". Five seem especially basic:

First, what is horizontal escalation supposed to do; what is the goal in an operational sense? Second, given some relatively concrete goal, how is the "proper" horizontal target selected? Related to that, in what ways might horizontal escalation affect the probability of vertical escalation by the U.S. or Soviet Union? Fourth, what are the risks of "counter-horizontal escalation" *by* the Soviets? Finally, are there otherwise avoidable diplomatic costs associated with the strategy?

Not only do these questions deserve thought, but the Administration's attraction to the strategy seems to rest on military premises that are questionable in their own right.

Having discussed these issues, the most important question of all—that of credibility—will be addressed. But, let us begin at the beginning.

THE QUESTION OF WARTIME OPERATIONAL GOALS

Without some sense of the operational goal of a military action, it is not possible to select its targets. Neither, *a fortiori,* is it possible to derive the forces required or to assess the adequacy of those already in being. While "carrying the war to other arenas" and "hitting the Soviets at their vulnerable outposts" may sound clear enough at first blush, such phrases in fact provide little guidance to the military planner, charged with designing a force, or to the public, charged with paying for it. What, exactly, is the goal of "horizontal escalation"?

Is it *to destroy something* in order *to punish* the Soviets, perhaps holding out the prospect of further punishment unless they comply with American terms, whatever those might be? Is it *to take something hostage,* hoping thereby to bargain a return to the pre-war status quo or some other political arrangement? Obviously, not both goals can be achieved: one cannot hold hostage what one has already destroyed.

Although it is hard to imagine many Soviet assets whose military acquisition would *compensate* the West for the loss of access to Persian Gulf oil, in principle, compensatory acquisition is another possible goal, one distinct from punishment or hostage-taking for bargaining purposes.

Perhaps the most intuitively appealing goals for horizontal escalation would be to *inhibit or to induce redeployments of Soviet forces,* thereby improving Western prospects for conventional defense in the original contingency. The appeal is natural enough: attacked at point A, one counters at point B in order (i) to "fix" Soviet forces at point B, preventing their use as reinforcements at point A, or (ii) to force the

Soviets to shift forces from A to B.

In the context of European war, the former has long been among the Navy's arguments for "opening up a second theater" by offensive fleet operations against Soviet Naval bases in the Western Pacific.[15] And, it is true that in a protracted conventional war between NATO and the Warsaw Pact, Soviet ground forces arrayed opposite China might be redeployed to the West as a third (or fourth) echelon of the Soviet European offensive. "Opening up a second theater" in the Pacific would allegedly tie down those Soviet forces, improving NATO's chances for conventional defense.

In fact, however, the Soviets' freedom to redeploy to Europe—or the Persian Gulf for that matter—their divisions on the Sino-Soviet border would depend primarily on the posture of the Chinese Army, not the US Navy. Admittedly, the Soviets might reinforce their Pacific Fleet's air forces with airpower normally deployed inland opposite China. But what real role could the corresponding Soviet ground forces play in either the Pacific sea battle or in defending Soviet naval shore facilities? A role significant enough to "fix" over forty ground divisions? That seems implausible.

Rather than inhibiting Soviet redeployments by "fixing" Soviet forces, geographical escalation could, in principle, induce Soviet redeployments. The object in that case would be to draw Soviet forces out of the original contingency, improving Western chances for success there. One open question in this regard is simply: when?

The Reagan five-year defense plan will, by definition, take half a decade to realize. At the end of that period, horizontal escalation might succeed in forcing Soviet wartime reallocations, but only if, in the interim, some ceiling on Soviet military growth had been reached. Otherwise, what's to prevent the Soviets from anticipating the strategy by simply adding forces in each theater over that interim period? After all, when the Sino-Soviet split presented them with "a new theater" (i.e., their Chinese frontier), the Soviets didn't shift many forces. True to Russian form, they essentially built. And, unless there's some "limit to growth," it may be hard to force Soviet reallocations, at least between theaters in the USSR.

To be sure, there may be military constraints in the Soviet offing. But if there are, the Administration has certainly not suggested them by its review of the Soviet military buildup and its projections of continuing growth as Soviet military investment[16] comes to fruition. In short, a reallocative goal for horizontal escalation seems to entail a

[15] See, for example, The Congressional Budget Office, *Navy Budget Issues for Fiscal Year 1980*, March 1979, p. xviii and *Sea Plan 2000 Naval Force Planning Study, Unclassified Executive Summary* (undated), p. 15.
[16] Investment is stressed over spending in *FY 83 Posture Statement*, p. II4–II7.

Soviet military growth ceiling, while the Administration's Soviet projections seem to deny the existence of any such limits.[17]

TARGETS: SOVIET VALUE, U.S. DIVERSION, AND VERTICAL ESCALATION

Punishment (destructive retaliation), hostage-taking, compensatory acquisition, fixing Soviet forces, or inducing their redeployment; these may not be the only possible rationales for horizontal escalation.

But, whatever its operational goal (punishment, hostage-taking, etc.), the compellent effectiveness of the horizontal action will surely depend upon the value placed *by the Soviets* upon its target. After all, the mere fact that a Soviet outpost is vulnerable doesn't make it valuable, as Secretary of Defense Weinberger recognizes: "If it (the counteroffensive) is to offset the enemy's attack, it should be launched against territory or assets that are of an importance to him comparable to the ones he is attacking."[18]

In practice, however, it may be difficult to identify a "horizontal target" which is at once of sufficient Soviet value to compel the behavior sought, but at the same time is not of such great value as to stimulate rash and grossly disproportionate (e.g., nuclear) Soviet responses.

It is an open question whether offensive sea control (attacking Soviet Fleets in their home waters) would be the most efficient way to secure Western sea lines of communication.[19] But, even if it otherwise were, such offensive naval operations could well run the nuclear risk, and not simply because they would involve hitting the Soviet homeland. Beyond that, in conducting offensive operations against either the Soviet Northern or Pacific Fleets, it might be difficult for the U.S. Navy to avoid sinking Soviet strategic ballistic missile submarines (SSBNs). And if American operations were to degrade, even inadvertently and by conventional means, the Soviets' strategic nuclear retaliatory capabilities, the Soviets might not *interpret* those operations as "conventional sea control," but as conventional precur-

---

[17] Some might argue that this criticism isn't fair because it presents horizontal escalation as a strategy toward which the US is building for the future when, in fact, they will claim, horizontal escalation is only an interim strategy until the U.S. can build up greater conventional defenses in the Gulf. But, if horizontal escalation is an interim measure with direct conventional defense the ultimate goal, then why is the Administration spending so much on carrier battle groups for "outyear" counteroffensives and so much less on programs directly related to Gulf defense (e.g., airlift and sealift) today?

[18] *FY 83 Posture Statement*, p. I-16.

[19] See *Navy Budget Issues* and Congressional Budget Office, *The U.S. Sea Control Mission: Forces, Capabilities, and Requirements*, June 1977. Still among the most concise essays on the factors involved in evaluating offense, defense, and requirements in each case is Arnold M. Kuzmack, *Where Does the Navy Go From Here?* (Washington, D.C.: The Brookings Institution, 1972).

sors to nuclear attack—conventionally executed nuclear damage-limiting first strikes, if you will.[20]

As for targets of too little value, were the Soviets to end up with control of oil fields in the Persian Gulf, they could certainly afford to buy a new merchant fleet,[21] had theirs been "swept from the seas" in bristling riposte to Gulf aggression. And regarding counteroffensives against Cuba, suppose, just for the sake of argument, that the Soviets were offered a straight trade: They "give up" Cuba and, in return, they get Iran's (or Saudi Arabia's) oil. Would Moscow turn it down? What assurance is there that, behind the compulsory fulminations, the Kremlin wouldn't be willing to let Cuba take a "horizontal beating" if it meant control of Gulf oil? And, if the Soviets would accept that trade, how "offsetting" would horizontal escalation against Cuba, in fact, be?

Not only may Administration strategists have exaggerated Cuba's value to Moscow, but horizontal escalation against Cuba was reportedly envisioned "if Moscow *or its surrogates* move into the Persia Gulf"[22] (emphasis mine). Are the Iraqis Soviet "surrogates?" Does that mean they have no goals of their own? Would the threat of American retaliation against Cuba (or anyone else for that matter) deter them? Would it deter Communist elements in Iran? The Syrians? The PDRY (South Yemen)?

Even if Moscow wished to bridle any of its surrogates lest we respond against "Cuba, Libya, Vietnam, or the Soviet Union itself," could they do it?

The main point, however, is that even with clear goals for horizontal escalation in mind, the selection of an appropriate target seems to require knowledge of the *Kremlin's* valuations. An uncertain affair even in peacetime, the problem would be compounded in war when, among other things, values change.[23] In addition to the problem of Soviet valuation, there is the problem of U.S. diversion.

Although contingency-counting has been rejected under the Administration's intellectual reforms, horizontal escalation nonetheless ensures that the U.S. confronts two contingencies (main plus horizontal) where it might have faced only one (main). And, even assuming that a horizontal target of the "proper" *Soviet* value were selected, the appropriate action against that target could require a significant

---

[20] By far the most comprehensive study of this important problem is Barry R. Posen, "Inadvertent Nuclear War? Escalation and NATO's Northern Flank," *International Security,* Fall 1982, Vol. VII, No. 2.

[21] Robert W. Komer, "Maritime Strategy vs. Coalition Defense," p. 1131.

[22] George C. Wilson, "U.S. May Hit Soviet Outposts," p. 1.

[23] This, and many other problems of conflict termination, are discussed in Fred Charles Ikle, *Every War Must End* (New York: Columbia University Press, 1971).

commitment of American forces, over and above those allocated to direct defense in the initial contingency.

The obvious question, therefore, is whether the U.S. would have to divert to horizontal offensives, forces that might otherwise have been applied (initially or as reinforcements) to the main defense, reducing the latter's prospects for success. If so, would not the strategy make it more likely that the U.S. find itself under pressure either (a) to concede defeat in the main contingency or (b) to use nuclear weapons there?

On the horizontal front, it should be noted that unless these counteroffensives are to be initiated preemptively; i.e., *before* the "provoking" Soviet attack—an option Mr. Weinberger has explicitly rejected[24]—then they will probably not achieve tactical surprise. Obviously, they might, but it would be imprudent to design forces on that assumption. And, on the prudent assumption that surprise would not be achieved, the horizontal target might enjoy a number of classical warning advantages (e.g., prepared defenses, cover, dispersal, etc.). These could well exacerbate the diversion problem and with it, the unpleasant problems of choice between humiliation and vertical (i.e., nuclear) escalation.[25]

Doubtless such considerations played a role in the Services' costing of the strategy: to avoid problems of diversion, one buys *much larger forces.*[26] But now that the Administration has essentially admitted that the forces necessary to hedge against the diversion problem are too expensive, retention of the strategy may be too risky.

Some, of course, argue just the reverse, that "because the development and acquisition of new weapons might be delayed, *more* emphasis would be placed on such flexible tactics as 'geographical escalation.' "[27] (Emphasis mine).

Admittedly, geographical escalation conjures up attractive images of "regaining the initiative", "turning the tables", and "making the Russians play by our rules." But this ought to suggest a further problem; namely, what if the Russians *do* decide to "play by our rules," and proceed to "counter-horizontal escalate" themselves?

[24] *FY 83 Posture Statement*, pp. 110–111.

[25] Indeed, in the worst of both worlds, the U.S. would divert so much force from the Gulf as to come under enormous pressure to use nuclear weapons there, while applying the large resultant counteroffensive force in such a way as to put the Soviets under equal pressure to use nuclear weapons on the horizontal front. Professor Huntington's proposal for a prompt conventional counteroffensive into Eastern Europe seems to invite this dangerous situation. See Samuel P. Huntington, "The Renewal of Strategy" in Samuel P. Huntington (Ed.), *The Strategic Imperative: New Policies for American Security* (Cambridge: Ballinger 1982).

[26] This is just the "flip side" of the Soviet solution discussed above. To avoid dangerous diversions (in the Soviet case, forced; in the U.S. case, self-imposed), build.

[27] Richard Halloran, "Reagan Aides see Pressure to Cut 1984 Military Budget," *The New York Times*, July 13, 1982, p. 1.

THE PROBLEM OF COUNTER-HORIZONTAL ESCALATION

Although the possibility was recognized by some Westerners at the time,[28] Khrushchev did not play "the Berlin card" in the Cuban missile crisis of 1962. Faced with an American "war-widening" move against Cuba, his successors might behave rather differently. One might imagine the following scenario: the Soviets invade Iran; we "hit" Cuba (or the Soviet brigade there); they "hit" West Berlin (or our brigade there). Then what? You got him to "play by your rules"; are you better off?

Is Cuba more valuable to the Soviets than West Berlin is to the Federal Republic? Would European leaderships dutifully "fall in" behind further American "initiatives" at that point?

Even assuming that the Soviets could attack the Berlin brigade "surgically," without killing West German citizens (the legal status of all West Berliners), would the U.S. allow it to be decimated without further response? If West Berlin had been sealed off, then at some point the brigade's survival might require airlift. Would the Soviets allow another Berlin airlift, or would they shoot down Western transports this time? Perhaps the airlift would "fight its way in," suppressing East German air defenses at a time of great tension and high military alert.

Whether or not one finds this particular scenario to be plausible, the point is that forcing the Soviets to "play by these rules" may not be in our interest; move and counter-move might quickly bring both sides to unforeseen and very unstable situations. And reversing the spiral might be exceedingly difficult.

DIPLOMACY FOR MILITARY PREMISES

Not only crisis management, but peacetime diplomacy as well may be compromised by a policy of "horizontal escalation."

The Soviets, Secretary Weinberger states, "can coerce by threatening—implicitly or explicitly—to apply military force".[29] But, mightn't a strategy of horizontal escalation, *predicated on the assumption that direct defense is infeasible,* facilitate that coercion?

In the Persian Gulf, one can only render Soviet threats the *more* credible, their local audiences the *more* compliant, by suggesting that direct conventional defense is unmanageable, "given the Soviets' inherent geographical advantages in the Persian Gulf region and their superior number of available ground forces."[30]

This, moreover, is a simplistic and misleading characterization of the Soviet-American conventional balance in the region. Geographical

---

[28] Herman Kahn, *On Escalation: Metaphors and Scenarios* (New York: Praeger, 1965), pp. 86–87.

[29] *FY 83 Posture Statement*, p. I–10.

[30] George C. Wilson, "U.S. May Hit Soviet Outposts," p. 1.

proximity does not *per se* constitute Soviet military access, and static pre-war "bean-counting" cannot reflect dynamic wartime effectiveness. The latter always depends on operational factors such as terrain, available avenues of advance (and their vulnerability), logistics, coordination, reconnaissance, flexibility, leadership, morale, combat technology, and troop skill. That fact is consistently bemoaned on the U.S. side, but is virtually neglected when assessing the Soviet threat. When such factors are accounted on *both* sides, in a balanced and systematic way, the prevalent assessment is seen to be overly pessimistic.[31]

Furthermore, while there are compelling reasons for the U.S. to avoid reliance on nuclear employment, the Soviets surely cannot ignore that possibility. And this, too, contributes to deterrence.

But does the attraction to "horizontal escalation" derive only from the unwarranted assumptions (a) that conventional defense is utterly infeasible and (b) that Soviet nuclear developments have stripped the U.S. strategic triad of deterrent value? Perhaps. But it often seems as though the true motivations run deeper—as though the advocates, at bottom, have turned away from the entire concept of limited war.[32]

WINNING

MacArthur said that "in war, there is no substitute for victory." Neither, of course, is there any substitute for national survival. While at various points, the Reagan Administration seems to have unqualifiedly adopted MacArthur's heroic dictum, at other points its strategists seem to be aware of the unheroic fact of nuclear life—"the difficulty that war invites the belligerents to regard the contest as mortal and to continue it until they are reduced to ruins."[33]

Over a decade ago, in an essay called "Peace Through Escalation?", Dr. Fred Ikle, now Under Secretary of Defense for Policy, put the enduring dilemma this way:

"If a nation can overwhelm all of the enemy's forces by escalating a war, the fighting will of course be brought to an end. . . . Short of inflicting such total defeat, successful escalation would have to induce the enemy

[31] Joshua M. Epstein, "Soviet Vulnerabilities in Iran and the RDF Deterrent," *International Security*, Fall 1981, Vol. VI, No. 2. See also Dennis Ross, "Considering Soviet Threats to the Persian Gulf," *International Security*, Fall 1981, Vol. VI, No. 2, and Keith A. Dunn, "Constraints on the USSR in Southwest Asia," *Orbis*, Fall 1981.

[32] In Secretary of the Navy John Lehman's view, the rapid growth of Soviet naval power has "eliminated the option of planning for a regionally limited naval war with the Soviet Union. It will be instantaneously a global naval conflict." Richard Halloran, "Reagan Selling Navy Budget as Heart of Military Mission," *The New York Times*, April 11, 1982.

[33] William W. Kaufmann, "Limited Warfare," in William W. Kaufmann (ed.) *Military Policy and National Security* (Princeton, New Jersey: Princeton University Press, 1956), p. 112.

government to accept the proffered peace terms. The trouble is, the greater the enemy's effort and cost in fighting a war, the more will he become committed to his own conditions for peace. Indeed, inflicting more damage on the enemy might cause him to stiffen his peace terms. . . . It is these opposed effects of escalation that make it so hard to plan for limited wars and to terminate them."[34]

In order, as Secretary Weinberger desires, "to prevent the uncontrolled spread of hostilities,"[35] it is obviously critical that the Soviets never see an advantage in opening new theaters or geographically widening a local war themselves. In that sense, a strategy of limited war, in fact does, and always has, required "horizontal" capabilities: 'you will not succeed at the initial point of attack and we will not be drawn off by attacks elsewhere; you must fight here and you cannot win here, so stop; indeed, don't start.'[36]

While multi-theater capabilities sufficient to *deny* the Soviets a war-widening strategy are thus essential to channel and limit conventional conflict should deterrence fail, it is far from clear that an American policy of *initiating* such expansions would foster military control or wartime diplomacy. It might, but having reviewed the risks, Dr. Ikle's observation is worth recalling:

"It is hard to say whether treason or adventurism has brought more nations to the graveyard of history. The record is muddied, because when adventurists have destroyed a nation they usually blamed "traitors" for the calamity.[37]

CREDIBILITY

If a strategy is to deter aggression, that strategy must be *credible.* We and our potential adversaries must believe at least two things about it. First, both sides must believe that, were deterrence to fail, the United States would actually operate its forces in accord with the strategy. Second, both must believe that such operations would be likely to achieve American wartime goals.

Failure on the second count often results in failure on the first. For example, Massive Retaliation, America's first great experiment in asymmetrical response, failed on the second requirement. The American goal was to contain Soviet expansion at military costs acceptable to the United States. But the strategy suggested that the U.S. would run a high risk of unacceptable damage in response to

---

[34] Fred Charles Ikle, *Op. Cit.,* pp. 41–42.
[35] *FY 83 Posture Statement,* p. III–101.
[36] For a fuller discussion, see Kaufmann, "Limited Warfare," in Kaufmann (ed.) *op. cit.*
[37] Fred Charles Ikle, *Op. Cit.,* p. 62.

even the most limited of Soviet encroachments. In the final analysis, not even the U.S. believed that we would operate our forces in such a way. And so, massive retaliation failed on the first count as well.[38]

Horizontal escalation—our most recent asymmetrical experiment—also fails to meet the basic requirements of credibility. It fails on the first count because it is not even clear what it would *mean* to operate American forces in accordance with the strategy: it is not clear what its targets would be or, more fundamentally, how one would go about determining them in wartime. Neither is it clear what military actions would be taken against the selected targets.

Horizontal escalation fails to meet the second requirement as well. It clearly runs daunting risks—of nuclear escalation or Soviet counter-horizontal—but the goals of horizontal escalation remain cloudy, in both the broader strategic sense (ultimate victory vs. limitation) and in the narrow operational sense (punishment, hostage-taking, etc.).

"The threat that leaves something to chance" may be credible. But threats that leave everything to chance most assuredly are not.

Now, as suggested at the outset, the Reagan Administration's early enthusiasm for the strategy seems to have cooled somewhat; it is certainly less vocal than it was. Logically, however, there are only two possibilities. Either horizontal escalation is the Administration's strategy or it isn't.

If it is, then the strategy is not credible. And if horizontal escalation is not the Administration's strategy, then *what is* the strategy? Given the economic costs allegedly required to support it, the American people surely deserve an answer.

---

[38] The seminal critique is Kaufmann's "The Requirements of Deterrence" in Kaufmann (ed), *Op. Cit.*

A Strategy for the Rapid Deployment Force

KENNETH N. WALTZ

Although it is widely believed that the United States needs a Rapid Deployment Force, no one has defined the purposes that an RDF can be expected to serve. Much has been written about the design of the Force: the speed with which it should be able to move, and the troops and equipment it should be able to deploy. Little has been written about the problem of devising a strategy for its use. Design will dictate strategy unless a promising strategy is first devised. If design dictates strategy, Americans may find themselves with a Rapid Deployment Force both over-built and ill-suited to its tasks. As a new Administration takes over the task of developing an RDF, it should ask itself two questions. What ends does the United States want an RDF to serve? What is the best strategy for its use?

WHAT ENDS SHOULD AN RDF SERVE?

The lesson of America's Vietnam venture is neither that we should intervene militarily abroad nor that we should not. Instead, it is that we should do so only when three conditions obtain: Vital interests are at risk; non-military measures cannot adequately serve them; the use of force can reasonably be expected to accomplish our purposes.

The ability to act militarily carries with it the temptation to take military action. The common quality of military advice is conservatism. Military weakness leads soldiers to advise politicians to be cautious, to avoid war, or to seek its postponement until strength can be gathered. Military strength leads soldiers either to counsel preventive war while the moment of military superiority lasts or to strike quickly to nip trouble in the bud. A sizeable RDF would provide the latter temptation. Former Secretary of Defense Harold Brown referred to the Force as one of the four pillars of our military power, along with the strategic deterrent, the forces contributed to NATO, and the Navy. Picking up the cue, General Edward C. Meyer, Army Chief of Staff, emphasized the importance of getting the right mix of forces for the RDF because, as he said, we are "not

From *International Security*, Spring 1981, pp. 49–73. Reprinted by permission of the MIT Press Journals.

just thinking of the Middle East or the Persian Gulf. Contingencies might arise in other areas, too." Developing the theme, General Maxwell Taylor, a former Chairman of the Joint Chiefs of Staff, looked toward a Force designed to deal in the next decade with threats "arising from continued Soviet malevolence supported by growing military power, the dependence of the United States and allies on Mideast oil and the turbulence of the developing world, where most of the overseas sources of imported raw materials are found." But since World War II, the malevolent activities of the Soviet Union, Eastern Europe aside, have produced gains that for the most part have been illusory and evanescent and are exceeded by the "loss" of such countries as Yugoslavia, China, and Egypt, countries in which the influence of the Soviet Union once seemed to be well established. Some political groups may want the Soviet Union's support while struggling to gain control of their governments. Once in power, they want to be as independent of the Soviet Union as they can manage to be and to reach this end will turn to the United States and other non-communist states. No state wants to be controlled by another. Angola is a recent illustration of this truth, and Algeria was an earlier one. We should avoid defining the Soviet Union's political-military activity in various parts of the world as automatically threatening American vital interests. Demonstrably, that has seldom been the case.

We should also view General Taylor's third threat with skepticism. He believes that turbulence in developing countries imperils us because most of our imported raw materials are found there. This is a simple error, and one easily fallen into. Oil aside, the industrial democracies produce about 45 percent of the world's raw materials; the less developed countries and the communist countries about equally account for the rest. In 1977, for example, two-thirds of our imports of roughly 25 critical materials came from Canada, Australia, South Africa, and other more developed countries, and over one-half from Canada alone. In classifying the third threat as being among the most dangerous we shall face, General Taylor exaggerates American dependence on less developed countries.

Moreover, the United States is markedly less dependent on imports, whatever their source, than most of the industrial noncommunist countries are. Exports plus imports in the year 1975, for example, ranged from 32 percent to 41 percent of GNP for France, Germany, Italy, and the United Kingdom. For the United States the comparable figure was 14 percent. These data do not show that we suffer from no dependencies other than oil. They do show that our dependencies are relatively easy to manage. States are the more independent if they have reliable access to important resources, if they have feasible alternatives, if they have the ability to do without, and if they have leverage to use against others. The extent of American dependency varies both with how much we need them and with how much they in turn need us. We are far and away the world's largest supplier of foodstuffs, of the technologically most advanced manufactures, and of capital. Those who have what others want or badly need are in favored positions.

Because the United States is so well endowed, and because in various economic and technological ways, we can protect ourselves from the disruption of supplies coming in from outside, we ordinarily need not think of using force to protect economic interests. We should guard against adopting expansive definitions of our vital interests, as great powers often do, and of then assuming that military force should be used to secure them. Most American interests are better served by means other than military force. By defining vital interests narrowly and by using force sparingly, we can avoid the unnecessary commitment of force that would risk our having force unavailable in those rare cases where it might be well to use it.

It is a vital interest of the United States, as of other countries, to have reliable supplies of all sorts of materials, from bauxite and chromium to nickel and oil. For most—indeed for all but one—of many important materials, the United States is able to take care of itself *without* using military force. Oil is the exception. For the foreseeable future, no technical means now known can reduce our dependence on oil to manageable proportions if the worst should happen. The "if" clause should be emphasized because even in the case of oil, the United States operates on fairly wide margins. We are not as dependent on imported oil as are countries closely associated with us. Table 1 makes this clear.

We import proportionately less oil than most other non-communist industrial countries do and get relatively little from the Middle East. Much of the production of oil for export is concentrated there, as Table 1 shows. In August of 1979, Persian Gulf countries produced 35 percent of the world's, and 45 percent of the non-communist world's, oil. Most of the oil produced elsewhere is consumed by the countries that produce it. Exported oil comes from Gulf states and from seven others. Production of the latter is about half that of the former and, Mexico aside, significant increases in production for export are likely to come only from the Middle East.

Countries are the more imperiled economically the greater their dependence on imported oil and the more their dependence concentrates on countries of the Persian Gulf. The United States is thus doubly fortunate. Our dependence is relatively low, and our suppliers are more dispersed geographically than those of our industrial competitors. Gulf countries can expect to experience political instability, and instability may spread from one country to another. Moreover, their proximity to the Soviet Union makes them susceptible to the military pressure and presence of the Soviet Union. In contrast, other oil exporting countries—flung across the map from Indonesia to Libya and Algeria, from Nigeria to Venezuela and Mexico—are not similarly vulnerable to the spread of internal unrest from one country to another or to military pressure from outside.

Oil is the only economic interest for which the United States may have to fight, yet interruption of oil exports from one or more OPEC countries would hurt the United States less and later than it would hurt most others. Former Secretary of Defense Harold Brown emphasized the point. "If the industrial democracies are deprived of access to those resources," he said in February of 1980, "there would almost certainly be a worldwide economic collapse of the kind that hasn't been seen for almost 50 years, probably worse." The shutting off of oil would create havoc among America's allies, who can do nothing "in the coming decades that would save them from irreversible catastrophe if it were cut off." Because the United States is less dependent on oil, he added sarcastically, "we would just face economic disruption, international chaos, and looming Soviet power." A major and prolonged reduction of oil exports would be damaging to us, would be even more damaging to some others, and would push the world toward economic ruin. To say that we should be prepared to act to prevent such damage is a statement that conforms to a modest definition of our vital interests.

Leaving aside the role others may play, the United States should be prepared to meet threats of three sorts: embargoes, disruption of oil production and export resulting from regional turmoil, and military attacks on, or subversion of, OPEC countries that would seriously interfere with the production and export of oil.

If we look at the RDF as part of a larger national security policy,

Table 1.

1978	United States	European Community	Japan
Oil as percent of total energy consumed	47%	55%	71%
Percent of oil imported	44	87	100
Percent of oil imported from Persian Gulf	30	57	73
Persian Gulf oil as percent of total energy consumed	7	28	51

Source: John M. Collins and Clyde R. Mark, "Petroleum Imports from the Persian Gulf: Use of U.S. Armed Force to Ensure Supplies," Issue Brief Number IB79046 (Washington, D.C.: Library of Congress, Congressional Reference Service, May 5, 1980), p. 2.

as surely we should, then our first concern must be to position ourselves so that we shall seldom have to use force suddenly. The passage of time reduces the chances of committing force needlessly. With the passage of time two questions can usually be answered. Is the threat severe enough to require the use of force? Will internal and external political developments moderate or contain the threat before we need to use force?

How can the United States afford itself the luxury of time? The answer is simple: by building a large stockpile of oil, as we are now too slowly doing. A billion-barrel stockpile would carry us for four to six months, depending on rates of consumption and on how strictly we rationed ourselves, without any imports at all. In the summer of 1980, the United States had 92 million barrels in the stockpile, barely equal to two weeks' imports, and had not added to its reserve since early 1979. To put high priority on building an RDF while having dallied for years in building an oil reserve is odd policy. If I had to choose between a billion-barrel stockpile and an RDF, I would choose the former. A large American stockpile would help to meet each of the three sorts of threats for which we need to prepare. In fact, it would enable us to foil the first one: namely, embargoes. Embargoes are hard to sustain, as the first oil embargo showed. OPEC countries are politically, culturally, and economically diverse. Diverse countries have trouble uniting to maintain costly policies. The economic and political interests of some of the states mounting an embargo will surely conflict. Thus, during the short term of the first embargo, Libya began to sell oil apparently because it thought OPEC countries too soft on Israel, and Iraq began to sell oil apparently because it wanted the money. Most OPEC countries, their oil riches aside, are weak economically as well as militarily and politically. All the more so because many of their interests diverge, one can safely bet on their inability to sustain punitive policies against the great and major powers of the world. A four- to six-month stockpile would provide a comfortable margin of safety. A large American stockpile would also tell our allies that we may not respond quickly to threats that endanger oil supplies and would thus give them strong incentive to build their own stockpiles. Once oil suppliers see that only long-sustained embargoes can be effective, they have little reason to mount them.

A large oil stockpile, although highly useful in dealing with the second sort of threat, would by no means eliminate it. The second threat is that oil exports be severely reduced for a prolonged period because of revolution or chaos in one or more of the major oil exporters or because of war among them. The one country that could cause international economic disaster by its inability to export is Saudi Arabia, producing 9.5 million barrels daily (MMBD) out of a world total of 63.1 MMBD in August of 1979. The one region that could bring this result is the Persian Gulf area, producing about 21 MMBD. The big producers there, in addition to Saudi Arabia, were Iraq (3.3 MMBD), Iran (3.0–3.6), Kuwait (2.2), and the United Arab Emirates (1.8). The comparable figures for big producers outside of the Gulf area were Venezuela (2.3), Nigeria (2.2), Libya (2.0), Indonesia (1.6), Mexico (1.4), and Algeria (0.9).

The threat of severe reduction of oil supplies concentrates in the Persian Gulf. This is unfortunate. The dispersion of numerous sources would lessen the likelihood that enough of them would dry up at any one time to cause serious problems. The concentration of sources does, however, mean that we can focus on the problem of increasing the security of our access to them in just one region. The expectation that one or another of the Gulf countries will experience political unrest and turmoil, whether or not in the style of Iran, is widely shared. Most observers believe the danger of major stoppages of oil exports lies within and among these states, rather than arising externally from the Soviet Union.

Radical regimes, whether of the left or of the right, want to continue to sell oil. We know this was true of Libya and Iraq. It has also been true of Khomeini's Iran, which lowered the price of its oil in July of 1980 to stimulate lagging sales. Although radical countries want to sell oil, they may not be very good at producing it. Should the exports of a country be internally disrupted, a large stockpile of oil would again prove its worth. It would give the luxury of time—the ability to wait to see whether the country in question can regain control of its affairs, the ability to wait to see whether a revolutionary movement in one country infects others. Abiding solutions to most of a country's political problems have to be found by its citizens; foreigners can seldom be of much help. Moreover, most problems find fairly good solutions without the use of force. If this were not so, the world would always be at war.

We should be slow to intervene militarily when countries are wracked by internal pain. We should also be slow to intervene militarily in others' wars. Intervention risks making a bad situation worse. Moreover, a certain amount of fighting may be prerequisite to a stable outcome, leaving both sides discontented yet satisfied that more fighting would be useless. Are we then to be at the mercy of crises that we cannot control, even of crises threatening to engulf a number of countries and to result in a prolonged denial of oil? We shall have to answer "yes" unless we can devise a strategy for using an RDF that promises a reasonable possibility that we can keep oil flowing. That is the problem to be solved in the next section of this essay.

Meanwhile, we have to consider the third sort of threat, the use of military force or pressure by a state outside of the Gulf area to appropriate oil or divert its shipment. The Soviet Union, so it is feared, might back one faction in a civil war and ride into control of somebody's government. Or needing oil for itself and Eastern Europe in some not-so-distant future, the Soviet Union might move over the mountains into Azerbaijan and bring pressure on Iran to ship its oil northward. Or the Soviet Union might drop airborne troops directly into someone's oil fields in order to control them.

Having gained control, the Soviet Union would presumably want to sell oil to the United States and to others outside of its bloc and might be a more reliable supplier than some of the OPEC countries have been. It would have good economic reason to be so; in recent years, more than one-third of its hard-currency earnings have come from the sale of oil and natural gas. We would nevertheless not want to become dependent, and see others become dependent, on the Soviet Union for major amounts of oil. More important than speculating on how the Soviet Union would behave after securing control of some oil fields, or after gaining influence over the disposal of their products, is weighing the chances that she would try to do so, whether by subversion or by force. In politically unstable regions, subversion of governments is a constant possibility. Nevertheless, the Soviet Union has not enjoyed much of a yield from the politically fertile soil around the Persian Gulf. The United States, on the other hand, has been able to maintain commercially satisfactory relations with unfriendly Moslem states even while strongly supporting Israel. (From 1977 to 1980, Algeria and Libya were our third, fourth, or fifth largest suppliers of imported oil.) The past, however, does not guarantee the future; and I shall ask in the second part of this paper whether a strategy for dealing with military intervention can also deal with the subversion of governments.

Compared to subversion, military intervention by the Soviet Union in Persian Gulf states is a remote possibility, partly because of difficulties the Soviet Union would face. But then we have to prepare militarily to meet remote dangers if their realization would be deeply damaging. We should prepare to deal with internal disruption and with external subversion and military invasion if they would bring major stoppages of oil supplies and thereby produce catastrophe on a world scale.

WHAT IS THE BEST STRATEGY FOR AN RDF?

An RDF should serve vital interests only and in serving them should be guardedly used. Force is a blunt instrument, costly to apply and difficult to control. The United States has many political and economic means for the furtherance of its interests, and they should be marshalled and used before force is brought into play.

Even in situations where non-military means do not suffice, we should act militarily only if a strategy promising success can be devised. We should avoid the temptation of resorting to force because nothing else will avail. We should use force only if we can see a way of doing so that will enable us to get our way.

Since the Mexican War, we have fought all of our international wars overseas. In the months following the Soviet Union's invasion of Afghanistan in December of 1979, World War III was talked about as though it would be fought by relatively small forces, mainly American and Russian, in the far-away Middle East. The problem is not to develop a strategy that will enable us to fight such a war. Instead, the problem is to develop a strategy that will help us to avoid having to do so. If military action in the Middle East nevertheless becomes necessary, our policy should seek to confine and limit it, while managing to keep enough oil flowing to meet the minimal needs of importing countries.

How can this be accomplished? Uncertainty about what kind of force we need arises from confusion about its tasks. Confusion about what we may need to do, and feelings of discomfort about our ability to do it, are evident in official and unofficial statements.

—For example, in his State of the Union Address on January 23, 1980, President Carter made a commitment to defend the Persian Gulf region. He later mentioned that we would need the help of allies, apparently without having consulted them. American officials believed that we would have to do most of the fighting, with some of them hoping that Australian, British, and French troops would join in if the going got rough. Grounds for the hope were not given.

—For example, officials of the Department of Defense talked loosely about using tactical nuclear weapons if we should be losing a conventional fight with the Soviet Union in the Gulf area, but just how that would be done and with what expected response was not made clear.

—For example, officials of the Department of Defense signalled that if the Soviet Union confronts us in the Middle East, we may spread the war to areas where we can fight better. The Republican Party's 1980 Platform spells this out. It calls for the limited and permanent presence of American troops in the Gulf area with provision for their rapid reinforcement. The strategy envisions "military action elsewhere at points of Soviet vulnerability—an expression of the classic doctrine of global maneuver." But we are not living in the classical military age. We are living in the nuclear age, and too many soldiers and politicians are still thinking conventional thoughts. Our appropriate aim is not to escalate force indiscriminately and spread wars widely but to de-escalate force and narrow the compass of military conflicts.

—For example, solutions are propounded that will work only if the Soviet Union forebears, at least for a time. The Department of Defense plans to have fourteen Maritime Prepositioning Ships, loaded with equipment for three Marine brigades, deployed in the Indian Ocean and wherever American troops may be needed. The first two ships were funded in FY 1981 and the last one will not be available for at least five years. Noticing this, Jeffrey Record proposed turning the Marines into a light armored, heavy fire-power force that could be moved to a theater quickly. The suggestion seems sensible, but such a force also lies some distance in the future.

Vague references to help from allies, loose talk about using tactical nuclear weapons, odd ideas about spreading wars from one part of the world to another, indulgence in solutions that can work only if the Soviet Union waits until we effect them: Such hesitations and false starts are the inevitable result of hazy notions about what an RDF can and should do.

An RDF should not aim to defeat the Soviet Union in the Middle East, or to fight the Soviet Union to a standstill unless doing so is necessary in order to keep oil flowing. Two quite different forces might accomplish the latter purpose.

One kind of force is a war-fighting, defensive force. Once equipped and ready to go, would a force small and light enough to be able to make a timely appearance on the battlefield be able to stand up to forces of the Soviet Union, say, in Iran? That appears to be the most difficult case and thus the most useful one to examine. I am slow to conclude that we cannot prepare a war-fighting force that would dissuade the Soviet Union from moving into Iran and that could put up a lively fight if dissuasion should fail. The balance of advantages and disadvantages is not as severely tilted in the Soviet Union's favor as is commonly thought.

Major advantages of the Soviet Union are the following:

DISTANCE. The Persian Gulf is about 7,100 miles from the United States and about 1,100 from the Soviet Union.

TROOPS AVAILABLE. The United States has designated 97,700 army and marine corps troops for the RDF, including support units for one airborne division and aviation and logistic support for three marine brigades. The Soviet Union has nine divisions of 80 to 90,000 men on Iran's northern border and a total of 23 mechanized divisions of about 200,000 troops in the Caucasas, Transcaucasas, and Turkmenistan military districts, with attendant air power. The United States has one airborne division and one air assault division of 33,200 troops. The Soviet Union has seven airborne divisions of 49,000 troops.

TIME. The Wolfowitz Report estimates that the United States

could place 20,000 troops in Iran in 30 days and that the Soviet Union in the same period could get 100,000 or more there.

The United States, however, would enjoy some important advantages, and the Soviet Union would suffer some serious disadvantages, if they met militarily in Iran. The United States used the "Persian Gulf corridor" during World War II to ship supplies to the Soviet Union. The Soviet Union can reverse the directions of movement and use the same corridor to bring troops and supplies to the south of Iran. Still, the route is a difficult one. Air cover would be hard to maintain. Roads and railroads are poor with narrow passes and bridges and in all more than 300 choke points. Supply stations and maintenance shops barely exist, and water is scarce. Although the Soviet Union has seven airborne divisions, it has the capability to lift only one of them over the 1,100 miles to the Persian Gulf. The Gulf is beyond the reach of most of the Soviet Union's fighter/attack aircraft, if those aircraft are based within the borders of the Soviet Union. Air dropped troops could not be supported by sea, could not be adequately supported by air, and could not be quickly supported by land. Even in the absence of national resistance, Russian troops and supplies would not enjoy easy passage through the Persian Gulf corridor. Nor would the Soviet Union gain advantage from its military occupation of Afghanistan. The Persian Gulf is 700 miles by straight line from Afghanistan. The Soviet Union would have to go through an even longer stretch of hostile territory if it came through Afghanistan than if it came through Iran's northern mountains.

The appropriate RDF for defensive use would be a highly mobile, light-armored, heavy fire-power force. It would be designed to take advantage of the Zagros Mountain barrier, which is 125 miles wide at Iran's northern border. It would also be designed for desert maneuvers that would further delay and deplete Russian forces on their way to the oil fields. Such a force might dissuade the Soviet Union from attacking and put up a good fight if dissuasion should fail.

The United States can build a defensive RDF, but it would not be a force that would best serve its interests in the long run or serve them at all in the short run. Speedy transport of the sizeable forces needed to fight the Soviet Union in the Middle East will be beyond our means until the middle 1980s. And we shall not have light and mobile forces of reasonable size able to use mountains and deserts to defensive advantage for some years to come. Even if the United States had them, climbing mountains and chugging through deserts are not what we want to do. Our interests do not concentrate in those areas, but on the shores washed by the Persian Gulf. We do not want control of countries, but only, if necessary, of the Gulf littoral. The oil is there, and it is there that our superior sea power gives us an advantage over the Soviet Union. We can gain further advantage if a force designed to meet external threats to the oilfields can also deal with internal disruptions.

We should first ask what course of action we will want to take, should disruptions in the Gulf area threaten oil supplies, a much likelier event than invasion by the Soviet Union. Secretary of Defense Brown sometimes spoke as if the problem to be solved were a relatively simple one. Feeling threatened from outside, a country invites us to add some of our force to its own. We do not intend, he said, "to threaten the sovereignty of any country or to intervene where we are not wanted. Rather, mobile, well-equipped, and trained conventional forces are essential to assist allies and other friends should conditions so dictate, and should our assistance be needed." Memories of World War I and II linger. The United States joins hands with an ally, uses its ports and airfields, and together they form a united front against a common enemy—a situation sometimes described as "supportive intervention within a permissive environment." But if our vital interests lie in the Middle East, we have to be prepared to solve the difficult problems there. To be prepared to deal with just the easy ones may not be enough.

RDF: A RESPONSE TO INTERNAL DISORDER?

The more difficult problem an RDF may face is that of establishing political order in someone else's country by using American troops. Military forces are not good at solving that problem. They are not instruments of government, something the United States recognized in World War II by preparing military government units to take over from soldiers in the governing of Germany and Japan once the war had been won. In a future oil crisis, the United States may face similar problems. Rather than being invited by a friendly government to give military help, it may be difficult to *find* a government or to know which of several factions promises to become one.

How can we use force with profit where the problem is posed not by someone's army but by someone's government? The answer is to occupy not a country but its oilfields. This changes the problem from one of governance, which we cannot reasonably expect to solve, to one of territorial control. The solution is not perfect, but it is probably the best we can do. The solution is imperfect for two reasons: because military forces from outside cannot prevent saboteurs from disrupting oil production before the troops arrive, and because the prospect of a strong country moving into a weak country's territory is distasteful. Even if military intervention succeeds in ensuring oil supplies in the short term, in undertaking such a course of action, the United States might incur such wrath from so many people that long-term losses would be greater than short-term gains. To avoid this is the task of diplomats, a more important one than the soldiers' because it is a prerequisite to useful military accomplishment. Politically, we should reduce hostility by proclaiming our limited aims, by securing the acquiescence of neighboring countries, and by gaining the open approval of oil-importing countries. After all, to avoid damage to oil fields and facilities is not in the American interest alone. It is in the interest of much of the world. We should also seek to convince countries experiencing disorder that our efforts to keep oil flowing and to keep fields and facilities undamaged are in its own interest and in the interest of whichever of the struggling factions may eventually gain political power.

If the threat to oil exports originates internally, our response should be slow and measured: slow because we want to give a country time to work out its political problems, measured because we want to keep hostility aimed at America as low as possible. Our response should be slow and measured above all because we want everyone to see that we waited as long as we could without risking the collapse of the world's economy. In the end, we shall have to say that for countries to deny their oil to starving economies is no more conscionable than it would be for us to deny food to starving people.

How would American troops operate in their presumably hostile environment? The RDF has to be prepared to force its way into the oil fields, to police them, and to secure the perimeter that encloses them. The perimeter to be defended may be a long one. Saudi Arabia's five principal oil fields cover about 10,000 square miles, or twice the area of Connecticut. The most serious threat, however, may not come from anyone's army or air force but from small bands of saboteurs. The Wolfowitz Report estimates that 65 percent of exported Gulf oil is shipped through three facilities, with eight "critical" pump sites. Ras Tanura and Juaymah are in Saudi Arabia, and Kharg Island lies off Iran. If plans are made, if replacement parts are stocked, and if technicians are available, repairs could in some cases be made "in a matter of weeks." Otherwise "repairs might take months or years." When the Report was written, the United States had no such plans. A properly equipped reserve corps of technicians is as essential to an RDF as are properly equipped troops.

RDF: A RESPONSE TO EXTERNAL THREATS

A second problem that an RDF would face is that of getting enough force into some part of the Middle East fast enough to stay the hand of the Soviet Union. How can the United States hope that a force able to defend a perimeter against the disorganized forces of a country in chaos or against the forces of some other Middle East country will be able to stand up to a determined attack by the Soviet Union? The answer is by linking a minimal defense to America's strategic deterrent. What we should strive for is an asset-seizing, deterrent force that can handle both internal and external threats. An asset-seizing, deterrent force is an alternative to a war-fighting, defensive force. The RDF should be designed to defend against countries of the Middle East and to deter the Soviet Union.

The deterrent solution has been alluded to by various officials. Secretary Brown, for example, thought that the United States could "deter the Soviets" if we kept our heads and supported "the tack the President has taken." Such statements raise more questions than they answer, beginning with the question of what is meant by deterrence. Much recent writing about deterrence lacks precision and clarity. Thus Brown defined the essence of "our countervailing strategy" as denying "an enemy any plausible goal, no matter how he might attempt to reach it." For deterrence to work, he continued, "our potential adversaries must be convinced that we possess sufficient military force so that if they were to start a course of action which could lead to war, they would be frustrated in their effort to achieve their objective or suffer so much damage that they would gain nothing by their action." Brown's usage compounds defense and deterrence. Defense aims to dissuade someone from doing something by placing obstacles in his way, by preparing to resist him. Defensive strategies tell a potential opponent that to overcome the resistance he will encounter will be forbiddingly difficult. Deterrence aims to dissuade someone from doing something by frightening him. Deterrent strategies tell a potential opponent that although he can seize his objective he may well have to pay a disproportionate price for it through the damage he can expect to suffer. Military strategies combine defense and deterrence in various proportions and ways (ref. introduction).

"Defense" is often confused with "deterrence." When the Wolfowitz Report refers to deterrence, defense is apparently meant. "In principle," the Report says, "a deterrent based on mountain defense should be feasible—especially if the objective is to guarantee delays and casualties for the attacker." Because defense is emphasized over deterrence, help from allies and the use of tactical nuclear weapons are contemplated, along with a mountain defense. Other defense officials have said that if American ground forces, even in small numbers, can get in position before Russian troops arrive, the Soviet Union would have to decide whether to risk confrontation with our troops. Such statements pull toward a strategy of using

conventional force as a tripwire and of signalling to the Soviet Union
that snapping the wire may activate some of our strategic missiles.
These two examples illustrate the sharp practical difference between
strategies that rely heavily on defense and strategies that rely
heavily on deterrence, as well as the lack of consensus among
political leaders and force planners on a strategy for the Rapid
Deployment Force.

Either way, dissuasion of the Soviet Union is what is wanted.
Can it be achieved in the Persian Gulf area more by deterrence than
by defense? How can we hope that deterrence will prevail in a
distant area populated by weak and unstable states when so many
have come to doubt whether deterrence covers even our European
allies? How can we hope that our deterrent will cover more areas
and more of our interests in an era of strategic parity than it was
thought to cover in an era of American superiority? Superiority in
strategic weapons is comforting; parity makes people feel uneasy;
and inferiority would be unsettling. Such reactions are psychologically understandable even though they have nothing to do with the
logic of deterrence and do not affect the military conditions under
which deterrence prevails: namely, the possession of second-strike
forces that can do severe damage. The credibility of deterrent
threats is insensitive to variations in the size of strategic forces
across wide ranges. Why this is true was understood better in the
earlier years of the nuclear age than it is now. The logic of deterrence was more clearly lodged in the minds of those who helped
develop the strategy than it is in the minds of those who now
casually recall it. Unless one country by striking first can reduce
another's strategic forces to the point where retaliation can be
tolerated, the relative size of opposing forces is irrelevant.

Some Americans are concerned about the vulnerability of our
strategic system because its land-based component can be struck
and perhaps largely destroyed by the Soviet Union in the middle
1980s. If the Soviet Union did that, the United States would still
have thousands of warheads at sea and thousands of bombs in the
air. The Soviet Union could not be sure that we would fail to launch
on warning or fail to retaliate. Uncertainty deters, and there would
be plenty of uncertainty about our response in the minds of the
Soviet Union's leaders. If no state can launch a disarming attack
with high confidence, force comparisons are irrelevant. That we
have 9,200 strategic warheads to the Soviet Union's 6,000 makes us
no worse and no better off than we were when the ratio was even
more in our favor. That the throw-weight of the Soviet Union's
missiles exceeds those of the United States by several times makes

the Soviet Union no better and no worse off than it would be were the ratio reversed.

A second-strike force is a necessary, but not a sufficient, condition for deterrence. Given only the military condition, no one can say whether deterrent threats are credible. Whether or not they are depends on what the threats are intended to cover. With second-strike forces, not military but political conditions determine the credibility of deterrence. Credibility does not depend on the ability to retaliate, which cannot be denied. Credibility depends on the will to do so. Deterrence gains in credibility the more highly valued the interests covered appear to be. Major and prolonged reduction of oil exports from the Persian Gulf would pose an absolute threat to the noncommunist world's economy and thus to the United States. With deterrent forces, the country that is absolutely threatened prevails.

That attacks on vital interests will provoke retaliation is not certain. But that does not matter. Uncertainty suffices because if retaliation occurs no one can be sure that limits will hold. In striking at a nuclear power's vital interests, one risks losing all not because thousands of warheads will immediately be fired but because there is some chance, however small, that force will get out of control. Who will risk losing all by attacking a nuclear power's vital interests? Lately, analysts have put too much emphasis on the retaliator's possible inhibitions and too little on the attacker's obvious risks. Credibility is not much of a problem because with vital interests at stake not much credibility is needed. Given an imbalance of interests, the attacker has to believe that the attacked *may* retaliate. That is enough to deter.

Once the military conditions for deterrence are met, the credibility of deterrence becomes a political question. What are the political conditions that must obtain if deterrent threats are to be credited? First, the would-be attacker must be made to see that the deterrer believes that the interests at stake are vital ones. Thus, by the presence of American troops, the United States stretches its deterrent to cover Western Europe. The presence of our troops makes the extent of American interest manifest. In a conflict between two countries equipped with second-strike forces, the balance of interests determines how the "balance of resolve," to use Glenn Snyder's apt phrase, is measured. Second, political stability must prevail in the area the deterrent is intended to cover. If the threat to a regime is mainly from internal factions, then an outside power may risk supporting one of them even in the face of deterrent threats. The credibility of a deterrent requires both that interests be seen to be vital and that it is the attack from outside that threatens them. Given these conditions, the would-be attacker provides both the reason to retaliate and the target for retaliation.

The first of the political conditions for credible deterrence is that the interest of the deterrer be seen to be a vital one. From the American standpoint, Persian Gulf oil meets this condition. The Soviet Union's gaining control of the Gulf area would be comparable to its seizing territory in Western Europe or Japan. American vital interests lie in these three areas, a fact that is easily seen by the Soviet Union as well as by others. If in a crisis, we were to put troops in the oil fields, it would make the depth of our interest, the extent of our determination, and the strength of our will manifest.

The deterrer needs a reason to retaliate, and the United States has reason enough. The deterrer also needs a target for retaliation. That we would strike if the Soviet Union tried to turn the Persian Gulf oil faucet off is sufficiently credible. But if saboteurs were to do it, who would we strike? The answer to that question helps to define the extent of the force required to serve as a tripwire. To rely on a tripwire force makes people uneasy. A thicker wire may make us feel more secure, but the point to emphasize is that the wire must be thick enough so that not a loose band of irregulars but only a national military force can snap it. This then gives the United States the target for retaliation and establishes the conditions under which deterrence prevails.

An asset-seizing, deterrent force solves the puzzles and problems discussed above. With an RDF designed for deterrence, the United States can achieve the rapid deployment that will enable the Force to live up to its title. Getting there first is more important than enlarging the Force beyond the point where it can perform its internal police and its external tripwire functions. Thickening the Force for the sake of our psychological comfort is less important than keeping the Force lean to aid its speedy deployment. On October 1, 1980, General P. X. Kelley, the first Commander of the RDF, told the House Committee on the Budget that although "we have a significant airlift capability in the Military Airlift Command, it is not sufficient to put a capital 'R' in 'Rapid'." To do so, he wisely added, "is one of my primary goals." Some deprecate the RDF by saying that "it will get there first with the least." But only that is required in order to implement a deterrent strategy against the Soviet Union. The effectiveness of a deterrent strategy depends on the credibility of threats and not on the ability to defend a position by force. Thus the 4,500 American troops in West Berlin cannot defend the city; they are there for the sake of deterrence.

With an RDF designed for deterrence, the United States can gain and hold the initiative. President Carter said, and others agreed, that we "cannot afford to let the Soviets choose either the terrain or the tactics to be used by any other country—a nation that might be invaded, their neighbors, our allies, or ourselves." With a defensive, war-fighting strategy how can we avoid letting the Soviet Union do the choosing? The answer that Secretary Brown, unnamed Defense officials, and the Republican platform gave is that we should strike the Soviet Union at places of our own choosing. The northern flank of NATO has been mentioned as a place we might choose. Surely the prospect of attacking there, if the Soviet Union should attack in the Middle East, neither delights the Norwegians nor scares the Russians. A defensive force calls for tactics of maneuver and diversion, with attendant risks that small and local confrontations become enlarged and spread. A deterrent force enables the United States to choose the territory to be seized and the strategy for holding it without enlarging and spreading the conflict.

With an RDF designed for deterrence, we can define and limit the conditions that call for the use of nuclear weapons. When military officials discuss their options, they are said to use "words like *horrendous* and *scary* and raise the specter of World War III." Secretary Brown and others, when they talked vaguely about using tactical nuclear weapons, invoked visions of force spiralling out of control. But nuclear weapons demand that their use be carefully planned, limited, and controlled. With a defensive strategy, the use of nuclear weapons is decided upon according to the fortunes of battle. With a deterrent strategy, the conditions for the use of nuclear weapons are clearly defined and advertised. A deterrent strategy, properly implemented, puts the Soviet Union on notice that maintaining a substantial flow of oil from Persian Gulf states is a vital American interest. Both the Soviet Union and the United States have been wary of direct confrontations over vital interests in all of the years since the Second World War. If such interference should ever occur, we need not engage in a riot of violence. Americans tend to emphasize their national vulnerabilities—the vulnerability of tankers going through the Strait of Hormuz to submarine attacks and the vulnerability of critical pumping sites to air attacks. The Soviet Union also suffers vulnerabilities. We need not threaten to destroy a country in order to deter it. Nothing about a deterrent strategy works against letting the punishment fit the crime. A deterrent strategy entails no use of nuclear weapons, if it succeeds, and can entail a limited and selective use, if it fails.

CONCLUSION

How well will an asset-seizing, deterrent strategy be liked? Probably not very well, despite its many advantages. Two questions should be asked. Can we improve it? Is a war-fighting, defensive strategy preferable? I can reply to the first question by saying that I hope others can improve the strategy I have described. The problem of developing a deterrent strategy to cover vital interests is well worked over. The problem of applying the strategy in areas of political instability and, if necessary, without the cooperation of local states has hardly been touched. More thought should be given to the possibilities.

The answer to the second question requires reflecting on the two strategies. For nine major reasons, I think that an asset-seizing, deterrent strategy is the better one.

—First, a force for fighting the Soviet Union would not be suited to the likeliest case: namely, political instability in Persian Gulf countries. A force for deterring the Soviet Union should be able to accomplish its three major tasks—coping with political disruptions, defending against attacks from within the Middle East, and deterring the Soviet Union.

—Second, a force for fighting would have to be much larger than a force for deterring the Soviet Union. The difficulties of achieving speed of movement, of maintaining logistic support, and of furnishing battlefield replacements would mount.

—Third, with an RDF designed for deterrence, the United States can avoid calling for help from reluctant allies except for naval support, the use of facilities, and enough cooperation to show that the enterprise is a collective one. The United States is a global power, and the task of a global power, sensibly defined, is to take care of regions where its vital interests lie if the countries in those regions cannot take care of themselves. West European countries and Japan can well do more to take care of themselves, while the United States tends to its own interests as well as theirs in the Persian Gulf. For the credibility of deterrence, situations should be kept simple and clear. The participation of allies in military operations would work against this.

—Fourth, for the United States to force its way into oil fields would be a politically costly and risky move. The cost and risk cannot be avoided no matter what strategy is followed. An RDF designed for deterring rather than for fighting the Soviet Union would, however, eliminate one cost and reduce risks. It would eliminate the need for a permanent military base in the Gulf region, a base that would be needed to prepare to fight a regional war against the Soviet Union. An American base in the region would draw opposition from many states and be a continual source of irritation. Moreover, a permanent American military presence would easily trigger action by the RDF even if in the absence of a base such action might have been avoided.

—Fifth, a defensive force could involve the United States in major fighting against the Soviet Union under conditions likely to be more difficult for us than for them. A war-fighting, defensive force may be able to keep Russian troops away from the oil fields, but this is a task added to that of securing the oil fields. The design of the RDF follows from its purpose and its tasks. The tasks are demanding, and we cannot make them less so. To keep oil flowing is the essential objective. Any objective added to it unnecessarily increases the demands on the Force.

—Sixth, both a defensive and a deterrent force would be at least somewhat dissuasive. Dissuasion is what we want to achieve by whatever combination of deterrence and defense. As the probability that a country's military moves can be effectively countered increases, the likelihood of its making those moves decreases. That statement suggests a credibility question that is seldom asked. Would a defensive force look strong enough to dissuade the Soviet Union from challenging it? Would Russian leaders believe that we would be willing and able to fight the Soviet Union to a standstill in the mountains and deserts of Iran? The Soviet Union is likelier to test an American defensive force than to test a deterrent force. The Soviet Union's leaders, operating in their own backyard, are in a good position to control escalation. They can reduce the scale of the fighting or withdraw behind their borders if force threatens to get out of control. Deterring the Soviet Union is less risky than fighting defensively against it.

—Seventh, an American deterrent strategy would be highly credible for reasons that I have suggested. We would be protecting a prize of undoubted value. In protecting it, we would not be able to fight to a very high level. If Russian forces challenged us directly, and if their force were about to overcome ours and take control of the oil fields, leaders of the Soviet Union would have to believe that in response, we might do something highly damaging to them. They do not have to believe that we will, but they do have to believe that we might—all the more so because if we pass, we lessen the credibility of American deterrence worldwide.

—Eighth, a defensive strategy cannot serve the United States while the forces for its implementation are being built. This, it is commonly agreed, will take five or more years. In the meantime, we will have to rely on deterrence. Even those less fond of deterrence than I am may be persuaded that deterrence, if not as reassuring as defense, is better than defeat. If we can rely on deterrence for five years, why not rely on it longer?

—Ninth, an RDF designed for deterrence would be an oil force, useful mainly for the protection of our vital economic interest. It would not be useful where a great deal of force is needed and less than vital interests are threatened. Deterrent threats would then not be credible. The best policy uses the least force that will achieve its objective. A single-purpose force is better than a multi-purpose one. The former is likelier to remain uncommitted until the moment of its intended use arrives and thus to be available when needed most.

Military planners will prefer a larger defensive force over a smaller deterrent force designed mainly for one purpose. Fighting for one's ends seems, misleadingly I have argued, less risky than relying on deterrence. And military planners believe they should give the President more rather than fewer options. Because the strategy I advocate does not give the military a traditional and congenial role, its adoption depends on civilians taking the lead. This is as it should be. Soldiers and sailors, like civil servants, follow their own interests and habits unless they are told what to do.

Where vital interests are at issue, an RDF should be used to create a situation in which deterrence applies. I have sought to show how this can be done even in situations customarily thought to be at least amenable to deterrent strategies—that is, where internal chaos makes it unclear how to retaliate and against whom. The strategy does this by physically staking out our claim to the vital resource, by establishing a perimeter, and by saying that if the Soviet Union attacks so hard that we cannot hold, we shall retaliate against appropriate targets. Our troops on the spot make our vital interest manifest, and thus deterrent threats become credible. This is a strategy. It leaves numerous practical questions unanswered. What should be the design of the Force for carrying the strategy out? How can the required speed be achieved? How big should the Force be? How heavily equipped? What is the best way to defend a perimeter against indigenous attacks? These are matters for discussion and decision. This essay is about the strategy of the RDF, and not about its design. Its design, though not its details, follows from the strategy. The strategy, if accepted, tells us what we need to do, but not just how to do it.

Naval Power and National Security

LINTON F. BROOKS

For the past five years, U.S. Navy officers and their civilian colleagues have been taking to heart the centuries-old dictum of the first great theorist of conflict, Sun Tzu: they have been studying war.* While military reformers have focused on the need for improved military strategy in a land campaign, a renaissance of strategic thinking has been taking place within the U.S. Navy. This renaissance has been marked by a series of internal and external discussions and debates in which naval strategy has received more attention than in any peacetime period since the days of Alfred Thayer Mahan. One important result has been to weave traditional naval thinking into a coherent concept for using early, forceful, global, forward deployment of maritime power both to deter war with the Soviet Union and to achieve U.S. war aims should deterrence fail. The concept, which has come to be called "The Maritime Strategy," was initially codified in classified internal Navy documents in 1982 and was gradually revealed to public scrutiny through Congressional testimony and public statements culminating in a January 1986 Supplement to the *Proceedings* of the United States Naval Institute. . . .

While the strategy represents the consensus of the Navy's military and civilian leadership on the best employment of maritime forces in war, it has been greeted with anything but consensus outside the Navy. . . . This article seeks to demonstrate that, far from being irrelevant or dangerous, the on-going renaissance in Navy strategic thinking offers a method of keeping the national

From "Naval Power and National Security: The Case for the Maritime Strategy" by Linton F. Brooks, *International Security*, Fall 1986 (Vol. 11, No. 2), pp. 58–88. © 1986 by the President and Fellows of Harvard College and of the Massachusetts Institute of Technology. Reprinted by permission of MIT Press, Cambridge, Massachusetts and the copyright holders. Portions of the text and some footnotes have been omitted.

*The author wishes to thank Rear Admiral William Pendley, Captains Thomas Daly, Michael Hughes, and Peter Swartz, Lieutenant Commander Joseph Benkert, and Mr. Bradford Dismukes for their assistance. All have contributed to the development of the Maritime Strategy as well as to this paper; none are responsible for the use I have made of their thoughts and insights.

strategy of the United States— which includes both global commitments and a commitment to the continental defense of Europe—viable in an era of nuclear parity and substantial imbalance in European land forces. Critics should welcome the new emphasis on forward maritime options as strengthening deterrence and aiding the nation in continuing the historic American guarantee of Western Europe's security while still denying the Soviets the initiative in other areas of the world.

THE STRATEGIC ENVIRONMENT

The Maritime Strategy cannot be considered unless we first understand the national military strategy it is intended to implement, the Soviet military strategy it is designed to counter, or the forces with which it would be undertaken.

National Military Strategy

Self-styled military reformers often assert that the United States has no national strategy. Such a declaration is understandable since no public document sets forth an overall military strategy except in generalities. . . . There is, however, a national security strategy, promulgated by the President on May 20, 1982 in National Security Decision Document (NSDD)-32. It designates the Soviets as the main military threat, rather than more common but less significant adversaries such as Libya. To counter this threat, the strategy calls for balanced conventional forces, expects a war to be global, envisions sequential operations during that global conflict, places increasing importance on allied contributions, and directs the forward basing of U.S. forces in peacetime. "In what was probably its most significant strategy innovation, the Reagan administration consciously and formally substituted the threat of escalation in space and time for the threat of escalation in weapons," thus leading to an emphasis both on prolonged conventional conflict and on denying the Soviets the ability to choose the geographic limits of that conflict.

In the development and refinement of the Maritime Strategy, Navy leaders took into account this NSDD, other Administration documents, the war plans of the Unified and Specified Commanders, and the treaties and other agreements the United States has with 43 nations, the most important of which is the North Atlantic Treaty. From this series of documents, many unavailable to the public, Navy leaders concluded that "our national strategy is built on three pillars: deterrence, forward defense, and alliance solidarity." This view of U.S. and NATO military strategy is the first factor shaping the Maritime Strategy.

Soviet Military Strategy

The second factor shaping the Maritime Strategy is Soviet military strategy and the role of the Soviet navy within that strategy. The Maritime Strategy is based on a Soviet strategy that assumes that any future war with the West "would be a decisive clash on a global scale . . . a coalition war"—a war that the Soviets would prefer to fight with conventional weapons, but one that is "still a 'nuclear' war in the sense that the nuclear balance is constantly examined and evaluated in anticipation of possible escalation" and in which the Soviets place "high priority on changing the nuclear balance, or as they term it, the nuclear correlation of forces, during conventional operations." Soviet war aims would be to defeat and occupy NATO, to neutralize the power of the United States and China, and to dominate the postwar world. The probable centerpiece of Soviet strategy in such a global war would be a "combined-arms assault against Europe, where they would seek a quick and decisive victory . . . . the Soviets would, of course, prefer to be able to concentrate on a single theater. . . ."

The most important Soviet navy roles in global war would be protecting (in Soviet terms, "ensuring the combat stability of") Soviet ballistic missile submarines (SSBNs) and protecting the approaches to the Soviet homeland. . . . Other traditional naval roles, such as attacking reinforcement and resupply shipping or supporting the Soviet army, are clearly secondary, at least at the start of a war.

To implement this strategy, the bulk of the Soviet navy must be used to protect defensive bastions near the Soviet Union, with only limited forces deployed into the broad ocean areas. This essentially defensive initial role for the Soviet navy is confirmed by the overwhelming majority of Soviet naval exercises.

Available Forces

The final factor shaping the Maritime Strategy is the structure of the military forces available to carry it out. As will be discussed more fully below, much public debate over strategy is really a debate over what forces the nation should procure for the future. While in theory strategy should determine forces, in practice the relationship is a reciprocal one, with available forces determining the limits of achievable strategy. . . .

THE MARITIME STRATEGY DESCRIBED

The strategy derived from these three factors is deliberately broad and general. Since it provides global guidance, rather than a detailed timetable, the strategy has no timelines attached. . . . it includes port visits and peacetime exercises to support alliances and short-notice response in time of crisis to deter escalation. While recognizing the importance of these aspects of the strategy, the Navy has devoted most of its attention—and critics have devoted almost all of theirs—to those aspects of the strategy dealing with global conventional war.

The Maritime Strategy foresees a global war as unfolding in three phases. In the first, *Deterrence or the Transition to War,* recognition that a specific international situation could lead to hostilities requires rapid, worldwide forward deployment of the Navy and Marine Corps (along with similar deployments by other services). Actions taken in this phase will include the surge deployment of anti-submarine warfare (ASW) forces (particularly submarines), forcing Soviet submarines to retreat into defensive bastions; the assembly and forward movement of multi-carrier battle forces; and embarkation of Marine amphibious forces. At the same time, execution of Presidential authority to call up reserves and to place the Coast Guard under Navy control will help prepare for the implementation of plans for sealift to Europe. The massive nature of the forward movement (indicating national will) and its global nature (indicating an unwillingness to cede any area to the Soviets, to defend only some U.S. allies, or to allow the Soviets their preferred strategy of concentrating on a single theater) are both designed to reinforce deterrence while being easily reversible if deterrence prevails.

Should deterrence fail, a second phase, *Seizing the Initiative,* comes into play. The object is establishment of sea control in key maritime areas as far forward and as rapidly as possible. U.S. and allied ASW forces will wage an aggressive campaign against all Soviet submarines, including ballistic missile submarines. Carrier battle forces will fight their way into the Norwegian Sea, Eastern Mediterranean, and Pacific approaches to the Soviet Union, depending on their location when hostilities begin. The integrated nature of modern naval warfare is especially relevant to this phase. For example, in the Norwegian Sea, air superiority is needed to permit operation of Maritime Patrol Air ASW aircraft, which in turn are needed to destroy Soviet cruise missile-carrying submarines, which in turn are necessary to protect aircraft carriers and missile ships required to ensure air superiority, which is essential for offensive operations. The strategy assumes that the use of amphibious forces or the strike power of carrier battle forces against targets ashore may also be appropriate in this phase, and Navy leaders specifically note that "the main threats to our fleet during this phase are . . . missile-carrying aircraft of Soviet Naval Aviation [land-based in the Soviet Union]. The United States cannot allow our adversary to assume he will be able to attack the fleet with impunity, from inviolable sanctuaries." The last essential aspect of this phase is the establishment of a logistics structure to support sustained forward operations, including advanced bases, sealift, and mobile logistics support forces.[1]

The final phase, *Carrying the Fight to the Enemy*, begins once sea control has been established and involves using carrier air power and Marine amphibious forces directly against targets ashore. At the same time, the vigorous ASW campaign, including the campaign against Soviet SSBNs, would continue. Direct conventional attacks on the Soviet homeland, while not ruled out (or required) in earlier phases, would be more likely in this phase in order to threaten the bases and support structure of the Soviet navy.

Throughout all phases of the strategy, close cooperation with allied navies and with other services, particularly the U.S. Air Force, is mandatory. . . . the strategy envisions global operations, with the Pacific equal in importance to other theaters. Operations within a particular theater may be conducted sequentially . . . .

The overall objectives of this strategy, in the words of Admiral Watkins, are to:

—Deny the Soviets their kind of war by exerting global pressure, indicating that the conflict will be neither short nor localized.
—Destroy the Soviet Navy: both important in itself and a necessary step for us to realize our objectives.
—Influence the land battle by limiting redeployment of forces, by ensuring reinforcement and resupply, and by direct application of carrier air and amphibious power.
—Terminate the war on terms acceptable to us and to our allies through measures such as threatening direct attack against the homeland or changing the nuclear correlation of forces.[2]

ASSUMPTIONS EXPLICIT AND IMPLIED

In addition to embodying a specific view of U.S. and Soviet strategy, the Maritime Strategy incorporates a number of inherent assumptions seldom made explicit by Navy spokesmen. Among the more important of these are:

AS A GLOBAL POWER, THE UNITED STATES HAS MILITARILY IMPORTANT INTERESTS BEYOND NATO. Europe and NATO are vital interests of the United States. . . .In addition, however, the United States

---

[1] There is an old military saying that "amateurs discuss strategy; professionals discuss logistics." One of the important and little noticed results of the growing prominence of the strategy within the Navy is a renewed interest in wartime logistics support.

[2] Admiral James D. Watkins, "The Maritime Strategy," Supplement to U.S. Naval Institute *Proceedings*, January 1986, p. 14.

has formal defense agreements of varying types with a number of nations outside of Europe. Demonstrating American readiness to honor commitments to, for example, Japan and Korea is also vital. An important function of any peacetime military strategy is declaratory; announcing a willingness to abandon Pacific allies in time of global war is unlikely to contribute to either deterrence or the furthering of peacetime foreign policy goals.

THERE WILL BE NO IMMEDIATE COLLAPSE IN CENTRAL EUROPE. Maritime power inherently requires time to take effect. If land and air forces in Germany are overrun in days, neither the Maritime Strategy nor any alternative use of seapower is likely to be able to prevent that event (although, as will be argued below, there is an implicit assumption that loss of Central Europe is the loss of a campaign, not a war).

THE BEST USE OF SEA-BASED AIRPOWER IS NOT DIRECTLY IN CENTRAL EUROPE. . . . . While Navy leaders stress that the flexibility of seapower allows many options, there is an implicit assumption that Germany is not the optimum location for employing carrier air power. The relatively small increase in air power from early arriving carriers, the command and control complexity of adding sea-based forces to a complex air war, and, above all, the fact that it is not in NATO's interest to allow Soviets the luxury of their preferred strategy, all argue for using sea-based air power to tie down and divert Soviet forces elsewhere rather than using such air power directly on the Central Front.

NUCLEAR WEAPONS USE IS NOT INEVITABLE. By altering the nuclear correlation of forces, the Maritime Strategy seeks to make nuclear escalation "a less attractive option to the Soviets with the passing of every day." Lacking the ability to directly influence the nuclear decision ashore, however, the strategy must assume that early use of nuclear weapons in Europe is not required, since nuclear use at sea will almost certainly follow.

THE APPROACH TO PROTECTING THE SEA LANES MUST BE DIFFERENT FROM THE PAST. It is arguable that the allies won the World War II Battle of the Atlantic, not by sinking submarines, but by building ships faster than they could be sunk. In that conflict, in both theaters, interdiction of strategic raw materials, the resources of war, was an important mission. It is tempting to use that experience as a model for the future. The strategy, however, recognizes that "we will neither be able to tolerate attrition typical of World War II nor provide adequate dedicated sealift to transport the strategic raw materials we will require." . . .

NATO IS NOT THE SAME AS THE CENTRAL FRONT. . . . the framers of the strategy clearly assume that defense of those allies on the flanks (Norway, Denmark, Iceland, Italy, Turkey, Greece) must have equal priority with defense against a Soviet thrust in Germany since, [in the words of Secretary of the Navy, John F. Lehman, Jr.]: "No coalition of free nations can survive a strategy which begins by sacrificing its more exposed allies to a dubious military expediency."

THE EUROPEAN CAMPAIGN IS NOT THE SAME AS THE WAR. The Maritime Strategy, like the overall military strategy it supports, recognizes that the defense of Europe is vital to the United States. But, [as Colin S. Gray has pointed out]: military leaders "need to consider unpleasant as well as satisfactory futures." Destruction of the Soviet fleet and establishment of maritime superiority are necessary to prevent defeat in Europe and provide leverage for war termination; they also enable the United States to ensure its own security and to enhance deterrence by demonstrating the ability to continue the conflict regardless of the outcome in Europe.

CONTRIBUTIONS AND LIMITATIONS

Containing Crises and Advancing U.S. Policy Goals

. . . Given innate Soviet conservatism and the lack of any plausible incentive for the Soviet Union to risk destruction in order to change the status quo, war in Europe is not likely to occur as a long-planned act of Soviet policy. Instead, a modern equivalent of the downward spiral of August 1914 during a European crisis, perhaps one growing out of an extra-European situation, offers the most plausible path to war. Containing extra-European crises is, therefore, of obvious importance to the West. As the chief agent for dealing with Third World crises, the Navy has a unique role to play in preventing escalation of a local problem to the point where war in Europe might seem necessary or inevitable to the Soviets. Navy spokesmen routinely emphasize that Navy and Marine Corps forces were used in 80 percent of the 250 instances of American military force employment since World War II, a point no less valid for being frequently stated.

Deterrence

The most important contribution any strategy can make is to deter, or help deter, major war. . . . How are navies and the Maritime Strategy relevant to deterrence?

First, maritime forces help demonstrate national will. Easy to move both physically and politically, the fleet can be deployed as a unilateral U.S. action, nonprovocative because reversible. Fleet movements in time of crisis can both demonstrate U.S. commitment to *all* its allies and, by their global nature, demonstrate that any war will not unfold along preferred Soviet lines. Such movements are an important *political* deterrent, precluding the Soviets from believing that they can coerce individual allies and fragment the alliance through what might be called a "political blitzkrieg."

Second, early forward fleet movements demonstrate that the Soviets will be able neither to cut off Europe from the United States nor to draw down remote theaters to reinforce Europe. Thus, they must win quickly in Europe or not at all. . . .

Finally, the Maritime Strategy recognizes that the United States must deter, not a collection of American theoreticians and scholars, but a Soviet leadership that constantly calculates the nuclear correlation of forces and uses those calculations in the decision-making process. By making it clear at the outset that Soviet SSBNs will be at risk in a conventional war, the strategy alters Soviet correlation of forces calculations, and thus enhances deterrence.

War-Waging

War is the ultimate test of any strategy; a strategy useless in war cannot deter. Since Soviet strategy views Europe as central, a counter-strategy must contribute directly or indirectly to the European battle. Maritime power can make four significant contributions:

PROTECTING THE SEA LINES OF COMMUNICATION (SLOCS). Any strategy for war in Europe must ensure the unimpeded flow of supplies to Europe, the overwhelming majority of which must go by sea. The potential threat to these lines of communication represented by the Soviet submarine force is immense. Sea lane interdiction, however, is a lower priority Soviet navy task than protecting sea-based strategic forces or homeland defense. Thus, early aggressive forward ASW operations directly protect the reinforcement and resupply of Europe, initially by tying down the Soviet submarine force in a pro-SSBN protective role and ultimately by destroying Soviet general purpose submarines.

DIRECTLY SUPPORTING THE LAND BATTLE ON THE EUROPEAN FLANKS. While Soviet literature suggests the Western TVD (NATO's Central Front) would be the scene of the decisive conflict, the Soviets also envision operations in the Northwestern TVD to seize northern Norway and in the Southwestern TVD to attack Thrace and to seize both sides of the Turkish straits. A considerable fraction of the available combat power to thwart these thrusts is in the form of carrier-based aircraft, with three or four aircraft carriers potentially available in each theater. Success in such defense serves both military and political aims by interrupting Soviet strategy and ensuring that alliance cohesion is not sacrificed by an apparent unwillingness to defend *all* members of an alliance that extends from Norway to Turkey.

TYING DOWN FORCES, ESPECIALLY AIR FORCES, THAT MIGHT

OTHERWISE BE AVAILABLE FOR THE EUROPEAN BATTLE. Some 1700 Soviet tactical aircraft are deployed in the Far East TVD, compared with 2300 Soviet and 1600 other Warsaw Pact tactical aircraft available in the Western TVD. While the more capable forces are in the European area, Far East tactical air forces could be made available to augment them if not pinned down by the necessity to defend against aggressive forward employment of American carrier and amphibious forces in the Pacific. There is no suggestion here that the Soviets necessarily *plan* on such a shift; rather, the result of maritime operations in the Pacific will be to limit Soviet flexibility to respond to changing conditions. Maritime forces are less likely to have an effect on a possible Soviet decision to shift ground forces from the Far Eastern to the Western TVD. Such forces are more difficult to transfer and are held in place by the constant Soviet need to consider the position of China. While it is exceptionally unlikely that China would find it in its interest to become an active belligerent, the active use of naval power, by demonstrating a clear U.S. intent to remain a Pacific power, may encourage a Chinese posture of armed neutrality rather than cooperation, thus complicating Soviet decision-making.

DENYING THE SOVIETS THEIR PREFERRED STRATEGY. Two-front wars are difficult. While the United States and its allies cannot open a "second front" through maritime power, the global use of such power can have a similar strategic effect on the minds of Soviet leaders, and it is in the minds of leaders that decisions to continue or terminate wars are made. Denying the Soviets their preferred strategy of a short, single theater war is an important, although intangible, contribution of maritime forces. . . .

War Termination

Should deterrence fail . . . maritime power may offer a unique form of war termination leverage through its ability to dramatically alter the nuclear balance, or, in Soviet terms, the nuclear correlation of forces. While Soviet doctrine may be shifting towards a conventional war option, Soviet leaders still assume a war between the two superpowers has a high probability of escalating and therefore place great importance on the constant calculation and evaluation of the nuclear correlation of forces.

The Navy can alter those Soviet calculations, most obviously by attacking SSBNs which, as a principal component of Soviet strategic reserves, are central to correlation of forces calculations. Such attacks offer significant war termination leverage. In addition to altering the Soviet estimate of their own nuclear capabilities, maritime forces can increase the magnitude of the nuclear threat that the Soviets must face. As the Soviet fleet is eliminated, both carrier strike aircraft (which the Soviets view as a significant nuclear threat) and nuclear Tomahawk missiles will be in a position to threaten the Soviet homeland. Objectively, the incremental increase in allied nuclear capability that these forces offer is small. Similarly, the destruction of even a large fraction of the Soviet SSBN force will result in only a limited decrease in total Soviet nuclear strike capability. But the Soviets, with their military conservatism and penchant for constant algebraic calculation of the correlation of forces, will not ignore either factor. They will evaluate the correlation of forces as growing constantly less favorable.

The fear that the war may escalate and the fact that such escalation is less and less attractive every day provide a powerful incentive for war termination. . . .

Limitations

. . . there are inherent limits in [the strategy's] applicability. . . . Among the most important are:

THE MARITIME STRATEGY (LIKE ANY OTHER USE OF MARITIME POWER) CANNOT ALONE BRING VICTORY IN A WAR AGAINST A MAJOR LAND POWER. . . .

THE U.S. NAVY ALONE CANNOT IMPLEMENT THE MARITIME STRATEGY OR ANY CONCEIVABLE ALTERNATIVE TO IT. . . .

THERE ARE INHERENT UNCERTAINTIES IN THIS OR ANY OTHER STRATEGY THAT . . . CAN NEVER BE RESOLVED SHORT OF WAR. . . . timely forward movement depends on receiving and reacting to warning. It is . . . impossible to be certain in advance such warning will be available, be recognized, and . . . be acted upon.

. . . no one can be certain that Soviet wartime strategy . . . will be what their prewar doctrine suggests. Finally . . . the Maritime Strategy . . . seeks war termination on favorable terms and shares the inherent uncertainties embodied in such a goal.

THERE ARE PLAUSIBLE CONFLICTS FOR WHICH THE MARITIME STRATEGY (BUT NOT NECESSARILY MARITIME POWER) IS INAPPLICABLE . . . [including] a major conflict (Vietnam War-scale) not involving the Soviet Union . . . [or] a regionally limited conflict outside Europe in which the United States and the Soviet Union are directly involved. . . .

CRITICISMS VALID AND OTHERWISE

Critics of the Maritime Strategy focus on three major issues: risk, relevance, and resources. They argue that the strategy will not accomplish anything important, is too dangerous, or costs too much, thus diverting resources from where they are really needed. In each case, a legitimate issue is buried in the criticism, but in each case the critics are, on balance, wrong.

Risk

Those who focus on risk have two concerns. The first is that the Navy is incapable of implementing such an aggressive and ambitious strategy. While the strategy deals with more than aircraft carrier operations, critics often frame their arguments as assertions about carrier vulnerability when operating in close proximity to the Soviet homeland. . . . Without actual combat, estimates of the Navy's ability to operate carrier battle groups in so-called "high-threat" areas are professional military judgments, best made not by those who must rely on experience with past fleet conditions, but by the men who would have to carry out such operations today. Chief among this latter group is the Commander of NATO's Striking Fleet Atlantic. Writing recently, the current Commander, Vice Admiral Henry Mustin, said;

> concern over our forward strategy is frequently couched in terms of whether U.S. aircraft carriers . . . can survive in the Norwegian Sea in a conflict with the Soviet Union. No one has ever said that war with the Soviet Union would be easy. In war, ships get sunk, aircraft get shot down and people get killed. The Soviet Union and the Warsaw Pact would be very formidable . . . they would not be invincible. The Striking Fleet can get . . . assistance in beating down Soviet air attacks through joint operations with NATO AWACS and Norwegian air defenses— including the U.S. Air Force—and we have demonstrated this capability in exercises. . . . The Soviets . . . acknowledge that a moving target ranging over thousands of square miles of blue water is much more survivable than a fixed airfield ashore. No one suggests that we should abandon all airfields in Norway at the start of hostilities, and yet some quake at the notion of less vulnerable carriers operating hundreds of miles at sea.

The second risk issue concerns escalation. . . . To many, deliberate attacks on SSBNs seem dangerously escalatory and destabilizing, and must be avoided. . . . Basing their logic on traditional theories of arms control, in which secure second strike strategic forces are indispensable to stability, such critics conclude that attacks on SSBNs raise the specter of a "use or lose" situation. While critics of the first sort fear the strategy cannot succeed, critics focusing on escalation fear it will, and in doing so lead to nuclear war, perhaps at sea, perhaps involving a strategic nuclear exchange.

The facts are not that clear. With regard to Pacific operations, critics and advocates are seeing opposite sides of the same coin. Forcing the Soviets to divert resources and attention from Europe is a strength of the strategy, not a weakness. Japan's central role arises not because the United States seeks to involve its allies in war, but because the United States has treaty obligations to defend

Japan, and there is good reason to believe the Soviets will threaten that nation regardless of what action the United States takes. Little in history suggests that removing U.S. naval forces will reduce the chance of attack on Japan or, for that matter, of a North Korean attack on U.S. and South Korean forces under cover of a more general war.

Concern that U.S. actions at sea could force the Soviets to use tactical nuclear weapons to counter American naval superiority, especially aircraft carriers, is based on a misreading of Soviet doctrine. The Soviets place nuclear weapons under the same tight political control as does the United States. . . .

> The decision to initiate tactical nuclear war at sea appears neither a Navy decision nor one that will hinge on Navy matters.

Simply put, a nation with a military dominated by artillerymen, a strategy focused on land, and a doctrine that suggests nuclear war cannot be limited is not going to cross the nuclear threshold based on at-sea tactical considerations.

This leaves the most difficult question: attacking SSBNs. The disagreement between those who see the risk of escalation in such attacks and those who see war termination leverage is based on very different models of escalation.* Those with intellectual roots in traditional arms control theory view threats to SSBNs, by general agreement the most secure component of strategic forces, as escalatory by definition. They further assume that this conclusion is universally valid, based on an objective reality that does not depend on the particular characteristics of the decision-makers involved. Even viewing escalation through this lens, it is not clear that the stability model is valid. The loss to conventional attack of one SSBN at a time over a period of days or weeks provides no single event sufficient to warrant the catastrophic decision to escalate to the strategic level.†

Advocates of the anti-SSBN facet of the strategy, however, reject the conclusion that traditional arms control theory offers the proper escalation model. They base their assessment of escalation risks not on arms control theory, but on Soviet military doctrine. Soviet navy acceptance of attacks on SSBNs as an integral component of conventional war has been made clear by such authoritative spokesmen as the former commander of the Soviet navy, Sergei Gorshkov, who

---

*I am indebted to Barry Posen for this point.

†Much of the discussion of Soviet response to SSBN losses is based on insights provided by Bradford Dismukes of the Center for Naval Analyses (CNA), both in personal discussion and in his unpublished CNA paper, "Pros and Cons of the Pro-SSBN Mission; What will the future bring?," June 1980.

noted several years ago that, among the "main efforts of a fleet," the "most important of them has become the use of the forces of the fleet against the naval strategic nuclear systems of the enemy with the aim of disrupting . . . their strikes . . . ." Such an approach is no more than the at-sea analogue of the priority, long recognized in the West, that the Soviets give to the destruction of nuclear weapons during the conventional phase of the land war.

Not only have the Soviets long accepted anti-SSBN operations as a legitimate military task (and one they would undertake were they able to do so); they have also long assumed that the United States will conduct such operations in time of war. Such an assumption is reasonable from the Soviet standpoint, both because of doctrinal mirror-imaging and because senior naval officers giving Congressional testimony have consistently stressed the practical difficulties of distinguishing between types of submarines and have indicated that all types of submarines would be legitimate wartime targets. Thus, while in the West the explicit acknowledgment that attacking SSBNs was a component of the overall Maritime Strategy was news, in the Soviet Union it was not.

Even if Soviet doctrine did not recognize the prospect of attacks on SSBNs as legitimate, escalation serves no useful Soviet purpose. A nuclear strike on the United States would result in immensely destructive retaliation. It is difficult to see why the Soviets would elect the physical destruction of their country unless the only alternative were its political destruction. If, therefore, allied war termination aims do not extend to the breakup of the Soviet state or the replacement of the Soviet leadership, but rather to some form of restoration of the status quo ante bellum, a Soviet nuclear strike is exceptionally unlikely.

Once again, critics and advocates are seeing two sides of the same coin. Almost by definition, any U.S. action important enough to exert war termination leverage carries some risk of escalation. But no war with the Soviet Union is without immense risk, and the escalatory risk associated with conventional attacks on SSBN forces at sea should be acceptable as a unique means of gaining war termination leverage. Threatening SSBNs by conventional means carries far *less* risk of escalation than does the use of tactical nuclear weapons to restore a declining battlefield situation, a risk that NATO has accepted for years.

Relevance

Quite apart from any notion of risk, some critics question the relevance of the strategy even if it should work and even if it were risk-free. As [Robert Komer], one of the more prolific critics asserts, the "basic flaw in any maritime strategy is that, even if we swept the other superpower from the seas and pulverized all its naval bases, this would not suffice to prevent it from dominating the Eurasian landmass.'' The short answer to this criticism is that no one ever claimed it would. Even the most vigorous advocates of maritime power do not suggest that it is a substitute for ground forces and air power in Europe. Wars are won on land, but they can be lost at sea.

In discussing the issue of relevance, the proper issue is whether some alternate employment of maritime forces is *more* relevant. The first alternative that critics propose deals with protecting the sea lanes to Europe. Critics and supporters alike agree with the need to protect U.S. resupply shipping. They differ over how such a mission should be accomplished. The Maritime Strategy seeks to discourage early Soviet forward deployments by adopting a declaratory strategy of threatening SSBNs, thus forcing the Soviets to withhold general purpose naval forces to protect those SSBNs, and to preclude later deployment by conducting a successful forward ASW campaign. In contrast, critics typically advocate what they term "defensive sea control," asking "why wouldn't a passive defense line across the Greenland-Iceland-United Kingdom gap protect our sea-lanes? Why are U.S. maritime strategists concerned . . . if the Soviet Navy stays home?"

Advocates of such a Maginot Line strategy miss several points. First, of course, there is no reason to assume that the Soviet navy, particularly its attack submarine component, will "stay home" once it is clear that the United States has no plans to challenge the bastions. Second, such a passive strategy cedes control of the Norwegian Sea (and of the coast of Norway) to the Soviets, violating the obligation of the United States to defend *all* its allies. Finally, such a strategy forgoes both the advantages to the ASW campaign of early deployments and the war termination and deterrent leverage attained by holding Soviet SSBNs at risk. . . .

While they take issue with using amphibious forces and carrier battle groups in forward power projection operations, critics have yet to come up with attractive alternatives. In theory, alternatives are available. Aircraft carriers could be deployed to engage Soviet clients and surrogates (Cuba, Vietnam), used to augment the air battle over the Central Front, or maintained as some form of strategic reserve. Amphibious forces, instead of being employed as envisioned in the Maritime Strategy, could be committed early in the war to augment defenses in Europe or used against Third World Soviet surrogates. On examination, none of these alternatives appears attractive.

Use of carriers against surrogates may be useful and necessary during the strategy's second phase (Seize the Initiative). One advantage of mobile, flexible forces is that they can be diverted to alternate tasks. But no operations against any surrogate appear to have as much prospect for direct influence over the Soviets as does the existing strategy. It is difficult to see how surrogates can be more relevant to a NATO battle than the NATO flanks themselves. Using carriers as a strategic reserve denies the early benefits of mobile forces. . . .

The remaining option, using Marine Corps or carrier air power (perhaps without the carriers) in Central Europe, is therefore the alternative that critics presumably prefer. Several problems arise. First, because carriers are the chief U.S. tool for responding to crises and because crisis control is an important aspect of war prevention, one cannot be certain where carriers would be at a war's start, thus making integrated European planning difficult. Second, the 50–60 fighter and attack aircraft per carrier are a relatively small addition to the 2100 ground attack and 900 interceptor aircraft already in place in Europe, but, by virtue of their ability to threaten different areas, they can tie down far more resources on the flanks and in the Pacific. Since Soviet aircraft in these areas are distributed across a wide battle area, carrier aircraft can be concentrated in numbers that *do* make a difference. Finally, while direct use of carrier air power in Germany may or may not be more relevant to the Central Front, it is less relevant to NATO as a whole. NATO's effectiveness depends on its solidarity, which in turn requires the defense of *all* its members. . . . Similar arguments apply to amphibious forces.

Maritime critics reserve a special form of criticism for Pacific forward operations. Accustomed to thinking in theater terms, critics doubt the relevance of global operations and urge against any form of horizontal escalation. Since Pacific operations are unlikely to draw ground forces from other theaters, they are deemed useless, even though the critics acknowledge that the Soviets "might reinforce their Pacific Fleet air forces." But air power is exactly what will be crucial in a European war. The result the critics denigrate would be a clear gain for NATO forces; indeed, even if the Soviets do not reinforce the Far Eastern TVD but simply fail to draw on its resources to augment the West, maritime power will have made a significant contribution. . . . even more so when the political impact on America's Asian allies is taken into account.

The most important criticism to analyze is the allegation that the Maritime Strategy is irrelevant to deterrence. . . . Mearsheimer, for example, in focusing on deterrence of large-scale conventional attack in Europe, concludes that denying the Soviets the ability to conduct a blitzkrieg is both necessary and sufficient for deterrence and that maritime forces are irrelevant to such denial.[3] This approach may be flawed. First, it ignores what was termed earlier a "political blitzkrieg," a fragmenting of the alliance in a crisis if the United States appears to be setting priorities among its allies. Second, conservative Soviet planners must consider unfavorable outcomes as well as favorable ones . . . . by demonstrating an ability to deny the Soviets their preferred strategy and to adversely alter the nuclear correlation of forces, an announced Maritime Strategy can make failure of a blitzkrieg even more unattractive and thus enhance deterrence.

A more general problem with the assertion that maritime forces are irrelevant to deterrence is that it considers only the deterrence of large-scale conventional attack in Europe. Such an attack is only likely to be considered after serious deterioration in the international situation. By responding to Soviet global encroachment, containing extra-European crises, demonstrating U.S. support for allies, and serving as a well-understood symbol of national will, maritime forces can deter the Soviets from the type of adventurism that could escalate into a grave crisis warranting Soviet consideration of war. This form of deterrence complements rather than substitutes for that provided by the ability to deny a blitzkrieg, just as wartime global maritime operations complement direct defense in Europe.

The most important problem with those who argue against the Maritime Strategy on grounds of its relevance is that they ignore the entire question of war termination. It often seems that, for all their stress on innovation at the theater level, at the strategic level critics are espousing a strategy whose components are: reinforce Europe, pray for a miracle, and be ready to use nuclear weapons if no miracle occurs. Ensuring alliance solidarity and providing war termination leverage appear to supporters of the Maritime Strategy to be eminently relevant.

Resources

Arguments about the relevance of the Maritime Strategy are often really arguments about resources, focusing not so much on how existing forces will be used as on what will be procured for the future. Much debate about any strategy is really a debate about money. This is as it should be; strategy should guide resource allocation. Thus, critics who recognize this fact attack the strategy precisely *because* it has helped justify the ongoing naval buildup.

---

[3] John Mearsheimer, Remarks at the Naval War College, May Conference on "Maritime Strategy: Issues and Perspectives," May 15–17, 1985. Mearsheimer also doubts that the strategy can be executed or that the President will permit it to be attempted.

They assert either that there is no strategy, only a budget document, or that the United States can not afford to buy the Navy required to implement such a strategy. Neither point is valid. . . .

Assertions that the Navy has no strategy are based on a misunderstanding of what strategy is . . . . the Maritime Strategy, whether one endorses or condemns it, clearly qualifies as a global strategy. Operational details . . . belong not in a global strategy, but in the theater campaign plans shaped by that strategy. . . . Some critics who might be prepared to accept the validity of the strategy for current forces still conclude that the United States cannot afford the type of future navy such a strategy implies. They argue that, if only the funds devoted to new carrier battle groups were shifted to Central Front defense, NATO would be capable of successful direct defense, preserving the territorial integrity of the Alliance without the need for risky attacks on Soviet strategic forces. The argument is superficially plausible. On closer examination, however, it is flawed.

The first flaw is the implicit assumption that funds "saved" from the Navy would be devoted to European defense in sufficient quantities to dramatically alter the situation. Little in recent history suggests that such a proposition is valid. NATO's unwillingness to devote sufficient resources to direct defense in Europe is a long-standing problem; there is no logical reason to assume that the Alliance would become more willing if the United States reduced spending on its Navy.

The second flaw in this argument is a blurring of time frames. If increased conventional capability is a solution at all, it is a solution for the future. But strategists have an obligation to decide how to fight a war *today*. While the Maritime Strategy logically requires the naval buildup that has come to be called the 600-ship navy, the strategy is valid today, before all of that navy is at sea. Alternatives are not.

Finally, those who would shift resources away from maritime capabilities have elected to compete with the Soviets almost entirely on their terms. Such an approach—opposing one of the largest land armies in history in a high intensity conflict on the territory of U.S. allies—carries with it the twin possibilities of the political collapse or the devastation of NATO, possibilities equally as grave as the escalation risks that critics deplore. . . .

The Maritime Strategy and Deterrence in Europe

JOHN J. MEARSHEIMER

. . . . This article explores the wisdom of the Reagan Administration's naval buildup by assessing the overall effect of the Maritime Strategy on deterrence in Europe.* America's central military objective, aside from deterring a direct attack on the United States, is to deter the Soviet Union from starting a European war. Strategically, Europe is the most important area of the world for the United States, and is the place where the Soviet Union has concentrated its most formidable military assets. A European war would therefore directly threaten America's vital interests. Such a war also could jeopardize the survival of the United States if it escalated to a nuclear exchange. Deterring the Soviet threat to NATO, especially the Soviet conventional threat, is therefore the baseline case against which the Maritime Strategy should be measured. This is not to deny the importance of other contingencies, but simply to point out that NATO is the most important and most demanding contingency confronting the American military. Indeed, the Navy itself has long recognized that its chief role lies in its contribution to a global conventional war against the Soviet Union and that such a war would be, above all, a war for the control of Europe. Accordingly, the Navy has argued that the Maritime Strategy would indeed

From "A Strategic Misstep: The Maritime Strategy and Deterrence in Europe" by John J. Mearsheimer, *International Security,* Fall 1986 (Vol. 11, No. 2), pp. 3–57. © 1986 by the President and Fellows of Harvard College and of the Massachusetts Institute of Technology. Reprinted by permission of MIT Press, Cambridge, Massachusetts, and the copyright holders. Portions of the text have been omitted; all referential and some explanatory footnotes have also been omitted.

*This article was originally prepared for the Naval War College's May 1985 conference on the Maritime Strategy. I would like to thank James Kurth, who was then Director of the Strategy and Campaign Department at the War College, for suggesting the topic to me, as well as the many conference participants who offered comments on my original draft. I also am deeply indebted to the following individuals for comments on later drafts of this article: Robert Art, Richard Betts, Daniel Bolger, Michael Brown, Owen Cote, Michael Desch, Benjamin Frankel, Charles Glaser, Karl Lautenschläger, Robert Pape, Barry Posen, George Quester, Rade Radovich, Jack Snyder, Peter Swartz, and Andrew Twomey. None bears any responsibility for the arguments offered here. Finally, I would like to thank the MacArthur Foundation for providing support.

contribute to NATO's European deterrent posture. In this article, I explore whether this is true.

I will offer four principal conclusions. First, the Navy has not defined the Maritime Strategy clearly and, moreover, has defined it in different ways at different times. The strategy therefore tends to have an amorphous and elastic quality about it. Nevertheless, it seems apparent that the strategy is a package of four different offensive postures. The Navy has occasionally shifted its rhetorical emphasis from one to another of these four postures, but all four have remained elements of the Maritime Strategy since it was formulated in 1981.

Second, the four offensive concepts encompassed by the Maritime Strategy contribute little to deterrence in Europe and may actually detract from it. Importantly, the latest variant of the strategy, which emphasizes using American attack submarines (SSNs) to strike at Soviet ballistic missile submarines (SSBNs) so as to shift the strategic nuclear balance at the start of a conventional war, is destabilizing in a crisis and potentially escalatory in a conflict, and therefore is a dangerous strategy.

Third, the Navy's main value for deterrence lies in the realm of sea control, where protection of NATO's sea lines of communication (SLOCs) might matter to Soviet decision-makers contemplating war in Europe. The Navy can counter this threat with a defensive sea control strategy. It is not necessary or desirable to adopt an offensive strategy to protect the SLOCs.

Finally, as a result of the Reagan Administration's policy of favoring the Navy over NATO's ground and tactical air forces, a significant opportunity to improve NATO's deterrent posture has been missed. Moreover, the seeds of future defense policy crises have been sown. In fact, if (as is widely forecast) future defense budgets do not grow significantly and if the Reagan Administration continues to favor the Navy at the expense of the forces in Europe, NATO's deterrent posture may actually be weakened. . . .

COMPETING VIEWS OF THE NAVY'S ROLE IN DETERRING WAR IN EUROPE

The U.S. Navy has four broad missions. The first is nuclear deterrence, for which the Navy relies mainly on SSBNs. The second mission is peacetime presence, which calls for maintaining naval forces around the world on a day-to-day basis. The aim is to use them to influence both allies and potential adversaries. The third mission is direct military intervention in Third World conflicts, while the fourth is deterring and fighting a large-scale conventional war with the Soviet Union. The first three missions, although certainly essential, are not directly relevant to the Maritime Strategy. Rather, the Maritime Strategy is concerned primarily with the fourth mission, which is largely synonymous with deterring a war in Europe. This fourth mission is the most demanding of the lot and therefore the baseline case against which the Maritime Strategy must be assessed.

The public debate about the Navy's role in deterring a European war is a confusing one. Basic concepts are not well defined, and arguments are often not clearly articulated. To impose order on this subject, it is helpful to think in terms of five alternative views about the role that the Navy might play.

The "Naval Irrelevance" Position

This first position holds that the Navy contributes very little to deterrence in Europe. The fundamental assumption here is that the Soviet Union is essentially a land power and, in deciding whether to initiate war with NATO, would pay little attention to naval considerations. The Soviets would instead focus almost wholly on calculations regarding those ground and air forces that would be directly engaged in the land battle. . . . The case for naval irrelevance is buttressed by the fact that blockade, a traditional naval weapon against land powers, has virtually no utility against a largely autarkic power like the Soviet Union. The principal implications of this position for NATO are that maintaining SLOCs should not be accorded a high priority and that the United States does not need a large navy.

The "Sea Control" Position

A second position holds that sea control *might* matter for deterrence. The Soviets, so the argument goes, would certainly focus on the balance of forces on the Central Front, asking themselves whether a blitzkrieg is feasible. A situation might arise, however, in which they conclude that their prospects for success in the ground war are slim, but that there is a good chance that they can sever the Atlantic SLOCs and thereby bring NATO to its knees. This would be a defensible option only if: there was tremendous political pressure on the Soviets to go to war and as a result they were willing to pursue a risk-laden military strategy; and it appeared that the SLOCs could be cut in some reasonably short period of time—say six to nine months. Although it is difficult to imagine the Soviets turning to their navy to provide the margin of victory in a European land war, this might happen. In such a case, the U.S. Navy would matter for deterrence. Therefore, NATO must ensure that the Soviets are never in a position where they might conclude that although a war of attrition on the Central Front is likely, they could win that war in some reasonably short time frame by cutting NATO's SLOCs.

To succeed, a sea control strategy must neutralize the Soviets' Northern Fleet, which poses the principal threat to NATO's SLOCs. This fleet is based on the Kola Peninsula, in the Arctic, east of northern Finland. Its principal elements are surface ships, attack submarines, ballistic missile submarines, and land-based aircraft. Of these forces, Soviet attack submarines comprise the main element of the threat to the SLOCs, although NATO must also be concerned about Soviet long-range bombers, Backfires in particular, that could reach the North Atlantic.

NATO could deal with this threat by either defensive or offensive sea control. Defensive sea control would involve three tasks: sealing off the Soviet attack submarines with a formidable barrier defense in the Greenland-Iceland-Norway (GIN) gap, a major choke point through which those submarines must pass to reach NATO's SLOCs; conducting open-ocean anti-submarine warfare (ASW) operations in the area of the Atlantic directly below the GIN gap to neutralize those attack submarines that penetrate the barrier; and providing troop and supply convoys with ASW assets.[1] The Backfire threat would be met with interceptor aircraft based in Britain, Iceland, Norway, and possibly Greenland. An offensive sea control strategy would include those same tasks but would add the task of moving north of the GIN gap to strike directly at Soviet SSNs, Soviet surface ships, naval bases, air bases, and aircraft located on the Kola Peninsula. This added task would be emphasized over the others.

Proponents of offensive sea control make their case on three grounds. First, they argue that the threat to move north forces the Soviets to hold their attack submarines in their home waters, thus keeping them away from the SLOCs. Second, they believe that it is militarily more efficient to defeat the Soviet SSN and Backfire threats in the far north than at the GIN barrier. The best way to deal with the threat to the SLOCs, in other words, is not to wait for the adversary to attempt to surge attack submarines into the North Atlantic, as mandated by defensive sea control, but to go directly to the root of the problem and eliminate it. Third, proponents suggest that an offensive strategy is essential to protect northern Norway from a Soviet attack. In this view, carrier operations in the Norwegian Sea are essential to fight off Backfire attacks against northern Norway and to provide air cover for NATO forces operating in that

---

[1] The GIN gap, which covers about 1000 miles of water and runs from Greenland to Iceland to the United Kingdom to Norway, is sometimes referred to as the GIUK gap. This is a misnomer, however, since the GIUK gap actually includes only the western part of the GIN gap—covering as it does only the 750 miles of water between Greenland, Iceland, and the United Kingdom, while excluding the water between the U.K. and Norway. The other key barrier in this area is the Bear Island–North Cape line which is north of the GIN gap and which essentially separates the Barents and Norwegian seas.

region. The Soviets would gain, without doubt, an important strategic advantage by capturing this area, since it would allow them to project power more easily into the lower reaches of the Norwegian Sea as well as against the SLOCs. There is, however, disagreement about whether offensive sea control is necessary to prevent that outcome.

Offensive sea control is the more demanding of the two strategies since it alone calls for taking offensive action against a powerful naval force that would have considerable assistance from land-based forces. The offensive, in its most ambitious form, would be comprised of two major operations. First, American SSNs would destroy the Soviet SSN force in the Norwegian and Barents seas. In what is called a "rollback campaign," attacking American SSNs would form themselves into lines in the Norwegian Sea and then move north to engage Soviet SSNs. The northernmost line might be located as far north as the Bear Island–North Cape gap, and even possibly in the Barents Sea. Second, after completion of the first operation, carrier battle groups would move into the upper reaches of the Norwegian Sea and launch air strikes or cruise missile strikes against naval and air bases on the Kola Peninsula. This operation would presumably eliminate the air threat to NATO's SLOCs. The Soviet Northern Fleet's surface navy, which would be involved in defense of the Barents Sea, would surely be sought out and attacked in both of these operations. Soviet SSBNs are another matter. They are not essential targets in an operation concerned with sea control and, in all likelihood, many of them would not be in harm's way. Nevertheless, as will be discussed, a successful offensive sea control strategy would pose a significant threat to these strategic nuclear forces. . . .

The force posture requirements of defensive and offensive sea control are quite different. Defensive sea control does not require aircraft carrier battle groups and cruise missile platforms. The emphasis instead is on attack submarines, land-based patrol aircraft, destroyers, and frigates. These weapons are ideally suited for barrier defense, convoying, and wide-area ASW operations in the North Atlantic. By contrast, an offensive sea control strategy requires aircraft carrier battle groups, cruise missile platforms, and a very robust SSN force, while it places less emphasis on destroyers and especially frigates.

The "Direct Naval Impact" Position

. . . A third position on the role of the Navy—direct naval impact—. . . [holds] that the U.S. Navy [should] strike Soviet targets and thereby directly lessen Soviet prospects of winning a conventional war in Europe. In essence, this is the classic task of power projection.

Such a strategy might include three components, which need not be accorded equal weight. First, the Navy and the Marines might launch amphibious attacks onto the European continent—specifically, the Soviet or Eastern European coasts. The aim would be to create a significant threat in the rear of the Soviet forces fighting on the Central Front. This would presumably divert ground and air forces from the battles along the intra-German border, thus decreasing the Soviets' prospects of winning the critical land and air battles in that area. Second, the Navy could introduce its carrier-based aircraft into the air war on the Central Front. Third, the Navy could mount carrier-based air attacks directly against the Kola Peninsula, which, if successful, might force the Soviets to shift air assets from the Central Front to the Northern Flank. The key assumption underlying the latter two components is that, in a closely contested air war over Europe, these actions by the Navy might provide the margin of victory for NATO.

Striking directly at the Kola Peninsula, the third component, is obviously congruent with offensive sea control. However, critical time constraints are involved when attacking the Kola for the purpose of drawing forces away from the continent. Specifically, the attacks must come early enough in the war to influence events on the Central Front. An air offensive against the Kola coming after NATO had lost the air war in Central Europe would matter little. The same principle applies, of course, to amphibious operations. In short, direct military impact, unlike sea control, involves time-urgent operations.

The force posture implications of direct military impact are similar to those of offensive sea control, since both are concerned with projecting power against the Soviet homeland. Both strategies require a very large and powerful navy with a substantial carrier battle group component. The most important difference is that direct military impact could call for a truly robust amphibious capability, which is not necessary for offensive sea control.

The "Horizontal Escalation" Position

A fourth position calls for using the Navy to threaten Soviet vital interests *outside* of Europe—for instance, Soviet Third World allies such as Cuba or Vietnam, or Soviet naval bases in East Asia. The Soviets, it is assumed, are particularly vulnerable in the Third World or on their own periphery. When struck there, they would be forced either to draw units away from Europe or simply to make concessions in Europe because of the grave threat to these other areas. Horizontal escalation would obviously require a navy built around a large number of carrier battle groups and with a substantial amphibious assault capability. In this regard, it would have much in common with the forces needed for offensive sea control and direct military impact. Horizontal escalation would differ from these two positions, however, in that it would place greater emphasis on strategic mobility assets than would the other two. This reflects the fact that horizontal escalation is a truly global strategy while the other two are focused mainly on Europe. Horizontal escalation, in other words, involves simultaneous operations around the world, while the other two call for sequential operations (which is shorthand for concentrating first on the European theater).

The "Counterforce Coercion" Position

A fifth position holds that the Navy can deter the Soviets from moving against NATO, or could persuade them to terminate the war, by threatening to use American SSNs to eliminate significant numbers of Soviet SSBNs. This policy would represent a counterforce attack against the Soviets' strategic retaliatory forces—although conducted with conventional weapons.

Advocates of this position suggest that the threat of such a counter-SSBN campaign could enhance deterrence in two ways. First, the United States could threaten to sink enough Soviet SSBNs to shift the strategic balance against the Soviets. The key assumption here is that they place so much importance on the nuclear balance that the threat to shift it significantly would deter them or compel them to halt their attack and withdraw.

Secondly, the Navy's counterforce campaign could produce deterrence simply by generating the risk of nuclear war, even if it did not necessarily change the strategic balance. Such a campaign would exemplify Thomas Schelling's notions of "manipulation of risk" or "rocking the boat"—actions taken that endanger both sides in order to deter one side. There is widespread agreement that striking directly at the Soviets' strategic forces in a conventional war would be a risky strategy, simply because of the threat of nuclear escalation. By threatening to pursue such a dangerous strategy—with its potential for events spinning out of control—the Soviets, so the argument goes, would be deterred from starting a war in Europe in the first place. Deterrence, it is said, is not based simply on calculations about the balance of nuclear forces, but also on the stark fear that the U.S. Navy's actions would precipitate a nuclear war. This is deterrence based on the threat of inadvertent or accidental escalation, rather than the threat of coercion based on American nuclear superiority.

The main targets of a counterforce coercion strategy would be Soviet SSBNs, although it is safe to assume that in executing this strategy American SSNs would also destroy large numbers of the Soviets' SSN force as well as a large portion of their surface navy.[2] After all, these forces would be attempting to protect the SSBNs. Thus, the principal targets of a counterforce coercion strategy (SSBNs) are different from those of offensive sea control (SSNs), are different from those of offensive sea control (SSNs), although in practice there would be considerable overlap in the actual target sets. However, the actual operational strategy associated with counterforce coercion is different from the rollback strategy needed for offensive sea control.

Counterforce coercion places a high premium on mobilizing the American SSN force early in a crisis and *inserting* large numbers of those attack submarines deep into the Barents Sea as quickly as possible. This operation is necessary because in a crisis the Soviets would surge large numbers of SSBNs—the principal target—out from their ports to hide under the polar ice cap. There, they would be difficult to find and destroy. The Navy would have to beat the Soviets to the punch by quickly getting attack submarines in positions outside of those ports so that they could pick up and trail the SSBNs as they head toward the ice. If American attack submarines do not move into the Barents before the SSBNs are surged, finding and destroying them would be a difficult task. Such a situation would threaten to undermine the counterforce coercion strategy, since it demands that the nuclear balance be shifted rather quickly— so as to have an impact on the Central Front. It would not make much sense for purposes of coercion for changes in the strategic nuclear balance to occur after Europe had been lost. Thus, the more pessimistic one is about the conventional balance in Europe, the more necessary it becomes to execute the strategy quickly. Since a rollback operation by its very nature would allow large numbers of Soviet SSBNs to get under the ice and would concentrate anyway on pushing back and eliminating the Soviet forces defending the bastion, it is not suited for coercion. The emphasis must instead be on a large-scale insertion operation.

This need to insert SSNs into the Barents Sea to destroy SSBNs notwithstanding, the American Navy would still have to strike at the Soviet SSNs, which would be attempting to protect the SSBNs. Thus, in the final analysis, counterforce coercion would require a large-scale insertion operation as well as a rollback operation. Obviously, this posture could only be executed with a large force of

---

[2] A counterforce coercion strategy would surely involve a major offensive against the 31 SSBNs and SSBs located with the Soviets' Pacific Fleet as well as the 41 SSBNs stationed on the Kola Peninsula. This coercion strategy therefore involves operations that are similar to those required by the variant of the horizontal escalation strategy calling for attacks against Soviet forces in the Far East. . . .

attack submarines. As defined here, counterforce coercion could be accomplished without aircraft carriers, although one could argue that destroying military targets on the Kola Peninsula would facilitate the Navy's efforts. This posture obviously requires a powerful navy with significant offensive capability.

The Maritime Strategy can best be understood in terms of the five positions outlined in [this] section. . . . The Maritime Strategy is, in effect, an inclusive package of four offensive postures: direct naval impact, horizontal escalation, offensive sea control, and counterforce coercion. (The Navy categorically rejects the naval irrelevance and defensive sea control postures.) . . .

DIRECT MILITARY IMPACT AND HORIZONTAL ESCALATION

Direct Military Impact

The Navy has not argued forcefully about the deterrent value of direct military impact, perhaps because the case is so weak. All three of the principal scenarios for using the Navy in this way lack plausibility.

Consider amphibious operations against the Soviet mainland, which would entail a major landing operation along the coast of either the Baltic or Black sea. The aim would be to create such a formidable threat in the Soviets' rear that they would have to pull a substantial number of forces away from the Central Front. This is a completely unrealistic scenario for three reasons. First, it would be essential that the attacking forces have control of the air and seas in and around the landing area. The landing forces must be protected from enemy air and naval strikes. Moreover, a major amphibious operation against the Soviet Union would require substantial fire support from air and naval forces, support that would not be forthcoming if those forces were themselves vulnerable to enemy air and submarine attacks. Thus, it would be imperative that the assaulting forces dominate the air and sea. This would almost certainly not be the case in the Baltic and Black seas. The Soviets have ground-based air defenses in these regions as well as large numbers of land-based anti-ship missiles. Furthermore, they maintain powerful fleets in both seas, and large numbers of land-based aircraft are within easy striking distance of these coasts. Also, it would be extremely difficult to achieve tactical surprise because the attacking forces would have to move through restricted routes of passage to get into either sea. Soviet surveillance would surely discover the assault forces early and move to destroy them before they reached the landing areas. The Baltic and the Black seas would be veritable hornets' nests in a war and hardly suitable for amphibious operations.

Second, the United States has a limited amphibious lift capability.

The Navy, which has long considered it a low-order priority, is now in the process of procuring enough ships to increase its amphibious assault capability by approximately one Marine brigade, from one Marine division to 1½ Marine divisions. These would be essentially light infantry forces which would be at a real disadvantage against Soviet heavy mechanized and armored divisions. This is hardly a formidable threat against a power like the Soviet Union, assuming, of course, that the Navy could insert that force into the Soviets' rear. To have a significant impact on the Central Front, where scores of divisions would be locked in combat, the Navy would have to insert more than a reinforced division. Instead for NATO to have any chance with an amphibious operation against the Soviet mainland would require a striking force of at least five divisions, something on the scale of the Allied force that landed at Normandy in June 1944. Furthermore, NATO would need reinforcements, most of which would have to be heavy divisions. NATO does not have and is not likely to develop such a capability, if for no other reason than because it would mean taking land forces away from the Central Front and naval forces away from their planned offensive against the Northern Fleet. No rational NATO planner would pull forces away from those main engagements to attempt a highly risky amphibious operation in the Baltic or Black sea. . . .

Finally, even if NATO were able to raise such a force of five or more divisions and somehow manage to land it in the Soviets' rear, it most likely would not be capable of presenting so serious a threat to the Soviets that they would have to draw forces away from the Central Front. First, it is not clear that NATO could maintain lines of communication with the attacking forces. The Soviets would bring substantial air and naval assets to bear to cut off the amphibious forces from their source of supply. Second, the Soviets should have adequate ground forces to check the amphibious forces without having to pull units from the Central Front. They have a large pool of divisions near the potential landing areas which they could draw upon to meet the attacking forces. If NATO were to develop a formidable amphibious capability, the Soviets would certainly make preparations to shift those forces in the actual event. Furthermore, because the Soviets would enjoy internal lines of communication and because they have good rail and road systems, they should be able to shift forces quickly enough to contain a NATO assault force. In sum, a major amphibious operation against the Soviet mainland is *not* a serious threat and offers little promise of enhancing NATO's deterrent posture.

What about the Navy's claim that carrier-based air might play a key role in the air war over Central Europe? This argument cannot be taken too seriously simply because neither the Navy nor NATO plans to use naval tactical air for this purpose. After all, the Navy's primary rationale for carrier task forces in a European conflict is that they are necessary for projecting power against the Kola Peninsula, not for helping win the air war on the Central Front. One certainly cannot rule out the possibility that carrier-based aircraft would be used in the air war over Germany, but it must again be emphasized that NATO's deterrent posture largely ignores that possibility and depends instead on Air Force tactical fighters.

There is a fundamental problem with relying on carrier-based air to provide the margin of victory in the air war over the Central Front. The cost of procuring a fixed number of naval tactical aircraft is much greater than the cost of procuring the same number of Air Force replacement aircraft. It is not the aircraft that account for the difference but the fact that, when calculating the price of naval air, it is necessary to include the enormous cost of the entire carrier battle group. In short, building naval air for the Central Front is a very inefficient way to buy tactical air power. If the purpose is to improve NATO's chances in the air war over Europe, it would make much more sense to use resources allocated to the Navy to buy additional Air Force fighters.

Finally, there is the issue that the threat of a successful naval offensive against the Kola Peninsula would cause the Soviets to pause when contemplating a blitzkrieg in Europe. Specifically, it has been suggested here that a naval victory on the Northern Flank might force the Soviets to transfer much-needed air units from the European heartland to the Kola—reducing their chances for success in the main land battles. Although Navy spokesmen do not often make this argument, it is important to consider.

The first problem with it is lack of credibility. It is not at all obvious that the national command authorities would allow the Navy to strike at the Kola Peninsula and, even if allowed to do so, it is not clear that the Navy would achieve a major success. These matters will be discussed in greater detail in subsequent sections. Suffice it to say here that the Navy, if sent to strike north, would face a very formidable task.

Second, if the Soviets were pressed to send additional air units to the Northern Flank, they could be drawn from units in regions not directly involved with the conflict on the Central Front.[3] Third, there is the time factor. The Soviets are likely to go to war only if they believe that there is a good chance that they can win a quick and decisive victory. Should they reach such a conclusion, it would

---

[3] The Soviets have a very large number of tactical aircraft as well as a formidable fleet of medium and long-range bombers. Air units from regions not directly involved in the fighting on the Central Front could be easily and quickly moved to the Kola Peninsula in a conflict. . . .

not be unrealistic for them to think in terms of effectively crippling NATO in 10–14 days. After all, NATO lacks strategic depth and employs most of its forces in forward positions. An American naval offensive, on the other hand, would probably take considerable time to execute. Carrier-based strikes against the Kola Peninsula, for example, would not take place until after the Northern Fleet's SSNs and surface navy had been rolled back; and that difficult task would probably take much time (several weeks or months) to accomplish. . . .

The key point here is that the Soviets' time frame for executing a successful blitzkrieg would, in all likelihood, be short enough that events on the Northern Flank would not upset it in any way.

Fourth, even if the Navy is capable of executing an offensive against the Kola Peninsula in a relatively short period of time, the resulting threat to the Soviet Union would not be very great. The Soviet Union is a great land power that cannot be hurt badly by naval strikes against its periphery. For the Soviets, and ultimately for NATO, Central Europe is where a major conventional war would be settled. The Navy could score a stunning victory on the Northern Flank, and it would be all for naught if NATO failed to check the Soviets in the land battle on the intra-German border. The Soviets, after consolidating their position on the continent, would then have little difficulty eliminating the threat on their northern flank. There would therefore be no compelling reason for the Soviets to pull units away from the Central Front. In short, a Soviet decision to launch a blitzkrieg would probably not be affected by the threat of naval strikes against the Kola Peninsula.

Horizontal Escalation

The Reagan Administration was initially attracted to horizontal escalation as a deterrent posture. However, except for the Navy, there no longer appears to be much interest in this strategy. This is probably because such a strategy does little to enhance deterrence— especially for NATO. One of the principal difficulties is finding an appropriate target. No area in the Third World compares in importance to Western Europe. Surely, the consequences for the Soviet Union of "losing" Angola, Cuba, or Vietnam would be nowhere near as great as the consequences to the United States of seeing Western Europe fall into Soviet hands. As a result, the Soviets would not be deterred by the prospect of the loss of those areas and probably would not move significant forces to defend them. The net result would be that American forces, but not Soviet forces, would be diverted from the crucial battle in Europe into campaigns that held little strategic significance. Furthermore, as the United States learned in Southeast Asia, America's ability to influence the course of events in the Third World is limited, so American horizontal escalations could develop into costly enterprises. It is, in short, simply not plausible to think in terms of threatening the Soviets with a tit-for-tat strategy in which they take Europe and the United States takes an area of comparable value in the Third World.

One might argue that the threat of a major military strike on the Soviet periphery would force the Soviets to pull units away from the Central Front. This kind of offensive would have to be directed at Soviet forces in the Far East, since this is the only important Soviet area *outside* of Europe that is vulnerable to attack by powerful naval forces. The logic here is analogous to the claim that direct strikes against the Kola Peninsula would weaken the Soviets' position in Central Europe. The flaws in the argument are similar. The Soviets could afford to absorb a temporary beating in the Far East while they were rolling up NATO's forces in Central Europe. A setback on the periphery would not weaken their European effort in any meaningful way and, moreover, once the Soviets had consolidated their position in Western Europe, they could move massive forces to deal with problems on their periphery. In any event, it is not clear that the Navy could inflict a significant defeat on Soviet forces in the Far East. The Soviets have formidable military forces in this area, and they could transfer forces from areas other than Central Europe to this theater. The Navy likes to emphasize the ease with which it could move forces around the Soviet periphery, giving the impression that it could bring greater force to bear at the point of attack than could the Soviets. This is a dubious claim. . . .

Finally, a major non-European offensive would employ forces that could otherwise be used in Europe. It takes NATO forces to divert Soviet forces, and there is no evidence, as implied in arguments for horizontal escalation, that NATO could force the Pact to divert more forces than NATO would divert. Thus, there is no evidence that NATO could improve the force ratio in Europe by pursuing a horizontal escalation strategy.

Sea Power In The Industrial Age

The inadequacies of direct military impact and horizontal escalation as deterrent postures extend beyond their particulars to include the general view of military power that underpins them. Advocates of both strategies tend toward a Mahanian view of military power. They believe that control of the seas is the key ingredient for great power status. . . . Underlying this belief is the core assumption that, in the competition between land power and sea power, the latter has distinct advantages that derive mainly from the flexibility inherent in naval forces. For these neo-Mahanians, offensively oriented naval forces provide the key for gaining advantage over a land power like the Soviet Union.

This view of power in the international system is fundamentally flawed and has little application to the U.S.-Soviet competition. Mahan's theories, as is widely recognized by scholars, were largely outdated when they were written. Furthermore, the notion that "the sea is . . . the major arena of competition" between great powers is probably an accurate description of the past conflict between Japan and the United States, but it is not an accurate assessment of the present superpower rivalry. Nor is it an accurate description of the British-German competition in the first half of this century. The Soviet Union, like Germany before it, is a continental power that threatens to take control of the Eurasian heartland, an area of tremendous strategic importance. Consequently, a rival power, be it Britain or the United States, has no alternative but to treat the Eurasian heartland as the principal arena of competition. . . .

The only suitable military lever that can bring pressure against a continental power is a strong army amply supported with tactical air forces. It is worth noting here that at the time of the infamous Munich accord the British chiefs of staff concluded that Britain, because it lacked an army that could be employed on the continent, had no choice but to appease Hitler. Britain's navy was simply not an effective instrument for confronting the likes of the Third Reich. The same is true with regard to the American Navy and the Soviet Union. The neo-Mahanian threats of horizontal escalation and direct military impact simply do not provide a satisfactory posture for deterring a formidable land power like the Soviet Union.

It would be a mistake to conclude from this discussion that NATO should not be concerned with the naval dimension of a conventional war with the Soviet Union. The evidence from both world wars makes it clear that a continental power with a robust submarine force can seriously threaten an insular power that is either heavily dependent on imports or has to project forces and materials across wide oceans. The Germans, in both wars, came dangerously close to knocking Britain out of the war with their U-boats, and although it is not widely recognized, American submarines greatly reduced Japan's warfighting capability by cutting its SLOCs.

The principal lesson to be derived from the historical record is *not* that an insular power with a large surface navy can use that force to threaten a continental power but, on the contrary, that a continental power armed with submarines is a very real threat to an insular power. It is the United States, not the Soviet Union, that must concern itself with falling victim to the other side's naval power. Thus, in the final analysis, the central question is not whether the United States can hurt the Soviets with its navy, but whether NATO can protect its SLOCs from Soviet submarines. Sea control is the key issue.

OFFENSIVE SEA CONTROL

It is not likely that Soviet calculations about the SLOC battle will have much influence on a decision to launch a war against NATO since that decision would probably be based on an assessment of their prospects in the ground war. Nevertheless, NATO must be concerned with the scenario in which the Soviets conclude that they are not likely to effect a blitzkrieg, but that there is a reasonable chance that they can defeat NATO by cutting its SLOCs in a few months' time. NATO must ensure that it has a sufficiently strong sea control capability that this situation never occurs. In this regard, the Navy matters for deterrence on the Central Front. The key issue, however, is whether offensive sea control is necessary to secure the SLOCs or whether that goal is best served by a defensive sea control strategy.

The balance of evidence suggests that offensive sea control is not an appropriate deterrent strategy for NATO. In the first place, it is not a credible strategy. Simply put, it is unlikely that the national command authorities would allow the Navy to pursue such a strategy in a conventional war. In addition, it is not necessary for the Navy to strike north to protect NATO's SLOCs. A robust defensive sea control posture would provide adequate protection.

The credibility of the Navy's threat to move north to protect the SLOCs depends on three factors. First is the matter of feasibility. It is not clear that the Navy, even a 600-ship navy, could roll back the Soviets' Northern Fleet navy and then launch devastating attacks against the Kola Peninsula. Second are the problems of inadvertent and accidental escalation. An offensive strategy carries a real risk of nuclear escalation, and NATO decision-makers will surely want to avoid a situation in which a conventional war escalates extempore. Finally, there is the matter of necessity. Policymakers might be willing to set aside the problems of feasibility and nuclear escalation if they conclude that NATO has no choice but to strike north to guarantee protection of the SLOCs. Since this is not the case, offensive sea control is neither credible nor necessary.

The Prospects for Successful Implementation

The Navy's prospects for rolling back Soviet naval forces in the Norwegian and Barents seas and then eliminating the important military installations and forces located on the Kola Peninsula are not good. This would not be an easy task in general, for it has become increasingly difficult in the 20th century for naval forces to strike effectively against powerful land-based forces. . . .

There are three specific reasons why it would be difficult for the Navy to roll back Soviet naval forces located in the Norwegian and especially the Barents seas. First, it is not apparent that the balance of forces would work to NATO's advantage. The Soviets have a large number of submarines in their Northern Fleet: 41 ballistic missile submarines and 140 attack and cruise missile submarines. Some of these submarines are old and would be of limited utility against modern American attack submarines. Still, approximately 75 percent of the Soviets' most modern attack submarines are in these northern waters. The American Navy, once it achieves the Maritime Strategy's goal of 100 attack submarines, would normally maintain about 56 of those SSNs in the Atlantic and about 44 in the Pacific. The Navy stresses that it would not swing forces from the Pacific to the Atlantic. It seems reasonable to assume that about six of those 56 submarines would be in overhaul at any one time. Furthermore, about 20 of the 50 operational attack submarines in the Atlantic would probably have to be used for defending the GIN barrier, protecting carrier battle groups, and possibly escorting high-value convoys across the Atlantic.[4] The Navy would therefore have about 30 attack submarines to send north against a total force of 181 Soviet submarines. Not counting Soviet SSBNs brings that number down to 140. There is no doubt that American submarines have a qualitative edge over their Soviet counterparts. Nevertheless, the Navy maintains that this qualitative edge has eroded markedly over the past decade and that the Navy now needs anywhere from 115 to 140 attack submarines to carry out its strategy. In short, it is not easy to assess what is likely to happen in a submarine war in northern waters. After all, there has never been a submarine versus submarine war, and military history demonstrates that outnumbered forces occasionally prevail in war. Nevertheless, it is difficult to be confident about the Navy's assumption that its submarines would score greater than 3:1 exchange ratios in Soviet waters.

Second, the Soviet submarine force will be assisted by an impressive array of land-based aircraft and surface combatants assigned to the Northern Fleet. These forces are specifically designed to participate in ASW operations.

Third, the Soviets have a huge arsenal of mines, which promises to complicate American efforts to move swiftly into this northern bastion. To compound these difficulties, the NATO navies, and

---

[4] This number, which is admittedly a rough calculation, is based on the assumption that the Navy would send ⅔ to ¾ of its available attack submarines north to strike at the Soviet fleet. This assumption is derived from interviews.

particularly the American, have a weak countermine capability.
. . . In sum, it will be difficult for the American Navy to roll back
the Soviet Northern Fleet.

It may be the case, however, that the American Navy is such a
superb fighting force that it would ultimately eliminate the majority
of the adversary's fleet. Let us assume that the Navy has successfully rolled back the Northern Fleet, driving the remnants of that
force into their bases on the Kola, and that the time has arrived to
move the carriers forward and strike directly at the Kola Peninsula.
This too would be a very difficult mission. The Soviets would
undoubtedly have had considerable time to augment their already
formidable forces and to fortify their defensive positions. These
forces would present two different problems for the carriers. First,
the Soviets would have a larger number of Backfire bombers, cruise
missiles, and other strike systems that could be used against the
carriers. Second, the Soviets would employ large numbers of fighter
aircraft as well as surface-to-air missiles (SAMs) and anti-aircraft
artillery (AAA) to defend the Kola Peninsula. Thus, even if the
carriers survive, their strike aircraft would be flying into the teeth
of a well-armed defender.

Other considerations cast doubt on the likelihood of the Navy
successfully silencing the Soviet threat on the Kola Peninsula. First,
the number of attacking aircraft that a handful of carriers could
muster for an air offensive is not great. There are limits to how
many aircraft could be placed on a carrier, and furthermore, a
substantial number of them would have to be used to defend the
carriers.[5] It is therefore not surprising that the Joint Chiefs of Staff
maintain that the Navy would need 22 carriers, not the currently
programmed 15, to execute its chosen strategy.

Second, even if the Navy enjoys great success with its initial air
strikes, Soviet air power in that region would not be "finished off"
in any meaningful sense. The Soviets would simply move air units
from other areas of the Soviet Union to the Northern Flank. It is
not possible to inflict a knockout blow against the Soviet air forces;
the air war would be a protracted one. This is one of the central
lessons of the air war in World War II. In that war, the United States
and its allies, despite inflicting a series of major defeats on the

[5] There are generally about 90 aircraft on a carrier, and about 34 of them are
designated attack aircraft. See Alan H. Shaw, *Costs of Expanding and Modernizing
the Navy's Carrier-Based Air Forces* (Washington, D.C.: U.S. Congressional Budget
Office, May 1982), p. 4. Thus, if three carriers were placed in the upper reaches of
the Norwegian Sea, the Navy would have only about 100 attack aircraft to strike
against a wide variety of heavily defended targets. This small force hardly generates
confidence. The Navy, if it is serious about launching a large-scale air offensive
against the Kola Peninsula, would surely have to augment its forces with *significant*
numbers of land-based fighters and bombers.

German and Japanese air forces in the early years of the war, were not able to establish complete dominance of the air until the late stages of the war. Earlier, the Luftwaffe scored a great victory against the Soviet air forces in the opening weeks of June 1941, but the Soviets nevertheless recovered.

Third, the Navy does not have many replacements or the capability of quickly generating replacements for either carriers or air wings lost in combat. The Navy, in short, is not well-suited to fight a protracted air war on NATO's Northern Flank. These considerations point up that there are substantial reasons for doubting whether the U.S. Navy could successfully execute its forward offensive strategy.

The Threat of Escalation

The majority of Soviet SSBNs are located with the Northern Fleet. There is widespread agreement in the Navy and the intelligence community at large that the principal mission of the Northern Fleet's other assets, its SSNs and surface forces, is to protect those SSBNs. Soviet forces in the Barents Sea, in other words, would be principally concerned with preventing American naval forces—especially SSNs—from reaching their SSBN sanctuaries. An offensive sea control strategy calls for strikes into the Barents, not for the purpose of eliminating Soviet SSBNs, but to destroy Soviet SSNs, which are the main threat to NATO's SLOCs. The aim would be to ensure that the Soviets cannot stage another "Battle of the Atlantic." There is, however, a major problem with this strategy: an offensive into the Barents Sea, regardless of intentions, would seriously threaten Soviet strategic nuclear forces, thus raising the specter of nuclear escalation.

The Navy, in pursuing a strategy of offensive sea control, might simply decide *not* to attempt to discriminate between Soviet SSBNs and SSNs, but to destroy all Soviet submarines. The rationale need not be linked to the counterforce coercion posture, but could instead include the following arguments: when a state goes to war, it should go all-out to defeat the adversary; because Soviet SSBNs are well equipped to destroy attack submarines, it would be dangerous to grant them immunity; the tactical situation facing the American attack submarines (i.e., the intermingling of Soviet SSBNs and SSNs) would not permit discrimination without placing the attacking SSNs in jeopardy; and the Navy simply does not have the intelligence capability to discriminate among Soviet submarines in a fast-paced conflict. There is little doubt that in this case an offensive sea control strategy would result in the destruction of some portion of the Soviets' strategic retaliatory forces.

There is, however, the possibility that the Navy would try to avoid striking Soviet SSBNs, but it is not clear that this would be possible in practice. Indeed, even if the Navy could technically discriminate SSNs from SSBNs, Soviet defensive strategy might call for co-mingling the two kinds of submarines. The attacking forces would then have no choice but to destroy SSBNs as well as SSNs. The best case that can be made for a discriminating strategy is that the Soviets would, in fact, accommodate it by placing their SSBNs under the polar ice cap, while locating the majority of their SSNs in the Norwegian and Barents seas to do battle with American attack submarines. Thus, the rollback strategy would largely involve a battle between rival SSN forces. Assuming this proves to be the case, successful execution of the strategy would still seriously threaten the Soviet SSBN force. The shield that protects the SSBNs would be destroyed, leaving them exposed to American attack submarines. Furthermore, the Navy plans to smash all military installations on the Kola Peninsula, which means elimination of the SSBNs' ports. . . . Thus, despite the best intentions, a discriminating strategy would probably not mean very much to Soviet decisionmakers intent on preserving their SSBN force.

In sum, an offensive sea control strategy would seriously threaten one leg of the Soviets' strategic triad. Whether intended or not, this deterrent posture would have the markings of a strategic ASW campaign and would therefore create risks of inadvertent nuclear escalation. The Soviets probably would not stand idly by while the strategic nuclear balance shifted against them. There would undoubtedly be pressure, which would grow as Soviet strategic assets were destroyed, to strike at American nuclear forces or to use Soviet nuclear weapons against selected NATO targets. Moreover, in addition to the risk of deliberate Soviet escalation provoked inadvertently by the United States, there would be the additional risk of accidental nuclear escalation against the wishes of both sides—meaning escalation in which individual commanders fire nuclear weapons before national command authorities on either side have decided to go to nuclear war. This could arise because of the uncontrolled or unforeseen interactions of local forces.

In a conventional war between the superpowers, American policymakers would almost surely go to great lengths to prevent nuclear escalation. Therefore, a good case can be made that they would not allow the Navy to launch an offensive against the Northern Fleet. Whether they are seriously tempted to overlook these risks and pursue such a strategy would depend on military feasibility and strategic necessity. As emphasized, there is good reason to doubt that the Navy could actually execute the strategy. Let us now consider whether offensive sea control is required for SLOC protection.

Is Offensive Sea Control Necessary?

The Navy's case for offensive sea control rests on three beliefs: (1) an offensive strategy forces the Soviets to keep their SSNs in their home waters, where they are not a threat to the SLOCs; (2) offensive sea control is militarily more efficient than defensive sea control; and (3) an offensive strategy is essential for keeping northern Norway out of Soviet hands. These arguments are flawed. NATO does not need an offensive sea control strategy. In fact, NATO's deterrent posture would be better served by the defensive alternative.

First, regardless of which sea control strategy the Navy adopts, only a small number of Soviet attack submarines at most are going to leave Soviet home waters and attempt to move into the Atlantic. The SSNs' primary mission is to protect SSBNs, *not* to attack NATO's SLOCs. Navy spokesmen are correct when they emphasize the importance the Soviets place on protecting their strategic nuclear forces. They fear, however, that if the Navy does not have an offensive sea control strategy, Soviet SSNs would be free to roam the Atlantic since there would be no threat of the American Navy moving north.

This fear is unfounded. The Soviet SSNs must remain in home waters to protect the SSBNs—regardless of American declaratory strategy—because of the threat posed by the mere presence of American attack submarines in the area around the GIN gap. They cannot risk leaving their SSBNs exposed to the formidable American SSN force.

For this reason, the Navy should always maintain a powerful attack submarine force with offensive potential. It is not necessary, however, to have an offensive sea control strategy. The best overall sea control strategy lies between pure offense and pure defense: the Navy should maintain an offensive punch but hold it in reserve to deter the Soviets from sending their SSNs to attack the SLOCs. . . .

Let us assume for argument's sake that NATO adopts a strategy of defensive sea control and, as a result, the Soviets attempt to cut NATO's SLOCs. Can they be confident that their navy can accomplish that end and emasculate NATO's fighting power in some reasonably short period of time?

The answer is almost surely no. First, Soviet attack submarines would confront not only the American Navy, but the not-insignificant navies of U.S. allies. NATO's combined navies represent a very formidable fighting force. Second, Soviet SSNs would have to pass through the GIN gap, which NATO has turned into a strong defensive barrier, on their way to *and* from the Atlantic. Third, NATO's land-based tactical aircraft can deal with the Backfire threat

in and around the GIN gap. Finally, NATO's dependence on reinforcement by sea in the early stages of a conflict is not great.
Massive amounts of U.S. equipment and many thousands of American soldiers and airmen are already located in Europe. Moreover,
much of the equipment that American reinforcements would need
in the early stages of a war is prepositioned in Europe. The manpower for those units could be flown in from the United States and
would not depend on sea transportation. It is not surprising, given
these factors, that NATO was confident in the 1970s that it could
protect its SLOCs with a strategy of defensive sea control. The
bottom line is that the Soviets could not be confident of winning the
SLOC war—much less winning it in a reasonably short period of
time—if NATO pursued a defensive sea control posture.

Even if one doubts the efficacy of a defensive sea control strategy, it still seems apparent that, on grounds of military efficiency,
defensive sea control is preferable to offensive sea control. Consider
dealing with the Backfire threat. It would be much easier for NATO
to destroy Backfires in the area around the GIN gap than near the
Kola Peninsula. The Backfires would have virtually no support in
the southern part of the Norwegian Sea, while NATO would have
numerous assets that it could use to target and destroy them. The
situation would be reversed if the battle took place near the Kola
Peninsula. There, the Backfires would be supported by fighter
escorts, while the American Navy's striking forces would surely be
under heavy pressure from the numerous Soviet naval and air forces
in that region. The same logic applies to the submarine war. NATO
could use a variety of assets at the GIN barrier that it probably
would not be able to use in the submarine war in the Barents Sea.
This would include land-based aircraft like the P-3, the American
surface navy, and the sophisticated listening devices that NATO has
deployed in the Norwegian Sea. Correspondingly, the Soviets could
not use their surface navy and their land-based aircraft to support
their submarines at the GIN barrier, while they could do so in the
Barents Sea. The choice between defensive and offensive sea control boils down to a question of whether the Navy is best served by
fighting air battles and SSN battles in the Soviets' backyard, where
the Soviet forces might outnumber NATO forces, or in NATO's
backyard, where NATO forces would outnumber the Soviets. There
is a strong case for preferring the latter location.

Proponents of offensive sea control also argue that offensive
operations are necessary to defend against the Soviet threat to
northern Norway. This is not the case. Close examination of the
terrain in that region and the disposition of forces reveals that NATO
has adequate ground forces for thwarting a Soviet ground attack
launched from the Kola Peninsula. Regarding air support, which the

Navy implies that only carriers can provide, NATO could rely on land-based air forces in Norway. Additional aircraft, if needed, could be flown into those bases. . . .

COUNTERFORCE COERCION

Deterrence is a function of both crisis stability and deterrence stability. It is essential to threaten an adversary with a formidable military posture so that he recognizes that he cannot use force to upset the status quo. At the same time, when dealing with an adversary who is not clearly bent on aggression, it is wise to avoid employing a strategy that gives him any incentive to launch a preemptive strike. The aim in such a situation should be to dampen tensions, not to exacerbate them. This matter of crisis stability was not an important issue for the previous three offensive postures, mainly because they do not require the Navy to take provocative action in a crisis. Counterforce coercion, however, could be quite destabilizing in a crisis. Of course, it is possible that counterforce coercion provides so much deterrence stability that it is worth accepting the danger of crisis instability. However, there is a strong case that this is not so. Counterforce coercion provides very little deterrence stability and is therefore a deficient naval strategy.

Crisis Stability

The root of the crisis stability problem is that a counterforce coercion strategy demands that the American SSN force be mobilized early in a crisis and that large numbers of those attack submarines be inserted deep into the Barents Sea as quickly as possible. If the SSNs are not moved into the Barents before the Soviets surge their SSBNs and move them under the ice, finding and destroying those SSBNs would be a difficult and time-consuming task. Inserting a large number of attack submarines into the Barents Sea during a crisis, however, would be very dangerous for several reasons. First, such a deployment would almost surely be interpreted by the Soviets as an offensive move, signalling offensive American intentions, even if the Americans meant it as a defensive measure that would buttress deterrence. After all, the United States will soon have, with Trident D-5, MX, Minuteman IIIA, nuclear-armed Tomahawk cruise missiles, and the Pershing IIs, a substantial counterforce capability against Soviet land-based ICBMs. This development, coupled with the fact that the Soviets have a small, antiquated, and vulnerable bomber force, means that the two land-based legs of their triad would be in good part vulnerable to an American strike. The survivability of their SSBN force would therefore loom as a much more important matter. Given this situation, the Soviets would almost certainly make worst case assumptions about American intentions if U.S. attack submarines began to position themselves to destroy the Soviet SSBN force. This would probably intensify rather than defuse a crisis.

A second dimension to the crisis stability problem lies in the risk that the Soviets would not stand idly by as American attack submarines moved into their bastion. They would undoubtedly use some of their SSNs to create a barrier defense at the Bear Island-North Cape line and maybe even at the GIN gap. Soviet attack submarines, because they are based closer to these two lines than their American counterparts, should be able to establish defensive positions there before large numbers of American attack submarines reach them. The Americans would then have to decide whether to penetrate these barriers, while the Soviets would have to face the question of whether to attempt to destroy any American submarines that cross the barriers. There would be several compelling reasons for the Soviets to fight at the barriers rather than allow American SSNs to reach the Barents Sea. First, it is important for them to keep the American SSNs far away from their SSBNs. Second, it would not be easy for the Soviets to find the American SSNs once they reached the Barents. They would be easier to locate and target at the barriers. Finally, it is probable that one-on-one SSN engagements, where each submarine knows of the other's presence, would occur at the barriers. There would be an incentive in these confrontations to fire at the opponent, since the side that got off the first shot would stand a good chance of destroying the adversary. It is a straightforward case of the classic gunfighter analogy. To make matters worse, the command and control of submarines is generally poor. It is not difficult in such a circumstance to imagine submarine commanders on either side interpreting their orders liberally and perhaps firing their weapons. This is, without a doubt, the kind of situation to avoid in a crisis.

Even if the Soviets failed to erect barriers or if the American SSNs penetrated them without prompting a naval battle, there would still be significant potential for crisis instability. The Soviets would surely send attack submarines to search the Barents for American SSNs and, moreover, Soviet SSBNs would certainly be on constant look-out for the American submarines. A deadly game of cat and mouse would ensue in which there would be the danger of one-on-one first-shooter-wins engagements as described above. There is the additional possibility that some American submarines would be lost to mines, which the Soviets would undoubtedly use at the barriers and in the Barents Sea. The United States, which would probably not know how these submarines were destroyed, might conclude that Soviet SSNs were responsible and that therefore a response in kind was in order. Finally, in a severe crisis, the Soviets might decide to declare a keep-out zone around their home ports, firing at unidentified submarines that enter. Again, these are the kinds of situations to avoid in a crisis.

Deterrence Stability

Thus, it is apparent that a counterforce coercion posture, when viewed in terms of crisis stability, weakens deterrence. Nevertheless, it might be argued that the strategy provides so much deterrence stability that it is worth accepting the danger of crisis instability. To evaluate this matter, it is necessary to answer three questions. First, how likely is it that the Navy would actually be allowed to execute this variant of the Maritime Strategy? Second, assuming that the Navy is turned loose, is successful execution of the strategy likely? Is an anti-SSBN campaign realizable? Finally, assuming the strategy is operationally effective, what is the Soviet response likely to be? In other words, is a successful anti-SSBN campaign or the threat of one likely to provide the leverage necessary for coercion? It should be emphasized that, since the focus here is on deterring the Soviets, the key issue is how *they* would answer these questions in a crisis. This is obviously impossible to determine with any precision because there is little information about Soviet thinking on these questions and also because it is difficult to predict how decision-makers will behave in an actual crisis. Still, one can make reasonable guesses about each question.

It is *not* likely that the U.S. national command authority would allow the Navy to surge submarines into the Barents Sea during a crisis with the Soviet Union, simply because American policymakers would almost surely try to dampen, not exacerbate, the crisis . . . . The key point, however, is that the deterrent value of the strategy would suffer if it is improbable that the Navy would be allowed to execute it. . . .

A second reason why national command authorities are not likely to allow the Navy to execute counterforce coercion is not related to crisis stability but to the threat of nuclear escalation during a war. There is a danger that a large-scale offensive against the Soviets' northern bastion would lead to nuclear war. American policymakers, who would surely go to great lengths to keep a conventional war from escalating to the nuclear level, would certainly have serious reservations about launching a submarine offensive that is laden with escalatory potential. . . .

It is not clear that the counter-SSBN campaign could succeed quickly if the Navy were allowed to move north. Counterforce coercion, with its emphasis on destroying large numbers of SSBNs in a short period of time, is a demanding strategy. The attacking forces, as emphasized in the discussion of offensive sea control, would be outnumbered and they would be operating in a heavily defended bastion. The Soviets have a variety of assets to protect their SSBNs. Furthermore, the SSBNs themselves could prove to be an elusive target. If, for example, in the very early stages of a crisis, the Soviets were able to move a large number of their SSBNs under the ice before the American attack submarines reached the Barents, those SSBNs would then be difficult to find. Finally, it should be remembered that the Navy has never conducted an operation of this kind under wartime conditions. . . .

Nevertheless, let us assume that in some future conflict the Navy is allowed to pursue a counterforce coercion strategy and, furthermore, that the Navy successfully destroys a large number of SSBNs, markedly shifting the balance of nuclear forces. What are the Soviets likely to do? In other words, is an operationally effective strategy likely to lead to coercion? The Navy assumes that the Soviets would be so disturbed by this shift that they would throw up their hands and agree, in the words of Admiral Watkins, "to end the war on our terms." Presumably, this means that on the continent they would, at the very least, retreat to the prewar borders.

But this is not likely. It is more likely that the Soviets would either ignore the shifting nuclear balance, refusing to be coerced, or would lash back militarily, themselves applying nuclear coercion against NATO.

If they chose to lash back, they would have three principal military options: (1) a strike against U.S. strategic nuclear forces, to redress the strategic balance; (2) a theater nuclear strike against U.S. anti-submarine forces, to cut the American noose before it closes completely on their SSBN force; or (3) a theater nuclear strike against American naval targets as a shot across the bow, or a "manipulation of risk," to introduce the threat of nuclear escalation unless NATO called off its counter-SSBN campaign.

A Soviet strategic strike against some portion of the American nuclear retaliatory force seems possible, although not likely. The Navy maintains that the Soviets would not attempt a strategic nuclear strike because the nuclear balance would be against them. This argument misses the essential point that the very attraction of a counterforce strike is that it would offer the prospect of redressing that balance. If the balance of nuclear forces is as important to the Soviets as the Navy claims, then there would undoubtedly be significant pressure on them to rectify the balance with a counterforce strike. This is not a likely response; it would involve a direct attack on the American homeland and they have other options.

A more attractive response would be to mount limited nuclear attacks against American naval forces and installations, for purposes of either noose-cutting or the manipulation of risk. Targets could include American aircraft carrier battle groups, which are vulnerable, and could be attacked without wide collateral damage. The Soviets should have no shortage of targets since the Maritime Strategy calls for ringing the Soviet Union with carriers and other ships carrying Tomahawk missiles. The Soviets also might consider nuclear strikes against those NATO naval installations in Norway, Iceland, Britain, and Greenland that contribute to the American anti-SSBN campaign or against high value targets in continental Europe.

Such strikes might not do much to cut the American noose, because its crucial element, the SSN force, is not directly vulnerable to nuclear attack. However, such attacks would signal seriousness of purpose and would make clear that the ante could be raised if the American Navy continued to destroy SSBNs. The Soviets could thereby put the last clear chance to avoid uncontrolled escalation on the United States.

As a final option, the Soviets could accept the SSBN losses and operate on the assumption that shifts in the strategic nuclear balance have no political utility. This is a viable strategy as long as the Soviet Union retains a secure assured destruction capability. The United States is unlikely to launch a first-strike against the Soviets as long as they have the capability to inflict massive damage on the American homeland. A counterforce coercion strategy will not eliminate the Soviets' assured destruction capability. The Navy, it should be emphasized, does not call for eliminating all Soviet SSBNs, but argues only for destroying enough SSBNs to shift perceptibly the nuclear balance. Even if the Navy were to eliminate this leg of the Soviet triad, the United States would still not be able to effect a splendid first strike against the triad's other two legs. The Soviets could adopt a launch-on-warning posture, and even if that failed, they could lose 95 percent of their land-based assets and still have a sufficient number of warheads left to wreak unacceptable damage on American society. As long as the Soviets maintain this capability, they can ignore an unfavorable nuclear balance. Those who doubt the logic of this argument should be reminded that little evidence exists that Soviet behavior in the first two decades of the Cold War was affected in any meaningful way by the fact that the balance of nuclear forces clearly favored the United States.

Thus three principal flaws are apparent in arguments that an anti-SSBN offensive would produce deterrence stability by shifting the strategic balance: (1) American political leaders may not allow the Navy to execute the strategy; (2) the Navy may not be capable of implementing it effectively; and (3) a successful anti-SSBN campaign may not coerce the Soviets into better behavior, since the Soviets would have options other than standing down, including escalation on their own part.

Advocates of a counter-SSBN strategy still might argue that such a campaign need not create a meaningful shift in the strategic balance in order to produce stability. Rather, in this view, such a campaign would deter the Soviets simply by generating or manipulating a shared risk of nuclear war. The Soviets, so the argument goes, would be given pause not by concern about the balance of nuclear forces, but by fear that the naval conflict would spin out of control and lead to a strategic nuclear exchange.

There is no question that NATO derives some deterrence stability from this threat, although not a great deal. The principal limiting factor is that, given the triple dangers of crisis instability, inadvertent escalation, and accidental escalation, it is again not likely that the Navy will be allowed to execute the strategy. Therefore, the threat may not be sufficiently credible to produce deterrence.

Is it worth pursuing a counterforce coercion strategy nevertheless, in order to gain the modicum of deterrence stability that its threat of escalation produces? The answer is no, for several reasons. First, this small gain in deterrence stability is far outweighed by the danger of crisis instability inherent in the strategy. Second, it would be the height of irresponsibility for NATO to begin purposely manipulating the risk of nuclear escalation *before* determining the fate of NATO's conventional forces on the Central Front; and a counterforce coercion strategy must be launched immediately upon the outbreak of war. Finally, if it becomes necessary for NATO to manipulate the risk of nuclear escalation, NATO already has forces in Europe that can perform this function in a safer and more credible manner. The express purpose of the American Pershing IIs, ground-launched cruise missiles (GLCMs), and other theater nuclear forces in Europe is to generate the risk of nuclear escalation if the Soviets overrun Europe.[6] These forces have the advantage of producing such risks at the appropriate time (after and only after NATO conventional forces are overrun), and they can do so more credibly than can sea-based forces, since "use or lose" dynamics could operate to persuade NATO commanders to use them. In contrast, an American anti-SSBN campaign generates risk too early and with less credibility.

The bottom line is that a counterforce coercion posture promises little deterrence stability. It is a strategy built on a number of suspect assumptions, and on close scrutiny it hardly generates confidence. When one then considers that the strategy also undermines crisis stability in important ways, the net conclusion is that counterforce coercion is a badly flawed deterrent posture.

---

[6] For an excellent discussion of NATO thinking about the employment of nuclear weapons, see J. Michael Legge, *Theater Nuclear Weapons and the NATO Strategy of Flexible Response,* R-2964-FF (Santa Monica, Calif.: Rand, April 1983), chapter 2.

CONCLUSION

The Maritime Strategy, which can best be described as a loose combination of four offensive concepts (direct military impact, horizontal escalation, offensive sea control, and counterforce coercion) does not contribute much to deterring a war in Europe. Direct military impact and horizontal escalation, which use the Navy to project power against the Soviet Union or its allies, simply have very little deterrent value. Counterforce coercion, the posture the Navy now stresses, actually threatens to undermine deterrence, mainly because implementation of that strategy in a crisis would be highly destabilizing. This problem, coupled with the threat of nuclear escalation that attends this posture, points up that this variant of the Maritime Strategy is potentially dangerous.

Sea control is where the Navy matters for deterrence in Europe. The Soviets must not be allowed to think they can cut NATO's SLOCs quickly. The Navy maintains that an offensive sea control posture is necessary for this purpose, but this is not so. A defensive sea control posture would satisfy NATO's needs on this count without the risks that attend offensive sea control. Very importantly, the force structure demands of defensive sea control are more modest than those of offensive sea control. Specifically, a defensive sea control strategy would allow the Navy to relinquish its requirement for 15 carrier battle groups. The Navy would still need large-deck carriers for its other missions—peacetime presence and direct intervention in Third World conflicts—but the overall number would be significantly less than 15—perhaps 10 would be enough. The Navy, however, should continue to maintain a powerful SSN force, which would not only be useful for executing a defensive sea control strategy, but would also provide the threat needed to keep Soviet SSNs concentrated in their home waters.

Moving to this smaller force structure would free up resources for the ground and air forces on the Central Front, which represent the nucleus of NATO's deterrent. This discussion points up that an assessment of the Maritime Strategy must consider the crucial issue of opportunity costs. . . .

In sum, the Maritime Strategy is fundamentally flawed, not only because it fails to enhance the deterrent posture in Europe, but also because it has meant spending large sums of money on the Navy that might have otherwise been spent on enhancing the fighting power of those forces that matter most for deterrence. While NATO is not any worse off in 1986 than it was in 1980, the more important point is that the Administration missed an excellent opportunity to improve NATO's deterrent posture. . . .

On the Objectives
of Arms Control

BERNARD BRODIE

The volume of literature on arms control contrasts sharply with the dearth of results in actual armaments limitation or control. Thus huge disparity between fullness of advice and leanness of practical results suggests a good deal about both the character of that advice and the magnitude of the practical difficulties—and especially about the failure of the former to adjust to the latter.

The ample quantity of the writing on arms control in the face of what would seem to be such poor prospects of realization reflects also an aspiration, amounting often to religiosity, in much of the motivation for that writing. Although we must be grateful for whatever propels motivation in what we feel intuitively to be a good cause, we must also be suspicious of that kind of motivation which corrupts the endeavor.[1]

All but a minute proportion of the works that I have seen on the general subject of arms control fail to be of any utility for the policymaker, and thus also for the student of policy making, except insofar as some of those writings conveniently provide for the interested layman some technical knowledge about weaponry. That failure is naturally due to various characteristics, but one common characteristic that I should put at the top of the list is *persistent failure to clarify and analyze objectives,* which of course precludes any rigorous and consistent adherence to the soundest objectives. Naturally, this clarification should not have to be done over and over again, but it would be useful to have it be done occasionally.

ARMS CONTROL OBJECTIVES AND PERCEPTIONS

An appropriate analysis of objectives would inevitably entail a pragmatic approach—we want our objectives to be mutually consistent, to be worth achieving, and to be in some degree achievable—and

From *International Security,* Summer, 1976, p. 17–36. Reprinted by permission of The MIT Press Journals.

[1] I can only hope that what I have seen is a fair and representative sampling. A manuscript for a bibliography of items related to and about arms control, prepared by Professor Richard Dean Burns, comes to some 900 pages of double-spaced typing. It will be published in 1976 or 1977 by the Clio Press of Santa Barbara, California.

that in turn entails a properly empirical utilization of our experience. We have had much relevant experience with arms control negotiations, with the armaments competitions that have stimulated efforts at control, and above all with war, the prospect of which ultimately dominates everything having to do with arms competitions and the efforts to control them.

Inasmuch as arms control efforts seek to affect future events, we have to be conscious of the degree of our uncertainty about the future, in which we are instructed by our experience with surprise in the past. Perhaps an appreciation for this uncertainty will inhibit our choice of arms control objectives, but if so, that is simply the way the ball bounces.

I am using the term "arms control" in a sense which accords with the popular conception but which some would regard as unduly restrictive. It was right once to make the point that the kind of arms control that may be most important in the long run is that which depends on tacit rather than explicit agreement—also that arms control for the purpose of enhancing security does not usually imply reducing the overall costs of our armaments but may in particular respects mean raising them.[2] Though of some perennial application, those points were more pertinent to the Eisenhower years than to the present. Anyway, the more common and narrower conception, which I accept, identifies the term "arms control" with some degree of limitation or reduction of particular armaments, and it implies also explicit rather than merely tacit international agreement. There is indeed substantial extra value in the relevant agreements being explicit.

The objectives of arms control are usually not stated, but when they are stated, they are only rarely if ever reflectively considered. Apparently this is because most writers feel that the merit of their implied or declared objectives is too obvious to need consideration.[3] Not only are some two, three, or four objectives usually held to be obviously desirable, but even the order of their priority seems to be a matter for declaration rather than examination. Among the numerous statements that might be quoted to illustrate this point, I choose one which I find specially provocative but which reflects fairly the view most commonly held by the vast majority of those who write on arms control. Herman Kahn and Anthony Weiner say that the purpose of arms control is:

[2] These ideas were prominent in the work of Thomas C. Schelling. See especially the book by him and Morton H. Halperin, *Strategy and Arms Control* (New York: Twentieth Century Fund, 1961).

[3] Hedley Bull's *The Control of the Arms Race* (New York: Praeger, 1961) does indeed devote the first chapter to "The Objectives of Arms Control," but I find it exploratory rather than analytical. This and the above-mentioned book by Schelling and Halperin, both published in the same year, both short, remain to this date the landmark books in the field.

. . . to improve the inherent stability of the situation, decrease the occasions or the approximate causes of war within the system, and decrease the destructiveness and other disutilities of any wars that actually occur. One may also add to this last, 'decrease the cost of defense preparation,' but we would argue that this would take a rather low priority to the first three objectives.[4]

This statement puts the aim of saving money not only last but in a separate sub-category of lesser worthiness than the other three. Those three in turn really boil down to only two, because the first two mentioned refer to the common aim of reducing the probability of war, and the third, which thus becomes the second, has to do with reducing the destructiveness of war if it should occur.

One notices in passing that giving priority to the twin aims of reducing the probability of war and of reducing its destructiveness if it occurs—the reference is almost always to war between the two superpowers—reflects an implicit appraisal of the existing probability of war. Some would protest that if war breaks out the penalties are so vast that *any* possibility of its occurring warrants whatever efforts we can make to counteract that possibility. Still, we know that few would greatly bestir themselves to cope with an evil that they regard as having only a miniscule probability of occurring. Individual views on armaments and arms control cover a wide range, and it is important to establish that one prime factor accounting for the differences is the individual's appraisal of the probability of war—an appraisal that is usually vaguely felt and nearly always implicit rather than explicit.

I find the Kahn-Weiner statement provocative because of their view of priorities. My own contrary view is that in a pragmatic approach to arms control the object of saving money really deserves a superior rating to that of saving the world. This conclusion must imply, among other things, either a high confidence that the probability of war between the two superpowers will continue to be extremely low, or the conviction that in any case we cannot do much about that probability through arms control. To make explicit and thus also to clarify what is otherwise ambiguous, let me record that I subscribe to both propositions.

Although one can defend a low expectation of superpower conflict by citing only objective factors, one must admit that the *weighting* of those factors depends upon a substantial increment of subjective and thus intuitive judgement.[5] Besides obliging one to be tolerant of differing opinions, this fact throws the main burden of the argument on the

    [4] Herman Kahn and Anthony Weiner, "Technological Innovation and the Future of Strategic Warfare," *Astronautics and Aeronautics* (December, 1967), p. 28.
    [5] I have dealt at greater length with the question of the probability of war between the United States and the Soviet Union in my *War and Politics* (New York: Macmillan, 1973), especially in chapters 6 and 9.

latter of the two above propositions—that arms control negotiations and the resulting agreements, if any, will rarely make important contributions to reducing either the probability of war or its destructiveness. There are several reasons for this, of which two stand out particularly: (1) each party is extremely suspicious of the adversary's efforts to disarm him in weaponry regarded as truly important, and (2) apart from a few simple and obvious devices like the "hot line" between Washington and Moscow, experience assures us that it is not at all a simple matter to determine objectively, let alone get international agreement upon, those arms limitation measures that will really advance the ends of greater stability and lesser destructiveness.

That leaves us with the mere matter of saving money, on which governments, unlike amateur observers, never look askance. Governments are at all times coping intensively with a number of recalcitrant economic problems, which in recent years have included marked inflationary pressures and also growing alternative demands for the monies raised from public restive about taxes. Competitive pressures from the chief foreign rival will at times force a commitment to expenditures which government leaders may feel to be of doubtful utility from the military point of view, or changed conditions will make less necessary or desirable what was previously considered essential. Yet political reasons may militate against cutting back unilaterally. Each government also finds itself pressed by its own military in a conflict where the rival government, which has similar problems, may occasionally be a useful ally.

We have already noticed that every participant in the national debate on arms control carries with him as part of his intellectual and emotional baggage some kind of appraisal of war-probability which inevitably affects his relevant attitudes. Obviously it will affect his feelings on how much one should try to accommodate to the views of the bargaining partner. It is an old story that one important reason why arms limitation conferences have so often failed or yielded only the most meager results is that both sides bring with them to the conference a contingent of experts, whether in uniform or not, whose whole professional predisposition is to look upon that bargaining partner as the prospective military adversary. They also feel a pronounced distaste for giving up any of those armaments with which they individually identify themselves and which they may have fought for on the domestic scene. There are also those left at home who can be counted upon to influence the debate that will precede any ratification. Depending on the moods of the time these experts may feel obliged to give lip service to arms limitation, but they will bring to the process a tight and often arbitrary measure of proportionality.

All that is of course familiar, but there is another less observed facet of the problem. Those who entertain a low estimate of superpower war probability will incline towards the idea that for deterrence purposes the fact of being powerful is much more important than the exact character or structure of that power. This attitude makes for more flexibility in the critical negotiations, and also for acceptance as a matter of course of the important distinction between deterrence capabilities and war-fighting capabilities. The former capabilities are those which are menacing enough, under expected conditions of low mutual motivation for war, to preclude the adversary's giving serious consideration to exploiting the means and paying the price of defeating them.

Those persons, on the other hand, who regard the danger of super-power war as appreciable are consistent in arguing that the best deterrence force is the optimum fighting force. They will run into difficulties with their insistence on this point when they contemplate the ultimate in strategic nuclear deterrence, where war-fighting capabilities seem to dissolve into irrelevance. Herman Kahn's well-known parable of the doomsday machine (designed by Americans to blow up the world if it should detect some five nuclear weapons exploding anywhere over the United States) demonstrated hypothetically that deterrence and war-fighting capabilities are *not* the same thing, at least at the maximum levels of warfare.[6] At theater levels of warfare, however, war-fighting capabilities are much more relevant to deterrence, and anyway, one wants the monies allocated to fighting forces to be spent efficiently, which means efficiently for fighting purposes. Even so, it is likely that an effort concentrated on deterrence will be less costly by wide margins than one concentrated on matching or outdoing the opponent in war-fighting capabilities.

All sorts of slogans get in the way of a reasonable handling of this problem, such as the common assertion that our efforts should be guided exclusively by the opponent's capabilities, not by our estimate of his intentions. This slogan is not likely to be fully followed in practice, because our sense of threat is inevitably qualified by our operating image of the opponent, which may be of one who wants to be strong but also wants desperately to avoid war. Nevertheless, the slogan does act to exacerbate competitive pressures.[7] These pressures certainly increase the disposition to match the rival's military efforts in degree, and they also to some extent dispose us to imitate him in kind. Obviously our military have their own ideas in some matters, but they and we will be uneasy with too radical a departure from the major pattern the rival is following. Thus both sides build up huge conventional forces in an age of nuclear weapons.

---

[6] See Herman Kahn, *On Thermonuclear War* (Princeton: Princeton University Press, 1960), pp. 145–151.

[7] I discuss the issue of "capabilities versus intentions" at greater length in my *Escalation and the Nuclear Option* (Princeton: Princeton University Press, 1966), ch. 7.

AGREEING UPON ARMS CONTROL OBJECTIVES

We turn now to some examples which will illustrate and perhaps also elaborate the various points made above. On the general issue of the difficulty of winning acceptance even of agreements that would seem to be obviously in the security interests of the participants, a recent and conspicuous example is the history of the effort to avoid proliferation of nuclear weapons. There is little overt dissension anywhere to the belief, which is almost universal within the United States, that the general proliferation of nuclear weapons among non-possessing nations would be a threat to world peace. This view seems to be held even by some governments that have refused to sign the Non- Proliferation Treaty of 1968, including the French government—which has, however, not hesitated to attempt to sell to governments like that of South Korea not only nuclear power plants but also plutonium reprocessing plants to go with them. In this case we do have a treaty, the achievement of which was one of the leading aims of American foreign policy for several years before its accomplishment. Still, the considerable resistances to the adoption of that treaty are well known. At this writing 98 nations are parties to it and 12 that have signed have not yet ratified. Both figures leave out some quite important states.[8] What is more, the treaty itself has more than its share of legal escape hatches, quite apart from the fact that it is more than usually subject to evasion or violation.

Ah, one protests, but is not this too blatant an example of inequality, where nations are being asked to sign a self-denying ordinance not subscribed to by some nations including our own, and where the compensation is all too abstract? No doubt, but when are the benefits of an arms limitation treaty not abstract—except insofar as they directly result in the saving of money? The fact remains that a proposition that commends itself overwhelmingly to virtually all interested citizens in the United States—and most arms limitation proposals do not meet that criterion—quite clearly does not commend itself universally. The treaty we do have is not worthless but neither is it worth very much. The actual plans of signatory nations concerning their own military nuclear programs have probably been little if at all affected by that treaty. The objective of the treaty is still worth pursuing, certainly in the direction of curbing the almost wanton distribution of nuclear power reactors and especially of plutonium reprocessing plants, but we have reason to be aware of the limited prospects of its success. In other examples we shall be considering, it is much less clear whether the objective is worth pursuing.

---

[8] Japan became the 98th party to the treaty with the deposit of its instrument of ratification on June 8, 1976.

DETERMINING WHAT IS NEGOTIABLE:
THE CASE OF TACTICAL NUCLEAR WEAPONS

One critical example of an arms limitation objective that we are in danger of pursuing too hastily involves tactical nuclear weapons (TNWs). These are commonly believed to be the most ill-begotten of a noisome race of weapons, particularly objectionable because they are unnecessary. In this view they should not be used even in the event of a major attack by the Soviet Union upon our own and allied forces in Europe and at sea. To use them, the argument goes, is to wipe out the only meaningful stop (or "firebreak") between theater warfare and the suicidal strategic kind. Why the slide from one to the other should be so steep and slippery is not explained, no doubt because the reasons are considered too obvious to require explanation.

The notion that TNWs are on the whole more dangerous than useful to their possessor derives from an idea developed and advocated in the early 1960s, mostly by a group of analysts then at the RAND Corporation.[9] If the United States and its NATO allies built up their conventional ground and air forces to something like parity with those of the Warsaw Pact, these men argued, the "nuclear threshold" would be raised to so high a level as virtually to eliminate the chances of its being breached even in an outbreak of major military action in Europe—which, everyone agreed, could be initiated only by a Soviet attack. They further insisted that inasmuch as everyone would understand that our European allies would be much more willing to resist Soviet aggression if they were highly confident that the resulting battle would remain non-nuclear, the proposed posture would greatly enhance real deterrence.

Thus, the 7,000 American TNWs reported to be stationed in Europe are held to be exceptionally available tokens to be offered in any arms reduction proposals to the Soviet Union. Secretary of State Henry A. Kissinger has already offered to reduce them by 1,000 if the Soviet Union will make an offsetting—though not similar—reduction in its armed forces in Europe. Whatever Kissinger's own beliefs on the subject may be—and he is on record as being dubious of the views of the conventional-war enthusiasts—he is aware that an offer of this kind meets the minimum of objections from the Pentagon, the Congress, and other relevant agencies. Alain Enthoven, however, would go much further than Kissinger. He would reduce their number unilaterally without offsetting concessions, and not *by* 1,000 but *to* 1,000.[10]

---

[9] Leadership of this group within RAND must be credited to Albert Wohlstetter, though Alain C. Enthoven has been the most frequent spokesman in print for their position. Others among them known for their publications include Malcolm Hoag, W. W. Kaufmann, and Henry Rowen.

[10] See Alain C. Enthoven, "U. S. Forces in Europe: How Many? Doing What?" *Foreign Affairs,* (April 1975), pp. 512–532.

To the layman 1,000 nuclear weapons will seem like an adequate number for any purpose, but if those retained are ever really adapted to tactical uses, which would mean among other things greatly reducing the yields on most of them, 1,000 would certainly not be adequate. Enthoven would reduce the number of TNWs in Europe primarily to free for conventional war purposes the men now assigned to guarding them, which he numbers at 30,000. And he would retain the 1,000 strictly to deter the Soviet Union from using TNWs in its attack.

Whether the Europeans could ever have high confidence that a major war in Europe would remain non-nuclear, or whether such confidence ought under any circumstances to be entertained, are among the vital questions which have not been scrutinized. The group that originated this mode of thought believed the logic of the new idea to be so compelling that it would be quickly accepted by the Soviet military leaders as well as allied ones, not to mention our own. To be sure, involved Americans were determined not to lose a war in Europe. There would be no first use by us *unless we found ourselves losing.* The Russians were apparently expected to accommodate to this rigidity on our part, which they would no doubt consider somewhat peculiar, and to do so without using nuclear weapons.

One notes a complete absence of empirical inquiry about various of the radical assumptions that went into this doctrine. *What* Europeans were meant by *the* Europeans who would supposedly resist under one set of circumstances but not under another? Did anyone try to find out whether that was really the opinion of those few Europeans who would make the critical decisions? Would the Russians launch a large-scale attack without the determination to win, swiftly, and would they expose themselves to the hazards of such a duel while leaving entirely to us the choice of weapons? What did their overt doctrine tell us on these matters? These and comparable questions which were subject to fruitful investigation were not in fact investigated. One notices also that the original protagonists of this view harbored a sufficiently high expectation of a Soviet attack in Europe to advocate with some urgency a considerable and costly improvement of NATO forces, though they seemed to find it forensically necessary to insist that in military manpower the NATO forces were already very nearly equal to those of the Warsaw Pact.[11]

The theory was attractive enough to win ready converts in the

---

[11] Dr. Enthoven has been consistently arguing this point in several publications, the most recent being his aforementioned *Foreign Affairs* article. On page 516 Enthoven holds that Warsaw Pact forces on M-Day plus 60 would be only 1,241,000 (as compared with NATO's 1,105,000). One wonders what happened to that Soviet Union which, without allies, suffered the loss of five to six million troops in the first 5½ months of war in 1941, and then went on to win. The estimate is Albert Seaton's in his *The Russo-German War, 1941–1945* (New York: Praeger, 1971), p. 208n.

highest reaches of the Kennedy Administration, including the President himself and his vigorous Secretary of Defense, Robert S. McNamara. And what was a novel and radical doctrine 15 years ago has now in the mid-1970s become the conventional wisdom of the interested public and of most of the defense community. Professional military officers tend today to be ambivalent on the use of TNWs, being ready in principle to use them if the other side uses them first, or, as something of an afterthought, in the event we find ourselves losing without them. But whether their forces are organized, equipped, and trained to make so swift a shift from one form of warfare to another is a pertinent question—to which the answer almost certainly is "no". The military did, after all, like that part of the theory which justified their requesting a good deal more of the kind of equipment they were accustomed to, albeit modernized. And, as some of them have frankly admitted, they have simply stopped thinking much about the problem. The most extraordinary example of how one service has adjusted to the idea that TNWs would surely not be used in a war with the Soviet Union is the manner in which our surface combat fleet has developed around huge attack carriers, any one of which could be volatilized by one small nuclear weapon, deliverable by aircraft, surface vessel, submarine, or even shore-based missile launcher.

Thus, a theory has been accepted almost without challenge simply because it is a seductive one. One wants to believe it, especially if one can be persuaded that forces organized for the non-use of nuclear weapons make for more rather than less deterrence. Some theories are of course self-fulfilling, and this one might be so if we were not talking about war—which always presupposes an adversary with intentions and drives of his own. Under the circumstances, however, it is a dangerous theory as well as a costly one. The conventional forces it calls for in NATO have not been provided, and would be of dubious utility if they were. Our NATO allies were never impressed with the American idea, and besides they felt the threat from the Soviet Union to be diminishing. That situation was not conducive to spending more on defense. Anyway, European policymakers have a long-standing fondness for nuclear *deterrence,* and if the strategic variety seems less dependable to them than formerly, as it clearly (and perhaps fortunately) does, they are that much less willing to relinquish the theater kind. Since 1967 they have found it expedient to give lip service within NATO to the concept of "graduated response," but they are far from fleshing our their purely conventional capabilities. They have indeed been tending in the opposite direction.

One of the primary ideas upon which the whole conventional war construct is based is that large-scale conflict between the superpowers can be the result of accident. By "accidental war" is presumably meant that which comes despite neither side wanting it, and with neither side realizing until war is actually upon it that the policy it is pursuing makes that war unavoidable. This notion has given rise to the concept of the "pause," intended to permit the enemy to reconsider his behavior before one introduces nuclear weapons against him.

Presumably this kind of accident is made possible by the very existence of nuclear weapons, for within the definition of the term given above, no such thing as accidental war has happened within the last three hundred years, if ever. And it really is bizarre to think that the presence of nuclear weapons can make nations more reckless and disportive in bearding their opponents than ever before, in a word more ready to risk war in the conviction that it will not come. Thus we pay heavy extra premiums in our defenses simply because most of those who currently philosophize about strategy have made no effort to acquaint themselves with the history of war.

In the context of TNWs, what about the aim of diminishing the destructiveness of war? The answers, in diminishing order of importance, are about as follows: First, the surest way of reducing the destructiveness of war is to deter it, and insofar as theater forces are required for deterrence they should be as effective in that role as possible. For *any* given sum of expenditures the best theater deterrence force is the most efficient fighting force, and that means a force organized, trained, and equipped for using the most modern weapons, certainly including nuclear ones. The prevailing assumption is, of course, that an attack upon it will *not* be an accident. Second, the decision to use nuclear weapons would in any case not be primarily ours to make, especially with the basic premise in all our war plans being that the opponent is the aggressor; defense plans have to consider not the most desired but the most likely mode of enemy attack. Third, there is no *prima facie* evidence that a battle fought with TNWs would be more destructive to the terrain over which it is fought or to noncombatants in the theater than the conventional battles we have known in the two world wars. It might well be the other way round. The critical factor in destructiveness to the terrain is usually the rate of movement of the contending armies, the destructiveness tending to be inversely proportional to the swiftness with which one side pushes back or destroys the other. Also, with nuclear weapons it is very much a matter of the types most used and the manner in which they are employed—something that should be studied intensively in advance, largely for the sake of minimizing undesired collateral damage.

DECIDING ON WEAPON NUMBERS

Leaving now the matter of TNWs, but pursuing the important objective of "limiting the destructiveness of war if it comes," we might briefly consider the views of Herbert York, who has been active in efforts to get agreements to reduce the size of nuclear stockpiles, especially of strategic nuclear weapons.[12] There can be little question that American and Soviet strategic nuclear weapons already deployed or otherwise available for use have grown in numbers far beyond any reasonable conception of military need and certainly of deterrence. This has been a result mainly of competitive pressures and of such technological advances as MIRV. The requirement to escape the threat of having one's retaliatory force obliterated by surprise attack is solved far better by the manner of its deployment than by multiplying its weapons. Though the long-term viability of our silo-protected ICBMs may be in doubt, alternative means of deployment, such as submarine-launched missiles, make it absurd to sound alarms about the imminent danger of the Russians developing a "first-strike capability"—a complaint frequently voiced by former Secretary of Defense Melvin Laird. Equally dubious were the public expressions of another recent Secretary of Defense, James R. Schlesinger, who argued that with the kind of accuracy that promises to become available in the cruise missile we should develop what was formerly called a "damage-limiting" capability, that is, limiting damage to ourselves by destroying enemy missiles in their silos.

Why then, has it been so difficult for York to get a sympathetic hearing for his views, even in such milieus as the Arms Control and Disarmament Agency (ACDA)? One of the reasons, no doubt, is that nuclear weapons already produced and deployed are so much sunk capital, not especially costly to maintain in their land-based missile configurations and certainly not when stockpiled. The budget for all American strategic nuclear forces, which includes bombers and missile submarines and all monies spent on related research and development, was in FY 1976 about 18 percent of our entire defense budget. Those costs would not be substantially reduced simply by phasing out warheads. Also, with the passing of the years the possibility of a strategic nuclear exchange seems to have become in most people's minds more and more remote, and one reason for that is precisely the horrendous number of weapons. It is one thing to say that we have far more than enough weapons for deterrence, but who is to say—and to persuade others—how far that number can reasonably drop before deterrence is in fact diminished? Who wants to rock the boat, especially since large numbers are also a protection against the alleged "destabilization" that tends to result from various kinds of technological innovation? Many people show a deep concern about "superiority," about relative "throw-weights" and all the rest, and although these fears do point to the importance of fruitful negotiation

---

[12] Of his many writings on the subject, one of the most comprehensive is *Race to Oblivion* (New York: Simon and Schuster, 1970).

to find mutual limits, they also reflect an abiding confidence in numbers which has to be, if not honored, at least humored.

Most important of all, however, in accounting for the lack of receptiveness to York's ideas is the fact that, precisely because the number of weapons is so huge, the realization of his ideas would require a *drastic* reduction in those numbers—not just 10 or 20 percent but something well over 90 percent! If the object is to retain the kind of deterrence which strategic nuclear weapons provide against any kind of war with the rival superpower, but to decrease materially the grimness that would follow a failure of deterrence—we should have to know how to draw the curve for the marginal utility of weapons. We should than have to hunt for something like an optimum balance between deterrence on the one hand, and on the other hand reasonable (?) limits to destructiveness if deterrence fails. We should then have to develop a consensus within the country, at least among relevant bureaucracies and the Congress, that we had found the optimum zone of figures, following which we should have to embark upon appropriate negotiations abroad. And because the figure to be aimed at is now so much lower than before, negotiations would have to include not only the Soviet Union but also China, France, and Britain. No one should presume to say that the day will never arrive when such a chain of events is possible, but it is certainly not on the horizon.

ASSESSING THE ARMS RACE

The competitive pressures mentioned above bring us to another of the alleged major causes of war which arms control is supposed to curb—the arms race. It is an article of faith among most of those who write on arms control that curbing the arms race in order to keep the peace of the world is what arms control is all about, or at least mostly about. Among these writers arms competitions or "races" are alleged to be by themselves the most potent—the word "inevitable" is frequently in evidence—of the causes of war.

The idea is on the face of it somewhat illogical. Why the pressures of an arms competition, however costly, irritating, or even alarming they may become, should move one of the competitors to try to resolve it all by resorting to the immeasurably more costly and hazardous arbitrament of war is not easy to see, unless he happens to be greatly superior, in which case the competition should not bother him. If the competition is downgraded to being only a potent contributing cause, then we should focus on what comes first and consider how much the arms competition really contributes. It may in fact derive from the prime cause, which we must assume to be political, in which case it is simply part of the working out of the animosity, that is, it is more an effect than a cause.

The arms competition we have been witnessing in the Middle East is clearly of the latter kind. We see both sides frantically attempting between wars to rearm themselves against another outbreak that both sides believe highly likely if not inevitable. In such situations, however, the major provocations to violence clearly lie outside the arms competition itself and almost totally account for that competition. Conditions of the moment which the aggressor finds favorable to himself *may* help to trigger a war, but that does not alter the basic quality we see in the competition, which is that it is entirely derivative from the hostility and not the other way round.

What may be called the "classical" arms race, on the other hand, follows a model where the rivals measure their arms progress against each other, out of considerations of status and of ultimate security against *conceivable* warlike situations, but where the focus is more on competition itself than on any high or imminent expectation of war. The latter situation fairly describes the competition between the United States and the Soviet Union during at least the last decade—which is in some contrast to the situation of the 1950s when the expectation of war was considerably higher.[13]

Arms races of this latter type are fairly recent phenomena. In older times the size of the military forces of the prince depended on his wealth, pride, and territorial ambitions, but a number of factors were missing then that seem to be essential in the modern type of competition. Among them are rapid technological progress and also a level of productivity of the national economy which makes for a good deal of "fat"—as contrasted with the subsistence-level economy that characterized most nations before the 19th century. There are in modern times vast resources free for competitive military buildups that were not comparably free at an earlier time.

Probably the most celebrated arms race in history is the Anglo-German naval race that began with the German naval laws of 1898 and 1900. It stands out as the stereotype of the modern arms race, and it was indeed hard and furious. It has for that reason often been charged with being a primary cause of Britain's entry into World War I.

There is much instruction in studying that race, particularly in seeing how the Germans rationalized a vain and improvident policy and how badly they misjudged the British. There can be no doubt that

---

[13] We should note here Albert Wohlstetter's denial that there is an arms race between the two superpowers, though he concedes there is an arms competition which raises costs on both sides. I have assumed above that the two terms were sufficiently imprecise to be virtually interchangeable. See Wohlstetter's "Is There a Strategic Arms Race?," *Foreign Policy*, No. 15 (Summer, 1974), pp. 3–20 and No. 16 (Fall, 1974), pp. 48–81. See also Michael L. Nacht's critique of Wohlstetter's view in the same journal, No. 19 (Summer, 1975), pp. 163–177, and Wohlstetter's reply to Nacht and others in No. 20 (Fall, 1975), pp. 170–198.

it caused much irritation and even some alarm in Britain. But we know now a good deal about the motivations of Britain's pre-war diplomacy and also about that week of groping in the Cabinet that finally brought Britain's declaration of war in August 1914. The evidence is overwhelming that the German naval competition was of far less than prime significance in provoking the British decision. It had had virtually nothing to do with Britain's departing "splendid isolation" to conclude its alliance with Japan in 1902 and its *entente* with France in 1904. In subsequent events, including the *entente* with Russia in 1907, it had loomed somewhat larger, but it was still only part of the whole image of Germany that the several pre-war crises and the posturing of a vainglorious kaiser helped to produce. Finally there was the clear and blatant violation of the Belgium Neutralization Treaty of 1839.[14]

No doubt the British tolerance for the German competition derived from their confidence that they could maintain the naval fighting superiority that was so important to them. To outbuild the Germans was costly but feasible, and far less costly than fighting them. That fact, too, points to something instructive about that race and especially to how it differed from any kind of armaments race that could possibly exist today between the United States and the Soviet Union.

The unit of account for fleet fighting power at the time of that race was the battleship—after 1906 the Dreadnought-type battleship— designed and built primarily for fighting its like on the high seas. Once built it might also be used for other purposes, like shore bombardment, but it was never put in hazard for such purposes if there was a chance that it might be needed for contending with enemy battleships. Because the British succeeded in building more battleships than the Germans and because they also built ships with bigger guns, they maintained a battle superiority which both sides knew to be overwhelming. When it came to the contest of battle fleets in World War I, the British Grand Fleet simply contained the German High Seas Fleet for four years of war and made the latter quite useless. It did so while being mostly silent and at anchor. On the one occasion that the two fleets met, off Jutland, the entire preoccupation of the German commander was with escape.

Thus, with surface fleets even more than with armies, the fact that the military units of each side fought comparable military units of the

---

[14] On official British attitudes towards Germany, a number of fascinating once-secret memoranda are reprinted in Kenneth Bourne's *The Foreign Policy of Victorian England,* 1830–1902 (London: Oxford University Press, 1970). Despite the terminal date in the book's title, the memoranda which are especially interesting cover the period from 1901 to 1914 (pp. 462–504). See especially the long extract from the major policy memorandum of 1 January 1907 by Eyre Crowe, who bore the misleading title of Senior Clerk in the Foreign Office, pp. 481–493.

other gave real meaning to a margin of superiority. Such meaning is lost in the present armaments rivalry with the Soviet Union, in which it is basic that we are dealing with weaponry where the units are *not* primarily intended to fight each other. Certainly that is characteristic of the whole family of nuclear weapons which, despite frequent allegations to the contrary, are the weapons most effective in keeping the two nations firmly on course—that is, on the course of avoiding war with each other. Also, there is between the superpowers nothing comparable now to the peculiar and one-sided vulnerability of Britain to the interruption of her sea-borne communications, a vulnerability which absolutely obliged her to insist on clear superiority on the seas.

That nuclear weapons are not intended primarily to fight each other may be denied by proponents of counterforce targeting. Until the conclusion of the SALT I agreements, some were excited also by the qualified capability of ABMs to destroy incoming nuclear warheads high above the ground—a possibility that seemed to promise to make warfare once more a duel, to be fought this time in space. However, few students of the problem can deny that success for a counterforce strategy must depend on some quite unpredictable variables and, especially because of the several alternative means of retaliatory attack, *is bound always to be critically limited.*

In the present situation there is even less reason than before to worry about the alleged provocatory nature of arms races. We may even allow ourselves some astonishment at how little such provocations seem to matter, either in diplomacy or in everyday life. Both superpowers have weapons aimed at each other that could spell for each something approaching obliteration. Neither side has anything remotely resembling a defense except its power of retaliation. It is a circumstance that, at the dawn of the nuclear age, people predicted would be quite intolerable. But the feared condition arrived gradually, and as people came to live with it, proved not only tolerable but also not without its own peculiar comforts. There developed a sense that no issue existed to induce the superpowers to go to war with each other when such a penalty for doing so hung over them mutually—a condition quite new in the world's history.

There are now, as there always have been, the habitual sounders of alarm about losing some margin of superiority, either in ships at sea, in throw-weight of missiles, or whatnot. But despite the jingoism on the far right evoked by the 1976 primaries, the national audience seems to be lacking something in responsiveness. When before has a secretary of state, who incidentally enjoyed a considerable and unusual reputation for understanding strategic issues, replied to some fulminations from the Defense Department, as Kissinger did in 1974, with the exclamation: "What in the name of God is strategic superiority? What is the significance of it politically, militarily, operationally, at this level of numbers?"

For our purposes we are not obliged to determine whether Kissinger is right or wrong in the sentiment reflected in his exclamation. What it does tell us incontrovertibly is that whatever arms race is going on currently, and however costly it may be, it is not in itself adding very much to the irritations and provocations that arise from time to time between the two major rivals. An arms race may indeed cause them to treat each other with more respect than they otherwise would, but that too has its net utilities.

We have learned over the three decades that nuclear weapons have been with us that the balance of terror is *not* delicate. For either superpower to attack the other because of an optimistic guess of the latter's vulnerabilities is obviously to take a risk of cataclysmic proportions. Neither can be seduced into such an error by some apparent shift in the relationship of forces—usually more apparent to technicians than to politicians. Nor will either superpower be seduced by the appearance of some new mechanical contrivance which at best affects only a part of the whole scheme of things, usually a small part.

The terms "destabilizing" and "stabilizing" have become fashionable in referring to various technological developments. Their use commonly reflects a limited perception of how each development alters or fits into the entire technological *and* political universe in which we live. No doubt a prolonged somnolescence by the United States concerning qualitative and quantitative changes in the arms balance would in time prove dangerous, especially if it were not accompanied by a drastic downward reassessment of our foreign policy interests. But the fate of ourselves and of the world is not going to hang on what we do or fail to do about some object like the cruise missile. Not long ago the alleged fate-determining object was the ABM. It sometimes helps to remember the several invasion panics in England in the mid-19th century, when the adoption of steam propulsion by warships was supposed to have created "a steam bridge across the Channel."

BUDGETING FOR DEFENSE

If arms competitions are not in themselves dangerous, which is to say significantly provocative of an inclination to war, they are certainly costly. An international agreement which succeeds in limiting that competition is an important and welcome way of limiting those costs. Naturally one does not wish to save money at the cost of a significant impairment of security, but the role for intelligent arms control is precisely to find and exploit instances where there is no such conflict.

There are some, to be sure, who argue that the arms race, if there is one, is not too costly. Many, including President Ford, have pointed to our current defense budget as being "only" 6 percent of our GNP, which they call an historically low proportion that should be considered a floor on our military expenditures. Some, like former Secretary of Defense Schlesinger, make statements arguing a positive value for their own sake in high military expenditures, claiming that any attempt to reduce them sends the "wrong signals" to the Soviet leaders. Reasoning from the 6 percent figure Schlesinger was looking forward with no apparent pain to annual defense budgets of $150 billion by 1980.

One might point out that 6 percent of GNP is historically a low peacetime figure for the United States only since the Korean War. One could suggest also that national and indeed worldwide trends make governments more responsible for social welfare than formerly, and these trends, which appear politically irreversible at least for the United States, make 6 percent of GNP for military expenditures considerably more burden than it used to be. This percentage currently represents approximately $100 billion. We are also becoming increasingly aware that percentage of GNP is a much less meaningful figure than percentage of the national budget, for the latter represents monies being raised by taxation and by deficit financing, and we are becoming acutely aware of the limits, disutilities, and special pains associated with both. The defense budget is still by far the largest single category in the national budget, and it accounts for roughly 35 percent of it.

But is all this relevant? The notion that it pays to spend extra billions just to send the "right" signals abroad ought to be rejected as most unlikely to be "cost-effective" compared with other means of signaling. What are the "right signals" supposed to be anyway? What signals are in fact sent by simply boosting military expenditures? If these and related questions are not in the narrow sense researchable, they are certainly worth more thought than they usually get by those who urge the Schlesinger view. That view, while not necessarily in conflict with efficient military expenditure, is not likely to be conducive to it either.

The merit of explicit, mutual agreements on arms control is that both sides are committed to the same course of action, usually for the same or at least similar reasons. That makes the signals mutual. Just as cost-effectiveness analysis was devised and pursued for the sake of avoiding sheer waste in military expenditures (it is usually expressed in other ways, but they amount to the same thing), so arms control should be conceived as an important and fruitful means of avoiding waste. For that we should not have to make apologies.

Two examples should suffice to illustrate the practical application of our argument. The first is the Washington Naval Limitation Treaty of 1922, later supplemented by the London Naval Treaty of 1930. These treaties are among the very few in history—if there are indeed others of comparable weight—in which the several great powers succeeded by free mutual agreement not only in limiting future building in a primary military category but actually in reducing significantly levels already reached. The motivation on all sides was entirely economic, though naturally in the speeches applauding the signing ceremonies the benign consequences for world peace were duly rung in.[15]

The other, more recent example was the effective demolition of the ABM programs of the United States and the Soviet Union as a result of the SALT 1 agreements of 1972. To anyone who had followed the ABM debate in the United States, this result was astonishing. Few historical debates on armaments had aroused the passions that this one did, with experts in the related technologies arrayed on both sides. The substance of the debate was mostly over the efficacy of the Sentinel system, a name changed to "Safeguard" by President Nixon, who showed himself to be one of its most ardent champions. In pushing the necessary supporting acts through a once-reluctant Senate, Nixon did indeed use the "bargaining chip" argument along with several others, but his obvious ardor for the system itself made it difficult to give credence to this explanation.

The fact that it ultimately did prove to be a bargining chip does not quite dispel one's doubts as to whether it was so conceived all along. It appears likely that President Nixon underwent a real change of heart about ABM, the rapidly growing problem with inflation no doubt having much to do with his change. Inflation clearly made him look harder at the data that brought into question the efficacy and utility of the system, including new developments like MIRVs, the cruise missile, and alternatives to fixed silos for ICBMs, especially land-mobile systems.

In any case, the motivation and justification for doing away mutually with the ABM (actually, in the first instance, limiting it) were almost entirely economic. It cannot plausibly be argued that it enhanced our security to accomplish this result; neither does it make much sense to say that it diminished it.[16] The ABM lent itself ideally to the action taken for the following basic reasons: (1) it was not yet acquired and deployed; (2) its efficacy was always questionable and becoming more so; (3) it would be an extraordinarily expensive system to build,

[15] The standard monograph on the first and most important of these treaties, that of Washington in 1922, is still Harold and Margaret Sprout, *Toward a New Order of Sea Power* (Princeton: Princeton University Press, 2nd ed., 1943.)

[16] One of the few hold-outs on the latter view is Dr. Donald G. Brennan, in his "When the SALT Hit the Fan," *National Review*, vol. 24, (June 23, 1972) pp. 685–692. See also his testimony in the ratification hearings of the SALT 1 agreements. It is important to notice that Dr. Brennan never thought that the ABM would be effective in protecting cities unless offensive forces were suitably limited. In his current view, the massive buildup of offensive forces since the late 1960s has diminished the feasibility (though not the desirability) of such a posture, at least based on current technology, to near the vanishing point.

deploy, and maintain; and (4) it would be difficult domestically to win a consensus on dropping it except through an instrument that obliged the Soviet Union to do likewise.

The original SALT agreement limited each side to two sites, one being the capital or "national command authority," the other being a single field site containing no more than 100 interceptor missiles of all types (in the United States the Spartan and the Sprint missiles). It quickly became obvious that the Congress would never support a system for the single city of Washington. An amendment in 1974 to the SALT agreement limited each side to one site only. The United States by then had built such a site, at Grand Forks, North Dakota, but in 1975 the Congress, facing the choice of appropriating $60 million to continuing it for another year or $40 million for liquidating it, chose the latter course. It is difficult to tell what the total expenditure had been at that time—it had cost about $4 billion to develop just the Spartan missile with its special nuclear warhead, of which some 30 were built—but there is no doubt that many times that sum was saved by abandoning it.

It retrospect the ABM may look like a system that virtually cried out for mutual abrogation, but it certainly did not look so at the time. The support for it within the defense community was intense. Now the ABM appears to have been a target of opportunity, torpedoed at just the right time and by the right means.

It should be the prime function of an intelligently directed arms control program always to be looking out for more such targets. They will be found especially among emerging systems, but also among those existing ones which are costly to maintain and of dubious marginal utility. One might, for example, nominate for consideration our aircraft bombing force, including both the proposed B-1 and the existing 400 B-52s. What is the marginal utility of this force *along with* our submarine-launched and our land-based missiles? If some bombers are desirable, do we need all those proposed? It would indeed take some stout-hearted men to explore this issue together with, or perhaps in the face of, the Air Force, but such a course is not unprecedented. The naval treaties of 1922 and 1930 were bitterly opposed by the chief naval officers and the navy leagues of virtually all the countries involved, which makes their achievement all the more remarkable. Perhaps the required stout-heartedness *is* what arms control is all about.

Arms Races:
Prerequisites and Results

SAMUEL P. HUNTINGTON

INTRODUCTION

Si vis pacem, para bellum, is an ancient and authoritative adage of military policy. Of no less acceptance, however, is the other, more modern, proposition: "Armaments races inevitably lead to war." Juxtaposed, these two advices suggest that the maxims of social science, like the proverbs of folklore, reflect a many-sided truth. The social scientist, however, cannot escape with so easy an observation. He has the scholar's responsibility to determine as fully as possible to what extent and under what conditions his conflicting truths are true. The principal aim of this essay is to attempt some resolution of the issue: When are arms races a prelude to war and when are they a substitute for war?

Throughout history states have sought to maintain their peace and security by means of military strength. The arms race in which the military preparations of two states are intimately and directly interrelated is, however, a relatively modern phenomenon. The conflict between the apparent feasibility of preserving peace by arming for war and the apparent inevitability of competitive arms increases resulting in war is, therefore, a comparatively new one. The second purpose of this essay is to explore some of the circumstances which have brought about this uncertainty as to the relationship between war, peace and arms increases. The problem here is: What were the prerequisites to the emergence of the arms race as a significant form of international rivalry in the nineteenth and twentieth centuries?

For the purposes of this essay, an arms race is defined as a progressive, competitive peacetime increase in armaments by two states or coalition of states resulting from conflicting purposes or mutual fears. An arms race is thus a form of reciprocal interaction between two states or coalitions. A race cannot exist without an increase in arms, quantitatively or qualitatively, but every peacetime increase in arms is not necessarily the result of an arms race. A nation may expand its armmaments for the domestic purposes of aiding industry or curbing

From *Public Policy,* 1958, pp. 41–83. Copyright © 1958 by John Wiley & Sons, Inc. Reprinted with permission of John Wiley & Sons, Inc.

unemployment, or because it believes an absolute need exists for such an increase regardless of the actions of other states. In the 1880s and 1890s, for instance, the expansion of the United States Navy was apparently unrelated to the actions of any other power, and hence not part of an arms race. An arms race reflects disagreement between two states as to the proper balance of power between them. The concept of a "general" arms race in which a number of powers increase their armaments simultaneously is, consequently, a fallacious one. Such general increases either are not the result of self-conscious reciprocal interaction or are simply the sum of a number of two-state antagonisms. In so far as the arms policy of any one state is related to the armaments of other states, it is a function of concrete, specific goals, needs, or threats arising out of the political relations among the states. Even Britain's vaunted two-power naval standard will be found, on close analysis, to be rooted in specific threats rather than in abstract considerations of general policy.

PREREQUISITES FOR AN ARMS RACE

. . . Certain conditions peculiarly present in the nineteenth and twentieth centuries would appear to be responsible for the emergence of the arms race as a frequent and distinct form of international rivalry. Among the more significant of these conditions are: a state system which facilitates the balancing of power by internal rather than external means; the preeminence of military force-in-being over territory or other factors as an element of national power; the capacity within each state to increase its military strength through quantitative or qualitative means; and the conscious awareness by each state of the dependence of its own arms policy upon that of another state.[1]

---

[1] Since an arms race is necessarily a matter of degree, differences of opinion will exist as to whether any given relationship constitutes an arms race and as to what are the precise opening and closing dates of any given arms race. At the risk of seeming arbitrary, the following relationships are assumed to be arms races for the purposes of this essay:

1.	France v. England	naval	1840–1866
2.	France v. Germany	land	1874–1894
3.	England v. France & Russia	naval	1884–1904
4.	Argentina v. Chile	naval	1890–1902
5.	England v. Germany	naval	1898–1912
6.	France v. Germany	land	1911–1914
7.	England v. United States	naval	1916–1930
8.	Japan v. United States	naval	1916–1922
9.	France v. Germany	land	1934–1939
10.	Soviet Union v. Germany	land	1934–1941
11.	Germany v. England	air	1934–1939
12.	United States v. Japan	naval	1934–1941
13.	Soviet Union v. United States	nuclear	1946–

Balancing power: external and internal means. Arms races are an integral part of the international balance of power. From the viewpoint of a participant, an arms race is an effort to achieve a favorable international distribution of power. Viewed as a whole, a sustained arms race is a means of achieving a dynamic equilibrium of power between two states or coalitions of states. Arms races only take place between states in the same balance of power system. The more isolated a nation is from any balance of power system the less likely it is to become involved in an arms race. Within any such system, power may in general be balanced in two ways: externally through a realignment of the units participating in the system (diplomacy), or internally by changes in the inherent power of the units. The extent to which the balancing process operates through external or internal means usually depends upon the number of states participating in the system, the opportunity for new states to join the system, and the relative distribution of power among the participating states.

The relations among the states in a balance of power system may tend toward any one of three patterns, each of which assigns somewhat different roles to the external and internal means of balancing power. A situation of *bellum omnium contra omnes* exists when there are a large number of states approximately equal in power and when there is an approximately equal distribution of grievances and antagonisms among the states. In such a system, which was perhaps most closely approximated by the city-states of the Italian Renaissance, primary reliance is placed upon wily diplomacy, treachery and surprise attack. Since no bilateral antagonisms continue for any length of time, a sustained arms race is very unlikely. A second balance of power pattern involves an all-against-one relationship: the coalition of a number of weaker states against a single *grande nation*. The fears and grievances of the weaker states are concentrated against the stronger, and here again primary reliance is placed upon diplomatic means of maintaining or restoring the balance. European politics assumed this pattern in the successive coalitions to restrain the Hapsburgs, Louis XIV, Frederick II, Napoleon and Hitler. At times, efforts may be made to bring in other states normally outside the system to aid in restoring the balance.

A third pattern of balance of power politics involves bilateral antagonisms between states or coalitions of states roughly equal in strength. Such bilateral antagonisms have been a continuing phenomenon in the western balance of power system: France vs. England, Austria vs. France and then Prussia (Germany) vs. France, Austria-Hungary vs. Russia, the Triple Alliance vs. the Triple Entente, and now, the United States vs. the Soviet Union. In these relationships the principal grievances and antagonisms of any two states become concentrated upon each other, and as a result, this antagonism becomes the primary focus of their respective foreign policies. In this situation, diplomacy and alliances may play a signifi-cant role if a "balancer" exists who can shift his weight to whichever side appears to be weaker. But no balancing state can exist if all the major powers are involved in bilateral antagonisms or if a single over-riding antagonism forces virtually all the states in the system to choose one side or the other (bipolarization). In these circumstances, the balancing of power by rearranging the units of power becomes dif-ficult. Diplomatic maneuvering gives way to the massing of military force. Each state relies more on armaments and less on alliances. Other factors being equal, the pressures toward an arms race are greatest when international relations assume this form.

In the past century the relative importance of the internal means of balancing power has tended to increase. A single worldwide balance of power system has tended to develop, thereby eliminating the possibili-ty of bringing in outside powers to restore the balance. At the same time, however, the number of great powers has fairly constantly decreased, and bilateral antagonisms have consequently become of greater importance. Small powers have tended to seek security either through neutrality (Switzerland, Sweden) or through reliance upon broadly organized efforts at collective security. The growth of the lat-ter idea has tended to make military alliances aimed at a specific com-mon foe less reputable and justifiable. . . . Alliances were perhaps the primary means of balancing power in Europe before 1870. Between 1870 and 1914, both alliances and armaments played important roles. Since 1918 the relative importance of armaments has probably in-creased. The primary purpose of the military pacts of the post-World War II period, with the possible exception of NATO, generally has been the extension of the protection of a great power to a series of minor powers, rather than the uniting of a number of more or less equal powers in pursuit of a common objective. In addition, the development of democractic control over foreign policy has made alliances more difficult. Alignments dictated by balance of power con-siderations may be impossible to carry out due to public opinion. Rapid shifts in alliances from friends to enemies also are difficult to execute in a democratic society. Perhaps, too, a decline in the arts of diplomacy has contributed to the desire to rest one's security upon resources which are "owned" rather than "pledged."

Elements of power: money, territory, armaments. Arms races only take place when military forces-in-being are of direct and prime im-portance to the power of a state. During the age of mercantilism, for instance, monetary resources were highly valued as an index of power, and, consequently, governmental policy was directed toward the ac-cumulation of economic wealth which could then be transformed into military and political power. These actions, which might take a variety of forms, were in some respects the seventeenth century equivalents of the nineteenth and twentieth century arms races. In the eighteenth century, territory was of key importance as a measure of power. The size of the armies which a state could maintain was roughly proportional to its population, and, in an agrarian age, its population was roughly proportional to its territory. Consequently, an increase in military power required an increase in territory. Within Europe, territory could be acquired either by conquest, in which case a surprise attack was probably desirable in order to forestall intervention by other states, or by agreement among the great powers to partition a smaller power. Outside of Europe, colonial territories might contribute wealth if not manpower to the mother country, and these could be acquired either by discovery and settlement or by conquest. Consequently, territorial compensations were a primary means of balancing power, and through the acquisition of colonies, states jealous of their relative power could strive to improve their position without directly challenging another major state and thereby provoking a war.

During the nineteenth century territory bacame less important as an index of power, and industry and armaments more important. By the end of the century all the available colonial lands had been occupied by the major powers. In addition, the rise of nationalism and of self-determination made it increasingly difficult to settle differences by the division and bartering of provinces, small powers and colonies. By expanding its armaments, however, a state could still increase its relative power without decreasing the absolute power of another state. Reciprocal increases in armaments made possible an unstable and dynamic, but none the less real equilibrium among the major powers. The race for armaments tended to replace the race for colonies as the "escape hatch" through which major states could enhance their power without directly challenging each other.

The increased importance of armaments as a measure of national power was reflected in the new emphasis upon disarmament in the efforts to resolve antagonisms among nations. The early peace writers, prior to the eighteenth century, placed primary stress upon a federation of European states rather than upon disarmament measures. It was not until Kant's essay on "Eternal Peace" that the dangers inherent in an arms race were emphasized, and the reduction of armaments made a primary goal. In 1766 Austria made the first proposal for a bilateral reduction in forces to Frederick the Great, who rejected it. In 1787 France and England agreed not to increase their naval establishments. In 1816 the Czar made the first proposal for a general reduction in armaments. Thenceforth, throughout the nineteenth century problems of armament and disarmament played an increasingly significant role in diplomatic negotiations.[2]

---

[2] Merze Tate, *The Disarmament Illusion* (New York, 1942), p. 7.

Capacity for qualitative and quantitative increases in military power. An arms race requires the progressive increase from domestic sources of the absolute military power of a state. This may be done quantitatively, by expanding the numerical strength of its existing forms of military force, or qualitatively, by replacing its existing forms of military force (usually weapons systems) with new and more effective forms of force. The latter requires a dynamic technology, and the former the social, political and economic capacity to reallocate resources from civilian to military purposes. Before the nineteenth century the European states possessed only a limited capacity for either quantitative or qualitative increases in military strength. Naval technology, for instance, had been virtually static for almost three centuries: the sailing ship of 1850 was not fundamentally different from that of 1650, the naval gun of 1860 not very much removed from that of 1560.[3] As a result, the ratio of construction time to use time was extremely low: a ship built in a few months could be used for the better part of a century. Similarly, with land armaments, progress was slow, and only rarely could a power hope to achieve a decisive edge by a "technological breakthrough". Beginning with the Industrial Revolution, however, the pace of innovation in military technology constantly quickened, and the new weapons systems inevitably stimulated arms races. The introduction, first, of the steam warship and then of the ironclad, for instance, directly intensified the naval competition between England and France in the 1850s and 1860s. Throughout the nineteenth century, the importance of the weapons technician constantly increased relative to the importance of the strategist.

Broad changes in economic and political structure were at the same time making quantitative arms races feasible. The social system of the *ancien régime* did not permit a full mobilization of the economic and manpower resources of a nation. So long as participation in war was limited to a small class, competitive increases in the size of armies could not proceed very far. The destruction of the old system, the spread of democracy and liberalism, the increasing popularity among all groups of the "nation in arms" concept, all permitted a much more complete mobilization of resources for military purposes than had been possible previously. In particular, the introduction of universal military service raised the ceiling on the size of the army to the point where the limiting factor was the civilian manpower necessary to support the army. In addition, the development of industry permitted the mass production and mass accumulation of the new weapons which the new technology had invented. The countries which lagged behind

---

[3] Bernard Brodie, *Sea Power in the Machine Age* (Princeton, 2nd ed., 1944), p. 181; Arthur J. Marder, *The Anatomy of British Sea Power* (New York, 1940), pp. 3–4.

in the twin processes of democratization and industrialization were severely handicapped in the race for armaments.

In the age of limited wars little difference existed between a nation's military strength in peace and its military strength in war. During the nineteenth century, however, the impact of democracy and industrialism made wars more total, victory or defeat in them became more significant (and final), military superiority became more critically important, and consequently a government had to be more fully assured of the prospect of victory before embarking upon war. In addition, the professional officer corps which developed during the nineteenth century felt a direct responsibility for the military security of the state and emphasized the desirability of obtaining a safe superiority in armaments As a result, unless one of the participants possessed extensive staying power due to geography or resources, the outcome of a war depended almost as much upon what happened before the declarations of war as after. By achieving superiority in armaments it might be possible for a state to achieve the fruits of war without suffering the risks and liabilities of war. Governments piled up armaments in peacetime with the hope either of averting war or of insuring success in it should it come.

Absolute and relative armaments goals. A state may define its armaments goals in one of two ways. It can specify a certain *absolute* level or type of armaments which it believes necessary for it to possess irrespective of the level or type possessed by other states. Or, it can define its goal in *relative* terms as a function of the armaments of other states. Undoubtedly, in any specific case, a state's armaments reflect a combination of both absolute and relative considerations. Normally, however, one or the other will be dominant and embodied in offical statements of the state's armaments goals in the form of an "absolute need" or a ratio-goal. Thus, historically Great Britain followed a relative policy with respect to the capital ships in its navy but an absolute policy with respect to its cruisers, the need for which, it was held, stemmed from the unique nature of the British Empire.

If every state had absolute goals, arms races would be impossible: each state would go its separate way uninfluenced by the actions of its neighbors. Nor would a full scale arms race develop if an absolute goal were pursued consistently by only one power in an antagonistic realtionship: whatever relative advantage the second power demanded would be simply a function of the constant absolute figure demanded by the first power. An arms race only arises when two or more powers consciously determine the quantitative or qualitative aspects of their armaments as functions of the armaments of the other power. Absolute goals, however, are only really feasible when a state is not a member of or only on the periphery of a balance of power system. Except in these rare cases, the formulation by a state of its armaments goal in absolute terms is more likely to reflect the desire to obscure from its rivals the true relative superiority which it wishes to achieve or to obscure from itself the need to participate actively in the balancing process. Thus, its Army Law of 1893 was thought to give Germany a force which in quantity and quality would be unsurpassable by any other power. Hence Germany

> was, in the eyes of her rulers, too powerful to be affected by a balancing movement restricted only to the continent. . . . From this time on Germany considered herself militarily invulnerable, as if in a state of splendid isolation, owing to the excellence of her amalgam army.[4]

As a result, Germany let her army rest, turned her energies to the construction of a navy, and then suddenly in 1911 became aware of her landpower inferiority to the Dual Alliance and had to make strenuous last minute efforts to increase the size of her forces. Somewhat similarly, states may define absolute qualitative goals, such as the erection of an impenetrable system of defenses (Maginot Line) or the possession of an "ultimate" or "absolute" weapon, which will render superfluous further military effort regardless of what other states may do. In 1956 American airpower policy was consciously shaped not to the achievement of any particular level of air strength relative to that of the Soviet Union, but rather to obtaining an absolute "sufficiency of airpower" which would permit the United States to wreak havoc in the Soviet Union in the event of an all-out war.[5] The danger involved in an absolute policy is that, if carried to an extreme, it may lead to a complacent isolationism blind to the relative nature of power.

The armaments of two states can be functionally interrelated only if they are also similar or complementary. An arms race is impossible between a power which possesses only a navy and one which possesses only an army: no one can match divisions against battleships. A functional realtionship between armaments is complementary when two

---

[4] Arpad Kovacs, "Nation in Arms and Balance of Power: The Interaction of German Military Legislation and European Politics, 1866–1914" (Ph.D. Thesis, University of Chicago, 1934), p. 159.

[5] For the most complete statement of the sufficiency theory, see Donald A. Quarles, Secretary of the Air Force, "How Much is 'Enough'?" *Air Force*, XLIX (September, 1956), pp. 51–52: ". . . there comes a time in the course of increasing our airpower when we must make a determination of sufficiency. . . .

"Sufficiency of airpower, to my mind, must be determined period by period on the basis of the force required to accomplish the mission assigned. . . . Neither side can hope by a mere margin of superiority in airplanes or other means of delivery of atomic weapons to escape the catastrophe of such a [total] war. Beyond a certain point, this prospect is not the result of *relative* strength of the two opposed forces. It is the *absolute* power in the hands of each, and in the substantial invulnerability of this power to interdiction."

See also H. Rept. 2104, 84th Cong., 2d Sess., p. 40 (1956).

military forces possessing different weapons systems are designed for combat with each other. In this sense, an air defense fighter command complements an opposing strategic bombing force or one side's submarine force complements the other's antisubmarine destroyers and hunter-killer groups. A functional relationship is similar when two military forces are not only designed for combat with each other but also possess similar weapons systems, as has been very largely the case with land armies and with battle fleets of capital ships. In most instances in history, arms races have involved similar forces rather than complementary forces, but no reason exists why there should not be an arms race in the latter. The only special problem posed by a complementary arms race is that of measuring the relative strengths of the opposing forces. In a race involving similar forces, a purely quantitative measurement usually suffices; in one of complementary forces, qualitative judgments are necessary as to the effectiveness of one type of weapons system against another.

Even if both parties to an arms race possess similar land, sea and air forces, normally the race itself is focused on only one of these components or even on only one weapons system within one component, usually that type of military force with which they are best able to harm each other.[6] This component or weapons system is viewed by the states as the decisive form of military force in their mutual relationship, and competition in other forces or components is subordinated to the race in this decisive force. The simple principles of concentration and economy of force require states to put their major efforts where they will count most. The arms race between Germany and England before World War I was in capital ships. The arms race between the same two countries before World War II was in bombers and fighters. The current race between the Soviet Union and the United States has largely focused upon nuclear weapons and their means of delivery, and has not extended to the massing of conventional weapons and manpower. In general, economic considerations also preclude a state from becoming involved at the same time in two separate arms races with two different powers in two different forms of military force. When her race in land forces with France slackened in the middle 1890s, Germany embarked upon her naval race with Great Britain, and for the first decade of the twentieth century the requirements of this enterprise prevented any substantial increase in the size of the army. When the naval race in turn slackened in 1912, Germany returned to the rebuilding of her ground forces and to her military manpower race with France.

---

[6] Other things being equal, this will probably be the "dominant weapon" in Fuller's sense, that is, the weapon with the longest effective range. See J. F. C. Fuller, *Armament and History* (New York, 1945), pp. 7-8.

Two governments can consciously follow relative arms policies only if they are well informed of their respective military capabilities. The general availability of information concerning armaments is thus a precondition for an arms race. Prior to the nineteenth century when communication and transportation were slow and haphazard, a state would frequently have only the vaguest notions of the military programs of its potential rivals. Often it was possible for one state to make extensive secret preparations for war. In the modern world, information with respect to military capabilities has become much more widespread and has been one of the factors increasing the likelihood of arms races. Even now, however, many difficulties exist in getting information concerning the arms of a rival which is sufficiently accurate to serve as the basis for one's own policy. At times misconceptions as to the military strengths and policies of other states become deeply ingrained, and at other times governments simply choose to be blind to significant changes in armaments. Any modern government involved in an arms race, moreover, is confronted with conflicting estimates of its opponent's strength. Politicians, governmental agencies and private groups all tend to give primary credit to intelligence estimates which confirm military policies which they have already espoused for other reasons. The armed services inevitably overstate the military capabilities of the opponent: in 1914, for instance, the Germans estimated the French army to have 121,000 more men than the German army, the French estimated the German army to have 134,000 more men than the French army, but both countries agreed in their estimates of the military forces of third powers.[7] Governments anxious to reduce expenditures and taxes pooh-pooh warnings as to enemy strength: the reluctance of the Baldwin government to credit reports of the German air build-up seriously delayed British rearmament in the 1930s. At other times, exaggerated reports as to enemy forces may lead a government to take extraordinary measures which are subsequently revealed to have been unnecessary. Suspicions that the Germans were exceeding their announced program of naval construction led the English government in 1909 to authorize and construct four "contingency" Dreadnoughts. Subsequently revelations proved British fears to be groundless. Similarly, in 1956 reports of Soviet aircraft production, later asserted to be considerably exaggerated, influenced Congress to appropriate an extra $900 million for the Air Force. At times, the sudden revelation of a considerable increase in an enemy's capabilities may produce a panic, such as the invasion panics of England in 1847–48, 1951–53, and 1959–61. The tense atmosphere of an arms race also tends to encourage reports of

---

[7] Bernadotte E. Schmitt, *The Coming of the War: 1914* (New York, 2 vols., 1930), I, 54n.

mysterious forces possessed by the opponent and of his development of secret new weapons of unprecedented power. Nonetheless, fragmentary and uncertain though information may be, its availability in one form or another is what makes the arms race possible.

ABORTIVE AND SUSTAINED ARMS RACES

An arms race may end in war, formal or informal agreement between the two states to call off the race, or victory for one state which achieves and maintains the distribution of power which it desires and ultimately causes its rival to give up the struggle. The likelihood of war arising from an arms race depends in the first instance upon the relation between the power and grievances of one state to the power and grievances of the other. War is least likely when grievances are low, or, if grievances are high, the sum of the grievances and power of one state approximates the sum of the grievances and power of the other. An equality of power and an equality of grievances will thus reduce the chances of war, as will a situation in which one state has a marked superiority in power and the other in grievances. Assuming a fairly equal distribution of grievances, the likelihood of an arms race ending in war tends to vary inversely with the length of the arms race and directly with the extent to which it is quantitative rather than qualitative in character. This section deals with the first of these relationships and the next section with the second.

An arms race is a series of interrelated increases in armaments which if continued over a period of time produces a dynamic equilibrium of power between two states. A race in which this dynamic equilibrium fails to develop may be termed an abortive arms race. In these instances, the previously existing static equilibrium between the two states is disrupted without being replaced by a new equilibrium reflecting their relative competitive efforts in the race. Instead, rapid shifts take place or appear about to take place in the distribution of power which enhance the willingness of one state or the other to precipitate a conflict. At least one and sometimes two danger points occur at the beginning of every arms race. The first point arises with the response of the challenged state to the initial increases in armaments by the challenging state. The second danger point is the reaction of the challenger who has been successful in initially achieving his goal to the frantic belated efforts of the challenged state to retrieve its former position.

The formal beginning of an arms race is the first increase in armaments by one state—the challenger—caused by a desire to alter the existing balance of power between it and another state. Prior to this initial action, a pre-arms race static equilibrium may be said to exist. This equilibrium does not necessarily mean an equality of power. It simply reflects the satisfaction of each state with the existing distribution of power in the light of its grievances and antagonisms with the other state. Some of the most stable equilibriums in history have also been ones which embodied an unbalance of power. From the middle of the eighteenth century down to the 1840s, a static equilibrium existed between the French and British navies in which the former was kept roughly two-thirds as strong as the latter. After the naval race of 1841–1865 when this ratio was challenged, the two powers returned to it for another twenty year period. From 1865 to 1884 both British and French naval expenditures were amazingly constant, England's expenditures varying between 9.5 and 10.5 million pounds (with the exception of the crisis years of 1876–77 when they reached 11 and 12 million pounds) and France's expenditures varying from 6.5 to 7.5 million pounds.[8] In some instances the equilibrium may receive the formal sanction of a treaty such as the Washington arms agreement of 1922 or the treaty of Versailles. In each of these cases, the equilibrium lasted until 1934 when the two powers—Germany and Japan—who had been relegated to a lower level of armaments decided that continued inferiority was incompatible with their national goals and ambitions. In both cases, however, it was not the disparity of power in itself which caused the destruction of the equilibrium, but rather the fact that this disparity was unacceptable to the particular groups which assumed control of those countries in the early 1930s. In other instances, the static equilibrium may last for only a passing moment, as when France began reconstructing its army almost immediately after its defeat by Germany in 1871.

For the purposes of analysis it is necessary to specify a particular increase in armaments by one state as marking the formal beginning of the arms race. This is done not to pass judgment on the desirability or wisdom of the increase, but simply to identify the start of the action and reaction which constitute the race. In most instances, this initial challenge is not hard to locate. It normally involves a major change in the policy of the challenging state, and more likely than not it is formally announced to the world. The reasons for the challenging state's discontent with the status quo may stem from a variety of causes. It may feel that the growth of its economy, commerce, and population should be reflected in changes in the military balance of power (Germany, 1898; United States, 1916; Soviet Union, 1946). Nationalistic, bellicose, or militaristic individuals or parties may come to power who are unwilling to accept an equilibrium which other groups in their society had been willing to live with or negotiate about (Germany and Japan, 1934). New political issues may arise which cause a deterioration in the relationships of the state with another power and which

    [8] See Richard Cobden, "Three Panics: An Historical Episode," *Political Writings* (London, 2 vols., 1867), II, p. 308; The Cobden Club, *The Burden of Armaments* (London, 1905), pp. 66–68.

consequently lead it to change its estimate of the arms balance necessary for its security (France, 1841, 1875; England, 1884).

Normally the challenging state sets a goal for itself which derives from the relation between the military strengths of the two countries prior to the race. If the relation was one of disparity, the initial challenge usually comes from the weaker power which aspires to parity or better. Conceivably a stronger power could initiate an arms race by deciding that it required an even higher ratio of superiority over the weaker power. But in actual practice this is seldom the case: the gain in security achieved in upping a 2:1 ratio to 3:1, for instance, rarely is worth the increased economic costs and political tensions. If parity of military power existed between the two countries, the arms race begins when one state determines that it requires military force superior to that of the other country.

In nine out of ten races the slogan of the challenging state is either "parity" or superiority." Only in rare cases does the challenger aim for less than this, for unless equality or superiority is achieved, the arms race is hardly likely to be worthwhile. The most prominent exception to the "parity or superiority" rule is the Anglo-German naval race of 1898–1912. In its initial phase, German policy was directed not to the construction of a navy equal to England's but rather to something between that and the very minor navy which she possessed prior to the race. The rationale for building such a force was provided by Tirpitz's "risk theory": Germany should have a navy large enough so that Britain could not fight her without risking damage to the British navy to such an extent that it would fall prey to the naval forces of third powers (i.e., France and Russia). The fallacies in this policy became obvious in the following decade. On the one hand, for technical reasons it was unlikely that an inferior German navy could do serious damage to a superior British fleet, and, on the other hand, instead of making Britain wary of France and Russia the expansion of the German navy tended to drive her into their arms and consequently to remove the hostile third powers who were supposed to pounce upon a Britain weakened by Germany.[9] One can only conclude that it is seldom worthwhile either for a superior power to attempt significantly to increase its superiority or for a weaker power to attempt only to reduce its degree of inferiority. The rational goals in an arms race are parity or superiority.

In many respects the most critical aspect of a race is the initial response which the challenged state makes to the new goals posited by the challenger. In general, these responses can be divided into four

[9] For the risk theory, see Alfred von Tirpitz, *My Memoirs* (New York, 2 vols., 1919), I, pp. 79, 84, 121, 159–160, and for a trenchant criticism, E. L. Woodward, *Great Britain and the German Navy* (Oxford, 1935), pp. 31–39.

categories, two of which preserve the possibility of peace, two of which make war virtually inevitable. The challenged state may, first, attempt to counterbalance the increased armaments of its rival through diplomatic means or it may, secondly, immediately increase its own armaments in an effort to maintain or directly to restore the previously existing balance of military power. While neither of these responses guarantees the maintenance of peace, they at least do not precipitate war. The diplomatic avenue of action, if it exists, is generally the preferred one. It may be necessary, however, for the state to enhance its own armaments as well as attempting to secure reliable allies. Or, if alliances are impossible or undesirable for reasons of state policy, the challenged state must rely upon its own increases in armaments as the way of achieving its goal. In this case a sustained arms race is likely to result. During her period of splendid isolation, for instance, England met the French naval challenge of the 1840s by increasing the size and effectiveness of her own navy. At the end of the century when confronted by the Russo-French challenge, she both increased her navy and made tentative unsuccessful efforts to form an alliance with Germany. In response to the German challenge a decade later, she again increased her navy and also arrived at a rapprochement with France and Russia.

If new alliances or increased armaments appear impossible or undesirable, a state which sees its superiority or equality in military power menaced by the actions of another state may initiate preventive action while still strong enough to forestall the change in the balance of power. The factors which enter into the decision to wage preventive war are complex and intangible, but, conceivably, if the state had no diplomatic opportunities and if it was dubious of its ability to hold its own in an arms race, this might well be a rational course of behavior.[10] Tirpitz explicitly recognized this in his concept of a "danger zone" through which the German navy would pass and during which a strong likelihood would exist that the British would take preventive action to destroy the German fleet. Such an attack might be avoided, he felt, by a German diplomatic "peace offensive" designed to calm British fears and to assure them of the harmless character of German intentions. Throughout the decade after 1898 the Germans suffered periodic scares of an imminent British attack. Although preventive action was never seriously considered by the British government, enough talk went on in high British circles of "Copenhagening" the German fleet to give the Germans some cause for alarm. In the "war in sight"

---

[10] On the considerations going into the waging of preventive war, see my "To Choose Peace or War," *United States Naval Institute Proceedings*, LXXXIII (April, 1957), pp. 360–62.

crisis of 1875, the initial success of French rearmament efforts aimed at restoring an equality of military power with Germany stimulated German statesmen and military leaders carefully to consider the desirability of preventive war. Similarly, the actions of the Nazis in overthrowing the restrictions of the Treaty of Versailles in the early 1930s and starting the European arms build-up produced arguments in Poland and France favoring preventive war. After World War II at the beginning of the arms race between the United States and the Soviet Union a small but articulate segment of opinion urged the United States to take preventive action before the Soviet Union developed nuclear weapons.[11] To a certain extent, the Japanese attack on the United States in 1941 can be considered a preventive action designed to forestall the inevitable loss of Japanese naval superiority in the western Pacific which would have resulted from the two-ocean navy program begun by the United States in 1939. In 1956 the Egyptians began to rebuild their armaments from Soviet sources and thus to disturb the equilibrium which had existed with Israel since 1949. This development was undoubtedly one factor leading Israel to attack Egypt and thereby attempt to resolve at least some of the outstanding issues between them before the increase in Egyptian military power.

At the other extreme from preventive action, a challenged state simply may not make any immediate response to the upset of the existing balance of power. The challenger may then actually achieve or come close to achieving the new balance of military force which it considers necessary. In this event, roles are reversed, the challenged suddenly awakens to its weakened position and becomes the challenger, engaging in frantic and strenuous last-ditch efforts to restore the previously existing military ratio. In general, the likelihood of war increases just prior to a change in military superiority from one side to the other. If the challenged state averts this change by alliances or increased armaments, war is avoidable. On the other hand, the challenged state may precipitate war in order to prevent the change, or it may provoke war by allowing the change to take place and then attempting to undo it. In the latter case, the original challenger, having achieved parity or superiority, is in no mood or position to back down; the anxious efforts of its opponent to regain its military strength appear to be obvious war preparation; and consequently the original challenger normally will not hesitate to risk or provoke a war while it may still benefit from its recent gains.

Belated responses resulting in last-gasp arms races are most clearly seen in the French and British reactions to German rearmament in the

---

[11] *Ibid.*, pp. 363–66.

1930s. The coming-to-power of the Nazis and their subsequent rearmament efforts initially provoked little military response in France. In
part, this reflected confidence in the qualitative superiority of the
French army and the defensive strength of the Maginot Line. In part,
too, it reflected the French political situation in which these groups
most fearful of Nazi Germany were generally those most opposed to
large armies and militarism, while the usual right-wing supporters of
the French army were those to whom Hitler appeared least dangerous.
As a result, the French army and the War Ministry budget remained
fairly constant between 1933 and 1936. Significant increases in French
armaments were not made until 1937 and 1938, and the real French
rearmament effort got under way in 1939. France proposed to spend
more on armaments in that single year than the total of her expenditures during the preceding five years. By then, however, the five-to-
one superiority in military effectives which she had possessed over
Germany in 1933 had turned into a four-to-three inferiority.[12]

Roughly the same process was going on with respect to the ratio between the British and German air forces. At the beginning of the 1930s
the Royal Air Force, although a relatively small force, was undoubtedly much stronger than anything which the Germans had
managed to create surreptitiously. During the period from 1934 to
1938, however, the strength of the RAF in comparison to the Luftwaffe steadily declined. In July 1934, Churchill warned Parliament
that the German air force had then reached two-thirds the strength of
the British Home Defense Air Force, and that if present and proposed
programs were continued, the Germans would achieve parity by
December 1935. Baldwin assured the Commons that Britain would
maintain a fifty per cent superiority over Germany. Subsequently,
however, Churchill's estimates proved to be more correct than those
of the Government, and the air program had to be drastically increased in 1936 and 1937. By then, however, two years had been lost.
In 1936 Germany achieved parity with Britain. In the spring of 1937
the Luftwaffe exceeded the RAF in first-line strength and reserves. By
September 1938 it was almost twice as large as the RAF, and the production of aircraft in Germany was double that in England. The
British vigorously pushed their efforts to make up for lost time:
British aviation expenditures which had amounted to 16.8 million
pounds in 1934–35 rose to 131.4 millions in 1937–38, and were
budgeted at 242.7 millions for 1939–40. The Germans were now on
top and the British the challengers moving to close the gap. The

---

[12] N. M. Sloutzski, *World Armaments Race, 1919–1939* (Geneva Studies, Vol. XII,
No.1, July 1941), pp. 45–46, 99–101. In 1933 the French army numbered approximately
508,000 men, the German army roughly 100,000. In 1939 the French army numbered
629,000 men, the German army 800-900,000.

readiness of the Germans to go to war consequently was not unnatural. As far back as 1936, the British Joint Planning Staff had picked September 1939 as the most likely date for the beginning of a war because in the fall of 1939 Germany's armed strength would reach its peak in comparison with that of the allies. This forecast proved true on both points, and it was not until after the start of the war that the British began seriously to catch up with the head start of the Luftwaffe. British aircraft production first equalled that of the Germans in the spring of 1940.

A slightly different example of a belated, last minute arms race is found in the German-French and German-Russian competitions of 1911–1914. In this instance, deteriorating relations between the two countries led both to make strenuous efforts to increase their forces in a short time and enhanced the willingness of each to go to war. For a decade or more prior to 1911, German and French armaments had been relatively stable, and during the years 1908–1911 relations between the two countries had generally improved. The Agadir crisis of 1911 and the Balkan War of the following year stimulated the Germans to reconsider their armaments position. Fear of a Franco-Russian surprise attack and concern over the quantitative superiority of the French army led the Germans to make a moderate increase in their forces in 1912. In the spring of 1913 a much larger increase of 117,000 men was voted. Simultaneously, the French extended their term of military service from two to three years, thereby increasing their peacetime army by some 200,000 men. The Russians also had an extensive program of military reorganization under way. During the three year period 1911–14 the French army increased from 638,500 men to 846,000, and the German army from 626,732 to 806,026 men. If war had not broken out in 1914, the French would have been faced with an acute problem in maintaining a military balance with Germany. The population of France was about 39,000,000, that of Germany 65,000,000. During the twenty years prior to 1914 the French trained 82 per cent of their men liable for military service, the Germans 55 per cent of theirs. As a result, the two armies were approximately equal in size. If the Germans had continued to expand their army, the French inevitably would have fallen behind in the race: the extension of service in 1913 was a sign that they were reaching the limit of their manpower resources. Their alternatives would have been either to have provoked a war before Germany gained a decisive superiority, to have surrendered their goal of parity with Germany and with it any hope of retrieving Alsace-Lorraine, or to have stimulated further improvement of the military forces of their Russian ally and further expansion of the military forces of their British ally— perhaps putting pressure on Great Britain to institute universal military service. The Germans, on the other hand, felt themselves menaced by the reorganization of the Russian army. Already significantly outnumbered by the combined Franco-Russian armies, the Germans could hardly view with equanimity a significant increase in the efficiency of the Tsarist forces. Thus each side tended to see itself losing out in the arms race in the future and hence each side was more willing to risk a test of arms when the opportunity presented itself in 1914.

The danger of war is highest in the opening phases of an arms race, at which time the greatest elements of instability and uncertainty are present. If the challenged state neither resorts to preventive war nor fails to make an immediate response to the challenger's activities, a sustained arms race is likely to result with the probability of war decreasing as the initial action and counteraction fade into the past. Once the initial disturbances to the pre-arms race static equilibrium are surmounted, the reciprocal increases of the two states tend to produce a new, dynamic equilibrium reflecting their relative strength and participation in the race. In all probability, the relative military power of the two states in this dynamic equilibrium will fall somewhere between the previous status quo and the ratio-goal of the challenger. The sustained regularity of the increases in itself becomes an accepted and anticipated stabilizing factor in the relations between the two countries. A sustained quantitative race still may produce a war, but a greater likelihood exists that either the two states will arrive at a mutual accommodation reducing the political tensions which started the race or that one state over the long haul will gradually but substantially achieve its objective while the other will accept defeat in the race if this does not damage its vital interests. Thus, a twenty-five year sporadic naval race between France and England ended in the middle 1860s when France gave up any serious effort to challenge the 3 : 2 ratio which England had demonstrated the will and the capacity to maintain. Similarly, the Anglo-German naval race slackened after 1912 when, despite failure to reach formal agreement, relations improved between the two countries and even Tirpitz acquiesced in the British 16 : 10 ratio in capital ships.[13] Britain also successfully maintained her two-power standard against France and Russia for twenty years until changes in the international scene ended her arms competition with those two powers. Germany and France successively

---

[13] Some question might be raised as to whether the Anglo-German naval race ended before World War I or in World War I. It would appear, however, that the race was substantially over before the war began. The race went through two phases. During the first phase, 1898–1905, German policy was directed toward the construction of a "risk" navy. During the second phase, 1906–1912, the Anglo-French entente had removed the basis for a risk navy, and the introduction of the Dreadnought opened to the Germans the possibility of naval parity with Britain. By 1912, however, it was apparent to all that Britain had the will and the determination to maintain the 60 percent superiority which she desired over Germany, and to lay "two keels for one" if this should be necessary. In

increased their armies from the middle 1870s to the middle 1890s when tensions eased and the arms build-up in each country slackened. The incipient naval races among the United States, Britain, and Japan growing out of World War I were restricted by the Washington naval agreement; the ten-year cruiser competition between the United States and England ended in the London Treaty of 1930; and eventually the rise of more dangerous threats in the mid-1930s removed any remaining vestiges of Anglo-American naval rivalry. The twelve-year arms race between Chile and Argentina ended in 1902 with a comprehensive agreement between the two countries settling their boundary disputes and restricting their armaments. While generalizations are both difficult and dangerous, it would appear that a sustained arms race is much more likely to have a peaceful ending than a bloody one.

QUANTITATIVE AND QUALITATIVE ARMS RACES

A state may increase its military power quantitatively, by expanding the numerical strength of its existing military forces, or qualitatively, by replacing its existing forms of military force (normally weapons systems) with new and more effective forms of force. Expansion and innovation are thus possible characteristics of any arms race, and to some extent both are present in most races. Initially and fundamentally every arms race is quantitative in nature. The race begins when two states develop conflicting goals as to what should be the distribution of military power between them and give these goals explicit statement in quantitative ratios of the relative strenghts which each hopes to achieve in the decisive form of military force. The formal start of the race is the decision of the challenger to upset the existing balance and to expand its forces quantitatively. If at some point in the race a qualitative change produces a new decisive form of military force, the quantitative goals of the two states still remain roughly the same. The relative balance of power which each state desires to achieve is independent of the specific weapons and forces which enter into the balance. Despite the underlying adherence of both states to their original ratio-goals, however, a complex qualitative race

---

addition, increased tension with France and Russia over Morocco and the Balkans turned German attention to her army. In 1912 Bethmann-Hollweg accepted as the basis for negotiation a British memorandum the first point of which was: "Fundamental. Naval superiority recognized as essential to Great Britain." Relations between the two countries generally improved between 1912 and 1914: they cooperated in their efforts to limit the Balkan wars of 1912–13 and in the spring of 1914 arrived an agreement concerning the Baghdad railway and the Portuguese colonies. By June 1914 rivalry had abated to such an extent that the visit of a squadron of British battleships to Kiel became the occasion for warm expressions of friendship. "In a sense," as Bernadotte Schmitt says, "potential foes had become potential friends." *The Coming of the War:* 1914, I, pp. 72–73; Sidney B. Fay, *The Origins of the World War* (New York, 2 vols., 1928), I, pp. 299ff.; Tirpitz, *Memoirs,* I, pp. 271–72.

produced by rapid technological innovation is a very different phenomenon from a race which remains simply quantitative.

Probably the best examples of races which were primarily quantitative in nature are those between Germany and France between 1871 and 1914. The decisive element was the number of effectives each power maintained in its peacetime army and the number of reserves it could call to the colors in an emergency. Quantitative increases by one state invariably produced comparable increases by the other. The German army bill of 1880, for instance, added 25,000 men to the army and declared in its preamble that "far-reaching military reforms had been carried out outside of Germany which cannot remain without influence upon the military power of the neighboring countries." These increases it was alleged would produce "too considerable a numerical superiority of the enemy's forces."[14] Again in 1887 Bismarck used Boulanger's agitation for an increase in the French army as a means of putting through an expansion of the German one. After the French reorganized their army in 1889 and drastically increased the proportion of young men liable to military service, the Germans added 20,000 men to their force in 1890. Three years later a still larger increase was made in the German army and justified by reference to recent French and Russian expansions. Similarly, the naval race of 1884–1905 between England, on the one hand, and France and Russia, on the other, was primarily quantitative in nature. Naval budgets and numerical strengths of the two sides tended to fluctuate in direct relation with each other.

A qualitative arms race is more complex than a quantitative one because at some point it involves the decision by one side to introduce a new weapons system or form of military force. Where the capacity for technological innovation exists, the natural tendency is for the arms race to become qualitative. The introduction of a new weapons system obviously is normally desirable from the viewpoint of the state which is behind in the quantitative race. The English-French naval rivalry of 1841–1865 grew out of the deteriorating relations between the two countries over Syria, Tahiti and Spain. Its first manifestation was quantitative: in 1841 the number of seamen in the French navy which for nearly a century had been about two-thirds the number in the British navy was suddenly increased so as to almost equal the British strength. Subsequently the large expansions which the French proposed to make in their dockyards, especially at Toulon, caused even Cobden to observe that " a serious effort seemed really to be made to rival us at sea."[15] The Anglo-French quantitative rivalry subsided with the departure of Louis Philippe in 1848, but shortly

---

[14] Kovacs, "Nation in Arms," p. 36.
[15] Cobden, "Three Panics," p. 224.

thereafter it resumed on a new qualitative level with the determination of Napoleon III to push the construction of steam warships. The *Napoléon*, a screw propelled ship of the line of 92 guns, launched by the French in 1850 was significantly superior to anything the British could bring against it, until the *Agamemnon* was launched two years later. The alliance of the two countries in the Crimean War only temporarily suspended the naval race, and by 1858 the French had achieved parity with the British in fast screw ships of the line. In that year the French had 114 fewer sailing vessels in their navy than they had in 1852, while the number of British sailing ships had declined only from 299 to 296. On the other hand, the British in 1852 had a superiority of 73 sailing ships of the line to 45 for the French. By 1858, however, both England and France had 29 steam ships of the line while England had an enhanced superiority of 35 to 10 in sailing ships. A head start in steam construction and conversion plus the concentration of effort on this program had enabled the French, who had been hopelessly outnumbered in the previously decisive form of naval power, to establish a rough parity in the new form. In view of the British determination to restore their quantitative superiority and the superior industrial resources at their disposal, however, parity could only be temporary. In 1861 the British had 53 screw battleships afloat and 14 building while the French had only 35 afloat and two building.[16]

By the time that the British had reestablished their superiority in steam warships, their opponents had brought forward another innovation which again threatened British control of the seas. The French laid down four ironclads in 1858 and two in 1859. The first was launched in November 1859 and the next in March 1860. The British launched their first ironclad in December 1860. The British program, however, was hampered by the Admiralty's insistence upon continuing to build wooden warships. The French stopped laying down wooden line of battleships in 1856, yet the British, despite warnings that wooden walls were obsolete, continued building wooden ships down through 1860, and in 1861 the Admiralty brought in the largest request in its history for the purchase of timber.[17] Meanwhile, in the fall of 1860 the French started a new construction program for ten more ironclads to supplement the six they already had underway. The British learned of these projects in February 1861 and responded with a program to add nine new ironclads to their fleet. In May 1861, the French had a total of fifteen ironclads built or building, the British only seven. From 1860 until 1865 the French possessed superiority or parity with the British in

---

[16] *Ibid.*, pp. 304–308, 392–93.

[17] *Ibid.*, pp. 343, 403; Robert G. Albion, *Forests and Sea Power* (Cambridge, 1926), p. 408.

ironclad warships. In February 1863, for instance, the French had four ironclads mounting 146 guns ready for action, the British four ironclads mounting 116 guns. Thanks to the genius and initiative of the director of French naval construction, Dupuy de Lôme, and the support of Napoleon III, there had occurred, as one British military historian put it,

> an astonishing change in the balance of power which might have been epoch-making had it not been so brief, or if France and Britain had gone to war, a reversal which finds no place in any but technical histories and which is almost entirely unknown in either country today. In a word, supremacy at sea passed from Britain to France.[18]

This was not a supremacy, however, which France could long maintain. By 1866, Britannia had retrieved the trident. In that year England possessed nineteen ironclads, France thirteen, and the English superiority was enhanced by heavier guns. Thereafter the naval strengths of the two powers resumed the 3 : 2 ratio which had existed prior to 1841.

In general, as this sequence of events indicates, technological innovation favors, at least temporarily, the numerically weaker power. Its long-run effects, however, depend upon factors other than the currently prevailing balance of military strength. It was indeed paradoxical that France should make the innovations which she did make in her naval race with England. In the 1850s and 1860s France normally had twice as much timber on hand in her dockyards as had the British, and she was, of course, inferior to England in her coal and iron resources. Nonetheless she led the way in the introduction of steam and iron, while the Royal Navy, which was acutely hampered by a timber shortage clung to the wooden ships.[19] In this instance, on both sides, immediate needs and the prospects of immediate success prevailed over a careful consideration of long-term benefits.

The problem which technological innovation presents to the quantitatively superior power is somewhat more complex. The natural tendencies for such a state are toward conservatism: any significant innovation will undermine the usefulness of the current type of weapons system in which it possesses a superiority. What, however, should be the policy of a superior power with respect to making a technological change which its inferior rivals are likely to make in the near future? The British navy had a traditional answer to this problem: never introduce any development which will render existing ships obsolete but be prepared if any other state does make an innovation to push ahead

[18] Cyril Falls, *A Hundred Years of War* (London, 1953), p. 102.
[19] Albion, *Forests and Sea Power,* pp. 406–07; Brodie, *Sea Power in the Machine Age,* p. 441.

an emergency construction program which will restore the previously existing ratio. While this policy resulted, as we have seen above, in some close shaves, by the beginning of the twentieth century it had become a fundamental maxim of British naval doctrine. Consequently, Sir John Fisher's proposal in 1904 to revolutionize naval construction by introducing the "all big gun ship" which would render existing capital ships obsolete was also a revolution in British policy. In terms of its impact upon the Anglo-German naval balance, Fisher's decision was welcomed by many Germans and condemned by many British. Although the construction of Dreadnoughts would force Germany to enlarge the Kiel Canal, the Germans seized the opportunity to start the naval race afresh in a class of vessels in which the British did not have an overwhelming numerical superiority. For the first few years the British by virtue of their headstart would have a larger number of Dreadnoughts, but then the German yards would start producing and the gap which had to be closed would be much smaller in the Dreadnoughts than in the pre-Dreadnought battleships. The introduction of the Dreadnought permitted the Germans to raise their sight from a "risk" navy (which had become meaningless since the Anglo-French entente in any event) to the possibility of parity with Britain. To many Britishers, on the other hand, construction of the Dreadnought seemed to be tantamount to sinking voluntarily a large portion of the British navy. The tremendous number of pre-Dreadnought capital ships which the Royal Navy possessed suddenly decreased in value. Great Britain, one British naval expert subsequently argued, had to write off seventy-five warships, the Germans only twenty-eight. British naval superiority fell by 40 or 50 per cent: in 1908 England had authorized twelve Dreadnoughts and the Germans nine; in pre-Dreadnought battleships the British had 63 and the Germans 26.[20]

Fisher's policy, however, was undoubtedly the correct one. Plans for an all-big-gun ship had been under consideration by various navies since 1903. The Russo-Japanese War underwrote the desirability of heavy armaments. The United States authorized the construction of two comparable vessels in March, 1905, and the Germans themselves were moving in that direction. The all-big-gun ship was inevitable, and this consideration led Fisher to insist that Britain must take the lead. While the superiority of the Royal Navy over the German fleet was significantly reduced, nonetheless at no time in the eight years after 1905 did the Germans approach the British in terms of numerical equality. Their highest point was in 1911 when their Dreadnought battleship and battle-cruiser strength amounted to 64 per cent of the

[20] Hector C. Bywater, *Navies and Nations* (London, 1927), pp. 27–28; Fay, *Origins of the World War*, I, p. 236.

British strength.[21] Thus, by reversing the nineteenth century policy of the British navy, Fisher avoided the British experience of the 1850s and 1860s when technological innovations by an inferior power temporarily suspended Britain's supremacy on the seas.

The very incentive which an inferior power has to make a technological innovation is reason for the superior power to take the lead, if it can, in bringing in the innovation itself. The British-Dreadnought debate of 1904–1905 had its parallels in the problem confronting the American government in 1949–1950 concerning the construction of a hydrogen bomb. Like the British, the Americans possessed a superiority in the existing decisive type of weapons system. As in the British government, opinion was divided, and the arguments pro and con of the technicians and military experts had to be weighed against budgetary considerations. As with the Dreadnought, the new weapons system was pushed by a small group of zealots convinced of the inevitability and necessity of its development. In both cases, humanitarian statesmen and conservative experts wished to go slow. In each case, the government eventually decided to proceed with the innovation, and, in each case, the wisdom of its policy was demonstrated by the subsequent actions of its rival. In an arms race, what is technically possible tends to become politically necessary.

Whether an arms race is primarily quantitative or primarily qualitative in nature has a determining influence upon its outcome. This influence is manifested in the different impacts which the two types of races have on the balance of military power between the two states and on the relative demands which they make on state resources.

Qualitative and quantitative races and the balance of power. In a simple quantitative race one state is very likely to develop a definite superiority in the long run. The issue is simply who has the greater determination and the greater resources. Once a state falls significantly behind, it is most unlikely that it will ever be able to overcome the lead of its rival. A qualitative race, on the other hand, in which there is a series of major technological innovations in reality consists of a number of distinct races. Each time a new weapons system is introduced a new race takes place in the development and accumulation of that weapon. As the rate of technological innovation increases each separate component race decreases in time and extent. The simple quantitative race is like a marathon of undetermined distance which can only end with the exhaustion of one state or both, or with the state which is about to fall behind in the race pulling out its

---

[21] I am indebted to a paper by Mr. Peter E. Weil on "The Dreadnought and the Anglo-German Naval Race, 1905–1909" for statistics on British and German naval strengths.

firearms and attempting to despatch its rival. The qualitative race, on the other hand, resembles a series of hundred yard dashes, each beginning from a fresh starting line. Consequently, in a qualitative race hope springs anew with each phase. Quantitative superiority is the product of effort, energy, resources, and time. Once achieved it is rarely lost. Qualitative superiority is the product of discovery, luck, and circumstance. Once achieved it is always lost. Safety exists only in numbers. While a quantitative race tends to produce inequality between the two competing powers, a qualitative race tends toward equality irrespective of what may be the ratio-goals of the two rival states. Each new weapon instead of increasing the distance between the two states reduces it. The more rapid the rate of innovation the more pronounced is the tendency toward equality. Prior to 1905, for instance, Great Britain possessed a superiority in pre-Dreadnought battleships. By 1912 she had also established a clear and unassailable superiority in Dreadnoughts over Germany. But if Germany had introduced a super-Dreadnought in 1909, Great Britain could never have established its clear superiority in Dreadnoughts. She would have had to start over again in the new race. A rapid rate of innovation means that arms races are always beginning, never ending. In so far as the likelihood of war is decreased by the existence of an equality of power between rival states, a qualitative arms race tends to have this result. A quantitative arms race, on the other hand, tends to have the opposite effect. If in a qualitative race one power stopped technological innovation and instead shifted its resources to the multiplication of existing weapons systems, this would be a fairly clear sign that it was intending to go to war in the immediate future.

Undoubtedly many will question the proposition that rapid technological innovation tends to produce an equality of power. In an arms race each state lives in constant fear that its opponent will score a "technological breakthrough" and achieve a decisive qualitative superiority. This anxiety is a continuing feature of arms races but it is one which has virtually no basis in recent experience. The tendency toward simultaneity of innovation is overwhelming. Prior to World War I simultaneity was primarily the result of the common pool of knowledge among the advanced nations with respect to weapons technology. The development of weapons was largely the province of private firms who made their wares available to any state which was interested. As a result at any given time the armaments of the major powers all strikingly resembled one another.[22] During and after World

---

[22] See Victor Lefebure, "The Decisive Aggressive Value of the New Agencies of War," in The Inter-Parliamentary Union, *What Would Be the Character of a New War?* (New York, 1933), pp. 97–101. See also Marion W. Boggs, *Attempts to Define and Limit "Aggressive" Armament in Diplomacy and Strategy* (Columbia, Mo., 1941),

War I military research and development became more and more a governmental activity, and, as a result, more and more enshrouded in secrecy. Nonetheless relative equality in technological innovation continued among the major powers. The reason for this was now not so much access to common knowledge as an equal ability and opportunity to develop that knowledge. The logic of scientific development is such that separate groups of men working in separate laboratories on the same problem are likely to arrive at the same answer to the problem at about the same time. Even if this were not the case, the greatly increased ratio of production time to use time in recent years has tended to diminish the opportunity of the power which has pioneered an innovation to produce it in sufficient quantity in sufficient time to be militarily decisive. When it takes several years to move a weapons system from original design to quantity operation, knowledge of it is bound to leak out, and the second power in the arms race will be able to get its own program under way before the first state can capitalize on its lead. The *Merrimac* reigned supreme for a day, but it was only for a day and it could be only for a day.

The fact that for four years from 1945 to 1949 the United States possessed a marked qualitative superiority over the Soviet Union has tended to obscure how rare this event normally is. American superiority, however, was fundamentally the result of carrying over into a new competitive rivalry a weapons system which had been developed in a previous conflict. In the latter rivalry the tendency toward simultaneity of development soon manifested itself. The Soviet Union developed an atomic bomb four years after the United States had done so. Soviet explosion of a hydrogen weapon lagged only ten months behind that of the United States. At a still later date in the arms race, both powers in 1957 were neck and neck in their efforts to develop long-range ballistic missiles.

The ending of an arms race in a distinct quantitative victory for one side is perhaps best exemplified in the success of the British in maintaining their supremacy on the seas. Three times within the course of a hundred years the British were challenged by continental rivals, and three times the British outbuilt their competitors. In each case, also, implicitly or explicitly, the bested rivals recognized their defeat and abandoned their efforts to challenge the resources, skill and determination of the British. At this point in a quantitative race when it appears that one power is establishing its superiority over the other, proposals

---

p. 76: ". . . the history of war inventions tends to emphasize the slowness and distinctively international character of peacetime improvements; no weapon has been perfected with secrecy and rapidity as the exclusive national property of any one state. At an early stage all nations secure access to the information, and develop not only the armament, but measures against it."

are frequently brought forward for some sort of "disarmament" agreement. These are as likely to come from the superior side as from the inferior one. The stronger power desires to clothe its *de facto* supremacy in *de jure* acceptance and legitimacy so that it may slacken its own arms efforts. From 1905 to 1912, for instance, virtually all the initiatives for Anglo-German naval agreement came from the British. Quite properly, the Germans regarded those advances as British efforts to compel "naval competition to cease at the moment of its own greatest preponderance." Such proposals only heightened German suspicion and bitterness. Similarly, after World War II the Soviet Union naturally described the American nuclear disarmament proposal as a device to prevent the Soviet Union from developing its own nuclear capability. A decade later a greater common interest existed between the Soviet Union and the United States in reaching an arms agreement which would permanently exclude "fourth powers" from the exclusive nuclear club. In disarmament discussions the superior power commonly attempts to persuade the inferior one to accept as permanent the existing ratio of strength, or, failing in this effort, the superior power proposes a temporary suspension of the race, a "holiday" during which period neither power will increase its armaments. In 1899 the Russians, with the largest army in Europe, proposed that for five years no increases be made in military budgets. In 1912–14 Churchill repeatedly suggested the desirability of a naval building holiday to the Germans who were quite unable to perceive its advantages. In 1936 the United States could easily agree to a six year holiday in 10,000 ton cruisers since it had already underway all the cruisers it was permitted by the London Treaty of 1930. Similarly, in its 1957 negotiations with the Soviet Union the United States could also safely propose an end to the production of nuclear weapons. The inferior participant in disarmament negotiations, on the other hand, inevitably supports measures based not upon the existing situation but either upon the abstract principle of "parity" or upon the inherent evil of large armaments as such and the desirability of reducing all arms down to a common low level. Thus, in most instances, a disarmament proposal is simply a maneuver in the arms race: the attempt by a state to achieve the ratio-goal it desires by means other than an increase in its armaments.

The domestic burden of quantitative and qualitative races. Quantitative and qualitative arms races have markedly different effects upon the countries participating in them. In a quantitative race the decisive ratio is between the resources which a nation devotes to military purposes and those which it devotes to civilian ones. A quantitative race of any intensity requires a steady shift of resources from the latter to the former. As the forms of military force are multiplied a larger and larger proportion of the national product is devoted to the purposes of the race, and, if it is a race in military manpower, an increasing proportion of the population serves a longer and longer time in the armed forces. A quantitative race of any duration thus imposes ever increasing burdens upon the countries involved in it. As a result, it becomes necessary for governments to resort to various means of stimulating popular support and eliciting a willingness to sacrifice other goods and values. Enthusiasm is mobilized, hostility aroused and directed against the potential enemy. Suspicion and fear multiply with the armaments. Such was the result of the quantitative races between the Triple Alliance and the Triple Entente between 1907 and 1914:

> In both groups of powers there was a rapid increase of military and naval armaments. This caused increasing suspicions, fears, and newspaper recriminations in the opposite camp. This in turn led to more armaments and so to the vicious circle of ever growing war preparations and mutual fears and suspicions.[23]

Eventually a time is reached when the increasing costs and tensions of a continued arms race seem worse than the costs and the risks of war. Public opinion once aroused cannot be quieted. The economic, military and psychological pressures previously generated permit only further expansion or conflict. The extent to which an arms race is likely to lead to war thus varies with the burdens it imposes on the peoples and the extent to which it involves them psychologically and emotionally in the race. Prolonged sufficiently, a quantitative race must necessarily reach a point where opinion in one country or the other will demand that it be ended, if not by negotiation, then by war. The logical result of a quantitative arms race is a "nation in arms," and a nation in arms for any length of time must be a nation at war.

A qualitative arms race, however, does not have this effect. In such a race the essential relationship is not between the military and the civilian, but rather between the old and the new forms of military force. In a quantitative race the principal policy issue is the extent to which resources and manpower should be diverted from civilian to military use. In a qualitative race, the principal issue is the extent to which the new weapons systems should replace the old "conventional" ones. In a quantitative race the key question is "How much?" In a qualitative race, it is "How soon?" A quantitative race requires continuous expansion of military resources, a qualitative race continuous redeployment of them. A qualitative race does not normally increase arms budgets, even when, as usually happens, the new forms of military force are more expensive than the old ones. The costs of a qualitative race only increase significantly when an effort is made to maintain both old and new forms of military force: steam and sail;

---

[23] Fay, *Origins of the World War,* I, p. 226.

ironclads and wooden walls; nuclear and nonnuclear weapons. Transitions from old to new weapons systems have not normally been accompanied by marked increases in military expenditures. During the decade in which the ironclad replaced the wooden ship of the line British naval expenditures declined from £12,779,000 in 1859 to less than eleven million pounds in 1867.[24] Similarly, the five years after the introduction of the Dreadnought saw British naval expenditures drop from £35,476,000 in 1903–04 to £32,188,000 in 1908–09. During the same period estimates for shipbuilding and repairs dropped from £17,350,000 to £14,313,900. The years 1953–1956 saw the progressive adoption of nuclear weapons in the American armed forces, yet military budgets during this period at first dropped considerably and then recovered only slightly, as the increased expenditures for the new weapons were more than compensated for by reductions in expenditures for nonnuclear forces.

Quantitative and qualitative arms races differ also in the interests they mobilize and the leadership they stimulate. In the long run, a quantitative race makes extensive demands on a broad segment of the population. A qualitative race, however, tends to be a competition of elites rather than masses. No need exists for the bulk of the population to become directly involved. In a quantitative arms race, the users of the weapons—the military leaders—assume the key role. In a qualitative race, the creators of the weapons—the scientists—rival them for preeminence. Similarly, the most important private interests in a quantitative race are the large mass production industrial corporations, while in a qualitative race they tend to be the smaller firms specializing in the innovation and development of weapons systems rather than in their mass output.

While the rising costs of a quantitative race may increase the likelihood of war, they may also enhance efforts to end the race by means of an arms agreement. Undoubtedly the most powerful motive (prior to the feasiblity of utter annihilation) leading states to arms limitations has been the economic one. The desire for economy was an important factor leading Louis Philippe to propose a general reduction in European armaments in 1831. In the 1860s similar motives stimulated Napoleon III to push disarmament plans. They also prompted various British governments to be receptive to arms limitation proposals, provided, of course, that they did not endanger Britain's supremacy on the seas: the advent of the Liberal government in 1905, for instance, resulted in renewed efforts to reach accommodation with the Germans. In 1898 the troubled state of Russian finances was largely responsible

---

[24] James Phinney Baxter, 3rd, *The Introduction of the Ironclad Warship* (Cambridge, 1933), p. 321.

for the Tsar's surprise move in sponsoring the first Hague Conference. Eight years later it was the British who, for economic reasons, wished to include the question of arms limitation on the agenda of the second Hague Conference.

The success of rising economic costs in bringing about the negotiated end of an arms race depends upon their incidence being relatively equal on each participant. A state which is well able to bear the economic burden normally spurns the efforts of weaker powers to call off the race. Thus, the Kaiser was scornful of the Russian economic debility which led to the proposal for the first Hague Conference, and a German delegate to that conference, in explaining German opposition to limitation, took pains to assure the participants that:

> The German people are not crushed beneath the weight of expenditures and taxes; they are not hanging on the edge of the precipice; they are not hastening towards exhaustion and ruin. Quite the contrary; public and private wealth is increasing, the general welfare, and standard of life, are rising from year to year.[25]

On the other hand, the relatively equal burdens of their arms race in the last decade of the nineteenth century eventually forced Argentina and Chile to call the race off in 1902. The victory of Chile in the War of the Pacific had brought her into conflict with an "expanding and prosperous Argentina" in the 1880s, and a whole series of boundary disputes exacerbated the rivalry which developed between the two powers for hegemony on the South American continent. As a result, after 1892 both countries consistently expanded their military and naval forces, and relations between them staggered from one war crisis to another. Despite efforts made to arbitrate the boundary disputes,

> an uneasy feeling still prevailed that hostilities might break out, and neither State made any pretence of stopping military and naval preparations. Orders for arms, ammunition, and warships were not countermanded, and men on both sides of the Andes began to declaim strongly against the heavy expenditure thus entailed. The reply to such remonstrances invariably was that until the question of the boundary was settled, it was necessary to maintain both powers on a war footing. Thus the resources of Argentina and Chile were strained to the utmost, and public works neglected in order that funds might be forthcoming to pay for guns and ships bought in Europe.[26]

These economic burdens led the presidents of the two countries to arrive at an agreement in 1899 restricting additional expenditures on armaments. Two years later, however, the boundary issue again flared

---

[25] Quoted in Tate, *Disarmament Illusion,* p. 281. See also pp. 193-94, 251-52.
[26] Charles E. Akers, *A History of South America* (New York, new ed., 1930), p. 112.

up, and both sides recommenced preparations for war. But again the resources of the countries were taxed beyond their limit. In August 1901 the Chilean president declared to the United States minister "that the burden which Chile is carrying . . . is abnormal and beyond her capacity and that the hour has come to either make use of her armaments or reduce them to the lowest level compatible with the dignity and safety of the country."[27] Argentina was also suffering from severe economic strain, and as a result, the two countries concluded their famous *Pactos de Mayo* in 1902 which limited their naval armaments and provided for the arbitration of the remaining boundary issues.

In summary, two general conclusions emerge as to the relations between arms races and war:

(1) War is more likely to develop in the early phases of an arms race than in its later phases.

(2) A quantitative race is more likely than a qualitative one to come to a definite end in war, arms agreement, or victory for one side.

ARMS RACES, DISARMAMENT, AND PEACE

In discussions of disarmament, a distinction has frequently been drawn between the presumably technical problem of arms limitation, on the one hand, and political problems, on the other. Considerable energy has been devoted to arguments as to whether it is necessary to settle political issues before disarming or whether disarmament is a prerequisite to the settlement of political issues. The distinction between arms limitation and politics, however, is a fallacious one. The achievement of an arms agreement cannot be made an end in itself. Arms limitation is the essence of politics and inseparable from other political issues. What, indeed, is more political than the relative balance of power between two distinct entities? Whether they be political parties competing for votes, lobbyists lining up legislative blocs, or states piling up armaments, the power ratio between the units is a decisive factor in their relationship. Virtually every effort (such as the Hague Conferences and the League of Nations) to reach agreement on arms apart from the resolution of other diplomatic and political issues has failed. Inevitably attempts to arrive at arms agreements have tended to broaden into discussions of all the significant political issues between the competing powers. On the other hand, it cannot be assumed that arms negotiations are hopeless, and that they only add another issue to those already disrupting the relations between the two countries and stimulating passion and suspicion. Just as the problem of armaments cannot be settled without

[27] Quoted in Robert N. Burr, "The Balance of Power in Nineteenth-Century South America: An Exploratory Essay," *Hispanic American Historical Review*, XXXV (February, 1955), 58n.

reference to other political issues, so is it also impossible to resolve these issues without facing up to the relative balance of military power. The most notable successes in arms limitation agreements have been combined, implicitly or explicitly, with a resolution of other controversies. The Rush-Bagot Agreement, for instance, simply confirmed the settlement which had been reached in the Treaty of Paris. The *Pactos de Mayo* dealt with both armaments and boundaries and implicitly recognized that Argentina would not intervene in west coast politics and that Chile would not become involved in the disputes of the Plata region. The Washington naval agreements necessarily were part and parcel of a general Far Eastern settlement involving the end of the Anglo-Japanese alliance and at least a temporary resolution of the diplomatic issues concerning China. As has been suggested previously, in one sense armaments are to the twentieth century what territory was to the eighteenth. Just as divisions of territory were then the essence of general diplomatic agreements, so today are arrangements on armaments. If both sides are to give up their conflicting ratio-goals and compromise the difference, this arrangement must coincide with a settlement of the other issues which stimulated them to develop the conflicting ratio-goals in the first place. If one state is to retreat further from its ratio-goal than the other, it will have to receive compensations with respect to other points in dispute.

While arms limitation is seldom possible except as part of a broader political settlement, it is also seldom possible if the scope of the arms limitation is itself too broad. One of the corollaries of the belief that arms races produce wars is the assumption that disarmament agreements are necessary to peace. Too frequently it has been made to appear that failure to reach a disarmament agreement leaves war as the only recourse between the powers. In particular, it is false and dangerous to assume that any disarmament to be effective must be total disarmament. The latter is an impossible goal. Military force is inherent in national power and national power is inherent in the existence of independent states. In one way or another all the resources of a state contribute to its military strength. The discussions in the 1920s under the auspices of the League conclusively demonstrated that what are armaments for one state are the pacific instruments of domestic well-being and tranquility for another. The history of general disarmament conferences persuasively suggests the difficulties involved in deciding what elements of power should be weighed in the balance even before the issue is faced as to what the relative weight of the two sides should be. At the first Hague Conference, for instance, the Germans were quick to point out that the Russian proposal for a five year holiday in military budget increases was fine for Russia who had all the men in her army that she needed, but that such a restriction would not prevent Russia from building strategic railways to her western border which would constitute a greater menace to Germany than additional Russian soldiers. The demand for total disarmament frequently reflects an unwillingness to live with the problems of power. A feasible arms limitation must be part of the process of politics, not of the abolition of politics.

The narrower the scope of a proposed arms limitation agreement, the more likely it is to be successful. Disarmament agreements seldom actually disarm states. What they do is to exclude certain specified areas from the competition and thereby direct that competion into other channels. The likelihood of reaching such an agreement is greater if the states can have a clear vision of the impact of the agreement on the balance of power. The more restricted the range of armaments covered by the agreement, the easier it is for them to foresee its likely effects. In general, also, the less important the area in the balance of power between the two states, the easier it is to secure agreement on that area. Part of the success of the Washington agreements was that they were limited to capital ships, and, at that time, particularly in the United States the feeling existed that existing battleships were obsolete and that in any event the battleship had passed its peak as the supreme weapon of naval power. Similarly, in 1935 Germany and England were able to arrive at an agreement (which lasted until April 1939) fixing the relative size of their navies—something which had been beyond the capability of sincere and well-meaning diplomats of both powers before World War I— because air power had replaced sea power as the decisive factor in the arms balance between Germany and England. Restrictions on land armaments have generally been harder to arrive at than naval agreements because the continental European nations usually felt that their large armies were directly essential to their national existence and might have to be used at a moment's notice.

Successful disarmament agreements (and a disarmament agreement is sucessful if it remains in force for a half decade or more) generally establish quantitative restrictions on armaments. The quantitative ratio is the crucial one between the powers, and the quantitative element is much more subject to the control of governments than is the course of scientific development. Furthermore, a quantitative agreement tends to channel competition into qualitative areas, while an agreement on innovation tends to do just the reverse. Consequently, quantitative agreement tends to reduce the likelihood of war, qualitative agreement to enhance it. In the current arms race, for instance, some sort of quantitative agreement might be both feasible, since the race is primarily qualitative in nature, and desirable, since such an agreement would formally prohibit the more dangerous type of arms race. On the other hand, a qualitative agreement between the two countries prohibiting, say, the construction and testing of intercontinental ballistic missiles, might well be disastrous if it should stimulate a quantitative race in aircraft production, the construction of bases, and the multiplication of other forms of military force. In addition, the next phase in the arms race, for instance, may well be the development of defenses against ballistic missiles. A qualitative answer to this problem, such as an effective anti-missile missile, would, in the long run, be much less expensive and much less disturbing to peace than a quantitative answer, such as a mammoth shelter construction program, which would tax public resources, infringe on many established interests, and arouse popular concern and fear. Continued technological innovation could well be essential to the avoidance of war. Peace, in short, may depend less upon the ingenuity of the rival statesmen than upon the ingenuity of the rival scientists.

The balancing of power in any bipolar situation is inherently difficult due to the absence of a "balancer." In such a situation, however, a qualitative arms race may be the most effective means of achieving and maintaining parity of power over a long period of time. The inherent tendency toward parity of such a race may to some extent provide a substitute for the missing balancer. In particular, a qualitative race tends to equalize the differences which might otherwise exist between the ability and willingness of a democracy to compete with a totalitarian dictatorship. The great problem of international politics now is to develop forms of international competition to replace the total wars of the first half of the twentieth century. One such alternative is limited war. Another is the qualitative arms race. The emerging pattern of rivalry between the West and the Soviet bloc suggests that these may well be the primary forms of military activity which the two coalitions will employ. As wars become more frightening and less frequent, arms races may become longer and less disastrous. The substitution of the one for the other is certainly no mean step forward in the restriction of violence. In this respect the arms race may serve the same function which war served: "the intensely sharp competitive *preparation* for war by the nations," could become, as William James suggested, *"the real war,* permanent, unceasing. . . ."[28] A qualitative race regularizes this preparation and introduces an element of stability into the relations between the two powers. Even if it were true, as Sir Edward Grey argued, that arms races inevitably foster suspicion and insecurity, these would be small prices to pay for the avoidance of destruction. Until fundamental changes take place in the structure of world politics, a qualitative arms race may well be a most desirable form of competition between the Soviet Union and the United States.

[28] *Memories and Studies* (New York, 1912), p. 273.

What Went Wrong With Arms Control?

THOMAS C. SCHELLING

. . . what follows is my interpretation of what has happened to strategic arms control over the past 30 years. I shall argue that the thinking on arms control was on the right track, and was effective, from the late 1950s to the early 1970s, culminating in the Anti-Ballistic Missile Treaty of 1972, but that things have derailed since. Maybe that loss of direction was natural and expectable, even inevitable. Even so, it is worth examining what went wrong.

II

The modern era of strategic arms control dates from the late 1950s. In 1957 the Gaither Committee examined the adequacy of U.S. strategic weapons and their deployment, and became alarmed at the vulnerability of the retaliatory force to surprise attack. Bombers were clustered, unprotected, on a few bases. Studies showed that Soviet bombers, too few to be identified by the Distant Early Warning Line, might be sufficient to destroy or disable our fragile aircraft, eliminating the prospect of the reprisal that was supposed to deter the attack in the first place. Announcement in 1957 of a Soviet flight test of an ICBM precursor further dramatized the vulnerability of a retaliatory force that offered only a small number of soft targets. The seriousness of bomber vulnerability was evidenced by the limited airborne alert during the last years of the Eisenhower Administration maintained to keep at least a small force safely in the air at all times.

It was agreed by President Eisenhower and Secretary Khrushchev that East-West talks on "measures to safeguard against surprise attack" should take place in the fall of 1958. It was not clear what they had in mind, but with a commitment to negotiations, the U.S. government had to collect its thoughts. A high-level group of officials met regularly and ultimately educated itself that a surprise attack was the central problem of strategic-force vulnerability.

The Geneva negotiations were to involve five participants from the West and five from the East; representatives of Canada, Great Britain, France and the Federal Republic of Germany gathered in

Reprinted by permission of *Foreign Affairs*, Winter 1985/86, pp. 219–233. Copyright 1985 by the Council on Foreign Relations, Inc. Portions of the text have been omitted.

Washington in the fall of 1958. By the time the team went to Geneva, after a few weeks of discussion in Washington, strategic-retaliatory-force vulnerability had been identified as the surprise-attack problem, and indeed as *the* problem of nuclear war.[1]

Nothing came of the negotiations on surprise attack (November–December 1958). But the occasion was crucial in identifying what was to become pivotal in arms negotiations for the next decade and, more important, in the design of strategic forces.

The large, above-ground, soft, slow-to-fuel Atlas missile was abandoned in favor of a new ICBM (intercontinental ballistic missile), dubbed Minuteman for its ability to fly instantly on warning. The navy's strategic future was assured with the development of the untargetable Polaris submarine. Secure, survivable forces were identified with what came to be called "strategic stability." Thus, in the event, the vulnerability problem was temporarily solved by unilateral action without any boost from arms control.

The idea that both sides could favor each other's strategic-force security was dramatized by Secretary of Defense Robert Mc-Namara's testimony to Congress that he would prefer the Soviet Union to invest in secure, hardened underground missile silos, rather than soft sites above ground, because the latter both invited and threatened preemptive attack while the former would encourage patience in a crisis.

Two technological developments of the 1960s came to endanger this strategic-force stability: one was ABM, the other MIRV. Antiballistic missiles at that time were thought of primarily as for area defense of populations, not for point defense of military targets, and were seen as potentially destabilizing. What was worrisome was that ABMs might offer a strong advantage to a first strike. The idea was that ABMs might work better when alert than when taken by surprise, might work poorly against a prepared attack but well against a damaged retaliatory force.

There was also the prospect that burgeoning defenses would require indefinite enlargement of the retaliatory force. Thus ABM systems deployed in both countries would make preemptive war more likely and the arms race more expensive. It was this conviction that led the Johnson Administration in 1966 to propose negotiations to forestall deployment of ballistic missile defenses.

The ABM treaty signed in 1972 had one characteristic that was

---

[1] An intellectual milestone was the publication of Albert Wohlstetter's "The Delicate Balance of Terror" in *Foreign Affairs,* January 1959. It had been available in manuscript to the Surprise Attack Team. My own "Surprise Attack and Disarmament," published in December in the *Bulletin of the Atomic Scientists* that same year, explicitly identifying arms control with reciprocally reduced strategic-force vulnerability, came out of those preparations for the Geneva negotiations.

incompatible with its philosophy but was probably a political necessity. The treaty was intended to preserve the efficacy of retaliatory forces by keeping them from being degraded by enemy defenses. Human and economic resources were hostages to be left unprotected. But ballistic missile defenses could also be used to protect military hard targets, indeed were generally thought superior in that mode of deployment. Land-based, fixed-site missiles were difficult and expensive to protect passively, by hardening or dispersing silos, while active defenses might have been cost-effective and compatible with the philosophy of the treaty, as long as there was a clear distinction between the technology of defending military targets and that of the forbidden defense of human resources. (This was acknowledged in the treaty provision allowing a very limited local active defense, a provision that in the end the United States chose not to take advantage of.)

I have always supposed that the disallowance of local hardpoint defense was partly due to the difficulty of guarding against upgrading, either surreptitiously or upon abrogation of the treaty, but also partly for political simplicity. It might have been hard to convince the American public, which had its own reasons for disliking an ABM system, that exceptions should be made for air force assets but not for people.

The other development of the 1960s that threatened stability was the multiple independently targetable reentry vehicle (MIRV). A missile with ten independently targetable warheads is a replica of an air base with ten aircraft. If it takes one weapon to destroy ten weapons (or two or three to destroy them with confidence), MIRVed but targetable forces equal in size are reciprocally vulnerable to an attack by only a fraction of an enemy's force. (For retaliatory forces that cannot be targeted, things that are hidden or mobile and cannot be found on short notice, the MIRV is merely an economical way of packaging warheads.)

There was no serious effort to constrain MIRVs until many years after a ban on ABMs became an objective in the Johnson Administration. The SALT II treaty signed in 1979 attempted to limit not only numbers of missiles but numbers allowed to be MIRVed.

That 15-year period from 1957 to 1972 is a remarkable story of intellectual achievement transformed into policy. Three books appeared in 1961 that epitomized an emerging consensus on what strategic arms control should be about. Each was a group effort, and each stimulated discussion even while being written. During the summer of 1960, Hedley Bull's manuscript, *The Control of the Arms Race*,[2] was circulated by the Institute for Strategic Studies in

[2] London: The Bradbury Agnew Press Ltd., 1961.

preparation for that institute's second annual conference. That same summer a study group met on the outskirts of Boston, and Morton H. Halperin and I produced a little book, discussed at numerous meetings of the Harvard-MIT Faculty Seminar on Arms Control during the fall of 1960, reflecting what we took to be a consensus, one that was wholly consistent with the ideas that developed around Hedley Bull's manuscript at the ISS.[3] And in the spring of 1960, Donald G. Brennan organized a conference that generated *Arms Control, Disarmament, and National Security.*[4]

Together those efforts were an intellectual achievement; a number of participants in the Harvard-MIT seminar took positions in the Kennedy White House, Department of State and Department of Defense; others from RAND and elsewhere, who had been part of this intellectual movement, moved into the government as well. So it is not completely surprising that those ideas became the basis for U.S. policy and were ultimately implemented in the ABM treaty. I consider that culmination of 15 years of progress not merely the high point but the end point of successful arms control.[5]

III

Since 1972, the control of strategic weapons has made little or no progress, and the effort on our side has not seemed to be informed by any coherent theory of what arms control is supposed to accomplish. Maybe right now there is nothing it can accomplish. But there has been retrogression in the doctrine.

A qualification needs to be added to this judgment that nothing constructive has happened. The five-year interim agreement governing offensive weapons that was part of the 1972 SALT I package was succeeded by the SALT II treaty of 1979, which was still unratified at the invasion of Afghanistan and never had a chance after that. Both sides have so far avoided going expressly beyond the limits contained in that treaty even though it has no formal standing. This is a powerful demonstration that restraints can be reciprocated without formal obligation.

One development since 1972 has been a hardening of the belief among diplomats and the public that arms control has to be embedded in treaties. In the 1960s, I used to believe that a tacit understanding might be arrived at regarding ballistic missile defenses: namely, that the United States would have to proceed at full speed unless

---

[3] Thomas C. Schelling and Morton H. Halperin, *Strategy and Arms Control,* New York: The Twentieth Century Fund, Inc., 1961, and reissued as a Pergamon-Brassey Classic, 1985.

[4] New York: George Braziller, 1961.

[5] Others would tell the story with more attention to the nuclear test treaty in 1963 or the nuclear nonproliferation treaty signed in 1969 and ratified in 1970. They were indeed important achievements but independent of strategic-forces development.

the Soviets stopped in their tracks, but the United States would happily forego the cost of building an ABM system if the Russians put a stop to theirs. I saw no advantage in a treaty. I later came to believe that the advantage of the treaty was to put the quietus on ABM in this country, especially in the Congress. But reciprocated restraint may often be as good as formal negotiations and treaties, sometimes better. This idea was better understood up until a dozen years ago than it has been since.[6]

Let me illustrate how something that deserves to be identified as arms control can come about informally and even without being recognized as arms control by the participants. This is the apparent understanding that a war in Europe should be kept non-nuclear if possible, and that reciprocated efforts should be made to ensure this. Secretary McNamara began an aggressive campaign for building up conventional defenses in Europe on the grounds that nuclear weapons certainly should not be used and possibly would not be used. (The no-first-use idea emerged later as a reflection of this same principle.) Throughout the 1960s, however, the official Soviet line was to deny the possibility of a non-nuclear engagement in Europe, even to deny that any nuclear war could be kept limited.

Yet the Soviets have spent enormous amounts of money developing non-nuclear capabilities in Europe, especially aircraft capable of delivering conventional weapons. This capability is not only expensive but utterly useless in the event of any war that is nuclear from the outset. It can only reflect a tacit Soviet acknowledgment that both sides are capable of non-nuclear war and interested in keeping war non-nuclear.

If "arms control" includes expensive restraints on the potential *use* of weapons as well as on their deployment, this reciprocated investment in non-nuclear capability has to be considered a remarkable instance of unacknowledged but reciprocated arms restraint. And it reminds us that the inhibitions on "first use" may be just as strong without declarations as with them.

IV

Until the emergence of a Strategic Defense Initiative (SDI) in 1983, for the last 13 years the focus of arms control has been on offensive weapons. I judge the proposals and negotiations on offensive weapons to have been mostly mindless, without a guiding philosophy. What guiding philosophy there used to be has got lost along the way.

[6] Kennth L. Adelman, Director of the Arms Control and Disarmament Agency, has resurrected the notion that not all arms restraint has to be formalized. "Arms Control With and Without Agreements," *Foreign Affairs,* Winter 1984/85, pp. 240–263.

The main difference between pre-1971 and post-1972 arms negotiations has been the shift of interest from the *character* of weapons
to their *numbers*. In the United States this is the common interest
that has joined left and right, leaving almost no room in between.
The proposals of the Carter and Reagan Administrations have been
for reduced numbers of offensive weapons. Simultaneously, the
programs of the Carter and Reagan Administrations have been to
match numbers. (This is matching in each category of weapons, not
merely in some aggregate index of firepower.) Sophisticates in the
freeze movement might talk privately about first-strike or second-
strike weapons, about vulnerability and survivability, but the simple
public goal has been freezing numbers and looking toward reduction. The last two administrations have been intent on matching
hard-target capabilities, number for number, almost without regard
to whether denying strategic-weapon targets to the enemy—such as
deploying untargetable weapons—was a superior alternative to
matching hard-target capability.

Thus there are two points to discuss: the interest that everybody
claims in ultimately reducing numbers through arms control, and
the interest in matching enemy capabilities whether we like them or
not.

On the "arms control" interest in reducing numbers, nobody
ever offers a convincing reason for preferring smaller numbers. (I
may exaggerate: saving money is a legitimate reason, and whether
or not smaller numbers would cost less, people may be excused for
thinking so.) And some people think that with fewer weapons there
is less likelihood that one will fall into mischievous hands or be
launched by mechanical error; this I think is incorrect, but may not
be worth refuting because it is no one's main motivation. For the
most part, people simply think that smaller numbers are better than
bigger ones. Those who believe we already have ten times what we
need never explain why having merely five times as many should
look better. If people really believe that zero is the ultimate goal it
is easy to see that downward is the direction they should go. But
hardly anyone who takes arms control seriously believes that zero
is the goal.

Furthermore, political and even professional discussion, to say
nothing of editorial and popular discussion, has great difficulty in
deciding which numbers matter. It is surprising how few people who
concern themselves seriously with arms control are aware that the
sheer explosive energy in American strategic weapons, the megatonnage of alert warheads, was several times greater 20 years ago than
it is now. Not that gross megatonnage is the important measure; my
point is merely that this is not an uninteresting fact, and people who
are unacquainted with it may be people who really do not know (or
do not care) what numbers they ought to be interested in.

In 1963 Lieutenant-General (then Colonel) Glenn Kent, of the United States Air Force, published an Occasional Paper of the Harvard Center for International Affairs in which he looked at the following question: if we were to have a limit of some kind on strategic missiles, what would be the most sensible limit?[7] He argued that we should want both sides to be free to proliferate weapons in whatever dimension would reduce their own vulnerability, but without increasing the other side's vulnerability. In those days missile accuracies were poor and megatonnage mattered more than today; big explosives, however, were less efficient than small ones because the lethal area was less than proportionate to the yield of the individual bomb or warhead. Kent concluded that the correct magnitude to limit was the sum of the lethal areas covered by all the warheads in the inventory; this would be calculated by using the two-thirds power of the yield of each weapon. In this formula, each party would then be free to proliferate smaller and smaller warheads on more and more missiles, thus becoming less and less vulnerable without acquiring any more preemptive attack capability. He further calculated that the weight-to-yield ratio went up as warheads got smaller, that the weight of the warheads would be roughly proportionate to the two-thirds power of the yields, and that no matter how many warheads were on a given missile, the physical volume of the missile would be approximately proportionate to that calculated index of lethality. And you could calculate the volume by looking at a missile from a distance, so monitoring would be easy.

Kent's specific formula may be somewhat obsolete technologically, but its virtue remains relevant; it attempts to answer the question, if you were to limit something, what would you want to limit?

The point of recalling Kent's investigation is that his question does not get the attention it deserves. In a very crude way, drawing a distinction between multiple- and single-warhead weapons moves in that direction; the Scowcroft Commission's advertisement for a single-warhead missile (Midgetman) to substitute ultimately for the MIRVed MX reflects a tardy and halting return to some inexplicit criterion in the spirit of Kent's proposal.

The SALT process tends to deal not only with numbers but with numbers in fixed categories. And the categories relate to things like land, sea and air, not strategic characteristics like susceptibility to preemption or capability for preemption, nor even relevant ingredients like warheads per target point, readiness, speed of delivery, accuracy or recallability after launch. The result has been that as fixed-site ground-based missiles have become more and more susceptible to successful attack (unless fired on warning), and as the

[7] *On the Interaction of Opposing Forces Under Possible Arms Agreements,* Cambridge: Harvard University Center for International Affairs, 1963.

SALT limits on MIRVed missiles invite building up to those limits, the process has moved exactly opposite to the direction that Kent pointed to.

What has been lost is the earlier emphasis on the *character* of weapons, and what has taken its place is emphasis on *numbers,* and specifically numbers within *fixed categories,* categories having nothing to do with the weapon characteristics that most deserve attention.

The rigidity of the emphasis on categories is illustrated by the MX controversy. The Scowcroft Commission was in a quandary: it apparently found little or no military virtue in the MX but felt it necessary to demonstrate, to the Soviet government and to allied governments, that the United States was determined to spend money to overcome any strategic-weapon deficiency vis-à-vis the Soviet Union, and specifically an apparent deficiency in large land-based missiles. The MX was alleged to be the only missile ready for procurement; and since quick procurement was essential, the commission recommended 100 MX, with a longing glance at an economical single-warhead missile (Midgetman) that was not even under development. Bemused by the SALT tradition, their horizon in searching for appropriate weapons was short of the oceans; they appear not to have considered as an alternative the scheduling of some equivalent number of Trident submarines. Perhaps Tridents were not considered quite equivalent militarily to the MX; but since the object was a demonstration of resolve to procure, and not the particular characteristics of the MX, and because the Trident solved the basing problem that had vexed the Carter and Reagan Administrations for most of eight years, the Trident solution at least ought to have been considered. (If it was, it does not show in the commission report.)

What a strange product of an arms-control mentality—to constrain the United States to purchase one of the least attractive weapons (in terms of what arms control is intended to bring about) and to preclude the procurement of a secure, non-targetable undersea system instead. What a lost opportunity to announce that the United States would compete by procuring weapons of its own choosing, not by matching, category by category, whatever the Soviets chose to deploy. Instead, we have "arms control" for its own sake, not for the sake of peace and confidence.

Arms control for its own sake is similarly implicated in the widespread abhorrence of submarine-based cruise missiles. The cruise missile, as advertised, is an economical retaliatory weapon, too slow for preemptive attack, yet difficult to defend against as it penetrates Soviet air space, impossible to locate on station because it can be based on submarines. It ought to seem a splendid answer to the problem of vulnerability in the retaliatory force. The widely voiced objection is a simple one. It is easy to hide; it can be got surreptitiously on board submarines. Because it can be fired from a torpedo tube and each submarine can have a reload capability, and because there are more attack submarines capable of carrying cruise missiles than any treaty limitation on the missiles would allow, there is no way to monitor a limitation on numbers of cruise missiles. The logic is that if you cannot find them you cannot count them; if you cannot count them you cannot have verifiable limits; if limits cannot be verified you cannot have arms control.

But who needs arms control if economical and reliable retaliatory weapons are available that are neither susceptible to preemption nor capable of preemption? There may be an answer to this question, but it has not been given. Again, arms control appears to get in the way of pursuing its own objective. Possibly there is some imperative in arms control to do something about offensive weapons, even when there is nothing constructive to be done; so something was done that could not be constructive and the result is confusion or worse. Possibly the first SALT agreement became a compelling model: Secretary of Defense Melvin Laird, after the signing of the SALT agreement, referred to it immediately as "SALT I," and looked forward to SALT II, freezing a procedural pattern with roman numerals. Perhaps the arms control bureaucracy nurtures itself on formal negotiations and ratified treaties, and has lost any subtlety it might have had. (Adelman's *Foreign Affairs* article is at least a hint at a less heavy-handed approach.) Perhaps an administration with no genuine interest in arms limitation finds in arms control the best pulpit from which to preach arms competition.

V

There is a separate development to weave into this story. Ten years ago, late in the Nixon Administration, secretaries of defense began to pronounce a new doctrine for the selection of strategic weapons. This doctrine entailed a more comprehensive target system than anything compatible with the McNamara doctrine. Its philosophical basis was that, if a war occurred, the president should have some alternative to mutual destruction, and the alternative proposed was a counterforce capability that could be operated purposively in a wartime environment, susceptible to control.

And there was a new strategic element: the threat of destroying a large part of the Soviet population and industrial capacity might no longer deter Soviet leaders, whose affection was for their own leadership and not for the people they served. The only effective deterrent threat might be the destruction of their entire military power base, including ground and naval forces. This required, of course, much larger and more versatile weapon capabilities for our forces.

The philosophy underlying the ABM agreement came under attack because it represented the mad notion that the only alternative to peace was mutual obliteration. The name of the strategy was abbreviated, and the acronym, MAD—Mutual Assured Destruction—has been brandished as a derisive slogan. Since 1964 the correct name of the strategy is not "assured mutual destruction," but "assured *capability* for mutual destruction," the difference being that the capability does not have to be ineluctably exercised at the outbreak of even an intercontinental nuclear war. The three crucial elements are an assured capability, restrained targeting and some capacity for war termination.

What has happened is that a capacity to maintain *control* over the course of war has come to be identified with a vigorous and extended *counterforce* campaign, while *retaliatory targeting* has been identified with what Herman Kahn used to call "spasm." The choice is presented as one between a counterforce campaign that is subject to control and a purely retaliatory campaign that is a total spasmodic response. I find it more plausible that the actual choice is between the two opposite alternatives. A controlled retaliatory capability seems to me supremely important, as these things go, and probably achievable, at least if somewhat reciprocated on the other side. But it is unlikely that "controlled" counterforce warfare on the scale typically envisioned could be sustained all the way to a termination that left populations and their economic assets substantially intact; indeed *uncontrolled* counterforce is probably what you would get.

But as long as the counterforce doctrine is governing, it will be hard to impose a reciprocal denial of substantial preemptive capabilities, since the capability to destroy hard targets, publicly eschewed by McNamara, has now become central to the doctrine. How this doctrine might be squared with arms control has never been clear to me, but it probably explains why the current arms control framework has become the one within which the numerical arms race is driven.

I should note briefly that the bargaining chip idea has again become transparent. The Administration, the Scowcroft Commission, and even Congressman Les Aspin have all publicly averred that an initial MX program was essential to drive the Soviets to the bargaining table. No one has given an estimate of the likelihoods of successful disarmament negotiations with and without MX: if the prospect were ten percent without MX and 30 percent with it—a differential I find implausibly large—it could still be a bad bargain if it is not the weapon we want. The Administration has never been altogether clear whether the MX itself is a definitive program whose completion will lead to arms control, or is a contingent program whose abandonment is up for discussion. Publicly acknowledging that Soviet intransigence can oblige the United States to procure an expensive weapon of admittedly little or negative military utility is embarrassing.

Another debating strategy that attempts to make things better by first making them worse is publicizing the argument that any perceived inadequacy of U.S. strategic weaponry vis-à-vis the Soviet Union, or even a perceived lack of competitive determination on the part of the United States, would invite the Soviets to press hard in the next confrontation in the confident belief that the United States must back down, much as Khrushchev did in 1962. In the face of Soviet hubris over strategic superiority, the United States will have no choice but to back down—a situation that invites confrontation. This may be a good argument for more armament if Americans believe it and Russians do not. It is a dangerous one if Russians believe it and believe that Americans do too. I find no logic in the argument, but it is one of those that could be self-fulfilling in a dangerous way. The argument could easily have been neutered by an administration that saw the danger in it and did not itself rely on such arguments to bolster support for its programs. One hopes that the Russians know better.

VI

Finally we come to the Strategic Defense Initiative—President Reagan's dream of harnessing technology to provide impregnable defenses against ballistic missiles sometime in the future, making nuclear weapons obsolete and permitting nuclear disarmament. How it can be thought that space-based defenses against ballistic missiles can completely deny the delivery of nuclear explosives to the proximity of U.S. population centers by land, sea and air, I do not know; but excusing the idea as an extravagance, let us try to see how the concept fits into arms control.

There is an easy way to fit it, even into the philosophy of the ABM treaty, but it is an interpretation that denigrates the President's dream and is nowhere near commensurate with the attention SDI gets. That is to argue that defending targetable U.S. missiles, like the MX, against preemptive attack through high-technology ABM is attractive and unobjectionable. It was a flaw in the ABM treaty that "good" ABM (protecting missiles) was disallowed along with "bad" (protecting cities). In consequence there is no way to protect the MX. A partial reversal of the ABM ban to permit defense of retaliatory weapons would bring us back to the McNamara spirit. This is a line taken by many defenders of SDI, although it is not clear to me whether it is an opportunistic rescue of ground-based missiles under the SDI umbrella, a minimally defensible foot in the door for SDI, a fillip to advanced research, or merely an attempt to rescue the President's image by showing that the concept of SDI, though overblown and oversold, is not quite empty.

There is, of course, the technical question of whether defenses good at protecting ground-based missiles are sufficiently distinguishable from defenses for population centers, so that rather than repairing the ABM treaty by inserting an exception we should be deciding whether or not to abandon it. There are so many interested parties with different interests that it is hard to find common ground even among those who share the same enthusiasm.

Let us leave aside the fact that cities are soft, unconcealable, and almost certainly unprotectable no matter how successfully ballistic missiles may be fended off, there being such a multitude of alternative means of wartime delivery or prewar positioning. There remains the question whether the President's dream is a good one.

He speaks of no longer depending on deterrence but of being unilaterally able to nullify any Soviet nuclear attack. Would we prefer to rely on defense, which is unilateral, or on deterrence, which is contingent and reciprocal? My question is whether we should wish away deterrence as the foundation of peace.

Those 40 years of living with nuclear weapons without warfare are not only evidence that war can be avoided but are themselves part of the reason why it can be; namely, increasing experience in living with the weapons without precipitating a war, increasing confidence on both sides that neither wishes to risk nuclear war, diminishing necessity to react to every untoward event as though it were a mortal challenge. I go further than that: a prudent restraint from aggressive violence that is based on acknowledgment that the world is too small to support a nuclear war is a healthier basis for peace than unilateral efforts to build defenses. I like the notion that East and West have exchanged hostages on a massive scale and that as long as they are unprotected, civilization depends on the avoidance of military aggression that could escalate to nuclear war.

Most of what we call civilization depends on reciprocal vulnerability. I am defenseless against almost everybody that I know, and while most of them would have no interest in harming me there must be some that would. I feel safer in an environment of deterrence than I would in an environment of defense. It is often said that terror is a poor basis for civilization, and the balance of terror is not a permanently viable foundation for the avoidance of war. Fear can promote hostility, and fear can lead to impetuosity in a crisis. I agree, but I do not equate a balance of deterrence with a balance of terror, even though the roots of "deterrence" and "terror" are the same. Twenty years ago I wrote and still believe:

> The extent of the "fear" involved in any arrangement—total disarmament, negotiated mutual deterrence, or stable weaponry achieved unilaterally by conscious design—is a function of confidence. If the consequences of transgression are plainly bad—bad for all parties, little dependent on who transgresses first, and not helped by rapid mobilization—we can take the consequences for granted and call it a "balance of prudence."[8]

People regularly stand at the curb watching trucks, buses and cars hurtle past at speeds that guarantee injury and threaten death if they so much as attempt to cross against the traffic. They are absolutely deterred. But there is no fear. They just know better.

[8] Thomas C. Schelling, *Arms and Influence*, New Haven: Yale University Press, 1966, p. 259.

*Toward Nuclear Peace**

KENNETH N. WALTZ

What will the spread of nuclear weapons do to the world? I say "spread" rather than "proliferation" because so far nuclear weapons have proliferated only vertically as the major nuclear powers have added to their arsenals. Horizontally, they have spread slowly across countries and the pace is not likely to change much. Sort-term candidates for the nuclear club are not very numerous, and they are not likely to rush into the nuclear business. One reason is that the United States works with some effect to keep countries from doing that. Nuclear weapons will nevertheless spread, with a new member occasionally joining the club. Counting India and Israel, membership grew to seven in the first 35 years of the nuclear age. A doubling of membership in the next decade would be surprising. Since rapid changes in international conditions can be unsettling, the slowness of the spread of the nuclear weapons is fortunate.

Someday the world will be populated by 10 or 12 or 18 nuclear-weapon states (hereafter referred to as nuclear states). What the further spread of nuclear weapons will do to the world is therefore a compelling question.

THE MILITARY LOGIC OF SELF-HELP SYSTEMS

The world has enjoyed more years of peace since 1945 than had been known in this century—if peace is defined as the absence of general war among the major states of the world. The Second World War followed the first one within twenty-one years. As of 1983, 38 years had elapsed since the Allies' victory over the Axis powers. Conflict marks all human affairs. In the past third of a century, conflict has generated hostility among states and has at times issued in violence among the weaker and smaller ones. Even though the more powerful states of the world have occasionally been direct participants, war has been confined geographically and limited militarily. Remarkably, general war has been avoided in a period of rapid and far-reaching changes—decolonization; the rapid economic growth of some states;

*A shortened and revised version of Waltz, *The Spread of Nuclear Weapons: More May Be Better,* Adelphi Papers, No. 171 (London: International Institute of Strategic Studies, 1981).

the formation, tightening, and eventual loosening of blocs; the development of new technologies, and the emergence of new strategies for fighting guerrilla wars and deterring nuclear ones. The prevalence of peace, together with the fighting of circumscribed wars, indicates a high ability of the postwar international system to absorb changes and to contain conflicts and hostility.

Presumably features found in the postwar system that were not present earlier account for the world's recent good fortune. The biggest changes in the postwar world are the shift from multipolarity to bipolarity and the introduction of nuclear weapons. In this paper I concentrate on the latter.

States coexist in a condition of anarchy. Self-help is the principle of action in an anarchic order, and the most important way in which states must help themselves is by providing for their own security. Therefore, in weighing the chances for peace, the first questions to ask are questions about the ends for which states use force and about the strategies and weapons they employ. The chances of peace rise if states can achieve their most important ends without actively using force. War becomes less likely as the costs of war rise in relation to possible gains. Strategies bring ends and means together. How nuclear weapons affect the chances for peace is seen by examining the different implications of defense and deterrence.

How can one state dissuade another state from attacking? In either or in some combination of two ways. One way to counter an intended attack is to build fortifications and to muster forces that look forbiddingly strong. To build defenses so patently strong that no one will try to destroy or overcome them would make international life perfectly tranquil. I call this the defensive ideal. The other way to inhibit a country's intended aggressive moves is to scare that country out of making them by threatening to visit unacceptable punishment upon it. "To deter" literally means to stop someone from doing something by frightening him. In contrast to dissuasion by defense, dissuasion by deterrence operates by frightening a state out of attacking, not because of the difficulty of launching an attack and carrying it home, but because the expected reaction of the opponent will result in one's own severe punishment. Defense and deterrence are often confused. One frequently hears statements like this: "A strong defense in Europe will deter a Russian attack." What is meant is that a strong defense will dissuade Russia from attacking. Deterrence is achieved not through the ability to defend but through the ability to punish. Purely deterrent forces provide no defense. The message of the strategy is this: "Although we are defenseless, if you attack we will punish you to an extent that more than cancels your gains." Second-strike nuclear forces serve that kind of strategy. Purely defensive forces provide no deterrence. They offer no means of punishment.

The message of the strategy is this: "Although we cannot strike back at you, you will find our defenses so difficult to overcome that you will dash yourself to pieces against them". The Maginot Line was to serve that kind of strategy.

Do nuclear weapons increase or decrease the chances of war? The answer depends on whether nuclear weapons permit and encourage states to deploy forces in ways that make the active use of force more or less likely and in ways that promise to be more or less destructive. If nuclear weapons make the offense more effective and the blackmailer's threat more compelling, then nuclear weapons are bad for the world— the more so the more widely diffused nuclear weapons become. If defense and deterrence are made easier and more reliable by the spread of nuclear weapons, we may expect the opposite result. To maintain their security states must rely on the means they can generate and the arrangements they can make for themselves. It follows that the quality of international life varies with the ease or the difficulty states experience in making themselves secure.

Weapons and strategies change the situation of states in ways that make them more or less secure, as Robert Jervis has brilliantly shown. (ref. Jervis article) If weapons are not well suited for conquest, neighbors have more peace of mind. We should expect war to become less likely when weaponry is such as to make conquest more difficult, to discourage preemptive and preventive war, and to make coercive threats less credible. Do nuclear weapons have those effects? Some answers can be found by considering how nuclear deterrence and nuclear defense improve the prospects for peace.

First, wars can be fought in the face of deterrent threats, but the higher the stakes and the closer a country moves toward winning them, the more surely that country invites retaliation and risks its own destruction. States are not likely to run major risks for minor gains. Wars between nuclear states may escalate as the loser uses larger and larger warheads. Fearing that, states will want to draw back. Not escalation but deescalation becomes likely. War remains possible, but victory in war is too dangerous to fight for. If states can score only small gains, because large ones risk retaliation, they have little incentive to fight.

Second, states act with less care if the expected costs of war are low and with more care if they are high. In 1853 and '54 Britain and France expected to win an easy victory if they went to war against Russia. Prestige abroad and political popularity at home would be gained, if not much else. The vagueness of their expectations was matched by the carelessness of their actions. In blundering into the Crimean War they acted hastily on scant information, pandered to their people's frenzy for war, showed more concern for an ally's whim than for the adversary's situation, failed to specify the changes in behavior that threats were supposed to bring, and inclined toward testing strength first and bargaining second. In sharp contrast, the presence of nuclear weapons makes states exceedingly cautious. Think of Kennedy and Khrushchev in the Cuban missile crisis. Why fight if you can't win much and might lose everything?

Third, the question demands a negative answer all the more insistently when the deterrent deployment of nuclear weapons contributes more to a country's security than does conquest of territory. A country with a deterrent strategy does not need the extent of territory required by a country relying on a conventional defense. A deterrent strategy makes it unnecessary for a country to fight for the sake of increasing its security, and this removes a major cause of war.

Fourth, deterrent effect depends both on one's capabilities and on the will one has to use them. The will of the attacked, striving to preserve its own territory, can ordinarily be presumed stronger than the will of the attacker, striving to annex someone else's territory. Knowing this, the would-be attacker is further inhibited.

Certainty about the relative strength of adversaries also makes war less likely. From the late nineteenth century onward the speed of technological innovation increased the difficulty of estimating relative strengths and predicting the course of campaigns. Since World War II, technology has advanced even faster, but short of a ballistic missile defense (BMD) breakthrough, this does not matter very much. It does not disturb the American-Russian military equilibrium, because one side's missiles are not made obsolete by improvements in the other side's missiles. In 1906 the British Dreadnought, with the greater range and fire power of its guns, made older battleships obsolete. This does not happen to missiles. As Bernard Brodie put it: "Weapons that do not have to fight their like do not become useless because of the advent of newer and superior types." They may have to survive their like, but that is a much simpler problem to solve.

Many wars might have been avoided had their outcomes been foreseen. "To be sure," Georg Simmel once said, "the most effective presupposition for preventing struggle, the exact knowledge of the comparative strength of the two parties, is very often only to be obtained by the actual fighting out of the conflict." Miscalculation causes wars. One side expects victory at an affordable price, while the other side hopes to avoid defeat. Here the differences between conventional and nuclear worlds are fundamental. In the former, states are too often tempted to act on advantages that are wishfully discerned and narrowly calculated. In 1914, neither Germany nor France tried very hard to avoid a general war. Both hoped for victory even though they believed their forces to be quite evenly matched. In 1941, Japan, in attacking the the United States, could hope for victory only if a series of events that were possible but not highly probable took place.

Japan would grab resources sufficient for continuing the conquest of China and then dig in to defend a limited perimeter. Meanwhile, the United States and Britain would have to deal with Germany, which, having defeated the Soviet Union, would be supreme in Europe. Japan could then hope to fight a defensive war for a year or two until America, her purpose weakened, became willing to make a compromise peace in Asia (ref. Sansom article).

Countries more readily run the risks of war when defeat, if it comes, is distant and is expected to bring only limited damage. Given such expectations, leaders do not have to be insane to sound the trumpet and urge their people to be bold and courageous in the pursuit of victory. The outcome of battles and the course of campaigns are hard to foresee because so many things affect them. Predicting the result of conventional wars has proved difficult.

Uncertainty about outcomes does not work decisively against the fighting of wars in conventional worlds. Countries armed with conventional weapons go to war knowing that even in defeat their suffering will be limited. Calculations about nuclear war are differently made. A nuclear world calls for and encourages a different kind of reasoning. If countries armed with nuclear weapons go to war, they do so knowing that their suffering may be unlimited. Of course, it also may not be. But that is not the kind of uncertainty that encourages anyone to use force. In a conventional world, one is uncertain about winning or losing. In a nuclear world, one is uncertain about surviving or being annihilated. If force is used, and not kept within limits, catastrophe will result. That prediction is easy to make because it does not require close estimates of opposing forces. The number of one's cities that can be severely damaged is at least equal to the number of strategic warheads an adversary can deliver. Variations of number mean little within wide ranges. The expected effect of the deterrent achieves an easy clarity because wide margins of error in estimates of the damage one may suffer do not matter. Do we expect to lose one city or two, two cities or ten? When these are the pertinent questions, we stop thinking about running risks and start worrying about how to avoid them. In a conventional world, deterrent threats are ineffective because the damage threatened is distant, limited, and problematic. Nuclear weapons make military miscalculation difficult and politically pertinent prediction easy.

Dissuading a would-be attacker by throwing up a good-looking defense may be as effective as dissuading him through deterrence. Beginning with President Kennedy and Secretary of Defense McNamara in the early 1960s, we have asked how we can avoid, or at least postpone, using nuclear weapons rather than how we can mount the most effective defense. NATO's attempts to keep a defensive war conventional in its initial stage may guarantee that nuclear weapons, if used, will be used in a losing cause and in ways that multiply destruction without promising victory. Early use of very small warheads may stop escalation. Defensive deployment, if it should fail to dissuade, would bring small nuclear weapons into use before the physical, political, and psychological environment had deteriorated. The chances of de-escalation are high if the use of nuclear weapons is carefully planned and their use is limited to the battlefield. We have rightly put strong emphasis on strategic deterrence, which makes large wars less likely, and wrongly slighted the question of whether nuclear weapons of low yield can effectively be used for defense, which would make any war at all less likely still.*

An unassailable defense is fully dissuasive. Dissuasion is what is wanted whether by defense or by deterrence. The likelihood of war decreases as deterrent and defensive capabilities increase. Nuclear weapons and an appropriate doctrine for their use may make it possible to approach the defensive-deterrent ideal, a condition that would cause the chances of war to dwindle. Concentrating attention on the destructive power of nuclear weapons has obscured the important benefits they promise to states trying to coexist in a self-help world.

WHAT WILL THE SPREAD OF NUCLEAR WEAPONS DO TO THE WORLD?

Contemplating the nuclear past gives grounds for hoping that the world will survive if further nuclear powers join today's six or seven. This tentative conclusion is called into question by the widespread belief that the infirmities of some new nuclear states and the delicacy of their nuclear forces will work against the preservation of peace and for the fighting of nuclear wars. The likelihood of avoiding destruction as more states become members of the nuclear club is often coupled with the question of who those states will be. What are the likely differences in situation and behavior of new as compared to old nuclear powers?

NUCLEAR WEAPONS AND DOMESTIC STABILITY

What are the principal worries? Because of the importance of controlling nuclear weapons—of keeping them firmly in the hands of reliable officials—rulers of nuclear states may become more authoritarian and ever more given to secrecy. Moreover, some potential nuclear states are not politically strong and stable enough to ensure control of the weapons and control of the decision to use them. If neighboring, hostile, unstable states are armed with nuclear weapons, each will fear attack by the other. Feelings of insecurity may lead to arms races that subordinate civil needs to military necessities. Fears are compounded by the danger of internal coups in which the control

---

* I shall concentrate on nuclear deterrence and slight nuclear defense.

of nuclear weapons may be the main object of struggle and the key to political power. Under these fearful circumstances, to maintain governmental authority and civil order may be impossible. The legitimacy of the state and the loyalty of its citizenry may dissolve because the state is no longer thought to be capable of maintaining external security and internal order. The first fear is that states become tyrannical; the second, that they lose control. Both fears may be realized either in different states or in the same state at different times (ref. Dunn article).

What can one say? Four things primarily. First, possession of nuclear weapons may slow arms races down, rather than speed them up, a possibility considered later. Second, for less developed countries to build nuclear arsenals requires a long lead time. Nuclear power and nuclear weapons programs, like population policies, require administrative and technical teams able to formulate and sustain programs of considerable cost that pay off only in the long run. The more unstable a government, the shorter becomes the attention span of its leaders. They have to deal with today's problems and hope for the best tomorrow. In countries where political control is most difficult to maintain, governments are least likely to initiate nuclear-weapons programs. In such states, soldiers help to maintain leaders in power or try to overthrow them. For those purposes nuclear weapons are not very useful. Soldiers who have political clout or want it are not interested in nuclear weapons. They are not scientists and technicians. They like to command troops and squadrons. Their vested interests are in the military's traditional trappings.

Third, although highly unstable states are unlikely to initiate nuclear projects, such projects, begun in stable times, may continue through periods of political turmoil and succeed in producing nuclear weapons. A nuclear state may be unstable or may become so. But what is hard to comprehend is why, in an internal struggle for power, the contenders should start using nuclear weapons. Who would they aim at? How would they use them as instruments for maintaining or gaining control? I see little more reason to fear that one faction or another in some less developed country will fire atomic weapons in a struggle for political power than that they will be used in a crisis of succession in the Soviet Union or China. One or another nuclear state will experience uncertainty of succession, fierce struggles for power, and instability of regime. Those who fear the worst have not very plausibly shown how those expected events may lead to the use of nuclear weapons. Fourth, the possibility of one side in a civil war firing a nuclear warhead at its opponent's stronghold nevertheless remains. Such an act would produce a national tragedy, not an international one. This question then arises: Once the weapon is fired, what happens next? The domestic use of nuclear weapons is, of all the uses imaginable, least likely to lead to escalation and to threaten the stability of the central balance.

NUCLEAR WEAPONS AND REGIONAL STABILITY

Nuclear weapons are not likely to be used at home. Are they likely to be used abroad? As nuclear weapons spread, what new causes may bring effects different from and worse than those known earlier in the nuclear age? This section considers five ways in which the new world is expected to differ from the old and then examines the prospects for, and the consequences of, new nuclear states using their weapons for blackmail or for fighting an offensive war.

In what ways may the actions and interactions of new nuclear states differ from those of old nuclear powers? First, new nuclear states may come in hostile pairs and share a common border. Where states are bitter enemies one may fear that they will be unable to resist using their nuclear weapons against each other. This is a worry about the future that the past does not disclose. The Soviet Union and the United States, and the Soviet Union and China, are hostile enough; and the latter pair share a long border. Nuclear weapons have caused China and the Soviet Union to deal cautiously with each other. But bitterness among some potential nuclear states, so it is said, exceeds that experienced by the old ones. Playing down the bitterness sometimes felt by the United States, the Soviet Union, and China requires a creative reading of history. Moreover, those who believe that bitterness causes wars assume a close association that is seldom found between bitterness among nations and their willingness to run high risks.

Second, some new nuclear states may have governments and societies that are not well rooted. If a country is a loose collection of hostile tribes, if its leaders form a thin veneer atop a people partly nomadic and with an authoritarian history, its rulers may be freer of constraints than, and have different values from, those who rule older and more fully developed polities. Idi Amin and Muammar el-Qaddafi fit these categories, and they are favorite examples of the kinds of rulers who supposedly cannot be trusted to manage nuclear weapons responsibly. Despite wild rhetoric aimed at foreigners, however, both of these "irrational" rulers became cautious and modest when punitive actions against them might have threatened their ability to rule. Even though Amin lustily slaughtered members of tribes he disliked, he quickly stopped goading Britain once the sending of her troops appeared to be a possibility. Qaddafi has shown similar restraint. He and Anwar Sadat were openly hostile. In July of 1977 both launched commando attacks and air raids, including two large air strikes by Egypt on Libya's el Adem airbase. Neither side let the attacks get out of hand. Qaddafi showed himself to be forbearing and amenable to mediation by other Arab leaders. Shai Feldman uses these and other examples to argue that Arab leaders are deterred from taking inordinate risks not because they engage in intricate rational calculations but simply because they, like other rulers, are "sensitive to costs."

Many Westerners who write fearfully about a future in which third-world countries have nuclear weapons seem to view their people in the once familiar imperial manner as "lesser breeds without the law." As is usual with ethnocentric views, speculation takes the place of evidence. How do we know, someone has asked, that a nuclear-armed and newly hostile Egypt or a nuclear-armed and still hostile Syria would not strike to destroy Israel at the risk of Israeli bombs falling on some of their cities? More than a quarter of Egypt's people live in four cities: Cairo, Alexandria, Giza, and Aswan. More than a quarter of Syria's live in three: Damascus, Aleppo, and Homs. What government would risk sudden losses of such proportion or indeed of much lesser proportion? Rulers want to have a country that they can continue to rule. Some Arab country might wish that some other Arab country would risk its own destruction for the sake of destroying Israel, but there is no reason to think that any Arab country would do so. One may be impressed that, despite ample bitterness, Israelis and Arabs have limited their wars and accepted constraints placed on them by others. Arabs did not marshal their resources and make an all-out effort to destroy Israel in the years before Israel could strike back with nuclear warheads. We cannot expect countries to risk more in the presence of nuclear weapons than they have in their absence.

Third, many fear that states that are radical at home will recklessly use their nuclear weapons in pursuit of revolutionary ends abroad. States that are radical at home, however, may not be radical abroad. Few states have been radical in the conduct of their foreign policy, and fewer have remained so for long. Think of the Soviet Union and the People's Republic of China. States coexist in a competitive arena. The pressures of competition cause them to behave in ways that make the threats they face manageable, in ways that enable them to get along. States can remain radical in foreign policy only if they are overwhelmingly strong—as none of the new nuclear states will be—or if their radical acts fall short of damaging vital interests of nuclear powers. States that acquire nuclear weapons will not be regarded with indifference. States that want to be freewheelers have to stay out of the nuclear business. A nuclear Libya, for example, would have to show caution, even in rhetoric, lest she suffer retaliation in response to someone else's anonymous attack on a third state. That state, ignorant of who attacked, might claim that its intelligence agents had identified Libya as the culprit and take the opportunity to silence her by striking a conventional blow. Nuclear weapons induce caution, especially in weak states.

Fourth, while some worry about nuclear states coming in hostile pairs, others worry that the bipolar pattern will not be reproduced regionally in a world populated by larger numbers of nuclear states. The simplicity of relations that obtains when one party has to concentrate its worry on only one other, and the ease of calculating forces and estimating the dangers they pose, may be lost. The structure of international politics, however, will remain bipolar so long as no third state is able to compete militarily with the great powers. Whatever the structure, the relations of states run in various directions. This applied to relations of deterrence as soon as Britain gained nuclear capabilities. It has not weakened deterrence at the center and need not do so regionally. The Soviet Union now has to worry lest a move made in Europe cause France and Britain to retaliate, thus possibly setting off American forces. Such worries at once complicate calculations and strengthen deterrence.

Fifth, in some of the new nuclear states civil control of the military may be shaky. Nuclear weapons may fall into the hands of military officers more inclined than civilians to put them to offensive use. This again is an old worry. I can see no reason to think that civil control of the military is secure in the Soviet Union, given the occasional presence of serving officers in the Politburo and some known and some surmised instances of military intervention in civil affairs at critical times. And in the People's Republic of China military and civil branches of government are not separated but fused. Although one may prefer civil control, preventing a highly destructive war does not require it. What is required is that decisions be made that keep destruction within bounds, whether decisions are made by civilians or soldiers. Soldiers may be more cautious than civilians. Generals and admirals do not like uncertainty, and they do not lack patriotism. They do not like to fight conventional wars under unfamiliar conditions. The offensive use of nuclear weapons multiplies uncertainties. Nobody knows what a nuclear battlefield would look like, and nobody knows what happens after the first city is hit. *Uncertainty* about the course that a nuclear war might follow, along with the *certainty* that destruction can be immense, strongly inhibits the first use of nuclear weapons.

Examining the supposedly unfortunate characteristics of new nuclear states removes some of one's worries. One wonders why their civil and military leaders should be less interested in avoiding their own destruction than leaders of other states have been. Nuclear weapons have never been used in a world in which two or more states possessed them. Still, one's feeling that something awful will emerge as new nuclear powers are added to the present group is not easily quieted. The fear remains that one state or another will fire its new nuclear weapons in a coolly calculated preemptive strike, or fire them in a moment of panic, or use them to launch a preventive war. These possibilities are examined in the next section. Nuclear weapons may also be set off anonymously, or back a policy of blackmail, or be used in a combined conventional-nuclear attack.

Some have feared that a radical Arab state might fire a nuclear warhead anonymously at an Israeli city in order to block a peace settlement. But the state exploding the warhead could not be certain of remaining unidentified. Even if a country's leaders persuade themselves that chances of retaliation are low, who would run the risk? Nor would blackmail be easy to accomplish, despite one instance of seeming success. In 1953 Russia and China may have been convinced by Eisenhower and Dulles that they would widen the Korean war and raise the level of violence by using nuclear weapons if a settlement were not reached. In Korea we had gone so far that the threat to go further was plausible. The blackmailer's threat is not a cheap way of working one's will. The threat is simply incredible unless a considerable investment has already been made. Dulles's speech of January 12, 1954, seemed to threaten massive retaliation in response to mildly bothersome actions by others. The successful siege of Dien Bien Phu in the spring of that year showed the limitations of such threats. Capabilities foster policies that employ them. But monstrous capabilities foster monstrous policies, which when contemplated are seen to be too horrible to carry through. Moreover, once two or more countries have nuclear weapons, the execution of nuclear threats risks retaliation. This compounds the problem of establishing credibility.

Although nuclear weapons are poor instruments for blackmail, would they not provide a cheap and decisive offensive force when used against a conventionally armed enemy? Some people think that South Korea wants, and that earlier the Shah's Iran had wanted, nuclear weapons for offensive use. Yet one cannot say why South Korea would use nuclear weapons against fellow Koreans while trying to reunite them nor how she could use nuclear weapons against the North, knowing that China and Russia might retaliate. And what goals might a conventionally strong Iran have entertained that would have tempted her to risk using nuclear weapons? A country that takes the nuclear offensive has to fear a punishing blow from someone. Far from lowering the expected cost of aggression, a nuclear offense even against a non-nuclear state raises the possible costs of aggression to uncalculable heights because the aggressor cannot be sure of the reaction of other nuclear powers.

Nuclear weapons do not make nuclear war a likely prospect, as history has so far shown. The point made when discussing the possible internal use of nuclear weapons, however, bears repeating. No one can say that nuclear weapons will never be used. Their use, although unlikely, is always possible. In asking what the spread of nuclear weapons will do to the world, we are asking about the effects to be expected as a larger number of relatively weak states get nuclear weapons. If such states use nuclear weapons, the world will not end. The use of nuclear weapons by lesser powers would hardly trigger them elsewhere, with the United States and the Soviet Union becoming involved in ways that might shake the central balance.

DETERRENCE WITH SMALL NUCLEAR FORCES

A number of problems are thought to attend the efforts of minor powers to use nuclear weapons for deterrence. In this section, I ask how hard these problems are for new nuclear states to solve.

The forces required for deterrence. In considering the physical requirements of deterrent forces, we should remark the difference between prevention and preemption. A preventive war is launched by a stronger state against a weaker one that is thought to be gaining in strength. Aside from the balance of forces, a preemptive strike is launched by one state when another state's offensive forces are seen to be vulnerable.

The first danger posed by the spread of nuclear weapons would seem to be that each new nuclear state may tempt an old one to strike preventively in order to destroy an embryonic nuclear capability before it can become militarily effective. Because of America's nuclear arsenal, the Soviet Union could hardly have destroyed the budding forces of Britain and France; but the United States could have struck the Soviet Union's early nuclear facilities, and the United States and the Soviet Union could have struck China's. Long before Israel struck Iraq's reactor, preventive strikes were treated as more than abstract possibilities. When Francis P. Matthews was President Truman's Secretary of the Navy, he made a speech that seemed to favor our waging a preventive war. The United States, he urged, should be willing to pay "even the price of instituting a war to compel cooperation for peace." Moreover, preventive strikes against nuclear installations can be made by non-nuclear states and have sometimes been threatened. Thus President Nasser warned Israel in 1960 that Egypt would attack if she were sure that Israel was building a bomb. "It is inevitable," he said, "that we should attack the base of aggression even if we have to mobilize four million to destroy it."

The uneven development of the forces of potential and of new nuclear states creates occasions that seem to permit preventive strikes and may seem to invite them. Two stages of nuclear development should be distinguished. First, a country may be in an early stage of nuclear development and be obviously unable to make nuclear weapons. Second, a country may be in an advanced stage of nuclear development, and whether or not it has some nuclear weapons may not be surely known. All of the present nuclear countries went through both stages, yet until Israel struck Iraq's nuclear facility in June of 1981 no one had launched a preventive strike. A number of reasons combined may account for the reluctance of states to strike in order to prevent adversaries from developing nuclear forces. A preventive strike would seem to be most promising during the first stage of nuclear development. A state could strike without fearing that the country it attacked would return a nuclear blow. But would one strike so hard as to destroy the very potential for future nuclear development? If not, the country struck could simply resume its nuclear career. If the blow struck is less than devastating, one must be prepared to repeat it or to occupy and control the country. To do either would be difficult and costly.

In striking Iraq, Israel showed that a preventive strike can be made, something that was not in doubt. Israel's act and its consequences, however, make clear that the likelihood of useful accomplishment is low. Israel's strike increased the determination of Arabs to produce nuclear weapons. Israel's strike, far from foreclosing Iraq's nuclear future, gained her the support of some other Arab states in pursuing it. And despite Prime Minister Begin's vow to strike as often as need be, the risks in doing so would rise with each occasion.

A preventive strike during the second stage of nuclear development is even less promising than a preventive strike during the first stage. As more countries acquire nuclear weapons, and as more countries gain nuclear competence through power projects, the difficulties and dangers of making preventive strikes increase. To know for sure that the country attacked has not already produced or otherwise acquired some deliverable warheads becomes increasingly difficult. If the country attacked has even a rudimentary nuclear capability, one's own severe punishment becomes possible. Fission bombs may work even though they have not been tested, as was the case with the bomb dropped on Hiroshima. Israel has apparently not tested weapons, yet Egypt cannot know whether Israel has zero, ten, or twenty warheads. And if the number is zero and Egypt can be sure of that, she would still not know how many days or hours are required for assembling components that may be on hand.

Preventive strikes against states that have, or may have, nuclear weapons are hard to imagine, but what about preemptive ones? The new worry in a world in which nuclear weapons have spread is that states of limited and roughly similar capabilities will use them against one another. They do not want to risk nuclear devastation anymore than we do. Preemptive strikes nevertheless seem likely because we assume that their forces will be "delicate." With delicate forces, states are tempted to launch disarming strikes before their own forces can be struck and destroyed.

To be effective a deterrent force must meet three requirements. First, a part of the force must appear to be able to survive an attack and launch one of its own. Second, survival of the force must not require early firing in response to what may be false alarms. Third, weapons must not be susceptible to accidental and unauthorized use.

Nobody wants vulnerable, hair-trigger, accident-prone forces. Will new nuclear states find ways to hide their weapons, to deliver them, and to control them? Will they be able to deploy and manage nuclear weapons in ways that meet the physical requirements of deterrent forces?

Deterrent forces are seldom delicate because no state wants delicate forces and nuclear forces can easily be made sturdy. Nuclear weapons are fairly small and light. They are easy to hide and to move. Early in the nuclear age, people worried about atomic bombs being concealed in packing boxes and placed in the hold of ships to be exploded when a signal was given. Now more than ever people worry about terrorists stealing nuclear warheads because various states have so many of them. Everybody seems to believe that terrorists are capable of hiding bombs. Why should states be unable to do what terrorist gangs are thought to be capable of?

It is sometimes claimed that the few bombs of a new nuclear state create a greater danger of nuclear war than additional thousands for the United States and the Soviet Union. Such statements assume that preemption of a small force is easy. It is so only if the would-be attacker knows that the intended victim's warheads are few in number, knows their exact number and locations, and knows that they will not be moved or fired before they are struck. To know all of these things, and to know that you know them for sure, is exceedingly difficult. How can military advisers promise the full success of a disarming first strike when the penalty for slight error may be so heavy? In 1962, Tactical Air Command promised that an American strike against Soviet missiles in Cuba would certainly destroy 90 percent of them but would not guarantee 100 percent. In the best case a first strike destroys all of a country's deliverable weapons. In the worst case, some survive and can be delivered.

If the survival of nuclear weapons requires their dispersal and concealment, do not problems of command and control become harder to solve? Americans think so because we think in terms of large nuclear arsenals. Small nuclear powers will neither have them nor need them. Lesser nuclear states might deploy, say, ten real weapons and ten dummies, while permitting other countries to infer that the numbers are larger. The adversary need only believe that some warheads may survive his attack and be visited on him. That belief should not be hard to create without making command and control unreliable. All nuclear countries must live through a time when their forces are crudely designed. All countries have so far been able to control them. Relations between the United States and the Soviet Union, and later among the United States, the Soviet Union, and China, were at their bitterest just when their nuclear forces were in early stages of development, were unbalanced, were crude and presumably hard to control. Why should we expect new nuclear states to experience greater difficulties than the old ones were able to cope with? Moreover, although some of the new nuclear states may be economically and technically backward, they will either have an expert and highly trained group of scientists and engineers or they will not produce nuclear weapons. Even if they buy the weapons, they will have to hire technicians to maintain and control them. We do not have to wonder whether they will take good care of their weapons. They have every incentive to do so. They will not want to risk retaliation because one or more of their warheads accidentally strikes another country.

Hiding nuclear weapons and keeping them under control are tasks for which the ingenuity of numerous states is adequate. Nor are means of delivery difficult to devise or procure. Bombs can be driven in by trucks from neighboring countries. Ports can be torpedoed by small boats lying offshore. Moreover, a thriving arms trade in ever more sophisticated military equipment provides ready access to what may be wanted, including planes and missiles suited to nuclear warhead delivery.

Lesser nuclear states can pursue deterrent strategies effectively. Deterrence requires the ability to inflict unacceptable damage on another country. "Unacceptable damage" to the Soviet Union was variously defined by Robert McNamara as requiring the ability to destroy a fifth to a fourth of her population and a half to two-thirds of her industrial capacity. American estimates of what is required for deterrence have been absurdly high. To deter, a country need not appear to be able to destroy a fourth or a half of another country, although in some cases that might be easily done. Would Libya try to destroy Israel's nuclear weapons at the risk of two bombs surviving to fall on Tripoli and Bengazi? And what would be left of Israel if Tel Aviv and Haifa were destroyed?

The weak can deter one another. But can the weak deter the strong? Raising the question of China's ability to deter the Soviet Union highlights the issue. The population and industry of most states concentrate in a relatively small number of centers. This is true of the Soviet Union. A major attack on the top ten cities of the Soviet Union would get 25 percent of its industrial capacity and 25 percent of its urban population. Geoffrey Kemp in 1974 concluded that China would probably be able to strike on that scale. And, I emphasize again, China need only appear to be able to do it. A low probability of carrying a highly destructive attack home is sufficient for deterrence. A force of an imprecisely specifiable minimum capacity is nevertheless needed.

In a 1979 study, Justin Galen (pseud.) wondered whether the Chinese had a force physically capable of deterring the Soviet Union. He estimated that China had 60 to 80 medium range and 60 to 80 intermediate range missiles of doubtful reliability and accuracy and 80 obsolete bombers. He rightly pointed out that the missiles may miss their targets even if fired at cities and that the bombers may not get through the Soviet Union's defenses. Moreover, the Russians may be able to preempt, having almost certainly "located virtually every Chinese missile, aircraft, weapons storage area and production facility." But surely Russian leaders put these things the other way around. To locate virtually all missiles and aircraft is not good enough. Despite inaccuracies, a few Chinese missiles *may* hit Russian cities, and some bombers *may* get through. Not much is required to deter. What political-military objective is worth risking Vladivostok, Novosibirsk, and Tomsk, with no way of being sure that Moscow will not go as well?

The credibility of small deterrent forces. The credibility of weaker countries' deterrent threats has two faces. The first is physical. Will such countries be able to construct and protect a deliverable force? We have found that they can quite readily do so. The second is psychological. Will deterrent threats that are physically feasible be psychologically plausible? Will an adversary believe that the retaliation that is threatened will be carried out?

Deterrent threats backed by second-strike nuclear forces raise the expected costs of war to such heights that war becomes unlikely. But deterrent threats may not be credible. In a world where two or more countries can make them, the prospect of *mutual* devastation makes it difficult, or irrational, to execute threats should the occasion for doing so arise. Would it not be senseless to risk suffering further destruction once a deterrent force had failed to deter? Believing that it would be, an adversary may attack counting on the attacked country's unwillingness to risk initiating a devastating exchange by its own retaliation. Why retaliate once a threat to do so has failed? If one's policy is to rely on forces designed to deter, then an attack that is nevertheless made shows that one's reliance was misplaced. The course of wisdom may be to pose a new question: What is the best policy now that deterrence has failed? One gains nothing by destroying an enemy's cities. Instead, in retaliating, one may prompt the enemy to unleash more warheads. A ruthless aggressor may strike believing that the leaders of the attacked country are capable of following such a "rational" line of thought. To carry out the threat that was "rationally" made may be "irrational." This old worry achieved new prominence as the strategic capabilities of the Soviet Union approached those of the United States in the middle 1970s. The Soviet Union, some feared, might believe that the United States would be self-deterred (ref. Nitze article).

Much of the literature on deterrence emphasizes the problem of achieving the credibility on which deterrence depends and the danger of relying on a deterrent of uncertain credibility. One earlier solution of the problem was found in Thomas Schelling's notion of "the threat that leaves something to chance." No state can know for sure that another state will refrain from retaliating even when retaliation would be irrational. No state can bet heavily on another state's rationality. Bernard Brodie put the thought more directly, while avoiding the slippery notion of rationality. Rather than ask what it may be rational or irrational for governments to do, the question he repeatedly asked was this: How do governments behave in the presence of awesome dangers? His answer was "very carefully."

To ask why a country should carry out its deterrent threat once deterrence has failed is to ask the wrong question. The question suggests that an aggressor may attack believing that the attacked country may not retaliate. This invokes the conventional logic that analysts find so hard to forsake. In a conventional world, a country can sensibly attack if it believes that success is probable. In a nuclear world, a country cannot sensibly attack unless it believes that success is assured. An attacker is deterred even if he believes only that the attacked *may* retaliate. Uncertainty of response, not certainty, is required for deterrence because, if retaliation occurs, one risks losing all. In a nuclear world, we should look less at the retaliator's conceivable inhibitions and more at the challenger's obvious risks.

One may nevertheless wonder, as Americans recently have, whether retaliatory threats remain credible if the strategic forces of the attacker are superior to those of the attacked. Will an unsuccessful defender in a conventional war have the courage to unleash its deterrent force, using nuclear weapons first against a country having superior strategic forces? Once more this asks the wrong question. The previous paragraph urged the importance of shifting attention from the defender's possible inhibitions to the aggressor's unwillingness to run extreme risks. This paragraph urges the importance of shifting attention from the defender's courage to the different valuations that defenders and attackers place on the stakes. An attacked country will ordinarily value keeping its own territory more highly than an attacker will value gaining some portion of it. Given second-strike capabilities, it is not the balance of forces but the courage to use them that counts. The balance or imbalance of strategic forces affects neither the calculation of danger nor the question of whose will is the stronger. Second-strike forces have to be seen in absolute terms. The question of whose interests are paramount will then determine whose will is perceived as being the stronger.

Emphasizing the importance of the "balance of resolve," to use Glenn Snyder's apt phrase, raises questions about what a deterrent force covers and what it does not. In answering these questions, we can learn something from the experience of the last three decades. The United States and the Soviet Union have limited and modulated their provocative acts, the more carefully so when major values for one side or the other were at issue. This can be seen both in what they have and in what they have not done. Whatever support the Soviet Union gave to North Korea's initial attack on the South was given after Secretary of State Acheson, the Joint Chiefs of Staff, General MacArthur, and the Chairman of the Senate Foreign Relations Committee all explicitly excluded both South Korea and Taiwan from America's defense perimeter. The United States, to take another example, could fight for years on a large scale in Southeast Asia because neither success nor failure mattered much internationally. Victory would not have made the world one of American hegemony. Defeat would not have made the world one of Russian hegemony. No vital interest of either super-power was at stake, as both Kissinger and Brezhnev made clear at the time (Stoessinger, 1976, ch. 8). One can fight without fearing escalation only where little is at stake. And that is where the deterrent does not deter.

Actions at the periphery can safely be bolder than actions at the center. In contrast, where much is at stake for one side, the other side moves with care. Trying to win where winning would bring the central balance into question threatens escalation and becomes too risky to contemplate. The United States is circumspect when East European crises impend. Thus Secretary of State Dulles assured the Soviet Union when Hungarians rebelled in October of 1956 that we would not interfere with efforts to suppress them. And the Soviet Union's moves in the center of Europe are carefully controlled. Thus her probes in Berlin have been tentative, reversible, and ineffective. Strikingly, the long border between East and West Europe—drawn where borders earlier proved unstable—has been free even of skirmishes in all of the years since the Second World War.

Contemplating American and Russian postwar behavior, and inter preting it in terms of nuclear logic, suggests that deterrence extends to vital interests beyond the homeland more easily than many have thought. The United States cares more about Western Europe than the Soviet Union does. The Soviet Union cares more about Eastern Europe than the United States does. Communicating the weight of one side's concern as compared to the other side's has been easily enough done when the matters at hand affect the United States and the Soviet Union directly. For this reason, West European anxiety about the coverage it gets from our strategic forces, while understand-able, is exaggerated. The United States might well retaliate should the Soviet Union make a major military move against a NATO country, and that is enough to deter.

The problem of extended deterrence. How far from the homeland does deterrence extend? One answers that question by defining the conditions that must obtain if deterrent threats are to be credited. First, the would-be attacker must be made to see that the deterrer considers the interests at stake to be vital. One cannot assume that countries will instantly agree on the question of whose interests are vital. Nuclear weapons, however, strongly incline them to grope for *de facto* agreement on the answer rather than to fight over it.

Second, political stability must prevail in the area that the deterrent is intended to cover. If the threat to a regime is in good part from internal factions, then an outside power may risk supporting one of them even in the face of deterrent threats. The credibility of a deterrent force requires both that interests be seen to be vital and that it is the attack from outside that threatens them. Given these conditions, the would-be attacker provides both the reason to retaliate and the target for retaliation. Deterrence gains in credibility the more highly valued the interests covered appear to be.

The problem of stretching a deterrent, which has so agitated the western alliance, is not a problem for lesser nuclear states. Their problem is to protect not others but themselves. Many have feared that lesser nuclear states would be the first ones to break the nuclear taboo and that they would use their weapons irresponsibly. I expect just the opposite. Weak states find it easier than strong states to establish their credibility. Not only are they not trying to stretch their deterrent forces to cover others but also their vulnerability to conventional attack lends credence to their nuclear threats. Because in a conventional war they can lose so much so fast, it is easy to believe that they will unleash a deterrent force even at the risk of receiving a nuclear blow in return. With deterrent forces, the party that is absolutely threatened prevails (Feldman 1980, ch. 1). Use of nuclear weapons by lesser states will come only if survival is at stake. And this should be called not irresponsible but responsible use.

An opponent who attacks what is unambiguously mine risks suffering great distress if I have second-strike forces. This statement has important implications for both the deterrer and the deterred. Where territorial claims are shadowy and disputed, deterrent writs do not run. As Steven J. Rosen has said: "It is difficult to imagine Israel committing national suicide to hold on to Abu Rudeis or Hebron or Mount Hermon." Establishing the credibility of a deterrent force requires moderation of territorial claims on the part of the would-be deterred. For modest states, weapons whose very existence works strongly against their use are just what is wanted.

In a nuclear world, conservative would-be attackers will be prudent, but will would-be attackers be conservative? A new Hitler is not unimaginable. Would the presence of nuclear weapons have moderated Hitler's behavior? Hitler did not start World War II in order to destroy the Third Reich. Indeed, he was surprised and dismayed by British and French declarations of war on Poland's behalf. After all, the western democracies had not come to the aid of a geographically defensible and militarily strong Czechoslovakia. Why then should they have declared war on behalf of a less defensible Poland and against a Germany made stronger by the incorporation of Czechoslovakia's armor? From the occupation of the Rhineland in 1936 to the invasion of Poland in 1939, Hitler's calculations were realistically made. In those years, Hitler would probably have been deterred from acting in ways that immediately threatened massive death and widespread destruction in Germany. And, if Hitler had not been deterred, would his generals have obeyed his commands? In a nuclear world, to act in blatantly offensive ways is madness. Under the circumstances, how many generals would obey the commands of a madman? One man alone does not make war.

To believe that nuclear deterrence would have worked against Germany in 1939 is easy. It is also easy to believe that in 1945, given the ability to do so, Hitler and some few around him would have fired nuclear warheads at the United States, Great Britain, and the Soviet Union as their armies advanced, whatever the consequences for Germany. Two considerations, however, work against this possibility. When defeat is seen to be inevitable, a ruler's authority may vanish. Early in 1945 Hitler apparently ordered the initiation of gas warfare, but no one responded (ref. Brown article). The first consideration applies in a conventional world; the second in a nuclear world. In the latter, no country will press another to the point of decisive defeat. In the desperation of defeat desperate measures may be taken, but the last thing anyone wants to do is to make a nuclear nation desperate. The unconditional surrender of a nuclear nation cannot be demanded. Nuclear weapons affect the deterrer as well as the deterred. All of the parties involved are constrained to be moderate because one's immoderate behavior makes the nuclear threats of others credible.

Arms races among new nuclear states. One may easily believe that American and Russian military doctrines set the pattern that new nuclear states will follow. One may then also believe that they will suffer the fate of the United States and the Soviet Union, that they will compete in building larger and larger nuclear arsenals while continuing to accumulate conventional weapons. These are doubtful beliefs. One can infer the future from the past only insofar as future situations may be like present ones for the actors involved. For three main reasons, new nuclear states are likely to decrease rather than to increase their military spending.

First, nuclear weapons alter the dynamics of arms races. In a competition of two or more parties, it may be hard to say who is pushing and who is being pushed, who is leading and who is following. If one party seeks to increase its capabilities, it may seem that the other(s) must too. The dynamic may be built into the competition and may unfold despite a mutual wish to resist it. But need this be the case in a strategic competition between nuclear countries? It need not be if the conditions of competition make deterrent logic dominant. Deterrent logic dominates if the conditions of competition make it nearly impossible for any of the competing parties to achieve a first-strike capability. Early in the nuclear age, the implications of deterrent strategy were clearly seen. "When dealing with the absolute weapon," as William T. R. Fox put it, "arguments based on relative advantage lose their point." The United States has sometimes designed its forces according to that logic. Donald A. Quarles argued when he was Eisenhower's Secretary of the Air Force that "sufficiency of air power" is determined by "the force required to accomplish the mission assigned." Avoidance of total war then does not depend on the "*relative* strength of the two opposed forces." Instead, it depends on the "*absolute* power in the hands of each, and in the substantial invulnerability of this power to interdiction." To repeat: If no state can launch a disarming attack with high confidence, force comparisons are irrelevant. Strategic arms races are then pointless. Deterrent strategies offer this great advantage: Within wide ranges neither side need respond to increases in the other side's military capabilities.

Those who foresee nuclear arms racing among new nuclear states fail to make the distinction between war-fighting and war-deterring capabilities. War-fighting forces, because they threaten the forces of others, have to be compared. Superior forces may bring victory to one country; inferior forces may bring defeat to another. Force requirements vary with strategies and not just with the characteristics of weapons. With war-fighting strategies, arms races become difficult, if not impossible, to avoid. Forces designed for deterring war need not be compared. As Harold Brown said when he was Secretary of Defense, purely deterrent forces "can be relatively modest, and their size can perhaps be made substantially, though not completely, insensitive to changes in the posture of an opponent." With deterrent strategies, arms races make sense only if a first-strike capability is within reach. Because thwarting a first strike is easy, deterrent forces are quite cheap to build and maintain. With deterrent forces, the question is not whether one country has more than another but whether it has the capability of inflicting "unacceptable damage" on another, with unacceptable damage sensibly defined. Once that capability is assured, additional strategic weapons are useless. More is not better if less is enough.

Deterrent balances are inherently stable. If one can say how much is enough, then within wide limits one state can be insensitive to changes in its adversaries' forces. This is the way French leaders have thought. France, as President Giscard d'Estaing said, "fixes its security at the level required to maintain, regardless of the way the strategic situation develops in the world, the credibility—in other words, the effectiveness—of its deterrent force." With deterrent forces securely established, no military need presses one side to try to surpass the other. Human error and folly may lead some parties involved in deterrent balances to spend more on armaments than is needed, but other parties need not increase their armaments in response, because such excess spending does not threaten them. The logic of deterrence eliminates incentives for strategic arms racing. This should be easier for lesser nuclear states to understand than it has been for the United States and the Soviet Union. Because most of them are economically hard pressed, they will not want to have more than enough.

Allowing for their particular circumstances, lesser nuclear states confirm these statements in their policies. Britain and France are relatively rich countries, and they tend to overspend. Their strategic forces are nevertheless modest enough when one considers that their purpose is to deter the Soviet Union rather than states with capabilities comparable to their own. China of course faces the same task. These three countries show no inclination to engage in nuclear arms races with anyone. India appears content to have a nuclear military capability that may or may not have produced deliverable warheads, and Israel maintains her ambiguous status. New nuclear states are likely to conform to these patterns and aim for a modest sufficiency rather than vie with one another for a meaningless superiority.

Second, because strategic nuclear arms races among lesser powers are unlikely, the interesting question is not whether they will be run but whether countries having strategic nuclear weapons can avoid running conventional races. No more than the United States or the Soviet Union will new nuclear states want to rely on executing the deterrent threat that risks all. And will not their vulnerability to conventional attack induce them to continue their conventional efforts?

American policy as it has developed since the early 1960s again teaches lessons that mislead. For two decades, we have emphasized the importance of having a continuum of forces that would enable the United States and her allies to fight at any level from irregular to strategic nuclear warfare. A policy that decreases reliance on deterrence increases the chances that wars will be fought. This was well appreciated in Europe when we began to place less emphasis on deterrence and more on defense. The worries of many Europeans were well expressed by a senior British general, in the following words: "McNamara is practically telling the Soviets that the worst they need expect from an attack on West Germany is a conventional counterattack." Why risk one's own destruction if one is able to fight on the ground and forego the use of strategic weapons?

The policy of flexible response lessened reliance on strategic deterrence and increased the chances of fighting a war. New nuclear states are not likely to experience this problem. The expense of mounting conventional defenses, and the difficulties and dangers of fighting conventional wars, will keep most nuclear states from trying to combine large war-fighting forces with deterrent forces. Disjunction within their forces will enhance the value of deterrence.

Israeli policy seems to contradict these propositions. From 1971 through 1978, both Israel and Egypt spent from 20 to 40 percent of their GNPs on arms. Israel's spending on conventional arms remains high, although it has decreased since 1978. The decrease followed from the making of peace with Egypt and not from increased reliance on nuclear weapons. The seeming contradiction in fact bears out deterrent logic. So long as Israel holds the West Bank and the Gaza Strip she has to be prepared to fight for them. Since they are by no means unambiguously hers, deterrent threats, whether implicit or explicit, will not cover them. Moreover, while America's large subsidies continue, economic constraints will not drive Israel to the territorial settlement that would shrink her borders sufficiently to make a deterent policy credible.

From previous points it follows that nuclear weapons are likely to decrease arms racing and reduce military costs for lesser nuclear states in two ways. Conventional arms races will wither if countries shift emphasis from conventional defense to nuclear deterrence. For Pakistan, for example, acquiring nuclear weapons is an alternative to running a ruinous conventional race with India. And, of course, deterrent strategies make nuclear arms races pointless.

Finally, arms races in their ultimate form—the fighting of offensive wars designed to increase national security—also become pointless. The success of a deterrent strategy does not depend on the extent of territory a state holds, a point made earlier. It merits repeating because of its unusual importance for states whose geographic limits lead them to obsessive concern for their security in a world of ever more destructive conventional weapons.

The frequency and intensity of war. The presence of nuclear weapons makes war less likely. One may nevertheless oppose the spread of nuclear weapons on the ground that they would make war, however unlikely, unbearably intense should it occur. Nuclear weapons have not been fired in anger in a world in which more than one country has them. We have enjoyed over three decades of nuclear peace and may enjoy many more. But we can never have a guarantee. We may be grateful for decades of nuclear peace and for the discouragement of conventional war among those who have nuclear weapons. Yet the fear is widespread, and naturally so, that if they ever go off, we may all be dead. People as varied as the scholar Richard Smoke, the arms controller Paul Warnke, and former Defense Secretary Harold Brown all believe that if any nuclear weapons go off, many will. Although this seems the least likely of all the unlikely possibilities, unfortunately it is not impossible. What makes it so unlikely is that, even if deterrence should fail, the prospects for rapid deescalation are good.

McNamara asked himself what fractions of the Soviet Union's population and industry the United States should be able to destroy in order to deter her. For military, although not for budgetary, strategy this was the wrong question. States are not deterred because they expect to suffer a certain amount of damage but because they cannot know how much damage they will suffer. Near the dawn of the nuclear age Bernard Brodie put the matter simply: "The prediction is more important than the fact." The prediction, that is, that attacking the vital interests of a country having nuclear weapons may bring the attacker untold losses. As Patrick Morgan more recently put it: "To attempt to compute the cost of a nuclear war is to miss the point."

States are deterred by the prospect of suffering severe damage and by their physical inability to do much to limit it. Deterrence works because nuclear weapons enable one state to punish another state severely without first defeating it. "Victory" in Thomas Schelling's words, "is no longer a prerequisite for hurting the enemy." Countries armed with only conventional weapons can hope that their military forces will be able to limit the damage an attacker can do. Among countries armed with strategic nuclear forces, the hope of avoiding heavy damage depends mainly on the attacker's restraint and little on one's own efforts. Those who compare expected deaths through strategic exchanges of nuclear warheads with casualties suffered by the Soviet Union in World War II overlook this fundamental difference between conventional and nuclear worlds.

Deterrence rests on what countries can do to each other with strategic nuclear weapons. From this statement, one easily leaps to the wrong conclusion: that deterrent strategies, if they have to be carried through, will produce a catastrophe. That countries are able to annihilate each other means neither that deterrence depends on their threatening to do so nor that they will do so if deterrence fails. Because countries heavily armed with strategic nuclear weapons can carry war to its ultimate intensity, the control of force, in wartime as in peacetime, becomes the primary objective. If deterrence fails, leaders will have the strongest incentives to keep force under control and limit damage rather than launching genocidal attacks. If the Soviet Union should attack Western Europe, NATO's objectives would be to halt the attack and end the war. The United States has long had the ability to place hundreds of warheads precisely on targets in the Soviet Union. Surely we would strike military targets before striking industrial targets and industrial targets before striking cities. The intent to do so is sometimes confused with a war-fighting strategy, which it is not. It would not significantly reduce the Soviet

Union's ability to hurt us. It is a deterrent strategy, resting initially on the threat to punish. The threat, if it fails to deter, is appropriately followed not by spasms of violence but by punishment administered in ways that convey threats to make the punishment more severe.

A war between the United States and the Soviet Union that got out of control would be catastrophic. If they set out to destroy each other, they would greatly reduce the world's store of developed resources while killing millions outside of their own borders through fallout. Even while destroying themselves, states with few weapons would do less damage to others. As ever, the biggest international dangers come from the strongest states. Fearing the world's destruction, one may prefer a world of conventional great powers having a higher probability of fighting less destructive wars to a world of nuclear great powers having a lower probability of fighting more destructive wars. But that choice effectively disappeared with the production of atomic bombs by the United States during World War II. Since the great powers are unlikely to be drawn into the nuclear wars of others, the added global dangers posed by the spread of nuclear weapons are small.

The spread of nuclear weapons threatens to make wars more intense at the local and not at the global level, where wars of the highest intensity have been possible for a number of years. If their national existence should be threatened, weaker countries, unable to defend at lesser levels of violence, may destroy themselves through resorting to nuclear weapons. Lesser nuclear states will live in fear of this possibility. But this is not different from the fear under which the United States and the Soviet Union have lived for years. Small nuclear states may experience a keener sense of desperation because of extreme vulnerability to conventional as well as to nuclear attack, but, again, in desperate situations what all parties become most desperate to avoid is the use of strategic nuclear weapons. Still, however improbable the event, lesser states may one day fire some of their weapons. Are minor nuclear states more or less likely to do so than major ones? The answer to this question is vitally important because the existence of some states would be at stake even if the damage done were regionally confined.

For a number of reasons, then, deterrent strategies promise less damage than war-fighting strategies. First, deterrent strategies induce caution all around and thus reduce the incidence of war. Second, wars fought in the face of strategic nuclear weapons must be carefully limited because a country having them may retaliate if its vital interests are threatened. Third, prospective punishment need only be proportionate to an adversary's expected gains in war after those gains are discounted for the many uncertainties of war. Fourth, should deterrence fail, a few judiciously delivered warheads are likely to produce sobriety in the leaders of all of the countries involved and thus bring rapid deescalation. Finally, war-fighting strategies offer no clear place to stop short of victory for some and defeat for others. Deterrent strategies do, and that place is where one country threatens another's vital interests. Deterrent strategies lower the probability that wars will begin. If wars start nevertheless, deterrent strategies lower the probability that they will be carried very far.

Nuclear weapons may lessen the intensity as well as the frequency of wars among their possessors. For fear of escalation, nuclear states do not want to fight long or hard over important interests—indeed, they do not want to fight at all. Minor nuclear states have even better reasons than major ones to accommodate one another peacefully and to avoid any fighting. Worries about the intensity of war among nuclear states have to be viewed in this context and against a world in which conventional weapons become even costlier and more destructive.

CONCLUSION

The conclusion is in two parts. After saying what follows for American policy from my analysis, I briefly state the main reasons for believing that the slow spread of nuclear weapons will promote peace and reinforce international stability.

IMPLICATIONS FOR AMERICAN POLICY

I have argued that the gradual spread of nuclear weapons is better than either no spread or rapid spread. We do not face a set of happy choices. We may prefer that countries have conventional weapons only, do not run arms races, and do not fight. Yet the alternative to nuclear weapons for some countries may be ruinous arms races with high risk of their becoming engaged in debilitating conventional wars.

Countries have to care for their own security with or without the help of others. If a country feels highly insecure and believes that nuclear weapons would make it more secure, America's policy of opposing the spread of nuclear weapons will not easily prevail. Any slight chance of bringing the spread of nuclear weapons to a full stop exists only if the United States and the Soviet Union constantly and strenously try to achieve that end. To do so carries costs measured in terms of their other interests. The strongest means by which the United States can persuade a country to forego nuclear weapons is a guarantee of its security, especially if the guarantee is made credible by the presence of American troops. But how many commitments do we want to make, and how many countries do we want to garrison? We are wisely reluctant to give guarantees, but we then should not expect to decide how other countries are to provide for their security. As a neighbor of China, India no doubt feels more secure, and can behave more reasonably, with a nuclear-weapons capability than without it. The thought applies as well to Pakistan as India's neighbor. We damage our relations with such countries by badgering them about nuclear weapons while being unwilling to guarantee their security. Under such circumstances they, not we, should decide what their national interests require.

Some have feared that weakening opposition to the spread of nuclear weapons will lead numerous states to make them because it may seem that "everyone is doing it." Why should we think that if we relax, numerous states will begin to make nuclear weapons? Both the United States and the Soviet Union were more relaxed in the past, and these effects did not follow. The Soviet Union initially supported China's nuclear program. The United States continues to help Britain maintain her deterrent forces. By 1968 the CIA had informed President Johnson of the existence of Israeli nuclear weapons, and in July of 1970 Richard Helms, Director of the CIA, gave this information to the Senate Foreign Relations Committee. These and later disclosures were not followed by censure of Israel or by reductions of assistance to her. And in September of 1980 the Executive Branch, against the will of the House of Representatives but with the approval of the Senate, continued to do nuclear business with India despite her explosion of a nuclear device and despite her unwillingness to sign the Nuclear Non-Proliferation Treaty.

Assisting some countries in the development of nuclear weapons and failing to oppose others has not caused a nuclear stampede. Is the more recent leniency toward India likely to? One reason to think so is that more countries now have the ability to make their own nuclear weapons, more than forty of them according to Joseph Nye.

Many more countries can than do. One can believe that American opposition to nuclear arming stays the deluge only by overlooking the complications of international life. Any state has to examine many conditions before deciding whether or not to develop nuclear weapons. Our opposition is only one factor and is not likely to be the decisive one. Many states feel fairly secure living with their neighbors. Why should they want nuclear weapons? Some countries, feeling threatened, have found security through their own strenuous efforts and through arrangements made with others. South Korea is an outstanding example. Many South Korean officials believe that South Korea would lose more in terms of American support if she acquired nuclear weapons than she would gain by having them. Further, on occasion we might slow the spread of nuclear weapons by *not* opposing the nuclear weapons program of some countries. When we oppose Pakistan's nuclear program, we are saying that we disapprove of countries developing nuclear weapons no matter what their neighbors do. Failing to oppose Pakistan's efforts also sends a signal to potential nuclear states, suggesting that if a country develops nuclear weapons, a regional rival may do so as well and may do so without opposition from us. This message may give pause to some of the countries that are tempted to acquire nuclear weapons. After all, Argentina is to Brazil as Pakistan is to India.

Neither the gradual spread of nuclear weapons nor American and Russian acquiescence in this has opened the nuclear floodgates. Nations attend to their security in ways they think best. The fact that so many more countries can make nuclear weapons than do make them says more about the hesitation of countries to enter the nuclear military business than about the effectiveness of American policy. We can sensibly suit our policy to individual cases, sometimes bringing pressure against a country moving toward nuclear-weapons capability and sometimes quietly acquiescing. No one policy is right for all countries. We should ask what our interests in regional stability require in particular instances. We should also ask what the interests of other countries require before putting pressure on them. Some countries are likely to suffer more in cost and pain if they remain conventional states than if they become nuclear ones. The measured and selective spread of nuclear weapons does not run against our interests and can increase the security of some states at a price they can afford to pay.

It is not likely that nuclear weapons will spread with a speed that exceeds the ability of their new owners to adjust to them. The spread of nuclear weapons is something that we have worried too much about and tried too hard to stop.

THE NUCLEAR FUTURE

What will a world populated by a larger number of nuclear states look like? I have drawn a picture of such a world that accords with experience throughout the nuclear age. Those who dread a world with more nuclear states do little more than assert that more is worse and claim without substantiation that new nuclear states will be less responsible and less capable of self control than the old ones have been. They feel fears that many felt when they imagined how a nuclear China would behave. Such fears have proved unfounded as nuclear weapons have slowly spread. I have found many reasons for believing that with more nuclear states the world will have a promising future. I have reached this unusual conclusion for five main reasons.

First, international politics is a self-help system, and in such systems the principal parties do most to determine their own fate, the fate of other parties, and the fate of the system. This will continue to be so, with the United States and the Soviet Union filling their customary roles. For the United States and the Soviet Union to achieve nuclear maturity and to show this by behaving sensibly is more important than preventing the spread of nuclear weapons.

Second, given the massive numbers of American and Russian warheads, and given the impossibility of one side destroying enough of the other side's missiles to make a retaliatory strike bearable, the balance of terror is indestructible. What can lesser states do to disrupt the nuclear equilibrium if even the mighty efforts of the United States and the Soviet Union cannot shake it? The international equilibrium will endure.

Third, nuclear weaponry makes miscalculation difficult because it is hard not to be aware of how much damage a small number of warheads can do. Early in this century Norman Angell argued that war could not occur because it would not pay (1914). But conventional wars have brought political gains to some countries at the expense of others. Among nuclear countries, possible losses in war overwhelm possible gains. In the nuclear age Angell's dictum, broadly interpreted, becomes persuasive. When the active use of force threatens to bring great losses, war becomes less likely. This proposition is widely accepted but insufficiently emphasized. Nuclear weapons have reduced the chances of war between the United States and the Soviet Union and between the Soviet Union and China. One may expect them to have similar effects elsewhere. Where nuclear weapons threaten to make the cost of wars immense, who will dare to start them? Nuclear weapons make it possible to approach the deterrent ideal.

Fourth, nuclear weapons can be used for defense as well as for deterrence. Some have argued that an apparently impregnable nuclear defense can be mounted. The Maginot Line has given defense a bad name. It nevertheless remains true that the incidence of wars decreases as the perceived difficulty of winning them increases. No one attacks a defense believed to be impregnable. Nuclear weapons may make it possible to approach the defensive ideal. If so, the spread of nuclear weapons will further help to maintain peace.

Fifth, new nuclear states will confront the possibilities and feel the constraints that present nuclear states have experienced. New nuclear states will be more concerned for their safety and more mindful of dangers than some of the old ones have been. Until recently, only the great and some of the major powers have had nuclear weapons. While nuclear weapons have spread, conventional weapons have proliferated. Under these circumstances, wars have been fought not at the center but at the periphery of international politics. The likelihood of war decreases as deterrent and defensive capabilities increase. Nuclear weapons, responsibly used, make wars hard to start. Nations that have nuclear weapons have strong incentives to use them responsibly. These statements hold for small as for big nuclear powers. Because they do, the measured spread of nuclear weapons is more to be welcomed than feared.

What Difference Will It Make?

LEWIS DUNN

THE BREAKDOWN OF NUCLEAR PEACE

A number of analysts and observers, noting that predictions at the dawn of the nuclear age of a nuclear apocalypse have proved exaggerated, argue that there is little reason to fear the consequences of the further spread of nuclear weapons. Frequently at the core of such optimistic assessments is the belief that the very destructiveness of those weapons will both instill prudence in their new owners, making them less willing to use even minimal conventional force out of fear that conflict will escalate to use of nuclear weapons, and lead to stable deterrent relationships between previously hostile countries. But such a fear of nuclear war was only one of the underpinnings of the first decades' nuclear peace. Other equally significant geopolitical and technical supports may be absent in the conflict-prone regions to which nuclear weapons are now likely to spread.

A SPIRALING THREAT TO PEACE

With the spread of nuclear weapons to conflict-prone regions, the chances that those weapons will be used again increase greatly. The heightened stakes and lessened room for maneuver in conflict-prone regions, the volatile leadership and political instability of many of the next nuclear powers, and the technical deficiencies of many new nuclear forces all threaten the first decades' nuclear peace.

Not least to be feared is nuclear war caused by accident or miscalculation. During an intense crisis or the first stages of a conventional military clash, for example, an accidental detonation of a nuclear weapon—even within the country of origin—or an accidental missile launch easily might be misinterpreted as the first shot of a surprise attack. Pressures to escalate in a last-ditch attempt to disarm the opponent before he completes that attack will be intense. Similarly, a technical malfunction of a radar warning system or a human error in interpreting an ambiguous warning might trigger a nuclear clash. Or fear that escalation to nuclear conflict no longer could be avoided

From *Controlling the Bomb* by Lewis A. Dunn. Copyright © 1982 by Yale University Press, pp. 69–95. Reprinted by permission of the publisher, Yale University Press. Portions of the text and some footnotes have been omitted.

might lead to a country to get in the first blow, so as partly to disarm the opponent and to minimize damage.

Unauthorized use of nuclear weapons by the military also is a possibility. For example, faced with imminent conventional military defeat and believing there is little left to lose anyway, a few members of Pakistan's military could launch a nuclear strike against India to damage that country as much as possible. Or a few hard-line, fanatic Iraqi, Libyan, or even Egyptian officers might use their countries' newly acquired nuclear weapons in an attempt to "solve" the Israeli problem once and for all. These officers' emotional commitment to a self-ordained higher mission would overwhelm any fear of the adverse personal or national consequences. Aside from the initial destruction, such unauthorized use could provoke a full-scale nuclear conflict between the hostile countries.

But the first use of nuclear weapons since Nagasaki may be a carefully calculated policy decision. The bomb might be used intentionally on the battlefield to defend against invasion. For example, faced with oncoming North Korean troops, a nuclear-armed South Korea would be under great pressure to use nuclear weapons as atomic demolition land mines to close critical invasion corridors running the thirty miles from the border to Seoul. Similar military logic could lead to Israeli use of enhanced radiation weapons—so-called neutron bombs—in the next Arab-Israeli war.

A calculated disarming nuclear surprise attack to seize the military advantage also is possible in these high-stakes, escalation-prone regional conflicts, particularly when one side has a decided strategic advantage. For example, in the 1980s, internal political instability in Pakistan and simmering unrest in Kashmir could erupt into a conventional military clash between India and Pakistan. A nuclear-armed India then would be under intense pressure to attack the more rudimentary Pakistani nuclear force to prevent its use—whether by accident or intention—against India. In a nuclear Middle East, as well, fear of events getting out of hand would fuel arguments in favor of an Israeli first strike once a conflict had begun.

Aside from the increased threat of actual use of nuclear weapons, the nuclearization of conflict-prone regions may have other costly or dangerous consequences. Given the stakes, some new nuclear powers will think seriously about a preventive strike with conventional weapons to preserve their regional nuclear monopoly. Israel already has taken such military action against Iraq's nuclear weapons program and has stated its readiness to take further action as needed. And notwithstanding the limited Iraqi reaction to Israel's preventive strike—in large part due to Iraq's being tied down in its war with Iran—it might not be possible to prevent escalation after similar or larger future attacks.

Possession of nuclear weapons also may be used as an instrument of blackmail or coercion. A country with nuclear edge may implicitly or explicitly threaten the use of nuclear weapons to enforce its demands in regional crises or low-level confrontations. Just as U.S. strategic superiority contributed to the Soviet Union's decision to back down in the 1962 Cuban Missile Crisis, so might possession of nuclear weapons by Iraq, Israel, India, or South Korea affect the resolution of crises with weaker opponents.

In addition, tensions among the countries of newly nuclearized regions are likely to be exacerbated. Pakistan's nuclear weapons activities, for example, already have heightened India's suspicion and have slowed efforts to improve relations between the two countries. Pakistani testing and deployment of nuclear weapons would further worsen relations between India and Pakistan, not least because such activity would affront India's claim to regional preeminence. Should India step up its nuclear weapons activities in response and achieve clear-cut nuclear superiority, Pakistan's fears of Indian nuclear blackmail would be increased as well. Even the anticipation of a country's "going nuclear" can have adverse political effects. For example, Iraq's efforts to acquire nuclear weapons have heightened Israel's siege mentality and stimulated efforts by Syria, Saudi Arabia, and even Kuwait at least to master basic nuclear theory and know-how.

The greater the scope, the quicker the pace, and the higher the level of proliferation, the more severe will be the threat of nuclear conflict. As more countries acquire the bomb, the number of situations in which a political miscalculation, leadership failure, geographical propinquity, or technical mishap could lead to a nuclear clash will increase. As the pace of proliferation accelerates, the time available for countries to adjust to living with nuclear weapons will grow shorter. As countries move to the more advanced levels of proliferation—from untested bombs to full-fledged military deployment, there is more chance that some of these new nuclear forces will be technically deficient. Further, nuclear weapons will cease to be isolated symbols and will become an integral part of international relations within these volatile regions.

The initial outcroppings of more widespread proliferation in and of themselves also will call forth efforts to reduce the resultant threat of nuclear conflict. But few of the possible measures for mitigating the consequences of proliferation offer a high promise of success, while domestic and international constraints may hinder implementation of even these more limited measures. And the greater the scope, pace, and level of proliferation, the more difficult and complex management efforts will become. Thus, the spiraling risk of regional nuclear conflict will not be entirely offset by these management efforts.

THE GLOBAL SPILLOVERS

While more widespread proliferation most likely will not overturn the existing structure of world politics, it will adversely affect the superpowers, and their relationship, as well as the great powers. The optimism among some analysts about the benign consequences of further proliferation again is likely to be proved wrong.

LIMITS TO STRUCTURAL CHANGE

The Soviet Union and the United States are involved in nearly all of the regions to which nuclear weapons may spread in the 1980s, frequently supporting opposite sides in long-standing disputes. Neither is likely to sever alliance ties, drop clients and allies, or phase out economic and military involvement after nuclear weapons spread to these regions. In all probability, the leaders of both countries will continue to believe that compelling national interests—whether, for example, Western access to Middle East oil, expansion of Soviet power toward the Persian Gulf or its containment, the protection of traditional allies, and maintenance of the military balance in East Asia—outweigh any new or enhanced risks of continuing involvement. Besides, because of the competitive nature of the superpower relationship, officials in each country may be reluctant to disengage from these regions in the absence of reciprocal action by the other country lest the opponent be given a "free hand." And an unwillingness to sacrifice past investments made in pursuit of regional influence and military-political advantage is likely to buttress these arguments against disengagement.

It is equally doubtful that more widespread proliferation will lead to a Soviet-U.S. condominium to prevent the further spread of nuclear weapons, ban their use by new nuclear powers, and restore the superpowers' absolute domination of world politics. The competing political, economic, and military interests of the Soviet Union and the United States in regions such as South Asia and the Middle East are likely to take precedence over joint efforts to reduce the risk of local nuclear conflict. The superpowers' reliance on the nuclear threat in their own defense postures also may constrain joint action, particularly since the threat of escalation to nuclear conflict is critical to NATO's defense posture. The international costs—political, military, and economic—of an attempt to restore superpower domination of regional politics also would be high, and quite possibly thought by U.S. and Soviet leaders to be excessive. For many countries, including U.S. allies in Western Europe, a superpower condominium for nuclear peace would be a grave threat to their current freedom of action. It is also doubtful that the military problems of reasserting control would be manageable at an acceptable cost in light of increased local capabilities for resistance, as exemplified by the Soviet experience in Afghanistan. Moreover, in the Middle East, the economic penalties of intervention at least for the United States, could be great. And while the domestic political constraints on active interventionism abroad may be less for the Soviet leadership than for U.S. policymakers, in neither country can they be overlooked.

The restoration of a more multipolar global political structure is even less likely to result from the further spread of nuclear weapons. The net impact on superpower strategic dominance of the emergence of a group of lesser nuclear powers will be quite limited. Even the deployment of nuclear forces by Japan and West Germany need not fundamentally upset the existing structure: should the nuclear forces of Japan and West Germany be equivalent to those of France and the United Kingdom, there still would be a considerable gap between the threat they could pose to the superpowers and the threat the superpowers would pose in return. The United States and the Soviet Union also could raise the threshold nuclear capability necessary for Japan or West Germany to mount a serious threat to either of their homelands by renegotiating the 1972 Treaty between the United States of America and the Union of Soviet Socialist Republics on the Limitation of Anti-Ballistic Missile Systems (ABM) to permit Soviet and U.S. deployment of defenses against Japanese or West German ballistic missiles. Besides, it is quite unlikely in any case that these countries will decide to acquire nuclear weapons.

This conclusion that widespread proliferation will not overturn the existing structure of world politics rests most of all on the assumption that even in that changed environment the leaders of the United States and the Soviet Union will continue to pursue their distinct national interests and objectives, utilizing force or the threat of force and relying on prudence, crisis management, and marginal adjustment to deal with the new risks. However, it is possible that following the use of nuclear weapons by a new nuclear power—especially if that use almost produces a nuclear confrontation between them—the United States and the Soviet Union may be far more ready to negotiate about joint disengagement and other steps to isolate newly nuclear regions. Alternatively, leaders in the Soviet Union and the United States could seek to reassert their countries' capability to dictate the rules of the regional nuclear game. The likelihood of such major adjustments clearly will depend on whether the superpowers' assessment of the direct risks to themselves and of the adequacy of traditional crisis management changes markedly. But particularly in light of the limited success of recent U.S. and Soviet efforts to reach agreement on reciprocal strategic restraints as well as their conflicting global interests, ideologies, and national styles, even after one or more small-power nuclear exchanges, the two superpowers probably will continue to pursue only prudent ameliorative measures to reduce the risks of competitive involvement in newly nuclearized regions.

REDUCED SUPERPOWER FREEDOM OF ACTION

Periodically during the past decades, the United States has intervened militarily in regional confrontations, disputes, and limited conflicts outside of the European arena. The decision in 1980 to create the Rapid Deployment Joint Task Force for Middle East and Persian Gulf contingencies reflects a continued willingness to project U.S. power into conflict-prone regions in order to protect U.S. interests, allies, and friends. But the presence of nuclear weapons in some future contingencies will increase the military and political risks of intervention, reducing U.S. freedom of action.

Notwithstanding the threat of U.S. retaliation, nuclear weapons might be used against U.S. intervention forces. A desperate leader, thinking there was nothing left to lose, might launch a nuclear strike against landing troops or close-in off-shore naval operations, both of which would be vulnerable to even a few rudimentary nuclear weapons. Or, in the heat of battle, a breakdown of communications could result in the use of nuclear weapons by a lesser nuclear power. Also possible is an unauthorized attack on U.S. forces by the military of a new nuclear power. If needed adaptations of the tactics, training, and structure of these U.S. intervention forces are not made, U.S. intervention could prove very costly, and U.S. forces might even suffer stunning reversals.

Admittedly, U.S. policymakers could launch a limited nuclear strike to disarm the hostile new nuclear power rather than seek to "work around" this regional nuclear threat and risk valuable military assets. But the regional and global political costs to the United States of such a strike are likely to be so high as to make policymakers very hesitant to authorize it.

These heightened risks also are likely to reinforce the lingering, although somewhat muted, national presumption against intervention derived from the Vietnam experience. Consequently, the stakes needed to justify involvement in a newly nuclearized region probably will be greater than in the past. U.S. policymakers may choose not to intervene militarily in some situations where they previously would have acted.

The risks and complexities of military intervention will increase for the Soviet Union as well. In the eyes of a Soviet leadership that has intervened militarily only when the balance of forces appeared clearly favorable, the possible use of nuclear weapons against Soviet troops in a newly nuclearized region could be an excessive risk. To illustrate, Yugoslav deployment of battlefield nuclear weapons might discourage Soviet military action in a future domestic political struggle in

Yugoslavia. Similarly, even a slight possibility that Israel or South Africa would use nuclear weapons against Soviet ground or naval forces might help deter Soviet military entanglement in those regions. And the political costs of a nuclear disarming attack on a new nuclear power are likely to appear nearly as excessive to the Soviet Union as to the United States.

The eventual development by a few new nuclear powers of even a limited last-resort capability to threaten the homeland of one or the other superpower with nuclear attack or retaliation also would reduce both Soviet and American freedom of action. For example, should Israel acquire the capability to strike Odessa, Kiev, and Baku, the Soviet leaders might not be as willing to risk direct military involvement in the Middle East to support their Arab clients. Such a capability in Yugoslav or South African hands might have a comparable restraining effect on the Soviets. Or, though less likely, a radical Arab government might threaten to destroy one or more American cities in an attempt to blackmail the United States into not resupplying Israel in the midst of the next Middle East war. Of course, the risk of carrying out such a threat to a superpower would be extraordinary. But neither superpower could ignore the possibility that a leader who thought he had nothing left to lose might do so.

However, this threat of direct attack by a new nuclear power is likely to be greater for the Soviet Union than for the United States. Hardly any of the next countries likely to acquire the bomb will seek to target the U.S. homeland. Moreover, the geographical remoteness of the United States from potentially hostile new nuclear powers in the Middle East and Persian Gulf, combined with the technological backwardness of these countries, makes American cities somewhat less vulnerable than Soviet cities to such a nuclear strike. At least in the 1980s, to attack a U.S. city, Iraq or Libya—the most plausible opponents—probably would either have to smuggle a weapon into the United States by plane or boat or use a converted Boeing 707 or 747 registered as a private or corporate jet to deliver a bomb, counting on subterfuge and the steady decline of U.S. air defenses to penetrate U.S. airspace. Though possibly feasible, such unconventional modes of attack would be less technically reliable, limited in magnitude, and subject to interception by intelligence agencies.

In contrast, Israel, Yugoslavia, and South Korea already possess long-range nuclear-capable aircraft that can reach the Soviet Union and may well be able to slip through Soviet air defenses. South Africa and Israel also are said to be developing a crude cruise missile that could increase their capability to hit Soviet cities. Should Japan or West Germany acquire nuclear weapons, they would have little trouble targeting Soviet cities. Barring unexpectedly rapid technological progress, the breakdown of current restraints on the sale of cruise missiles and advanced missile guidance systems, or widespread traffic in space-booster technology and boosters themselves, the United States will continue to be less vulnerable to nuclear attack by a new nuclear power than will the Soviet Union—at least into the 1990s.

The constraining effect of more widespread possession of nuclear weapons of the superpowers should not be exaggerated. The superpowers' readiness and capability to control events abroad have already been lessened by the decreased legitimacy of using force, rising nationalism, the difficulties of bringing applicable force to bear in limited disputes, the availability of advanced weapons systems to regional powers, and the strengthening of countervailing economic instruments of power. So viewed, the further spread of nuclear weapons only contributes to a continuing, longer-term relative decline of superpower freedom of action. Moreover, as long as the two superpowers are ready to pay the necessary price, they could preserve a significant gap between their military capabilities and those of any new medium and lesser nuclear powers, including even Japan and West Germany. Further, in those situations where U.S. or Soviet interests are seen to justify either the military costs of working around lesser nuclear forces or the political costs of suppressing them, the superpowers most probably will be impeded but not prevented from realizing their objectives.

INCREASED RISK OF SUPERPOWER CONFRONTATION

Continued U.S. and Soviet pursuit of their respective interests in these newly nuclear conflict-prone regions also will entail acceptance of a higher risk of a U.S.-Soviet political-military confrontation. With the acquisition of nuclear weapons by long-standing regional enemies, there will be many more flashpoints for such a superpower clash. For instance, a preventive attack with conventional weapons, a surprise disarming strike, use of nuclear weapons on the battlefield, nuclear blackmail, a conventional attack backed by the threat of recourse to nuclear weapons, in each case by one superpower's ally against an ally of the other, all could trigger superpower involvement and confrontation. Both the Soviet Union and the United States would be under great pressure to "do something" to help their allies. While aware of the risks, Soviet and U.S. leaders might nonetheless be drawn into the conflict for fear that otherwise their past political, military, and economic investments in the regions would be wasted, their interests sacrificed, and their "reputations for action" ruined. But by responding, the superpower could set in motion an upward spiral of response and counterresponse, of initial entanglement and increased commitment, that may result in a direct confrontation between them.

Though present already, the risk of miscalculation on the part of the two superpowers also may be higher in situations involving newly nuclearized regions—again enhancing the chances of unwanted confrontation. In this new environment, either superpower may modify in unexpected ways its traditional assessment of the stakes, its preferred responses, or its readiness to run risks. Thus, whatever lessons about the other superpower's thinking and responses have been learned from prior regional crises may no longer be fully applicable. And this uncertainty could be most pronounced and most dangerous in the uncharted territory after the next use of nuclear weapons.

But concern about even indirect entanglement in crises or confrontations that could involve the use of nuclear weapons may make policymakers in Western Europe more cautious in extending existing political, economic, or military ties. Domestic pressures against heightened involvement could grow as well. Moreover, because of this fear, these policymakers might be even more reluctant to support U.S. military initiatives and may not permit use of facilities and bases on their territories, or agree to reallocate or transship material and supplies, or provide military forces.

As well, these Western European countries might be the targets of nuclear blackmail intended to make them stand aside in such clashes or withdraw previously offered assistance. For example, in the midst of an Arab-Israeli conflict in the late 1980s, Egypt, Iraq, or Libya could anonymously threaten to detonate a nuclear weapon previously smuggled into Portugal unless that country rescinded landing rights at air bases in the Azores for U.S. planes on their way to Israel with needed military equipment. Or West Germany might be the target of such an anonymous nuclear threat in an indirect effort to prevent the United States from shipping military equipment from NATO stocks to the Middle East. Besides, once nuclear weapons are more widely available, it could be quite difficult to distinguish a hoax from a serious threat, and, thus, even a hoax might suffice to disrupt such U.S. operations for a time.

Under certain conditions further proliferation also would increase considerably the cost and difficulty for France and Britain of maintaining a credible nuclear deterrent against the Soviet Union. Confronted by a growing threat to their homelands from new nuclear powers, or believing that such a threat was likely to emerge by the 1990s, the superpowers might renegotiate the 1972 ABM Treaty and deploy ballistic missile defenses. But to counter that change, these medium nuclear powers would have to develop and deploy costly and technically demanding systems able to penetrate those more extensive Soviet missile defenses. Failure to do so would lead to the increasing obsolescence of the French and British nuclear forces.*

---

*China's nuclear force would be similarly threatened with obsolescence by a Soviet missile defense capability.

DOMESTIC POLITICAL REPERCUSSIONS
NUCLEAR-ARMED TERRORISTS, IRREDENTISTS, AND SEPARATISTS

A considerably greater risk that terrorist and dissident groups will gain access to nuclear weapons will be another adverse consequence of the further spread of nuclear weapons. As more countries seek to acquire a nuclear weapons option by initiating sensitive reprocessing or enrichment activities, or set up actual weapons programs, the number of sites from which these groups could steal nuclear weapons material for a bomb will increase. The ensuing transportation of such material between a growing number of sites will further increase the risk of theft. Once a group possesses nuclear weapons material, the technical hurdles of processing that material and fabricating a nuclear weapon still would have to be overcome, but at least for some groups these difficulties would not be insurmountable. More important, a subnational group might opt for stealing the bomb itself, taking advantage of the probably less-than-adequate physical security measures of some new nuclear forces.

Hit-and-run clandestine terrorist groups, such as the Japanese Red Army, extreme left-wing Palestinian factions, the Italian Red Brigade, the Irish Republican Army (IRA), or successors to the Baader-Meinhof gang, may well regard a nuclear weapon as a means of extorting money or political concessions from a government, much as taking hostages is now. The countries of Western Europe, Japan, and the United States will be especially vulnerable to terrorist threats or attack because of their open societies. A group such as the IRA, claiming to represent a legitimate alternative government and dependent on popular support, might stop short of carrying out a nuclear threat even if its demands were not met. But members of the more radical and nihilistic fringe movements, such as the successors to the Baader-Meinhof gang and the Japanese Red Army, might think otherwise. To them, carrying out the threat might appear justified as a means of bringing down corrupt bourgeois society in a spasm of violence. Or, in the eyes of the most extreme Palestinian groups, use of a nuclear weapon might be thought justified as a way of mortally wounding Israel. Yet again, with the police closing in on them, these more radical, isolated terrorists could conclude that, since all was lost, it would be preferable to fall in a nuclear *Götterdämmerung*. Such a decision would be consistent with the near-suicide mentality shown in some past terrorist actions.

In contrast, the theft and threatened use of nuclear weapons may not appear a worthwhile tactic to a group such as the Palestinian Liberation Organization (PLO). Even though the PLO's freedom of action has been reduced by the Lebanese civil war, it still controls territory, administers to its refugee population, has a military force, and has been recognized by international bodies and foreign governments.

Rather than enhancing the PLO's claim that it is a legitimate government in exile, possession of a few stolen nuclear weapons could have the opposite effect. Theft of nuclear weapons would reinforce the PLO's reputation for extremism and unwillingness to accept minimal norms of international behavior and would make it harder for those Western European governments moving closer to the PLO's position on the Middle East to sustain that shift. Besides, should Israeli intelligence manage to locate these nuclear weapons, pressures to carry out a preventive strike, disregarding the risk of Soviet counteraction, would be intense. If Israel could not locate the nuclear weapons but knew that the PLO had them, the result is not likely to be Israeli acceptance of the need for a Palestinian state but Israeli unwillingness to compromise on that PLO demand. On balance, therefore, the costs to the PLO of stealing nuclear weapons appear to outweigh the benefits. Still, that conclusion reflects a Western weighing of costs and gains, which may prove as unfounded in this instance of Middle East maneuverings as it has on earlier occasions.

Separatist movements such as the Kurds or Arabs in Iran, the Baluchis in Pakistan, the Bengalis in India, the Moslems in the Philippines, or even the Basques in Spain might be more inclined to steal and threaten to use a nuclear weapon. For example, a separatist Baluchi movement might threaten to use stolen Pakistani nuclear weapons if the Pakistani central government mounted a new military campaign to restore its authority. Though extreme, such a threat would not be out of line with the bitter fighting so characteristic of these struggles for greater autonomy. Fearful of the consequences of cracking down on the separatists and under international and domestic pressure to find a "reasonable" settlement, the central government might come to terms with that group. Conversely, the central government could conclude that the costs of yielding to the separatists' demands were so great that it had no choice but to strike back, even using its own nuclear weapons against those of the separatists. But with little to lose, the Baluchis—and other separatist groups in other countries—might be ready to take that chance.

THE NUCLEAR COUP d'ETAT

In the 1980s and early 1990s, politically unstable new nuclear powers—such as Argentina, Brazil, Chile, Egypt, Iran, Iraq, Libya, Nigeria, Pakistan, South Korea, and Syria—might be vulnerable to nuclear coups d'etat. Particularly if the balance of political and military power between the rebels and the government were unclear, control of nuclear weapons—as compelling a symbol and instrument of national power as control of the airport, capital city, or radio and television stations—could greatly enhance the rebels' bargaining position. Control of nuclear weapons would change the psychological climate and afford rebel groups a means not only of demoralizing opponents but also of rallying supporters. The specter of nuclear destruction—should the situation get out of hand—quite possibly might lead civilian and military fence-sitters to come out in favor of a coup and even change the minds of some anti-coup forces. Moreover, just a few nuclear weapons in rebel hands could suffice to deter attack against them, assuming that the government was both unwilling to overwhelm the rebels with conventional force lest they retaliate with nuclear weapons and reluctant to use nuclear weapons first on its own territory in a surprise disarming attack. Consequently, more so than in past coups, efforts to dislodge such rebels would remain a test of wills and bargaining strategy. Nevertheless, nuclear weapons might be employed, either intentionally, by accident, or out of contempt and hatred.

Already on at least one occasion during the first decades of the nuclear age, access to nuclear weapons has figured in a domestic political upheaval. In April 1961, French army forces stationed in Algiers rebelled, demanding that the government in Paris reverse its decision to grant independence to Algeria. At the time, French scientists were preparing to test a nuclear weapon at the French Saharan test site in Reganne, Algeria, not too far from Algiers. Noting the proximity of the rebellion, the scientists called on the general in charge at Reganne to authorize an immediate test and thus avoid the possibility that the nuclear device would be seized by the rebel troops and used for bargaining leverage. Three days after the outbreak of the revolt, the order to detonate the device came directly from French President de Gaulle; there was no attempt to undertake precise experiments, only to use up all the available fissionable material.

THE CORROSION OF LIBERAL DEMOCRACIES?

At least some of the measures required to deal with the threats of clandestine nuclear attack—whether from a terrorist group or a new nuclear power—and of nuclear black marketing will be in tension with or in outright violation of the civil liberties procedures and underlying values of Western liberal democracies. Because of the stakes, there will be strong pressures to circumvent or set aside—in the United States and elsewhere—various constitutional and legal restrictions on invasions of privacy or other traditional civil liberties. Unauthorized, warrantless emergency searches based on skimpy evidence or tips might be made. Or broad neighborhood—even city-wide—searches may become legitimate in these instances, although existing laws in many countries, particularly the Fourth and Fourteenth Amendments in the United States, prohibit searches without specific definition of the site and evidence sought. The use of informants, warrantless or illegal wiretaps, and the secret detention and questioning of suspects for days or even weeks might follow, all motivated by the need to acquire information as fast as possible.

However, it may prove possible to contain this challenge to liberal democratic procedures and values. Within the United States, both rigorous administrative supervision of any emergency measures and strict judical review after the fact would help prevent those measures from spilling over their boundaries and corrupting procedures in other areas of law enforcement. Authorizing legislation and official policy statements also could stress the extraordinary character of those restrictions as a response to an exceptional threat while reemphasizing the more basic American belief in the worth, dignity, and sanctity of the individual that underlies respect for particular civil liberties.

But if the frequency of proliferation-related threats grows, and if violations of traditional civil liberties cease to be isolated occurrences, it will become more difficult to check this corrosion of liberal democracy here and elsewhere. For that reason, as well, concern about the many adverse consequences of increasingly widespread nuclear weapons proliferation is well founded.

Suggestions for
Further Reading

The literature on the uses of force in international relations is extensive. This list of books is by no means comprehensive, but it should be useful to those who wish to give more thought to the subjects covered in this book.

Raymond Aron, *The Great Debate.* New York: Doubleday, 1965.

Desmond Ball, *Politics and Force Levels: The Strategic Missile Program of the Kennedy Administration.* Berkeley: University of California Press, 1980.

Leonard Beaton and John Maddox, *The Spread of Nuclear Weapons.* New York: Praeger, 1962.

André Beaufre, *Deterrence and Strategy.* New York: Praeger, 1966.

Richard K. Betts, *Surprise Attack.* Washington, D.C.: The Brookings Institution, 1982.

————, *Nuclear Blackmail and Nuclear Balance.* Washington, D.C.: The Brookings Institution, 1987.

Geoffrey Blainey, *The Causes of War.* New York: The Free Press, 1973.

Donald G. Brennan, editor. *Arms Control, Disarmament, and National Security.* New York: George Braziller, 1961.

Bernard Brodie, *Sea Power in the Machine Age.* Princeton: Princeton University Press, 1944.

————, *Strategy in the Missile Age.* Princeton: Princeton University Press, 1959.

Ashton B. Carter and David N. Schwartz, eds., *Ballistic Missile Defense.* Washington, D.C.: The Brookings Institution, 1984.

Abram Chayes and Jerome B. Wiesner, editors. *ABMs An Evaluation of the Decision to Deploy an Antiballistic Missile System.* New York: New American Library, 1969.

Edward Meade Earle, editor. *Makers of Modern Strategy.* New York: Atheneum, 1966 (first published in 1941).

Lawrence Freedman, *The Evolution of Nuclear Strategy.* New York: St. Martin's Press, 1982.

Paul M. Kennedy, *The Rise and Fall of British Naval Mastery.* London: Macmillan, 1983.

J. F. C. Fuller, *Armaments and History.* New York: Scribner's, 1945.

B. H. Liddell Hart, *Deterrent or Defense.* London: Stevens and Sons, 1960.

————, *Strategy*. New York: Praeger, 1962.

Gregg Herken, *Counsels of War*. New York: Alfred A. Knopf, 1985.

David Holloway, *The Soviet Union and the Arms Race*. 2nd ed. New Haven: Yale University Press, 1984.

Herman Kahn, *On Thermonuclear War*. Princeton: Princeton University Press, 1961.

Fred Kaplan, *The Wizards of Armageddon*. New York: Simon and Schuster, 1983.

William W. Kaufmann, *The McNamara Strategy*. New York: Harper and Row, 1964.

Klaus Knorr and Thorton Read, editors, *Limited Strategic War*. New York: Frederick A. Praeger, 1962.

Robert A. Levine, *The Arms Debate*. Cambridge: Harvard University Press, 1963.

Guenter Lewy, *America in Vietnam*. Oxford: Oxford University Press, 1978.

Edward N. Luttwak, *The Grand Strategy of the Roman Empire*. Baltimore: The Johns Hopkins University Press, 1976.

Salvador de Madariaga, *Disarmament*. New York: Coward-McCann, 1929.

Arthur J. Marder, *The Anatomy of British Sea Power*. New York: Alfred A. Knopf, 1940.

Thomas L. McNaugher, *Arms & Oil: U.S. Military Strategy in the Persian Gulf*. Washington, D.C.: The Brookings Institution, 1985.

Etling E. Morison, *Men, Machines and Modern Times*. Cambridge: Massachusetts Institute of Technology Press, 1968.

Lewis Mumford, *Technics and Civilization*. New York: Harcourt, Brace and World, 1963 (first published in 1934).

John U. Nef, *War and Human Progress*. New York: W. W. Norton, 1968 (first published in 1950).

John Newhouse, *Cold Dawn—The Story of SALT*. New York: Holt, Rinehart and Winston, 1973.

Robert E. Osgood, *Limited War*. Chicago: The University of Chicago Press, 1957.

Gerhard Ritter, *The Schlieffen Plan*. London: Oswald Wolff, 1958.

Theodore Ropp, *War in the Modern World*. New York: Collier Books, 1962.

Thomas C. Schelling, *The Strategy of Conflict*. Cambridge: Harvard University Press, 1960.

Strobe Talbott, *Endgame—The Inside Story of Salt II*. New York: Harper and Row, 1979.

J. W. Wheeler-Bennett, *The Pipe Dream of Peace*. New York: W. Morrow, 1935.

Quincy Wright, *A Study of War*. 2 vols. Chicago: University of Chicago Press, 1942.

Contributors

Robert Art is Herter Professor of International Relations at Brandeis University.

Barry M. Blechman is President of Defense Forecasts, Inc.

Bernard Brodie was affiliated with the RAND Corporation and was Professor of Political Science at the University of California at Los Angeles.

Linton F. Brooks is a Captain in the United States Navy.

Frederic J. Brown served in the United States Army.

Zbigniew Brzezinski was National Security Advisor to President Jimmy Carter and is Professor of Political Science at Columbia University.

McGeorge Bundy was National Security Advisor to President Kennedy and is Professor of History at New York University.

Lewis A. Dunn is Senior Analyst at Science Applications International Corporation.

Joshua M. Epstein is a Senior Research Associate at the Brookings Institution.

John Lewis Gaddis is Professor of History at Ohio University.

Raymond L. Garthoff is a Senior Research Associate at the Brookings Institution.

Charles S. Glaser is Assistant Professor of Political Science at the University of Michigan.

Colin S. Gray is President of the National Institute for Public Policy.

Ernst B. Haas is Robson Professor of Political Science at the University of California at Berkeley.

Morton H. Halperin is Director of the Center for National Security Studies.

Douglas M. Hart is a defense analyst for the Pacific Sierra Corporation.

Samuel P. Huntington is Eaton Professor of the Science of Government at Harvard University.

Robert Jastrow is Professor of Earth Sciences at Dartmouth College.

Robert Jervis is Professor of Political Science at Columbia University.

Max M. Kampelman is a Washington, D.C. lawyer and served as Head of the United States Delegation in Geneva on arms control talks with the Soviet Union under President Reagan.

Karl Kaiser is Director of the Research Institute of the German Society for Foreign Affairs.

Edward L. Katzenbach, Jr., was Vice President of the University of Oklahoma.

George F. Kennan is Professor Emeritus of the Institute for Advanced Study at Princeton University.

Georg Leber was Minister of Defense under Chancellor Schmidt and is a Social Democratic member of the West German Bundestag.

Robert S. McNamara was Secretary of Defense under Presidents Kennedy and Johnson.

John J. Mearsheimer is Professor of Political Science at the University of Chicago.

Alois Mertes is a Christian Democratic member of the West German Bundestag.

Louis Morton was Professor of History at Dartmouth College.

Paul H. Nitze has served in high posts in the American Government in the national security field for over forty years.

Barry R. Posen is Associate Professor of Political Science at the Massachusetts Institute of Technology.

Sir George Sansom was a writer and a British diplomat with extensive experience in the Far East.

Thomas C. Schelling is Lucius N. Littauer Professor of Political Economy at the John F. Kennedy School of Government at Harvard University.

Franz-Joseph Schulze was Commander in Chief of Allied Forces, Central Europe and Deputy Chief of Staff, Allied Command, Europe.

Gerard Smith has served in high posts in the American Government in the national security field.

Glenn H. Snyder is Professor of Political Science at the University of North Carolina.

Stephen Van Evera was Managing Editor of the journal *International Security*.

Kenneth N. Waltz is Ford Professor of Political Science at the University of California at Berkeley.

Albert Wohlstetter was with the RAND Corporation and is Professor of Political Science Emeritus at the University of Chicago.

Roberta Wohlstetter is the author of *Pearl Harbor: Warning and Decision*.